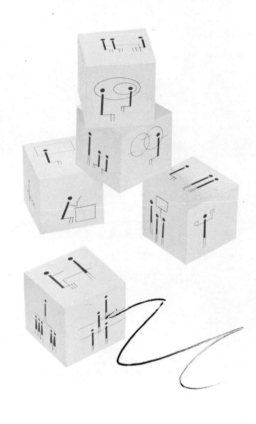

HUMAN BEHAVIOR

Prentice-Hall, Inc., Englewood Cliffs, New Jersey

IN ORGANIZATIONS

Leonard R. Sayles

Professor of Business Administration, Graduate School of Business,
Columbia University

George Strauss

Professor of Business Administration,
School of Business Administration
and Associate Director, Institute of Industrial Relations,
University of California, Berkeley

In Memory of Douglas McGregor

SEP 2 0 1978

LIBRARY
FLORIDA S TE UNIVERSITY
TALLAHASSEE, FLORIDA

Current printing (last digit):

11   10   9   8   7   6

HUMAN BEHAVIOR IN ORGANIZATIONS

Sayles and Strauss

© *Copyright 1960, 1966 by* GEORGE STRAUSS *and* LEONARD R. SAYLES. *All rights reserved. No part of this book may be reproduced in any form—by mimeograph; by photocopying; by electronic recording, or information storage or retrieval systems; or by any other means—without permission in writing from the publisher. Some of the material in chapters 1, 2, 11, and 14 appeared, in modified form, in Human Relations and Personnel Administration, Vol. I, copyright 1957, University of Buffalo Bookstore. Library of Congress Catalog No. 66-19281. Printed in the United States of America.*

Design by John J. Dunleavy

44470   C

PRENTICE-HALL INTERNATIONAL, INC., *London*
PRENTICE-HALL OF AUSTRALIA, PTY., LTD., *Sydney*
PRENTICE-HALL OF CANADA, LTD., *Toronto*
PRENTICE-HALL OF INDIA PVT. LTD., *New Delhi*
PRENTICE-HALL OF JAPAN, INC., *Tokyo*

Preface

Unfortunately, the human problems of administration in contemporary organizations have often been dealt with in a fragmentary way in a wide variety of academic courses. Courses titled Management, Human Relations, Personnel, Industrial Sociology, Social Psychology in Industry, to name but a few, have been devoted primarily to a better understanding of the effective management of human resources. Each has had its own special perspective. Recently there has been a tendency for many of these diverse approaches to coalesce in the field of *organizational behavior*.

This book endeavors to focus both the methods and findings of the behavioral sciences on the persisting human problems of administering modern organizations.

We find that many courses in administration still show little recognition of the full spectrum of relevant recent research. They tell the manager what he "ought" to do in a logical, rational fashion, not what problems he will face with real, often illogical, people and what methods of implementation are likely to be most successful. On the other side, many behavioral scientists show scant knowledge of the operating problems of organizations, nor do they have an intimate acquaintance with the realities of modern business. Often they appear to be presenting stereotypes of what the outsider thinks business is like, just as the management specialist stresses what business organizations ought to be like.

We have tried to avoid both extremes. Our objective has been to give the student a realistic view of the dynamic interplay of people and structure. Thus, rather than merely present tables and research "findings," we have endeavored to integrate the knowledge about organizations into a systematic framework. It is our hope that the reader will get a feeling for what it is like to work, to manage, and to resolve conflicting pressures inside real institutions. To this end we have intermixed behavioral descriptions, actual quotations and case examples, statistical survey findings, and empirically derived generalizations.

Our focus, however, is not just on understanding for its own sake, but also on the managerial problems of integrating the efforts of individuals and groups into effective, productive work. We do not assume that all workers are unmotivated and that all managers are oriented to the goals of the enterprise. We want the student to get to know highly motivated professionals, scientists and engineers, as well as machine-tenders; to see the conflicts that take place within management and among staff technicians; to see the world through the eyes of accountants and engineers; at other times, to identify with purchasing agents. We try to take him with us into "white-collar factories," automated plants, assembly lines, labs, and executive suites.

While we have tried to present a well-rounded and up-to-date survey of the leadership field, we do not concentrate on face-to-face problems of supervision to the exclusion of managerial uses of organization structure, policies, lines of authority and controls. A great deal of recent research suggests that the type of technology makes a big difference; there are no absolute rules of good management or human relations. Thus, participative management has its place and also its limitations. The organizational hierarchy is important; it is also often bypassed. Oftentimes structure plays a more important role than interpersonal skills, and sometimes leisure outweighs work, even in the eyes of a manager. The environment of business can hardly be ignored, and we endeavor to consider how community values influence the manager and affect some of the critical choices he must make. Under the best of circumstances, introducing organizational change is difficult; we suggest a variety of managerial skills that may be of assistance in making the important decisions.

In preparing for this book, we are fortunate in having done a good deal of field research over the past twenty years. Both authors have spent much of their professional careers studying the operations of large and small organizations, often by extended periods of observation. Our research has been relevant to psychology, sociology, and applied anthropology. Although most of our discussion relates to business, our work with administrators in hospital, educational, military, governmental, and social-work organizations suggests that the materials are relevant to these institutions as well. Finally, we have been greatly helped by the work we did for our previous text, *Personnel,* and many parts of this volume are based on that text.

Professors Vaughn Blankenship, Raymond Miles, and Lyman Porter generously provided critical comments. The Faculty Research Fund of the Graduate School of Business, Columbia University, aided Sayles in some of the research background for the chapters for which he was responsible. Our secretaries Janet Gehl, Judy Cowan, and Joyce Phelan helped us greatly.

Having collaborated since the 1940's, we are often asked, "How?" A good question and perhaps some clarification is in order. Author order on the title page was determined by the toss of a coin. Both authors share responsibility for the total book since we have evolved the unfortunate habit of exchanging all our materials (often endlessly, or so it would seem). However, Sayles had primary responsibility for Chapters 3-5, 10, 15-19 (although Chapters 17 and 19 are built around major field studies by Strauss). Strauss was responsible primarily for Chapters 1, 6-9, 11-14, and he did the original draft of Chapter 2, which was later enlarged and revised by Sayles.

We have dedicated the book to the memory of Douglas McGregor who, as our teacher at MIT in 1947, first stimulated our interest in this field. Through the years, until his recent untimely death, his enthusiasm and work was a source of inspiration.

Morningside Heights, New York City   Berkeley, California   April 30, 1966

Contents

INDIVIDUALS, JOBS,

AND GROUPS

Studying the human problems of organizations can be exciting but frustrating too. As with so many problems in behavioral science, one often feels the need to know everything before one can know something. Human organizations are organic in the sense that the various parts are interdependent. For example, you can't understand why an engineer complains about the work he receives from the model shop without knowing something about his needs (and those of his counterpart in the other department), the structure and policies of the larger organization, small group norms, how various supervisors behave, and many other things.

But one has to begin some place to build knowledge and understanding. We think that it is easier to start with some of the building blocks of the organization—individuals, jobs, and groups—and then look at the complex interrelationships involved in administration.

Individuals place a variety of demands on their work; in fact, the workplace is one of the most important institutions for providing human satisfactions. What motivates people? Do individuals differ in the relative importance they place on various needs and how stable are these demands? These are some of the questions which Chapter 1 ("The Meaning of Work") endeavors to answer by mustering relevant research findings.

But individual demands or needs are just one side of the equation. Different kinds of jobs provide more or less of various human satisfactions. In other words, management ought to be able to predict the impact of technological decisions on human reactions to work. Chapter 2 ("Technology and Job Satisfaction: Blue-Collar Work") contrasts the effect of craft, machine-tending, and assembly-line work.

These three categories include the more traditional types of manual jobs. Automation and the growing importance of administrative, professional, and service work introduce quite distinctive new job patterns. The reactions of employees to these developments are examined in Chapter 3 ("Technology and Job Satisfaction: Automation and White-Collar Work").

Motivation and on-the-job behavior are influenced profoundly by still another factor: group identifications. In a sense, every organization gets fractionated over time into a number of smaller groups because people need the close, more personal associations these groups provide in contrast to the effects of the more impersonal, larger institutions. In turn, these informal groups come to modify both individual needs and objectives, the character of the job and the organization. The dynamics of small group elaborations are analyzed in Chapter 4 ("Work Groups and Informal Organization").

Another type of group which has an impact on the larger organization is the labor union, which is, of course, a much more formal, complex entity than the work group. Not every firm has union relations, but because of their crucial importance to the human problems of management and their pervasive influence, it would be unrealistic to endeavor to understand the functioning of organizations without some knowledge of union structure and behavior. Chapter 5 ("Unions and Labor Relations") only endeavors to introduce the subject; you must depend on other sources for a more complete treatment of this technical problem.

The Meaning of Work

1

It's hard to imagine the changes in human life that have come about in western civilization over the past century and a half. For thousands of years the material conditions of our existence (the way food, clothing, and shelter were produced) remained relatively unchanged. And then, since 1800, at an ever faster pace, we have had steam engines, cotton gins, locomotives, the telegraph, automobiles, airplanes, radio, atomic energy, and space explorations. Our way of life has changed unbelievably—but perhaps in no area has the change been greater than in the way men earn their living.

Let us look for a moment at the "industrial relations" of yesteryear—for only by examining the past can we bring into focus the problems of today. Back in 1800, 90 per cent of the American people lived on farms, and the percentage was not much lower in Europe. Although there were large plantations in some sections of the country, most men owned and worked their own farms, receiving aid at harvest time when neighbor helped neighbor. The family was the basic economic unit. Father worked in the fields. Mother processed the food (in a way housewives rarely do in this age of supermarkets), cooked the meals, spun the wool, made the clothes, and did the household chores. Brother and sister were assigned simple tasks almost as soon as they could walk. Labor relations and family relations were the same.

Economically, the farm was almost self-sufficient. Of course, with a cash crop the farmer might buy an ax, a flintlock, gunpowder, and such luxuries as dishes, sugar, shoes, and books (though luxuries could be either fashioned at home or done without). If the crop was poor, life was less comfortable, but few people worried about unemployment.

A man was his own boss. No one could tell him when to plant or harvest, or could give him a written warning if he started work three minutes late. True, nature and the weather might prove more tyrannical than any foreman, but what a man produced was his own. His motivation was clear: If he was lazy, his own family suffered.

Furthermore (in contrast to what prevails in many jobs today) his efforts brought tangible fruit. Looking at his growing fields, he could say with real satisfaction, "Look what *I* have created." He, his family, his life, and his job were all tied together in a rich oneness that many look back on with nostalgia. (Few farmers today, however, would give up the benefits of tractors or electricity, nor would their wives long enjoy dipping candles and spinning wool. The earlier farmer's hours were long and his frustrations many. The continuing exodus from farm to city over the last century indicates that, for all its disadvantages, many prefer our urban civilization to the simple country life.)

Even in earlier days, in the city perhaps the farmer had a younger brother, a journeyman wagon-maker. He was a wage-earner, not his own boss. And yet, how different the meaning of his job was to him than to his great-great-grandson who tightens bolts on the final line of Chevy No. 3! In the first place, he knew he would not be a journeyman for long. If he saved his money, he might expect to set himself up in business within a few years.

Relations between himself and his boss were simple and easy—at times almost like the relations between father and son. The older man taught the younger what he knew and together they performed the same job. The work was creative and satisfying. Building a wagon required skill, and when the job was finished the worker could see what he had done. He could be proud of his craftsmanship and sure of his place in the world.

Such was the way some men earned their living not so many years ago—even though our picture is admittedly somewhat idyllic. After all, a slave on a plantation or a peasant in Europe was often just a working beast, and few wage-earners had the sense of skill enjoyed by our journeyman wagon-maker. In fact, it may well be "that in modern society there is a far greater scope for skill and craftsmanship than in any previous society, and that far more people are in a position to use such skills." [1]

---

[1] J. A. C. Brown, *The Social Psychology of Industry* (Baltimore: Pelican, 1954), p. 207. See also Robert Blauner, "Work Satisfaction and Industrial Trends in Modern Society," Walter Galenson and S. M. Lipset, eds., *Labor and Trade Unionism* (New York: Wiley, 1960).

The Impact of the Industrial Revolution

The last century and a half has brought a dramatic revolution, not only in what we make, but in how we make it. The industrial revolution has been a revolution not only in technology but also in human relations. As technology grew more and more complex, people became more dependent on one another and the problems of working together became more troublesome. Today the typical American is no longer his own boss; he is not a farmer, but a city dweller. Furthermore, the industrial revolution has brought major changes in what it means to be an employee.

SPECIALIZATION

The journeyman wagon-maker did a whole job from beginning to end. But one of the distinguishing marks of the industrial revolution is specialization. Here is Adam Smith's famous description of the changes that were taking place in pinmaking almost two centuries ago, at the dawn of the industrial revolution in England:

> A workman not educated to this business . . . could scarce, perhaps, with utmost industry, make one pin a day, and certainly not make twenty. But in the way in which this business is now carried on, not only the whole work is a peculiar trade, but it is divided into a number of branches, of which the greater part are likewise peculiar trades. One man draws out the wire, another straightens it, a third cuts it, a fourth points it, a fifth grinds it at the top for receiving the head; to make the head requires two or three distinct operations; to put it on is a peculiar business. . . . I have seen a small manufactory of this sort where ten men only were employed and where some of them consequently performed two or three distinct operations. But though they were very poor, and therefore but indifferently accommodated with the necessary machinery, they could, when they exerted themselves, make upwards of forty-eight thousand pins in a day.[2]

Economically, specialization has brought great advantages. But it has brought many disadvantages as well: boredom and the loss of a sense of individual importance, of accomplishment, of pride in work. How much satisfaction can a man obtain from spending his entire day pointing pins?

Further, workers feel that they are shackled to work processes they have had no hand in developing. The Industrial Engineering Department frequently determines every detail of the job, depriving the individual of any chance to show initiative or originality. Specialization has sharpened the dividing line between workers and management.

Specialization has also developed within management. Instead of a single owner-manager with complete control over the plant, or a foreman with complete control over his department, we have staff departments such as engineering, production scheduling, purchasing, and personnel. No man performs more than a small part of the whole job; no man has significant control over what he

---

[2] *The Wealth of Nations* (New York: Modern Library, 1937), p. 4.

does. A dozen staff agencies may be involved in making a simple decision, and the worker is at the very bottom: "Everybody gets consulted but me. I just carry out their orders."

OPPORTUNITY TO GET AHEAD

To make the industrial revolution possible, elaborate machinery was necessary—and machinery requires money. The journeyman craftsman needed little more than his own tools to set himself up in business, but the man on the automobile assembly line cannot hope to compete with General Motors. Unless he wants to operate a small store or a gas station, the modern worker has far less chance to be his own boss than did his great-grandfather.

Even after the average man's chance to become an *independent* industrialist had vanished, the avenue of promotion within a company remained wide open for many years. Fifty years ago an able and ambitious man might conceivably work himself up from sweeper to president. Today, as our technology and business life become more and more complicated, opportunities for the noncollege man become increasingly limited. Sociologists call this phenomenon *blocked mobility*. A man can still get ahead through hard work, but unless he is a college graduate it is a much more arduous task than it used to be.

INCREASING SIZE OF BUSINESS ORGANIZATION

The industrial revolution has made business organizations larger and the boss more remote. The journeyman wagon-maker had no trouble talking to his boss; communication was easy. Today, however, a man may spend his lifetime in a steel mill and never talk to the plant manager, let alone the president.

The owner of a wagon shop could easily supervise all phases of manufacture. In a business like AT&T, supervision and coordination require the services of thousands of executives. All this leads to the process of bureaucratization, the making of rules that restrict individual discretion even to the point where top executives find themselves tied down.

CONSTANT CHANGE

In the simple society of the early 1800's, changes were rare. Behavior was governed by tradition: There was no need to tell a man what to do—all he had to do was follow the patterns laid down by his ancestors.

Modern industry is subject to constant change. The very fact of change creates two types of problem: (1) Less can be left to routine; careful planning, deliberate orders, and elaborate communications are essential. Since personal experience and tradition are less valued, there is a correspondingly greater need for rules and regulations. (2) People normally resist change, particularly when it is imposed upon them. Consequently the problems of motivating people to work together have grown more complex.

In short, the industrial revolution has done wonders to make life easier for all of us, but at a serious cost in terms of the rewards and enjoyments that individuals derive from their jobs.

The rest of this chapter will be concerned with three questions: What sorts of needs are satisfied through work? How can these needs be ranked in relative importance? And how important as a source of satisfaction is one's *job*, compared with other means of satisfaction available in life? [3]

Needs Satisfied by Working

Although the authors recognize that all attempts to categorize needs are somewhat artificial, in this book we shall speak of three forms of need satisfaction:

1. *Physical and security needs.* These relate to the satisfaction of bodily functions, such as hunger, thirst, shelter, and the like, as well as the need to be secure in the enjoyment of these.

2. *Social needs.* Since human beings are dependent on each other, there are some needs which can be satisfied only when the individual is helped or recognized by other people.

3. *Egoistic needs.* These relate to man's desire to be independent, to do things on his own and to sense accomplishment.

Another way of categorizing needs is in terms of the means by which they are satisfied. Some forms of satisfaction are enjoyed *off the job*—for example, a man spends his pay check after work and away from the job. Other needs are satisfied through having a happy, satisfying work environment *around the job*. A third form of satisfaction can be obtained only through the process of working and so can be called intrinsic or *through-the-job* satisfaction. As we shall see in later chapters (Chapter 6 in particular), this three-way distinction is critical for the motivation of employees. When management emphasizes off-the-job satisfactions, it assumes, in effect, that work is a punishment which employees endure in exchange for rewards to be enjoyed after work. Managers who stress around-the-job satisfactions seek to make the work environment a pleasant one, but do not provide direct, positive motivation for men to work harder. To the extent that through-the-job satisfactions are provided, employees work hard; the harder they work the greater their satisfaction.

As will be seen, both sets of categories—types of needs and ways in which needs are satisfied—overlap a bit and many needs can be placed in more than one category. Nor is there any hard-and-fast relationship between the sets of categories. To a considerable extent, however, physical needs are satisfied off the job, social needs are satisfied through personal contacts around the job,

---

[3] We are indebted to our teacher, the late Douglas McGregor, for many of the concepts discussed in this chapter.

whereas egoistic needs are chiefly satisfied through the job. There are, of course, many exceptions to this "rule." For example, safe working conditions satisfy an important physical need, yet they are enjoyed on the job; status is a social need, yet the status derived from holding an important position is enjoyed away from work as much as on the job; praise is another social need, yet praise from one's boss is often best obtained through doing one's job well; a salesman may satisfy his social needs through his work—the more sales he makes, the greater his opportunity to meet people.

With the above warnings in mind, let us now look at the various forms of need satisfaction obtained from work, starting with physical and security needs.

Primarily Physical and Security Needs

MONEY

Ask a man why he works and chances are he will tell you, "to make money." Certainly the need to earn a living is the most powerful single reason why people work, though, as we shall see, nonmonetary incentives are also important.

Money satisfies all types of needs. Its principal use may be to provide the physical necessities of life as well as security; however, social status in our society depends largely on the size of one's earnings; and earning a good income provides many people with an egoistic sense of accomplishment.

The first demand most people make of a job, then, is that it provide them with enough to enjoy a "proper" standard of living. But what we accept as "proper" tends to rise over time. Today we consider a house substandard if it lacks running water or central heating; this was not so a hundred years ago. To many people today, an automobile and a TV set are among the essentials of life. Moreover, our concept of the proper standard of living depends a good bit on what our neighbors have. If the man next door buys a shiny new Buick, our five-year-old Chevy becomes less adequate.

This tremendous interest in material goods is not a natural characteristic of man but a special trait of our own culture. Many other societies ascribe far less importance to material goods than to holiness, wisdom, and physical and military power. The individual's place in society may be determined purely by who his ancestors were; displays of wealth may be regarded as poor taste. Among certain tribes competitiveness is socially tabu; when the missionaries taught these people how to run races, they insisted that every race must end in a dead heat.

Even in our own culture, money is ordinarily more important to the salesman than to the teacher or the minister. Some men refuse a promotion with a higher salary simply because it involves "too much responsibility." And there are people without much "get up and go" who are satisfied to live on a subsistence level and to spend the rest of their time fishing or building model airplanes.

Although, in the larger community, income may be only a rough measure of status, within a plant it measures very precisely the importance of a job. Even the difference of a penny in hourly rates may assume great significance. If one job pays $2.62 an hour and another $2.63, workers feel (a) that the $2.63 job is more important, or (b) that the $2.62 job should be more highly paid.

Who is more important, the plumber or the electrician? If the plumber gets a 20-cent raise, the electrician wants the same—otherwise he feels he is suffering a cut. The National War Labor Board perhaps only slightly exaggerated when it said: "There is no single factor in the entire field of labor relations which does more to break down morale, create individual dissatisfaction, encourage absenteeism, increase labor turnover, and hamper production than obviously unjust inequalities in the wage rates paid to the same individuals in the same labor group within the same plant."

SECURITY

Job security is a fundamental human need; for many people it is more important than either pay or advancement. The forces driving toward unionism, the most serious problems of superior-subordinate relations, the fears surrounding changing technology—all revolve around the need for security.

It is not enough for a man to have his physical needs satisfied from day to day; he wants to make sure they will continue to be satisfied in the future. In some cases, seniority offers the unskilled worker a sense of security akin to that of the farmer who owns his property or the craftsman who possesses special skills. In recent years, however, automation and other economic changes have brought unemployment to many who once thought their jobs secure. Older men, members of minority groups, and those with limited education or outmoded skills find it extremely hard to find steady work again. As a consequence, losing a job can be a catastrophe, both physically and psychologically. No wonder workers' desires to hold on to their "property rights" to their jobs have led to labor-management disputes over working rules and featherbedding, particularly in industries with declining employment.

Illness and old age provide similar threats to security. Understandably, many companies and unions now seek to provide employees with "total" or "employment-to-grave" security against all forms of income interruption.

ADVANCEMENT

The urge to advance, "to get ahead," is particularly strong in America. In many other societies a man is born to a rigidly defined class and follows his father's occupation without question; bootblack or king, he fullfills as best he can "the station to which God has called him."

Deep in the heart of every "true" American lies the Horatio Alger dream of unlimited occupational mobility, the belief that every man, no matter how humble his birth, can rise to the highest positions in the land. Indeed, our fondest stories concern men like Abe Lincoln who through honesty and hard work make their way from log cabin to White House.

Children are taught that any virtuous man can work his way to the top. "Your future is strictly up to you," [4] said a National Association of Manufacturers pamphlet in 1951. "Your opportunities will be limited only by your vision of what your future may become, your abilities and how you use them, your character and your determination." At one time it was believed that poverty was largely due to moral weakness, that failure was the fault, not of the system, but of personal character.[5]

Historians and sociologists are finding increasing evidence that the "sweeper-to-president" phenomenon has always been something of a myth.[6] Even a century ago opportunities to get ahead were considerably limited. Yet for a long time this myth of unlimited opportunities for "upward mobility" was generally believed and provided hopes for millions. Today this dream may be fading.[7] True, a child born in the 1960's has as good a chance to advance in social status as did his grandfather. But once a man reaches the age of 25 without having gone to college, his chances for advancement in the old-fashioned sense are limited. Such men may still want to get ahead, but they must redefine what they mean by getting ahead in terms that are realistically related to their actual opportunities.

A generalization of this sort, however, is much too broad, and needs careful qualification. In fact, as we shall discuss in future chapters, the very meaning of advancement differs substantially from one segment of the population to another: whether more security, more responsible jobs, higher incomes, greater status, or recognition from one's colleagues. The measure chosen depends in part on the kind of work one does.

In addition, an individual's level of aspiration depends to a great extent on personality and family background. The son of underprivileged parents who have never known security is likely to be content with less "success" than someone from a middle-class background. An ex-farmer is more likely to try to get ahead on his own than someone with a city upbringing. Similarly, for a girl from a middle-class urban background, waiting on table may seem a defeat, whereas for a girl from a farm, "The restaurant becomes . . . a foothold in the life of the city, and it may also make it possible for her to rise in the world." [8]

---

[4] *Your Future and What You Make of It,* fourth of the "You and Industry Series" (New York: National Association of Manufacturers, 1951), p. 3, as quoted in Ely Chinoy, *The American Automobile Worker and the American Dream* (New York: Doubleday, 1955), pp. 9-10.

[5] For an excellent discussion, see John William Ward, "The Ideal of Individualism and the Reality of the Organization," in Earl F. Cheit, ed., *The Business Establishment* (New York: Wiley, 1964), pp. 37-76.

[6] Seymour Martin Lipset and Reinhard Bendix, *Social Mobility and Industrial Society* (Berkeley: University of California Press, 1960).

[7] Chinoy, *op. cit.;* Bennett M. Berger, *Working Class Suburb* (Berkeley: University of California Press, 1960), p. 88.

[8] William F. Whyte, *Human Relations in the Restaurant Industry* (New York: McGraw-Hill, 1948), p. 153.

Management must recognize the existence of these differences in dealing with individual employees. A rising member of middle management may find it difficult to understand why piece-workers are more likely to restrict production than to earn all they can and win a promotion. Certainly competition is much less effective in motivating production workers than it is in motivating white-collar employees or executives. Indeed, many of the difficulties among these groups arise from failure to understand one another's motivations.

Primarily Social Needs

Man is a social animal. He craves *friendship*, is unhappy when left alone for too long, and often associates with his fellows just because he is hungry for companionship. Particularly for employees who have an unsatisfactory home life, the job provides a large part of their social-need satisfaction.

It is social banter that makes many jobs bearable. If there is nothing more constructive to talk about, small issues can be magnified and boredom can be relieved through circulating rumors. In the informal social life of the plant, too, many a worker has a chance to demonstrate skill and initiative. And even the work itself may be socially rewarding for some employees, such as telephone operators and salesclerks who gain great satisfaction from talking to customers.

The job frequently satisfies other social needs besides the need for friendship. Belonging to a clique provides employees with a sense of *identification* and belonging, and they insist on forming "informal groups" even in the face of management opposition. When they are unable to achieve such identification, the job becomes less desirable. Indeed, there is evidence that workers who belong to small, integrated work groups have higher morale than those who work either alone or among large masses of employees with whom they have few social ties. One study explains why steelworkers are more satisfied with their job than automobile assembly-line workers partly on the grounds that steelworkers typically work in small teams; in contrast, on an assembly line a worker can talk only to the two men flanking him, thus making cohesive social groups difficult to form.[9]

Merely working together, *teamwork*, helps to build morale. Most people like *helping others*. Also, when we need it, we like to be *helped* by others.

Another set of social needs develops out of the subordinate's relationship to his supervisor. Naturally the subordinate wants *to be treated fairly:* He wants a fair hearing when he thinks his supervisor has made a wrong decision, and he wants the right to appeal over the supervisor's head. Most people like *praise* when they do something well (though sometimes praise from a fellow worker is more meaningful than praise from management). The average worker also expects acceptance from his supervisor—that is, understanding and consideration when he makes a mistake. Finally, he wants to *know where he stands*.

---

[9] Charles R. Walker, *Steeltown* (New York: Harper & Row, 1950); Charles R. Walker and Robert H. Guest, *Man on the Assembly Line* (New York: Harper & Row, 1952).

Regardless of whether he is doing badly or well, the typical worker wants some *attention* from his boss. Individuals differ in the amount of attention they desire, however, for some want to be left strictly alone and others constantly run to the boss for reassurance. The supervisor must adjust his supervisory practices accordingly (and yet avoid charges of favoritism). But we shall have more to say about this later on.

Primarily Egoistic Needs

ACCOMPLISHMENT

"The trouble with this work is that I don't have any feeling of accomplishment. I'm just nobody, doing nothing, getting nowhere. I'm just a cog, so small I'd never be missed." So one worker explained his dislike for his job, even though it was one of the highest-paying jobs in the plant.

One of man's strongest needs is the need for a sense of accomplishment, for the feeling that he is getting something done, that his work is of importance. The work "accomplishment" is rather nebulous, however, for it means many things to different people. Let us examine some of the dimensions of this term.

Importance of the work. Work that seems pointless is bound to lead to frustration. One of the most unpleasant forms of punishment used by the military is to have men dig holes and then fill them in again. Compare this with the rich reward that people who perform even menial tasks in a hospital get from "helping people."

Two English researchers, in a study of a candy factory, once found that the greatest dissatisfaction centered in a small work group whose job consisted of unwrapping defective chocolates as part of a salvage operation.[10] The workers felt that their job was far less constructive than that of the other operators. Telephone supervisors report that production and morale are always higher during an emergency. As one said, "It's amazing. An operator may be a low producer and a disciplinary problem, often tardy and absent, but come a blizzard when the highways are closed, she will walk long distances to come to work."

The satisfied worker takes pride in the product he makes: "I get a big kick every time I see it in the store," he may say, or "Our widgets are made to the finest tolerance in the industry." The various forms that this sense of accomplishment may take are suggested by the following quotations: [11]

> *Responsibility for the welfare of others:* "I am very proud of my job because I examine the mine to make sure it is safe. I save a lot of lives by taking chances for them."—*Miner.*

---

[10] S. Wyatt and J. N. Langdon, *Fatigue and Boredom in Repetitive Work*, Industrial Health Research Council, Report No. 77 (London: H. M. Stationery Office, 1938).

[11] Eugene A. Friedmann and Robert J. Havighurst, *The Meaning of Work and Retirement* (Chicago: University of Chicago Press, 1954), pp. 77, 110, 119.

Service to others: "There is a lot of satisfaction out of putting something on a man you know looks well on him, and that he is going to get a lot of compliments and he's going to be pleased and all that."—*Salesclerk.*

Satisfaction in product: "When you are selling sterling silver, you've got something to talk about and you talk about it truthfully. It's something that turns into an heirloom—never wears out."—*Salesclerk.*

The elevator operator, the janitor, and the groundskeeper—all *want* to feel that their job is important, and good supervision can do much to enhance their sense of accomplishment and their feeling of self-respect, as we shall see in later chapters.

Studies suggest that there is a close correlation between an occupation's prestige and the satisfaction people get from working at it. "Jobs that have high prestige will tend to be valued for their status rewards even when 'objective' aspects of the work are undesirable; similarly low-status jobs will tend to be undervalued and disliked." [12] Low-status work is considered unimportant. "The best way to improve the job may often be, in fact, to change what the outside public thinks about it and its doers." [13]

How the work fits into the whole. During World War II, the morale in a small plant was very low and turnover was high. Most of the employees were women who spent their days producing a small metal part that had no obvious importance. The women had no idea what it was used for, nor would management tell them. Then one day they were taken by bus to a nearby aircraft plant where they were shown that the part was an important component of the tail assembly of the B-29. For a while at least, production and morale soared.

For a soldier, one of the most important causes of low morale is the feeling that he, as an individual, is unimportant. Since secrecy must be maintained during a military campaign, the soldier, ignorant of the significance of his activities, concludes that they are pointless. Officers may claim that "there is a reason for everything you do in the Army," but enlisted men can't help but be skeptical.

Similarly, in modern industry it is often extremely difficult for the worker "to see his place in the scheme of things, to appreciate his contributions to the total process. Too often the individual job is like the isolated pieces of a jigsaw puzzle. And because there are so many 'pieces,' those at the work level generally have only the haziest notion of the total pattern. . . . In a real sense, therefore, the job loses its meaning for the worker—the meaning that is in all terms except the pay envelope." [14]

Skill. All of us enjoy the sense of creativity that springs from doing something well, from being "on top" of our job. The housewife is proud of her clean-

---

[12] Robert Blauner, *Alienation and Freedom* (Chicago: University of Chicago Press, 1964), p. 63.
[13] Whiting Williams, *The Mainsprings of Man* (New York: Scribner's, 1925), p. 63.
[14] James C. Worthy, *Some Observations on Frederick W. Taylor and the Scientific Management Movement,* paper delivered before the Society for Applied Anthropology, Columbia University, New York City, April 9, 1954.

liness or her shortbread, the safe-cracker of his sensitive fingers, the professor of his brilliant lecture or his searching questions.

We also like to imagine that our job requires unusual skill, and as a consequence we tend to exaggerate its importance. When describing his job, a worker often stresses its difficulty, complexity, and the length of time required to learn it. Every machine seems to have special quirks in the eyes of its operator.[15] Every trade has its tricks which require skill, ingenuity, and expertise. Even the janitor feels he has developed a number of special techniques (knowing that Executive A likes his desk dusted, but that Executive B never wants his desk touched) that raise him above the level of unskilled labor. "The bricklayer as a rule is more than a workman. He is a craftsman," says the Bricklayers' Union journal.[16] "His work endures and stands the gaff of years ... I have worked with a certain bricklayer who takes great pride in telling you one of his ancestors used to take his son to Buckingham Palace and point out some of the stately arches which he himself had built. ... When a bricklayer has finished with a day's work there is something real to compensate for it. He can go home feeling that he has created something that will last longer than he will."

Employees resent any implication that they can be easily replaced by untrained workers. Partly, of course, such an implication threatens their job security. But there is more to it than that: If anybody can do your job, what can you say that you have accomplished in your working life? What more significant sign of utter failure? True, many workers feel that they contribute nothing to their job that a completely untrained man could not contribute, but they are dismally discouraged by this realization. As individuals, they feel they are accomplishing nothing.

This sense of frustration helps explain the popularity of do-it-yourself projects, many of which involve no economic saving for the home craftsman but do provide a sense of skill and creativity. A worker may come home tired from the factory or office and "rest" by working hard in his basement or garden.

For the skilled craftsman the feeling of skill is particularly important; he resents anything that threatens it. Many companies have discovered that it is harder to get employees to lower their standards of quality than to raise them. When management decides that customers will accept lower quality, and that looser tolerances can be maintained, skilled workers stubbornly resist the consequent reduction in skill required. They take real pride in their job and have no desire to make it less difficult. Looser standards mean less sense of accomplishment.

It is for this reason that many companies are plagued by running battles between engineers and top management. The engineers insist on close toler-

---

15 See Nancy Morse, *Satisfactions With White Collar Jobs* (Ann Arbor: Institute for Social Research, University of Michigan, 1953).

16 *The Bricklayer, Mason and Plasterer,* Vol. 30 (May 1927), p. 134.

ances and top quality; they try to delay a new model from being put into production until all the "bugs" have been eliminated. Top management regards this desire for perfection as financially ruinous.

Progress and completion.   If an employee is to have a feeling of achievement, he must have some way of measuring his progress. Everyone wants to know "How am I doing?" People like "feedback" even when there is no reward or penalty attached to failure or success. Thus, when a man idly throws a piece of paper at a wastepaper basket, he is interested in whether it goes in (even if he doesn't have to clean up afterward). Only if he can set up some goal and know that he has reached it can he feel this sense of achievement. Many routine jobs are considered boring and monotonous precisely because they give the worker no way to check his progress.

Productiveness.   Perhaps all that we have been saying adds up to one point: most people have a genuine desire to be productive, to keep busy.[17] Certainly our observations cast doubt on the common assumption that most workers prefer to "goldbrick" than to work. In fact, it is harder to look busy than to work. Time passes more quickly when a worker is absorbed in what he is doing than when he is trying to avoid work. In our society, a healthy individual feels lost without some sort of job or hobby. Normally, expending mental and physical energy is a pleasant, not a painful, experience.

But if all this is true, how can we explain why people often do loaf on the job and go to extraordinary extremes to avoid work? Usually such behavior is a sign of dissatisfaction with the job, with supervision, or with the company as a whole. Workers who feel that they have been treated unfairly direct their energies to beating the system and show high skill in doing as little work as possible. This response, however, is a sure sign that the organization is beset by severe problems.

The sense of productivity and accomplishment is particularly important to executives. One study, which made extensive use of psychological tests, reported:

> They conceive themselves as hard working and achieving people who must accomplish in order to be happy. . . . They obtain continual stimulation from the pleasure of immediate accomplishment. They feel the necessity to move continually upwards and to accumulate the rewards from increasing accomplishments.[18]

---

[17] One astute student suggests that once people have started to work they have a virtual compulsion to keep on going, an urge that he calls "traction." W. Baldamus, *Efficiency and Work* (London: Tavistock Publications, 1961).

[18] William E. Henry, "The Business Executive: A Study in the Psychodynamics of a Social Role," *The American Journal of Sociology*, Vol. 54, No. 4 (January 1949), p. 287.

AUTONOMY

> "You know, it's a funny thing. I work all day at the plant and then I come home and what do I do? I work some more—I mean in the shop in the basement. I love to do things with my hands. Funny, that's what I do at work—only it's different.
>
> "You see at work I don't have any freedom. That's the difference. The company tells me when to start working, when I get time to go to the john, when I get my lunch and how long (I get .7 hours—that's 42 minutes for anyone who isn't an engineer). They tell me how fast to work and exactly what motions to make. About the only thing I'm free to do is to think how damn lousy the job is.
>
> "Now, at home I'm my own boss—and believe me, that's a wonderful feeling."
>
> —*Autoworker*.

Most people like being their own boss. Yet in modern industry only a few employees really have this feeling. The process of specialization has deprived the individual worker of his freedom to plan and organize his own job and has transferred initiative and responsibility to management. As Frederick Taylor, father of the scientific management movement, once put it, "Each man must learn how to give up his own particular way of doing things, adapt his methods to the many new standards, and grow accustomed to receiving and obeying directions covering details, large and small, which in the past have been left to his individual judgment." [19] The effect of this approach has been to strip many jobs of every opportunity for spontaneity and creativity.

Sometimes the tall stories told by workers are indicative of their hidden desires to do things in their own way. For instance, there is the tale of the assembly-line workers who fixed their cars so that when you stepped on the accelerator the windshield wiper started flapping and the horn blew "honk-honk." Then there is the story about the skilled glass blower who for years had been making glass rabbits with straight ears. One day he decided to let the ears droop. "I thought it might be a nice change," he told an amazed management.

Initiative and imagination are essential to any sense of autonomy; yet too often management fails to use the creative abilities of employees. As a consequence, they display their initiative and imagination in forms of which management disapproves, such as sabotage, union activity, and horseplay. Often the creative individual is considered a troublemaker. [20]

We must not paint too black a picture, however, for on many jobs workers do have a good deal of freedom. We have all seen janitors who really felt they were kings of all they surveyed—and behaved accordingly. Skilled workers, guards, inspectors, and many production workers frequently have this same feeling of independence. For example,

---

[19] Frederick W. Taylor, *Shop Management* (New York: Harper, 1919), p. 113.

[20] Some observers report that the trend toward conformity is causing the same thing to happen on the management level. W. H. Whyte, Jr., *The Organization Man* (New York: Simon and Schuster, 1956).

Because everywhere in the industry buildings are regarded as being essentially different from one another, building craftsmen as a group do not have a mass production outlook in which they view their work as hammering out so many feet of lumber or of connecting miles of pipe. The craftsman regards his activities as special work, and his job as a special order. He is likely to feel that with each new unique job, conditions and technical problems are bound to arise which will make that job different from all others.[21]

How a man feels depends on both the type of work he does and how he is supervised. Mineworkers, truckdrivers, and railroaders all have above-average job satisfaction, which has been explained by "the absense of close supervision" and the fact that "the contact between employees and supervision is so much less than in factory work." [22] Of course, no one can be boss of everything, but within limits an employee can feel that he is his own boss. This is particularly true if he can feel that what he does is determined by the objective requirements of the situation rather than by human orders. (From an objective point of view, the substation operator in a public utility has almost no freedom; he must constantly make adjustments to meet the changing demands for power. Yet he feels quite independent, since he gets his orders from dials rather than from people.)

Many jobs demand such a high degree of teamwork that the individual worker is deprived of all opportunity to make decisions by himself. But in a situation like this it is often practicable to have the decisions made by the group as a whole. *Participation* in decision-making by the group is the equivalent of autonomy for the individual.

KNOWLEDGE

The desire for knowledge is a basic impulse in human beings. People like to know not only "what" is happening to them but "why." They want both to understand the present and to predict the future. Arbitrariness, caprice, and unexpected events all make it hard for us to fashion an orderly, reasonable explanation of the events that shape our lives. To be at the mercy of people and forces that we can neither understand nor control is a serious threat to our sense of security. Take, for example, the unrest that prevails in a shop after a familiar, well-known supervisor is replaced by a new man with unknown preferences, attitudes, and idiosyncrasies.

People want to know about things that are directly important to them, and also about those that are not. Satisfying idle curiosity is a way of spending one's time. The village busybody and the bored receptionist have nothing better to do than to pry into other people's business. The desire for information is so strong that if the truth is not available, appropriate substitutes will be fashioned.

The quest for knowledge has more constructive elements as well. Many

[21] Richard R. Myers, *The Building Trades Workers, A Study of an Industrial Sub-Culture* (Unpublished Ph.D. thesis, University of Michigan, Ann Arbor, Michigan, 1945), pp. 42-43.
[22] Blauner, *op. cit.*, p. 348.

people find that learning gives them a sense of achievement. Being an expert on something—whether it is baseball, trout flies, the fine points of one's job, or the ramifications of union politics—gives the individual a sense of uniqueness and progress.

Relative Importance of Various Needs

Obviously, all the previously mentioned needs are important, but which is most important? Which can be used most effectively to motivate employees to work for organizational objectives?

This question has been the subject of extensive research.[23] The answer has been found to vary with the individual concerned, his job, the general economic climate, and a host of other factors. Several generalizations seem to be at least partly valid, however, as we shall discuss below.

NEEDS HIERARCHY

According to one hypothesis,[24] human needs can be ordered into a hierarchy, with physical needs being the "lowest" and most basic, followed, in ascending order, by security, social, egoistic, and self-actualization[25] needs. In this hierarchy, a higher, less basic need does not provide motivation unless all lower, more basic needs are satisfied; but once a lower-level need is satisfied, it no longer motivates.

Thus, once physical needs for food, clothing, and shelter are reasonably well satisfied, individuals become relatively more concerned with other needs. First, they seek to satisfy their safety or security needs for protection against danger, threats, and deprivation. (As we have seen, physical and safety needs are usually satisfied through pay, seniority, fringe benefits, and the like.) When the standard of living rises so that security is assured, then social needs take first priority, followed by egoistic needs. Finally, according to this hypothesis, only when most of the less pressing needs are satisfied will individuals turn to the ultimate form of accomplishment, self-actualization, which has been described as "the desire to become . . . everything that one is capable of becoming," to make the very most of one's potentialities.[26]

The message for management in this theory is that as long as employees' lower-order needs are unsatisfied, it will be difficult to motivate them with

---

[23] For one comprehensive survey, see Fredrick Herzberg, Bernard Mausner, R. Peterson, and Dora Capwell, *Job Attitudes: A Review of Research and Opinion* (Pittsburgh: Psychological Service of Pittsburgh, 1957).

[24] This hypothesis has been developed at length by A. H. Maslow, *Motivation and Personality* (New York: Harper & Row, 1954), chapters 6-8.

[25] In our discussion of needs in the previous section we have not included self-actualization as a separate need largely because we find it difficult to distinguish this need from such egoistic needs as accomplishment.

[26] A. H. Maslow, "A Theory of Human Motivation," *Psychological Review*, Vol. 50 (July 1943), p. 372.

those of a higher order. But once those lower needs *are* reasonably well satisfied, management will have to shift its emphasis to the higher needs if it is to provide continued motivation.

This point is nicely illustrated by two studies of job satisfaction. In an investigation in Nashua, New Hampshire, workers were asked why they wanted to stay on their present job and were requested to list any reasons why they might like to leave it.[27] In a similar study in New Haven, Connecticut, workers were asked to give the reasons why they were satisfied or dissatisfied with their present work.[28] Notice in the chart that the relative importance of the various needs was the same whether the workers were responding in terms of staying or quitting, or in terms of being satisfied or dissatisfied. But between the groups

---

[27] Charles A. Myers and George P. Shultz, *The Dynamics of a Labor Market* (Englewood Cliffs, N.J.: Prentice-Hall, 1951), pp. 130-131.

[28] Lloyd G. Reynolds and Joseph Shister, *Job Horizons* (New York: Harper & Row, 1949).

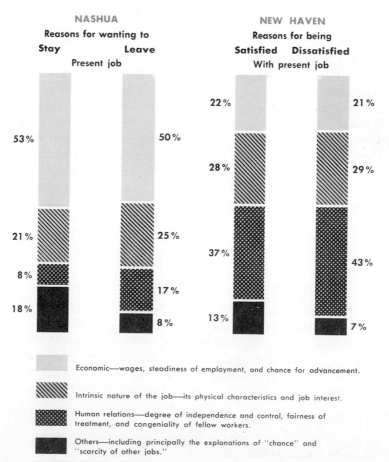

Relative importance of various reasons for job satisfaction (or dissatisfaction) as reported by two studies.

there was a significant difference. In Nashua, half the workers emphasized economic reasons; in New Haven, only about one-quarter of them did. Why such a difference?

The answer can be found in the economic conditions existing in the two communities when the studies were made. New Haven was enjoying a period of full employment when jobs were plentiful and minimum economic needs were being met. Consequently, social and psychological factors gained importance. In Nashua there was substantial unemployment, created by the closing of a large textile plant. In effect, the men here were saying, "Better a bad job than no job at all."

> The attractiveness of any one job factor (such as wages) . . . , is a consequence of the extent to which other job satisfactions or expectations are being fulfilled at the time. When a worker enjoys a steady job paying good wages, he is understandably more concerned about the treatment he gets from his supervisors, the degree of independence and control he has on the job, and whether the job is interesting. But when he loses his high-paid job he is more concerned about regaining steady, well-paid employment.[29]

The needs-hierarchy hypothesis has been subjected to a good deal of criticism. The two most telling points are the following:

1. People seem to differ greatly in the extent to which a need must be satisfied before they are willing to move on to a higher level. Furthermore, for some people egoistic needs may be more basic than social ones. A scientist's physical needs, for example, may be very easily satisfied, his social needs may be minimal, and his consuming passion for research may involve egoistic and self-actualizing needs. By forcing the facts, one might say that the scientist conforms to the needs hierarchy, but doing so does not help us understand his behavior.

2. As we have seen, the various categories of need overlap, and a given need may be fitted into more than one category. Money is perhaps the most important single source of need satisfaction; yet depending on the circumstances, it may satisfy any of the needs listed.

For all these reasons, it is very hard to put the hypothesis in operational form and to test whether or not it is true. Yet, despite its limitations it does present some useful insights into human behavior. Other factors must also be considered, however.

Opportunities for satisfaction. People strive to satisfy needs only to the extent that there is a reasonable chance of success. Needs that are already being satisfied or that are impossible to satisfy do not seem important. For example, when a group of hospital doctors were asked what they wanted most from their jobs, they mentioned prestige and advancement.[30] What about their sense of accomplishment in curing the sick? That was taken for granted. In general, the

---

29 Myers and Shultz, *op. cit.,* pp. 132-133.

30 We are indebted to Temple Burling, Edith Lentz, and Robert Wilson, who permitted us to read the interview notes collected in a study published as *The Give and Take in Hospitals* (New York: Putnam, 1956).

motivations reported were more self-centered than idealistic. Hospital maids, on the other hand, emphasized the satisfactions they derived from helping people. Why? The maid's job in itself has little prestige—but she does work for the hospital and that does have prestige. Cleaning rooms requires little skill, but the maid derives a feeling of accomplishment from her work because it obviously helps the patients. The important point, then, is what needs workers feel they can satisfy in the present situation, not what they might want in a totally different situation.

Substitution of one need for another.   To some extent, people will give up one source of need satisfaction for another. Once job security is obtained, workers will accept loss of social and egoistic satisfaction only in return for a significant increase in pay.[31] Conversely, many will accept lower wages in return for a more desirable job. As one worker put it:

> "Sure this job doesn't pay much. But nobody pushes you and you are your own boss. I could get more in the mills, but I would hate myself for doing it: push, push, and bosses. Life is too short. I like the guys here."

Role of money.   Management is sometimes deceived by workers' demands for money, because money has many meanings in terms of need satisfaction. If we looked solely at union demands on management and at the overt causes of strikes, we might well conclude that workers were interested in money alone. Yet, as we have seen, this is not the whole picture.

There are two reasons for this overemphasis. In the first place, workers may regard higher earnings as a partial compensation for the lack of other forms of need satisfaction. Second, money has a symbolic value. Money earnings are tangible; psychic earnings are not. If one is going to gripe, one seizes on something tangible to gripe about. Dissatisfaction with the job in general is often semiconscious and hard to put into words. If workers went to the boss demanding that he provide them with more interesting work, they would feel pretty foolish; but a demand for an increase of 10 cents an hour can be put in writing.

From the union's point of view, of course, the size of the pay check is a measure of the union's strength and the officers' bargaining skill. Wage improvements can be obtained for everyone at one fell swoop around the bargaining table, but the union can improve human relations only piece-meal through the grievance procedure.

Relationship among needs.   The types of satisfactions emphasized by various occupational groups will vary, depending on what opportunities for satisfaction are available to them, what they have come to expect, and which needs have already been satisfied.[32] Attitude surveys suggest that unskilled blue-

---

[31] The overwhelming majority of employees in an automotive assembly plant indicated that they liked their pay but disliked the job as such. They took the job only for the extra income. Walker and Guest, *op. cit.*, p. 143.

[32] See, for example, Elizabeth L. Lyman, "Occupational Differences in the Value Attached to Work," *American Journal of Sociology*, Vol. 55, No. 2 (September 1955), pp. 138-144;

collar workers, who have relatively little chance for autonomy or advancement, give relatively strong emphasis to job security and physical working conditions. Craft workers emphasize the *kind* of work they do, while white-collar workers are more likely to mention autonomy and the nature of their job. Service workers stress the social satisfactions derived from the people they work with and meet. Accountants have relatively less opportunity for being creative on their jobs than do engineers, whereas engineers, in many cases, are concerned with looking well in the eyes of their colleagues. Thus, we should not be surprised that one study shows engineers to be relatively more concerned with achievement, and accountants with advancement.[33] Along the same lines, another finds that "managers mention salary much more frequently than do professsionals . . . who stress the content of the job itself." [34] In a government laboratory, "junior investigators," who had college degrees, were relatively more interested in egoistic, on-the-job satisfactions than were laboratory technicians, who did slightly less skilled work and did not have degrees.[35] Interestingly, the junior investigators gave relatively little emphasis to advancement unless they had been denied promotion; then advancement became a primary goal for them. Finally, we have a study of executives which indicates that although executives at all levels are relatively well satisfied with their job security, lower-level executives are considerably more dissatisfied with their opportunities for autonomy and creativity than are those further up the ladder.[36]

How Important Is Job Satisfaction?

How important is it for any individual to have satisfying work? This question can be divided into two parts: (1) What does dissatisfying work do to the individual? And (2) what does it do to organizational efficiency and productivity? We shall deal briefly with the first question here. The second question will be discussed in later chapters, particularly Chapter 6.

The question of what role work plays in human life is a concern not only of management. It is a psychological, philosophical, moral, and even theological question, one about which scholars have debated endlessly. There is no clear answer, but let us state some of the issues in terms of a debate.[37]

Nancy Morse and Robert S. Weiss, "The Function and Meanings of Work and the Job," *American Sociological Review*, Vol. 20, No. 2 (April 1955), pp. 191-198; Blauner, *op. cit.*

[33] Fredrick Herzberg, Bernard Mausner, and Barbara Snyderman, *The Motivation to Work* (New York: Wiley, 1959).

[34] Morse and Weiss, *op. cit.*, p. 197.

[35] Stephen T. Boggs, "The Value of Laboratory Workers," *Human Organization*, Vol. 22, No. 3 (Fall 1963), pp. 207-215.

[36] Lyman W. Porter, *Organizational Patterns of Managerial Job Attitudes* (New York: American Foundation for Management Research, 1964).

[37] For a more complete statement of the debate, see George Strauss, "Notes on Power Equalization," in Harold Leavitt, ed., *The Social Science of Organizations* (Englewood Cliffs, N.J.: Prentice-Hall, 1963), pp. 45-57.

THE CASE FOR WORK BEING VERY IMPORTANT

One group argues that mature human beings require high levels of egoistic and self-actualizing need-satisfaction from their jobs. The process of growing up involves accepting more and more challenge and autonomy and becoming more independent. Those who do not have these opportunities (in particular those who are unable to express themselves meaningfully through work) never reach psychological maturity.[38] Since the average man spends nearly a third of his waking hours on the job, if that job does not provide challenge and autonomy he may suffer real frustration, with results that are costly both to himself and his employer. Thus, the fact that many individuals have boring, meaningless jobs may lead to severe social problems.

Indeed, the very act of working satisfies basic human needs. In a survey of work attitudes, a highly affirmative response was given by all occupations and brackets polled. Eighty per cent of those employees questioned in the survey replied that they would continue to work even if they "inherited enough money to live comfortably without working." [39] "Working gives them a feeling of being tied into the larger society, of having something to do, of having a purpose in life." [40] The existence of the Peace Corps suggests that many seek meaning in their work and, indeed, through their work may seek a meaning in life.

The importance of work in modern life is indicated by the impact of unemployment and retirement on persons who have been active and productive for decades.[41] Unless the retired employee can find some other kind of work (a hobby, for instance), the psychological effects of idleness may be extremely upsetting. All of us have heard comments of this sort: "After Dad was pensioned off he just fell apart. He didn't know what to do with himself." Unemployment can be even more demoralizing.

Recent evidence suggests that workers on unskilled (and presumably boring) jobs are significantly more likely to suffer from personality disturbances (as measured by interviews) and psychosomatic illnesses (as measured by dispensary visits) than are skilled workers.[42] Individuals who move from unskilled

---

[38] For a classical statement, see Chris Argyris, *Personality and Organization* (New York: Harper & Row, 1957). A later extension of this work is Chris Argyris, *Integrating the Individual and the Organization* (New York: Wiley, 1964).

[39] Morse and Weiss, *op. cit.*, p. 192 and p. 197. Interestingly, a substantial proportion (though not a majority) of middle-class employees mentioned "interest in work" and "accomplishment" as reasons for wanting to keep on working; by contrast blue-collar workers emphasized the importance of "keeping occupied."

[40] *Ibid.*, p. 191.

[41] W. Wight Bakke, *Citizens Without Work* (New Haven: Yale University Press, 1940); Eugene A. Friedmann and Robert J. Havighurst, *The Meaning of Work and Retirement* (Chicago: University of Chicago Press, 1954).

[42] Arthur Kornhauser and Otto M. Reid, *Mental Health of the Industrial Worker: A Detroit Study* (New York: Wiley, 1965); John R. P. French, Robert L. Kahn, and Floyd Mann, eds., "Work, Health and Satisfaction," *Journal of Social Issues*, Vol. 18, No. 3 (July 1962).

to skilled work tend to become better adjusted after the move, and vice versa.

In addition, as we shall discuss in later chapters, low morale and poor motivation may lead to inefficiency and low productivity. In sum, so the argument runs, the existence of unrewarding jobs creates an unhealthy situation, which is harmful to the individual, to the organization which employs him, and to society generally.

THE CASE FOR JOB SATISFACTION NOT BEING IMPORTANT

The opposing argument is that many people adjust easily to dull work. They center life away from the job, expect relatively few satisfactions from it, and so are not disappointed when it offers them little in the way of challenge or sense of creativity.[43] Indeed, some suggest that many people would not want a high level of challenge and autonomy on the job, even were it available. Possibly such individuals are immature, but their immaturity is due far more to family environment than to the job; they have learned to be dependent in childhood, and are unlikely to change this pattern in later life. (See Chapters 6 and 7.)

It is claimed that most of the evidence designed to show the importance of need satisfaction is misleading, showing in fact that in our culture people want *some* sort of job (and preferably one with high status) but not that the job itself must provide higher orders of satisfaction.

According to some studies, retirement in itself does not bring on the rapid deterioration of physical and mental health as was once supposed; health tends to improve after retirement.[44] Further, evidence on the impact of unskilled work on mental health is still incomplete. Apparently, not everyone suffers equally from unskilled work, and some adjust more easily than others. And it is not clear whether mental ill health results from the intrinsic nature of unskilled work or from the fact that such work pays poorly and has low status both off and on the job.[45] Insofar as mental disturbances are caused by economic and social pressures at home, higher wages may be a better solution than improved satisfaction on the job.

---

[43] Lower-class people "tend to accept the unpleasantness of work in order to bring home a pay check. Work is not enjoyable nor is it supposed to be." Argyris, *Integrating the Individual and the Organization,* p. 79.

[44] W. E. Thompson and G. F. Streib, "Situational Determinants: Health and Economic Deprivation in Retirement," *Journal of Social Issues,* Vol. 14, No. 2 (April 1958), pp. 18-34.

[45] In fact, a hasty glance at the research in this field [for example, see Stanislov V. Kasl and John R. P. French, "The Effects of Occupational Status on Physical and Mental Health," *Journal of Social Issues,* Vol. 18, No. 3 (July 1962), pp. 67-89; and Victor H. Vroom and Norman R. F. Maier, "Industrial Social Psychology," in Paul Farnsworth, ed., *Annual Review of Psychology* (Palo Alto: Annual Reviews, 1960)] makes it abundantly clear that unskilled workers are not the only ones to suffer from poor mental health. Depending on which study one looks at or what mental health index is used, one can conclude that executives, clerical personnel, salespeople, and lower-level supervisors *all* suffer from below-average mental health. The evidence makes one sympathize with the old Quaker who said, "All the world is queer except me and thee, and sometimes I suspect thee."

Attitude surveys suggest that most people expect relatively little from work, and so adjust rather easily—though professionals and executives, whose work is more satisfying, find such adjustment easier than do factory workers.[46] Thus, a typical poll, taken by *Fortune* in 1957, indicated that even among factory workers 54 per cent found their jobs interesting (compared to 94 per cent among professionals and executives and 72 per cent among salaried employees).[47] On the other hand, other studies suggest that the proportion of those who would choose the same kind of work if they were beginning their career again varied from 91 per cent among mathematicians and 82 per cent among journalists to 52 per cent among skilled printers and 16 per cent among unskilled autoworkers. In other words, workers in general seem to have adjusted to their present jobs, though many would prefer other kinds of work, were it available.

Ideally, it would be better if everyone could lead a fully satisfying life, both on and off the job. Possibly job satisfaction would be greater were we to return to the idyllic preindustrial conditions pictured at the beginning of this chapter —if, for example, cars were made on a handcraft basis rather than on an assembly line. But the cost of doing so would be the abandonment of our modern technological efficiency and a substantial reduction in our standard of living. Few would be willing to pay this price. Or so the argument runs.

WORK AND LEISURE

Perhaps the issues will seem less confused if we step back and examine them from both a historical and a cultural viewpoint. Remember that our present attitude toward work is culturally based. Work has not always been so important as it is today, nor is it likely to be so important in the future. In centuries past, particularly when civilization was flourishing in Greece and Rome, work did not occupy an exalted position. In fact, those of higher social status did not expect to work, for work was primarily restricted to slaves and to free citizens who lacked independent resources.

During the Protestant Reformation, work took on many religious connotations. Work was clearly a duty, a duty to fulfill one's predestined "calling." It was also regarded as an ordained punishment for the sins of man. To fail to work was immoral. Our present feeling about the idle—that they are somehow not behaving morally—is a reflection of this religious emphasis. To maintain respect in our society, rich men must work.

---

[46] The discussion which follows is adapted from Robert Blauner, "Work Satisfaction and Industrial Trends in Modern Society," Walter Galenson and S. M. Lipset, eds., *Labor and Trade Unionism* (New York: Wiley, 1960).

[47] Another major study concludes, "The distribution of alienation and freedom in the typical score card [of the typical workers] is probably consonant with the values and aspirations of the blue-collar labor force today." Blauner, *Alienation and Freedom*, p. 183. Another study suggests, however, that since white-collar workers start out with much higher levels of expectations than do blue-collar workers, white-collar workers end up feeling more frustrated. G. Gurin *et al.*, *Americans View Their Mental Health* (New York: Basic Books, 1960).

Today, attitudes toward work differ greatly among occupational groups. For some, "work has now become the main business of life" [48] and the chief function of recreation is to recuperate to do more work. Certainly many professionals and executives feel this way. Indeed, some corporations seem to feel that their executives should behave as "Organization Men" twenty-four hours a day. But the central focus of other people's lives is not the job (which is merely a "way of getting a living") but the home or community. Such people find a large measure of challenge, creativity, and autonomy in raising a family, pursuing a hobby, or taking part in community affairs. An eminent sociologist concluded: [49]

> Work, for probably a majority of workers, and even extending into management, may represent an institutional setting that is not the central life interest of the participants. The consequence of this is that while participating in work a general attitude of apathy and indifference prevails. . . . Thus the industrial worker does not feel imposed upon by the tyranny of organizations, company or union.

Further, in many occupations people spend less time on the job today than in the past. A half-century ago the six-day week (for, in some instances, ten to twelve hours a day) was the rule, and vacations and holidays were far from common. Today few people work more than five days a week, and the average worker has at least a two-week vacation and perhaps eight paid holidays a year. Not far over the horizon is the 30-hour, four-day week (already the New York City electricians' contract calls for a 25-hour week), while the Steelworkers' union may be establishing a new trend through negotiating a 13-week "sabbatical" for its members every five years.[50] In addition, our life span grows longer while the retirement age tends to come earlier. All these influences are eroding the key position held by work in our daily lives.

A recent study which summarizes trends throughout the world predicts that work in the future will become increasingly routine and provide fewer and fewer opportunities for creativity and discretion.[51] On the other hand, as working hours grow shorter, there will be a new "bohemianism" off the job as people seek self-expression away from work.

> Leisure will be the happy hunting ground of the independent spirit . . . The new slavery to technology may bring a new dedication to diversity and individualism off the job.[52]

---

48 Charles R. Walker, *Modern Technology and Civilization* (New York: McGraw-Hill, 1962), p. 439.

49 Robert Dubin, "Industrial Relations Research and the Discipline of Sociology," *Proceedings of the 11th Annual Meeting* (Madison: Industrial Relations Research Association, 1959).

50 On the other hand, there are large numbers of moonlighters who seem to prefer work and its monetary rewards to leisure.

51 Clark Kerr, John T. Dunlop, Frederick H. Harbison, and Charles A. Myers, *Industrialism and Industrial Man* (New York: Oxford, 1964).

52 *Ibid.,* pp. 237-238.

From such predictions, some conclude that perhaps the best use of our resources is to accelerate automation, shorten the work week as fast as possible, forget about on-the-job satisfactions, and concentrate our energies on making leisure more meaningful.

Others argue that it is impossible to compartmentalize work and leisure activities and that expanded leisure activities will never substitute for what is missing on the job. Indeed, it is suggested that work routines spill over into leisure routines, and that those who have routine jobs tend to engage in passive, routine types of recreation.[53]

Nevertheless, the line between work and nonwork activities is drawn much sharper today than it ever was in the past. Prior to large-scale commuting, people lived and played with the same people they worked with, and a whole series of ceremonies and other social activities tended to integrate work, family, and community life into a seamless web. In those days, people felt little need to "get away" from work (and, of course, less opportunity to do so). Today, since work and play occupy separate spheres in our lives, we feel under pressure to decide which is most important.

Summary of the Argument

JOB SATISFACTION IMPORTANT	JOB SATISFACTION UNIMPORTANT
1. People want self-actualization.	Some people prefer unchallenging work.
2. Those who don't obtain job satisfaction never reach psychological maturity.	Individual personality becomes fixed before people start working. Work is not to blame.
3. Those who fail to obtain job satisfaction become frustrated.	Most people have relatively low levels of aspiration for job satisfaction and expect only routine work.
4. The job is central to man's life.	This is a professor's value. Many people focus their lives on family and community.
5. Those without work are unhappy. People want to work even when they don't have to.	Even though there are social pressures to have *a* job, this does not mean the job must be challenging, etc.
6. Lack of challenging work leads to low mental health.	Poor mental health may be due to low income or low status of routine jobs. Anyway, research findings are not conclusive.
7. Work and leisure patterns spill into each other. Those with uncreative jobs engage in uncreative recreation.	A new bohemianism off the job will make up for increasing boredom at work.
8. Lack of job satisfaction and alienation from work lead to lower morale, lower productivity, and an unhealthy society.	We can provide challenging work for everybody only at the cost of eliminating our mass production technology and high standard of living—and society is unwilling to pay this price.

---

[53] Eric Fromm, *The Sane Society* (New York: Holt, Rinehart and Winston, 1955), p. 136.

Conclusion

Management can do its job only through motivating people to work for management's objectives. But it is impossible to understand motivation without considering what people want and expect from their jobs.

Since people spend about a third of their waking hours at work, it is not surprising that they should expect work to satisfy many sorts of needs—physical, social and egoistic—and that, further, these needs may be satisfied in a wide variety of ways—off the job, around the job, and through the job. Though there is some evidence that these needs can be ranked in a hierarchy, it is fairly clear that the various forms of need satisfaction can be substituted for each other.

There is considerable debate about the importance of satisfaction enjoyed on the job, as opposed to satisfactions derived elsewhere in life. Professors (and they are the ones who do most of the writing in this field) in general place high value on autonomy, creativity, and the quest for maximum self-development. As much as any other group in society, their existence is work-oriented; for them creative achievement is an end in itself and requires no further justification. As a consequence, they are inclined to equate true happiness with interesting work and assume that everyone should be as work-involved as professors are. Perhaps those professors who give such a major role for job satisfaction are right—but the case is not black-and-white.

As for the present authors, we hold a middle-of-the-road position. A man's work is one of the most important (if not the most important) activities in his life. Those who do not have satisfying jobs rarely have fully satisfying lives. As we shall discuss in future chapters, dissatisfying work can lead in many (but not all) circumstances to lower production and friction on the job, so that it may be in management's economic interest to reduce such dissatisfaction. But even where this is not true, management has a certain degree of social responsibility (as we shall discuss in our concluding chapter) to provide work opportunities which are psychologically meaningful. Regardless, we must bear in mind that work is not man's only objective, nor is work satisfaction the sole objective of management.

A safe conclusion is that people differ not only in the importance they assign to work but also, as we shall discuss in Chapters 2 and 3, that jobs differ themselves in the types of satisfactions they offer.

P R O B L E M

Engineering Construction Company

This company designs and supervises the erection of chemical and petroleum processing plants. It employs a large number of engineers with college degrees, most of whom work in the Field Division or the Drafting Division.

The approximately 1000 engineers in the Field Division supervise the erection of plants throughout the world. As of 1956 (the date of this case), new college graduates received $425 a month. After five years they might reasonably expect $800 a month; after 20 years, $1500. However, few reach these higher salaries. By the end of two years over half have either quit or been discharged. Top management engages in frequent purges, weeding out those it thinks are incompetent. Fierce competition is encouraged for the top jobs. Men are often transferred from one part of the country to another with as little as one week's notice, a policy that creates particular hardships for children who must be constantly uprooted from school. Working conditions on the job are usually poor, with wind, rain, heat, and cold being common.

The Drafting Division contains approximately 500 graduate engineers. Prior to 1935, when the company was much smaller, high school graduates were hired to do drafting, but during the depression, men with college diplomas could be obtained for very little money and the policy of hiring them was started. Pay starts at $2.90 an hour and reaches $3.85 after two years, the highest drafting pay in the city. No one has been laid off for lack of work since the early depression days and discharges for incompetence are rare. There is one section head for every 20 men (salary $8500). Promotions to this job are normally obtained through seniority.

The drafting work on a single project may take as long as two years to complete, and prior to 1950 each project was given to a small group of men who would work on it from beginning to end. Beginning in 1950, substantial changes were made in organization. Individual offices were eliminated and all operations were placed in one large, well-lighted, air-conditioned room. Each man was given a specialty such as heating or wiring, and work now proceeds from one department to another on an assembly-line basis.

In both divisions liberal vacations, sick leave, and a retirement plan are provided. As yet neither division is unionized.

1. List separately for each division the needs which are and are not satisfied.
2. In which division will the engineers be easiest to unionize?
3. What recommendations would you make to management to improve morale and motivation in each division?

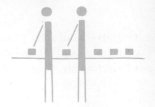

Technology
and Job Satisfaction:
Blue-Collar Work

2

The previous chapter explored what employees want from work and the meaning they give to work. This chapter and the next look at the other side of the coin: the impact of differences in work on employee need satisfaction. Many managers and students err in assuming that, even if individuals differ in their preferences, one job is basically like another or that the only important distinctions are those between managerial and nonmanagerial jobs. In this chapter we shall see first that the technology, or work method, selected by management has an overriding effect on the types of satisfactions and dissatisfactions which employees derive from their jobs. And second, we shall describe the techniques by which employees, given the limits that are set by the methods of production, adapt jobs to make them more compatible to their needs. Management ought to understand both processes. For often, alternative job designs may be possible and an important consideration will be the impact of a given job design on employee attitudes.[1] In addition, managers should anticipate the techniques by which workers seek to improve their work environment.

[1] Some of our analysis is derived from Robert Blauner, *Alienation and Freedom* (Chicago: University of Chicago Press, 1964).

Here we shall deal just with "blue-collar" jobs, those involving manual work, saving the so-called "white-collar" jobs and automation for Chapter 3. We shall contrast two kinds of blue-collar work: (1) craft work (skilled tradesmen) and (2) machine-tending and assembly line (mass-production jobs)—though, of course, most types of work do not fall neatly within one of these categories. For the sake of exposition, we shall compare the extremes and consider how craft and mass production jobs differ in:

1. Interest, variety, and the opportunities for moving around and changing pace.
2. Opportunities to derive a sense of accomplishment (in both psychological and economic terms), of autonomy, and identification with the work.
3. Job pressures and relations with management.
4. Social relations.

These categories, which are related to the physical, egotistic, and social satisfaction discussed in Chapter 1, will become clearer as we observe various examples of men at work.

Craft Work

Craft work has a long history. The term craft work applies to certain tasks that resist mechanization and that require long and arduous training of their practitioners. Craftsmen still predominate in such industries as entertainment, transportation, construction, and printing, to name a few, although they have almost disappeared from many other fields, such as the manufacturing of clothing and glass. Even industrial plants, though, utilize craftsmen in such jobs as maintenance work and model-building.

INTEREST, VARIETY, AND MOVEMENT

The craftsman's job provides abundant variety. Unexpected problems constantly crop up, the solutions to which cannot be programed by management. Thus, the employee must be allowed to choose his tools, methods, and even pace to conform to the ever-changing work requirements *as he sees them.* "Traditional skill thus involves the frequent use of judgment and initiative, aspects of a job which give the worker a feeling of control over his environment." [2]

In addition, unlike most factory workers, craftsmen generally move around a good deal, both to perform widely dispersed jobs and to obtain tools, instructions, materials, or assistance. This ease of movement gives a sense of freedom and diversity (also enjoyed by a salesman or a landscape gardener, both of whom prize their mobility). And since the employee is not "tied" to a machine

---

[2] *Ibid.*, p. 43.

or an assembly line, he can set his own pace. When he must figure out a difficult job problem, he can muse and putter for a time, taking breaks as he sees fit. On the other hand, when the work is going well he can accomplish a great deal quickly, whereby he gains both a little spare time and a sense of competence.

ACCOMPLISHMENT, AUTONOMY, AND IDENTIFICATION

The craftsman has a rich sense of accomplishment; what he has done, he has done for the most part on his own. The machinist can see the model he has built; the plumber can point to his operating sanitary system. Each can be proud not only of his day-to-day work, but also of what he has made of himself. Most skilled jobs require lengthy training. In addition, in most craft work "age-grading," as the anthropologists call it, prevails. That is, an employee gains greater status and recognition with age.

> Because his experience and knowledge accumulates, the old printer at the end of his career maintains his usefulness and is often the most respected man in the shop, unlike the old automobile worker, who may skid to the lowest job in the plant hierarchy.[3]

This sense of accomplishment is enhanced by community recognition. Whereas many factory jobs have no real identity outside the plant, such skills as those of electrician, machinist, and printer are widely recognized as skilled work and thereby accorded a certain status. The extent of craft identification shows itself in stronger loyalty to (and pride in) the trade than to any single employer, especially in industries where work is unstable and employees move from employer to employer.

A craftsman's ego-satisfaction has been well expressed by a toolmaker:

> "As a tool and die maker, I feel that I have ability that the average man don't have. I can look at almost anything even in this room, tell you how it was made, and if I had to turn around and make the dies to duplicate it, I believe I could. I think it's got all other skill trades beat a hundred miles. In the apprenticeship training—you had to spend 9000 hours in the shop, 9000 hours to become a journeyman tool and die maker, and when you get a job say like on a big molding die, where you've already put say four or five hundred dollars in it, just one slip and it's wrecked, so you got to stop and think. Got to make sure you know what you're doing, and you don't want nobody bothering you when you're doing it. You got to be in good frame of mind, and I believe that when . . . you get the job done, why, you gotta pat yourself on the back. . . ."[4]

JOB PRESSURES AND RELATIONS TO MANAGEMENT

There is a counterbalance to work autonomy—responsibility. Since a craftsman works on his own in a relatively unprogramed fashion, he can be held responsible for mistakes—from leaky plumbing to a wrecked train! Much anxiety

---

[3] *Ibid.*, p. 53.

[4] Eli Ginzberg and Hyman Berman, *The American Worker In The Twentieth Century* (New York: The Free Press of Glencoe, 1963).

can be generated by a job: "... where you've already put say four or five hundred dollars in it [meaning hours of labor], just one slip and it's wrecked ..." Of course, the ability to take pressures is a source of pride.

Management can have trouble in supervising craftsmen. Such men feel they know how their job should be done and are therefore reluctant to accept very much direction. They resist being rushed or taking short cuts that violate their conception of correct method. This resistance to close supervision is often reinforced by strong craft unions that have their own work rules (which management is pressured to accept).

This arrangement reverses the traditional situation in which management imposes its rules on the worker. However, well-trained craftsmen who identify with their craft may require less supervision. They are used to accepting responsibility and being held accountable.

Their independence is furthered by management's recognition that craft skills are scarce and that craftsmen cannot easily be replaced by a more compliant employee. Knowing and controlling the work, the methods, the pace, and the tools, the employee is not likely to feel dominated by management.

In short, craftsmen generally feel secure. Their only serious fears arise from economic instabilities and the threats of massive technological change which will render their skills obsolete (for example, computers that will do typesetting).

SOCIAL RELATIONS

Though craftsmen typically work alone or with a single helper, they identify with fellow employees who share the same training and job experiences. If you visit a construction site during work breaks, you will see clusters of men from a single craft swapping stories of job problems met and conquered and sharing "tricks of the trade." Off-the-job social groups often consist of men who share a common trade. Where the craft involves unusual working hours (as with many newspaper printers or theatrical entertainers) almost all off-the-job friends may be fellow craftsmen (who share the same work schedules). These social groupings reinforce craft identification and are a significant source of job satisfaction. At the same time, the minimal need for interaction on the job, the relative autonomy of the craftsman, also makes it easier to get along with one's fellow workers.

SUMMARY

One study of the craftsman's world concludes:

> When work provides opportunities for control, meaning, and self expression, it becomes an end itself, rather than simply a means to live. ... Work for craft printers is a source of involvement and commitment. ... It is almost the expression of an inner need rather than the grudging payment of a debt imposed by external sources.[5]

---

[5] Blauner, *op. cit.*, p. 53 and p. 56.

Machine-Tending and Assembling

Many blue-collar workers are machine-tenders or assemblers. Machine-tenders watch and facilitate the operation of semi-automatic equipment; assemblers combine parts by hand or with small tools. Assemblers are often tied together by a moving belt; each takes the partly completed work of the preceding worker as it comes to him on the line, attaches additional parts, and replaces the unit on the line for passage to the next work station.

The way these jobs are now performed has been influenced by the scientific-management movement, best typified by the recommendations of its chief proponent, Frederick Taylor. Taylor believed in: (1) high specialization—breaking down jobs into very small parts, and (2) specifying in advance exactly how the job should be done—in a sense separating the physical work from the thinking. Taylor also favored payment by results or piece work. As Taylor himself put it:

> Each man must learn how to give up his own particular way of doing things, adapt his methods to the many new standards, and grow accustomed to receiving and obeying directions covering details, large and small, which in the past have been left to his individual judgment.[6]

This is what is now called "programing," and it is the primary characteristic of *mass-production* technology.

We shall talk about the impact of specialization on organizational structure later. Now we want to see what effect the Taylor movement and accompanying mass-production mechanization had on employee attitudes toward their jobs.

INTEREST, VARIETY, AND MOVEMENT

Machine-tending and assembly jobs provide little opportunity for initiative, ingenuity, and variability. By means of engineering studies, management carefully predetermines the exact motions and pace for each employee. This procedure insures that the work will be done quickly in a uniform, predictable fashion, and precisely coordinated with other jobs. The employee is confined to a fixed work station and is expected to leave it only with permission. What effects will such restrictions have on a man's attitude toward his job?

Short job cycle.   An important determinant of job satisfaction is the length of the job cycle: how long it takes to perform a job operation before having to start it all over again. For a college professor the work cycle may be a semester; for a skilled craftsman, if may be several days or weeks. But for the man on a machine or assembly line the work cycle may last less than a minute. At the extreme, he may be simply tightening one or two bolts. Then he has to repeat the same cycle over and over again, with a deadening lack of variety.

---

[6] Frederick W. Taylor, *Shop Management* (New York: Harper, 1919), p. 113.

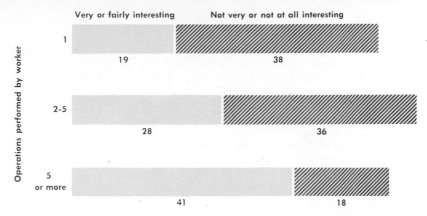

	Very or fairly interesting	Not very or not at all interesting
1	19	38
2-5	28	36
5 or more	41	18

Operations performed by worker

Number of workers reporting on job

Correlation between job interest and job complexity on an automobile assembly line.

"The job gets so sickening—day in and day out plugging in ignition wires. I get through with one motor, turn around, and there's another staring me in the face. It is sickening." [7]

On jobs of this sort all mental challenge has been eliminated, and in most cases only a few muscles are involved. Life seems one endless procession of bolts to tighten. A study of the automobile assembly line found a high correlation between the number of operations a worker's job called for and his level of interest in his job.[8] (See chart above.)

In this same study, employees who worked off the assembly line remarked frequently about how much better their jobs were. For example: [9]

"I move a few cars around. I perform quite a few things actually. That's enough variety to satisfy me. It's not like turning a screw all day on the production line."

Inability to control pace. Although some of these jobs allow an employee to stop and start machines, most give him little control over the work pace. For instance, in a textile factory the employee may tend dozens of machines which function automatically. He moves from one to another as they require attention: the mending of a break in the yarn, a maladjustment, the need for new supplies, and so on. His pace is a function of the number and type of machines he has been assigned and the frequency with which his particular skills are required, all of which depend on the engineering of the job—over which he has no control.

The most extreme example of machine control of work pace, of course, is the assembly line. Listen to this auto worker describe his job: [10]

"My job is to weld the cowl to the metal underbody. I take a job off the bench, put it in place, and weld the parts together. The job is all made up and

---

[7] Charles R. Walker and Robert Guest, *The Man on the Assembly Line* (Cambridge: Harvard University Press, 1952), p. 55.

[8] *Ibid.*, p. 54.

[9] *Ibid.*, p. 56.

[10] Ginzberg and Berman, *op. cit.*, p. 77.

the welds are made in set places along the metal. Exactly twenty-five spots. The line runs according to schedule. Takes me one minute and fifty-two seconds for each job. I walk along the line as it moves. Then I snap the job off, walk back down the line, throw it on the bench, grab another just in time to start on the next car. The cars differ, but it's practically the same thing. Finish one— then have another one staring me in the face.

During each day I get a chance for a breather ten minutes in the morning, then a half-hour for lunch, then a few minutes in the afternoon. When I'm working there is not much chance to get a breather. Sometimes the line breaks down. When it does we all yell "Whoopee." As long as the line keeps moving I've got to keep up with it."

Research indicates that workers grow less fatigued and enjoy their work more when they can work at their own rhythm,[11] avoiding abrupt movements and jerky stops and starts. Everyone has a natural tempo at which he works best. Some will be quite happy on a job on which they work relatively fast; others find it impossible to maintain a fast pace.

Before the industrial revolution, work songs were a popular device for establishing a recurrent, rhythmic work pace. In the medieval world, for instance, weavers "were well known by the name of *Lollards*, because, in fact, while working they 'lolled' (mumbled), singing some cradle song in a low voice."[12] Sea shanties and marching songs are still part of our folk lore, though they are seldom used for their original purpose. These rhythms have an effect similar to that of a "pacer" in racing. Here and there we still find work chants, even in modern industry. In mass-production work, however, the relentless rhythm of the assembly makes such natural pacing difficult or impossible.

Most people also like to vary their work rhythm; they may work fast for a while, and then slow down gradually as the day wears on. This variety in pace helps to reduce both fatigue and boredom on the job. The assembly line, however, makes no provision for the preference of individual workers. It sets the pace for him and never lets him change it. Thus the machine may be a worse autocrat than any foreman.

Fortunately, on most mass-production jobs workers do have a slight opportunity to vary their pace through "building a bank" or "getting into a hole." On some jobs a worker can hurry up a bit and build up a reserve or "bank" of completed work and then take a break for a few seconds while the work slides by. By pushing 15 seconds ahead and then falling 15 seconds "in a hole," an energetic worker can earn himself a 30-second break.

Limited attention required.   Another factor affecting the degree of satisfaction a worker derives from his work is the amount of attention it requires. A doctor enjoys his work because his job is constantly new and challenging and

---

[11] Georges Friedmann, *Industrial Society* (New York: The Free Press of Glencoe, 1955), p. 159.

[12] Michelet, *Le Peuple,* 2nd ed. (Paris: 1846), pp. 84-85; cited in Friedmann, *op. cit.,* pp. 158-159.

absorbs all his attention. Jobs like this are said to require *depth attention.* At the other extreme are the so-called *no-attention jobs,* which are so routine that the worker's mind is free to wander at will. Dishwashing is an example of such work; so, too, is driving over a straight highway with little traffic. Your mind is a thousand miles away, although subconsciously you are still watching the road.

The least-satisfying of all are jobs that require *surface attention.* Here the worker is obliged to perform a routine, unchallenging chore but at the same time to remain relatively alert. "... The mind, though not wholly absorbed by work, cannot free itself entirely from it." [13] Examples of this sort of work are watching control gauges, inspecting parts, grading exam papers, or adding up columns of figures. These jobs do not provide the challenge, interest, and sense of autonomy provided by depth-attention jobs; nor do they permit the employee to daydream as he can on a no-attention job.

These classifications, of course, are simply points on a continuum, for there are relatively few cases of, say, a purely no-attention job. Further, the attention demanded by a particular job depends largely on the abilities of the individual employee. A very bright employee may find that a job requires only surface attention, while a less able employee may find that the same job requires depth attention. (The implications for employee selection are obvious.)

Similarly, the amount of attention required varies with the worker's experience. Learning a new job always requires depth attention; then for a while only surface attention is needed; and finally, the job may require almost no attention. When you first learn to drive a car, driving demands depth attention. Later you show surface attention. Only when the routine aspects of driving are purely automatic can you be called a good driver. Yet, even for a good driver, maneuvering into a tight parking space calls for depth attention.

As a worker gains experience on a job, a semiconscious monitor seems to take over to sound the alarm when trouble develops. As one girl described her job: "I used to give full attention to the machine. However, now I can tell what is wrong by the sound."

ACCOMPLISHMENT, AUTONOMY, AND IDENTIFICATION

Inadequate sense of accomplishment. "This job is endless. It just goes on and on. You don't feel that you are getting anywhere."

We all feel that we are accomplishing something when we can break our work down into units that can be completed successively. If we have two assignments to complete, we breathe a sigh of relief as soon as we finish one. When we are driving a long distance, we break the trip down into sections and feel great satisfaction as we pass by each check point.

Mass-production work characteristically fails to provide this sense of completion, or even a feeling of progress toward a goal. Each employee does only

---

[13] Friedmann, *op. cit.,* p. 146.

a small, specialized part of the total job. Rarely does he have a chance to look at the finished product and say, "Mine, all mine."

Automobile-assembly-line workers often comment that they would like to do the whole job from beginning to end.[14] Work on the assembly line has been compared with work in a steel tube mill as follows:

> On the assembly line, only a small fraction of the "product" is ever seen or handled by most workers. In the tube mill, the whole product, from billet to finished product, as it moves through a series of machines, is worked on by everyone and can be followed by the eye of the members of the crew. Workers frequently go to the cooling and inspection tables to look over for their own satisfaction the job which they have just done.[15]

As a further drawback, mass-production jobs have titles which lack meaning and status in the community. Who knows what a smash hand or battery filler does? (Jobs in the textile industry.)

Excessive specialization deprives the worker of any real sense of skill. Work that has been so subdivided and simplified that it takes almost no time to learn provides little challenge or interest. The worker has no sense of doing a whole job—he sees only part of the total process—and thus his contribution seems negligible and unimportant. Workers who exercise skill take pride in their achievement, but a man who has learned his job in a few hours knows that he can be replaced by almost anyone who happens along. This is one explanation of the tendency of mass-production workers to exaggerate the complexity of their jobs: It is just too humiliating for them to admit how simple their work actually is.

Walker and Guest found a great deal of dissatisfaction among workers who had a genuine desire to do "quality" work but who were prevented from doing so.[16]

> "I try to do quality work, but I'm too rushed. This keeps me from getting pleasure from the work. They say 'haste makes waste,' and they're getting plenty of both."

By contrast, workers who could fulfill their desire for "quality" expressed considerable satisfaction with their work:

> "You can take time to get quality. It's not like on the line when you have to rush so much. And I get work satisfaction. It makes me feel good when I put in a good day's work and get no kickbacks."

Lack of autonomy.   Mass-production workers have little sense of autonomy. We have already spoken of the desire of most employees to be their own boss, to exercise some control over the work situation. Yet opportunities for

---

14 Walker and Guest, *op. cit.*, pp. 154-155.

15 Charles R. Walker, "Work Methods, Working Conditions, and Morale," in Arthur Kornhauser, Robert Dubin, and Arthur Ross, eds., *Industrial Conflict* (New York: McGraw-Hill, 1954), pp. 353-354.

16 Walker and Guest, *op. cit.*, p. 55.

discretion and judgment, or even for determining one's work methods, are at a minimum in mass-production work.

There is an implicit assumption in specialization that some people will do the thinking and others the work. As Henry Ford put it, "The average worker, I am sorry to say, wants a job on which he does not have to put forth much physical energy—above all, he wants a job on which he does not have to think." [17] But this approach to what the "average worker" wants has been criticized as destructive of morale and wasteful of human abilities:

> Scientific management has failed to utilize properly the greatest resource at its command: the complex and multiple capacities of people. On the contrary . . . it has deliberately sought to utilize as narrow a band of personality and as narrow a range of ability as ingenuity could devise. The process has been fantastically wasteful for industry and society.[18]

It should be noted, however, and we shall return to this point later, that workers differ in their desire to exercise skill and autonomy. Some have no desire for creative challenge on the job—they are happy enough to daydream. Others are deeply disturbed because their work provides so little interest and meaning.

Little opportunity for advancement.   One of the significant dissatisfactions associated with most factory jobs is the inability to advance. For one thing there are few promotional steps open; most jobs in the factory require almost the same skill level and provide almost the same pay. Thus, the semiskilled factory worker has to satisfy the need for a sense of advancement very differently from the craftsman.

> The worker learns to set bounds to occupational ambitions. If in his early years he had any illusions about a rapid rise to independence and wealth, these hopes soon wither before the realities of industrial employment. He learns to limit his aspirations to modest and attainable objectives: a change from a second shift, from hourly rated work to incentive work, from a job in labor grade "7" to labor grade "8," or even to another job in the same labor grade which is more desirable for one reason or another. Beyond this most workers have little expectance of going.[19]

Many younger men start to work on an unskilled job expecting that it will be only temporary; they hope to earn a little money and perhaps buy a car, but one day they expect to go to college or start a business of their own. As they get caught up in marriage, family, and mortgages, however, their dreams begin to fade away.[20] Gradually they come to accept their limitations.

[17] Henry Ford, *My Life and Work* (New York: Doubleday, 1922), p. 22.
[18] James C. Worthy, "Some Observations on Frederick W. Taylor and the Scientific Management Movement," Address given to the Society for Applied Anthropology, New York, April 19, 1954.
[19] Lloyd G. Reynolds and Joseph Shister, *Job Horizons* (New York: Harper and Row, 1949), p. 89.
[20] For a discussion of these dying hopes, see Ely Chinoy, *The Automobile Worker and the American Dream* (New York: Doubleday, 1955), pp. 9-10.

In theory, most companies give outstanding workers an opportunity to rise to the top. Yet the technical requirements of modern industry mean that many supervisory jobs can be handled only by men who have had special training. Increasingly, the highest job to which a production worker can aspire is a "factory clerical" position such as expediter or clerk, a position that carries with it slightly higher pay and status, and slightly more freedom from supervision.

It is hard for management today to determine who among the rank and file does have promise and ability, for many jobs offer the worker little chance to display initiative. The docile, submissive worker may be regarded as the good worker. The man with ideas is restless and the union is often more likely than management to give him a chance to express himself. (There is some tendency, however, for management to consider active union members as potential foremen.)

At the same time the unions have done much to reduce the chances of a man to forge ahead on the basis of individual ability. They have emphasized seniority rather than merit, and management has tended to go along with their emphasis. In addition, pay grades have been compressed in many companies so that the range between the top- and bottom-paid jobs among unskilled and semiskilled workers is quite narrow. Skilled jobs, such as that of tool and die maker, are often filled through an apprenticeship program, and few men are accepted for such training after 30. Once a man reaches this age, his chances of rising out of the semiskilled class are slight.

Advancement redefined.   Some opportunities for upward mobility are, of course, still open to the average worker, but these are somewhat limited (most, but not all, involve seeking off-the-job satisfactions).

1. He can establish a small business, such as a bar, a gas station, or repair service. A substantial minority have made this attempt and failed—though not all fail [21]—and many more dream, with various degrees of seriousness, of going into business for themselves. A great many carry on small business ventures after work as a side line which gives them extra income and a chance to express themselves in a manner they cannot enjoy on the regular job. (This practice is called "moonlighting.")

2. If he is still young, he can go to college or school at night, in the hope of being able to move ahead after graduation.

3. If he realizes that he cannot advance on his own, he may transfer his aspirations to his children. Many factory workers make great financial sacrifices in order to send their children through college.

4. Over the years he may come to regard seniority as a way of getting ahead. After all, unions emphasize seniority as a determinant in layoffs and promotions,

---

21 Seymour Lipset and Reinhard Bendix, "Social Mobility and Occupational Career Patterns, II, Social Mobility," *The American Journal of Sociology*, Vol. 57, No. 5 (March 1952), pp. 494-504. Almost half the manual workers in the study had attempted to start their own business.

and management concurs, with such symbols as long-service pins and testimonial dinners.

5. For some workers, the union provides a chance to "get ahead." Although there are few full-time union jobs with regular salaries, there are many part-time posts, such as steward or executive board member. Negotiating with management, handling grievances, and dealing with day-to-day union business offer many opportunities for creative expression and personal satisfaction.

6. Many workers feel they are advancing when they move to a job that may not be better-paying but that seems "better" in the sense that the work is cleaner, the pace is slower, or the location is away from the assembly line.

7. Finally, if the individual cannot advance by himself, the group to which he belongs may be able to advance the interests of its members. So long as his union can win him a 10-cent hourly wage increase each year, he feels that he has tangible evidence of progress.

8. Many workers interpret "getting ahead" in terms of security and material possessions. As one man put it, "If you've got security, if you've got something to fall back on, you're getting ahead." [22] They measure success not in terms of what they do, but in terms of what they own—a bigger car or a new TV set.

Some workers, however, seem to reject completely the idea of getting ahead —no matter how it is defined. A study of a gypsum mill compared the motivation of "surfacemen" with that of miners:

> It was, for example, frequently possible to predict which houses belonged to the miners simply by noting their unpainted and unrepaired exteriors; this, despite the fact that miners' take-home pay always averaged higher than surfacemen. Miners' work habits were more likely to be directed to the satisfaction of their immediate needs. Surfacemen, however, believed in "steady" work practices and they insisted money should be saved, "not burned up" . . . To the miner, however, money was a source of "independence," and an instrument for satisfying desires often forbidden by middle-class values. If the surfaceman wanted to compete with and impress his neighbors by buying a new car, the miner preferred to "set one up for the boys." He wanted to be a good fellow, not a better one.[23]

JOB PRESSURES AND RELATIONS TO MANAGEMENT

The factory employee has a carefully engineered quota of parts to finish or the requirement that he keep up with the line. Because his job is relatively simple and his methods and output readily observable, he is easy to supervise closely. Management exerts constant pressure to maintain a regular pace and thus maintain productivity. But what of the employee's view?

> *Assembler:* You're always behind. When you get too far behind, you get in a hole. . . . All hell breaks loose. . . . The foreman gets sore and they have to rush in a relief man to bail you out.[24]

---

[22] Chinoy, *op. cit.,* p. 126.

[23] Alvin Gouldner, *Patterns of Industrial Bureaucracy* (New York: The Free Press of Glencoe, 1954), p. 125.

[24] Ginzberg *et. al., op. cit.,* pp. 283-284.

> *Machine-tender:* When breaks occur in the yarn which stop a machine or cause material waste, the worker must respond immediately or he will fall behind in his production quota. There is a constant strain and necessity to keep on the move. . . . Relatively large numbers of textile workers complain of working too fast and getting too tired. . . .[25]

New employees, particularly, who find themselves falling behind, become anxious about their ability to keep up with the line or make the quota. Being replaceable they worry about being discharged, especially when there is no union or when as new employees they are on a *trial period*. Gradually, though, most develop those patterns of skill and coordination which enable them to meet the engineered standards.

Some workers even prefer machine-paced jobs or assembly lines. At least the "line" controls them impersonally; it keeps the foreman from breathing down their necks. Further, it eliminates the need to pay attention to how fast they are working and thus makes it possible for them to daydream. In effect, the machine sets a rhythm which their body seems to accept.

Unlike craft jobs in which the worker maintains considerable autonomy, most machine and assembly-line work tends to pit workers against managers.[26] As we have suggested, it is tempting to supervise closely since both work methods and output are easy to observe. In mass-production factories, management is constantly trying to reduce labor costs and increase productivity by upping work standards and improving methods, thus forcing the employee to adopt new working procedures and perhaps to change his tempo. Although many engineering changes do *not* require additional physical effort on the part of the worker (in fact, they frequently reduce physical effort), the employee views the increasing output and the necessary changes in his work methods as burdensome and threatening.

Low-skilled employees often fear technological changes that will require them to relearn a job and to struggle to regain adequate quickness. Other anxieties are aroused by the fear that new machines may mean fewer jobs and fewer workers.

Not only are job pressures maximized, but mass-production employees, in contrast to skilled craftsmen, tend to have rather formal relations with management, being unlikely to have any contact with anyone above their immediate supervisor. The status gap between workers and managers tends to be great since such employees, as we have seen, rarely become managers or have significant careers in the firm. Thus, they tend to see the world very differently from their managers who do have career possibilities, and whose success depends on their ability to maintain productivity levels among reluctant employees.

---

25 Blauner, *op. cit.*, p. 67.

26 A large-scale survey of British companies shows clearly that both labor relations and human relations are least amicable in the type of technology we are now discussing. Joan Woodward, *Management and Technology* (London: HMSO, Department of Scientific and Industrial Research, 1960), p. 18.

SOCIAL RELATIONS

The physical confinement of many factory jobs reduces the opportunity for social relations. In industrial plants employees socialize on the basis of physical proximity rather than occupational status. Congenial on-the-job relationships are important as a means of both reducing boredom and expressing one's total personality since the job requires such a small segment of the individual's mental and physical abilities. Yet, feeling little identification with their occupation, workers are relatively unlikely to make friendships on the job which carry over after work. In fact, most are anxious to get away from every aspect of the job at quitting time.

Assembly-line workers are restricted to a very small area and can only talk with those directly on either side or, occasionally, across the line. Machine operators have somewhat more flexibility in making social contacts although a high noise level may make necessary various ingenious facial expressions, grimaces, and hand signs as a substitute for words. And, of course, work breaks provide an opportunity for social contacts.

Social games provide a form of diversion. Gambling of various sorts is common in many factories, from flipping coins to see who pays for coffee, to World Series pools, to bookmaking, and numbers games. Horseplay (mock fighting, high jinks, and brawling) combines social activity and a chance to release aggression. (Accidents often result.)

These on-the-job social activities have become extremely important to workers in mass-production industries. Two astute observers have remarked,

> "Workers seem to want to buy leisure inside rather than outside the plant. ... They may, like many of us in business and professional strata, prefer to complain at home of their hard day's work while secretly profiting from its trivialities." [27]

ADJUSTING TO MASS-PRODUCTION WORK

Aside from elaborating social relations, how do employees adjust to mass-production work? Many learn to ignore the job through daydreaming or to modify the job by various "games at work." Others take more decisive action, either leaving or sabotaging the work.

Daydreaming. Daydreaming is a common means of escaping from the boredom of a no-attention job. As one observer notes, "The revolt against work is widespread and takes manifold forms in the United States. First and foremost it appears in the constant evasion of thought about work, the obsessive reveries

---

[27] David Riesman and Warner Bloomberg, Jr., "Work and Leisure: Fusion or Polarity," in Conrad Arensberg, *et. al., Research in Industrial Human Relations* (New York: Harper & Row, 1957), pp. 72-73.

while on the job." [28] An employee told us: "If I thought about the job all the time I'd go nuts. I think about vacation and going hunting. You don't even know you are working."

The sort of daydream in which workers indulge varies with the individual and the situation.[29] The man who is unhappy with his job and bitter over life in general is likely to brood over his miserable lot. If the work group as a whole is dissatisfied with the job and with the group's relationship with management, the workers tend to dream up grievances and engage in so called "obsessive thinking." "Day-dreaming emphasizes the worker's grievances and, especially if he is already depressed, crystallizes around them all his irritation with the conditions of his life." [30] These feelings may be expressed aggressively through what Roethlisberger calls "compulsive complaints," endless grumblings about unimportant matters that serve as symbols for bigger ones. Eventually, this behavior can mean trouble for management.

Yet in one study made by the authors, casual observation suggested that workers who daydreamed worked at a more constant pace than those who did not.[31] Most of the complaints about being machine-paced and "tied to the line" came from those who reported they did not daydream on the job.

Whether daydreaming is a practice that should be encouraged seems to depend on the nature of the job. "If day-dreaming does not interfere with good work it is probably a desirable adjustment, but if constant alertness is imperative, it may cause errors and accidents." [32]

Who adjusts to monotonous work?   Almost all workers regard a job that requires surface attention from them as boring, mentally exhausting, and undesirable.[33] (This is true even if the same work might require depth attention or no attention from someone else.) But there are some workers who can adjust moderately well to monotonous, no-attention jobs. These workers seem to have little need to derive satisfaction from the job itself and spend their working days in daydreaming.

Whether or not a worker succeeds in adjusting to monotonous work depends in part on his level of aspiration and the importance of the job to his over-all goals. Men as a whole seem less satisfied than women with monotonous work. Single women seem less satisfied than married women, who often spend their work hours thinking about family activities. Among men, the most contented are oldsters approaching retirement, boys awaiting induction into the armed services, and farmers who take a job to supplement their income. One study

---

[28] Daniel Bell, "Work in the Life of an American," in William Haber, *et. al.*, eds., *Manpower in the United States* (New York: Harper & Row, 1948), p. 15.

[29] See S. Wyatt and J. N. Langdon, *Fatigue and Boredom in Repetitive Industrial Work*, Industrial Health Research Board, Report 77 (London: HMSO, 1937), p. 10.

[30] Friedmann, *op. cit.*, p. 146.

[31] See also Wyatt and Langdon, *op. cit.*, p. 35.

[32] Norman R. F. Maier, *Psychology in Industry*, 2nd ed. (Boston: Houghton Mifflin, 1955), p. 470.

[33] Possibly some workers with serious emotional problems may prefer surface-attention work which keeps them from thinking about these problems.

found that the relative lack of education and aspiration among Southern textile workers caused many to call "objectively dull" jobs interesting.[34]

Another study concludes: "The groups satisfied with relatively routine work appear to be deriving satisfaction from other aspects of the work situation, rather than the work content itself." [35] There is evidence that the "monotony-susceptible worker tends to be less contented with life in general than the worker who is non-susceptible (and) . . . more poorly adjusted in her relations to family and home. The non-susceptible liked better the routine kinds of housework, and preferred the quieter forms of recreation." [36] Other studies suggest that extroverts and those with higher intelligence are likely to be bored with monotonous jobs.[37]

For many people the desire to do an interesting, worthwhile job, and to have a voice in determining how they do their work, is so compelling that they experience acute frustration when that desire is blocked.

Making a game out of work.   In spite of the obvious inefficiency of the practice, some people like to mow their lawns in fancy figure eights. Making a game out of work, as with other "around-the-job" satisfactions, provides variety, gives the worker a chance to show his creativity, and supplies goals to work toward.

On jobs that are not tightly machine-paced, the worker may experiment with various speeds and set himself various output goals. Workers on piece work are particularly likely to set goals for themselves (sometimes called "bogies") and to engage in elaborate calculations to make sure that they produce neither more nor less than the bogey.[38] Although the primary purpose of these calculations is to avoid overproduction that might lead to a cut in the piece rate, they also provide a satisfying diversion from the monotony of work.

Fantasy is another form of game-playing. A female assembly-line worker who had wanted to be a nurse said, "These (pieces) are always getting in trouble. They are sort of helpless, like sick people." Another woman commented, "This job is like cooking. It's something to do with your hands. It keeps you busy."

Changing job requirements.   Workers sometimes reduce the monotony of their jobs by introducing variations in their work that are unplanned by management. They may exchange work, modify parts of the job, and avoid others altogether. They drag out set-ups, find excuses to pick up parts more frequently

---

[34] Blauner, *op. cit.*, pp. 82-84.

[35] Nancy Morse, *Satisfactions in White Collar Jobs* (Ann Arbor, Mich.: Institute for Social Research, University of Michigan, 1953), p. 65.

[36] Reported in Thomas A. Ryan, *Work and Effort* (New York: Ronald, 1947), p. 205.

[37] Wyatt and Langdon, *op. cit.*, pp. 19-20. There is also evidence that those with higher intelligence are more likely to quit monotonous jobs than those with lower intelligence. But this may be due only to the fact that those with higher intelligence have greater opportunity elsewhere. A. G. Brills, "Fatigue in Mental Work," *Psychological Review*, Vol. 17 (1937), pp. 436-453.

[38] This practice is called "making out." For an excellent discussion, see Donald Roy, "Work Satisfactions and Social Rewards in Quota Achievement," *American Sociological Review*, Vol. 18, No. 5 (October 1953).

Extent of mass-production characteristics

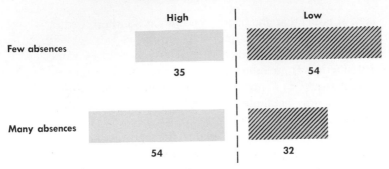

**Absenteeism related to mass-production characteristics of job
(175 workers).** *High and low mass-production characteristics
are measured in terms of the job's (1) degree of repetitiveness,
(2) degree of mechanical pacing, (3) skill, as measured by
learning time, (4) frequency as to break in job routine, (5) frequency of social interaction, and (6) size of interacting group.
Charles R. Walker and Robert Guest, The Man on the Assembly
Line (Cambridge: Harvard University Press, 1952), p. 120.*

than necessary, and perhaps let the machine break down in order to create a
slight change in pace.

Absenteeism and turnover. Another means of adjusting to unpleasant
work is to avoid it as much as possible. In practice this leads to absenteeism,
frequent visits to the dispensary, excessive time spent in the washroom, feigned
illness, and even quitting. Some have argued that employees may unconsciously
seek an accident.

Walker and Guest found correlations between short absences and the "mass-
production characteristics" of jobs on the assembly line. Absenteeism was highest on the jobs that required the least skill, were most repetitive, gave workers
the least chance to express themselves, and so forth.[39] (See chart above.)

Antimanagment activities. In a sense, antimanagement activities are an
overt reaction to the frustration of mass-production work. Active union participation, for example, provides an opportunity to release aggression and to enjoy
a sense of skill and accomplishment that is denied on the job. Similarly, sabotage and wildcat strikes enable a demoralized work group to let off steam.[40]
In Detroit, for instance, after long periods of overtime work on boring assembly-
line jobs, employees appear pleased with the prospect of a strike!

[39] Another careful research effort showed much the same thing: Absenteeism is higher on
the less complex, less demanding jobs: Arthur Turner and Paul Lawrence, *Industrial Jobs
and the Worker* (Boston: Division of Research, Harvard Business School, 1965), pp. 35-48.
However, still another study indicates that repetitious work has no relationship to turnover:
Maurice D. Kilbridge, "Turnover, Absenteeism, and Transfer Rates as Indicators of Employee
Dissatisfaction with Repetitious Work," *Industrial and Labor Relations Review*, Vol. 15,
No. 1 (October 1961), pp. 21-32.

[40] Leonard Sayles, "Wildcat Strikes," *Harvard Business Review*, Vol. 32, No. 6 (November 1954), pp. 42-52.

**SUMMARY: JOB SATISFACTIONS
IN TRADITIONAL FACTORY WORK**

Management pays a price for the work simplification, routinization, and ease of supervision inherent in mass-production work. The cost is largely in terms of apathy and boredom as positive satisfactions are engineered out of jobs. Being confined physically and limited socially to contacting his own immediate supervisor, the factory worker sees very little of the total organization and even less of the total product being manufactured. It is hardly surprising that there is frequently little pride in work or identification with the job. However, employees have put back some of the satisfactions they require by informal modifications of work methods (such as games and trading-off of jobs) and by concerted group activities (these will be detailed further in Chapter 4). Further, many employees have low levels of aspiration which are consistent with the initiative required on these jobs and others have redefined the meaning of advancement to compensate for the absence of significant careers.

Perhaps the most serious problem associated with these jobs is the high frequency of worker-management conflict over technological change and the question of what is a fair day's work. As we have seen, these conflicts are greatest where job pressures are greatest.

Positive Management Actions
To Improve Mass-Production Jobs

Since mass-production jobs are among the most common industrial jobs and represent the most serious problems in human relations, it is worth considering what steps management can take to ameliorate the situation.

Traditionally, technological decisions are made purely on the basis of mechanical efficiency and short-run labor costs. The heritage from scientific management is that employees with simple jobs can be trained and controlled easily. But a heavy price is paid in terms of utter indifference to work, extending from escapist daydreaming to purposeful sabotage.

In the next chapter we shall see that a different technology, like continuous-processing automation, provides very different employee attitudes and job behavior. Management may wish to consider whether this technology cannot be more widely applied. However, many industrial situations still require machine-tending and assembly work. Thus, the question becomes: What modifications in existing job design can produce more favorable employee reactions and perhaps greater motivation? Let us review the various methods that have been proposed.

JOB ENLARGEMENT

Specialization in mass production has been pushed to the point where the smallest possible band of a worker's ability is being utilized. Already efforts are being made to reverse this process, and with some success.[41] To accomplish this reversal, the engineering factors involved in each individual job must be carefully analyzed. Perhaps the assembly lines can be shortened so that there will be more lines and fewer workers on each line. Instead of assigning one man to each job, a group of men can be assigned to a group of jobs and then allowed to decide for themselves how to organize the work. Such changes permit more social contacts and greater control over the work process. Some companies have experimented with letting machine operators do their own set-ups (formerly done by skilled maintenance personnel) and their own quality control, and sometimes several jobs are combined into one, thus increasing employee responsibility.

> A recent example at the Polaroid Corp. involved operators and assistant operators who worked on a major film assembly machine. They felt that their work was repetitive, that they were in effect "chained to the machine." They also resented being told by the inspection and quality control departments when the film they produced did not meet quality standards.
> The solution to relieving their frustrations was to change the operation so that they are now responsible for their own quality. In addition to feeding and controlling the flow of materials through the machine, they take photographs and make graphs to determine quality. It's possible for them to determine immediately if anything is not operating properly and take the necessary corrective action. . . .
> Results have been impressive—as operators have taken more interest in the quality of their work, costs per roll of film have gone down and quality yields have gone up. It's also been possible to eliminate several inspecting jobs and transfer the inspectors to more challenging jobs in the company.[42]

Care must be exercised, however, not to convert a job which has become automatic (and that allows daydreaming and unlimited socializing) into one that makes employees tense. Many employees have not only grown used to a no-attention job, but they may actually prefer it to one which requires additional learning, surface attention, and responsibilities.[43]

JOB ROTATION

Some companies are seeking to reduce boredom through systematically moving workers from one job to another. This practice provides variety, lets the employee see more of the total operation, and gives workers a chance to learn additional skills. The company also benefits, since the workers become able to perform a number of different jobs in the event of an emergency.

---

[41] For an excellent résumé of the literature in this area, see Chris Argyris, *Integrating the Individual and the Organization* (New York: Wiley, 1964).

[42] "Job Enlargement and Job Rotation," *Personnel Management Bulletin*, Report No. 157 (May 15, 1962), p. 1.

[43] *Cf.* Maurice Kilbridge, "Do Workers Prefer Larger Jobs?" *Personnel*, Vol. 37, No. 5 (September 1960), p. 45.

On an automobile assembly line, for example, the utility man (sometimes called a "floater") is qualified to handle a number of jobs and takes over for workers who are absent or taking a break. These men seldom complain of monotony or lack of job interest.[44] At least four reasons can be given for their satisfactory work adjustment: (1) They are constantly changing their job, (2) they make use of a wide range of skills, (3) they get to know every operation and feel more involved in the final product, and (4) they get to know all the workers on the line.

Yet in one situation we studied, some of the workers objected to being rotated from job to job and jolted out of their routine. They looked upon their job almost as a piece of personal property; being an "expert" on one particular type of work gave them a feeling of status and importance that they lost when they were moved around.

In general, those who opposed job rotation worked on no-attention jobs and enjoyed daydreaming. Being shifted from spot to spot converted these no-attention jobs to surface-attention jobs and made reverie more difficult. On the other hand, workers whose regular job prevented them from daydreaming endorsed rotation as a relief from monotony.

Thus, the choice between job rotation and permanent assignment depends on the nature of the job and on the people who work on it. In some cases the decision can be made by the workers themselves. Having made the decision themselves, they will be more likely to accept it.

Change of pace. Anything that will give the worker a chance to change his pace when he wishes will make him feel less like a robot and more like a human being—and will lend variety to his work.[45] Further, if workers are permitted to change pace they can often build "banks" and thus obtain visible evidence of accomplishment.

At present there is some controversy surrounding the question of whether it is more efficient to allow an employee to rest some of his muscles by changing his pace (or changing his work method) or to rest all of his muscles by taking a break.[46]

Scheduled rest periods. Extensive research on the impact of rest periods indicates that they may increase both morale and productivity. Scheduled rest periods bring many advantages:

1. They counteract physical fatigue.
2. They provide variety and relieve monotony.

---

[44] Walker and Guest, *op. cit.*, p. 58.

[45] One of the most insistent demands of the United Automobile Workers has been for the right to control the speed of the assembly line. This and safety are the two areas about which the union has the right to strike at any time. For two experiments in which workers substantially increased their output when given control over their work pace, see John R. P. French, "Field Experiments: Changing Group Productivity," in James G. Miller, ed., *Experiments in Social Psychology* (New York: McGraw-Hill, 1950), p. 86; and William F. Whyte *et. al.*, *Money and Motivation* (New York: Harper and Row, 1955), Chapter 10.

[46] James March and Herbert Simon, *Organizations* (New York: Wiley, 1958), p. 18.

3. They are something to look forward to—getting a break gives a sense of achievement.
4. They provide opportunities for social contacts.

Research also suggests that the most beneficial rest periods are those that come just after the rate of output starts to decline—that is, relatively near the peak of the output curve. Needless to say, unduly frequent rest periods lead to an inefficient number of stops and starts.

Even where there are no formal rest periods, technology permitting, every worker takes a break once in a while, perhaps just by slowing down a bit, or going to the washroom or the coffee machine. If management tries to forbid this practice, workers will still "bootleg" breaks into the work schedule, although the value of the breaks in reducing fatigue will be impaired. Management must recognize that many of the rest periods workers take are minor goals that they set for themselves and rewards they give themselves for making certain quotas, rather than just the result of a desire to get away from work.

Scheduled rest periods seem to reduce the incidence of unscheduled ones. But on the other hand, as we have seen, many jobs fall into natural work units, and the natural time to take a break is at the end of a unit. Indeed, a few moments of relaxation at this point accentuate the feeling of accomplishment. Rest pauses scheduled for the whole department may tend to destroy these natural units, interrupt the work, and reduce the pulling power of the job. Further, when management *tells* workers when to rest, they have less feeling of autonomy than if they were to make the decision for themselves.

These work breaks are more complex than they first appear. If management is sensitive to the problem, however, it can decide, for any given situation, whether the department as a whole, or certain groups within the department, should take rest periods together, or whether individual decisions are more desirable.

GIVING A FEELING OF ACCOMPLISHMENT

There are many ways in which management can give employees a feeling of accomplishment, though few are appropriate to every situation.

Greater autonomy. Possibly the single effective way of increasing job satisfaction is to give workers more freedom to do their work in their own way—or, if that is impossible, to let the work group as a whole make this decision or at least be consulted when decisions are made. Since this whole area is closely related to the supervisor-worker relationship, however, we shall postpone detailed discussion of it to a later chapter.

Setting goals. In order to satisfy the natural desire for specific assignments, and in order to provide definite goals toward which to work, some companies permit workers to leave early (without loss of income) when they have finished their job. Other plants set daily production quotas which are announced to the entire work force. When these quotas are "accepted" as being "fair," they may well provide motivation for higher production. In a sense, working to achieve a quota makes a game out of the work. On the other hand, employees may regard quotas as a form of management pressure. They will work hard for goals that they have set for themselves, but strongly oppose "unfair" goals set by management.

In any case, psychologists tell us that goals are much more effective (1) if they are realistic, if there is a reasonable chance of attaining them, and (2) if they can be achieved in the relatively near future. Finishing a chapter in an hour is a far more compelling goal than reading a whole book in an evening.

Breaking the work down into meaningful units. Earlier we pointed out that most people get a sense of accomplishment from completing a whole job. But just what constitutes a "whole job" and precisely what is meant by "completion" are matters that can be manipulated by management. By breaking the work down into units or batches, management can give the employee a feeling of completion every time he finishes one batch. The desire to finish a unit has a strong "pulling power" and also enhances the worker's efficiency.

If the natural work unit is too big, the goal of completion seems too remote to elicit a strong desire to achieve it. On the other hand, the natural unit may be too small to entice the worker into additional effort. The man who tightens bolts on an assembly line gets little satisfaction from having completed the tightening of an individual bolt; there are just too many to tighten in a day.

Work units that are too large should be broken down and those that are too small should be lumped together. How large is the optimal unit? One study suggests that it should last for an hour or an hour and a half, depending on the situation.[47]

Maier reports an ingenious example of how the boring work of telephone maintenance in the central office was broken down into smaller units:[48]

> There is no challenge of diagnosing trouble, and the job is very confining since a man can work for hours within the space of a few feet. There is never a real experience of progress. When the job is finished the worker starts all over again.
>
> In one office the frames on which the men worked were subdivided by means of chalk lines. . . . Each block required between one and a half and two hours to complete. The worker made his choice of . . . unit. . . . The benefits of this pattern of work were immediately apparent. . . . Once a man selected a block he worked until it was finished.
>
> Every time a man completed a unit he took a smoke or a stretch. Even lunch and quitting time found no untagged units. The men liked the plan and the supervisors reported that complaining decreased and the trouble with meeting work schedules was eliminated.

---

[47] D. Cox and K. M. D. Sharpe, "Research on the Unit of Work," *Occupational Psychology,* Vol. 25, No. 2 (April 1951), pp. 90-108.

[48] *Op. cit.,* p. 489.

You can probably think of dozens of instances in which you have set up subgoals to make a large job easier—for example, dividing the lawn up into small sections when you mow the grass.

An English researcher uses the concept of "traction" to distinguish those jobs which serve to pull the worker along toward completion.[49]

Similarly, smaller jobs can be grouped together. In one plant, parts used to be sent on to the wrapper by means of a conveyor belt. Now that they are delivered in trays of a hundred, production has increased substantially. Completing a unit has even more significance if it is marked by a rest pause or by some special sign of recognition (a notation is made on a board), or even by a momentary change in activity (the worker wraps up a package).

Avoiding interruption of natural units. A man who is engrossed in his work resents being disturbed and wastes a good bit of time trying to pick up his work again. Secretaries object to being asked to do something else when they are in the middle of a letter. It is almost a matter of simple courtesy to say, "When you get a break for a minute, could you do this?"

Similarly, workers object to starting a new job just before quitting time, although if they are behind schedule on an existing job they will spurt to finish it up. There is often trouble between shifts when one shift leaves unfinished work for the next shift to complete.

Other forms of goals. On some jobs the worker tends one or more machines and can see no visible accumulation of product. Here management may be able to provide other forms of goals, such as producing x amount per shift, reducing the time required for repairs by a given percentage, or avoiding breakdowns for an entire shift. Or management may change the form of goal altogether.

> One of the most interesting human relations studies arising out of World War II related to the Royal Air Force. Fighter pilots at a certain air base were growing discouraged because an almost perpetual fog kept them from contacting enemy bombers. Their discouragement was reflected in careless flying and high accident rates. When the pilots accepted as a goal the conquering of the weather, which became their new enemy, morale was substantially raised and accidents declined. Thus their need for accomplishment was no longer frustrated.[50]

Providing information on progress. Even where production has nothing to do with incentive earnings or opportunities for promotion, employees like to know how they are doing. When you drive along a turnpike on a foggy night, you feel anxiety because you don't know how far you are from your destination.

> In a plant that manufactured a large number of small items at high speed, management installed counters on each of the lines, just for supervisory pur-

---

[49] W. Baldamus, *Efficiency and Effort* (London: Tavistock Publications, 1961).
[50] See T. T. Paterson, *Morale in War and Work* (London: Max Parish, 1955).

poses. Soon the employees were spending so much time sneaking a look that additional counters were installed at each work place. Informal competition developed both between lines and between shifts on the same line. Then the foreman brought in a blackboard and chalk and the men began posting their records. (*Question:* What might have happened had management deliberately tried to foster competition?)

An aircraft manufacturer posts bar graphs showing the length of time actually taken to complete various components of the plane as compared to the time planned.[51] A telephone company uses indices of efficiency, particularly among its white-collar employees.[52]

Building career lines. Management can promote a sense of progress and commitment to the organization by fitting jobs together into promotional ladders. As we have seen, mass-production work typically provides "no place to go," and this lack of opportunity discourages those employees who may be most worth promoting.

Selection. A good deal of attention is already devoted to endeavoring to preselect those employees whose psychological dispositions are likely to be consistent with the available job satisfactions. More research, however, needs to be done in this area.

Stressing the importance of the job. If the job becomes too specialized, the worker loses his feeling for the relationship between his work and the overall process. He would like to feel both (1) that he plays a significant part in the work process as a whole, and (2) that the process itself is important.

Many companies take new employees on a trip through the plant to show them how the work they will be doing fits into the total picture. During World War II war heroes were invited to visit war plants, and demonstrations were staged to dramatize what happened when a part misfunctioned. In indoctrinating new employees the telephone company impresses on them the importance of their jobs in saving lives and in helping people in trouble.

PROVIDING SOCIAL SATISFACTIONS

On jobs that lack other satisfactions, provisions for social relationships often produce very favorable reactions. Partitions can help identify a social group in what would otherwise be a huge amorphous department. Employees who work in isolation or among strangers (for example, packers who are

---

[51] John Walsh and Max Shousen, "Scoreboards Boost Production," *Supervisory Management,* Vol. 1, No. 5 (May 1956), p. 4.

[52] Of course, such indices may be regarded as a method of exerting pressure. Or they may encourage quantity at the expense of quality. We shall discuss some of these factors later. See Peter M. Blau, *The Dynamics of Industrial Bureaucracy* (Chicago: University of Chicago Press, 1955), Chapter 3.

"farmed out" on a daily basis to production departments) can be given a home base by allowing fellow employees who share the same occupational status to get together first thing in the morning or at the end of the shift. Where this is impossible, shared relief time or group meetings may help.

Employees gain enormous satisfaction from being able to exercise some control over the actions of others, particularly when most of their day is spent responding to others.

> Laborers on a construction project occupy a very low status position. Everyone orders them about to get materials, to help out and do the "dirty" work. A group of men helping on cement pouring got enormous satisfaction when pushing heavy wheelbarrows filled with fresh cement that had to be transported quickly from the trucks to the pouring site. When they did so, everyone else had to get out of their way, and they yelled to claim this priority to all the craftsmen they were subordinate to at other times.

Many times a job element gives an employee the opportunity to feel some self-importance in relation to others, and this fleeting exercise of dominance makes up for what is otherwise a low-status job. Supervisors can help by accepting advice or responding to requests from employees concerning their very special area of competence.

PHYSICAL CONTEXT OF WORK

We have been concerned largely with the psychological and social setting of work, and the reactions of employees to this context. But there is also a physical context. Some craft jobs have to be performed in dangerous settings (consider the iron-workers who erect the superstructure of skyscrapers). Many factories (say, smelters) are hot and dirty! Some operations involving chemicals have acrid fumes; textile plants tend to be hot and damp (in part because thread doesn't break easily with high humidity). There are still many jobs which are physically exhausting on the auto assembly lines in Detroit. Many workmen have to be on their feet a good deal; cranemen sit in one place for long, fatiguing hours; and some generator assemblers have to crouch. We could extend this list, but it should be obvious that there are substantial sources of dissatisfaction to be found in the physical conditions under which jobs are performed.

Employees do like clean, comfortably cooled, light and airy workplaces in which they can sit and walk at will and where physical fatigue is at a minimum. Most managers know this, but some jobs are difficult to adapt to these rather universal desires.

Some observers who would argue that certain employees gain satisfaction from doing heavy—even dangerous—work under difficult circumstances. Their sense of "maleness" is enhanced and they poke fun at other men doing "women's" work. On the other hand, women are more likely to be disturbed by "unpleasant" working conditions.

Music. In recent years many companies have begun to play recorded music during work hours. Brisk marches are recommended for certain times of the day, more soothing melodies for others. Claims have been made that music leads to higher production and that some types of music (marches, for instance) have a more beneficial effect than others. Other studies show that although the effects on production are negligible, workers generally enjoy listening to the music, provided it isn't too loud or incessant. Obviously the effect of music varies from one industrial situation to another.[53]

Shorter hours. How long should the work-day be? During World War II the British discovered that a shorter work-day sometimes led to higher production. After the shock of the Dunkirk disaster, the work-week of British factory workers was increased from an average of 56 hours to 69.5 hours. After an initial spurt, production started to fall off until at last it was 12 per cent lower than it had been before the change in hours. Then, when the shorter work-week was restored, production increased to a higher point than ever before. In one case when the work-day was reduced from 12 to 10 hours shop accidents dropped 70 per cent—indicating that fatigue may also create serious safety problems.

Conclusion

We are not surprised to find the enormous contrast in job satisfactions derived from craft as compared to mass-production work. What really are more interesting and useful to recall are the various dimensions of these jobs which elicited strong employee reaction. Although most typical industrial jobs will tend to be an admixture of craft and machine operation, one will be able to assess the contribution of many of the following elements to employee reactions.

Interest, Variety, and Movement

    Intrinsic variability of the work, length of job cycle, and repetitiveness
    Depth-, surface-, or no-attention requirement
    Opportunity to develop own work methods, to vary pace and rhythm, to move around and utilize different body muscles, to take breaks
    Ability to adjust job requirements to personality

Accomplishment, Autonomy, and Identification

    Opportunity to exercise discretion, initiative, and self-expression
    Duration and intensity of training required
    Availability of a career line, sense of progress in status and earnings

---

[53] A comprehensive review of research on the effects of music is provided by Richard S. Urhbock, "Music on the Job: Its Influence on Morale and Production," *Personnel Psychology,* Vol. 14, No. 1 (Spring 1961), pp. 9-38.

Degree to which work results appear to depend on personal ability and skill
Commitment to and identification with some end result or total process
Sense of completion, of being responsible for a finished product or service
Identification with a recognized and prestigious occupational group

Job Pressures and Relations to Management

Tightness of work standards, type of pressure exercised by supervision
Variability of work load through the day
Potential cost of failure
Personal vulnerability, the degree to which mistakes can be "assigned" to individuals
Interpersonal pressures for improved performance from peers
Ability to contact more than one level of management
Apparent congruity between interests of managers and employees
Job security—ease of replacement by others, relative importance of labor costs to total costs

Social Relations

Required by work process itself
Available within the work environment
Impact of hours of work on community social relations

Physical Conditions of Work

Heat, noise, temperature, humidity, and odors
Posture imposed, effort required
Relative cleanliness and attractiveness of work setting
Length of work-day and work-week

Often the alert manager can relate his observations of employee behavior and the sentiments they express to these various job factors. He is thus in a better position to interpret the underlying source of satisfaction or dissatisfaction. At times, as we have seen, the manager can go one step farther. He can make modifications at the margin of the job, so to speak, by changing the length of the cycle, the opportunity for social relationships, and so on. In a few cases the manager may actually be able to influence the over-all character of the job, whether it tends to fit toward the craft or toward the mass-production end of the continuum. Again, knowing something about employee reactions may improve the quality of such decisions.

PROBLEM ONE

The Headliner Group [54]

The headliner group is located in the Passenger Trim Department; it is their job to place the fabric covering on the inside of the car roof, stretch it to a fit, smooth out the wrinkles, and glue it into place. Though the job might, at first observation, seem to be rather simple, it is actually something of an art, for far

---

[54] We are indebted to a former student, James T. Bennett, for this case.

more skill is required to handle the pliable fabric than is needed in working with unyielding metal, the major component of an automobile. To train a man to do the work with any degree of proficiency requires at least a week of constant instruction. For this reason, it is difficult to replace a headliner on short notice and few are trained to do the job.

The seven men who filled the job were not unaware of this modest skill requirement. They considered themselves superior to most of the assemblers who worked with metal parts, although their job, too, was highly repetitive. They also felt free to complain about anything and everything: heating, lighting, ventilation, the tools with which they worked, and supervisory prejudice.

Although each man performed the same job, the group did not actually work together on a car. Each installed the headliner on every seventh automobile. A worker would get into a unit, remain in it until he finished the work, and then go to the seventh unit back and repeat the cycle. Therefore, the work of a given man was not dependent on the work of any other. The amount of effort required might vary, however. For example, a station wagon would require more work, for it has more interior to be covered by the headliner than a two-door automobile. Similarly, a two-door requires less work than a four-door. Although attempts were made to keep the proportion of each type of unit produced constant during each hour, it was indeed rare when no variation occurred. Difficulties in scheduling, errors, and problems in other departments made the maintenance of a constant "mix" almost impossible. Since these variations had an impact on the work time of the headliners, they were quick to seize on the smallest fluctuations, pressure the foreman for relief, and threaten the foreman with union action.

The major bone of contention of the workers was the time standard imposed on them. It was consistently argued that the job could not be time studied and that there was no "standard time" for the work. The group complained that there were too many variables to consider and even went so far as to assert that changes in the weather (humidity) would have noticeable changes on the material with which they worked. It was claimed that judgment was required for every unit was a little different. Resentment was also strong against their rate of pay. Although they were well-paid and within a few cents of the highest-paid jobs in the plant, the workers believed that their jobs required more effort than that of the door-fitters, the best-paid group. Because their work necessitated that they climb into the automobile, perform the operation with their hands above their heads, and remain stooped over in the unit until the headliner was installed, they contended that the task was the most tiring in the plant. It was also protested that not enough allowance was given for fatigue and contingencies, and that an extra worker should be trained and placed in the group to assist. Although the headliners had complained about the job and the work load, it was possible for them to give each other an extra break during some part of the day. While six men kept up the work, one could leave the job and go for a cup of coffee and a cigarette.

Since the foreman had to get the work from these men to maintain production, he had to have their cooperation. Checks were made on the cost which each foreman's area incurred as well as the quality of his production. Data were recorded daily on these two control items and were given to the foreman, the general foreman, and the department superintendent. Costs and quality were the determinants of the foreman's bonus and directly affected his chances for promotion.

If the foreman placed new pressure on the group to speed up, the quality would drop, the workers would slowly fall further behind, and the utility man would be required to help the men catch up, thus diverting him from his regular duties of relieving others and disrupting the whole relief schedule. Complaints were sure to arise from the others when this occurred.

1. If you were instructing a new foreman in this department, what are the things you would tell him about the "headliners?"
2. What do you know about technology and job satisfaction that would be useful in managing such a group?
3. Do "gripes" and pressure provide any satisfaction? How?

PROBLEM TWO

Dirty Bottles

The Milwaukee Brewing Company has been plagued with trouble among its *bottle inspectors*, whose job is to check each bottle carefully to make sure that it is absolutely clean as it leaves the bottle-washing machine. Though there have been many attempts to develop mechanical inspecting devices, none of these has worked with 100 per cent accuracy. As a consequence, each bottle must be visually inspected as it passes by the inspector on a conveyor belt. Although this job is highly paid, it is hard to find men to take it and many quit after working on a few months.

1. What seems to be the basic problem here?
2. What suggestions can you make for solving it?

PROBLEM THREE

Candy Wrappers

All candy made by the Quality Candy Company is wrapped by hand. Candy is brought to each wrapper by chute. She wraps each piece and then drops it into another chute which leads to packers in another room.

Each girl handles a different kind of candy and their work locations are isolated from each other.

1. How will the girls react to this sort of work?
2. What can be done to increase their morale and output?

Technology
and Job Satisfaction:
Automation
and White-Collar Work

3

Two occupational trends have received a great deal of attention in the 1960's. One is the onrush of automation in manufacturing, the other is the growing importance of nonfactory jobs, of service industry, and white-collar work. Both have important implications for job satisfaction and give us a more well-rounded view of the world of work and its impact on the employee. Since it most directly affects what has been described in the previous chapter, let us look first at the jobs created by automation.

Automation and Continuous-Process Technology

Perhaps a definition of automation is in order since the term has come into such widespread use. Although there is no single definition, most authors stress the following components: (1) use of high-speed computers for data processing or control, (2) use of "closed-loop feedback" techniques to facilitate self-control by machines themselves, (3) mechanization of transfer operations, (4) increased use of multiple-purpose equipment, and (5) the combination of jobs and work units in larger self-contained processes.[1]

DETROIT AUTOMATION

Much "automation" leaves the intrinsic characteristics of jobs unchanged. Workers merely operate more productive machinery that positions the work, checks its accuracy, and transports materials from stage to stage automatically. But the operator continues to be a machine-tender, and a sharp status line continues to separate him from the engineers who install and maintain the equipment and the managers who supervise it. For the most part, this is what is called "Detroit Automation." Jobs may be somewhat less physically demanding, but there is also more pressure associated with the complicated, expensive and potentially very vulnerable processing techniques.[2] Should something go wrong, a great deal of production is lost. As a consequence, supervision may be even closer than before the changes.

CONTINUOUS-PROCESS TECHNOLOGY

Something close to true automation does, however, exist today in some plants in the chemical and petroleum industries and in electrical power generation and steel manufacturing. Automation of this sort is most easily adapted to industries in which the product can flow continuously (particularly as a liquid or gas) from entering raw material to finished product through a number of interlinked stages. Continuous steel strip mills and electrical generating plants, where fuel or water power is used to make steam or is applied directly to power turbines, approximate the continuous flows of a chemical plant. In all such factories an employee spends much of his time monitoring gauges and control instruments, and his major physical activities come only during break-downs, and start-up and change-over periods.

Such work contrasts sharply with that of craftsmen and machine operators. As we have seen, a craftsman utilizes manual, motor, perceptual and conceptual skills. He manipulates materials, his own body, and ideas. Engineers have eliminated the conceptual and perceptual element from the job of the semi-skilled machine-tender and the assembly-line worker, though they must still develop some manual dexterity and motor skill, but far less than the craftsmen.

---

[1] James Bright, *Automation and Management* (Boston: Harvard Business School, Division of Research, 1958); Floyd Mann and L. Richard Hoffman, *Automation and the Worker* (New York: Holt, Rinehart and Winston, 1960), p. 3; Charles R. Walker, *Toward the Automatic Factory* (New Haven, Conn.: Yale University Press, 1957).

[2] *Cf.* William Faunce, "Automation in the Automobile Industry," *American Sociological Review*, Vol. 23, No. 4 (August 1958), pp. 401-407.

Automated employees, however, need few physical skills, but they are expected
to use their "heads." [3]

TYPE OF WORKER		SKILLS REQUIRED		
Craftsman	Manual	Motor	Conceptual	Perceptual
Machine-tender and assembly-line worker	Manual	Motor		
Automation worker			Conceptual	Perceptual

INTEREST, VARIETY, AND MOVEMENT

Most jobs in continuous-process plants require an irregular combination
of surface attention and depth attention. The *job cycle* is a relatively long one.
Dials have to be checked and adjustments made when readings are "off
standard." In one case in a chemical plant, 50 different instruments are
monitored every two hours.[4]

The pace of work is uneven, but in part it can be adjusted to the comfort,
convenience, and natural "rhythms" of the employees. Although the checking
operations must be periodic, they need not be done precisely on time:

> "Sometimes when it's close to the time for 2 o'clock readings, we might have
> soup on the stove. You can eat the soup first and do the work later or take the
> readings at 1:45 and then eat your soup." [5]

In utility generating stations and in some parts of a refinery, the operators
may be confined to a control room. In a chemical plant, however, they must
take lengthy walks through widely dispersed equipment.

Aside from monitoring operations, the other part of automated jobs consists
of handling unexpected breakdowns (and sometimes assisting in regular
starting-up and shutting-down activities). In this phase depth attention is
called for, and time is of utmost importance. Because of the enormous costs
involved in idle equipment, management expects everyone to pitch in ener-
getically when there is trouble. But if there are going to be sufficient personnel
available for such emergencies, when things are going smooth, there is of
necessity going to be a good deal of idle time.

Unlike a typical mass-production plant where a breakdown is a welcome
relief, here a stoppage is a sign of failure. It is also a period of excitement,
even drama. The unexpected breaks up the monotony. Locating, diagnosing,
and fixing troubles can be absorbing, even though breakdowns also call for
very hard work.

---

[3] The table is adapted from Joan Woodward, *Industrial Organization: Theory and Practice* (London: Oxford University Press, 1965), pp. 63-64.

[4] Robert Blauner, *Alienation and Freedom* (Chicago: University of Chicago Press, 1964),
p. 134.

[5] *Ibid.*, p. 138.

ACCOMPLISHMENT, AUTONOMY, AND IDENTIFICATION

"Continuous-processing technology may serve to reverse the historic trend toward the greater division of labor and specialization."[6] It is this involvement in a tangible, complete activity (refining oil, producing electric power) that produces job interest and the satisfaction which grows out of meaningful activity. Employees feel *responsible* for keeping highly expensive technology going. Rather than concentrate on a small, essentially meaningless task, the employee develops a sense of commitment to the total process. Thus, he gains the satisfaction of knowing that in some measure he contributes to an observable, finished product:

> The worker's role changes from providing skills to accepting responsibility ... the very definition of responsibility as a job requirement involves a meaningful connection between the worker's own function and the goals of entire enterprise.[7]

In contrast to the mass-production factory, there are not endless, impersonal rows of people repeating small tasks. Instead, relatively few men patrol and control a vast array of massive equipment, or they oversee a control room which is like a command post. Here employees accept some of the functions that supervisors exercise in other technologies.

Their sense of growth and development and importance is further enhanced by the career ladders that develop naturally. A refinery still or a production unit in a chemical plant is handled by a small crew which is differentiated in skill and experience; the lowest-ranking employee is usually called a helper and the top-skilled person can be a head operator stillman or crew chief. Because of the close interdependence of their jobs and the need to be familiar with a variety of complex tasks, new employees are brought in as part of general labor gangs and progress through a series of jobs as their experience increases and they evidence willingness to accept responsibility. Each successive job enables them to get a broader view of operations.

And here management, far more than in craft or mass-production industries, is willing to invest in continuing training. Hence, most employees experience a sense of steady progress in status and earnings. Highly important by-products are, for the employee, substantial job security and, for management, a workforce showing unusually high identification with the company. Evidence of this opportunity to enjoy a real career and to progress is provided by wage differentials. In continuous-processing plants, unlike mass-production with its inherent limitations, jobs are arrayed in ascending ladders and there are considerable opportunities for promotions and steps upward in earnings.

The top skilled crew-chief positions involve enormous responsibility and challenge in these industries. As an example, let us look at the chief melter in a

---

[6] *Ibid.*, p. 143.
[7] *Ibid.*

newly computerized oxygen-furnace steel plant. Premixed, preweighted ingredients are transported to a huge pressure cooker (the furnace's converter), which heats them for about an hour and is then tapped. Here is a description of the work of the employee who handles the operation, Mr. Peral:

> Mr. Peral directs operations with the computer from a control room several feet from the vessel. He is in touch with his eight men through a loudspeaker system. . . . To make a batch of steel, called a heat, Mr. Peral first has his computer figure out the ingredients, based on orders for specific grades of steel. Then the vessel is tilted to the "charging" side. The press of a button sets off 75 to 80 tons of scrap—. . . . How does Mr. Peral know when it's time to tap? "You've got to know your end points," he says. "You notice how the carbon flame above the vessel is dying? It's about ready." . . . Mr. Peral orders the vessel tilted again toward the charging side. Protected by a metal shield, two of his assistants insert a long pole called a thermocouple into the vessel. . . . If the mixture is not hot enough, the vessel is turned upright again and heated some more. If it is too hot, Mr. Peral will have to have a look at it. . . . There is no device yet that will tell the melter about the heat that Mr. Peral can discover merely by peering into it through purple-tinted cobalt glasses. To Mr. Peral the process is "fascinating." . . . "On this process," he says, "I learn something new about steelmaking every day." [8]

Here, as elsewhere, machines do not completely displace employees; a number of critical jobs can still be performed more effectively by human beings.

The psychological satisfactions associated with these jobs has been highlighted by a recent study of an automated electricity-generating plant:

> It would appear that company managements through their design engineers are now in a position to restore to our working population some of the pride and satisfaction that stems from performing interesting and challenging jobs. Rather than making men adjuncts to machines, automation seems to be capable of utilizing workers as human beings with a capacity for intellectual understanding. [9]

JOB PRESSURES AND RELATIONS TO MANAGEMENT

Under automation the speed-up that occurs during breakdowns or changeover periods is not resented as efforts by management to get more work done. Here the employees can see for themselves when hard work is required and the supervisor doesn't have to push them. Also, as we have seen, the technical leadership in these situations often is provided by the top-ranking member of the crew, the chief operator. Since he works right alongside the other members of the gang and shares their values and difficulties, his demands are likely to be interpreted as reasonable. [10]

---

[8] *The New York Times*, March 18, 1965, p. 43 and p. 50.

[9] Mann and Hoffman, *op. cit.*, pp. 205-206.

[10] One article suggests that leadership exercised by working, "inside" leaders was characteristic of man's earliest work groups: F. L. W. Richardson, "Managing Man's Animal Nature," *Pittsburgh Business Review*, Vol. 34, No. 11 (December 1964), p. 4.

Mistakes can be terribly expensive, so employees cannot be rushed or excessively pressured by management. Although a craft worker can redo poor-quality work and an assembler's mistakes can be remedied by a repairman farther down the line, an error by a continuous-process employee may cost thousands of dollars before it can be rectified. Checking and repairing involve mental processes which cannot be coordinated by stop watch.

In many circumstances, management is pleased when employees are not working hard—this indicates that things are going well. If the employees work wisely and effectively, there are few or no breakdowns. Under these conditions both employee relaxation and company product are maximized! One company considered developing an incentive payment plan under which employees would receive bonuses in proportion to how *little* time they had to work. Their work time was almost directly proportional to the amount of breakdown and loss of production, much of which reflected lack of employee foresight.

There are other reasons why management seldom appears oppressive to employees under this type of technology. Since at least the top-ranking workers are highly experienced and well informed, their opinions are often sought out by supervisors and by engineers. Particularly when pilot-plant operations are conducted, employees are likely to have contact with levels of management above their immediate supervisor and with staff engineers. Thus, in a modern continuous-process steel mill, there is less status distinction between skilled hourly workers and management and more personal relationships than are found in an automobile assembly plant, where relationships are highly formal and primarily limited to order-giving by the immediate manager.

Continuous-process industry is characterized by better human relations between management and employees over-all than those that prevail in other technologies. Since workers only indirectly control output, pressure on people is at a minimum. "The process foreman's job was to arrange things within limits, set by the plant, which both he and the operators understood and accepted." [11] And the small number of subordinates per manager helps improve human relations.

Since labor costs make up a much smaller percentage of total costs in automated plants than in nonautomated plants, management can provide more generous wages and fringe benefits. More important, since these plants are designed to operate with a minimum of employees, nearly all of whom are required no matter what the scale of operations, employees are less expendable during periods of recession. Furthermore, management as we have noted has a major investment in the career training of its workforce. The employees sense that they are not dealt with as a "variable cost," something that can be let go if business activity declines. Instead, they see themselves as having careers that will last their working life.[12]

---

[11] Joan Woodward, *Management and Technology* (London: HMSO, 1960), p. 30.

[12] Of course, this assumes that the employee exhibits reasonable energy and learning ability. In recent years some oil refineries have had to cope with what they termed "obsolete" employees, often through early retirement.

HOURS OF WORK

Many automated jobs require shift work and this is a source of dissatisfaction. To get maximum use of expensive equipment, it must be used round-the-clock. And, chemical plants and utilities operate day and night because their processes can't be turned "on" and "off" except at great cost.

Though a few employees like shift work, because it enables them to make alternative use of the daytime, most find that late hours interfere with normal family and social life. Many firms rotate shifts. This procedure avoids charges of discrimination and prevents jockeying for favorable schedules, but it requires employees to get used to constantly changing sleeping and waking hours, not an easy thing to do as anyone knows who has flown across a number of time zones.[13]

SOCIAL RELATIONS

Most employees in automated industries work in teams. On some chemical operations there may be only two or three employees per shift; on others ten or so. The employees work closely together and must develop the ability to coordinate their efforts and help each other. In turn, close social relations develop on the team which may carry over into the community.

Whereas social-group boundaries are often ambiguous and vague in traditional industrial plants, they are more clear-cut here. Where hundreds of employees do similar operations under one roof or where an assembly line snakes for a mile or two past thousands working side by side, it is difficult for employees to identify with a specific group of fellow workers. The limited number of employees under automation and their specific relationship to a given process serves to unite a social group which has the same boundaries as the work unit.[14]

We should not exaggerate the beneficial effects of automation on social relations, however. Some automated plants have only a small number of employees, widely dispersed, who rarely see each other. Isolated locations plus noise may make difficult all but limited conversation.

SUMMARY: AUTOMATION AND JOB SATISFACTION

It would be a mistake to assume that all job-satisfaction problems are solved by the introduction of continuous-process automation. For there is

---

[13] For a more complete treatment of the total subject of working hours see Clyde Dankert, Floyd Mann, and Herbert Northrop, eds., *Hours of Work* (New York: Harper and Row, 1965).

[14] In Chapter 16 we shall see that many work frictions are caused by work environments in which the social group contains other members than the work group which must coordinate itself.

substantial monotony associated with watching and waiting. Future research will likely emphasize the psychological reactions to this *surface-attention problem* since many military (for instance, missile bases and space ships) as well as civilian activities require "dial-watching" tasks to be performed over long periods of time.

> Automation often requires a very high-level person for one hour a week and somebody who is capable of doing nothing for the other 39 hours. . . . You are going to have trouble keeping people from getting a kind of "turnpike fatigue" running one of these machines.[15]

In addition employees are likely to feel substantial anxiety about making costly errors.

More than balancing these dissatisfactions, however, are the through-the-job satisfactions derived from the relatively long work cycles, flexible work rhythms, and the opportunities to work as a team in emergencies. In fact, the entire relationship between management and workers is improved over what obtained in traditional manufacturing: There is more two-way communication and mutual understanding. People handle problems as they arise and there is little need for management to impose quotas and work standards. Employees can see themselves progressing over time on a career through a series of graded job steps. Relatively small numbers and management's investment in training give a sense of individualism which contrasts sharply with the impersonality of the traditional sprawling factory.

True automation is really the opposite of Taylorism and scientific management's mass-production methods. The former involves looking at work processes as a whole and giving employees a broader view and wider responsibilities. Mechanization and mass production foster a piecemeal approach: speeding up a machine here, eliminating an arm motion there, saving an operation some place else. It is hardly any wonder that employee reactions to these widely different technologies vary so dramatically.

A NOTE: UNSKILLED WORK AND FLOATING LABOR

Automation is having one of its most profound effects in helping to eliminate some of those jobs that used to be filled by completely unskilled, often temporary, employees. Jobs such as those of yard gangs, sweepers, and loaders used to be reserved for "floating labor" who move endlessly from job to job and sometime from region to region. Lacking education, or handicapped by membership in a minority group, they are disqualified from the better jobs. Experience has "taught" them that they have little chance to get ahead, that there is no point even in trying. Just to hold on to what they have is hard enough. When they find a job they work until they get enough to meet their

---

15 P. L. Cook, Jr., "Social and Economic Effects of Automation," *Twenty First Annual Midwest Conference on Industrial Relations* (Chicago: Graduate School of Business, University of Chicago, 1955), p. 10.

minimum needs, and when they are unemployed their friends support them. Immediate pleasures are their only goal. They show little "drive" or "ambition."

> [Indeed,] only when one knows where his next week's or next month's shelter will come from, can he and his children afford to go in for long-term education and training, the endless search for opportunities, and the tedious apple polishing that the attainment of higher skills and occupational status requires.[16]

Since security and economic advancement mean little to these workers, they look for jobs that provide independence and a feeling of being one's own boss. They may not amount to much by middle-class standards, but they retain the freedom of telling off the boss and quitting their job whenever they want to.[17] Thus, in terms of commitment they represent the antithesis of the employee attitudes that can be fostered by continuous-process automation and its career lines.

White-Collar Work

Economists have observed the following trend as industrialization proceeds. Primary industry (mines and farms) requires a decreasing proportion of the labor force as secondary industry (manufacturing) becomes more important. In its turn, tertiary industry (services) becomes increasingly significant. With increasing incomes, people want and can afford to pay for more services. And service industries (banks, hospitals, stores, and so on) tend to provide a high proportion of white-collar jobs. Even in our factories, the ratios of managers, engineers, clerks, and technicians (all white-collar workers) to production workers grow as more sophisticated technologies are utilized and as more attention is paid to research, design, marketing, finance, and other nonmanufacturing activities.

Although the future is uncertain and economists are not agreed, the table on page 68 suggests what may happen to various jobs in the next decade.

WHITE VS. BLUE COLLAR

Prestige advantages. In almost every country white-collar carries more prestige than blue-collar. In fact, some developing nations have great difficulty improving their productivity because the educated citizens all want to work in offices (as bank or government employees, lawyers, accountants, and so on) and not in factories. The reasons for the difference in status are not difficult to identify.

The names alone suggest an important difference. Blue-collar workers pre-

---

[16] Allison Davis, "The Motivation of Underprivileged Workers," in William F. Whyte, ed., *Industry and Society* (New York: McGraw-Hill, 1946), p. 89.

[17] See Richard Centers, "Motivation Aspects of Occupational Stratification," *Journal of Social Psychology*, Vol. 28 (November 1948), pp. 187-217.

sumably get their hands and clothes soiled while working; the others can wear spotless white shirts. White-collar jobs are thought to have individuality in contrast to the mass character of factory work, to be "middle class" as distinct from "working class"! They are also "closer," both physically and psychologically, to management, and it is assumed that promotions come easier and salaries are higher in office work than in the plant. For many people whose fathers worked on farms, in mines, or factories, just getting a white-collar job is a major step forward. Finally, the traditional difference in prestige between these two types of jobs reflects assumed differences in the relative difficulty and complexity of brain work as against manual work.

Projected Employment Growth for the Next Decade by Occupation [*]

PERCENTAGE OF LABOR FORCE, 1970 [**]	OCCUPATION	PROJECTED GROWTH				
		Decline	No Change	Less Than Average	Average	More Than Average
14	Service workers (*e.g.*, hairdressers, hospital attendants)					X
23	Clerical workers					X
	Sales workers				X	
24	Professional and technical (*e.g.*, engineers)					X
	Managers and proprietors				X	
13	Craftsmen				X	
17	Operatives: semiskilled workers			X		
5	Laborers (nonfarm)		X			
5	Farm workers	X				

[*] U.S. Department of Labor, *Manpower Report of the President* (March 1963), Table 28.
[**] U.S. Department of Labor, *Manpower Report of the President* (March 1965), Page 54.

Some have said that white-collar "psychology can be understood as the psychology of prestige striving." [18] Managers have to learn that very substantial ego and social rewards are derived from what may appear to be unimportant differences between jobs. For example, a job title like "staff assistant" may provide a sense of advancement to an employee who was doing the same work when it was called "chief clerk." An invoice checker who works for Saks Fifth Avenue derives much pleasure from the superiority of her position compared to her counterpart at Macy's. The secretary of the general manager

---

[18] C. Wright Mills, *White Collar* (New York: Oxford University Press, 1953), Chapter 4.

knows she is much more important than the girl with the same task requirements who assists the division manager.

Exaggerated differences.   But it should be noted that the differences between blue- and white-collar work are declining. At least some factory work
is as clean as office work, some much cleaner (for instance, the spotless,
temperature-controlled manufacturing facilities where delicate instruments are
made and tested). Some factory jobs (like the previously described chief
melter in a steel mill) have a larger component of "brain work" than do most
routine clerical office jobs. And there is some long-run tendency for the pay
differential between blue- and white-collar work to disappear.

White-collar factories.   The almost complete disappearance of differences
between white- and blue-collar work can be observed in what could best be
described as a "white-collar" factory. On a single work floor, there might be an
acre of desks and work tables stretching as far as the eye can see. Minutely
described, mechanized short-cycle jobs, requiring such "tools" as card punchers
or typewriters, are being performed by clerical personnel, all of whom receive
very similar wages.

Identification with management has been much reduced on such jobs.
Promotions to the supervisory level tend to be reserved for college graduates
who come into special training programs that bypass the great majority of
lower-skilled office jobs. As a consequence, many white-collar workers substitute the goals of security and prestige for personal advancement.[19]

Of course, the introduction of computers is changing the office scene.
Whether or not computers have increased or decreased the number of low-
skilled, routine jobs is still being debated. Most modern, "automated" offices
are really at a very primitive stage of automation; indeed, the stage is very
like mass-production work. Employees who punch data on to computer cards or
who place the magnetic ink numerals on the bottom of bank checks are
doing finely divided, highly circumscribed, short-cycle jobs. To be sure, there
are additional programmers, console operators, and maintenance personnel
required, whose jobs are more interesting.[20]

Thus, we find the reactions of many white-collar workers to their jobs very
similar to those described in the previous chapter. Here below, for example,
is a self-description provided by an office worker in a large insurance company:

> "As an operator I had to complete 720 units in 4 hours with no more than 11
> errors. This quota was often very difficult to meet, especially on nights when
> the packs were of more than average difficulty. The job was extremely boring.

---

[19] Roland J. Pellagrini and Charles H. Coates, "Executives and Supervisors: Contrasting
Definitions of Career Success," *Administration Science Quarterly,* Vol. 1, No. 4 (March
1957), pp. 506-512.

[20] For a good review of the impact of mechanization on office jobs see Floyd C. Mann,
"Psychological and Organizational Impacts," in John T. Dunlop, ed., *Automation and Technological Change* (Englewood Cliffs, N.J.: Prentice-Hall, 1962).

"Each pack usually contained 180 policyholders' account cards. About 150 of these had to be billed on 'short forms.' There were two types of short forms— a #1 form and #4 form. The number of each type that was billed was recorded on a digital index on the machine. Usually, each pack had about the same number of each of the two types, and I played games of 'basketball' with each pack with the #1's vs. the #4's. Usually the scores were quite close, and on a couple of occasions the game went into overtime—that is, was continued in the next pack. Punching in the seven numbers that made up the policyholder's account number was my way of 'dribbling the ball down the floor,' and pushing in the button that rang up the total was 'the ball going through the basket.' "

Thus, workers in white-collar factories make a game of routine work just as do machine-tenders in factories.

Distinctive "white-collar" jobs. While differences in prestige and the physical characteristics of the work may have been exaggerated, there are white-collar jobs which provide distinctive satisfactions because of their unique properties. These are the jobs which embody major elements of:

1. Human-relations activity
2. Intellectual effort
3. Managerial responsibility

To be sure some positions require all three, but we shall treat them separately. In addition, we shall see that there is an important trend toward professionalization in white-collar work which has profound implications for the supervision of these types of employees.

WHERE WORK IS HUMAN RELATIONS

The social satisfactions which blue-collar workers are able to obtain are enjoyed for the most part *around* the job; for receptionists, salesmen, waitresses, and others in similar jobs, satisfactory social relations are the essence of their work. Thus, these employees enjoy the opportunity to gain social satisfaction *through* work, but, as a consequence they are subject to much potential frustration when these relations become pressureful.

In these human-relations occupations, employees are often required to fit into closely timed relationships with other employees, many of whom may be under great stress just at the time they are asked for their cooperation. This problem can be most easily observed in restaurants where the waiter feels under great pressure to serve his customers quickly and thus earn more tips. Waiters struggle with bus boys to get their tables cleared and set up quickly to be ready for the next customer. The waiter also may compete with other waiters to get scarce silverware or particular food items in short supply. Conflicts also occur between waiters and personnel in the serving pantry, kitchen and the bar.

Obviously, the need to cooperate under pressure can provide human-relations conflicts where personalities are poorly matched. Many individuals break down under such severe interactional strain: the constant bickering and the need to accommodate to others. For them the relative peace and quiet of a factory job, where "if you do your job no one bothers you," may be far more appealing. Other employees thrive on the hectic pace and the demands of fellow employees and customers alike; for them, interaction under pressure is highly satisfying and only the idleness associated with a slow day or slow season is painful.

A case example: retail selling. Retail selling is typically a fast-paced, unprogramed, demanding occupation and the pressures often exceed those in production work. As in any activity involving a customer, who is not a member of the organization, we find the need to adjust quickly to the whims and fancies of the person who is spending his money and expects *service*.

An example of the human-relations pressures and satisfactions of retailing is provided by the following description of a women's high-fashion specialty store.

> Markhams has three branches in a large midwestern city.[21] It deals in very expensive clothes and has a wealthy clientele. The downtown store is managed by Miss Stoler and her assistant, Sylvia. Frances, Ruth, and Betty are all salesgirls, working on commission.
>
> Whenever Mrs. von Jones and her daughter appear in the store, everyone jumps to attention; they are very good customers. One afternoon, Frances saw them first, greeted them, and used the intercom to call Ruth since they enjoyed having Ruth serve them.
>
> In a minute or two Ruth was on the floor; she took her customers to an alcove which contained a separate large fitting room for each of the women. Within minutes the floor was bustling. Coffee was brought. Miss Stoler joined the elder lady for a chat on a sofa, and Ruth brought dresses from the stockroom for her.
>
> At one point Ruth said to Betty, who now had a customer, too, "Betty, run to the [other] stockroom and get me that size 14." Betty answered that she couldn't right now, she was busy. Ruth, obviously irritated, turned to Sylvia with her request. Sylvia complied.
>
> Ruth soon exhausted the stock of suitable dresses to show Mrs. von Jones. She slipped out to take the back elevator to the Receiving Room, and, peering through the wiremesh security wall, spied several expensive pieces just being unpacked. Upon asking, she was informed that they were destined for a branch store, and would not be ready for transportation until late in the day. She returned in a few minutes with Sylvia, pointed to them, and said, "See, those are the ones." Sylvia, declaring that Miss Stoler had OK'd their removal from the Receiving Room, picked several items for Mrs. von Jones from the rack for the East Side branch, obtained the cost of the dresses from the Receiving Agent, and told Ruth what the price on each would be. Together they went back up the freight elevator.
>
> All the girls were busy on the second floor. No one except Ruth had had a chance to get a bite to eat. Then Mrs. von Jones exclaimed, "But Ruth, don't you have *anything* more for me? And what about my daughter? She needs a dress, too."
>
> The harassed Ruth located Miss Stoler in a stockroom and asked for help.

---

[21] We are indebted to our former student, Mr. M. D. Strickler, for this description.

She then used the phone to call to the main floor for some things to be sent up for the daughter. The floor manager promised help, but, since all her girls were busy, she was obliged to take some things up herself. Ruth called the shoe department, described what had been sold thus far, and told the department head to "get up here now, before she leaves. Your customer will wait." Next Ruth went to get an additional fitter, and became quite angry when the Cashier told her, "Your saleslip isn't completed, and I can't process these charges until you get Mrs. von Jones' signature." Ruth took them back to the floor to get her customer's signature.

Miss Stoler began "closing the sale" with both the von Joneses for several garments, and since they wished to take two items with them, had them packed at the Cashier's desk. The Cashier called to the Credit Department for the OK, and was informed to "hold everything." It seemed that the account was 90 days overdue, in a large sum. When Ruth discovered the garments weren't being packed, she called the Credit Department, and demanded that it be OK'd at once. "She's in a hurry and she'll be mad. Besides, she always pays."

[Note particularly the large number of diverse, unpredictable, and stressful contacts handled by Ruth in response to her customer's demands. In turn, many people in the store must adjust their behavior to meet Ruth's job requirements.]

WHERE WORK IS MENTAL EFFORT

An increasing number of jobs demand intellectual rather than physical effort. Copywriters, laboratory personnel, engineers, and programers all require creative talents that cannot be programed. Satisfactions on these jobs stem from the ability to do challenging work and find solutions to unique problems. Almost all involve depth attention and a highly variable work pace. As a talented designer explained:

> "When ideas come easily and I feel myself making progress, I can work up to 24 hours at a stretch. I often forget meals and don't really know whether it is night or day out or the weekend. Then there are long periods—maybe weeks— in which I can't seem to get anything done. I am always looking for an excuse for a break. If anyone comes near my office I start talking with them and am always going out for food."

When the work is going badly, deadlines are approaching, or an obstacle can't be overcome, tremendous internal tensions are generated. Even slight inconveniences or frictions cause blow-ups:

> The three programers responsible for finishing the work were a month behind; they could not debug what had been written so far. Worse, the computer was always "over them"; it was perfection and it taunted them by finding even the slightest mistake they made. One night when a supervisor came into the machine room and simply asked, "How are things going?" one of the programers flew into a rage.

Often such employees are restless, constantly seeking new assignments even though they might learn more on their present work or will have more to contribute where they have built up a backlog of experience. Endlessly, they try out new methods—even when the old ones have worked and might be quicker to adapt.

Such people usually have an enormous sense of possessiveness. The drawing or copy or program being worked on is "theirs." Although this attitude brings forth extraordinary effort, it can also make it difficult for such people to accept aid, ideas, and advice from others or to modify their work so that it better fits into the work of others.[22] Many take these jobs so that they can work almost alone, with minimum requirements for supervision or coordination.

In this type of work credit for successes and failures is easy to assign. Completion of a difficult assignment leads to elation, even euphoria. Failure leads to depression.

The nature of their work means that these persons frequently know much more about their subject than does their supervisor.

> "When one of my people gets stuck on a problem, I know I can't provide them with technical assistance. A supervisor fools himself who thinks he can. They're prima donnas. Many of those guys have received so much praise that you have to handle them with kid gloves. So the only way I can help them is to get them to step back a little from what they are doing, by asking the right questions. Often they have just been so intensely immersed in the work that they have missed some little point. Once you get them to take a different tack or step back they find their own mistake quickly enough."

MANAGERIAL JOBS

Although the jobs of no two managers are exactly alike, certain characteristics sharply distinguish managerial from nonmanagerial jobs.

Let's look at a typical series of activities constituting a few hours in the life of a manager:

> When Henry came in at 9 A.M. there were already six telephone messages on his desk. He first called back the Employment Office and told them it was all right to hire two temporary secretaries to fill in for vacations. . . . Then he called one of the supervisors in the plant and told him to hold back on the Pickney Order because a parts shortage had turned up yesterday that would delay final assembly work. As his secretary came in to indicate that one of the more nervous expediters was outside waiting to see him, he waved to her their standard signal which meant he was too busy to see anybody. Then he called up Engineering and told them in no uncertain terms that no matter what happened they had to get those drawings done by the afternoon. He ignored the other calls.
>
> As a breather he began glancing at his mail which his secretary had arrayed on the right-hand side of his desk. He soon had picked up a dictating machine to answer those deserving quick attention; several others he handed to the secretary to answer with a "pleasant 'no.'"
>
> To get ready for a meeting with the head of the Division he used a slide rule to work up some figures on comparative costs of contracting-out and doing internally several maintenance jobs. Then he telephoned the Art Department to have the figures placed on large charts for display at the meeting. (He was

---

[22] In such organizations one often hears: NIH, meaning "not invented here," as an explanation of why an idea is rejected.

anxious to make a good impression, since the man responsible for his next promotion was going to be there.)

He remembered that at 9:30 he was scheduled to interview a new engineer and he walked out to escort him into his office. It took 20 minutes to learn something of his background and personality.

Next, another supervisor came in to request that the cost accounting department redo last month's "variance analysis" since he was sure that his groups costs were stated incorrectly. Henry spent ten minutes looking over the figures with the man before agreeing to have them checked. And in the next few minutes, he took a call from a vending-machine company that wanted to install some equipment in the cafeteria, agreed to meet with a union grievance committee at the end of the week, and told an employee that he could not change his vacation date since others were already scheduled.[23]

Within the short space of an hour this executive had been in contact with ten people, engaged in a variety of different types of activity extended from mathematical and mental tactical calculations to interviewing, negotiating, and order-giving. Although he had to respond to other people, the how and when he responded and how he scheduled his day were largely up to him. The unpredictable and ever-changing nature of his job required constant alertness. In that dizzy array of contacts and activities, there was a great deal of challenge and the requirement for real depth attention. For many managers this pace is maintained through a ten- or twelve- (not an eight-) hour day and there is no time to daydream or seek social relationships for their own sake. And yet managers get the same pleasure from the "fielding" of the ever-changing variety of problems that a baseball player gets from a championship game.

Accompanying this pressure are numerous satisfactions derived from having the status of a manager. It is not just the secretary who comes when the buzzer is pressed, but the large number of people whom he can call and who will give him a respectful hearing and who are dependent on him. And, of course, there are his immediate subordinates who accept him as their leader.

Particularly at higher levels of the organization, the manager derives enormous satisfaction from power, knowing he can influence critical decisions and may control the expenditure of tens or hundreds of thousands of dollars. And indeed the success or failure of new ventures may well be dependent on his personal acumen and decision-making skill.

In addition, managerial work pays well. In our society, salary is an index of success, a measure of accomplishment. For the executive, salary is the score card that tells him how far and how fast he has moved ahead. What he does with money is less important than the mere fact of earning it.

There is a price to be paid for these satisfactions: heavy responsibilities and anxieties. Mistakes are easy to make, in part because the manager has to please other people, particularly those above him in the organization. Further, the

---

[23] For more extended descriptions of managerial life, see Leonard Sayles, *Managerial Behavior* (New York: McGraw-Hill, 1964); and Walter Guzzardi, Jr., *The Young Executives* (New York: New American Library, 1966).

success of his activities depends upon many people he does not directly control (for instance, the staff departments within the company). Since so much of his job involves decision-making and human-relations skills, the evaluation of which tends to be subjective, most managers feel themselves especially vulnerable to criticism, even to severe penalties (such as demotion) for making decisions which higher management does not like. Further, there is fierce rivalry for promotion at managerial levels—by fair means and foul.[24] Still, most managers thrive on competition.

Unfortunately, successful executives are seldom aware of how different their jobs are from those of nonmanagerial subordinates.

> "These workers don't want to give a fair day's work; they're always looking for a chance to get out of work, to talk or loaf or fool around. They don't want to take responsibility and show what they can do, even though it could lead to a promotion or a raise sometime."

What this manager is forgetting is that these other employees cannot obtain the same intrinsic satisfactions he obtains. They cannot see the same rewards for themselves in the future nor can they get so involved in and committed to the future of the company. Neither participating in the key decisions nor able to see their impact, they view the company as something separate from themselves. For many managers, in contrast, the success of the organization and their own success are inextricably interwoven. And this identification in itself is enormously gratifying.

Professionalization

An increasing number of employees in jobs requiring high orders of mental ability conceive of themselves as professionals. By this we mean that they identify more with their field of competence than they do with any specific employer. Primarily they seek job opportunities which will enlarge their knowledge and broaden their skills. The same high expectations may increasingly be characteristic of managers who jump with alacrity from company to company to find opportunities to gain a greater sense of fulfillment by dealing with more challenging assignments.

Of course, at least some of these rising aspirations and feelings of independence stem from an extended period of high employment and affluence, at least for those with scarce expertise. The very opposite of the assembly-line worker, who feels himself expendable with every slight shift in demand or technological change, is the professional. Just a few years ago an advance-degree "egg head" on the payroll was considered pure overhead and a luxury. Now such professionals are often working at the core of the business. Many

---

[24] There is a vast literature on besting one's rivals in this intra-management competition. For example: Chester Burger, *Survival in the Executive Jungle* (New York: Macmillan, 1964).

employers make no secret of their growing dependence on "knowledge workers," who constitute an ever larger proportion of the typical payroll. The head of one very successful company explained why his firm had paid such a premium for another company they had taken over: "Why they had 200 Ph.D.s working for them and we needed that talent. We bought the people as much as the company!"

STATUS AND PROFESSIONAL AUTONOMY

Most of us tend to think of professionalism as being a characteristic of those very few occupational groups to which society has accorded the highest status: doctors, lawyers, ministers, professors, and the like. Their high status gives them special benefits. Most importantly they do not have to accept many orders; their expert skill makes them immune to pressures from others. They have great autonomy. Further, they expect that when they ask someone else for assistance, it will be forthcoming immediately and without question. (When a doctor makes a request, the nurse typically jumps to serve.)

A profession has an integrated and distinctive body of knowledge which only its members can lay claim to mastering. There is a long, carefully supervised learning period for neophytes; only those who can pass a difficult series of tests are admitted to full-fledged membership. They, in turn, are committed to a lifetime career in their specialty. Also, professionals subscribe to high ethical standards (such as the doctor's Hippocratic Oath) to serve the interests of the broader society rather than selfish goals. These standards are enforced by the professional group itself, which typically has special review and disciplinary procedures to evaluate questionable behavior on the part of its members. Further, professionals expect to be supervised, if at all, by a peer, someone with comparable technical training.

DUAL LOYALTY AND SOURCES OF CONFLICT

Professionals have their own standards of what constitutes advancement. To be sure, they are interested in higher incomes and status titles (though they sometimes deny this).[25] Still, many professionals place less value on salary than on other satisfactions. For example, many chemists would not give up a challenging assignment in an organization that had prestige in the profession (say, a highly regarded Foundation-sponsored laboratory) for a higher paying job with an organization that lacked these attributes.[26]

Professionals seek recognition primarily from their fellow professionals. Thus, they are tied to a criterion of excellence that exists outside the organization for which they work. In a way they have a dual loyalty. This dual loyalty

---

[25] See Robert Weiss, *Process of Organization* (Ann Arbor, Mich.: Survey Research Center, Institute for Social Research, 1956), p. 48.

[26] John Thibaut and Harold Kelley, *The Social Psychology of Groups* (New York: Wiley, 1959), see Chapter 12.

may both help and hinder the administration. A man's feeling of professional pride may motivate him to work harder and to maintain higher standards than he would otherwise.[27] A study of hospitals found that this motivation was an important element in explaining the doctors' high level of voluntary cooperation in accepting many unpleasant administrative procedures.[28]

On the other hand, conflict arises when a man is more interested in winning recognition from his professional colleagues than from the organization for which he works. For example, the medical profession has a tendency to look down on physicians who take administrative jobs in hospitals, and for this reason highly qualified men may refuse such assignments. Similarly, engineers, scientists, and professors sometimes turn down promotions that require administrative work which may interfere with their research.

> Management believes that an individual's success is primarily a product of his position on the management ladder. . . . [Yet] many technicians in this environment, though not all, still cling to their belief that success for an individual should be as a result of his technical achievements.[29]
> They are more interested in approbation by their colleagues than in the promotions offered by management. Such a radically different way of thinking is often completely foreign to the manager; his values are too different and he finds it difficult to understand what makes professionals in technical fields behave so "queerly." [30]

Engineers and scientists with professional orientations may resent work assignments that do not offer challenge and the opportunity to make some kind of break-through. They may prefer seeking new solutions to "tried and true" old methods, preferring basic research to applied research. They can resent accepting orders from supervisors who do not have comparable professional training and find standard rules of conduct within the organization needlessly confining and nothing more than "bureaucratic red tape." [31] As one manager described them: "They are bright, belligerent, and independent."

THE NEW PROFESSIONALS

Many groups are striving to professionalize themselves and thus join the ranks (and get the privileges) of the older established professions.[32] For

---

[27] Donald Pelz, "Social Factors Related to Performance in a Research Organization," *Administrative Science Quarterly,* Vol. I, No. 3 (December 1956), p. 312.

[28] Temple Burling, Edith Lentz, and Robert Wilson, *The Give and Take in Hospitals* (New York: Putnam, 1956), p. 86.

[29] Further, the fact that a man is a good scientist or engineer does not necessarily make him a good administrator. In promoting such a person, management may gain a poor administrator and lose a good professional.

[30] Charles Orth, "More Productivity for Engineers," *Harvard Business Review,* Vol. 35, No. 2 (March 1957), pp. 54-55.

[31] *Cf.* Simon Marcson, *The Scientist in American Industry* (Princeton, N.J.: Princeton University, Industrial Relations Section, 1960); and Charles Orth, Joseph Bailey, and Francis Wolek, *Administering Research and Development* (Homewood, Ill.: Irwin, 1964).

[32] For studies of professionalism, see A. M. Carr Saunders and P. S. Wilson, *The Professions* (Oxford: Clarendon Press, 1933); Everett C. Hughes, *Men and Their Work* (New

example, security analysts, hospital administrators, purchasing agents, programers, and industrial engineers are attempting to establish standards that will set themselves apart—and, hopefully, above—individuals who claim some competence in these fields but who lack formal preparation or adequate experience. Understandably, these staff specialists, whose claim to authority is based on formal professional training, often come into conflict with line managers whose knowledge and skill derive primarily from long years of on-the-job experience, intuition, and good common sense.

At times, the claim to the title of "professional" may be a tactic in an intergroup struggle. Managers whose promotions have been blocked or who see themselves losing influence may take refuge in professionalism as a source of job satisfaction. A safety director rationalized:

> "Safety is a real profession as good as any of them. We can't all be chiefs . . . I have lots of contacts with other companies presumably with men having similar specialties. I belong to two societies and also panels and community organizations." [33]

In some cases management may even encourage individuals who, for one reason or another, are unlikely to raise their organizational status through the normal route of promotions to conceive of themselves as professionals. As professionals, it is hoped, they will be more interested in technical expertise than increased managerial responsibility. [34]

THE ORGANIZATION VS. THE PROFESSIONAL

It would be a mistake to exaggerate, however, the restlessness of the typical professional working in industry. Many possess scarce, respected skills to which both fellow employees and management are deferential. They often receive special treatment, and their requests for services and assistance are honored before the requests of less prestigious employees. The modern organization provides a wealth of interesting assignments, and many people feel that "real-life" problems, where stakes are great, are much more exciting than problems in a cloistered academic atmosphere. The professional's goals of increased knowledge and skill and the solution of difficult problems are often company goals as well. Thus, the professional may see little conflict between his needs and the company's needs. For professionals, relationships with like-trained supervisors are usually informal, approaching relations between colleagues, and thus more satisfying than those enjoyed by other occupational groups.

York: The Free Press of Glencoe, 1958); William Kornhauser, *Scientists in Industry* (Berkeley: University of California Press, 1962); George Strauss, "Professionalism and Occupational Associations," *Industrial Relations*, Vol. 2, No. 3 (May 1963), pp. 7-31; and Harold Wilensky, "The Professionalism of Everyone?" *American Journal of Sociology*, Vol. 70, No. 2 (September 1964), pp. 137-158.

[33] We are indebted to our colleague Dr. Fred Goldner for this example.

[34] Fred Goldner and Richard Ritti, "Professionalization As Career Mobility" (Unpublished Manuscript, 1965).

Conclusion

With the exception of "white-collar factories" we have noted that newer technologies do hold forth the promise of significantly greater through-the-job satisfactions than many of the more traditional jobs associated with manufacturing. In truly automated factories (what we have called process production) as well as in many of the growing white-collar occupations, employees obtain very real ego rewards, derived from identification with the work and opportunities for autonomy, advancement, and a sense of accomplishment. In addition, social relations are a part, not an escape from, the work.

But as we have seen in our discussion of professionalization, these opportunities are more than matched by the rising aspirations of job holders. An increasing number of employees identify more strongly with their occupation than with any employer. In later chapters, when we discuss supervisory and organizational structure problems, it will be with these groups in mind. They do have high motivation, growing out of the depth-attention jobs they fill, but it is not always simple to direct these energies in such a way that they mesh with larger organization goals.

Thus, specialization does not inevitably lead to routine, monotony, and job insecurity. Modern industry calls for specialized persons as well as specialized jobs. The former, both highly trained and self-confident, bear little resemblance to the employees conceived by Taylor and his scientific management.

One of the most valued sources of satisfaction in many of the jobs created by the new technologies is the sense of doing work that is obviously important. Both managers and the highly trained "brain workers" in industry see themselves as contributing to key decisions that shape the well-being of the organization. Also, many service-industry employees and those in process manufacturing can view a *total operation* which is the heart or close to the heart of the business. Those who control expensive automation machinery, just as those who work at the customer-organization interface in a store or bank or restaurant, can observe the relationship between their efforts and business success.

PROBLEM ONE

The New Waiter

When I first came to work as a waiter for the Krautter Restaurant, I was sure I would not stay for very long; there seemed to be so much animosity.

Waiters were supposed to get "set ups" for their table (silver and glassware) from the pantry, but by mid-evening there were always shortages. Many waiters would take more than they needed in order to be sure they would not run out, and some would go into the kitchen to get things directly from the dishwashers, although this was against the rules. Many times there were arguments over hoarding of silver, and the dishwashers frequently chased waiters out of their area of the kitchen.

Busboys cleared tables, but I soon learned that one had to add something extra to the normal share of the tips received by the busboys if one expected to get fast service. Similarly, when customers asked for a special item (for instance, very rare beef) and the restaurant was busy, it was difficult to get the serving chefs to oblige. If you asked twice for something, they took this as an insult to their skill or intelligence, and giving something back to them could cause a mighty uproar. They seemed to have a real "chip on their shoulders."

I noticed that most of the old timers had "paired off" so that one waiter could ask his "buddy" for help when he fell behind. As a newcomer, however, I had difficulty getting anyone to cooperate with me. The result was that I often could not provide the service that customers expected and they would get upset and complain. Often this meant a very low tip and in some cases no tip at all, which is the worst insult a waiter can receive. However, at times I had the feeling that the hostess was sending people to my tables who had a reputation for being poor tippers. This, too, hurt my feelings.

All this was very puzzling to me. Waiting on table had looked so easy. I liked people and was willing to work hard, but this job was much more difficult than I had anticipated.

1. Which of the human-relations problems described here are typical of all service-industry jobs and which represent poor management?
2. What are the potential positive sources of need satisfaction that this new waiter is not describing and that may become more important when his "initiation" period is over.

P R O B L E M   T W O

The Life of the Programer [35]

The Western Insurance Company, a large casualty insurance writer, had more than 5,000 employees. Several years ago it had established a separate computerized data-processing section. The center of activity in this department was the computer itself along with the programing group which developed new computer programs to handle the company's payroll, premium and policy-holder records, billings, and so forth. In addition, the department stored computer tapes which contained great quantities of data that were relevant to these activities of the firm.

Unlike most of the clerical personnel in the company, programers did not have to punch a time clock, could take their lunch hour whenever they desired, and had no set coffee breaks. In total, there were about 25 in the group, most of them quite young. Almost all had college degrees, although a few were still attending evening classes. Even so, the programers had also been extensively trained by the company for their specialized work and continued to attend regular company training programs as new techniques and problems were introduced into their division.

The supervisor seemed to have the full confidence of the employees since he himself was an expert in their field. The more skilled and experienced programers were often sought out by the supervisor and other members of management for their advice on highly technical problems. Programing was the type of work in which some of the more routine tasks could be assigned to the youngest, least experienced workers (for example, the coding).

There was actually a good deal of work tension in the group. Although

---

[35] This description was written by one of the programers at Western Insurance.

schedules could not be precisely set for the completion of a new program, because of all the uncertainties involved, the company was often in a hurry to finish the program so that data could be processed. Thus, there were pressures to meet deadlines. Further, large programs were divided up among a number of programers, and the work of each individual depended on that of his fellows. The computer itself was a source of tension because it demanded perfect work; and discrepancies or mistakes in logic would show up every time.

As a result, the successful testing of an important program was cause for general celebration throughout the group. Furthermore, a good deal of joking and light-heartedness was utilized to lessen the tension when one or more programers were having difficulties. There was an enormous sense of unity in the group since each man could understand exactly the problem another was facing and the tensions he was working under.

As we have seen the department was physically separate from the rest of the organization. While most of the company worked, particularly in the summer, under sweltering conditions, the programers, because of the needs of the computer, worked in refreshing air-conditioning.

Whereas most employees regarded Western Insurance as "a job," the programers thought of themselves as being specialists. They realized that their task was highly important to over-all company operations, and they had a sense of both responsibility and dedication. They were proud of the fact that they had successfully and jointly overcome a number of difficult schedules to develop the crucial programs that were the underpinning of the company's data-processing operations. This was a highly prestigious and strategic accomplishment. They felt the company could not operate without them.

Although pressure was often high and the work difficult, the constant impersonal push associated with factory work was lacking. And although there were set procedures underlying programing, much was left to the programer's skill, judgment, and discretion. There were no unalterable time tables or precisely defined methods that could be laid out for each project. The coordination came out of the closely timed human-relations patterns that the employees evolved as a means of working together.

Many of the programers often voluntarily remained overtime to complete a project; some worked right through a weekend when they were behind or felt that the work was going especially well. Some of the enthusiasm, of course, stemmed from having been instrumental in the establishment of an important new division and getting in, so to speak, "on the ground floor."

Also, the group seemed to have set its own goals and aims concerning the projects it hoped the company would eventually undertake and the course which data-processing would follow over the next few years at Western Insurance. This interest gave the programers something more personal and more concrete than the vague company goals that were supposed to motivate other employees. Each person became so important on a new programing assignment that he couldn't even take a vacation without expecting to be telephoned at least once during the period.

Recognition in the group was bestowed on the basis of ability and accomplishment—and a newcomer soon knew where every programer stood in terms of his ability. High-status programers got the desks enclosed by partitions, had both an "out" and an "in" mail basket on their desks, and enjoyed the privilege of keeping their graphic tools rather than having to return them to a central pool.

The programers had a sense of a career, the feeling that their skill and knowledge were being constantly broadened and refined and that the future promised new and exciting jobs and unlimited advancement possibilities in a dynamic growing field. While the career line of jobs was limited within their present department, the company was expanding data-processing procedures in its other branches; and if a programer did not desire to remain in this line of work indefinitely, the experience he gained was highly useful in achieving other jobs in the company.

1. List each of the elements in the job of the programer that appears to contribute to high motivation.
2. How unique or distinctively related to programing are these and which might be found in most white-collar jobs?
3. Which suggest possible job modifications that management can make in other types of technology to achieve comparable motivational effects?

PROBLEM THREE

En Route [36]

Each newspaper delivery driver was required to make two trips each day with a jumper assigned to his truck as he left the paper's main garage. The stops were outlined on a sheet of paper along with the amount to be delivered at each stop. Drivers knew the time allotment for all routes and would never come back to the plant before that time allotment expired.

One of the most attractive aspects of working as a jumper or a driver was that usually at least six hours of the eight-hour day were spent away from the plant and immediate supervision. Invariably, the men would "pull the route" the quickest way, taking advantage of all short cuts, rearranging the list, and accepting help in unloading from the waiting newsboys. Some did so just to prove that they knew routes better than the men who assigned them.

They would finish unloading all papers and then proceed to a place where the truck could be effectively hidden away from the prying eyes of an occasional newspaper executive who might happen by. The driver and jumper would then pass at their leisure an hour or more in a bar, poolroom, or lunchroom, until it was time to return to the plant.

If you worked as a manager in this newspaper, are there changes you would make in these jobs? Justify your "yes" or "no" answer.

---

[36] We are indebted to a former student, Donald C. Waite III, for this case.

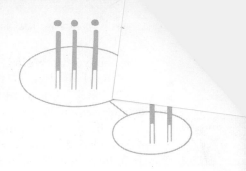

Work Groups
and Informal Organization

4

We have seen that social needs are among the most powerful and compelling on-the-job motivations. The people who make up organizations behave as members of groups, and their membership helps shape their work behavior and attitudes toward the organization and the job. Groups may exercise far stronger control over their members than does management. Since management can achieve its ends only through working with people, it must also work through groups. But before considering the problems of supervising groups, we must first understand why groups develop and how they function.

Why Groups Are Formed

COMPANIONSHIP

Psychologists may argue about whether man is born with the need for society or acquires it early in life; yet the need for relationships with other people is one of the strongest and most constant of human drives.

As we have discovered, many jobs call forth only a small fraction of a person's total abilities. To management he may be just another unit of labor or a time-clock number; to his friends on the job he is an individual. To these colleagues an employee can be himself and express his true feelings.

Research indicates employees who have no opportunity for close social contact find their work unsatisfying, and this lack of satisfaction often reflects itself in low production and high turnover and absenteeism. Many years ago Elton Mayo observed that employees in a textile plant who worked at isolated jobs were highly dissatisfied and consistently failed to meet production standards. Staggered rest periods helped a little. But when the company permitted these workers to take rest periods *as a group,* production and satisfaction both increased.[1] Another company, where the girls worked in small, isolated booths, had the same experience. When management put glass partitions between the booths, the rate of turnover and the number of grievances both dropped sharply. Similarly, researchers in hospitals have discovered that maids feel uncomfortable when they work only in the company of high-status personnel (doctors, nurses, etc.) with whom they cannot associate with ease. Several hospitals have found that when three or four maids are grouped together as a team, turnover falls and a much better job is done.[2]

IDENTIFICATION

The difference may be subtle—but people want more than just to have friends, they want to *belong.* One can sense that he is part of a larger organization only by indirection, but the shared experiences of one's immediate colleagues are among the most meaningful and potent sources of job satisfaction.

Extensive studies during World War II indicated that soldiers' willingness to show bravery and make sacrifices was correlated not with loyalty to country or understanding of the war issues, but with loyalty to the immediate group. In other words, men committed acts of heroism that were motivated largely by the desire not to let their buddies down.[3]

Having learned this lesson, the army abandoned its system of bringing individual replacements into combat units and instead began rotating units as a whole.

During the same war the rapidly growing West Coast aircraft industry was troubled by extremely high turnover. No sooner was a worker partially trained

---

[1] Elton Mayo, *The Human Problems of an Industrial Civilization* (Boston: Graduate School of Business Administration, Harvard University, 1946), pp. 42-52. It should be noted that other factors were introduced that contributed to the improved morale and productivity. The work was broken up into self-contained tasks, and the rest periods themselves helped combat fatigue and monotony.

[2] Temple Burling, Edith Lentz, and Robert Wilson, *The Give and Take in Hospitals* (New York: Putnam, 1956), pp. 181-192.

[3] E. A. Shils, "Primary Groups in the American Army," in R. K. Merton and P. F. Lazarsfeld, eds., *Continuities in Social Research: Studies in the Scope and Method of the American Soldier* (New York: The Free Press of Glencoe, 1950), pp. 16-39.

than he quit. Research indicates that this pattern was associated with the absence of stable work groups. Since new employees never became part of a stable group, they developed no loyalty to the group and either quit or asked for a transfer at the slightest dissatisfaction.[4]

Other studies indicate that smaller groups tend to enjoy higher morale. Employees working in large departments where everybody does the same job find it hard to form stable social groupings and often have low morale. Many companies with large secretarial pools are putting up waist-high barriers on the office floor to encourage the development of social groups and team spirit.

UNDERSTANDING FROM FRIENDS

The daily work routine is rich in opportunities for frustrations and tension. Whether we are harassed by an overbearing customer, an obstreperous typewriter, or a picayune inspector, we all seek a sympathetic ear, preferably from someone who has had similar experiences and can thus share and understand our troubles. Organizations that lack this outlet sometimes rely on the clumsy and expensive system of employee counseling, in which outsiders "hear out" employee troubles.

GUIDE TO ACCEPTABLE BEHAVIOR

Whenever we are thrown into a new social situation, we are uncertain about how we are expected to behave. Our work days are filled with ambiguous situations. How much time should I take for a coffee break? Is it all right to talk to fellow employees while the boss is in the room? Must all copy be shown to the advertising manager? Even where there are established rules, one question remains: Is everybody expected to live by the letter of the law? Most employees don't want to violate the generally accepted "rules of the game"; at the same time they don't want to conform to restrictive rules that everyone else ignores. They want to know the "right" thing to do. The group fills an important need by providing all its members with a kind of "guide to correct behavior"—correct not in terms of any written policies, but in terms of what is actually acceptable.

OPPORTUNITIES FOR INITIATIVE AND CREATIVITY

Many jobs which appear superficially dull and routine are made more interesting by the individual ingenuity and spontaneity encouraged and protected by the group. Although it may appear to the casual observer that management has defined a rigid series of job requirements, work groups

---

[4] Elton Mayo and George F. F. Lombard, *Teamwork and Labor Turnover in Aircraft Industry of Southern California* (Boston: Graduate School of Business Administration, Harvard University, 1944).

provide a setting which spurs the individual to modify the job situation more to his own liking:

> Extra work breaks can be obtained because employees spell one another. Unpleasant tasks assigned to one man can be rotated or shared by group agreement.

> Clever techniques for "beating" a difficult incentive formula can be worked out with the collusion of fellow group members.

The key point here is that all of these new activities take initiative and energy. Thus, on jobs which appear to require little of either, an outlet can be found in the informal modifications of the environment that are sanctioned by the group.[5]

HELP IN SOLVING WORK PROBLEMS

A new sales clerk may not be sure about how to handle a complicated problem of returning some merchandise. A lab technician may be hesitant about asking his boss to repeat instructions, yet he is afraid that he may ruin the experiment unless he receives additional information. In each case the employee turns to his fellow workers for assistance, often preferring this source of help.[6]

The group's solution to a problem may differ from what management expects, and it may even be more efficient. Red tape is eliminated; shortcuts are evolved; informal channels of communication are established to cut across department boundaries. By the same token, work groups may also engage in featherbedding and work-restriction.

Certain jobs can be done by isolated workers, but working as a group often results in higher individual motivation and a faster work pace. Some groups observe regular rituals (such as a coffee break when a given task is done) which serve to emphasize the group nature of the task.[7] Even schools are experimenting successfully with teaming students together rather than allowing each pupil to work alone or wait his turn to recite. Team members provide mutual help which increases the rate of learning.

Obviously, in most cases management must take the responsibility of making specific work assignments, but there are work situations in which a cohesive group can do a better job of fitting individual personalities to the work process

---

[5] A good over-all description of this process is Ivar Berg's "Some Unlikely Sources of Initiative and Creativity," in Leonard Sayles, ed., *Individualism and Big Business* (New York: McGraw-Hill, 1964), pp. 35-46.

[6] A study of government employees found that they consistently preferred getting assistance from fellow employees to going to the manager, and this ability to provide aid was a source of substantial prestige for the giver. Peter Blau, *Dynamics of Bureaucracy* (Chicago: University of Chicago Press, 1955).

[7] For example, see Donald F. Roy, " 'Banana Time': Job Satisfaction and Informal Interaction," *Human Organization*, Vol. 18, No. 4 (Winter 1959-1960), pp. 158-168.

and making expedient job assignment changes as new problems arise. The manager's decisions, since they must encompass a longer time period, are often less flexible and timely than the group's.

Where the technology imposes extreme interdependence, and precise and instant coordination is required, for example in military fighting crews, the organization depends on the group to control and specify the individual's contribution to the total effort.[8]

PROTECTION FOR THE MEMBERSHIP

Groups help protect their members from outside pressures. As we shall discuss later on, groups often resist management demands for additional output, longer work hours, and higher quality. Most dynamic organizations have a tendency to introduce changes in work methods and routines at a faster rate than the individual can adjust to them. The pace at which these changes are introduced can be materially altered by a determined work group.

Without a sense of group allegiance, individual workers may behave in ways that will injure their fellow workers. The work group often disciplines members who try to earn the supervisor's favor by "squealing" on fellow employees or by turning out too much work, or who fail to help their fellow workers on the job.

> A market-analysis office was required to prepare reports for top management. As time passed, the men made these reports increasingly elaborate, using colored graphs, photographic reproductions, and ever-more detailed data. Some of this window-dressing had real value, but most of it was designed to catch the boss' attention. At last, the men realized that they were spending tremendous amounts of uncompensated overtime in their efforts to outdo one another. Finally, they got together and agreed on standards to limit their competitive efforts.

In some groups the members actually agree on the level of output each will put forth so that no one member will out-perform the others.

The most common target of group power is the immediate manager. Most managers are quick to recognize that although they have the authority to make a wide range of decisions, to make certain decisions would be downright foolhardy (see Chapter 8). The members of the group can express their displeasure by cutting down their work pace, sabotaging the work (discreetly, of course, so that blame will be hard to place), or making their boss look inept to his own superiors.

---

[8] It has been suggested that turnover of membership in an airline crew can increase the safety hazard since almost instantaneous collaboration is required in emergencies. Such collaboration can only result from working together as a team for a long time. Team members have to be trained as a group as well; it is less useful to train them as individual performers. William Karraker, "Teamwork and Safety in Flight," *Human Organization*, Vol. 17, No. 3 (Fall 1958), pp. 3-8.

How Work Groups Are Formed

When an engineer designs the plans and technology for a new factory, and when an architect designs the office layout, they are also designing the social relations that will prevail within the organization. Management determines where men will work and what opportunities they will have to contact each other during the day. It also determines rates of pay, conditions of work, and the various symbols that are associated with each job. Given these basic elements, a sophisticated observer can predict the social relations that will exist within the organization long before the first employee enters the building.[9]

In telling men where and how they are to work, management is also telling them with whom they will come into contact. Normally, individuals develop friendships with the people they see most often. In fact, employees who have the greatest opportunities to make contacts on the job make the largest number of friends and are in the best position to become leaders of the group.

> A study of a housing project for married students indicated that friendship patterns were determined by apartment locations. Most families made a majority of their friends within their own building and especially on their own floor. Furthermore, those whose apartments were located on the ground floor nearest the building entrance had the best chance of becoming social leaders. Those who were physically isolated in end units were also most socially isolated and least liked.[10]

MULTIPLE GROUP-MEMBERSHIPS

Rarely do participants in an organization belong to just one group. Take Adam Kopka, a mechanical engineer in the W Company. He has one group of friends whom he works with on a development project: two electrical engineers, a technician, and a chemist. In addition, he is identified with all those who report to Alex Fisher, the manager of the Special Projects Department, which includes two other project groups. He also feels close to other mechanical engineers who are scattered through the laboratory. His lunch group and after-hours bowling associates may include still other people. Now each of these groups has a different membership, although there may be a great deal of overlapping. For some purposes one group is the most important to Adam; for others, another. The mere fact that he belongs to several groups, however, may subject him to considerable stress when their respective interests come into conflict.

---

[9] For two such predictive studies, see A. Zaleznik, C. R. Christensen, and F. J. Roethlisberger, *The Motivation, Productivity and Satisfaction of Workers: A Prediction Study* (Boston: Graduate School of Business Administration, Harvard University, 1958); and Leonard Sayles, *Behavior of Industrial Work Groups* (New York: Wiley, 1958).

[10] See Leon Festinger, Stanley Schachter, and Kurt Back, *Social Pressures in Informal Groups* (New York: Harper, 1950).

Suppose, for instance, that the mechanical engineers grow concerned that their jobs and point of view are assuming less significance in the laboratory. The engineers agree among themselves to exert greater pressure for higher mechanical-engineering standards in their design work. As long as Adam is in the company of his fellow mechanical engineers, he feels this is a fine decision. Back in his project group, however, he may find that this is a minority position and he is under pressure to emphasize other project goals. Now he feels under cross pressures; he can't be loyal to both groups.

THE GROUP BECOMES AN ORGANIZATION

Employees form friendship groups based on their contacts and common interests—and these groups arise out of the life of the organization. Once these groups have been established, however, they develop a life of their own that is almost completely separate from the work process from which it arose. This is a dynamic, self-generating process. Brought together by the formal organization, employees interact with one another. Increasing interaction builds favorable sentiments toward fellow group-members. In turn, these sentiments become the foundation for an increased variety of activities, many not specified by the job descriptions: special lunch arrangements, trading of job duties, fights with those outside the group, gambling on paycheck numbers. And these increased opportunities for interaction build stronger bonds of identification.[11] Then the group becomes something more than a mere collection of people. It develops a customary way of doing things—a set of stable characteristics that are hard to change. It becomes an *organization* in itself.

SUBOPTIMIZATION: GROUP GOALS

From the point of view of management, what are the major characteristics of these new suborganizations? So far, we have just illustrated that they perform a psychological function for the individual: providing support and permissiveness. Most importantly, the group sets goals for itself that become important motivators for the individual.

In the large organization, everyone—manager and nonmanager—is supposed to be working toward the same objectives. But individuals are likely to put their own need satisfactions ahead of these goals. In addition, groupings of individuals set goals for themselves and these goals take precedence over the total organization's objectives. Here is one example:

> The installation of a new computer in the Y Corporation was delayed two years by an interdepartmental struggle over who would control this new equipment. The Finance group claimed that it should be under their jurisdiction but Production and Sales both wanted a new "Computation and Programing" department to be created. Finance felt it would lose prestige if a separate department was created while Production and Sales believed that the new com-

---

11 The best theoretical description of this process is George Homans, *The Human Group* (New York: Harcourt, Brace and World, 1950), pp. 48-155.

puter would not be as helpful to them if it was placed in an existing department. Thus, a very costly piece of equipment was wasted for two years, from the point of view of the total organization, because of these special interest groupings.

In a sense, then, the organization pays some price in divisiveness for the help of the group in attaching and holding the individual. This has come to be called the *suboptimization* problem, where small group objectives tend to conflict with or take precedence over the larger organization's goals. Members are motivated primarily by small group goals, not by large organization goals. (For more examples see Chapter 16.)

Internal Structure of Groups

To perpetuate themselves, to move in the direction of accomplishing their goals, and to provide the protection and support their membership needs, work groups require an internal structure. "Structure" here means a set of unique characteristics that determine the members' relationships to one another and to supervision, the standards of conduct that are approved and enforced by the group, its system of rewards and punishments, and its system of communication.

All these aspects of group life are in balance with one another, or, as the social scientist would say, they are in equilibrium: (1) They are all interrelated, (2) a change in any one of them has an immediate effect on all the others, and (3) the members strongly resist changes in any part of this interrelated system. What, specifically, are these characteristics that dictate the internal organization of the group?

LEADERSHIP

Every group has informal leaders—individuals who have a special sort of status which results in their being followed by other members of the group. The informal leader is a very different sort of leader from the supervisor appointed by management. The formally appointed leader is followed because directly or indirectly he has the power to discharge those who refuse to obey his orders. The informal leader has no such power. Why, then, is he followed? He is followed because the members learn that the group will not provide them with the benefits they seek unless they have some established leadership. Someone has to take the initiative in getting people to recognize that there is a common problem to be solved. The leader circulates through the group to urge a united front against a new threat from management, or to devise punishment for an uncooperative fellow member. In the process of developing consensus on what needs to be done, a successful leader is careful to sound out the members and to smooth over internal differences of opinion by personal persuasion and suggested compromises. He also serves as the group's representative in contacting the supervisor, or the union, or other work groups.

In summary, the leader performs vital functions that contribute to the group's ability to survive in its environment:

1. He initiates action.
2. He facilitates a consensus.
3. He provides a link or liaison with the outside world: managers, other work groups, the union.

Most observers have a tendency to refer to *the* informal leader, as though a single leader could be identified in every group. Actually, unless the group is very small, the functions we have described are usually shared by several active individuals who together comprise the leadership of the group. Although the supervisor is most aware of the employee who contacts him as the group's representative, he must recognize that within the group, in less obvious positions, there may be other equally influential leaders adept in the use of human-relations skill as well as members who seek leadership but are rejected by the group.[12] The manager needs to be aware of these differences among the more active members of any group to be in a position to influence the group. Often, as we shall see later, it is easier to accomplish change by dealing with the group through its leaders than by attempting to persuade or order individuals to change.

Many studies have been conducted to determine the personality traits that characterize the effective group leader, but none of these studies has been altogether successful. It appears that each group requires a type of leadership suited to its own particular needs. These studies do suggest one important generalization, however: The group leader must live up to the group's idealized conception of what a group member should be. In the study of the bank-wiring room at the Western Electric Company, the informal leader of the group was described as follows:

> He was a key member of the superior clique and . . . one of the two men whose output conformed most closely and consistently to the accepted idea of a proper day's work. . . . In every way, indeed, he embodied the norms the group had adopted as its own. He never broke a rate, "chiseled," "squealed," or took a superior tone. . . .[13]

Some members of a group may aspire to a position of leadership without ever winning group acceptance. Outsiders may assume that these men are more influential than they actually are, when they are particularly active in contacting others. It is important to distinguish between the two types of leader, since the false leader rarely represents the true feelings of the group he pretends to lead.[14]

---

[12] In fact some studies suggest that every stable group has at least two leaders, a task leader whose function it is to drive the group toward its goal, and a human-relations leader who keeps the group from falling apart.

[13] Homans, *op. cit.*, pp. 147-149.

[14] A good description of these leaders can be found in T. T. Paterson, *Glasgow Limited: A Case-Study in Industrial War and Peace* (Cambridge: Cambridge University Press, 1960), p. 171.

GROUP STANDARDS OF BEHAVIOR

The urge to conform to group standards pervades most social life. Teenage boys must be careful not to act too differently if they want to be accepted by the gang. Adolescent girls must dress like the other girls in their crowd, even if their parents object. There are group standards in industry as well. Some of these standards exist for the sole purpose of making life more enjoyable for the group members: The accounts receivable department always goes out together for lunch; the maintenance gang spends its breaks playing gin rummy. If you don't do these things—you don't *belong*.

Other customs serve to make the job easier or to heighten the quality of workmanship. Waiters agree among themselves to share all tips equally and to help one another serve and clear tables during rush hours; if a college professor has to miss a class, his colleagues will try to stand in for him; retail clerks "spell" one another so that all the counters will be covered while one clerk is taking a break. All these customs reflect the expectations of group members with respect to one another's behavior.

Probably the most important group standards are those that protect the members of the group against real or imagined outside dangers, particularly from upper management. Production workers may agree on a level of output and exert pressure on those who deviate from it—especially on those who produce more than the accepted "bogey." "Eager beavers" in the classroom are frequently reminded that "C" is the "gentleman's grade." Group standards of good workmanship and high quality often make management's task easier; for the group, by taking "troublemakers" in hand, reduces the need for management to impose discipline.

Thus, from management's point of view, the pressure to conform to group standards may be most desirable. A standard that a worker can be five minutes late also means that the group will prevent him from abusing this privilege.

A group of white-collar employees was frequently given the afternoon off when the ball team played a home game. Without any prompting from management, the employees agreed among themselves to come in an hour early to compensate for the short days. Employees who were unenthusiastic about this informal change in the schedule were pressured into conforming, and management gained the extra work time.

Larger groups, particularly in professional pursuits, often maintain ethical standards designed to further the goals of the over-all membership. A study of hospitals, for example, noted that the high level of teaching competence maintained by the senior medical staff, and the high quality of patient care maintained by the junior staff members, could be largely explained in terms of the allegiance felt by both groups to standards of professional conduct.[15]

---

[15] Burling, Lentz, and Wilson, *op. cit.*, pp. 79-80.

Many a professional, whether he is an attorney, an accountant, or a scientist, undoubtedly is tempted to take short cuts that would save him time and money, and he may be absolutely certain that these short cuts would go undetected. And yet the standards that he has "internalized" during years of training and association with a professional group hold him to certain fixed patterns of behavior. (For other examples see Chapter 3.)

Even work groups performing menial occupations often adopt a "code" that contribute to the organization. One such self-imposed standard that has been observed is the effort to "save the people in the next higher position above from their own mistakes." [16] This code also serves a psychological function for the group: It gives them a sense of greater power and skill and importance than they might otherwise enjoy. On the other hand such standards may make it harder for management. For example, they may be a handicap to an engineering administrator who finds it difficult to dissuade his staff from "gold-plating" their work, setting higher-quality standards than are necessary.

It would be a mistake, of course, to assume that all group standards are consistent with the objectives of the larger organization. We have stressed the positive aspects because so much of the literature only emphasizes the negative results of the group effort. But many times groups do urge their members to produce less than they might otherwise accomplish, do try to reject new assignments because they do not approve of the work, and do even coalesce in opposing a new supervisor.

GROUP ATTITUDES AND VALUES

In addition to group standards of behavior there are also group standards of attitude or values. People who work closely together naturally adopt common points of view that everyone is expected to share: "Ours is a good job (or a bad one.)" "Most people don't realize how difficult our job really is." "Inspection is trying to make our job rough." "You've got to be a college man to make supervisor."

Many of these standards of attitude are without factual basis, of course. They are simply myths that have risen from the group's fears or wishes. Yet the group's acceptance of them *is* a fact—a fact that management must take into account.

> Some years ago, the job of heater in a steel crew was dangerous and difficult. Primarily a hand operation, it required great skill to lift large bars of metal into the furnace via a pulley system. The intense heat made the job even more unpleasant. Now the worst part of the job is handled by automatic equipment, and the operator works some distance away from the furnace. But heaters still feel that their job deserves special financial consideration. Fellow workers support them in this claim, even though it means that more difficult jobs are paid less.

---

[16] Everett Hughes, *Men and Their Work* (New York: The Free Press of Glencoe, 1958), p. 46.

As we have said, the individual becomes wedded to the group as a result of constant association and socializing. Members begin to think and act alike, not only in order to enjoy the fruits of group membership, but because the very process of living together reinforces certain feelings and attitudes in the mind of each member. These attitudes may have existed only weakly before, if at all. Before going to work in XYZ Company, for instance, a recently graduated chemical engineer considered himself only moderately well-trained and useful. After working in a research group composed entirely of chemical engineers, however, he decided that chemical engineers are the most skilled and valuable group in the laboratory. Through constant interaction with a group, certain predispositions are reinforced, or even distorted, in the minds of the members. Further, the goals of the group gradually become as important to each member's feeling of accomplishment as his own individual needs. Once the group has become truly established, the individual members come to identify themselves with its successes and failures.

PRESSURES TO CONFORM

Why is it that most people are so anxious to conform to group standards? In the first place, as members of the group, they look at things from the group point of view; they tend to identify with the group and, since it helps meet their needs, they accept its goals. Even those who have misgivings about the validity of the standards go along anyway, because they want to be well regarded by their fellows. Finally, the group has effective means of punishing those who insist on doing things their own way.

Ostracism is one of the most effective forms of group punishment for deviant behavior. A member who overproduces, who fails to share important information, or who is officious may find himself isolated from his fellow workers. In extreme cases, no one will talk to him or even acknowledge his presence. In less extreme cases, the deviant may be excluded from ordinary social activities, such as getting the morning coffee, or may be greeted coldly when he reports for work. When he has trouble, no one will come to his aid. Or his connection with the "grapevine" may be rudely cut off. Over a period of time the work situation can become intolerable for the victim.

Sometimes the group resorts to more direct techniques. Someone may "accidentally" let management know about some of the deviant's mistakes. Fellow workers may be slow in giving him the parts or the information he needs. His equipment or desk may be "adjusted" while he is away. In the bank-wiring-room study, one of the inspectors failed to live up to certain group norms. The other workers flooded his inspection station with work so that he could not possibly keep up with it, and they "adjusted" his testing equipment so that it failed to work properly.[17]

---

[17] Roethlisberger and Dickson, *op. cit.*, p. 487.

The punishments devised to enforce group standards are sometimes highly ingenious. In one office, supervision was lenient in permitting employees to arrive late for work. When one man began to abuse this privilege by arriving very late every day, the group was afraid that management would start to crack down on tardiness. Whenever this employee came in late, his fellow workers applauded him warmly. This gesture served to emphasize their displeasure, and, it was hoped, would encourage management to deal with him on an individual basis.

It would be a mistake to assume that all group members conform. Not only do groups differ in their cohesiveness, in the "hold" they have over their membership, but individuals differ in their response to group pressures. Interesting experiments have been designed to assess the susceptibility of given individuals to group pressure. At one extreme are those who will deny what their own sense organs tell them to be consistent with group opinions. At the other end of the spectrum are those who are unshakable in their own beliefs, even in highly ambiguous situations when the group provides useful information.[18]

STATUS SYSTEMS

Just as soon as a loose aggregation of individuals develops into a genuine group, subtle status differences begin to arise. Roughly defined, status is a measure of a person's prestige within the group. It is an index to how important he is, to his position in the "pecking order."

Status is generated by group interaction. It provides a sense of security, and failure to have one's status recognized generates insecurity. Think of the senior who is mistaken for a sophomore, or the professor who is introduced as a student. Moreover, status provides a reassuring guide to the members of the group in their contacts with one another. A man with high status expects and receives greater deference than a man with lower status.

How is status determined? What criteria do groups use in assigning higher standing to Mr. A than to Mr. B? Some status decisions are based on the attitudes and behavior of management; others are entirely the product of the informal organization of the group.

Status often depends on *job title*. Obviously a superintendent is more important than a general foreman and a general foreman outranks a foreman. Engineers outrank technicians, secretaries are "above" stenographers. In almost every organization the job titles are subtly graded according to levels of status, and the status of each individual depends in part on the job he holds.

Pay, of course, is one of the most important determinants of the status according to each job. Higher pay means higher status, and even a difference

---

[18] *Cf.* Solomon Asch, "Effects of Group Pressure upon the Modification and Distortion of Judgements," in E. Maccoby, T. Newcomb, and E. Hartley, eds., *Readings in Social Psychology* (New York: Holt, Rinehart and Winston, 1958), pp. 174-183.

of a few cents per hour may have a significant effect on a job's status. The new manager may find this bewildering and unreasonable.

> Take the case of the checkers and the loaders in one newly unionized plant. The checkers received $1.70 an hour, the loaders $1.60. The checkers insisted that since keeping records involved greater responsibility and required a high-school education, they should receive a pay increase of at least 30 cents. The loaders felt that since their job required considerable skill and physical effort, they should be paid as much as the checkers. The union succeeded in getting 20 cents for the checkers, but won 30 cents for the loaders—and the checkers were more unhappy than ever.

Understandably, many companies encourage their employees to keep their pay scale secret.

How one is paid also helps to determine status. Some companies have monthly, semi-monthly, and weekly payrolls. Being a salaried man on the monthly payroll may be less convenient, but it carries much more prestige than getting a weekly *wage* (which may be computed on an hourly rather than an annual basis). Sometimes, unskilled casual workers receive their pay by the day.

Work schedules are also a useful index. The hourly-paid man comes in at 7:30, the office clerks at 8:30, and the executives dribble in from 9:00 on—but the executives often work late at night. The freedom to choose one's hours, or being excused from punching the time-clock, is a mark of distinction. (Henry Ford once made all his executives punch the time-clock—thus lowering even further what was already rock-bottom morale.)

In which company lunchroom can you eat? Are tables reserved for you? Can you leave the building for morning coffee? Do you receive a daily copy of the *Wall Street Journal?* The allocation of these *special privileges* follows status lines.

Then there's the question of *where one works*. In the field or in the home office? In the new building where the important operations occur—or over in the "boneyard"? In some offices, the closer a man works to the big boss the more status he enjoys. To be able to say "I work on the fourteenth floor" may be the pinnacle of prestige.

> We once interviewed a girl whose eyes were still red from crying. Her problem: She had worked her way up till her desk was right next to the office manager, and she thought she was next in line when the office manager retired. Now the boss had shifted her to the back of the room. What were her future possibilities? What would the other girls think of her?

In factories, higher status is often accorded to the man who works near the focal points of employee interaction than to the man who works in an isolated position. Working near the end of the production line carries more status than working near the beginning—for the finished product is more valuable and the job more responsible.

Among the job factors that affect status are: cleanliness, freedom from

supervision, amount of training and skill required, and opportunity for promotion. A study of the restaurant industry revealed substantial differences in
the status enjoyed by employees who worked with various vegetables:

> At the top were luxury or decorative items such as parsley, chives and celery.
> At the top of the regular vegetables were green beans. Next came spinach and
> carrots. Next to the bottom were sweet and white potatoes, and onions were
> considered the most undesirable of all. . . .
>
> Comments of the workers showed that they valued highly in vegetables
> lack of odor, crispness, and cleanness in handling, whereas the vegetable that
> had an odor and that stained the hands or was sloppy to handle was held in low
> esteem. The low standing of potato peeling is too well known to require com-
> ment, but here at least the workers said they preferred potatoes to onions be-
> cause they did not smell or stain the hands. . . .[19]

Most jobs carry with them certain *symbols* that bestow varying degrees of
status. In the army, shoulder insignia denotes officer rank. Paratroop boots,
berets, or wings indicate that enlisted men belong to elite outfits (and for this
reason, during World War II, many men wore them without authorization).

In industry, too, there are countless widely recognized symbols. Take
clothing, for example. Executives (and often, office people) wear coats. Foremen wear white shirts. Hourly-paid workers wear work clothes. The chef's
hat and the machinist's apron are more specialized symbols of prestige.[20]

> Even though there was no plant rule, in one company only the higher-paid
> machinists wore white coats, the rest had white aprons. One lower-paid man
> wore a coat for a week—but social pressure forced him to discard it.

> Some time ago, one of the authors conducted a series of interviews in a plant.
> Wanting to make it clear that he was primarily interested in studying the union
> and the work force—and that he was not connected with management—he was
> careful to wear T-shirts whenever he was in the plant. One day he made the
> mistake of coming in with a regular shirt and tie. Several workers asked, "What's
> wrong—sold out to management?"

Among executives, the *type of office* a man has bears strongly on the amount
of status he enjoys. Does he have his own office? How large is it? Does he have
his own secretary? Does she have a separate office? What type of desk does he
have? Does he have a phone? Or, even better, *two* phones? As one carpet
company puts it, "A title on the door rates a Bigelow on the floor." [21]

> The story is told of a vice-president who suffered a nervous breakdown after
> his company moved into new office quarters. The accommodations were fine,
> but his desk was smaller than those of the other VP's, so obviously he was going
> to be eased out—or so he thought.

---

[19] William F. Whyte, *Human Relations in the Restaurant Industry* (New York: McGraw-
Hill, 1948), p. 36.

[20] Abraham Zaleznik, *Worker Satisfaction and Development* (Boston: Graduate School
of Business Administration, Division of Research, Harvard University, 1956), p. 21.

[21] For a sensitive discussion of executive status problems, see J. P. Marquand's novel,
Point of No Return (Boston: Little, Brown, 1949).

Status depends on *who one is* as well as what one does—that is, on the attributes or characteristics that the employee brings with him from his community and home. The boss' son has status in the plant regardless of what he does—and so does the captain of the plant baseball team. Among the qualities that confer status are education, age, seniority, sex, and ethnic background. Typically in business women are ranked below men. Unfortunately, in our society Negroes are often accorded lower status just because of the color of their skin. The same holds true in some places of Mexicans, Indians, and Asiatics. Other ethnic groups are also arranged according to a regular status hierarchy, with Anglo-Saxons usually at the top and people of southern European background near the bottom. The relative positions on this status ladder may vary from one community to another (for instance: in some places Poles may rank higher than Italians; in other places the reverse may be true), but in every case there is some kind of ranking, together with a struggle among groups to pull themselves up the ladder and others down.

Individual behavior also seems to have some influence on status. People with pleasant personalities, specialized skills, or leadership traits ordinarily enjoy high status, as do individuals who conform closely to the behavioral standards of the group. The man who just doesn't know "how to behave" is likely to lose status—either in an exclusive club or on the factory floor.

It would be a mistake to conceive of status as merely a complication added by the members of an organization. Status systems facilitate the operation of any organization by:

1. Providing ego rewards and social satisfactions to people. As we have seen in Chapter 1, individuals will work hard and make sacrifices to obtain greater prestige.

2. Status provides some security and predictability (and answers at work) by helping people know where they and others "stand."

3. Status makes contacts, particularly between relative strangers, easier. Insofar as the relative status of each is known, individuals know who should defer or accommodate to whom. Symbols of status (such as insignia) can provide quick and unquestioning response to request.

> Our colleague Dr. Ivar Berg has told us of the very progressive mental hospital that endeavored to function by eliminating all outward distinctions in dress between patients and staff. The result was chaos; important identifications could not be made, particularly when bizarre behavior was being manifested. In violation of the formal rules of the hospital, the staff began carrying their keys in easy-to-observe places on their person so that they could distinguish patients from fellow staff members.

STATUS INCONSISTENCY AND AMBIGUITIES

Thus there are several different indicators of status—title, pay, type of work performed, symbols, and others. In a sense, each of these is a thermometer which measures a different aspect of status. So long as all these status "thermometers" give approximately the same readings, status is not likely to cause trouble in the organization. But when they read differently, when the various indicators of status give inconsistent or ambiguous measures, personnel unrest and dissatisfaction occur.

For example, more prestigious group members occupy the more prestigious jobs. The longer-service, better-educated employee in a restaurant kitchen would resent being assigned to onion-peeling, particularly if junior employees were chopping greens and celery. The violation of a group standard would produce a disturbing status inconsistency. The same problem prevails when an employee is promoted to a department manager's job but is not given the type of office usually assigned to men of that rank. The university is not immune to these problems. In university towns, the assistant professor who moves into a section of the community normally regarded as the preserve of full professors is considered "strange" or aggressive.

Often a supervisor is unaware of the subtle distinctions drawn by the group among various jobs, work locations, and types of equipment. Seemingly innocent changes in job assignment or work location may precipitate ill feeling and resentment.[22]

> The metal-drawing department had four kinds of machines. Though work on each machine paid the same wages, there were noticeable differences in ease of operation. From the group point of view, it was a promotion to move to a Z machine and a demotion to move to an X machine. This attitude made it much harder for management to transfer men as production needs dictated and led to many grievances, particularly when management tried to move informal leaders to "lower-ranking" jobs.

Thus, the group's conception of what is right and fair is of critical importance in understanding employee reactions to the work situation. We would anticipate that "status anxiety" would show itself where there was status inconsistency. An employee with a prestigious family background and education working on a low-status job would be uncomfortable and likely to demonstrate aggression. The engineer without a college degree working with colleagues who all have a degree would be less sure of himself and might interpret a critical comment by his supervisor as being much stronger than it was intended. Thus, "status anxiety" can mean hypersensitivity, a condition which explains many problems of communications and morale in organizations.

---

[22] Professor George Homans of Harvard University has developed what he calls a "theory of distributive justice": First, there are certain elements that a member brings to his job from his past or puts into his work on the job. Examples are age, seniority, sex, ethnicity, responsibility, and education. Homans calls these "investments." Second, there are other status factors the worker expects to get out of his job. Examples are the material rewards (pay, etc.), the interest of the job, and status itself, the prestige accorded him by his fellows. These Homans called "rewards" or "returns."

According to Homans, when the "investments" of an individual member or of one subgroup are higher than those of another, *distributive justice* requires that their "rewards" should be higher, too. When "distributive justice" does not prevail—*i.e.*, when investment is not equal to reward—Homans predicts there will be trouble on the job. (Zaleznik, Christensen, and Roethlisberger, *op. cit.*, pp. 53-56.)

Ambiguous situations in which the status position of an individual or group has not been clearly established can be troublesome. Often periods of organization change provide such situations. Take this example:

> The bookkeeping-clerical operations of a large bank always occupied a status position beneath that of the "front office" groups that dealt with the public (for example, in handling loans and deposits). With the addition of expensive, powerful computers the "back room" operations took on added importance. In fact, some of the key computer and systems specialists had to be paid higher salaries than the loan officers and other "front office" personnel.
>
> When these computer people began requesting some of the special perquisites that had been enjoyed in the past only by the high-status officers (such as executive dining room privileges), there was resentment in the latter group. It took several years for top management in the computer area to attain accepted high status.

In a sense, group relations are characterized by a "culture lag": Status relationships do not keep up with technological and organizational changes. In another company a group of highly trained mechanical engineers could not attract the respect of production supervision because the engineers filled jobs (now expanded) that in the past had been filled by low-status clerical personnel.

Newly created groups (for instance, a special task force or a new department) obviously suffer status anxieties, which are demonstrated through aggressive reaching out for recognition and symbols of prestige (such as office space). Once such groups are established and have been relatively successful in gaining recognition, they are not easily disbanded, even though their original function may have been served. The members of the group, through the process of having fought together for status, now identify with the future of the group. Thus, many committees continue to meet and work groups to function when their work no longer contributes to the objectives of the organization.

Cases like the bank example confront management with a dilemma. Management argues that each group should be treated "equally," but if status distinctions are ignored, this policy is bound to generate trouble. The manager's problem is complicated by the fact that "underdog" departments may be struggling to get ahead and raise their relative status in the organizational community.

Competition for improvements in working conditions and benefits appear to be most frequent among groups that are more than halfway up the status ladder. Their position is somewhat ambiguous; they are almost the best, but not quite. Members of these groups seem to be carrying a chip on their shoulders. They seize on real or imagined slights that they can protest through the grievance procedure, and never miss a chance to put pressure on both union and management. They are always looking for ways to improve their position: making the job a little easier, loosening the incentive standard, or perhaps eliminating some of the less desirable operations. Their special sensitivity marks them off as sources of danger for both union and management, who must treat them with extra care if turmoil is to be avoided. We will go into this problem in more detail in the next chapter.

However, a note of caution must be added. Status systems can be too static for dynamic organizations and thus cannot nor should not always be observed. For example, employees whom the group ranks low in status may well be equipped to handle more responsible jobs. And undue emphasis on status may hinder communications between superior and subordinate.[23] (This problem will be discussed further in Chapter 8.)

Group Cohesion

Just as the work groups are internally differentiated, so there are also significant differences *among* groups. One of the most important is the degree of unity or cohesion within the group. All the elements of group behavior that we have mentioned are influenced by this factor.[24] The more united the group, the greater the likelihood that all members will conform strictly to group standards (in part as a result of heightened pressures to conform) and the greater the likelihood that a small leadership core will represent without challenge the feelings of all members. By definition, cohesive groups are internally consistent in their measures of status and are more likely to act in unison when their expectations are violated, either by management, by one of their own members, or even by another group.

New employees may find it difficult to get accepted by highly cohesive groups, and this can create problems for management endeavoring to fill a vacancy. There may be a "trial period"—not unlike a fraternity initiation—in which the newcomer has to prove himself. He must show that he is willing to live up to the norms of the group, that he has an acceptable personality, and that he accepts his status within the group. Exclusiveness can come as an unpleasant shock to the unprepared employee.

For management, it isn't enough simply to recognize that such differences among groups exist. It also wants to be able to predict the conditions that will produce either united or disunited groups. From our own research and that of others, the following factors emerge as some of the determinants of group cohesion.

Status of the group. Other things equal, people are more likely to feel loyalty toward a high-status group than towards a low-status group. Social climbers, for example, are more careful to conform to the norms of the group

---

[23] *Cf.* Louis Barnes, *Organizational Systems and Engineering Groups* (Boston: Harvard University Graduate School of Business, Division of Research, 1960).

[24] For two excellent discussions of cohesion, see Dorwin Cartwright and Alvin Zander, eds., *Group Dynamics: Research and Theory* (New York: Harper & Row, 1953), pp. 73-91; and Stanley Seashore, *Group Cohesiveness in the Industrial Work Group* (Ann Arbor: Survey Research Center, University of Michigan, 1954).

to which they aspire than to the norms of a group from which they want to escape. Indeed, there is a kind of circular process at work here: A high-status group elicits greater loyalty from its members, which in turn makes the group even stronger and more likely to gain increased status.

What determines the status of a group? All the factors noted above as determining individual status contribute, though interrelations between these factors become quite complex at the group level. For example, when we asked some employees in a public utility to compare their importance relative to that of other groups in the same organization, among the factors they mentioned were these:

1. The company has recognized the difficulty and responsibility associated with our jobs by establishing a special test which new employees must pass before they can do our type of work.
2. Because of the difficulty and dangerous nature of our jobs, no one else can touch our work—although in an emergency we can fill in on other jobs.
3. Our job is a good training ground for high responsibility. Over the years a number of our men have gone on to top management posts.
4. Our office used to be located in company headquarters. Now we are in an isolated building where no one goes unless he has to.
5. Before the company made any major decision our old boss used to be consulted. He was a very important man. Our present boss isn't thought of too highly and doesn't carry much weight in company affairs.

In effect, these employees were listing a number of status criteria: the intrinsic nature of the work, their level of responsibility, their opportunities for promotion, the boss' standing, and even their physical location. Several organization changes (noted in factors 4 and 5) had recently led to a substantial reduction in the status of this group. As a result, the members took less interest in informal company activities and even in the union, and they showed less satisfaction in being identified with the department.

Similarly, employees working at the very bottom of the organization's promotional ladder seldom develop a strong attachment to their work groups.[25] In fact, they sometimes regard themselves as only temporary members of their group.

Size.   Small departments are more closely knit than large ones. Loyalty, as we have seen, is a product of constant, face-to-face contacts. Naturally it is easier to have close relationships with all the members of a small group than with all the members of a large one.

Homogeneity.   Groups whose members have different interests and backgrounds are often less effective in promoting their own interests than groups whose members are more homogeneous. When, for example, people with sharp

---

[25] Howard Vollmer, *Employee Rights and The Employment Relationship* (Berkeley: University of California Press, 1960).

differences in rates of pay and job duties work near one another, the resulting informal group is seldom cohesive. This lack of homogeneity may reflect itself in the formation of competing subgroups or cliques, and conflict between these cliques may become so intense that any area of common interest is almost obliterated.

However, cohesiveness can be destroyed in groups composed of people doing similar work who are in competition with one another. A group consisting of store clerks competing actively for scarce customers and merchandise or of vice presidents competing for promotion and the attention of the chief executive would hardly be likely to have much solidarity. In fact, where the likelihood of interpersonal conflict is high, one finds that social groups tend to consist of people working for different bosses and doing different kinds of work.[26]

Communications. Groups in which the members can communicate easily with one another are more likely to be cohesive. Internal group unity can be thwarted in noisy steel mills or along assembly lines.[27] Even scattered groups, like maintenance crews, may become tightly knit if the technology of work requires or permits them to interact frequently with one another. We have observed one highly cohesive group whose members never saw each other on the job and yet were sufficiently cohesive to dominate the union and win substantial wage increases: These were electrical utility substation operators whose jobs required them to communicate by phone. Indeed, one of the determinants of group cohesion is the speed with which rumors or other messages can be transmitted through the group, for rumors contribute to the feeling of common identity.

Isolation from other groups. Physical isolation from other groups of workers tends to build cohesiveness. Employees on night shifts find it difficult to make nonwork friends. Miners among others have demonstrated in countless lengthy strikes that they will stick together more stubbornly than workers who are more socially integrated with the rest of the community.[28]

Where there is no sharp line between one group and another, cohesion is difficult to achieve. For example, on the assembly line, B may interact with A on his left and C on his right, while D may interact with C on his left and with E on his right. Thus, a chain of interactions develops but little group solidarity.[29]

---

[26] *Cf.* Edward L. Gross, "Social Integration and Control of Competition," *American Journal of Sociology*, Vol. 67, No. 3 (Nov. 1961), pp. 270-283.

[27] Charles R. Walker, Robert Guest, and Arthur N. Turner, *Foreman on the Assembly Line* (Cambridge: Harvard University Press, 1956), pp. 131 ff.

[28] Clark Kerr and Abraham Siegel, "The Interindustry Propensity to Strike—An International Comparison," Arthur Kornhauser, Robert Dubin, and Arthur Ross, eds., *Industrial Conflict* (New York: McGraw-Hill, 1954), pp. 191-193.

[29] Zaleznik *et al., op. cit.,* pp. 120-121.

Supervisory practices. The customary behavior of the supervisor has a direct influence on the degree of cohesion that exists within a group. By fostering competition, and by constantly comparing one employee with another, he may make close relations impossible. On the other hand, he can build solidarity by rewarding cooperative behavior. Among members of management, where there is often sharp competition for promotion and recognition, there is less cohesion than among hourly-paid employees who look to the union for protection against management and have much less expectation of promotion.

Outside pressure. Group members draw together when they are threatened by a common danger. A group of employees may forget their personal differences and close ranks against a new supervisor who is regarded as a threat to the group. The speed with which long-standing feuds are healed under pressure from a common enemy is sometimes wondrous to behold.

What happens when the pressure is removed? Group solidarity may diminish somewhat, but the cooperative patterns that arose during the time of crisis may well persist. Thus, the supervisor who inadvertently produces a strong anticompany clique may find that it survives long after the original grievances have been eliminated.

> In order to introduce a new incentive program, a large manufacturing company hired several new time-study men. As the program got under way, the men met intense opposition from the older industrial engineers, who felt the new program would endanger their relationships with their subordinates, and among the employees themselves who feared that the new program would mean "tighter" work standards. As the hostility mounted, the time-study men drew closer together. Then management capitulated to a strike called to protest the new standards, and the whole program suddenly collapsed. Some of the men in the defunct time-study department were offered other jobs in the organization; still others were helped to find jobs in the adjacent area. Even though the members now work in widely scattered locations, the group continues to meet regularly for dinner and a "chat about old times." Welded together by the pressure they shared, they became a closely knit group.

Changes in accustomed ways of doing things and sudden cancellations of prerogatives may also draw employees together. Management opposition to their new solidarity may serve only to strengthen the group.

Success. A group is likely to be stronger and more cohesive if it has engaged successfully in cooperative action in the past. This is the familiar circular pattern: Cohesive groups are more successful and successful groups are more cohesive. Success, however, is largely a matter of luck and depends on many other factors; for example, whether the group occupies a strategic position in the flow of work.

If a small group discovers that it can cripple a plant by refusing to work, it can use this leverage to win special concessions in the future. Once the group loses this strategic advantage, however, it may fall apart.

The machine polishers had a reputation for winning grievances and exercising control over the union. A new invention caused the company to cut down on the number of machine polishers employed. The company also failed to loosen up what the polishers felt was an outmoded incentive plan.

Members of the group began to blame their informal leaders for what had happened. With the recognition of failure came an unwillingness to stick together any longer. Workers began to squabble with one another, particularly over who should have priority to certain jobs. Personal recriminations followed and gradually the men began to request transfers to other departments.

Naturally, when members find that their own group is not successful in protecting them or winning benefits for them, they are unlikely to abide consistently by group standards. In fact, members may begin to seek other affiliations that offer more security and status. This defection further weakens the group, and it becomes less and less successful.

Conclusion

In this chapter we have sought to analyze one important component of every organization: the aggregations of employees we have called groups. Although the boundary lines that determine group membership are affected by management's job assignments and supervisory practices, each group develops a momentum of its own. As a result, there is a constant elaboration of informal organization which does not appear on any chart or plan of the company's operations.

People seek membership in existing groups and form new groups for a wide variety of reasons. But at the bottom there always seems to be a search for satisfactions that are not provided directly by the job or by the supervisor —satisfactions such as companionship and protection.

Informal groups have a life of their own; they have customary ways of doing things and of looking at things; they have their own leaders and a minutely defined status hierarchy. These are the stable, enduring components of group life. In other words, informal organization is a *reality* that management can ignore only at its own peril.

Management sometimes tries to evade this reality by emphasizing the organization as a whole, even to the point of trying to break up what it regards as destructive cliques. Yet loyalty to the face-to-face group, to one's fellow workers, is much stronger than loyalty to the larger entity. Indeed, management can develop over-all loyalty only by encouraging teamwork and informal relations. The group may exercise far stronger control over its members than does management itself.

Other managements seek to by-pass the group by telling supervisors they should concentrate on dealing with each employee as an individual. It is certainly true that the supervisor must spend much of his time dealing with the personal needs and idiosyncrasies of his subordinates, yet he is completely missing the realities of the situation if he fails to see that the group is something more than the sum of the individuals concerned.

A good supervisor must understand the social organization with which he works, just as he must be familiar with tools, materials, and technological processes. If he is to avoid making unwitting mistakes, he must know the status structure of the group, its informal leaders, its standards and values. This knowledge will strengthen his tools of leadership immeasurably.

Does this mean that management must *accept* group standards as they are—for example, that it should do nothing to overcome a thoroughly unacceptable "bogey"? No, we think not. In later chapters we shall discuss ways in which management can work through the informal organization instead of fighting it.

First, however, we shall examine an organization that often grows out of the informal organization and exercises strong influence over it: the union.

P R O B L E M   O N E

The Frustrated Salesmen [30]

Over the years, salesmen in the ABC Company had developed the habit of perusing office records. Management was anxious to discourage this practice for fear that a salesman who had become intimately familiar with company costs and customers might go over to a competitor. The problem was intensified when new offices were constructed separating the salesmen's quarters from those occupied by the office staff. The salesmen were now expected to request necessary information from the office staff over a four-foot counter, and were never to enter the new premises. Here is the way one observer described the salesmen's determination to preserve the practice of looking at the records:

> "At first the salesmen would try to think of every conceivable way to 'break the barrier.' It became a matter of pride to see if they could enter the office and walk around. They said they had to speak to the accountant, to consult with the president, to check an order with a clerk, to pick up some clean towels—almost any excuse."

Management reacted by making the rules against infiltration even more rigid. All salesmen were absolutely forbidden to enter the office except for exceptional reasons. This time the reaction was even more severe. The salesmen began to complain about every sort of petty detail in the office. Their favorite complaint was that the switchboard operator was not giving them all their messages. Next they began to find all sorts of fault with their new quarters. The ceiling tile was installed improperly, the phones were on the wrong side of the desk, the lighting was inadequate, the floor was not cleaned regularly. Fights broke out between the salesmen and the sales manager, and the salesmen began to make aggressive remarks about the office force. They became more clannish and self-conscious.

1. Basically, the changes management introduced were modest ones, and they did not "hurt" the salesmen. Why, then, were they exhibiting such aggressive behavior?
2. What group factors were affected by the change?
3. To what extent were these predictable reactions and of what value would such predictions be to supervision?

---

[30] We are grateful to a former student, J. J. Nerenberg, for the outline of this case.

PROBLEM TWO

The "Old Girls" [31]

Every summer, the Children's and Infants' Department of Hackett's Department Store had been plagued by friction between the regular full-time clerks and the temporary summer replacements.

The regular clerks had developed close social ties in the years they had spent together. They had a common ethnic background and all but two were unmarried or widowed. Whenever possible, they took their coffee and lunch breaks together and often saw each other after work. Further, the department had frequent slack periods when the clerks could sit around and talk together.

The replacements were drawn either from a "flying squad" of full-time employees who were assigned to different departments as need dictated, or from young high-school girls who took the jobs for the summer. Both groups were extremely unhappy at being sent to the Children's Department, and two of the high-schoolers asked for transfers after a short stay. The reasons became quickly evident. The independent work-structure evolved by the regulars had resulted in a department pattern which violated the store rulebook. There was, for example, a definite "pecking order" governing who could take coffee breaks when, and there were frequent unexplained disappearances and early preparations for departure at closing time. The regulars made little effort to assist or advise the newcomers, and criticized them constantly behind their backs. There were seldom more than two part-time girls in the department at any one time, and since they were unlikely to have known each other before, there was little opportunity for them to develop any relationship.

The major difficulties occurred in the area of commission sales. Although the full-timers had an unspoken agreement not to "push hard" for sales achievements, they bitterly resented any commission earned by replacements. They argued that as senior workers they deserved the lion's share of the commission income. The part-timers didn't need it as much as they did, nor had they worked to build up the department. Furthermore, the full-timers thought of themselves as embodying all the sales know-how in the department; the part-timers "didn't know how to sell." Catastrophe occurred when one of the part-timers made a substantial sale and "sabotaged" the commission of one of the regulars. The high-school girl came to the assistant buyer in tears; she had sold a crib when the full-timer in her area was absent from the department, and had been roundly berated for making the sale! She was told that she did not understand the merchandise, and that the other clerk could have made a larger, more profitable sale.

The part-timers were naturally anxious to build up a good sales record. They were motivated to do a good, capable job—either with a view to winning permanent employment, or, in the case of the "flying squad," to convince management that they were worthy of promotion.

As a result, the "old girls" gave either misleading or incorrect information about merchandise or department policies to the part-timers, in order to slow them down and make their job performance less impressive. When a replacement turned to a full-timer for help while serving a customer, the full-timer would frequently take over and consummate the sale. Part-timers were often sent to the stockroom for more goods or were asked to rearrange displays. The full-timers were directing their energies into undermining the part-timers instead of into trying to improve their own sales records.

---

[31] We are indebted to a former student, Eben W. Keyes, II, for this case.

1. How do you explain the behavior of the full-time clerks in this department?
2. Was management gaining any compensating advantages from the increased cohesiveness of the full-timers?
3. Is it realistic or typical to find employees doing average or below-average work and still viewing themselves as top-notch salesmen, as in this case?
4. What would you do if you were the buyer (department head) in this case?

PROBLEM THREE

New Against Old [32]

The old "standard" spinning machines in a large manufacturing plant were operated chiefly by high-seniority men paid on an hourly rate. For nine years the company had been experimenting with new machines that were faster and easier to run. During the experimental period, the machines had been operated by younger men with low seniority. After a two-year tryout, these operators had been put on incentive rates.

To obtain the union's approval, management granted a "loose" rate (one on which it is easy to obtain high earnings). The union readily accepted, believing that unless the long-run productivity of this particular department was improved, the company would move its operation to another plant.

The old spinners, however, who were politically powerful in the union, resented the incentive system. They feared that it would set a precedent for working too fast and perhaps even reduce the amount of work available to them. Eventually this could mean fewer jobs.

Even before the incentive plan was accepted, the men on the old spinners derided the younger men as "damn fools for working themselves to death." In turn, the younger men were resentful of the old spinners' "creamy jobs" and were upset that the seniority system forced them to take what was then less desirable work, with little chance of obtaining jobs on the old machines.

After the incentive plan was put into effect, the men began to compare their paychecks in neighborhood bars. It became obvious that the younger men, on incentive, were earning a great deal more than the older spinners on their hourly rate. Since the two types of machine were located right next to each other, the old spinners were able to watch the ever-increasing production on the other line. With growing anxiety, they saw the differential in earnings grow larger and larger.

Some of the high-seniority spinners considered these jobs as rightfully theirs:

> "Why should some young guy that has been in the plant less than a year be taking home 30 dollars more a week than guys like us that have been here more than 15 years? We'll be the laughing stock of the plant."

The two lines had never been friendly, but now they began to exchange angry threats. An informed leader among the top-seniority spinners told the "youngsters":

> "You guys better save what you are earning because you're not going to be on these jobs very long. We're coming over to take them. They're ours because we're the oldest men in the department."

---

[32] This case is adapted from the authors' earlier book, *The Local Union* (New York: Harper & Row), pp. 43-58.

His counterpart in the young spinner group answered:

"Don't start anything because if you try to bump us [use the seniority provisions of the contract to take their jobs] we're going to fix those jobs so no one wants them.

"We took these jobs when no one else wanted them. We stuck to them through a two-year trial period when everyone else was laughing at us, and you fellows have no right to come over and bump us off."

Three of the more vocal old-timers submitted a formal grievance to their steward outlining their right to the new job and demanding that the union do something about the threat of the youngsters to use production increases to "ruin the new job."

In the meantime, the incentive workers made good their threat to accelerate production, hoping thereby to discourage the older men from any further interest in the job. Their logic was this: if they worked very hard, management would expect much more production than the older men, who had been "spoiled" by their hourly rates, would be willing to put out.

The older men responded by calling a departmental meeting, as authorized by the union constitution. The younger men boycotted the meeting but learned of the results the next day. They, too, submitted a formal grievance in writing, enunciating their claims to the incentive jobs.

1. Analyze the sources of this conflict in terms of the type of group factors involved.
2. Assess the likelihood that struggles *between* employee groups will be an important personnel problem in most organizations.
3. Where these intergroup problems exist, to what extent is management also a participant? Why?

Unions and Labor Relations

5

Over 17 million Americans belong to unions. This simple fact has profound implications for management. Although we cannot treat union-management relations in depth in this chapter, we will consider why employees join or don't join unions, how unions function within the organization, and what their impact on management is. First, however, let us note that labor relations do *not* represent as distinct a problem in relationships for the organization as we might first assume.

Why Union Problems Are Not Unique

COMMONNESS OF OCCUPATIONAL ASSOCIATIONS

As described in Chapter 4, when employees work together and share common experiences they tend to develop into a group and to acquire goals of their own which may differ sharply from the goals of the total enterprise.

Most times these groups never go beyond the stage of informal organization (with informal leaders and unwritten objectives). Sometimes, however, where there is a great deal of common occupational identification, employees form occupational associations. There are such associations for purchasing agents, nurses, industrial engineers, and the like. These groups may begin largely for social reasons, then move on to aid members to advance themselves and the status of the occupation. Finally, some begin to consider bargaining directly with the employer for improved salaries and working conditions. For example, the American Nurses Association took on aspects of a bona fide union when it decided to engage in collective bargaining.

BARGAINING

It is easy to believe that without unions, everyone would work together in harmony for common organizational objectives. Actually, bargaining is a way of life in nearly all organizations, even where there are no unions. As we shall see later, supervisors often exchange favors or make "deals" as a means of gaining cooperation from their subordinates. Large organizations include many different specialized groups even within management itself, and these groups negotiate with one another, "trading off" one advantage for another (see Chapter 16).

OUTSIDERS

The typical management fears the union as an outside force with different goals from those of the firm. After all, the union is interested primarily in its own growth and survival. However, companies have grown used to dealing with many "outsiders." For example, government officials, recommend (or demand) special accounting or quality control procedures, outside contractors work inside firms, and countless examples could be cited of places where an organization's boundaries have become permeable.

DIFFERING PERCEPTIONS

Management often argues that there are no real conflicts of interest between workers and the company. Both stand to gain if profits and productivity improve. This is often true, but the significant point is that employees *believe* that there is a conflict of interest, say, between profits and wages. Although their over-all interests may not always be in conflict, workers and management tend to see problems from a different vantage point. To the manager a new machine may represent a saving in labor cost, but to the employee it will appear as a threat to his job.

> It is now a well-established uniformity of organizational behavior that wherever groups of people occupy widely differing positions in a hierarchy (vertically arranged organization structure) and carry out different activities, they are bound to see their interests as being different.[1]

[1] William F. Whyte in an unpublished paper, "Models for Building and Changing Organizations" (mimeo, 1965).

CONFLICT

At one time it was believed that a harmonious consensus within an organization was normal and that only unions introduced intergroup conflict. Yet given the inevitable differences among groups within an organization (between production and sales, for example), conflict and differing objectives permeate modern organizations. Of course, these internal conflicts do not result in the actual breaks in relationship that occur in strikes, but they are similarly obstructive to organizational effectiveness.

The Course of Union Development

Unions are not a new phenomenon in American life. There were scattered efforts to form trade unions early in the nineteenth century and, by the close of the century, the American Federation of Labor was well established in a number of skilled crafts. Yet until the 1930's union membership outside these crafts was highly unstable. Though unskilled workers sometimes joined unions in time of prosperity, they abandoned them when hard times returned. This pattern began to change drastically during the great depression of the 1930's, when a relatively large, permanent trade-union membership emerged not only in the traditional crafts where workers had found it easier to organize, but also in mass-production industry.

Certain changes in the American economic and political environment coincided with this growth:

1. The depression cost American business a great deal in terms of prestige and employee confidence. The unions, on the other hand, gained in prestige. Many observers regarded them as a healthy check on business power (a check that might help to moderate the business cycle). Gradually, unions began to escape the stigma of being somehow un-American.

2. Government at both the state and federal levels, which had traditionally handicapped union organization (for example, by unfavorable court decisions and the use of injunctions), became more favorably disposed to labor. In fact, new legislation like the Wagner Act (1935) actively encouraged union organization.[2]

3. A substantial segment of the working population began to accept as permanent the role of wage-earner, realizing that it was not just a temporary stop on the road to owning one's own business. As we observed in Chapter 1, the American dream of moving constantly along to better jobs had lost its

---

[2] The basic federal statute protecting the right of workers to join unions and prohibiting employers from interfering with the organization of unions is the National Labor Relations Act of 1935 (the Wagner Act) as amended by the Labor-Management Relations Act of 1947 (the Taft-Hartley Act) and the Labor-Management Reporting and Disclosure Act of 1959 (the Landrum-Griffin Act).

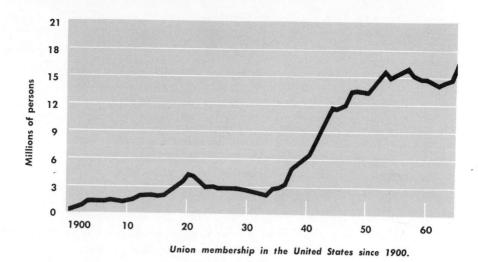

Union membership in the United States since 1900.

luster for some and was replaced by a desire to protect the present situation. With this acceptance came an interest in improving one's lot as an employee through union membership.

4. The decline in immigration and the rise in educational standards tended to make our population more homogeneous. Relatively high standards of education raised the level of employee aspirations. No longer satisfied with just having a job, they demanded more and more from their jobs. And they regarded the union as a valuable ally in getting what they wanted.

5. The unions' growth provided some of its own impetus. Greater acceptance of unions by the community, and increased union prestige as a result of participation in civic and governmental affairs, increased the attractiveness of membership, as did identification of the steadily rising wage level since the beginning of World War II with increasing union strength.

Why Employees Join Unions

Almost every union member is also an employee and has joined his union because he hopes it will better his relationship with his employer. Why does he feel this move is necessary? Many managers have two oversimplified explanations of why workers join unions: The first is that the company has been foolish or selfish, or both. By providing unsatisfactory working conditions and wages, by permitting supervisors to play favorites, management has actually encouraged its employees to seek out a union. Such conditions undoubtedly stimulate the growth of unions. But what about the many well-managed organizations that have been unionized? What has motivated the workers of these companies to join unions?

Here is where the other explanation comes into play. Unionization, it says, must be the result of outside agitators, rabble-rousers, and radicals, who by lies and deceit stir up an otherwise satisfied work force. This reason also is an oversimplification. To be sure, professional organizers from the outside have a great deal to do with bringing workers into the union fold. And they often make use of a small number of strategically located insiders who are willing to take on the task of agitating for the new union. But this is only a small part of the total explanation. Below we have summarized the opinions of many careful observers of union organization.

DESIRE FOR BETTER ECONOMIC AND WORKING CONDITIONS

Most people want to increase their income—even in top-paying companies. Seldom do we find a man who is convinced that the economic returns and physical satisfactions provided by his job are perfect and quite beyond improvement. In the United States, the greatest growth period of unions coincided with a rapidly rising income level for workers. Whether the unions have really obtained higher wages and better pension, insurance, and other benefits for their members, or whether these would have come anyway through normal economic and social processes, is not the point. The point is that an impressive number of employees *believe* that unions are responsible for improving their economic lot.

DESIRE FOR CONTROL OVER BENEFITS

In our society, many employees are unhappy when they are completely dependent on someone else for the satisfaction of their needs. Even when that "someone else" is very good, as many managements have been, and provides good wages, steady employment, and desirable working conditions, workers tend to be uneasy when they have no power to control the benefits received. In fact, management makes matters worse by emphasizing how much it has "given" its employees (that is, benefits provided at the discretion of the company, not offered because they *had* to be). In telling people that they should be thankful for what has been voluntarily given them, a company is also saying that what it has given can also be taken away. In such cases, employees also wonder what they are going to have to give in return for these gifts—how much extra effort, what display of loyalty.

Even in organizations where employees have always been treated with complete fairness and justice, stories circulate that John Jones over in Department 16 has been severely penalized for something he didn't do because a supervisor "had it in for him." In any situation where we lack the power to control what happens to us, we are more than ready to believe these "atrocity" stories and think, "Next time that could happen to us." The truth or falsity of the rumor may be unimportant.

Furthermore, in a large company where top management is many levels removed from the individual employee, the individual's sense of dependency and lack of control over what happens to him is magnified.

DESIRE FOR SELF-EXPRESSION AND
COMMUNICATION WITH HIGHER MANAGEMENT

Many an employee feels that, as far as his company is concerned, he is nothing more than a time-clock number. Though many would not want the responsibility of management, they would like greater opportunity to express themselves. In part, this is just the desire to complain when hurt. But more importantly, as individuals we all have a need to express our point of view— not just to "get more" for ourselves, but to enjoy the feeling of being a whole person instead of a pair of hired hands.

Without a union, most employees feel they have no means of "safely" going over the head of their boss with a problem. After all, they must rely on this man to do many things for them. There are a hundred and one ways in which a supervisor can make their working life unpleasant and unrewarding. Discretion is frequently the better part of valor; when the supervisor says "No," most employees accept it as the final word.

This feeling of helplessness is particularly acute when the immediate supervisor is unsympathetic to their demands, either because he has no decision-making authority of his own (a point that will become clearer when we discuss organizational problems in Chapter 15), or because he has a natural unwillingness to reverse his own decisions. If only they can gain access to higher levels in the organization, employees reason, they may find someone with the authority to satisfy their requests.

The union promises a worker an opportunity to protest inequities, to believe that if something goes wrong he will have a chance to be heard. The union offers a direct road to participate, for its leaders have access to the top decision-making levels of the organization.

THE UNION SHOP

Many employees, of course, do not have a choice about joining a union. Approximately nine-tenths of unionized blue-collar workers labor under a "union shop" agreement, that is, they are required to maintain their union membership in their present employment.

PRECIPITATING CAUSES

We have been describing some of the underlying reasons for the growth of unions. But how can we explain why a union is organized in a particular company at a specific time? Here are some typical precipitating causes:

1. A change in the top management of the plant. Employees fear that the new management will be less friendly and will not preserve the favorable conditions they are used to.

2. Specific problems arising from incentive-payment systems, particularly new standards or new work assignments.

3. The cutting off of promotional ladders—for example, requiring that all new supervisors have college degrees.

4. Sudden cutbacks and layoffs.

Why Some Workers Don't Join Unions

In recent years union growth has slowed almost to a halt. Unions have been more successful in the older and more heavily populated industrial centers of the East and Midwest. They have been less successful in the South. Small towns in that region have been hostile to unions for a variety of historical and social reasons. On an industry basis, manufacturing, mining, transportation, and public utilities have been relatively well organized. Approximately 80 to 90 per cent of the eligible employees in manufacturing and public utility plants in the more heavily industrialized sections of the country are union members. On the other hand, office workers and those in the service industries and in wholesale and retail trade have not been receptive to union organization. Except in the largest cities, the proportion of employees unionized in these industries hovers around 10 per cent. Women and professional workers have also tended to shy away from union membership.

Yet the greatest growth in employment in recent years has taken place in service industries (schools, stores, banks, insurance companies, government work) where white-collar work predominates. Not only has relative employment declined in manufacturing, the stronghold of union organization, but many companies have had absolute decreases in employment as a result of technological improvements.

Since union membership is associated with blue-collar work, many white-collar employees fear that joining a union would lower their social status. Many of these employees work in close proximity to management and hope to move into management positions themselves. Further, the fact that they are broken down into small, uncohesive groups makes it difficult for them to develop the kind of consensus necessary for union organization.[3] Professional and technical employees tend to believe that they can get along "on their own" and that their individual chances for advancement should not be tied to the status of the whole group.

Nevertheless it should be noted that a heavy proportion of the relatively small recent union growth has been in the white-collar area. Unions of government employees (teachers, among others) have expanded their membership significantly. And professional and occupational associations which do not call

---

[3] Interestingly, engineers join unions when they work closely together in large undifferentiated groups, as in some of the huge aircraft and electronics plants.

themselves unions have been taking on union-like functions. Indeed, these "quasi-unions" seem to be growing much faster than have unions of the orthodox sort.

Organizations of functional staff groups, such as the National Association of Purchasing Agents, though not engaging in bargaining, have become increasingly active in advancing their members' occupational interests.

The recent slowdown in union expansion may also be attributed to the exposure of corruption in a small number of unions. Corrupt leaders threaten strikes and boycotts if company officials refuse to hand over sums of money for their personal use. They can also organize unions and collect dues, yet do nothing to aid the membership; this small number of unscrupulous leaders may also tap accumulated dues and premiums paid to health and welfare funds by employees and employers. As a result of such disclosures, the union movement lost some of its reputation for crusading for improvements in the status of the common man.

At the same time, the legislation encouraging union growth has been modified, and in some ways organization has been inhibited. In addition, many employees have forgotten the preunion period of the 1930's when management personnel techniques were less well developed and unions had a larger number of obvious grievances to win and contract gains to acclaim.

Of course, employees have new worries: increasing company mobility and automation are threats to jobs. Further, there has been sharp management resistance to union demands for improved economic benefits and to increased union decision-making in matters affecting day-to-day production. Management opposition to union gains, emanating in part from increased competitiveness in product markets and decreased shortages in labor markets, has also served to detract from the union's momentum and prestige.

Internal Organization of the Union

THE LOCAL UNION

Now let us look at the rather complex structure of the unions themselves. Some employees are organized on the basis of the company or plant in which they work—for example, all the employees of the Carter Chemical Company's Atlanta plant are eligible to join a local industrial union whose membership is restricted to these employees. Frequently the white-collar clerical employees of such a company, or its most highly skilled maintenance employees, may belong to separate local unions. Industries that employ several clearly defined trades are usually not organized by unions on a plant or company basis. Rather, all employees in a given geographic area, usually a community, who have the qualifications to practice the trade, are eligible for membership in a local craft union—for example, all unionized bricklayers in Rochester, New York, belong to the same local, regardless of which employer they work for.

Community-wide locals are also found where the employer unit is relatively small (for example, all the dry-cleaning plant employees in town might belong to a single local of the Teamsters), or where employees are likely to shift from one employer to another (for example, in the needle trades).

Why do we emphasize this difference between unions that are organized on the basis of an employer unit and unions that are organized on the basis of a geographic area? Because the governments of these two types of local union are quite different. Where the membership is derived from many different companies in a clearly defined geographical area, the union is likely to vest a great deal of authority in an elected business agent, who works full time on the negotiation of contracts, grievance problems, and the protection of the union's job jurisdiction.[4] Since these agents service many widely dispersed members who work for a variety of employers, they are very powerful, and management must be willing to deal regularly with them. Unfortunately, most of the corruption mentioned above has arisen in this type of union, and, because of the growth of so-called service industries in the United States, this type is expanding at the expense of unions organized by employer units.

By contrast, in unions organized on a company or plant basis, authority usually is dispersed among a number of leaders, many of whom continue to work at their regular jobs.

THE LOCAL LEADERSHIP

The local union has two types of officer: *Executive-board members* handle the union's internal business—finances, administration of election procedures, appointment of committee members, social functions, and so forth.[5] *Grievance officials* handle relationships with management—the union's collective-bargaining business. These latter officials have a variety of titles, depending on the union and their rank—business agents, committeemen, stewards, grievancemen, chief stewards, and so forth. Most of these officials continue to work for the company in their regular jobs while they are serving in their union capacity, and the company often pays for the time they spend handling employee grievances. Larger and wealthier locals, however, may engage full-time elected officials to handle their grievances and negotiations.

THE MEMBERSHIP

The most active union members—the elected officers—are employees who have more energy and ambition than they can expend on their jobs. Essentially discontented and anxious to get ahead, they often turn to the union when

---

[4] Unions organized on the basis of an employer unit are usually not active in getting jobs for members, nor are they concerned with making sure that no job in the community for which one of their members is qualified is filled by a nonmember.

[5] In some unions, the executive board is involved at some stage of the grievance procedure as well.

their drives are frustrated elsewhere.[6] Many of these men may also be excellent workers, and management frequently finds that leadership in the union may provide a clue to supervisory ability.

This active group, together with members who do not hold office but who attend union meetings and participate in the local's political life, is likely to include no more than 5 per cent of the membership, and frequently a good bit less. Most of the members prefer to "let George do it" when it comes to taking an active role. They pay their dues as they would pay premiums on an insurance policy and they have little to do with the organization except when a grievance arises or when a strike takes place.

Few members seem to feel that union membership conflicts with their loyalty to the company that provides them with job and wages. For many, the union is a way of "making the company better." Of course, unions also attract members with deep-seated hostility toward management, workers who seek to embarrass their supervisors through union activity. Such persons are likely to be most active in the original organization of the union. Advocating a union where none exists typically requires stronger emotions than accepting it after the union has become established. However, many of the "firebrands" who helped bring in the industrial unions during the 1930's and 1940's are nearing or have reached retirement. Newer members may feel less commitment to an organization they did not help or observe get started.

THE INTERNATIONAL UNION [7]

Most local unions are affiliated with an international union that provides them with certain services. You are probably familiar with the names of many of these organizations: The Steelworkers, the Autoworkers, the Teamsters, the Carpenters [8] (all with close to a million members each!). Primarily, the internationals deal with union problems that are out of reach of the local, such as company-wide bargaining problems, government relations, and organizing the unorganized.

The international union usually hires "international representatives" to help the local union get established and to present local bargaining problems directly to management. These officials often participate in the later stages of the grievance procedure (which is described in the next section). Their most important job, however, is usually the handling of contract negotiations. The decision-making body for the international union is the convention, which is held once every year or two, or even more infrequently.

A large number of American international unions have joined together in

---

[6] Leonard Sayles and George Strauss, *The Local Union* (New York: Harper & Row, 1953), pp. 99-132.

[7] Many a national organization is usually referred to as an "international" union in recognition of the fact that it may have members in Canada.

[8] These are not the formal names of these international unions, but the unions are commonly referred to in this fashion.

the AFL-CIO, which serves as a general trade union organization.[9] It has almost no direct power over collective-bargaining matters, for most of its activities concern problems of the labor movement and relationships with government. There are other units in the union movement, such as city councils and state federations, which are organized to deal primarily with various levels of local and state government. The international union, however, is by far the strongest unit.

THE UNION AS A POLITICAL BODY

If management is to deal with a union successfully, it must recognize that the union is a *political* body. Nearly all union officials—at both the local and international levels—are elected, and many union decisions, particularly at the local level, are made by direct vote of the membership. Thus, most decisions do not necessarily flow from top down as they do in management; officers cannot guarantee that the members will do as they are told, particularly in democratic unions, and members can always engage in wildcat strikes. Consequently, in order to win elections, officers must always win something in their negotiations with management. For this reason, they sometimes go through the motions of pressing grievances in which they do not believe.

Still, there is widespread apathy among union members—for example, the local union meeting, which is the major decision-making forum for the local, is usually very poorly attended. And yet, in spite of this apathy, management must recognize that what the union leaders do must at least appear to the members as satisfying their needs. Failure to recognize this fact may lead to a serious miscalculation of the behavior of union leaders. Whereas a top-management official in a negotiation may be able to make firm decisions on his own, a union negotiator may have to get membership approval before he can make a binding commitment. Unions are certainly not models of pure democracy, but in most unions an aroused membership can turn out its leadership in favor of another group. Discontent of this sort contributed to the defeat, in 1965, of David McDonald and James Carey, long-time presidents of the Steelworkers and the International Union of Electrical Workers, respectively.

INTERGROUP CONFLICTS

An important component of the political life of the union is struggle *between* groups within the rank and file: Each wants improved benefits for itself and each wants to protect itself from the encroachments of other groups. Members of each group feel the union is theirs. It is easy to be misled into thinking that the local union is a single, cohesive unit with a leadership that can speak for all members. But look at the kinds of issues on which there can be coercive comparisons leading to internal disagreement:

> Younger employees want their leaders to get higher wages while the older employees want negotiating efforts to go into improving pensions.

---

[9] However, several important international unions are not included in the AFL-CIO, such as the West Coast Longshoremen, the Teamsters, and the Mineworkers.

Higher-paid workers want "percentage" wage increases and lower-paid work-ers want the same hourly increase to go to everyone "across the board." [10]

Management adds a new finishing process. Workers in Department 35 claim jurisdiction over this work while the employees in Final Assembly insist that the new work ought to become part of their department.

Such conflicts are not surprising when we reflect on the degree to which job satisfactions or dissatisfactions are felt in relative, not absolute terms (see Chapter 1). Thus, the leadership must balance off the claims of one group against those of another in the light of their relative political strength as well as the real equities. For example, some groups, if they don't get their way, will be able to defeat the officers at the next election or even to mount an illegal wildcat strike that will embarrass the officials in their dealings with manage-ment. Other groups put up no resistance if they lose their demands.

VARIETIES OF WORK-GROUP PRESSURE

Work groups seem to react to problems in different ways, depending on the kinds of jobs they do. At least four varieties of groups may be identified: [11]

Apathetic Groups are least likely to pressure the union into fighting for them. They are often made up of men with low-status, relatively unskilled jobs who lack internal cohesion and leadership.

---

[10] For example, with a 5 per cent increase, employees earning $2.00 per hour would get 10¢ and those earning $3.00 per hour would get a 15¢ increase.
[11] Leonard Sayles, *Behavior of Industrial Work Groups* (New York: Wiley, 1958), p. 39. The other material in this section is also drawn from this source.

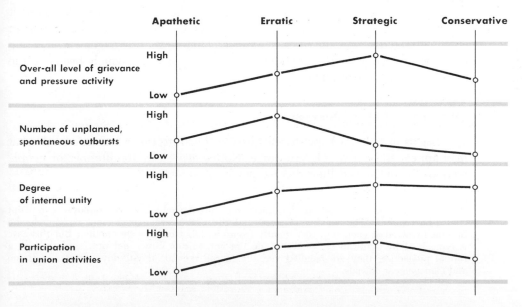

Summary of work-group differences.

Erratic Groups at times exhibit very bellicose behavior, even walking off the job. Other times, with just as important problems facing them, they seem to be uninterested in any union actions on their behalf. These groups often include assembly line and crew workers, where there is a great deal of interdependence in work operations.

Strategic Groups are the most calculating and self-conscious groups within the rank and file and frequently exert pressure for more benefits for themselves. They are never satisfied, always feel "relative deprivation" and know how to exert effective political pressure on the union leadership. The most typical workers in such groups are individual machine operators who work independently, not in crews. They also hold jobs near, but not at, the top of the plant's status ladder.

Conservative Groups are seemingly content with their high-status position. These groups only occasionally feel the need to pressure the union to do battle for them. When they are dissatisfied, they are restrained and very rational in their approach. Often, maintenance workers and other skilled craftsmen demonstrate this pattern.

The Union-Management Relationship

Union-management relations are seen most dramatically during contract negotiations, when the parties meet together to determine the wages, fringe benefits, and working rules that will prevail until a new contract is negotiated one, two, or more years thereafter. But the negotiation of labor agreements takes much less time than the handling of grievances.

Even when a union exists, management continues to make most of the personnel decisions: who shall be hired, disciplined, promoted, given an increase in pay, have his working conditions or hours of work changed, and so on. Very few such decisions are ever made jointly, although the contract is designed to establish certain limits or checks on the decisions that management can make in these areas. After a manager takes action, however, the union can challenge the decision and file a grievance claiming that management is acting in violation of either the contract or of past practice (which becomes the equivalent of the contract).

JOHN JONES HAS A GRIEVANCE

Let us examine a hypothetical case to illustrate the ramifications of what may appear to be a simple grievance. Notice especially the number of people who are involved and their diverse points of view.[12]

---

[12] This case does not describe the exact procedure by which every employee complaint would be handled. The number of steps and the union and management personnel who become involved at each step vary greatly from one labor contract to another. But this case is typical. Many "grievances," however, do not get written down and processed through a formal procedure; they are handled verbally in the regular, day-to-day contacts of union and management officials.

The employee's problem.   John Jones works as a laboratory assistant in the animal experimentation station of a large drug company. His work involves feeding, washing, and weighing animals, building cages, and occasionally cleaning them. Recently, Jones has noticed that he is required to spend much more time cleaning cages than are the other assistants. Since this is the least pleasant and lowest-status of all his tasks, he thinks it is unfair that he should have to do so much of it.

The supervisor's reaction.   When Jones discusses his problem with the supervisor, Brown, he is told that job assignments are arranged in order to use the work force most efficiently. All assistants are hired with the under-standing that they will be doing one or all of the tasks noted above. Brown feels that some of the other men are more skilled in handling the animals and doing minor construction work. So it seems a better use of manpower to have Jones spend more of his time cleaning cages.

Enter the union.   Unsatisfied by Brown's answer, Jones considers calling in the union for help. He hesitates for a while, for fear that such a step may antagonize his supervisor and win him the reputation of troublemaker. Then he decides that, after all, help is what he pays dues for. So Jones contacts the union steward for the laboratory, who happens to work in an adjacent building. The steward discusses the problem with Brown and reports back to Jones the next day:

> "Brown refuses to do anything. He says it's his job to make decisions like this one, and he is not trying to discriminate against you. I'm not satisfied with his answer. I'll see the chief steward tonight at the union meeting and see what he says."

Note what has happened: The steward has tried unsuccessfully to represent the worker and now has turned the case over to a higher level in the union which can contact higher management.

The union's reaction.   The steward goes to the chief steward and describes the case. Here is the chief steward's reaction:

> "This is not a simple case; we have to be careful. In the first place we have to consider the reaction of the other men in the department. Jones is the newest employee; they may get pretty sore if more of this cleaning work is thrown at them. Secondly, the whole thing may backfire. Our present contract is weak on this point. There is actually nothing to prevent the company from changing a man's work, and if they start giving him a lot of the dirty jobs if they want to be mean about it, they might be able to justify paying him less money since his work may now be less skilled than before. Our only chance to win would be if we could show that the supervisor was doing this to Jones because he didn't like him. That would be covered by Clause 14. Discuss it with Jones and, if he has some evidence on this, get him to sign a grievance."

Note the implication behind this reaction: The union is not just the repre-sentative of the individual worker. It also has to think of its total membership.

Actually, as you have already learned, many grievances and worker demands are directed against other employees, not against management. The union depends on the support of its total membership; dissatisfied members may succeed in ejecting officers or in overthrowing the union itself. Clearly, the union must consider the over-all implications of each grievance and demand.

Moreover, the union has to consider its strategic position vis-à-vis management. The union has certain institutional objectives. For example, it is seeking to strengthen its own position in the company somewhat independently of particular employee or group needs. Creating a fuss about Jones' complaint might lead management to insist on its contractual right to change jobs as it sees fit. Of course, the union might be aroused to seek a stronger contract at the next negotiations.

The middle steps of the grievance procedure.   Jones agrees to sign the formal grievance papers charging Brown with discrimination. He notes on the printed form that his assignment to excessive cleaning duties followed an argument with Brown over new coveralls. "When I complained that my coveralls (supplied by the company) were too torn, Brown said I was always complaining and ought to have something to really complain about for a change." The grievance is also signed by the steward; the supervisor himself signs it, but only after adding this note: "Grievance refused—employee has not been discriminated against." Then the chief steward sends the grievance to the laboratory manager, asking for an appointment to talk the matter over.

Management's reaction.   After the manager receives the grievance, he calls in the supervisor, Brown, to get his version of the case; he also checks with the personnel director to see whether similar cases have established precedents in this area that would affect the settlement.

The manager is at first concerned that this might be a case of discrimination. The company has a firm policy that no supervisor is to allow personal feelings to enter into personnel decisions. Having satisfied himself that Brown was right, the manager feels that he cannot grant the grievance. To do so would be to open the door to a stream of union challenges of work assignments. The manager tells the chief steward that, even though a man may feel he is getting more than his share of the unpleasant jobs, it is up to the supervisor to make such decisions in accordance with his own work requirements and the available manpower. So, while he will caution Brown to make sure such assignments are dictated by work needs and not by his personal feelings toward particular employees, the grievance will have to be refused. He writes: "No contract violation, supervisor was acting within normal management prerogatives."

Higher levels of the grievance procedure.   The next move is clearly up to the union. The chief steward and the steward explain to Jones that he has a weak case. No one has heard the supervisor threaten Jones and, even if the supervisor admitted using threats, that would not prove he was discriminating. Well, yes, there are some other steps that might be taken. The union's business agent could take the case up with the division manager of the drug company. If the company still refused to agree to divide the work up more equitably, the case could then be taken to arbitration.[13]

The chances of winning, however, are not good, Jones is told. The chief steward advises Jones to be alert for other evidence of discrimination that would enable the union to reopen the case. He promises that the union will also try to obtain a contract clause next year to prohibit, without specific union approval, changes in work assignments that are equivalent to job transfers.

Even though the chances of success were very slight, the chief steward might have decided to push the case anyway. Grievances provide interesting, challenging work and relieve the monotony of his highly routine job in the company. And yet most union leaders are not anxious to build up a reputation for pressing "poor cases" too vigorously. They want their opposite numbers in management to believe that they are sensible men who can tell the difference between just and unjust claims—but that they are also tough, of course.

Impact of the Union on Management

What over-all effect does the existence of a union have on the organization as a whole and on the management of personnel? The following discussion, which goes beyond the specific grievance problems we have described, will also suggest some of the reasons why many companies have resisted unionization.

CHALLENGES TO MANAGEMENT DECISIONS

The existence of a union means that all personnel decisions are subject to close scrutiny and, perhaps, active challenge. In a nonunion situation, employees may grow dissatisfied and harbor a sense of injustice or injury, but they are not necessarily willing to express their attitudes. The union gives them a means of taking action, not only by approaching the immediate supervisor, but also by reaching higher in the management structure with their demands. For the manager who relishes unchecked authority, this is an unpleasant experience. Almost any manager would prefer to have his orders and decisions go unchallenged.

---

[13] Most union-management agreements provide for the introduction of a third party, an impartial outsider, to decide grievance issues that have not been resolved through the normal grievance procedure. Arbitration is designed to preclude the use of strikes or lockouts in the grievance procedure, although these economic pressure weapons are retained for use during disputes over new contracts.

COMPETITION FOR LOYALTY

Furthermore, the union is in a strategic position to compete with management for the loyalty of employees. For example, it may try to claim credit for any improvement in wages or vacations—even implying that these benefits had to be wrung from an unwilling management. Particularly in the organizational stage, when the union is trying to establish itself, it may caricature company executives and their "desire to sweat labor." Such charges of dishonesty and high-handed tyranny come as a rude shock to executives, particularly to those who think of themselves as benevolent, thoughtful employers. These managers are likely to fear that the union will deprive them of the opportunity to serve as protectors of their employees.

REVIEW OF PERSONNEL POLICIES

The awareness that the union is ready to challenge its actions stimulates management to exercise more care in shaping personnel policies. Mistakes can be costly, not only in terms of the time and goodwill lost through grievance-processing, but also in terms of the new contractual demands that are likely to spring from employee dissatisfaction. For example, in one company the supervisors made a habit of asking workers just before quitting time to work overtime and pressured those who had other commitments either to stay or face the consequences. Here the union later demanded and won a clear-cut contractual prohibition against mandatory overtime work. At times this policy handicapped management.

Over-all, the growth of unions has been an impetus to the development of better personnel policies.

THREATS TO EFFICIENCY

Management fears that the union may want to introduce barriers to efficient work methods, reduce work loads, and, in general, hold back productivity. For example, the union usually wants to introduce rigid rules preventing one man from doing another man's work. If a manager is prevented from assigning work in a way that will take advantage of the employees' aptitudes and experience, management reasons that labor costs are bound to go up.

Some observers argue that the increased costs that result from union pressures "shock" management into finding more efficient work methods.

CENTRALIZATION OF DECISION-MAKING

A manager who fails to understand the contract may inadvertently prompt an embarrasing grievance. It may set a precedent that will be very costly to the company for a long period of time in other departments and strengthen the union's argument that the company is "unfair." For example, in our hypothetical case above, the laboratory manager was anxious to avoid establishing the precedent that work assignments were not a management prerogative. Fearing such contingencies, many companies have withdrawn from lower-level supervisors the authority to make certain personnel decisions. This authority has been delegated to higher levels of management and, in many cases, to staff departments with specialists trained in labor relations.[14]

INTRODUCTION OF "OUTSIDERS" INTO LABOR RELATIONS

As we have seen, an "international" union usually embraces members from a number of different firms.[15] Not only does the union have institutional goals distinct from those of the company (it wants to grow and prosper and its officers want to be re-elected), but it is also concerned with more than one employer. The union seeks wage increases in one company to set a precedent that will make it easier to negotiate a favorable contract elsewhere. Frequently, arbitration decisions set precedents affecting labor relations in many companies. As a result, many company officials feel that the problems to which union officers force them to devote time are not restricted to the interests of the particular organization and its employees.

Business agents and international representatives are not employees of the firms with which they negotiate. Although, in principle, many managers resent the fact that the union brings "outsiders" onto the scene, in practice, they often find that the outsiders are more dispassionate and better able to understand the company's side of a grievance than their own employees would be.[16]

Evolution of Sound Union-Management Relations

There is little question that the introduction of a union may prove a traumatic experience for management. At the outset, the union may try to dramatize every company mistake, and the early days may be spent in destructive warfare rather than in the constructive solution of problems. In

---

[14] The problems created by the changing organizational position of the supervisor and the growing importance of staff departments are analyzed in Chapter 16.

[15] Many independent unions, however, which are not affiliated with international unions, have no organizational relationships beyond the company in which they are organized.

[16] Managers even find themselves facing this dilemma: Some unions which are not democratic, where the officers are not directly responsive to the demands of the membership, are easier to negotiate with than more democratic unions. Because the leadership in the latter group must face constant political criticism, they must be more careful of the agreements when the political pressure becomes great—e.g., when a wildcat strike seems to be gaining widespread membership support.

many firms this period may drag on for years in a kind of "armed truce," with both sides trying to capitalize on the other's mistakes. While grudgingly accepting the existence of the union, managers may seek to sharply limit its influence in the company and compete actively with the union for the loyalty of the membership.[17] Yet many companies and their managements develop a more harmonious relationship and admit that the union can have a beneficial effect on the organization if dealt with properly.

OPPORTUNITIES FOR IMPROVED HUMAN RELATIONS

The most important factor contributing to sound labor relations is the recognition by management that its own actions and policies have a major impact on union behavior. Some observers even go as far as to generalize that "a management gets the kind of union it deserves."

To the management that is willing to explore new techniques, the introduction of a union into the organization need not be a catastrophe. The union can actually help management improve employee relationships.

Labor relations involve a problem that every company must face, whether or not its workers are unionized: this is the problem of adjusting the needs of the individual to the needs of the organization. Without a union, employees may find other means of protesting what they think is unfair: slowdowns, sabotage, or quitting. The union provides a peaceful means of resolving such disputes or differences in a way that will maintain productivity and preserve the work force intact.

Increasingly, managers are recognizing the merits of informal discussion of common problems. Even on subjects solely within the area of management prerogatives, they are learning that the union can serve as a channel of communication with the work force and can provide an aid in discovering and correcting weak spots in the plant.

Supervisors who are sensitive to human relations prefer to obtain group agreement before initiating changes in work procedure. Rather than deal with a large number of individuals with diverse points of view, they realize that it is far more efficient to sit down with a responsible union leader. He is the single spokesman who presumably represents the unified opinion of the entire work group and can subsequently sell his analysis to the group. In a sense, strong local unions are a guarantee that agreements will be honored.

Management learns that it can introduce changes in working conditions with much less friction if it consults with the union beforehand. Rather than sit back and wait for the union to raise problems, the company can make the first move and involve union officials in clearing up potential trouble areas.

---

[17] In recent years this type of active opposition to increasing union power has come to be called "Boulwarism" after the former head of labor relations of the General Electric Company. Its tactics and point of view are best described in Herbert Northrop, *Boulwarism* (Ann Arbor, Michigan: Bureau of Industrial Relations, University of Michigan, 1964).

"We knew we were going to have a lot of squawks over new job assignments when we brought automation into the department. This could have meant a hundred grievances and months of wasteful talk. Instead we went to the union and told them what our plans were, how many of what kinds of jobs there would be after the change. We got them to work with us in deciding who was going to stay in the department and how transfers would be arranged. We also negotiated the rates on the new jobs."

Consulting with the union prior to the development of grievances often produces a valuable by-product. As we have seen, union officials are typically active men who want to keep busy. If they can be involved in handling constructive questions, they are less likely to seek out problems and grievances.

THE MANAGER'S ROLE

The chances of converting hostility-ridden, destructive labor relations into a constructive pattern depend largely on the manager's ability to adapt to the existence of the union. When a union is first established, the manager may have difficulty dealing with subordinates who are also active union organizers. At the outset, he needs to distinguish between the outspoken rabble-rouser and the genuine informal leader. The free-wheeling organizer may be motivated by deep-seated personality problems or personal grievances. Often he does not have the confidence of the group as a whole.

Instead of assuming that aggressive talk and behavior are in themselves evidence of valid leadership, the supervisor should give the members of the group an opportunity to decide whether the man who tries to usurp leadership is in fact the man they want as a leader. If they perceive that he is prompted by selfish motives and is overbearing and clumsy in his approach, they may reject him voluntarily. On the other hand, if the supervisor attempts to punish him, he may become a martyr and actually gain the group's support.

The supervisor should recognize that most employees experience no serious conflict between loyalty to the union (which they see as a sort of insurance program to protect them against future contingencies) and loyalty to management (to whom they owe appreciation for their jobs and economic well-being). So, if the manager rejects or becomes suspicious of everyone who expresses pro-union sentiments, he may alienate a number of very capable employees who, were they accorded responsibility and trust, might have identified themselves strongly with the company.

The manager also should be alert to the special problems affecting the union leader's behavior: He may be under conflicting pressures, one group wanting him to do one thing, another group insisting on something else. The manager should recognize the political position of the union leader and learn how to cope with him intelligently rather than bemoan the fact that unions are political institutions.

Management representatives quickly learn to differentiate between the grievances on which the union leaders face strong political pressures and those which they are merely "going through motions" of pressing. . . . A shrewd management learns not to embarrass union officials before a close election. . . .

We have observed many episodes such as the following telephone call by a union leader to a personnel director:

"Look, Bill, we'll admit that Charlie Jones was drunk last week. Frankly we don't have a leg to stand on. If you'll take it easy on him—after all this is his first offense—we'll waive the formal hearing. And that'll save you a lot of time and money. . . ."

These are not collusive dealings but rather part of the flexible process by which both sides adjust to new problem situations which could not have been foreseen when the contract was written.[18]

Thus, as time passes, the union abandons its role as a *competitor* for the loyalty of the worker. It takes on the role of a *policeman* who calls "halt" when a company representative makes a mistake, but who also keeps the member-employee within the bounds of legal decisions and practices. In some companies, this evolutionary process advances to the point where the union becomes a genuine *collaborator*, sharing with management the problems of improving efficiency and productivity.

Conclusion

The problems of labor relations are not distinct from other human-relations problems that arise in an organization. Although the union cannot eliminate management's responsibility for the conduct of personnel administration, it can become an integral part of the employment relationship. Even though its roots lie outside the organization, its existence reflects employee needs and dissatisfactions. Some human-relations problems, particularly in larger organizations, may be almost beyond the ability of management to solve, and the manager need not feel that the establishment of a union is evidence of his own failure. Thus, it is unrealistic to think of personnel administration as an *alternative* to unionization.

Unions have, in fact, been a part of American life for more than a century, but they did not gain in numbers and strength until the 1930's, when social, economic, and political developments combined to enlarge their role. Workers join unions for many reasons, not necessarily because of bad management or outside agitation, but because they want to improve their working conditions or their pay, to satisfy their needs, to express their individuality, and to communicate with management, and they feel that the unions provide a way of doing so. Despite earlier impressive gains, union growth has slowed down, however, partly because of regional hostility, disgust with instances of corruption, and the reluctance of white-collar workers and professionals to join.

The heart of unionism is the local, whether industrial or craft, which is run by elected officers; grievance officials deal directly with management. Most

---

[18] Sayles and Strauss, *op. cit.*, pp. 18-19.

members are inactive, though in form the locals are democratic, and many decisions are made by membership vote. The local rank and file are not necessarily close-knit, and many conflicts among groups can and do arise, which the union leaders must deal with as well as with management.

Union-management relations provide another challenge for management. In many companies, the necessity of working through these problems is just as much a part of the managerial job as developing budgets and work schedules, and issuing orders. While negotiation and consultation are time-consuming, frequently frustrating, and certainly threatening, they require some of the same supervisory skills and persistence that are necessary to carry out other management functions. These responsibilities cannot be avoided, nor would it be healthful for the organization if they could.

PROBLEM ONE

Union and U.N.

Following is a description of the functioning of the United Nations. How comparable is the role of the union in the organization?

> There are, to be sure, other important functions which the U.N. performs. One of them is that is provides a public forum in which the weak nations can talk to the great powers and get back some kind of accounting. Although the debates in the General Assembly do not produce the purest candor or the highest wisdom, and are in fact often ignorant and foolish, it is better that the grievances and accusations be brought into the open than that they should be left to fester in the dark. But, while the public forum is useful and indeed necessary, the indispensable activity of the United Nations is what goes on privately and off the record. It goes on in the corridors and lounges of the U. N. . . .
>
> There is no other place where conversation is possible at any time of the day or night among the contending and quarreling peoples of the world. . . .
>
> This network provides an element which, while it has always been indispensable in the conduct of diplomacy, has become rare and difficult under the white lights of modern publicity and of democratic government. This indispensable element is the ability to try out proposals without being publicly committed to them, of letting them be accepted or amended or rejected without public debate, without any need to explain them or justify them if they do not work.[19]

PROBLEM TWO

Wildcat Strike

During the 20 years Harold Keller has worked for the James Company, he has risen to the top of his promotion ladder: a machinist first-class and one of the highest-paid nonsupervisory employees in the company. About five years ago, the workers in the company were organized by a union; Keller played no active part in the organizing campaign. About a year ago, Keller developed an illness that was difficult to diagnose; although he lost strength and energy, he was able to continue at work. Because of his good record and long service, the company found a number of special assignments for him and maintained his wages until he regained his health.

---

[19] Walter Lippmann, "The Indestructibility of the U.N.," *Newsweek* (October 25, 1965), p. 27.

Just recently, the men in the machine shop in which Keller worked staged a wildcat one-day walk-out that did not have the formal authorization of the local union. Employees in other departments were not involved. The men in the machine shop claimed that their wages had declined relative to wages in many other departments because they had had no opportunity to work more than 40 hours a week. Men in many of the other departments were working 45 hours and 50 hours a week.

Much to the surprise and disappointment of the machine-shop supervisor, Keller not only participated in this protest demonstration, but actually appeared to be one of the leaders.

1. Does Keller's action seem reasonable in light of the consideration management accorded him during his illness?
2. What should the supervisor do with Keller now?
3. How typical do you think this case is?
4. What is your reaction to the complaint of the men in the machine shop?

PROBLEM THREE

A Change in Schedule

The company guards at the Rembrandt Company were among the last groups to join a union, but they had always expressed a great deal of dissatisfaction over their work schedules. For many years there had been charges of favoritism in the assignment of work hours. Guard work had to be carried on around the clock, and employees who were assigned to the less desirable shifts or to week-end duty complained that they should have better working hours.

The issue of "fair working schedules" was plugged hard by the new union in signing up new members, and it was one of the first questions raised by the union leaders when they met with management to negotiate their first labor contract. In fact, this issue took up the first two weeks of negotiation.

When the issue was finally settled, management discovered that the agreement with the new guard union specified a work schedule that was almost identical with the one that had existed prior to unionization. Nevertheless, the union and the membership seemed satisfied with the agreement, and there was no longer the heavy stream of complaints about work assignments.

1. How do you explain this strange development? Were the employees dissatisfied before and, if so, why did they appear satisfied after the agreement was made?
2. What scheduling difficulties may the union leaders have become aware of during their two-week discussion with company representatives?

LEADERSHIP

AND MOTIVATION

Up to this point we have been dealing with the "ingredients" of the business organization: people and their needs, technology and its impact, groups, and unions. In the following chapters we shall talk about the manager, the person whose job it is to blend all these ingredients in such a way as to enable the organization to satisfy its basic needs for production and profit.

What is a manager? A manager is one who is responsible for getting a job done that is too big to do by himself—a job that he can accomplish only through other people. True, he must have some technical ability. But it is the fact that *he must get his work done through others* that sets him apart as a manager and that creates the problems that we shall discuss in this section.

Clearly, management is not just a matter of giving orders or overseeing subordinates to make sure they follow rules. Management means building an effective work force and motivating each member of it to turn in his best performance. This is the job of every manager whether he is president of the company, a regional sales manager, or a foreman on the line.

To be sure, managers have other functions besides dealing with subordinates. Depending on their level in the hierarchy, they may have to make decisions relating to finance, marketing, production, research, advertising, scheduling, quality control, or public relations. Technical, analytical, and imaginative skills may be as essential as human-relations skills. The manager may have to deal with customers, suppliers, government agents, superiors, staff representatives, and other supervisors on his own level. Yet one of the most critically important skills of any manager is skill in leadership, and in this section we shall emphasize the manager as leader.

What is the difference between a good leader and a bad one? Styles of leadership vary greatly from one situation to another. The techniques used by "a maid to control her man" are very different from those used by a drill sergeant. The political demagogue, the parish priest, the president of the senior class, the father of a family—all are leaders. And so are the unofficial, informal leaders we met in an earlier chapter.

Each uses a style of leadership appropriate to his own situation. As we shall see, in business, too, there is a wide range of leadership behavior.

Every manager, however, faces the problem of motivation. When a man works for himself, either at his job or at a hobby, he works with enthusiasm and energy. How can we get him to work in the same way in our complex mass-production society, where men work not for themselves, but for others, and where the satisfaction derived from the work itself is often meager? As we shall see in Chapter 6, there are various means of "Motivating People to Work," some appropriate to one situation, others to another. Nevertheless, the most generally positive form of motivation, in circumstances where it is applicable, is what is called internalized motivation.

The effective manager has three tasks: he must decide how much to delegate and in what manner; he must exercise his authority in such a fashion as to maximize acceptance of his orders; and he must act as leader of his work team.

1.) The manager should delegate decision-making authority to subordinates to the maximum extent the subordinates' abilities and the needs of the organization permit. Instead of issuing detailed instructions, he will lay down rules, set goals, and seek to indoctrinate subordinates in organizational objectives. All this is involved in "Delegation" (Chapter 7).

2.) In the "The Exercise of Authority" (Chapter 8), the manager must develop effective day-to-day relations with his subordinates. He must also take into account their conceptions of what they feel to be the legitimate use of authority.

3.) The manager and his subordinates are members of the same work group. The effective manager is in effect a team leader. His job is to strengthen the group (provided the group's objectives are not opposed to those of management), to consult with group members, both formally and informally, and to work through the informal group structure (Chapter 9, "The Manager and the Group").

Before we go on to discuss these three aspects of leadership, we must point out that no one form of leadership is equally good in all situations. What form is best suited to a given situation depends on many factors: the type of work; the cohesiveness of the group; the group's attitude toward management; the individual needs and personality of the subordinate; and the personality, experience, and technical ability of the manager. The best manager is the one who is sensitive to the needs of each situation and adjusts his style of management accordingly.

Motivating People to Work

6

One of the basic problems in any society is how to motivate people to work. In a mass-production society this is not an easy task, since many people derive only slight personal satisfaction from their jobs, and enjoy little sense of accomplishment or creativity. In large organizations people must work together, following orders they may neither understand nor approve, and obey instructions from superiors whom they had no part in selecting and may never see. Few have the opportunity for self-expression or the freedom from control enjoyed by the farmer or the independent businessman or the professional man. How can one motivate people who have boring jobs, little freedom to make decisions on their own, and the normal human quota of laziness and stubbornness? How can we create a situation in which employees can satisfy their individual needs while at the same time working toward the goals of the organization?

In this chapter we shall consider five alternative methods for motivating people: (1) the "be strong" approach, (2) the "be good" approach, (3) implicit bargaining, (4) competition, and (5) internalized motivation. (We make no claim to have exhausted the list of possible forms of motivation, and in practice most managers use combinations of all five.) [1]

Be Strong

The traditional form of motivation in industry (and the one that seems to come easiest to most supervisors) emphasizes authority. At its crudest, this method consists of forcing people to work by threatening to fire them if they don't. The assumption behind this approach, of course, is that the only reason people work is to earn money, and that they will work only if driven to it by fear of losing their jobs. It ignores the fact, mentioned in Chapter 1, that people also want around-the-job and through-the-job satisfactions. Off-the-job, economic satisfactions are not enough.

This approach further assumes that since no one likes work, people will try to get away with doing just as little as they can. To prevent them from doing so, there must be close supervision. Management must tell every worker exactly what he is to do every minute of the day; it must spell out every rule and give the worker the narrowest possible range for discretion. Often rules are promulgated just to "show who's boss." Individuals are kept busy "to keep them out of trouble."

This thinking is inherent in some of the less sophisticated versions of scientific management: Men are hired to work rather than think, and the smallest possible segment of human ability should be used on the job. It is also related to what has been called the "commodity" or "contractual" theory of labor, which holds that labor can be bought and sold just like material supplies—and can be treated in the same way.

This approach paid off fairly well in the early days of the industrial revolution when workers and their families were so close to starvation that the material, off-the-job needs for food, clothing, and shelter were paramount. In recent years, however, people have begun to expect more from their jobs than sheer punishment. As a consequence, the "be strong" policy has become less effective as a motivating device. There are three major reasons for the decline of the authoritarian approach.

1. In the first place, as we discovered in Chapter 1, as our standard of living has gone up and our physical needs have become better satisfied, people have begun to look for social and egoistic satisfactions higher up on the need hierarchy. This is particularly true in times of full employment. (Or, to put it another way, we have used part of our increased productivity to provide ourselves with more material goods, such as bigger houses, better cars, and fancier cuts of meat; part to provide us with more leisure off the job, shorter hours,

---

[1] Our thinking in this chapter has been greatly influenced by Douglas McGregor.

and longer vacations; and part to provide ourselves with a more decent work environment, which means among other things a slower work pace and less tyrannical supervision.)

2. Fifty years ago children were taught, both at home and at school, to show strict obedience to their elders. And so the child-grown-man found little difficulty adjusting to stern discipline in the office or factory. Recent years have seen a revolution in the way children are brought up. Freedom and self-expression are encouraged in the home; schools emphasize spontaneous discussion and individual expression. As a consequence, the young worker of today finds it hard to accept autocratic leadership on the job.

3. Basic to the philosophy of "be strong" is the expectation that if a man doesn't do what the boss tells him to do, he will be fired. Unions, however, have made it more difficult to fire a man; in effect, they have lowered the minimum a worker can get by with.

APPLICATION TO WHITE-COLLAR WORKERS

We all know how "be strong" techniques are used by the bullying foreman. But the same policy may also be applied to executives, supervisors, and white-collar workers. With no union to protect them and with a keen interest in advancement, the fear of punishment (either through discharge or denial of promotion) may be quite effective in motivating these individuals.

It is common practice for top management to set goals (increased sales, lowered costs, and so forth) for their executives, and then to exert constant pressure to insure that these goals are met. The penalty for not doing so is usually the withholding of promotions or salary increases, if not outright discharge. Some companies deliberately set their goals too high. Every time a goal comes close to being met, management raises it even higher, hoping as a consequence to stir employees to work harder and harder. As one supervisor remarked, "My philosophy is, always give a man more than he can finish. That way you can be sure you are getting the most out of him."

This is one reason we hear so much about "pressure" in many business offices. A top executive described his use of the "be strong" approach this way:

> As soon as we examine the budget results and see a fellow is slipping, we *immediately* call the factory manager and point out, "Look Joe, you're behind on the budget. What do you expect to do about it?" True, he may be batting his brains out already on the problem but our phone call adds a little more pressure.[2]

The consequent feeling of frustration is intensified because the white-collar employee typically does not have the channels of redress or the opportunities to express aggression that are available to his blue-collar brother.

---

[2] Chris Argyris, *The Impact of Budgets on People* (New York: Controllership Foundation, 1952), p. 5.

IMPACT ON PEOPLE

The trouble with "be strong" as a form of motivation is this: It ignores the fact that people are not passive, inert machines and that they often react in ways not intended by management.

1. This policy normally provides no incentive to work harder than the minimum required to avoid punishment. The minimum may be fairly low in the case of unionized workers who are promoted on the basis of seniority and who have a union to protect them if they are fired. (On the other hand, the minimum may be relatively high if the work is closely programed and if it is easy to see whether a man is falling down on the job. And in the case of executives whose chances of promotion and winning substantial salary increases are quite great, the policy of "be strong" may seem quite effective. However, as mentioned above, executives often find it difficult to work creatively when subject to the pressures which "be strong" involves.)

2. The essence of "be strong" is the application of pressure. But when subjected to *too much* pressure, employees fight back. When they can, they fight through their union. Even if they have no union, they engage in slow-downs, sabotage, and spoilage.[3] As one worker commented, "In my shop there is an undeclared war of nerves. If management won't treat us like men, we aren't going to show much respect for them."

Part of this "war of nerves" consists of workers' efforts to get away with doing as little as possible; there is no incentive for doing more than the minimum, but there is a great deal of satisfaction in making management look silly. Naturally, management reacts by deciding, "We have to watch these men like hawks if we are to get anything done at all." Both sides spend a tremendous amount of energy trying to outsmart the other. Production is lower than it might otherwise be, and management, in frustration, often strikes back irrationally, perhaps by imposing needless restrictions or by firing alleged ringleaders. Thus, a vicious cycle is set in motion, a cycle of restraints and evasions, more restraints and more evasions.

As J. S. Mill said a century ago, "Nor are the greatest precautions more than very imperfectly efficacious, where, as is now almost invariably the case with hired laborers, the slightest relaxation of vigilance is an opportunity eagerly seized for eluding performance of their contract."[4]

3. To protect themselves from pressure, employees organize groups and cliques, as we saw in Chapter 4. And already-existing groups may be drawn closer together and take on a new purpose, that of protecting themselves

---

[3] See Stanley B. Mathewson, *Restriction of Output Among Unorganized Workers* (New York: Viking, 1931).

[4] J. S. Mill, *Principles of Political Economy*, People's Edition (London: Longmans, Green, 1891), p. 68.

against management pressure. As we have seen, work groups frequently establish "bogeys" or standards of output that no member is expected to exceed—in spite of what management wants. Group members may even conspire to "cover" each other's mistakes and to punish "squealers." As a result, higher management is kept ignorant of what is happening on subordinate levels and therefore cannot inflict the discipline that is necessary if "be strong" is to succeed.

This policy of self-protection is openly practiced by hourly-paid workers; even executives, however, often band together in an implicit alliance to protect themselves against their own superiors. Such an alliance may be highly effective even though it is never actually talked about.

4. Probably the most serious trouble with "be strong" is that it ignores a basic factor in human behavior: When people are put under too much pressure they become *frustrated*. (Note: we say *too much* pressure. Most of us respond well to some pressure, but all of us have a critical point—which differs from one person to another—beyond which frustration sets in.[5])

When people become frustrated they react in strange ways that tend to reduce the effectiveness of the organization in its main task of getting out production. Often their behavior seems quite irrational, in the sense that it cannot be understood in terms of the apparent stimulus.

> Superintendent Jones' secretary usually does a fine, conscientious job. Today she forgot to type an important letter. Jones bawled her out unmercifully.

Jones is normally a kind man. Why did he act this way today? Certainly his behavior was not designed to get the letter out more quickly, or even to prevent his secretary from making mistakes in the future. The fact is that he had been trying to meet an important deadline with an inadequate staff of men, and his boss had just called him up to spur him on.

One response to frustration is *aggressiveness*, which expresses itself in many ways. Instead of bawling out his secretary, Jones might have picked a fight with another supervisor, had a hassle with his wife, or whammed a small, defenseless white ball around the country-club park. If his frustration became too intense, it might have led to psychosomatic illnesses, such as high blood pressure or ulcers:

> Once we observed a group of working supervisors who had been strongly pressured to increase production under difficult circumstances with no backing from management. There were nine men regularly assigned to the day shift. One had a nervous breakdown, another had a fatal heart attack that was generally attributed to overwork and fatigue. Of the remaining seven, five had serious illnesses and in most cases no organic cause could be determined. All this happened during a period of twelve months. Meanwhile, the men on the night shift, where pressure was much less, had an almost perfect health record.

---

[5] Evidence suggests that, up to a certain point, anxiety facilitates the performance of all tasks, but that anxiety is more effective with simple than with complicated tasks.

There are many other reactions to frustration. Some people *repress* their feelings for a long time and then suddenly blow up without notice. Others *regress* to less mature levels of behavior. Everyone is familiar with the three-year-old who reverts to thumb-sucking when a baby brother arrives on the scene. Similarly, adults who are frustrated by excessive pressure may find it difficult to make decisions or react intelligently and may engage in juvenile (and aggressive) activities such as horseplay. Though employees may be dragooned into submission by the "be strong" approach, the consequent frustration may lead to a serious reduction in the quality of their decision. Under extreme frustration, they may simply fall into *resignation* and give up trying altogether. Possibly the underprivileged, floating employees mentioned on page 66, who despaired of trying to improve themselves economically, had reached a state of resignation.

Frustration may also lead to *scapegoating*—that is, picking on those who are weak and defenseless. It is not accidental, for instance, that racial tensions in plants are higher when times are bad and layoffs are pending. Another response is *fixation*, in which the individual persists in some fruitless activity, such as Lady Macbeth's handwashing, even though it obviously accomplishes nothing. When assigned a difficult problem, some supervisors spend their time shuffling papers rather than trying to work out a realistic solution.

Finally there is *sublimation*, in which the individual seeks to satisfy his frustrated needs in some more effective fashion. Thus, the executive who has been denied promotion may become active in a social club, just as the girl who has been jilted may seek to express her love in nursery school work.

The collective reaction of a group of workers to frustration may have a devastating effect on the entire organization. It may disrupt group solidarity and cooperation, turning departments, groups, and individuals against one another. It may lead to rumor, mistrust, and suspicion. It may result in un-explained wildcat strikes or a general state of snarling irritability. In most cases, the basic objective of the organization—*production*—is bound to suffer.

To put this whole problem another way, when a rider whips his horse he must remember that the horse may dash off in any direction. A high degree of control is required to make sure it goes where the rider wants. If the only form of incentive operating is the employee's desire to escape punishment, there is no guarantee that he will perform his job in the way management desires unless *all* alternative courses of action are blocked.

THE VALUE OF BE STRONG

Thus, the effectiveness of the "be strong" technique of motivation is subject to significant limitations: (1) It motivates employees to do only enough work to keep from being fired (except where there are significant opportunities for promotion); (2) it motivates them to "get away" with as much as possible (often making a game of it), thus leading to a vicious cycle of further management restrictions and employee evasions; (3) it motivates them to band together in self-protection; and (4) it leads to frustration and in turn to a whole series of deleterious side-reactions that jeopardize production.

And yet, as we shall see, there are times when "be strong" works fairly well. It works better in the short run than in the long run. It generally works better with white-collar workers than with blue-collar workers. It is most effective in nonunionized situations, during depressions when men are desperate for work, with members of minority groups who find it a difficulty to find work elsewhere, and in highly programed work where deviation from rules may be easily spotted.[6] Even in these situations, though, there are undesirable side-reactions.

There are times when a manager, because of his position, must use threats, either implicitly or explicitly. But a manager who relies solely on threats as a means of motivation is likely to develop a group of subordinates who at best are cowed into fearful rigidity and at worst are openly rebellious.

Be Good

As a substitute for "be strong," many managements have adopted the philosophy of "be good." They have sought to raise employee morale by providing good working conditions, fringe benefits, employee services, high wages, and decent, fair supervision.

We may distinguish between two forms of "be good," which may be called *paternalism* and *hygienic management*. The argument for paternalism holds that if management is good to employees, they will work harder out of loyalty and gratitude. The argument for hygienic management ignores the question of gratitude; it holds that liberal benefits, good working conditions, and friendly supervision make for satisfied employees, and that satisfied employees work harder.

PATERNALISM

Paternalism is pretty much outdated, having had its heyday in the 1920's. In part, its wide adoption at that time was the result of genuine interest by employers in their employees, as well as the belief that "be good" was a more effective form of motivation than "be strong." In part, too, its popularity was a reaction to the rise of unionism during and immediately after World War I. In any case, under the banner of the "New Industrial Relations," management became interested in a wide variety of projects, varying from cafeterias and recreation programs for employees to cooking classes for their wives. Some of these programs were designed to change the employees' personal lives as well

---

[6] For a case study of a situation where "be strong" worked with a group of marginally qualified employees who would have found it difficult to find work elsewhere, see William J. Goode and Irving Fowler, "Incentive Factors in a Low Morale Plant," *American Sociological Review*, Vol. 14, No. 6 (October 1949), pp. 619-624.

as their on-the-job performance. The Sociology Department of the Ford Motor Company of an earlier day went further than most programs. Headed by a Protestant minister, this department was manned by 30 investigators.

> In what amounted to a brief reign of benevolent paternalism, these gentlemen and their house-to-house canvassers imposed . . . a set of rules which blended good sense with Ford whims and Puritan virtues.
>
> On the positive side, the men . . . behaved like the home visitor of the modern public welfare agency. They doubtless helped to "Americanize" Ford's vast body of immigrant workmen. Their charges were encouraged to start savings accounts and to budget their incomes. They were given elementary lessons in hygiene and home management. . . .
>
> At worst . . . its agents became, to some extent, collectors of tales and suspicions. . . . Hearsay as well as fact found its way into a card catalogue where a record was kept of every worker's deviations. . . . Frittering away one's evenings "unwisely," taking in male boarders, sending funds to the "old country"—these things came to be regarded as earmarks of "unwholesome living." The use of liquor was forbidden . . . as was marital discord that resulted in a separation or divorce action.[7]

Ford's program was shortlived, but similar patterns of paternalism were developed in other companies. There is little evidence that any of them were particularly successful in eliciting gratitude, in motivating workers to do a better job, or even in staving off the development of unions. In fact, some of the companies with the best-known histories of paternalism later became scenes of bitter labor-management strife.

There are good psychological reasons for believing that if management expects employees to work harder out of gratitude for benefits, then paternalism will fail to accomplish its purpose. What actually happens may be this:

1. Paternalism may engender resentment rather than gratitude. People don't like to feel dependent on someone else. They prefer to decide for themselves what they want. Letting others decide what is good for them makes them feel infantile and lowers their sense of importance. In spite of stories to the contrary, most people prefer earning things for themselves to having everything handed to them by others. Unearned rewards given out of the kindness of the employer's heart often are regarded as slights to the employee's sense of self-esteem. Instances of "biting the hand that feeds one" are quite common.

> A dramatic example of "ingratitude" was shown in a branch factory of a nation-wide company located in a small hill town in the South. As was typical of the area, most of the houses in town were owned by the company.
>
> Some years back, the company president's wife, Mrs. X, passed through and was shocked by the poverty of the town and the ugliness of the factory. A religious woman, she convinced her husband that something should be done—and she was given a free hand to do her best.

[7] Keith Seward, *The Legend of Henry Ford* (New York: Holt, Rinehart & Winston, 1948), p. 59.

Her first step was to attack the diet problem. A dietician was imported from the North. When no one showed up for her classes, Mrs. X complained to the factory manager. Next session an impressive number of women "voluntarily" signed up for the program.

Heartened by this victory, she made similar efforts in other directions. A model home was set up, and attractive (by big-city standards) modern furniture was offered for sale at wholesale prices. Mrs. X had little success as an order-taker until the factory manager accompanied her on her visits through the town.

The next step was to paint the factory equipment in bright cheerful colors. Then one day potted geraniums appeared at the factory windows. This was the last straw. The men went on strike, threw the geraniums out the windows, and joined the union.

2. As time passes, the novelty of being given free "hand-outs" wears off, and employees begin to take their benefits for granted. Once they come to regard benefits as part of their regular compensation, management is obliged to provide increasingly impressive gifts. Otherwise the workers will turn resentful, and management will get no credit at all.

3. Paternalism incorporates some of the basic assumptions of "be strong." People are expected to be docile in return for their gifts, and work is still regarded as a form of punishment that people undergo only in return for a reward. Moreover, many of the rewards must be enjoyed *off* the job. Little effort is spent on making the job itself more rewarding.

Although paternalism emphasizes the positive nature of the gift, it also carries with it a negative threat: "If you don't do your job as ordered, your gifts will be taken away." In most instances, since the rewards are distributed without discrimination to everyone on the payroll, there is little incentive for the individual worker to do more than the minimum required to keep from being fired.

HYGIENIC MANAGEMENT

Today paternalism is seldom resorted to, except by smaller companies. Hygienic management, which, in a sense, is a more subtle version of paternalism, is quite common, however. Management showers workers with high wages, fringe benefits, good working conditions, good supervision, and all the rest, in the hope that they will have higher morale and *therefore* work harder.[8] The only trouble with this assumption is the *therefore*. Since everyone shares equally in these benefits, there is no reward for good work and no incentive to increase output.

The term *morale* has been used in many different ways; but if morale means the employees' attitude toward the company as a whole, there is little evidence

---

[8] In psychological terms this hypothesis suggests that morale is an intervening variable between management behavior and productivity.

that high morale is necessarily associated with high productivity.[9] Just the reverse may be true. Morale may be very low in a concentration camp, yet production very high. Similarly, workers may be well satisfied to "goof off" in a department where the work pace is extremely slow. A confidential study of a nationwide manufacturing company showed that the plant with the highest production rate had the highest morale, while the plant with the next-highest production rate had the lowest morale. Most studies indicate a rather low correlation between morale and productivity. Apparently, efforts by management to raise morale do not necessarily raise productivity.

A significant, but controversial, study has given us a new insight into the effectiveness of the "be good" approach.[10] In this study, accountants and engineers were asked to "think of a time when you felt exceptionally good or exceptionally bad about your job" and then asked to describe what happened and why they felt as they did. Interestingly, the factors which made people satisfied with their jobs were not the same (or the opposite either) as those which made them dissatisfied. Apparently, the presence of so-called "satisfiers" would act to increase an individual's satisfaction, but their absence would not make him actively dissatisfied, only apathetic. Similarly, the presence of so-called dissatisfiers made people feel they had a "bad" job; but the absence of dissatisfiers did not make a "good" job.

What were these satisfiers and dissatisfiers? The satisfiers were: achievement, recognition, work itself, responsibility, and advancement. Note that all these forms of satisfaction arise *out* of work. The dissatisfiers were: interpersonal relations (both with one's superiors and peers), the technical ability

[9] One careful scholar concludes that there is little convincing evidence that individuals, within any group who have more favorable attitudes toward the company do a better job. See Arthur H. Brayfield and Walter H. Crockett, "Employee Attitudes and Employee Performance," *Psychological Bulletin*, Vol. 52, No. 5 (September 1955), pp. 396-424. Another survey of research suggests there may be a slight positive correlation between morale and productivity: Frederick Herzberg, Bernard Mausner, Richard Patterson and Dora Capwell, *Job Attitudes: A Review of Research and Opinion* (Pittsburgh: Psychological Service of Pittsburgh, 1957). For a study which lists some of the conditions in which low morale and high productivity may go together, see Harold Wilensky, "Human Relations in the Workplace," in Conrad Arensberg, *et al.*, eds., *Research in Industrial Human Relations* (New York: Harper & Row, 1957), p. 25.

[10] Frederick Herzberg, Bernard Mausner, and Barbara Snyderman, *The Motivation to Work* (New York: Wiley, 1960). There have been a number of attempts to replicate this study with various degrees of success. See M. Scott Myers, "Who Are Your Motivated Workers?" *Harvard Business Review*, Vol. 42, No. 1 (January 1964), pp. 73-88. The research techniques have been subject to quite serious (and we think justifiable) criticism. Victor Vroom suggests that (1) the findings are inconsistent with other evidence and (2) people are "more likely to attribute the causes of satisfaction to their own achievements and accomplishments on the job. On the other hand, they may be more likely to attribute their dissatisfaction, not to personal inadequacies or deficiencies, but to factors in the work environment." *Work and Motivation* (New York: Wiley, 1964), pp. 127-29. The authors of this present volume feel that despite the drawbacks of the research technique, the Herzberg study does point to a suggestive new way to examine the problem of motivation. For a review of recent studies of this controversial topic, see Lyman Porter, "Personnel Management," *Annual Review of Psychology*, Vol. 17 (1966).

of the supervisor, company policy and administration, physical working conditions, and the individual's personal life off the job. Note that all these factors relate to the *context* or the *environment* within which the job is performed, but not to the job itself. (Interestingly, salary ranked both as a satisfier and a dissatisfier. In general, when a man indicated that salary helped make his job a bad one, he was referring to the system by which salaries were set; when salary was mentioned as making a job a good one, salary was looked on as a sign of achievement and recognition.)

What is the relationship between these factors and productivity? The evidence is quite tentative, but Herzberg suggests that the presence of satisfiers leads to higher productivity (and for this reason satisfiers have also been called motivators). Dissatisfiers, on the other hand, do not lead to lower production nor does their elimination tend to raise it. Their elimination may reduce active resistance to the job, but promote only a passive acceptance of it. This attitude is illustrated by an interview we once held with a blue-collar worker on a routine job. This worker said:

> "I got a pretty good job."
> Q: "What makes it such a good job?"
> A: "Don't get me wrong. I didn't say it is a *good* job. It's an OK job—about as good a job as a guy like me might expect. The foreman leaves me alone and it pays well. But I would never call it a *good* job."

The experimenters called the factors which lead to this rather sterile, non-involved attitude "hygienic factors" (since they are used to avoid trouble). We shall accordingly call management which emphasizes these factors "hygienic management." Such a "be good" policy may provide a pleasant environment in which to work and a considerable amount of around-the-job satisfaction, but little satisfaction through the job, and little sense of enthusiasm or creativity.

THE VALUE OF "BE GOOD"

We have applied the term "be good" to the philosophy which holds that high wages, good treatment, and so forth will automatically motivate employees to work harder. And we have suggested that this is an oversimplified theory of human behavior. Does this mean that it is a complete waste of money to try to make the company a better place in which to work? Of course not. Properly presented, fringe benefits and employee services are an important part of any personnel program. Such benefits bolster the company's reputation in the community and attract better workers. They also help to reduce turnover, for good workers are less likely to leave the company's employ. Further, a feeling of security serves to reduce tension among employees and thus, to some extent, contributes to higher productivity.

Without question, efforts to make the company a better place in which to work do pay off in terms of better workers and more harmonious relations on the job. But they provide little *direct* motivation for workers to contribute more than a minimum effort. Thus, they provide only a partial answer to the problem of how to motivate workers most effectively.[11]

Implicit Bargaining

One of the most common forms of motivation today (though some managers may hate to admit it) is bargaining. In this approach, management encourages workers to put out a "reasonable" volume of work by making an agreement to provide, in return, "reasonable" supervision (though the bargain is usually a matter of implicit "understanding" rather than any explicit agreement on terms).[12] In a sense, management agrees not to use all the pressures at its command if the employees will agree not to restrict output unduly. The chief difference between this approach and the two forms of motivation already discussed is that the terms of the bargain (namely, what constitutes *reasonable* supervision, and what constitutes *reasonable* output) are agreed upon more or less voluntarily by both parties.

Thus, in practice the level of output and the conditions under which men work are not determined unilaterally by the supervisor, but through unwritten agreement between supervisor and subordinate. There is an assumption that the parties are more or less equal in power, so that the terms of the "effort bargain"[13] are agreed upon voluntarily. Just how favorable the final agreement is to each of the parties is determined by their respective bargaining power. Let us look for a moment at the weapons in the possession of each party.

The workers' major weapon is this: Either they can display cheerful cooperation and maintain high production or else they can indulge in excessive clumsiness, misunderstanding, or overt slowdowns or strikes.

The manager's most obvious weapon is his power to discipline workers who fail to produce. In practice, in the typical unionized situation, formal discipline is difficult to impose unless the worker's production is completely out of line. Still, the supervisor has at his disposal a whole arsenal of minor weapons: small but highly prized "plums," minor concessions, and petty but very real punishments. He can assign easy jobs or hard ones. He can make concessions in terms of time off and accept obviously false excuses for absenteeism or tardiness—or he can nag employees for minor offenses. He can

---

[11] In terms of organization theory, "be good" provides motivation "to participate" but not motivation "to produce." James G. March and Herbert A. Simon, *Organizations* (New York: Wiley, 1958), Chapters 3 and 4.

[12] At times, of course, management does engage in explicit bargaining with the union over the level of production.

[13] Maurice D. Kilbridge, "The Effort Bargain," *Journal of Business*, Vol. 33, No. 1 (January 1960), p. 12.

provide the help that makes a job easier—or he can make work almost impossible (this is a particularly telling weapon where piece-work is involved).

Sometimes the immediate supervisor permits minor violations of rules as part of the bargain. Superintendents in one gypsum mill allowed workers to punch the clock a little early so they could make more overtime, and to take limited amounts of material home with them for their own repair work.[14] In other situations, employees are permitted to take coffee breaks, make personal calls on the company phone, or take home company pencils. In return for this "indulgency pattern," [15] they implicitly agree to work harder. Although such agreements are never put into words, they are tacitly understood by everybody concerned. As one worker put it:

> "Our policy is to live and let live. We give the foreman reasonable production. He protects us from the time-study man who tries to jack up the output rate and looks the other way if we take a smoke. We look out for each other."

These privileges are extended only so long as the supervisor feels that the subordinates are doing a satisfactory job. Otherwise they are withdrawn.

> A case in point was the "no-floating around rule" which specified that workers must stay at their workplace, except to go to the washroom or eat. When foremen felt that things were going smoothly in their group, that their men were "doing a day's work" and were friendly and "cooperative," they would allow their workers to "sneak off" for a smoke, and they would make no caustic remarks if they wandered over to talk to a friend. If, however, a man or a group was felt to be "goofing off," or was being "snotty," foremen were more likely to invoke the "no floating" rule.[16]

An analogy may be drawn between the indulgency pattern and bank deposits. Both subordinates and supervisors build up credits by doing favors for the other party, and both expect to draw on their account when they need a favor for themselves.

Perhaps this bargaining approach can best be understood in negative terms: The supervisor agrees not to push the men if they will agree not to restrict production. The fear that the other side will break the bargain provides motivation for living up to it. Just as a supervisor can withdraw his indulgency if he fails to get cooperation from his subordinates, so they can withdraw their cooperation if the supervisor fails to be indulgent.

In many situations this policy of "live and let live" is the most realistic approach available to the supervisor. For all its disadvantages, it does make possible a reasonably satisfactory level of production and reasonably harmonious worker-supervisor and labor-management relations. Employees enjoy a

---

[14] Alvin Gouldner, *Wildcat Strike* (Yellow Springs, Ohio: The Antioch Press, 1954), pp. 19-20.

[15] *Ibid.*

[16] Alvin Gouldner, *Patterns of Industrial Bureaucracy* (New York: The Free Press of Glencoe, 1954), p. 173.

sense of independence that they are denied under "be good" and "be strong." To be sure, they are motivated in part by the fear that if they fail to produce the supervisor will withdraw their petty benefits. Probably equally important is the feeling that since the supervisor is "fair" to them, it is only proper that they put out a "fair day's work."

The picture we get from this point of view is not that of the worker crushed by the organization, but of one who fights it, copes with it, and retains his autonomy—making deals with it which satisfy both the individual and the organization. Yet unless bargaining is coupled with more positive forms of motivation, it suffers from many of the disadvantages of "be good" and "be strong." Work is still considered a punishment that one endures only for the sake of receiving the benefits that may accrue from living up to the agreement. Each side does something unpleasant in return for something pleasant. From management's point of view, bargaining offers little opportunity to raise production. Indeed, production is often stabilized at a fairly low level. On the other hand, as we shall discuss later, in some cases this may be the most that management can realistically expect.

Competition

Another form of motivation is competition for the pay increases and promotions that go to the men who do outstanding jobs. Competition furnishes several forms of need satisfaction. The prospect of winning a promotion or a pay increase provides a meaningful goal to work toward. And actually attaining the goal means that the employee enjoys an economic reward, as well as a sense of accomplishment and completion, a sense of progress, and added social prestige. Less supervision is required on jobs where competition provides a reasonably satisfactory source of motivation, since each man is on his own to do the best job he can. There is no need to push him.

Competition is not particularly successful as a motivating device among factory workers, however. In union plants the principle of seniority substantially decreases the possibility of winning a promotion on the basis of hard work alone. The trend to reserve foremen's jobs for college-trained men has further reduced the factory worker's chance of rising into management. In theory, the incentive (piece-work) system does provide an opportunity for workers to compete with one another. In practice, however, they usually cooperate to restrict output and prevent competition.

Among blue-collar workers (or white-collar workers in mass-production offices), competition is often more effective among *groups* than it is among *individuals*. We have observed numerous incidents where competition has arisen almost spontaneously between groups to see who will put out the most work, make the biggest reductions in scrap losses, and so forth. Workers seem to enjoy the increased sense of group belonging, the excitement of the game, and the thrill of winning.

Competition among individuals is much more widely accepted on the white-collar and managerial levels. Indeed, among salesmen, it is the traditional form of motivation. Yet even among nonfactory employees competition as a means of motivation suffers certain limitations and undesirable side-effects:

1. Not everybody is equally interested in advancement. Some people are highly ambitious, but others—who may be just as competent and hardworking —seek to avoid situations where they have to "cut the other man's throat" to get ahead. Indeed, if books such as William H. Whyte's *Organization Man* are correct, competition among members of management is no longer as socially acceptable as it once was. And many people, reasonably satisfied with their present job and earnings, do not want to expend the extra effort necessary to win a promotion.

Many engineers and scientists are more interested in professional advancement than in promotions, particularly if the higher-rated job takes them from their laboratory and saddles them with administrative chores. In a sense, these men are competing, but they are competing for professional recognition rather than for the goals management has set for them.

2. Excessive competition has been known to disrupt an entire organization. "A football team may compete successfully with other teams, but it does not follow that it will compete best if its members are in competition with one another." [17]

As we shall see in Chapter 16, the modern industrial organization is being broken down more and more into specialized activities, such as credit, sales, advertising, engineering, product development, and so forth, none of which can be carried on without continuous cooperation from people who are performing other activities. There are fewer and fewer one-man operations, particularly at the higher levels of management. As a consequence, cooperation is vital to sustained productivity.

3. On many jobs it is difficult to measure who has been most successful, since it is impossible to identify the output of each employee. Even when objective measures are appropriate they are hard to formulate, and using them as the primary basis for distributing rewards may itself lead to a distortion of effort through an overemphasis on the factors being measured (see Chapter 15). Yet unless there is some purely objective way of determining who should receive promotions and rewards, competition may make subordinates overly dependent on their boss. They may be more anxious to look good than to actually do a good job.

Overdependence tends to transform the subordinate into a "yes man" and "apple polisher" who is so fearful of making mistakes that he never has a chance to learn from them. The supervisor who is constantly looking upward toward his boss rather than downward toward his subordinates is likely to do a

---

[17] Harold Leavitt, *Managerial Psychology* (Chicago: University of Chicago Press, 1958), pp. 258-259.

poor job of supervision, and he is certain to inhibit upward communication. But more of this in Chapter 15.

4. Efforts to encourage competition are often regarded as pressure, and, as we have seen, excessive pressure is frustrating. Aggression and regression are common by-products of the contests conducted by sales organizations. *Time* magazine writes that:

> Many firms have . . . enlisted salesmen's families in ulcer-building campaigns to spur the breadwinner on. One company regularly sends cards to the home showing the salesman's standing in the current company contest, gives wives tags to hang on furniture around the house to remind their husbands of the furnishings they can earn. Some firms have even sent buzzers and shrill whistles to salesmen's children; when dad asks what the noise is all about, the kids are instructed to tell him it's only a reminder to straighten up and sell harder. . . . Such constant pressure from home and office is bound to take its toll on even the strongest salesman. . . . "You can carry this business of pounding away at a salesman too far," says Republic Steel's General Sales Manager L. S. Hamaker. "It can be too demoralizing." [18]

Excessive emphasis on competition is particularly frustrating to the loser. Since most promotional hierarchies are shaped like a pyramid, with fewer jobs at the top than at the bottom, there are always more losers than winners.

Many work groups actually band together to protect themselves from attempts to encourage competition, either by formulating group standards of "fair competition" or by banning competitive practices altogether. (For examples, see Chapter 4.) This response is most common among hourly-paid workers, but employees at all levels apply pressure on the "eager beaver."

In conclusion, excessive competition may do more harm than good. In its pure form, the philosophy of competition as a motivating device seems to assume that work is itself uninteresting. When used in moderation, however, and in conjunction with other forms of motivation, competition among individuals may be useful, particularly with certain groups (salesmen, for example), and in situations where teamwork is not essential.

Internalized Motivation

A fifth approach to the problem of motivation is to provide opportunities for need satisfaction through doing the job itself, and thus internalize motivation so that people will enjoy doing good work. Here, the better job an employee does, the higher his level of job satisfaction will be. This approach requires management to discard the assumption that work must be objectionable. It also de-emphasizes economic motivation and off-the-job and around-the-job need satisfactions.

Note how this approach differs from "be good." In that method the employee is *given* need satisfaction; here he *obtains* satisfaction *through his own work*—

[18] *Time*, Vol. 72, No. 2 (July 14, 1958), pp. 75-76.

work that he enjoys and work that helps management. In "be good" it is assumed that greater satisfaction leads to harder work. Here the relationship is reversed: It is assumed that the harder work is the element which leads to greater satisfaction.

We have seen that in informal groups people work together and accept the orders of their leaders in order to achieve group objectives. In the same way, it is management's task to create conditions under which people "will willingly and voluntarily work toward organizational objectives" [19]—because they enjoy their work and feel it important to do a good job. This desirable attitude has been called by various authors "spontaneous cooperation" [20] and "Theory Y." [21] As J. S. Mill put it, "Nor are the greatest outward precautions comparable in efficacy to the monitor within." [22]

The preceding chapters have already given some hints about how these opportunities can be provided. Later chapters will make other suggestions, but we shall list the major themes here.

1. We have already seen how intrinsic job satisfaction can be increased through redesigning the job—through job enlargement, job rotation, greater understanding of how the work is coming along, feeling of the whole, and so forth.

2. We have also considered the importance of social satisfactions on the job. Opportunities can be provided to develop friendships and to work together as a team. When members of the group can participate in solving work problems, they may become more involved in the job itself so that their productivity rises.

3. Equally, if not more, important is the style of leadership shown by management. In the next chapter we shall suggest ways in which the supervisor may engage in "general supervision." Workers may be given an opportunity to enjoy a feeling of accomplishment in their work and, in so far as possible, to be their own boss. Under such circumstances supervisors conceive of their job as a way of helping their subordinates rather than as a means of pushing them.

Glance back for a moment at Chapter 1 and notice some of the needs we listed there:

skill	understanding	acceptance
autonomy (being one's own boss)	knowledge of where one stands	attention self-confidence
achievement	praise	

These are the needs that the policy of internalized motivation seeks to harness.

---

[19] Douglas McGregor, *The Supervisor's Job.* Mimeographed; undated.

[20] See Elton Mayo, *The Social Problems of an Industrial Civilization* (Boston: Graduate School of Business Administration, Harvard University, 1945).

[21] Douglas McGregor, *The Human Side of Enterprise* (New York: McGraw-Hill, 1960).

[22] Mill, *op. cit.*, p. 111.

Striking a Balance

For all its merits, internalized motivation is not a panacea, though some observers are more optimistic about it than the authors are. To our minds, those who are most unreserved in its praise tend to overestimate the possible gains from its use and to underestimate the costs involved in making it work.

As we have just discussed, the policies of "be strong," "be good," and implicit bargaining provide little motivation to produce more than a certain minimum amount of work. Yet on many routine jobs this minimum may be enough, since management may have no need for outstanding performance. What is outstanding performance in the case of the assembly-line worker? That he work faster than the line? That he show creativity and imagination on the job? Management needs none of these. *Adequate* performance (as set by implicit bargaining, perhaps) is all that can be used on the assembly line and on many other jobs in our society. Here the conforming, dependent worker (who is not *dis*satisfied) may well be the best.

Further, as we have seen in Chapter 1, many individuals center their lives off the job and have little desire for the challenge internalized motivation provides. There are those who argue that such individuals are immature personalities, and that they have adjusted to techniques such as hygienic supervision or "be strong" by becoming apathetic and dependent: Were the organization environment healthy, were internalized motivation available, the argument goes on, these individuals would react differently. But in many cases, these people's limitations stem from childhood or are present in the general culture. Even if the argument is valid, such individuals may be "too far gone" to react well to internalized motivation, and their attitude is not likely to be changed short of intensive psychotherapy.

In addition, the reliance on internalized motivation can be quite costly to the organization. To increase intrinsic job satisfaction may require the use of job processes which are technologically inefficient. Increased teamwork may not be useful to the organization if employers unite to keep production low. To make general supervision work, many of the old-line autocratic supervisors must be retrained or replaced; this is an expensive process which may result in the demoralization and elimination of the organization's technically most competent individuals.

Since it is extremely difficult to develop internalized motivation on many routine jobs, once the traditional, external sanctions (implicit bargaining, fear of discharge, and so forth) are removed, *net* motivation may, on balance, fall. Furthermore, it is fairly meaningless to talk of permitting exercise of discretion to assembly-line workers or girls on punch-card operations; the very nature of technology requires that all essential decisions be centrally programed. There are those who suggest that such programed jobs should be redesigned to permit job enlargement, and thus greater challenge and discretion. Yet, as we have discussed, such technological changes can be made only at a substantial cost in terms of productivity.

Internalized motivation works best where the nature of the job permits the employee to enjoy autonomy (there may be little opportunity for it on the assembly line, but a good deal in professional work); where employees accept the organization's objectives (it might work better with managerial than blue-collar employees); and among those who make the job their central life focus (it might work poorly with women whose primary interest is finding a husband or bringing up their children).

In any case, the philosophy of internalized motivation is somewhat idealistic. It assumes that somehow the needs of the organization and needs of the individual can both be maximized at the same time, so that what is good for one will be good for the other. Clearly, this is rarely if ever, the case. Normally there must be some sort of trade-off, that is, if organizational needs are to come first, the individual will suffer to some extent, and vice versa. The most the manager can expect to provide is a reasonable satisfactory level of satisfaction for both parties. Conflicts of interest will continue to exist between management and employees and it is totally unrealistic to expect to eliminate them altogether. Employees will want more satisfaction, management will want more production, and where the balance is to be poised between the two "is a matter to be solved by bargaining, not by scientific evidence." [23]

Conclusion

One of the central problems of any organization is to motivate its members to work for the organization's over-all objectives. In the family, the primitive society, or the voluntary social club, this may be a relatively easy matter. But in the larger organization of our society, motivating employees is a difficult problem.

Traditionally, management has resorted to "be strong." With the growth of unions, a rising standard of living, and changing patterns of discipline in home and school, this approach has become less effective. It motivates people only to produce the minimum necessary not to get fired (though in some cases this minimum may be adequate). Moreover, it creates frustration and other undesirable side effects. In practice it is often tempered with a large dose of implicit bargaining.

"Be good" removes some of the harshness of the authoritarian approach. It may help recruit employees and make them more willing to accept their jobs. As a consequence they may not be dissatisfied. But "be good" alone provides little motivation to do more than the minimum amount of work to avoid being discharged.

Implicit bargaining seems a somewhat more realistic approach, particularly

---

[23] Herbert A. Simon, "Authority," in Conrad Arensberg, *et al.*, eds., *op. cit.*, p. 114.

where there is a union situation. It provides an atmosphere of live-and-let-live, but it rarely furnishes any motivation to *increase* production.

Competition has only limited effectiveness as a motivating device on jobs where there is little opportunity for promotion or where seniority prevails. Excessive competition may actually disrupt teamwork and lead to frustration and a host of undesirable side effects.

From many points of view, internalized motivation is the "best" form of motivation, since it provides the greatest opportunity for individuals to satisfy their needs and to develop their personalities. Yet internalized motivation can rarely be applied alone, and it is considerably more appropriate with some sorts of people and jobs (for example, jobs which require individual discretion and commitment) than it is with others.

(Since all chapters in this supervisory section are closely related, we have grouped all the relevant problems together at the end of Chapter 9.)

Delegation

7

A manager makes decisions in some areas by himself; in other areas he delegates to his subordinates. In this chapter we are concerned with the means by which the manager delegates and with the conditions under which delegation is feasible. Our next chapter will deal with how the manager may exercise authority in the areas where he makes decisions on his own.

Delegation on the face-to-face, supervisor-subordinate level is often called *general supervision;* [1] on the organization-wide level it is called *decentralization.* General supervision involves giving increased autonomy to individuals; decentralization involves giving it to organizational subunits. The discussion in this chapter is primarily concerned with the face-to-face level, but much of what we have to say will apply to organization-wide decentralization as well.

---

[1] Some scholars think of general supervision in terms of a pattern of interaction (or face-to-face contacts) and define delegation in terms of the location of formal decision-making powers. For our purposes here we will look upon delegation and general supervision as equivalents.

The Meaning of Delegation

In applying delegation a manager makes relatively few decisions by himself and frames his orders in broad, general terms. Delegation is really a form of job enlargement, for it gives each subordinate a sense of being his own boss and exercising control over his own work environment. Thus, it seeks to provide internalized motivation, and tends to offset the monotony and lack of autonomy that technology has built into many jobs.

The manager who delegates is interested primarily in results, and he permits his subordinates to work out the details for themselves. He sets goals, tells his subordinates what he wants accomplished, fixes the limits within which they can work, and (in cases where the subordinates are adequately trained) lets them decide how to achieve these goals. Instead of rattling off a list of orders, he is likely to communicate helpful information or make suggestions. He explains *why* he wants things done and points out how the subordinate's contribution fits into the over-all plan. In other words, he gives each subordinate the maximum freedom he can handle consistent with the aims of the organization. A successful plant manager exaggerated only a bit when he said:

> "I never make a decision by myself. Oh, I guess I have one or two since I have been here. If people know their job, I believe in letting them make their own decisions. Of course, if there is anything which affects the entire plant, the assistant managers, the staff chiefs, and sometimes the assistant staff chiefs come in here and we discuss it. But I don't believe in saying, 'This is the way it is going to be done.'"

Other managers seem to be unable to take this approach. They are inclined to give detailed instructions telling subordinates exactly how, and in what sequence, they want things done. They "were found to check up on their employees more frequently, to give them more frequent instructions, and in general to limit their freedom to do their work in their own way." [2]

Compare, for example, the difference in approach used by two office managers as they handed out the same assignment.

> *Office Manager A:* "Call Jones Office Equipment and the Wilson Supply Store. Get them to quote you prices on all the office dictation equipment they will. Ask them to give you a demonstration. Invite two managers to the demonstration, Ellis and Conrad, and let them try it out. Get them to put their reactions on paper. Then prepare me a report with the costs and specifications of all the equipment. Oh, yes, be sure to ask for information on repair costs...." (And so on.)

> *Office Manager B:* "I'd like to do something about our stenographic system. A lot of the executives who don't have secretaries of their own are complaining

[2] Daniel Katz and Robert L. Kahn, "Human Organization and Worker Motivation," in L. Reed Tripp, ed., *Industrial Productivity* (Madison, Wisc.: Industrial Relations Research Association, 1951), p. 157.

that it takes them too long to get a girl who can handle their dictation. Could you check up on some of the various kinds of dictating machines, find their prices, advantages and disadvantages, and give me a recommendation as to what we should do? I think we can spend $2,000. Possibly you could talk to some of the executives to get their ideas."

Office Manager A tried to think of all contingencies, and in doing so, gave his subordinate the feeling that she was little more than an errand girl. Moreover, he took so much trouble in trying to think of all the possibilities that he might as well have done the work himself.

USE OF PRESSURE

One difference between what might be called close and general supervision lies in the use of pressure. Note how these managers "push" their men:

"I handle the amount of work given each clerk, watch the dates and time the work so that everything gets out on schedule. If a letter comes in late, we have to speed up handling it—give it special attention. It has to be rushed along —handled in a different fashion than the usual run. I have to watch this to see that we make up time lost in other departments." [3]

"A factory is not a kindergarten. We've got schedules to meet and my job is to make sure that we meet them. . . . If you start babying the men, they will take advantage of you. They expect you to be tough."

Apparently, the supervisors quoted here have little trust in their subordinates' initiative or judgment, and feel that they have to check up on them constantly to make sure that they carry out instructions.

Note the difference in attitude reflected by this comment made by a supervisor who did exactly the same job as the first supervisor quoted above.

"If you keep your employees from feeling hounded, they are more likely to put out the necessary effort to get the work done on time. . . . I tell them, 'if you feel the job is getting you down, get away from it for a few minutes.' " [4]

Implicit in these different attitudes towards subordinates are distinct assumptions about human motivation. The close supervisor often seems to believe in the philosophy of "be strong," in effect, "Work is punishment. If I were to leave the shop, everyone would stop work." (And, no doubt, in his case, exactly this would happen.)

But the general supervisor seems to be saying, "As far as I am concerned, the average man wants to do a good job—at least until proven otherwise. If I walk away, production will continue as usual." (And in his case, this, too, will

---

[3] Daniel Katz, Nathan Maccoby, and Nancy C. Morse, *Productivity, Supervision, and Morale in an Office Situation* (Ann Arbor: University of Michigan, Institute for Social Research, 1950), p. 18.

[4] Rensis Likert and Daniel Katz, "Supervisory Practices and Organizational Structure as They Affect Employee Morale," in Schuyler Hoslett, ed., *Human Factors in Management,* 2d. ed. (New York: Harper & Row, 1951), p. 92.

probably happen.) One study of supervisors with such attitudes comments as follows: "These foremen clearly believed in the willingness and capacity of their men to do a good job, and accordingly acted towards them with this assumption in mind. The men, therefore, tended to react in ways which justified the expectation held of them." [5]

It should be emphasized that the absence of pressure does not mean that subordinates are free to set their own standards. As we shall discuss shortly, delegation is rarely possible unless subordinates are given some sort of direction. High standards are essential if the organization is to be effective. They are also important from the standpoint of morale, since most people derive satisfaction from completing a difficult task. "In an organized production situation, workers expect to be asked to produce and be helped to reasonable levels of output. Furthermore, if the supervisory pressure is not excessive, workers' morale goes up with increasing pressure!" [6] By setting exalted standards the leader indicates that he has confidence in his men. Throughout history, effective leaders have inspired their followers to strive for seemingly impossible goals.

In one sense, the general supervisor does apply pressure when he sets the goals he expects his subordinates to achieve. This is a very different kind of pressure, however, from the nagging, "breathing down a man's neck" type of pressure exerted by close supervisors. If subordinates accept the goals of the organization as valid, they tend to feel that the pressure to do a good job *originated* from the goals themselves, rather than from the supervisor. But we shall discuss this point later on.

THE ADVANTAGES OF DELEGATION

What are the advantages of delegation?

1. Few supervisors have the time to handle both their own job and the jobs of their subordinates. The close supervisor who tries to make every decision by himself frequently exhausts himself physically and mentally. Furthermore, his decision may not be as good as those of his subordinates, since the man who is closest to a problem usually understands it better than anyone else. [7]

2. A subordinate can take pride in results that are directly attributable to his own judgment. He feels little involvement in his work when someone else makes all the decisions.

---

[5] Charles R. Walker, Robert H. Guest, and Arthur N. Turner, *The Foreman on the Assembly Line* (Cambridge: Harvard University Press, 1956), p. 16.

[6] Robert Dubin, "Supervision and Productivity: Some Empirical Findings and Theoretical Considerations," in Robert Dubin and others, *Leadership and Productivity* (San Francisco: Chandler, 1965), p. 28.

[7] As we shall discuss in Chapter 15, the spread of computers has somewhat reduced this advantage of delegation. Provided information can be translated into computer language, electronic data-processing makes it possible to communicate the information quickly and accurately from subordinates to the data-processing center, and the computer itself never becomes exhausted from making too many decisions.

3. Delegation helps to develop the talents and abilities of subordinates. It is hard to train people to take the risks of decision-making without putting them in a position of making decisions on their own. Over-close supervision makes it difficult for people to learn, even by making mistakes.

Substitutes for Decision-Making by the Boss

Effective delegation does not mean that subordinates are permitted to do exactly what they want. Quite the contrary. Delegation is feasible only when there are means available (other than the superior's making the decision himself) which can insure that subordinates will make decisions which are at least "adequate" from the viewpoint of the organization. To use a fashionable term, subordinates must be "programed" (or directed) to insure that they conform to patterns of behavior which are consistent with organizational needs.

The extent of programing necessary, whether it is tight or loose, may depend on a number of factors which we shall discuss later. First, however, we shall consider four types of programing (or four means of avoiding direct orders) which are available to management. The first three are *rules, goals,* and *indoctrination*. The fourth, on a somewhat different level, is the influence of *technology and work-flow*. Let us look at these in turn.

RULES

Rules are a means by which the decision-making activities of subordinates are programed so that it is unnecessary for every decision to be referred to the supervisor. Thus, rules save time for the executive. His subordinates do not have to consult him on routine matters, for the rules lay down principles in advance. Decisions can, therefore, be made more quickly and at lower levels.

Rules set up standard operating procedures. They may be written or unwritten; they may be established by supervisory edict, by training, by implicit bargaining, or through consultation. The significant points are that rules (1) restrict subordinate behavior, and (2) are enforced, in one way or another, by management (and, as we shall see in Chapter 9, sometimes by the subordinate's peers as well). Though many people disparage rules (particularly written rules) as "red tape," they are essential if an organization is to operate effectively.[8]

Rules serve to limit the freedom of subordinates. Naturally, the greater the area of freedom given the subordinate, the greater the feeling of autonomy he will have. Unfortunately, the subordinate cannot be given authority to do *everything* he wants: Well-understood limits or rules make it possible for

---

[8] For an excellent discussion of the relationship between rules and organizational efficiency, see Alvin Gouldner, *Patterns of Industrial Bureaucracy* (New York: The Free Press of Glencoe, 1954), pp. 167 ff.

him to exercise freedom within these limits. Sometimes, of course, these rules are implicit and need not be spelled out in detail.

> Suppose you are the office manager and the Big Boss tells you: "Go ahead, use your discretion in redecorating the office. Anything you say, goes!" Beware! He doesn't really mean that. There are certainly clearly understood rules within which you must work. You must abide by the city building codes and the union contract. You cannot exceed your budget. Further, you must go through the purchasing department, fill out the proper forms, and so forth.
>
> Also, if you are smart, you know that redecorating must play second fiddle to keeping production going. Unless you are on Madison Avenue, the office better wind up looking like an office, not a ladies' lounge or a Japanese garden.

Where there is room for doubt, the supervisor should state the rules clearly, sometimes even in writing. As we shall note later, it often seems that people are objecting to responsibility, when they are really objecting to uncertainty. Rules have both advantages and disadvantages, as the following sections discuss.

Establish consistency.   Particularly in large organizations, rules serve to make the behavior of the parts consistent with the needs of the whole. They reduce the possibility that personal feelings rather than organizational objectives will predominate in decision-making. For instance, in an effort to achieve uniformity, management frequently promulgates standard lists of penalties for disciplinary infractions. Thus, excessive absenteeism will result in the same penalty in every department, even though managers may not agree about the seriousness of this offense. The alternative would be to have one man handle all discipline.

Reduce personal dependency.   Rules are impersonal and, in effect, reduce the power of both the boss and the subordinate. This makes it easier for the subordinate to obey and for the boss to exercise authority. An office manager put it:

> It sure helped me when top management put in a rule that everyone must fly tourist class. This way when I turn down expense accounts with first class fare, the men know it isn't my fault (and almost no one puts it in any more).

Rules also protect the subordinate from arbitrary actions on the part of his boss. They are useful in defining employees' duties and responsibilities. They enable subordinates to predict the consequences of their actions—an ability that is essential to personal security. Well-thought-out rules establish limits within which employees are free to act on their own. Persons on higher levels step in only when one of these limits is violated, or when a question comes up which is not covered by existing policy. As a result, the position of employees is strengthened all down the line.

Permit routinization.   Rules require the manager to initiate orders only once—when he lays a rule down. Most people prefer not to receive constant initiation, particularly when they cannot return it. But once rules are established for how a man should do his job (and once he is adequately trained in the meaning of these rules), then the job can be reduced to a routine. And "routinization protects the ego of those who would otherwise be continually ordered around." [9]

The value of rules in establishing routine was brought sharply to our attention in a training class for telephone supervisors. We asked a chief operator if she found it hard to delegate or give autonomy to operators since the nature of their job provided them little opportunity for discretion. "Oh, no," she said, "once a girl is trained, I let her completely alone. She knows her job and knows what she is supposed to do. She has complete freedom as long as she does her job."

Many employees apparently do experience a feeling of autonomy under such circumstances. Usually it is a situation characterized by constant change that requires most direction:

> In their drive for change and progress, many executives overlook the stabilizing nature of work routines that can be built up and carried on by workers without constant attention from their supervisors. They fail to see that frequently imposed changes not only upset work habits of individuals, but also have a disturbing effect on the pattern of human relations that ties workers to each other and their supervisors.[10]

Excessively rigid rules.   Rules may be too specific and detailed, however, and they may be applied too rigidly by subordinates who fail to use good judgment in handling specific cases. This is one symptom of what some people call "bureaucracy" (though sociologists apply this term to any hierarchical organization that makes use of uniform policies).

Unnecessary rules are difficult to enforce, and inadequately enforced rules may lead to a general breakdown of discipline. Even when they are enforced, if there are too many rules, men may live up only to the minimum requirements of the rules, feeling they have done all the company can reasonably require. Particularly when the reasonableness of the rules is neither self-evident nor well explained, they tend to make a man feel restricted, to breed resentment and aggressiveness, and at times to provoke a desire to break the rules just to prove one's independence.

Excessively rigid rules also discourage individual discretion and initiative, and make it difficult for an organization to adapt to changing conditions. They give the petty tyrant a shield behind which he can vent his vindictiveness. They provide the inept supervisor with a crutch to lean on and enable him to avoid the conflicts and uncertainties of making decisions on his own. They subject the able supervisor to endless frustration and make it impossible for him to operate with the flexibility required for peak efficiency. At the very

[9] Henry Landsberger, "The Horizontal Dimension in Bureaucracy," *Administrative Science Quarterly*, Vol. 6, No. 3 (December 1961), p. 309.

[10] William F. Whyte, *Human Relations in the Restaurant Industry* (New York: McGraw-Hill, 1948), p. 263.

least, they lead to red tape and wasted effort. Here is the way the personnel director of a small branch plant described the effect of excessively rigid rules:

> "The company employment procedures require us to check all references. This may be OK for some of the big plants with operations different from ours. But in this community with our type of work it is silly. We have written the top office a dozen times asking for an exception to be made for us. All they say is that it has to be uniform throughout the company. Why? Well, we go through the motions, but it really is a waste of time. *And in my job this kind of thing happens again and again.*"

Rules give the insecure supervisor a means of "passing the buck" for unpleasant decisions: "The office just issued a strict new policy—no more days off unless a man is sick; my hands are tied." The supervisor hopes, by blaming higher managers with whom the subordinate does not have any regular contact, to maintain his own good relationship with his subordinate. The result is a general weakening of the immediate supervisor's leadership position as well as damage to the employee's respect for the organization.

Rules have a tendency to become ends in themselves, particularly if those who carry them out forget the reasons for which they were promulgated in the first place. Consider this case:

> In order to prevent salary increases from getting out of hand, top management decides that one per year is the limit for any employee. An exceptional employee does an outstanding job. To prevent him from accepting a better offer from another company, his supervisor tries to offer him an extra salary raise. The personnel department automatically turns the supervisor's request down and the man quits.

We have no way of knowing, of course, whether this particular man should have been given an extra increase; we would need additional facts before deciding that. But it is clear that further investigation was called for before a decision was made.

Rebellious employees can cripple an organization by following every rule to the letter. In recent years, for example, "follow-the-rules" campaigns have been successfully used by employees of the British Post Office and the Long Island Railroad as alternatives to strike as means of putting pressure on management.

Correct use of rules. Rules are designed to set a general direction, to insure some measure of uniformity and consistency. But the basic reason for rules is not to restrict the individual, but to further the general welfare of the organization and the attainment of its goals. When a particular rule prevents this organizational objective from being attained, then it must give way, an exception must be made.

The important point is that an exception must be clearly identified as such. Establishing a rule is like setting the course of a ship.[11] There may be times

---

[11] Peter Drucker, *The Concept of the Corporation* (New York: John Day, 1956).

when the ship runs off course—in bad weather, for example—but the ship's officers need to know when and by how much they are departing from the prescribed course if the ship is to reach its destination.

In summary, intelligently devised rules grant the individual in a large organization considerable freedom to make decisions on his own. To insure that his decisions are not completely unfettered, however, his actions need to conform to the goals of the total organization. This insurance is provided through setting limits—that is, through establishing rules. These rules or policies can free higher-level managers from the necessity of handling many time-consuming aspects of the routine business of the organization. Subordinates do not have to check back with their boss each time an action or a decision is called for—they know the limits within which they can operate. The higher manager need step into a problem situation only when one of the pre-established limits has been violated by a subordinate or when a case comes up that is not covered by existing policies. The danger is that the existence of rules makes it possible for the inept or autocratic supervisor to avoid his responsibility for making difficult personnel decisions by interpreting rules in an excessively narrow fashion and "passing the buck."

GOAL-SETTING

By setting goals the manager can avoid the necessity for either making specific decisions or laying down detailed rules. This approach, which is in sharp contrast to detailed, minute-by-minute supervision, is often called "management by exception." It permits the subordinate to experiment, to adjust to novel situations.

Definite assignments. The manager who practices close supervision gives his subordinates detailed orders but sets no over-all goals towards which to work. As soon as the subordinate finishes one task, the manager gives him another. The manager's only goal seems to be to "keep the men busy." Few practices can be so destructive to morale.

> The engineers studying a factory operation said the men could produce 500 units a day. The men said this was impossible. But one day, under the plant manager's urging, they really made an effort and reached their quota 30 minutes before the end of the shift. While they were congratulating themselves on their accomplishment, the plant manager saw them "loafing" and sent them back to work, saying that if they could complete 500 units in 7½ hours, they ought to be able to get up to 550 or 600 tomorrow. And that is what he was expecting! Next day, production went down to 350.

When employees have the experiences of this sort day after day, they develop attitudes that have disastrous effect on output. "Work hard and what rewards do I get? More work. I might as well just *look* busy." [12]

---

[12] Although employees often resist time-study and other forms of work measurement as means of "speed-up," a report from IBM suggests that work measurement and the estab-

Delegation can be more effective when subordinates can be given definite assignments in terms of results expected. If an employee knows exactly how much he is expected to do, he has a goal to work for. He knows if he works hard now, he will have the reward of an easier time later on. He won't have to look busy just to keep out of trouble. (Once an employee told us, "I'm always in trouble because I work hard and finish up, so the boss sees me doing nothing. The man next to me has no trouble with the boss; he's slow and it looks like he is always working.")

On jobs which provide little satisfaction, leisure may be a strong reward. Some organizations allow employees who have finished their days' work to go home and still collect eight hours' pay. In England this practice is known as "job and finish." In America, electric-meter readers, postmen, and garbagemen often work on this basis. In all these occupations close supervision is almost impossible. (Of course, if a man finishes much too soon, the supervisor has an indication that the work has been assigned inequitably. Still, management must be careful not to kill incentive by using a few free minutes as an excuse to give a man extra work.)

On managerial levels, goals are also used. Thus, in many companies each department is considered a "profit center" for accounting purposes, and the departmental manager is given the goal or making the "planned profit" or of not exceeding "planned costs." Sales quotas are, of course, frequently assigned to salesmen. In each of these cases management must be careful not to destroy incentive by raising the goals too quickly after they have been reached.

Naturally, many assignments cannot be as specific as "Process 150 forms a day" or "Sell $500 worth of toothpaste a month." Some must be more general, such as "Wait on all customers who come to your counter" or "Handle all union grievances which come to your level." The latter sort of assignment does not, in itself, constitute a definite goal to work toward (unless it is put this way: "Take care of all these customers or grievances and you will have a few minutes break till the next group comes.") Still, a general assignment (such as "take care of all customers") provides more autonomy than does a host of specific instructions. There is real satisfaction in knowing "This is my job. Here I am in charge. As long as I do it adequately, no one will interfere with me. I will be judged on how well I do."

A number of companies have experimented recently with goals which are jointly set by the boss and his subordinates or by the subordinates themselves. Many of these experiments have been on the management level. There is considerable evidence that goals set in this fashion are at least at high as those set by the boss alone—and that subordinates are more likely to feel such goals are fair and to be motivated to meet them.

---

lishment of output standards may actually result in higher morale, where such standards are seen as providing "stability of work expectations" and a protection against managers who would otherwise constantly cry for "more, more." David Sirota, "A Study of Work Measurements," *Proceedings of the Sixteenth Annual Meeting* (Madison: Industrial Relations Research Association, 1963), p. 160.

Supervision by results. Typically, when supervision by goal-setting is practiced, management interferes very little, so long as the goals are met, except perhaps to give subordinates praise, promotion, or some financial reward. Only when serious trouble develops does higher management step in. The establishment of standards has advantages from the point of view of both management and the individual employee.

1.) The very fact that employees know their efforts are being measured may stir them to work harder. Statistical measures are sometimes more effective in insuring high output than are specific rules. To require each supervisor to make a monthly report on scrap loss may be more effective than a whole series of regulations or exhortations on avoiding waste. Such controls may also provide a swift means of altering the behavior of subordinates. Notice how this approach worked with interviewers in a public employment agency:

> Formerly, statistics were kept only on the *total* number of interviews carried on per month by each interviewer. This system motivated the interviewers to make a large number of *interviews,* but it gave them no incentive to find *jobs* for applicants. There was an immediate change in their behavior when statistics were also kept on the percentage of applicants who actually got jobs. In a two-month period the percentage of jobs filled jumped from 55 to 67. As one interviewer put it: "There is no tendency to get rid of an applicant as there was before. . . . Since they are measured by placements, everybody tried to get a job for every applicant." [13]

2.) Supervision by results makes each man feel that he is his own boss. He understands what is expected of him and is encouraged to show initiative and develop his potentialities. He has a goal to work for and a feeling of completion when he reaches it. This approach encourages competition between individuals and groups—though excessive competition has certain disadvantages, particularly when individuals are expected to work together.

3. The existence of a clear-cut set of performance standards makes it easier for superiors to criticize the shortcomings of their subordinates. Employees are often resentful when their boss talks about their personal failings: It is quite another matter when the criticism is couched in terms of helping them improve their record. In fact, the mere existence of such records tends to reduce the need for the supervisor to prod employees; they know automatically when they have fallen down on the job.[14]

4. This approach to supervision makes it possible for higher management to discover when departments are having trouble and to take remedial measures quickly. As we shall discover in Chapter 15, this is a form of feedback, or upward communication.

5. Similarly, supervision by results makes it possible to evaluate the effective-

---

[13] Peter M. Blau, *The Dynamics of Bureaucracy* (Chicago: University of Chicago Press, 1955), p. 37.
[14] For further discussion of this point, see *ibid.,* p. 40. Also, George Odiorne, *Management by Objectives* (New York: Pitman, 1966).

ness of employees and supervisors and to decide who should get promotions or pay increases.

On the other hand, supervision by results can be attacked as over-emphasizing the individual at the expense of the group; as encouraging competition and passing the buck rather than fostering cooperation; as substituting for the single boss the more pervasive control of a number of "auditing departments" (such as accounting and quality control—see Chapter 16); and as placing excessive emphasis on immediate measurable results, as opposed to significant but immeasurable intangibles such as morale, good will, and employee development. Some of these problems, particularly as they relate to statistical controls, are discussed at greater length in Chapter 15.

INDOCTRINATION

When employees fully accept the goals and values of the organization for which they work, they are said to be indoctrinated. Such persons are willing to subordinate their personal views to the higher interests of the organization as a whole. Indoctrination, in a sense, is a means of establishing organizational loyalty and commitment.[15] Indoctrination makes it easier to delegate authority, since highly indoctrinated individuals all think in roughly the same terms and make their decisions on the basis of the same premises as their superiors. In other words, if a manager's subordinates are indoctrinated, he can feel sure that they will solve their problems in roughly the same way that he would himself. As a consequence, he has little need to be specific about rules or goals which his subordinates know as well as he does himself. They also know which goals are important and which can be broken when they conflict with others of higher priority. Ideally, then, with indoctrination, an organization can permit innovative flexibility as to *means*, knowing that there will be uniformity as to *ends*.

Many of the most effective organizations—such as the Marine Corps or the Catholic Church—rely on indoctrination to a high degree. A well-trained Marine can be relied on to "fight like a Marine" even in situations where he cannot be supervised by his superior officer. The Catholic Church operated for centuries on a decentralized world-wide basis, long before the advent of modern communications, largely because the strength of its priests' faith made it unnecessary for them to receive constant instructions from Rome. To a lesser degree many large corporations try to train their employees so that everyone in the organization can take a more or less consistent point of view towards their job. (Large corporations develop characteristic modes of operations and ways of thinking among their employees, and a General Electric man may well approach problems in a very different fashion from that of a man from Jersey Standard.)

---

[15] Philip Selznick, *Leadership and Administration* (New York: Harper & Row, 1957).

As we pointed out in Chapter 3, professionals are also indoctrinated, but in terms of professional, not organizational, values. As long as the two are consistent (for example, as long as the company wants the scientist to engage in pure research or the company doctor to do his best to maintain employee health), decision-making power may be delegated to professionals with little need for external controls. But when professional and organizational objectives conflict (for example, when a scientist oriented towards pure research [16] is told to work on applied research), then some sort of closer control may be necessary. Skilled craftsmen are indoctrinated in much the same way. Their internalized sense of pride in craft motivates them to maintain high standards of workmanship as well as to put out a fair day's work.[17]

Indoctrination usually requires a long period of hard training: The Catholic Church has its seminaries, the Marine Corps has boot camps, many companies have management training programs,[18] professionals, for the most part, learn their values in universities, and craftsmen in apprenticeship. Indoctrination is usually most effective, however, in organizations with high purposes and long traditions.

Indoctrination is far from being a universal cure-all for every management problem. Indoctrination can be really effective only when individuals internalize management's objectives and make them their own.[19] The Church, the Marine Corps, and other such noneconomically oriented organizations have ideological appeals which make it possible to demand almost complete loyalty from their members; but business firms will rarely, if ever, win such perfect dedication.[20] Religious zealots may be willing to sacrifice their personal ambitions to advance the True Faith. But the typical corporate manager seeks to advance only *himself;* faced with a choice, personal success is more important to him than are corporate profits. And the typical worker has less interest in

---

[16] We do not subscribe to the myth that every scientist wants to do pure research. Many find considerable satisfaction working in the applied area.

[17] See, for example, Robert Blauner, *Alienation and Freedom* (Chicago: University of Chicago Press, 1964), pp. 175-76.

[18] The function of management schools in providing managers with a common point of view has been described by IBM President Thomas J. Watson, Jr., as follows: "These schools were not only to teach general management, but—most important—they were to give our managers a feeling for IBM's outlooks and beliefs. After a time we found that the schools tended to put too much emphasis on management, not enough on beliefs. This, we felt, was putting the cart before the horse. We felt it was vital that our managers be well grounded in our beliefs. Otherwise, we might get management views at odds with the company's outlook." *A Business and Its Beliefs* (New York: McGraw-Hill, 1963), p. 91.

[19] As a sociologist puts it, "Compliance in normative organizations in which there is a high personal commitment not based on force or possible economic gain rests principally on the internationalization of directives accepted as legitimate." Amitai Etzioni, *A Comparative Analysis of Complex Organization* (New York: The Free Press of Glencoe, 1961), p. 40.

[20] In addition, the Church and the Marine Corps are able to isolate their members from conflicting pressures and values in a way which most businesses cannot. However, frequent transfers may reduce the strength of the business executives' loyalties to relatives, community, and social organizations.

advancing the company's interests, particularly when he sees them as conflicting with his own. Thus, indoctrination in business may have a meaning considerably different from what it has in nonprofit institutions.

Still, indoctrination may be useful for instilling in organization members a common approach to problems which may reduce the need for restrictive rules. It is more effective, however, on the management level than among rank-and-file white- or blue-collar workers.

TECHNOLOGY AND WORK FLOW

The nature of the work to be done restricts subordinates in much the same way as do direct orders, rules, and other supervisory techniques.[21] The auto assembler's pace is set by the speed of the assembly line; the bank teller's by his customers; the tool crib attendant's by his fellow workers. In none of these cases does the superior have to tell his subordinates *how fast* to work; in each case controls are very simple: It becomes immediately obvious when a man falls down on the job.

Also, customers, fellow workers, and the demands of the work situation may tell the employee *what* to do; there is no need for the supervisor to initiate orders. This is true, for example, in a hospital operating room:

> Although innumerable orders have been precisely responded to, most of them have flowed from the dictates of the patient's presence and condition. In a very real sense, few of the directives during surgery are arbitrary decisions on the surgeon's part. Rather, in the last analysis, the patient's needs have been the controlling element in the entire situation. Thus the person who seems to be the least capable of exerting authority—the supine, unconscious object—has in fact assumed the star role and preponderant influence in the course of the drama.[22]

Electric utility substation operators, who often work completely by themselves, report feeling that they are completely their own bosses, when in fact they have to respond to "orders" issued by dials and meters. In the same way, factory maintenance men work only when equipment breaks down, and how they do their work is normally determined by the nature of the emergency, not by the boss's instructions. As long as the subordinates are adequately trained and the technology remains relatively constant (two determining constraints), the boss intervenes only when there is obvious trouble. The most important problems involve lateral rather than boss-subordinate relations (we shall discuss lateral relations in Chapter 16).

---

[21] A recent study suggests that, particularly in process industries, technology imposes obvious directives which all can see, thus reducing the necessity for higher management to give orders. Joan Woodward, *Industrial Organization: Theory and Practice* (London: Oxford University Press, 1965).

[22] Temple Burling, Edith Lentz, and Robert Wilson, *The Give and Take in Hospitals* (New York: Putnam, 1956), p. 262.

When a man knows his job well, the mere giving of information serves as a substitute for an order. Note the difference between these two statements: "Bill, bring some parts over to Machine 16," and "Bill, Machine 16 is down to six parts." The second provides Bill with the information he needs to make his own decisions—and it assumes that he will make the correct one. It enables him to serve Machine 3 first if it has fewer parts than Machine 16. In addition, providing a man with abundant information (all that he seeks and requests) has a positive effect on morale, even if he doesn't need all the information to do a good job.

Jobs can be rearranged so as to reduce the number of "human orders." We once observed a factory in which there was constant friction between operators and inspectors; the main trouble was the operators' resentment of what they felt was the inspectors' constant badgering to keep up quality. Only one inspector was able to keep up good relations. The secret of his success was that he rarely *told* a man he had made a mistake; instead, he showed him the offending part with the proper dimensions marked in chalk.

It should be emphasized that the various forms of programing just discussed are, in effect, substitutes for one another and for close supervision. As one form is strengthened, another may be weakened. For example, in times of rapid change, close supervision may be required, since goals are no longer well defined, the requirements of technology are not clearly understood, and new rules have yet to be devised and accepted. If indoctrination breaks down, then new rules must be enforced. When work becomes routine, then there may be less need for elaborate measurement of results because bottlenecks become immediately obvious, and perhaps just as immediately straightened out by those involved without need for intervention by higher management.

General Supervision in Practice

By our definition, general supervision involves a high degree of delegation of authority and, in most cases, requires some indirect means in insuring that employees' behavior conforms to management's needs. We have emphasized that the general supervisor does not give constant orders nor does he spend a large part of his time checking up on employees or putting pressure on them to keep working.

What does the general supervisor do with his time then? As we shall discuss in Chapter 18, spending less time giving orders to each individual subordinate may permit a general supervisor to manage larger numbers of subordinates (in terms which we will discuss later, he can expand his *span of control* and have a *flatter organization*). Even where this does not occur, the activities of the general supervisor may differ substantially from those of close supervisors. General supervisors are more likely (1) to do work different from that of subordinates, (2) to concentrate on long-range rather than short-range problems and, (3) to engage in training. Let us look at these activities in turn.

DIFFERENT WORK
FROM THAT DONE BY SUBORDINATES

There is an old tradition that the good supervisor is the one who rolls up his sleeves and works alongside his subordinates, often setting an example by his efforts. The evidence suggests that this is a myth. Of course, in an emergency the good supervisor will always pitch in to help. And there are certain supervisory jobs that require close technical coordination, jobs such as that of orchestra conductor or engineering project manager. With these exceptions, however, research indicates that the high-productivity supervisor devotes much of his time to activities that pay off only in the long run, such as planning, improving human relations, and co-ordinating activities with other departments.[23] The low-productivity supervisor is more likely to do the same sort of work as his men, and to concentrate on paper work and short-term activities such as checking up on his subordinates or arranging for materials.

How can we explain these differences? In the first place, the close supervisor may seek to avoid the personal contacts required for effective leadership. He may feel more secure working with his hands or mind than trying to cope with human-relations problems. This is particularly true of the man who has come up through the ranks and to whom the supervisory position has been given as a reward for hard work, technical competence, and seniority rather than as a recognition of leadership abilities. Faced with an entirely new and confusing set of problems that he is ill-equipped to handle, he retreats to a behavior pattern in which he feels secure. The following account describes what happened to head nurses in a hospital—but it applies equally well to business situations:

> In some hospitals women were raised to positions of authority over nursing floors because they had worked there the longest and had proved to be excellent craftsmen. Sometimes they had no experience whatsoever in organizing the work of others. Such a person, since her field of competence lay in the art of nursing rather than in supervision, tended to do what she was best at, which was to give direct bedside care. She put off the other parts of her job, resenting the time spent on paper-work, supervision and teaching. Sometimes a head nurse would have so much pride in her command of nursing skills that she found great difficulty in accepting the less perfect work of subordinates. She would follow each student or auxiliary around, picking up where they left off and finishing the job for them. . . .

---

[23] Much of the most interesting work in this area has been done by the Institute for Social Research, University of Michigan. For summaries of this work, see Robert L. Kahn and Daniel Katz, "Leadership Practices in Relationship to Productivity and Morale," in Dorwin Cartwright and Alvin Zander, eds., *Group Dynamics, Research and Theory* (New York: Harper & Row, 1953), pp. 612-627; and Rensis Likert, *New Patterns of Management,* (New York: McGraw-Hill, 1961).

Another type of retreat was that taken by the head nurse who centered all her attention on paper work. Sometimes this was an older woman who looked upon her promotion to this post as a graduation from hard labor, a kind of semi-retirement from the strains of bedside nursing.[24]

The very fact that the supervisor works alongside his men means that he must engage in close supervision. His presence provides a form of "pace-setting," and his men may well feel that his directions and example are a reflection of his belief that they cannot be left to do the job on their own.

True, it is difficult for a manager to avoid close supervision of this sort. Every supervisor feels a strong temptation to fix up a subordinate's mistakes himself rather than explain what should have been done.[25] Doing something oneself is usually easier than teaching. As a supervisor in an engineering laboratory put it:

> "Frankly, I've had a lot more experience than anyone in my section. Most of the time when I hand out a problem I can get the solution very easily. It requires superhuman control to let those guys take three times as long as I would to get the answer. But how else can they learn?"

The close supervisor either keeps nagging his subordinates, feeling that constant pressure is the best way to get results—or does the work himself and thus tries to avoid personal contacts.[26] The general supervisor, however, tries to provide explanations and motivate his employees to improve their perform-ance. Instead of rushing in and taking the job into his own hands, he is patient enough to help a subordinate who has failed.

CONCENTRATION
ON LONG-RANGE PROBLEMS

There is a significant difference between the way the general supervisor and the close supervisor spend their time on their job. The close supervisor is a man who runs from crisis to crisis putting out fires. He is concerned exclusively with the here and now (or perhaps checking on the past). He has no time for anything but short, specific instructions. Often he dispenses even with these, and pitches in to do the job himself. The general supervisor, on the other hand, looks to the future. He spends more time on planning, working to im-prove relations with other departments, setting goals, and training subordinates so they can meet emergencies without coming to him. In a sense he is making

---

[24] Burling, Lentz, and Wilson, *op. cit.,* pp. 113-114.

[25] For a discussion of some of the personality problems involved in obtaining effective delegation, see Chapter 18.

[26] The term "close supervision" may seem inappropriate when applied to the man who avoids personal contacts and shuns supervising. Yet when this individual does supervise, he is likely to supervise in detail.

a capital investment of his time from which he will derive gains in time saved over the long run.

When employees are well trained and when work is delegated, the supervisor has time to concentrate on the over-all problems of his department and to develop new, more permanent solutions rather than just to cope with each crisis as it comes along. For instance, how does the supervisor react when a severe problem suddenly arises that calls for several men to work overtime? Does he go to each man in the department to ask him whether he is willing to stay late? Or does he develop a method of getting people to indicate in advance when they want extra work? The time the supervisor saves by adopting the second approach can be used for many useful purposes, including the improvement of relations with his boss, with staff sections, and with other departments with which his own department has to cooperate.

A study at General Electric reported this observation:

> The least effective foremen spent the greatest percentage of their time finding immediate solutions to short-range production problems, while the most effective foremen spent the greatest percentage of their time on activities which involved planning and organizing the longer-range aspects of the job. The less effective foremen spent more time checking on work progress or status, securing materials, supervising materials or production movement, and similar activities which successful managers apparently delegate. Probably because of their greater emphasis on training employees, their belief in their abilities to carry out their assigned tasks without checking, and greater success in organizing the work of their groups, better foremen did not find it necessary to continuously check the conditions in their area.[27]

Here is a summary of the findings on how the two groups of GE foremen spent their time.[28]

	FOREMEN	
Activity	*Effective*	*Ineffective*
Production	20%	40%
Personnel administration	23	12
Equipment and methods	14	8
Quality	6	6

There were similar differences in the pattern of communication between supervisors and their work groups: [29]

---

[27] General Electric Company, Public and Employee Relations Service, *The Effective Manufacturing Foreman* (processed, 1957), p. 47; see also Quentin D. Ponder, "The Effective Manufacturing Foreman," in *Proceedings of the Tenth Annual Meeting* (Madison: Industrial Relations Research Association, 1957), pp. 41-54. Findings roughly similar to the General Electric study are reported in Paul R. Lawrence, *The Changing of Organizational Behavior Patterns* (Boston: Harvard University, Graduate School of Business Administration, 1958), and in Emanuel Kay and Herbert M. Meyer, "The Development of a Job Activity Questionnaire for Production Foremen," *Personnel Psychology,* Vol. 15, No. 1.

[28] Ponder, *op. cit.*, p. 47. The percentages do not add up to 100 because a number of miscellaneous activities are omitted.

[29] *Ibid.,* p. 52.

| | FOREMEN | |
Type of Communication	Effective	Ineffective
Giving *specific* work orders	3%	15%
Giving *general* work orders	5	1
Passing information to the group or engaging		
in two-way discussions with members of the		
work group	67	47
Receiving information from workers	25	37

The study comes to this conclusion:

> When the more effective foremen found it necessary to give direction to the work of their employees, they would do so in a general way, giving explanations and suggestions, but leaving details of method and sequence up to the worker. The less effective foreman, on the other hand, gave a far greater number of direct work orders, without explaining why a job should be done, or how the specific order related to the over-all work pattern.[30]

General supervisors seek to develop an atmosphere in which workers feel free to bring their problems to them. In this atmosphere subordinates ask for help and information when it is needed, thus reducing the supervisor's need to give instructions. As one foreman told us:

> "As far as getting action is concerned, it doesn't make much difference whether you *tell* a man what to do or he *asks* you. But it makes all the difference in the world in how he feels. So I try to be available for questions instead of telling people."

The GE study found that effective foremen were aware of this difference: "The lower-rated foremen spent more time seeking information from others, while the higher-rated foremen spent more time answering requests for information." [31]

The General Electric study revealed that there was little difference in the *total* amount of time spent by the two types of supervisor with their subordinates, but that the effective supervisors had fewer and therefore longer contacts than ineffective supervisors. The short contact is sufficient for an abrupt order or a question; more time is required if there is to be a meaningful explanation or a two-way discussion. The very fact that the general supervisor permits his subordinates greater freedom means that fewer contacts are required.[32]

In addition, this study found that more effective supervisors spent a greater proportion of their time improving their relations with their bosses, staff sec-

---

[30] *Ibid.*, p. 52.

[31] *Ibid.*, p. 51.

[32] The average length of a supervisor's contact depends in part on the technology of the work he is supervising. Supervisors on an assembly line, for example, may well have shorter average contacts than maintenance supervisors. See Walker, Guest, and Turner, *op. cit.* We would hypothesize, however, that if technology is held constant, high-production supervisors in most cases will have fewer and longer contacts.

tions, and other departments. Here is a summary of how these supervisors spent their time.[33]

People Dealt With	FOREMEN	
	Effective	*Ineffective*
Staff and Service People	32%	20%
Own Subordinates	19%	17%

This distribution is consistent with other findings that one of the most important functions of the supervisor is to represent his work group to other groups in the organization.

What picture of the general supervisor emerges from all these observations? The picture of a man who is abreast of his job, who gives his subordinates a broad range of freedom, and who is regarded by them as being available for help rather than being a source of pressure. In the studies cited, the supervisors who exhibited these characteristics were also the ones who had the most effective, productive subordinates.

TRAINING

We have already mentioned that the manager who engages in general supervision places considerable emphasis on training his subordinates. Well-trained men have no need for detailed instruction. It has been said that the test of a good manager is what happens when he is away from his department. If his men have been trained well, everything goes so smoothly that he is hardly missed. Even where there is a formal training department in the organization, the most valuable training still comes from one's immediate boss, for he is the one who provides the on-the-spot cues to what should or should not be done.

The close supervisor and the general supervisor adopt very different approaches to training. The close supervisor tends to equate training with the never-ending issuance of specific instructions; to him training and detailed supervision are identical. He has no interest in helping his subordinates learn so they can do without close supervision.

The general supervisor explains the *why* of his instructions; he gives his subordinates the theory, the over-all framework within which this particular instruction fits. Provided with this framework, subordinates can cope with unusual problems without having to run to their boss for new instructions every time a problem arises. Patient explanation and demonstration by the manager is frequently an essential first step.

But in many areas it is more effective if the trainee is given an opportunity to think out his problems by himself—under guidance. For instance, when giving a new assignment the manager should try to avoid saying, "I want you to do it this way." Instead he might ask, "Do you have any ideas how this

[33] Ponder, *op. cit.*, p. 50.

should be done?" and then encourage the subordinate to work out the problems involved. Possibly the manager can listen to the subordinate as he thinks through the problems out loud. If the subordinate cannot arrive at a satisfactory solution on his own, of course, the manager offers suggestions. But he is careful to give the subordinate maximum opportunity (consistent with his ability) to figure things out by himself.

This approach to training is substantiated by two psychological principles: (1) Active learning is more effective than passive learning in bringing about a change in attitude and behavior. People learn more easily when they work out solutions for themselves than when they are provided with ready-made answers. (2) Learning is more effective when they see the results of their actions and can correct their own mistakes. In other words, "feedback" is an important element in learning.

When Does General
Supervision Work Best?

We have spent our time so far contrasting close and general supervision, but, with the exception of the GE study, we have said very little about what sort of supervision is most effective, principally because this is still a highly uncertain area. There has been a good deal of research in the area, but much of it is inconclusive and the most we can say is that there is no simple answer.[34] It does seem that a broad range of people (but not everyone) finds delegation satisfying. But this does not mean that delegation necessarily results in higher productivity. About all we can say is that the extent to which delegation will be effective varies with the circumstances. What are the circumstances? Here, the research data is very scanty and the best we can do is to offer some hypotheses only partly supported by evidence.[35]

It would seem that general supervision works best (1) where the work provides intrinsic job satisfaction; (2) where the work group accepts management's objectives; (3) where worker and union-management reactions are harmonious; (4) where consistency and coordination are relatively unimportant; (5) where technology permits individual discretion; (6) where subordinates desire responsibility; (7) in the long run rather than in the short run; and (8) where the pattern of supervision is consistent throughout the organization.

---

[34] One reason for caution in this area is that the relationship between cause and effect is rarely clear. A study may find that close supervisors have less efficient departments, but this does not prove that close supervision *causes* low efficiency. It may be that in departments where efficiency is low, close supervision is the most intelligent way of getting it back to normal.

[35] For an excellent discussion, see Harold Wilensky, "Human Relations in the Workplace," in Conrad Arensberg, and others, eds. *Research in Industrial Human Relations* (New York: Harper & Row, 1957), pp. 25-50.

WHERE THE WORK PROVIDES
INTRINSIC JOB SATISFACTION

There is some evidence that general supervision is most effective where the job is challenging, where the work cycle is long, and where there is an opportunity for intrinsic job satisfaction. In contrast, where there is little opportunity for creativity and internalized motivation, employees are less likely to perform effectively when left by themselves.[36] One study suggests that, compared to unskilled workers, skilled workers feel more involved in their jobs and are more anxious for an opportunity to participate in making decisions relating to it.[37] Another indicates a less positive relationship between general supervision and productivity on jobs where the work is machine-paced than on jobs where the men pace themselves.[38] Thus, in some cases, job enlargement may be a precondition for effective delegation.

General attitudes toward work are relevant here. Journeymen printers, for example, are very proud of their craft. They have internalized management's objectives of putting out high-quality work, and have a long tradition of self-regulation. With such a group anything but general supervision would be resented. On the other hand, relatively less benefit might be derived from general supervision in the textile industry, where workers generally have low aspirations, place little value in self-expression, display an "indifferent attitude toward the meaningfulness of work," [39] and do not have work as a central life interest.

The fact that a given job may offer *some* people intrinsic job satisfaction is not enough to motivate *everyone* to work hard at it. If a man does not feel his job offers challenge to *him*—if he does not value the skills the job requires—then delegation is not likely to lead to higher productivity.[40] One would imagine, for example, that a musician who is working temporarily as a salesman would react less well to general supervision than would someone who considers himself a career salesman.

WHERE THE WORK GROUP ACCEPTS
MANAGEMENT'S OBJECTIVES

The general attitude of the work group towards management's objectives is also significant in determining whether delegation is realistic. If the group

---

36 Nancy Morse, *Satisfactions in White Collar Jobs* (Ann Arbor: Survey Research Center, University of Michigan, 1953), p. 46.

37 Howard Vollmer, *Employee Rights and the Employment Relationship* (Berkeley: University of California Press, 1960), Chap. 4.

38 Michael Argyl, Godfrey Gardner, and Frank Cioffi, "Supervisory Methods Related to Productivity and Labor Turnover," *Human Relations*, Vol. 9, No. 1 (1958), p. 38.

39 Blauner, *op. cit.*, p. 176.

40 Victor Vroom, "Ego Involvement, Job Satisfaction, and Job Performance," *Personnel Psychology*, Vol. 15, No. 2 (Summer 1962), pp. 159-178.

is indoctrinated to support these objectives, then a high degree of delegation may be feasible. But, as we shall discuss in Chapter 9, if the group does not support these objectives, then more autocratic techniques must be used to get the work done. A higher degree of delegation is possible in a hospital or a social agency, where presumably the organizational objectives are highly valued by the participants, than might be possible in a jail or concentration camp.[41]

WHERE WORK AND UNION-MANAGEMENT RELATIONS ARE HARMONIOUS

Obviously, general supervision is difficult to practice in the face of a militantly antimanagement union or where subordinates are bitterly divided on ethnic or other grounds. Similarly, it is hard to elicit cooperation in communities where there is a long tradition of hostility to management and where everything a "boss" does is automatically looked upon with suspicion.

WHERE CONSISTENCY AND COORDINATION ARE UNIMPORTANT

In many instances the nature of a job requires that subordinates follow a uniform pattern of behavior, for example, where the job permits outsiders to compare behavior among employees. Thus, in a firm that deals with hostile unions, responsibility for labor relations is far more likely to be centralized than is training (which is a purely internal matter). Similarly, internal revenue agents are checked closely by top management in the Treasury Department to insure that there is a common, nationwide policy toward interpreting the law.

The nature of internal work-flow is another important factor. More delegation is feasible where there is "parallel" specialization than where specialization is "interdependent."[42] Parallel specialization occurs where work activities are assigned so as to minimize the amount of coordination required, that is, where there is relatively little work-flow among individuals and departments. Interdependent specialization exists where the day-to-day functioning of the job of one individual or department is closely related to that of other individuals or departments. For example, in the programing of computers there may be a number of programers who each do part of the job. Since their respective activities must fit perfectly into one another, the manager must specify in great detail how each is to proceed.

An automobile assembly line, with its closely coordinated work flow, is a prime example of interdependent specialization, whereas a university repre-

---

[41] Etzioni, *op. cit.*

[42] Interdependence is related to what some organizational theorists call complementarity. See, for example, Jacob Marshak, "Efficient and Viable Organization Forms," in Mason Haire, ed., *Modern Organization Theory* (New York, Wiley, 1959), p. 317.

sents parallel specialization. Indeed, academic freedom is possible largely because each professor can proceed on his own in research or class with only a minimum of coordination with others in the university.

WHERE THE TECHNOLOGY PERMITS
INDIVIDUAL DISCRETION

Technology often limits the amount of discretion which subordinates can be given. Some equipment can be operated only in one way; once it is put in place employees have no choice but to follow the prescribed routines. In some work, mistakes can be so expensive that higher management feels obligated to check subordinates constantly.[43]

The need for decisive decision-making on many jobs leaves little room for delegation. The conductor of a symphony orchestra must exercise strong leadership and there is little opportunity for delegation or participation (a jazz combo on the other hand may practice considerable participation). Decisive decision-making is also required of a surgeon in the operating room, an aircraft pilot, and a ship's captain. In each of these cases subordinates are likely to get their satisfactions from the excellence of their performance as a team rather than from the opportunity to exercise discretion. As we shall discuss in Chapter 8, in these cases human-relations ability may well be subordinate, in the eyes of subordinates, to technical ability.

Technology also determines how managers might best interact with subordinates. A study of parcel delivery service indicated that drivers, who see their boss only for a few minutes each day, are more likely to prefer bosses with strong authoritarian attitudes, whereas positioners, men who handle parcels on the dock and who work in close contact with their boss all day long, prefer those who are not authoritarian. Since drivers spend only a short time with their boss, apparently they prefer someone who is decisive.[44]

WHERE SUBORDINATES DESIRE RESPONSIBILITY

There are substantial differences in the amount of responsibility people are willing to accept on the job.[45] One person may flourish under supervision that another might find extremely restrictive. One of the authors learned this lesson

---

[43] For a study which suggests that continuous-process technology requires closer supervision than batch or unit technology, see Robert Dubin, "Supervision and Productivity: Empirical Findings and Theoretical Considerations," in Robert Dubin and others, *Leadership and Productivity* (San Francisco: Chandler, 1965).

[44] Victor Vroom and Floyd C. Mann, "Leader Authoritarianism and Employee Attitudes," *Personnel Psychology*, Vol. 13, No. 2 (Summer 1960), pp. 125-140.

[45] People may also differ in the areas in which they wish responsibility. Some individuals may accept a great amount in their home life and in community organizations, yet not wish much on the job.

the hard way when he was working in a government agency some years ago and was assigned an elderly secretary. Imbued with the principles of good human relations, he explained in detail the background of every letter he dictated, asked for her comments on style, and even suggested that, if she wished, she could draft some of the letters herself. At last she burst out. "I'm not paid to do that kind of work! That's your job."

Psychological research provides evidence that the nature of a person's personality affects his attitude toward supervision. There are some employees with a low need for achievement and high fear of failure who shy away from challenges and responsibilities.[46] Many seek self-expression off the job and ask only to be allowed to daydream on it. (For example, women who look upon their job as only a brief interlude before marriage may have relatively little desire for autonomy.) [47] One study, for example, suggests that people who have a high need for independence and weak authoritarian attitudes are likely to respond to consultation with their supervisors by being more satisfied with their work and turning out a better performance; those with low needs for independence and strong authoritarian values are much less likely to respond in this manner.[48] In addition, there are many who have become so accustomed to the authoritarian approach in their culture, family, and previous work experience that they regard general supervision as no supervision at all. They abuse the privileges it bestows on them and refuse to accept the responsibilities it demands.

Consider the case of two hospital floors supervised by two very different head nurses.[49] The first head nurse (Miss Smith), though extremely courteous, was strict and uncompromising with nurses who violated regulations. She insisted that conversations be kept to a minimum and handed out detailed, unambiguous work assignments to her nurses.

The second head nurse (Miss Rogers) had a much more informal, almost kidding relationship with her subordinates and patients. She consulted with her nurses about problems and changes, and succeeded in developing a strong feeling of camaraderie on the floor.

Now you might suppose that all the nurses would have preferred Miss Rogers' floor to Miss Smith's—but they didn't. The hospital let nurses choose which floor they wanted to work on; both floors were quite popular, but with different groups of nurses. In general the older women liked the security of Miss Smith's floor, where everything went according to predetermined routine. As one older nurse put it:

---

[46] For a study which suggests that there are substantially different needs for achievement among various classes, cultures, and ethnic groups, see D. C. McClelland, *The Achieving Society* (Princeton: Van Nostrand, 1961).

[47] Howard Vollmer, "Supervising Women is Different," *Personnel Journal*, Vol. 34, No. 7 (December 1955), pp. 261-263.

[48] Victor H. Vroom, *Some Personality Determinants of the Effects of Participation* (Englewood Cliffs, N.J.: Prentice-Hall, 1960).

[49] This case is based on the research of Dr. Edith Hamilton.

"I honestly feel I need a responsible person nearby to supervise me. I need guidance and therefore I prefer to work where there is fairly close supervision. . . . I like to do things in an orderly way. . . . (on Miss Rogers' floor) things are done too sloppily."

Most of the younger girls preferred the independence allowed them by Miss Rogers.

Why these differences? For one thing, nurses' training in recent years has become less strict than it once was, and the younger nurses have never experienced close supervision. More important, these differences may reflect an attitude toward authority that the younger girls developed in their formative years at home and at school, an attitude influenced by the wide range of freedom permitted to modern children. Indeed, subordinates' feelings toward their boss are often colored by the relations they had with their parents and the emotional maturity and security they developed as children.

Different groups develop different attitudes toward work. College graduates, for example, expect a great deal of responsibility and freedom. Certain ethnic groups, on the other hand, have trouble accepting the concept that people should make decisions for themselves, particularly decisions concerning work.[50] Some Indian tribes are brought up in a cultural tradition which teaches one not to take the initiative. "In their passivity, restraint and expectation of immediate results . . . there is scant evidence that the average adolescent, once he leaves [the reservation] will acquire the inner ambition that helps to produce a high standard of living." [51]

Americans have often run into trouble trying to apply general supervision abroad. Peasants from Latin countries who have worked for years under the control of *patrons* may find a sudden dose of independence extremely unsettling. Since the employees are not prepared for this kind of treatment, they think something is wrong with a boss who doesn't act like a boss.

A recent study compared a group of "Town" workers in rural or small-town surroundings with a group of "City" workers (mostly with Italian and French-Canadian backgrounds).[52] The Town workers tended to react positively to work requiring greater skill and the acceptance of greater responsibility. The City workers, on the other hand, preferred simpler, less challenging tasks. This surprising contrast is hard to explain. It does seem that work and achievement (the so-called Protestant ethic) are more central to the life interests of those with a rural background than they are to those from certain ethnic groups in the city. Certainly those brought up on a farm are introduced to

---

[50] For examples from various countries see Heinz Hartmann, *Authority and Organization in German Management* (Princeton: Princeton University Press, 1959); James Abegglen, *The Japanese Factory* (New York: The Free Press of Glencoe, 1958); and Frederick Harbison and Eugene Burgess, "Modern Management in Western Europe," *American Journal of Sociology*, Vol. 60, No. 1 (July 1954), pp. 15-23.

[51] Frank C. Miller and D. Douglas Caulkins, "Chippewa Adolescents: A Changing Generation," *Human Organization*, Vol. 23, No. 2 (Summer 1964), p. 159.

[52] Arthur N. Turner and Paul R. Lawrence, *Industrial Jobs and the Worker* (Boston: Harvard University, Graduate School of Business Administration, 1965).

chores (now a rarity in city families) at an early age. For them work and discipline are easily taken in stride. The City workers, on the other hand, seem to value more highly social satisfaction on and off the job.[53]

IN THE LONG RUN RATHER THAN THE SHORT RUN

Even under close supervision a work group may be highly productive, particularly in times of widespread unemployment when men are fearful of losing their jobs. In fact, management has often found that the best way to get an immediate increase in production is to increase pressure and to impose close supervision. In the long run, however, close supervision may well lead to a deterioration of morale and productivity and to what one author calls "a liquidation of human assets." [54]

> One experiment involved four divisions of a large company, each of which had about 100 clerical employees.[55] In two of these divisions managers and supervisors were trained in the principles of general supervision. In the other two divisions management cut the number of employees by 25 per cent without reducing the work load and systematically intensified the pressure and closeness of supervision. By the end of twelve months both groups had increased productivity. But the closely supervised group had increased theirs by 25 per cent compared with a 20 per cent increase for the group under general supervision. The employees under general supervision, however, showed significant improvements in measures showing loyalty, feeling of responsibility, and involvement in work. In the other group these same indices declined dramatically.

Of course, lowered morale need not lead to a decline in production. But increased pressure may well result in resistance on the part of individuals, informal work groups, and the union; in restriction of output; and in all the familiar symptoms of aggression that we discussed earlier. Under these circumstances management is often tempted to enter into the vicious cycle of closer and closer supervision, to which the employees reply by sabotage, wildcat strikes and ever-tightening output restrictions.

On the other hand, the sudden introduction of general supervision is unlikely to lead to an immediate increase in production where the individuals involved have become accustomed to close supervision. If, because of their previous experience, workers expect to be pushed into work, chances are that they will abuse any relaxation of pressure unless the process is handled with great skill. They may look upon the manager who tries to apply general super-

---

[53] The evidence so far is slim, but see for example B. C. Rosen, "Race, Ethnicity, and the Achievement Syndrome," *American Sociological Review*, Vol. 24, No. 1 (Feb. 1959), pp. 47-61; Melville Dalton, "The Industrial Rate Buster: A Characterization," *Applied Anthropology*, Vol. 7, No. 1 (Winter 1948), pp. 5-18.

[54] Rensis Likert, "Measuring Organizational Performance," *Harvard Business Review*, Vol. 16, No. 2 (March-April 1958), pp. 41-50. See also Nancy Morse and Everett Reimer, "The Experimental Change of a Major Organizational Variable," *Journal of Abnormal and Social Psychology*, Vol. 52, No. 1 (January 1956), pp. 120-129.

[55] *Ibid.*

vision as weak and flabby.[56] At times the manager who is being trained to use general supervision is regarded by his subordinates as threatening because his behavior is unpredictable. Employees sometimes find it easier to work for a hard-bitten so-and-so whose behavior is more predictable than one who seems to be changing his behavior every day.

WHERE THE PATTERN OF SUPERVISION IS CONSISTENT THROUGHOUT THE ORGANIZATION

The *over-all pattern* of supervision is more important than any one aspect of it. There is a danger that managers may adopt certain features of general supervision and disregard others. A manager who delegates authority but neglects to train his subordinates to exercise it intelligently may well have worse results than the manager who retains all authority for himself.

More important than any particular manager's style of leadership is the general pattern of human relations that prevails in the organization. It is very difficult for a supervisor to practice general supervision if his boss and his fellow managers all practice and expect close supervision, particularly if the boss fails to back him up and show tolerance for his mistakes.

Conclusion

General supervision is an approach to management which is based on delegation to subordinates of wide authority to make decisions. It assumes that people will work harder if they are given freedom to make their decisions, and it relies on internalized motivation, the satisfactions people get from being free to do a good job more or less in their own way.

Delegation is rarely absolute. Delegation is possible only under conditions when management can be reasonably sure that subordinates will behave in a relatively satisfactory fashion and, if they make mistakes, that these will not be too dangerous to the organization. To insure that subordinates do behave adequately, management must provide some sort of guidance. Rules, goals, indoctrination, and even the requirements of technology tend to provide such guidance.

There is a good deal of research which suggests that general supervision results in higher productivity. As we have indicated, this is not always true. The feasibility of delegation depends on a number of factors: the nature of the work, individual personality and background, over-all management practices, employee acceptance of management goals, union-management relationships, and the organization's needs for coordination and consistency. Unless these factors are favorable to delegation, delegation may not increase motiva-

---

56 For an excellent discussion of some of the problems involved in introducing general supervision into an organization, see Lawrence, *op. cit.* The point made above is discussed on pp. 196-197.

tion substantially. Even if it does, the cost to the organization in terms of impaired coordination, and so forth, may be greater than the gains in terms of motivation.

Clearly, there is no one best method of supervision applicable to all situations.[57] There are a number of means of delegations, some of which are applicable to routine work, for example, and others of which work best where a high degree of initiative is required. Only in rare instances is delegation enough in itself. Even the general supervisor must exercise authority. The problems this involves will be discussed in the next chapter.

---

[57] See, for example, Warren G. Bennis, "Leadership Authority and Administrative Behavior," *Administrative Science Quarterly*, Vol. 4, No. 3 (December 1959), pp. 259-301. Also, Robert Tannenbaum and Warren Schmidt, "How to Choose a Leadership Pattern," *Harvard Business Review*, Vol. 36, No. 2 (March 1958).

The Exercise of Authority

8

The manager must make many decisions on his own. He must do so when he sets the rules and goals previously discussed. And if the rules are violated or the goals unmet, it is the manager who must somehow restrain or reprimand the subordinates responsible for falling short. In some cases, subordinates may not be competent to make decisions because of lack of information, training, or understanding of over-all organizational needs. In other cases, as we have seen, subordinates may not be motivated to make the proper sorts of decisions or to exercise freedom in a manner consistent with organizational objectives. Often the manager must arbitrate disputes among subordinates.

In all the above situations the manager must exercise authority. But being given the right to do so doesn't mean that he will be effective. To get subordinates to respond to his authority requires that the manager both skillfully handle his relations with subordinates *and* establish himself as a legitimate source of authority. These are two separate considerations. The manager must have effective day-to-day relations, but more than this is required. Based on previous experiences, subordinates have developed perceptions of what leadership should be like. They expect that anyone to whom they give their allegiance will have characteristics and behave in a fashion consistent with this image.

Thus, this chapter will approach the exercise of authority from two points of view. First, we shall look at the day-to-day relations or interaction patterns between bosses and subordinates. Second, considering the problem from a longer-run point of view, we shall examine the conditions under which subordinates will view the manager's exercise of authority as legitimate.

Developing Effective Relations

Subordinates can hardly be expected to forget that their boss (or someone at a higher level of management) has the power to discharge them or withhold benefits and promotions. Regardless of how effectively the relationship between subordinates and superior is cloaked in democratic procedure, no one forgets for a moment that there are very real differences in power between them. In every work situation, problems of reward and discipline inevitably arise, and these problems often lead to frustration and bad feeling. One of the manager's goals should be to minimize this frustration and to try to create conditions in which people will accept authority with the maximum of enthusiasm and the minimum of resentment.

AMBIVALENCE TOWARD AUTHORITY

The manager's job is always complicated by the fact that people feel a certain ambivalence toward authority. In Chapter 1 we talked about egoistic and social needs, or independent and dependent needs. Among the many independent ones we listed was the need for a sense of accomplishment, autonomy, and skill. To illustrate dependent needs we mentioned the need for praise, fair treatment, and approval.

As Eric Fromm has suggested, most of us have complicated, mixed feelings toward independence and dependence. We value freedom but sometimes feel lost and anchorless when we have too much. We like protection but we don't like interference.

If management fails to provide enough independence on the job, employees will exercise independence on their own by resorting to absenteeism, union activity, slowdowns, and the like. On the other hand, employees find it difficult to adjust to too much independence, for no one can stand completely by himself. Most of us like to be assured that we are doing the right thing and that we will receive help when we are in trouble. On occasion we even like to have people make tough decisions for us.

To put it another way: People are generally willing to tolerate, and may even be anxious for, a few areas of their life which are unpredictable and exciting, but they insist that most events occur as expected. A research scientist, for example, may relish the novelty and uncertainty of laboratory work, but he insists that his secretary be always on call, that his technician give predictable responses, and that his car start with complete regularity.

The policy of "be strong," under which employees know that they are expected to do exactly what they are told, minimizes the sense of independence. The policy of "be good" fosters dependence, for it regards the ideal employee as the "loyal worker" who follows instructions to the letter without a thought of his own. Delegation, on the other hand, helps satisfy the need for independence that is present to some extent in everyone. Even so, some accommodation must be made to the people who require the security and assurance of knowing that someone is interested in them, and to others who must be restrained lest they abuse their freedom.[1]

Working in a large-scale organization requires that every subordinate be to some degree dependent on the organization generally and on his supervisor in particular; individual independence must be sharply restricted. But dependence should not stifle the individual or impair his chances for self-development.

We shall now consider some of the ways in which the manager can exercise authority effectively, but without being unduly restrictive. The kind of personal relations he develops, the way he gives orders, his fairness in handling problems, and his manner in handling mistakes—all have a significant impact on subordinates' attitudes toward authority.

Personal Relationships

The personal, man-to-man relationships between a boss and his subordinates have a lot to do with the way subordinates view their jobs. Since employees are dependent on their boss, it is all-important for them to feel that he approves of both their work and themselves as individuals. A feeling of approval is an adult version of the child's feeling that his parents love him. It is the assurance that "though the supervisor may chastise me for my mistakes, he values me as an individual. He is not out to get me. He is out to help me."

CREATING A FEELING OF APPROVAL

The supervisor can foster a feeling of his approval of subordinates in many different ways: taking an active interest in subordinates, listening to their problems, giving praise when justified, showing tolerance when mistakes are made, and so forth. Notice that we say *feeling* of approval. We are talking about the over-all supervisory pattern rather than about any one specific act. In fact, the existence of such a feeling helps determine how individual acts are interpreted. *If* such a feeling exists, employees may tend to excuse their boss's

---

[1] For a strong statement of this view, see Robert N. McMurray, "The Case for Benevolent Autocracy," *Harvard Business Review,* Vol. 36, No. 1 (January 1958), pp. 82-90.

mistakes; if it does *not* exist, they may exaggerate his mistakes out of all proportion. For instance, in the absence of a feeling of approval, a boss's attempt to show interest in his employees may be seen as meddling.

> When the supervisor is interested in the welfare of his subordinates and is accepted by them as a member of their "team," then his close attention to what his subordinates are doing is welcomed by them. When the supervisor is around and showing interest in what they are doing, subordinates may be eager to please him and win his approval. On the other hand, when the supervisor is held by subordinates as indifferent to their welfare, or even as a hostile outsider, then his close supervision will probably meet with apathy and resentment.[2]

Thus, the over-all pattern of the supervisor's behavior is infinitely more important than any specific gesture. Take kindness and courtesy as an example. Obviously, saying "please" and "do you mind" is important, but employees soon see through superficial gestures if they conflict with the rest of the supervisor's behavior. In some situations cusswords are better evidence than icy courtesy that the boss likes you. Although most human beings like approbation, they are suspicious of indiscriminate praise.[3] Further, praise for good work is not enough. People have bad days as well as good; a real feeling of approval assures the individual that his boss will show tolerance for an occasional mistake.

In short, the existence of a feeling of approval means that the supervisor has demonstrated a personal loyalty to his subordinates. Until he has done so, he cannot expect loyalty to flow the other way.

Note, though, that approval means different things to different people.

> We once interviewed two lacquer-mixers who worked pretty much by themselves at opposite ends of a long factory floor. They did the same job and were under the same foreman (who said both did a good job). The first mixer said: "I've got a good boss. He knows I know the job so he leaves me alone, he never bothers me." The second mixer said: "My foreman doesn't care whether I'm dead or alive. He's a bum foreman who doesn't show any interest in his men or how they are doing."

Obviously, these two men looked upon supervision very differently. The first saw supervision as restrictive, to be avoided if possible. The second expected help and reassurance from his boss. Both men were anxious to win approval and acceptance, but what came through clearly as acceptance to one man seemed outright rejection to the other. The manager must be alert to these subtle differences in the manner in which his behavior—however well intentioned—is interpreted; he should try to adjust his behavior pattern to his subordinates' individual personality needs.[4]

---

[2] Martin Patchen, "Supervisory Methods and Group Performance Norms," *Administrative Science Quarterly*, Vol. 7, No. 3 (December 1962), p. 290.

[3] Praise given in public may give rise to charges of favoritism—and those who are not praised may feel that the supervisor is resorting to an undercover form of criticism against which they cannot defend themselves.

[4] For further discussion of this point, see Leonard Sayles, *Managerial Behavior* (New York: McGraw-Hill, 1964), pp. 152-153.

DEVELOPING PERSONAL RELATIONS

A feeling of approval is more likely to result if the boss shows personal interest in his subordinates. Consequently, an effective manager "makes" time to get to know his subordinates and to help them with their problems both on and (to a limited extent) off the job.

Need for personal relations. People like being treated as individuals. Yet, as far as the typical company is concerned, the average employee is nothing more than a time-card number or a job specification. The company is impersonal; only the immediate boss can make management personal. Particularly to a new employee, the immediate supervisor *is* the company, and what he does helps mold the individual's conception of the company as a whole. An insensitive manager can easily counterbalance all the company's efforts to create a good impression through public relations and fringe benefits.

Home problems affect efficiency on the job. So a good manager listens to his employees' problems, and in some areas actually offers assistance. Ordinarily, all he can do is listen, but even this interest provides some relief to an individual in distress. In any case, the more the manager learns about the people who work for him, the better he can understand their behavior and how to deal with it. (Of course, the manager should not seem to pry or meddle, as we shall discuss in Chapter 11.)

Even more important, good informal relations on matters that are not directly related to the job set the stage for better communication between manager and subordinate on problems related to work. Any social barrier will create a communications barrier. An employee rarely feels completely free and easy when talking with the boss about the work in hand, for he is quite aware that the boss is the one who hands out rewards and punishments. But when they talk about the employee's fishing trip, the employee is an *expert* for the time being, even if there is no true feeling of equality between them. Some of the air of permissiveness and informality created in discussing baseball or the weather may carry over to on-the-job affairs. Once the manager and the subordinate know each other as individuals, both will feel freer to bring up mutual problems.

To put it another way: As we said earlier, the good manager tries to reduce the number of orders he gives by encouraging people to ask him questions rather than by telling them what to do. For this approach to succeed, however, the subordinates must feel confident and secure enough to go to their boss when difficulties arise.

Setting the tone. Obviously, it is the superior who sets the tone of the relationship, not the subordinate. First, the manager must make himself available to all comers. The boss who barricades himself behind a wall of formality or is always "busy, busy, busy" is not likely to develop satisfactory informal relationships. Nor is it enough to be a good fellow a few times a year. In most companies the permissive atmosphere of the annual Christmas party stands out in sharp contrast to the distant relationship that is normal for the rest of the year.

The manager must take the initiative by maintaining regular and frequent contacts with subordinates. Some managers make periodic "howdy rounds," talking to each employee in turn. Even if these encounters consist only of idle chatter, still they provide an opportunity for employees to bring up problems that are bothering them. In other words, the manager opens up the contact and lets the subordinate decide what topics should be covered.

Certain very real dangers are likely to arise when the manager develops excessively close personal relations with his subordinates, particularly in circumstances where he must rely on close rather than general supervision. There are situations where a manager is forced to rely largely on formal authority to maintain discipline. Then he can hardly afford to be a "good guy." As we shall discuss later in this chapter, one reason for the carefully maintained social barrier in the armed forces is that officers do not want their men to question decisions or initiate action.

In any case, there is more to being a good boss than being a nice fellow. Although many employees respond favorably to the "glad-hand" approach, most are suspicious of insincerity. After all, the manager must develop a *long-term* relationship, and over a period of time it is easy for subordinates to detect whether his apparent interest is sincere. It is better for an introvert to be naturally reserved than artificially friendly. In today's cynical world, people are highly suspicious of overfriendliness: They are constantly afraid of being manipulated. They easily see through what has been variously called "false personalism" or a "skin-deep relationship." Unless the manager combines good informal personal relations with good job-oriented relations, he will be judged a hypocrite: "He'll try to butter you up. But watch out, he'll stab you in the back."

Job-Oriented Relations

Some early studies of managerial behavior contrasted "job-centered" with "employee-centered" supervision. The job-centered manager is interested almost exclusively in getting his job done; the employee-centered mangager is interested chiefly in satisfying the needs of his subordinates. In the terms used in some studies, the job-centered manager is high in what was called "initiating structure" (running the job), whereas the employee-centered manager is more concerned with "consideration." Regardless of what terms were used, it was believed that these two qualities are on opposite ends of a continuum. Later research suggests that these characteristics are not mutually inconsistent.[5] An

---

[5] For a good discussion of this point, see Robert L. Kahn, "Productivity and Job Satisfaction," *Personnel Psychology*, Vol. 13, No. 3 (Fall 1960), pp. 275-287.

effective manager is interested both in his employees as individuals and in the work they do. An interest in one does not preclude an interest in the other. A good manager, then, has effective job-oriented relations with his subordinates.

In one sense, this entire volume is concerned with job-oriented relations. At this point we wish to stress that, where feasible in directing the job, an effective manager will keep open the lines of communications with his subordinates, both upward and downward. He will provide them with information, consult with them, and listen to their suggestions. Let us consider each of these points in turn, although we have already seen something of the over-all pattern in our discussion of the General Electric study in the previous chapter.

PROVIDING INFORMATION

Few of us are content to be at the mercy of forces we do not understand. We all tend to feel insecure in poorly defined situations. Research indicates that high-production supervisors tend to give their subordinates as much information as possible about what is expected on the job and what is likely to happen to them in the future. This information helps the subordinate do better work by enabling him to make wiser decisions; moreover, it heightens his sense of security.

Understandably, employees are keenly interested in knowing what they are required to do on the job. For some, this need is satisfied only when they receive explicit direction in every aspect of their work. You will remember the nurse who said, "I need guidance and therefore I prefer to work with a fairly strict supervisor."

> The older girls on Miss Rogers' floor complained because they did not receive enough detailed instructions; the younger girls on Miss Smith's floor felt insecure because Miss Smith failed to provide enough information for them to make decisions on their own, and had a habit of issuing unexpected and seemingly arbitrary orders.

Even those who value the freedom to make decisions themselves feel more self-confident in a well-structured situation. When they are given an order, they want some explanation of what is to be done, why it is to be done, and what limits will be set on their freedom—as well as any background information necessary to help them do a better job or to satisfy their natural curiosity.[6] They prefer that the boss be easily available to answer questions or to provide assistance when asked.

The subordinate is especially curious to know *where he stands with his boss.* For white-collar workers in particular, "getting ahead" is of paramount importance. The subordinate constantly asks himself, "How am I doing?" and

---

[6] For a good discussion, see Robert L. Kahn and John R. P. French, Jr., "A Summary and Some Tentative Conclusions," *Journal of Social Issues,* Vol. 18, No. 3 (July 1962), p. 122.

tries to divine from the boss's tone of voice or facial expression whether his performance is finding favor. The subordinate is directly dependent on his boss, he wants to please him, and he wants some sort of feedback or evaluation to indicate how his efforts are being received.

Finally, employees are keenly interested in knowing about anything that will have an effect on their future prospects or their work. "What's the production level likely to be next week?" "Has the supply room received the forms I need?" "Are the rumors true that this department will be automated?" "How will this affect me?" "How bad are the squawks down the line about the bum job I did yesterday?" To the employee who is deprived of this sort of information, the future seems uncertain and sinister. Relegated to unrelieved ignorance, he develops what psychologists call a short-term perspective and loses all sense of involvement in his work.

CONSULTING WITH SUBORDINATES

The way a manager issues an order influences the way it is received. With routine orders there is usually little trouble. But before a manager issues an order that will have a major impact on his subordinates, or an order that they are likely to resist, it is better for him to discuss it with them than to impose it unilaterally with no opportunity for questions or objections. Even if the manager may wish to make the final decision himself, he may wish to increase the subordinate's sense of involvement through permitting him to influence the final decision.

The wise supervisor explains such "critical" orders orally at first, though later he may put them in writing for permanent reference. To be sure, it may take more time to issue instructions orally than in writing. Yet, as we will see in Chapter 10, voice communication is often more effective than the written word. It permits the supervisor, if necessary, to present a detailed explanation of what he wants and why he wants it—and in a way that is tailor-made to the needs of the individual subordinate.

The effective supervisor also permits the subordinate to comment and to ask questions (at least within the limits set by other demands on the supervisor's time). This gives him a chance to judge how the subordinate is reacting to the proposed order and enables him to answer objections, explain points that are not clearly understood, or make arrangements for exceptional circumstances that may require special procedures. Moreover, the subordinate may come up with suggestions that will make the proposed order more workable—or he may object so strenuously that the supervisor will decide to withdraw the order altogether.

Doesn't the supervisor lose respect when he modifies or withdraws an order in face of his subordinate's objections? Yes—if his original instructions were stated in terms of "this is what I order you to do." No—if he has said, "I have been thinking about this and would like your reaction." There is a gain even if the supervisor eventually decides that he must impose an order over his subordinate's objections, for at least the subordinate has had a chance to be heard and to let off steam.[7]

Finally, a subordinate is more likely to carry out an order if he has specifically agreed to do so, for he is then committed to take some action. If the supervisor closes the discussion with the question, "Are you willing to give it a try?" he is likely to get assent. Even though this assent may be enforced, there has been an explicit agreement to go along. Suppose the subordinate refuses to assent? In most instances it is better to bring the resistance out in the open at the outset than to assume that the order will be carried out when in fact it will be sabotaged.

LISTENING TO SUGGESTIONS

Although there are many areas in which the manager cannot give his subordinates freedom to make decisions by themselves, he can encourage them to make suggestions. This practice provides the manager with many useful ideas and a more accurate feeling for what his subordinates are thinking. It provides subordinates with an opportunity to express themselves and to feel that they have made a valuable contribution to the operation of their organization.

The manager should not only listen to the suggestions that are brought to him; he should actively seek them out. There are many areas in which the manager doesn't have all the facts that he needs to make important decisions. Or perhaps he feels perfectly confident that he can make a good decision, but has some doubts about whether his subordinates will accept it. Under such circumstances it may pay for him to ask for suggestions. This approach will certainly result in better acceptance of the decision, and it may improve its quality as well. There is no obligation for the manager to accept all the ideas presented, so long as he considers them seriously. If he rejects all suggestions out of hand, however, his subordinates will soon see through his pretense.

Many of the suggestions made by subordinates are remarkably valuable. Understandably, the man who works close to a job day after day often knows more about it than his boss.

Management in a small steel plant was facing an unusually stubborn problem. Product quality had fallen off and none of the engineering staff was able to come up with a solution. Expensive consultants also failed to stem the increasing flow of scrap. Finally, the plant manager called some of the old-timers together, explained the problem, and told them the firm would face bank-

---

[7] To prevent misunderstanding, let us make clear what we are *not* saying: First, we are not saying that a supervisor should never issue an order. On the contrary. But *how* he issues the order *is* important. Second, we are not saying that the supervisor should *always* consult with subordinates before issuing orders or always propose them first in a tentative form ("I am thinking of...."). Obviously such an approach is not always required—and even where consultation might be useful in itself, the supervisor may not have time to do so.

ruptcy if the problem wasn't solved. After a few minutes' discussion, one of these workers suggested the cause of the trouble and how to solve it. When asked why he hasn't produced this important information before, he answered, "I wasn't asked." [8]

People derive great satisfaction from knowing that their suggestions are being considered and even more if they are actually put into use. Everyone is enthusiastic about implementing his own ideas.

But what happens when management is obliged to reject a suggestion? Even here the suggestion has served a purpose. First, the subordinate did have a chance to express himself and to be heard. Second, by explaining why the suggestion was rejected, the supervisor can improve the subordinate's understanding of the problem and perhaps stimulate him to produce better suggestions in the future.

Fair Treatment

Since subordinates are directly dependent on their bosses, they are understandably anxious to receive fair treatment from them. "The highest praise a worker can give his foreman is to say 'he's fair.' " [9] The boss can demonstrate his sense of fair play by letting each employee know exactly what is required of him, and by exercising consistent discipline. He can base his decisions on grounds that are accepted as legitimate by his subordinates, he can provide an appeals procedure (see Chapter 15), and, above all, he can make an all-out effort to treat them equally, so that the rewards he dispenses seem proportional to their contributions. [10]

"Treating people equally" is not as simple as it sounds. The conscientious manager is torn between two conflicting, though universally accepted, platitudes: "Avoid favoritism" and "Treat people as individuals, in accordance with their special needs." He can never forget that each individual has special needs, but at the same time he must realize that what appears to be inconsistent treatment will create endless bad feeling within the group.

With all the good will in the world, the manager may begin to play favorites unconsciously and to follow the normal tendency of either favoring the passive, dependent, "good" employee or paying the most attention to the aggressive individual who fights for his demands, to "oil the wheel that squeaks the loudest." The manager must avoid both extremes.

The manager should be careful to bestow favors only when the employee needs them. If, for instance, the boss decides to lend a hand at a time when the subordinate feels he is doing his job adequately, the subordinate may

---

[8] From the experience of Joseph Scanlon, as told to the authors.

[9] George Homans, "Effort, Supervision and Productivity" in Robert Dubin, *et al., Leadership and Productivity* (San Francisco: Chandler, 1965), p. 65.

[10] George Homans calls this meeting the requirements of "distributive justice." See his *Social Behavior: Its Elementary Forms* (New York: Harcourt, Brace & World, 1962).

either look upon his help as meddling or accept it as the normal thing and complain when he doesn't get it.

Making exceptions.   What about making exceptions in special situations? Obviously, treating people fairly does not mean treating everyone in exactly the same way. It does mean that when an exception is made, it must be accepted as legitimate by all members of the group. There is a general rule, for example, that vacations must be taken during the summer months. Bill Lawrence's wife is sick, so the boss lets him have February off to take her to Florida. Is this favoritism? Only if Bill Lawrence's fellow employees think so. An exception of this sort will be accepted as fair if the group (1) knows why it was made, (2) accepts it as justified, and (3) is confident that another employee in the same situation would receive the same treatment.

Granting special favors when the circumstances permit not only lessens a subordinate's feeling that the organization is arbitrary and "heartless"; but it may also lead to an "exchange of good turns." As a worker in an assembly plant described it: [11]

> "My foreman knows the traits of human nature and acts accordingly. . . . He came in one morning and it was bitterly cold. He went out to the cafeteria and brought two big cans of hot coffee and gave it to the men. While we can't be bought the thought was there and we appreciated it. As a result the men picked up lots of jobs that ordinarily they would have let go through to be picked up by the repair man."

The assumption behind this approach is that if the manager does more for his men than is absolutely required, they will respond in kind. It means, for instance, that if Jack comes to work with a sprained ankle, the foreman will find him some work that he can do sitting down; if a waitress is suddenly deluged with customers, the hostess will relieve some of the pressure by setting up tables and pouring water. The hope is that when an emergency arises the subordinates will reciprocate by doing more than is normally required, by working overtime or by producing more than the usual "bogey." Thus, an atmosphere is created in which both supervisor and subordinate exhibit a flexible attitude toward their mutual obligations.

Handling Mistakes

In the previous chapter we suggested that managers should set realistic goals for their subordinates, train them to do the best job they are capable of doing, and then give them a wide margin of freedom. But this does not mean that management should sit idly by when employees violate rules, turn out

---

[11] Arthur N. Turner, "Foreman—Key to Worker Morale," *Harvard Business Review*, Vol. 35, No. 5 (September 1956), p. 77.

sloppy work, or fail to do their job. Quite the contrary. Not only is such laxity bad for production (after all, the company exists to make a profit); it is also unfair to the conscientious worker who carries out his assignments effectively, and it even serves to encourage the "culprit" in his bad work habits.

The manager cannot ignore mistakes. But the manner in which he handles them may determine whether his subordinates will resent his use of authority or will come to look upon him as a source of help.

BLAME OR HELP?

Research studies reveal that the difference between high-production and low-production managers lies not in their interest in eliminating mistakes, but in their *manner* of handling mistakes. Note the difference between these two comments: [12]

> "My boss thinks that whenever anything goes wrong it's always my fault. . . . He never says what he can do to help you, but he always picks your job apart. He tries hard, but he is too ready to condemn rather than help."

> "My boss is the best man I have ever worked for. He finds out what's troubling you before he tells you what to do, and he'll ask why. . . . Other supervisors come down here and start yelling at you before they find out what's wrong. But not him."

When something goes wrong, the low-production manager is interested above all in fixing blame and bawling out the person responsible. ("Well, what sort of excuse do you have?") He has a tendency to look to the past, to "cry over spilt milk," and to assume that all negligence is deliberate. What is the effect of such an approach? The subordinate denies responsibility, tries to pass the buck to someone else, or at least to find some sort of excuse to show that he really wasn't at fault. This approach encourages the "stool pigeon" and tends to make the development of harmonious groups almost impossible. If the group *does* succeed in working together in such an atmosphere, it directs its efforts *against* the manager.

The policy of blame-placing often defeats its own purpose: It makes employees so tense and insecure that they make even more mistakes. And it motivates them to cover up errors and spend their time trying to avoid *looking* wrong. As a result, upward communications is impaired and higher management can never get a clear picture of what is really happening below. A kind of game develops: In an effort to uncover the deceptions of subordinates, higher management sets up inspection systems and elaborate control reports, while the subordinates become increasingly adept at hiding mistakes.

In contrast, high-production managers tend to look forward, rather than backward. They are interested in discovering what happened, why it happened,

---

[12] Charles R. Walker, Robert H. Guest, and Arthur N. Turner, *The Foreman on the Assembly Line* (Cambridge: Harvard University Press, 1956), p. 45.

and what can be learned rather than in fixing responsibility. They look upon mistakes as an opportunity to provide training.[13]

Mistakes as a means of learning.   If the manager insists that subordinates must never make a mistake, he is also insuring that they will never assume any real responsibility. Not that the subordinate should be encouraged to make mistakes. Far from it. But if he feels that one mistake is disastrous, he will be completely inhibited from taking any responsibility or initiative. The boss who feels that every mistake is a calamity must abandon all hope of improving the performance of his subordinates.

Actually, doing something wrong is often the most effective way of learning to do it right. Getting "burned" a few times may be the only way for us to learn that some of our pet ideas really won't work. In effect, a subordinate should have freedom to fail. A superior should weigh very carefully the cost of a mistake against the value of having the subordinate learn both (1) that he has the freedom to act on his own, even to make mistakes, and (2) that the particular way he has chosen was wrong. Overprotection by the superior means underdevelopment by the subordinate.

In effect, when mistakes are overpunished by severe criticism, people learn not just to avoid *specific* behavior, but to avoid *any* situation where a mistake is possible. When a subordinate has taken the initiative and his action has turned out badly, the supervisor can buttress his sense of independence by saying, "You made some mistakes in handling this, but I am glad you were willing to experiment and to take responsibility on your own." Of course, if the subordinate continues to make mistakes or exceed his authority, then it may be necessary to take disciplinary action.

Some managers react to a subordinate's mistake by taking the job over themselves because they find this course easier than training the subordinate so he won't make the mistake again. Obviously, with an approach like this the subordinate will never learn, and he will become increasingly reluctant to take on responsibility on his own.

CALLING MISTAKES TO SUBORDINATE'S ATTENTION

When to call a mistake to a subordinate's attention depends both on the situation and on the subordinate's personality.

"Many times workers recognize their own mistakes and take steps to remedy them before the supervisor steps in. If, then, the manager pushes his criticism anyway, the worker becomes resentful. It is only when workers are unaware

---

[13] For two studies which show that supervisors who engage in nonpunitive handling of mistakes have higher production, see Michael Argyl, Godfrey Gardner, and Frank Cioffi, "Supervisory Methods Related to Productivity, Absenteeism and Turnover," *Human Relations*, Vol. XI, No. 1 (1958), p. 38; and Robert L. Kahn and Daniel Katz, "Leadership Practices in Relation to Productivity and Morale," *Group Dynamics*, Dorwin Cartwright and Alvin Zander, eds. (Evanston, Ill.: Harper & Row, 1953), p. 621.

of their mistakes or seem not to be profiting from them that the supervisor should step in." [14]

On the other hand, it is clearly foolish to let a subordinate continue to make mistakes when he is obviously making no progress in solving them or when they are causing great harm to the organization. Leaving a subordinate in the dark when he is doing a poor job is unfair both to him and to the organization as a whole.

Some managers find it temperamentally difficult to correct their subordinates. They are unsure of the soundness of their own judgment; or they resist accepting the responsibility of "playing God" and judging other men; or they are reluctant to risk injuring the personal relations they have established with their men. As a consequence, one often hears managers defending their failure to offer constructive criticism: "You shouldn't correct anyone until you are 100 per cent sure you are right. You have got to get all the facts." But this is an exaggeration of the problem. There is no need to prove the other man *wrong*. The question of guilt is irrelevant. What *is* relevant is to discuss the trouble in terms of "What happened? What can be done about it?"

Investigating mistakes.   Some observers say that a manager should never try to correct a subordinate unless he can offer a better alternative. The cautiousness implied in this approach is commendable, and yet little harm is done when the manager says, "There seems to be something wrong here. Frankly, I don't know the answer, but perhaps we can work it out together." Certainly this is better than letting anger and suspicion mount until one has "all the facts." Lack of frankness between superior and subordinate cannot help but generate tension and misunderstanding.

> When a mistake is made, ask the worker how it happened. *Let him tell you.* If his explanation is weak, he'll recognize it in telling the story, and so will you. You won't have to rub it in, in most cases, because he knows what is expected of him and is willing to recognize his own failings—when he isn't pushed and prodded with them.
> Then ask him to *tell you* how the mistake can be avoided in the future. You don't have to accept his solution but, with this approach you are more likely to get him to accept responsibility for his actions and to try to do something constructive.[15]

Letting the subordinate explain what went wrong and then work out his own solution has a definite educational value. As one manager put it, "When you go to them that way and let them explain, they feel a lot better. Sometimes they will come to you and tell you when they make a mistake, and you can really talk it over. That's very important." [16]

---

[14] William F. Whyte, *Human Relations in the Restaurant Industry* (New York: McGraw-Hill, 1948), p. 270.
[15] *Ibid.*, p. 269.
[16] *Ibid.*, p. 268.

Often the problem involves the entire group and can best be handled by group discussion. But there, too, the manager can refrain from trying to pin the blame on one or two individuals and concentrate instead on working out a solution for future activities that is satisfactory to everyone.

CRITICISM

Most mistakes are due to ignorance or lack of skill, and can be handled through training without resort to overt criticism. Some mistakes, however, are clearly due to negligence; here the manager has no choice but to let the subordinate know that he is dissatisfied with the subordinate's level of performance. But unless the manager is tactful in making his criticism, he will jeopardize his relationship not only with the subordinate but with the whole work group as well. Whyte suggests some useful rules:

(1.) The criticism should be voiced in a matter-of-fact manner. Emotional heat on the part of the critic seems to beget a defensive reaction on the part of the subordinate. Only when the subordinate refuses to act on the criticism does it seem advisable to apply the heat.

(2.) The criticism should be focused on the job operation and should, as much as possible, avoid placing of personal blame.

(3.) After it has been stated, the criticism should be dropped—unless the mistake has not been corrected. Men speak of the emotional tensions they have been under when working for a [supervisor] who would not only criticize you but would then seem to be "down" on you for a long time thereafter. One man described the more effective approach in this way:

> "Ed will tell you right to your face how he wants it done. Oh, sometimes we might have a little argument about it, but when the argument is over, it is really over and forgotten. He never gets down on you. You like to work for a fellow like that."

(4.) Criticism should be balanced by giving credit for good work. No matter how skillfully a man makes his criticism, if he has only critical remarks to make, he destroys cooperation.[17]

It should be added that criticism of this sort is best offered in private.

Some mistakes, of course, are due to improper training, failure to understand instructions, or severe problems at home. In situations of this sort, the manager may be able to get at the root of the trouble only through skillful interviewing. And he may have to resort to formal discipline if the subordinate fails to respond to criticism and training. The problems of interviewing and discipline will be discussed in Chapters 11 and 14.

In our discussion to this point we have dealt with day-to-day manager-subordinate relationships. But in doing so, we gave a somewhat oversimplified picture. Having read this far, you might well conclude that there is one sort of

---

[17] William F. Whyte, *Leadership in the Work Team* (mimeographed, 1956), pp. 12-13.

boss-subordinate relationship which is best for all conditions. Obviously this isn't so. Let us look at the exercise of authority from a broader perspective and examine why subordinates follow their superiors in the first place. In so doing, we will gain some insight into how the means by which authority is effectively exercised may well differ from one situation to another.

Legitimacy

From a purely formal point of view, the manager receives his authority from above, from his superiors, who define his powers and responsibilities and who sometimes put a statement of these in an organization handbook. Another view is that the manager receives much of his *real* authority from below, from his subordinates, and that the statement of authority which he receives from above is merely a hunting license; for in spite of his statement of formal powers, if his subordinates are not willing to obey him, then he has no real authority.[18]

How can the manager induce subordinates to obey him? Of course, he can use bluster, force, and the policy of "be strong." If enough pressure is applied, then his subordinates will comply. But as we saw in Chapter 5, their compliance may well be grudging and resentful.

Alternatively, subordinates may wish to comply because the organization is doing what they want to do themselves. Individuals lost in the wilderness gladly take directions from a leader who seems to be taking them back to civilization. Orchestra members exercise little autonomy, but they follow their conductor willingly because they want to create good music. Similarly, a junior research scientist will obey his boss with enthusiasm if he sees his boss's directions as helping him solve his own research problem. Note that in all these cases the subordinates would have followed their boss's instructions even if he didn't have the formal title. They obey because their ends are identical with those of their leader.

Relatively few cases involve either sheer coercion or the boss telling subordinates to do what they really wanted to do in the first place. Most situations occupy a middle ground: Subordinates obey their boss because they respect the legitimacy of his order, that is, because according to their norms and values it is expected and proper for the boss to give his particular order and for them to obey it.

Thus, the leader must establish a series of relationships with subordinates which support his legitimacy. But he must also recognize that the process of legitimization occurs in a group and cultural setting, for what any one individual perceives as legitimate depends largely on the views of his associates. The

---

[18] For a recent summary of the literature on authority, see Amitai Etzioni, *Modern Organizations* (Englewood Cliffs, N.J.: Prentice-Hall, 1964). For a somewhat different approach, see T. T. Patterson, *Glasgow, Ltd.* (Cambridge: Cambridge University Press, 1960).

group makes it easier for the boss, though, for it often informally disciplines those who violate group expectations by not obeying legitimate orders.

As we mentioned in Chapter 4, every group has customs, proprieties, and expectations that its members believe are proper. A manager who violates these standards acts in an "illegitimate" fashion, and does so at his peril: Subordinates can retaliate in numerous ways, ranging from refusal to do more than their normal share in time of emergency, to wildcat strikes and sabotage. In contrast, the manager who respects the group's standards often wins its cooperation and, at times, finds that the group will modify its standards in management's favor. To take an example of the impact of such standards:

> Train crews in a marshaling yard were handling 150 trains a day. Through short cuts (often violating safety rules) they were able to finish their work in six hours. The rest of the time they could sleep or read.

We can identify several standards in this situation: (1) 150 trains a day represent a proper work load; (2) the remaining time can be spent as the men wish; and (3) certain rules will not be enforced.

> Then management decided that since the men had so much free time they could handle 200 trains. Immediately the men began to follow all the rules. They would never move a train even a few feet without having someone to go to the rear and wave a red flag. As a result, the men put in a full day's work, but productivity fell to 50 trains a day. Soon management gave up its demands for 200.

Here management violated group standards and acted in what the group felt was an illegitimate fashion, and the men retaliated in a way that left management helpless.

In the remainder of this chapter we shall consider what the group views as the legitimate use of authority. In the next chapter we shall consider how the manager can best deal with the group. First, however, a word of warning: though we shall use the word "group" rather freely here, you should remember that social groups tend to overlap and that any given employee may belong to several groups with varying expectations (see Chapter 4).

How can a manager exercise power legitimately? The answer seems to depend on at least three factors: (1) his job legitimacy, that is, on his right to hold his power in the first place; (2) the way be behaves on the job; and (3) the demands he makes on subordinates. These three factors are obviously interrelated; for example, the manager can ask more from subordinates if his right to hold his job is legitimate, and if he makes his demands in a legitimate fashion.

JOB LEGITIMACY

To some extent people obey leaders just because they are invested with the symbols or titles of authority. Soldiers are trained to obey those who wear officers' insignia, regardless of the individual merits of the wearer. Royal coronations and presidential inaugurations are ceremonials which symbolize the transfer of a certain "magic" to kings and presidents.

Nevertheless, every group has definite expectations about what qualifications their leader should possess. If the leader fails to live up to these expectations, then his subordinates feel that he is not "fit for his job"—and this holds true whether he is a foreman or President of the United States. The important thing is that the leader be respected.[19]

Background. Certainly there are expectations about the leader's background. He may be expected to belong to a certain ethnic group, to be a graduate of a certain college, or to have a certain degree (thus a Dean without a Ph.D. or a hospital director without an M.D. can find it harder to win support from subordinates). Recall our discussion of status incongruence in Chapter 4. It is hard for a person who has low status in terms of sex, age, seniority, ethnic background, and so on to win respect as a supervisor.

The nature of the qualifications subordinates expect in their leaders will, of course, vary substantially from job to job. Thus, in many American companies the fair-haired boy who is promoted solely on the basis of family connections will find it hard to win cooperation. On the other hand, family connections are almost essential if one is to be considered a legitimate king (and, in some European firms, a legitimate company president). In some organizations a man is expected to work his way up through the ranks, and an outsider who is brought in over the head of someone subordinates feel deserves the job will have to face strong resentment (though "proper" behavior may ultimately win him respect). In other cases, it is traditional for leaders to be brought in through special channels; thus, for a long time in the Army, officers won greater respect if they started their careers in West Point, rather than as privates. But traditions can change: In recent years the Army has made it easier for enlisted men to become officers; on the other hand, many large companies have increasingly reserved management ranks for college graduates.

Technical ability. In the old days, on some construction projects and steel mills the foreman was expected to be the biggest and strongest man on the job, and was not infrequently called upon to defend his position with his fists. Today physical skill is less crucial, but it is important for the supervisor to be technically skilled in his work, even if he rarely practices this skill on the job.[20] Indeed, subordinates often subject a new supervisor to a period of testing and initiation to determine whether he measures up to their standards.

The feeling that the boss should show technical skill is particularly strong among men who take pride in their work and closely identify with their

---

[19] Respect need not mean liking. As Machiavelli advised his Prince, it is often better to be feared than to be loved.

[20] The leader's technical skill need not duplicate that of his followers. A pilot can't overhaul an engine; perhaps a conductor can't play all the instruments in an orchestra; yet both derive status from their technical ability.

occupation (building tradesmen, for example, or college professors). Supervisors who do not possess the relevant skills have a hard time, indeed.

> Take the situation in certain Air Force control towers during World War II. Some of the senior enlisted men had years of experience as controllers. But many of the officers were "wash-outs" from pilot training, still in their teens or early twenties. A workable arrangement often developed in which the officers confined their activities to signing papers prepared for them by enlisted men.
>
> In one case, however, the officer-in-charge (age 19) insisted on taking a more active role. The enlisted men tried to keep him out of the tower by the simple expedient of insisting that whenever he was there, he would have to make all the technical decisions himself. After a few horrible mistakes (fortunately no one was injured) and a severe reprimand from the base commander, the young man confined his activities to the officers' bar.

If subordinates feel their supervisor is master of skills they themselves regard as important, then in a way he has beaten them in a fair race—he has earned his job and is respected for doing so.

Technical skill is very important in certain types of work where close co-ordination is required between members of the work team—as in flying a plane, conducting an orchestra, or operating on a patient. In such cases, "unpleasant personal characteristics are often overlooked if competence is high enough. The irascible surgeon who is, nevertheless, highly respected for his skills is almost a legend. Colleagues and nurses judge doctors according to the mastery they exhibit." [21]

To summarize, we are discussing here what Herbert Simon calls the "authority of confidence." [22] Or, to put it another way, the manager will find his authority more easily accepted if he is an authority *on,* as well as an authority *over.*

A manager needs more than technical skills to win legitimacy. He also needs human-relations skills, as we shall discuss next.

MANAGERIAL BEHAVIOR

Subordinates normally have well-defined expectations about how a "good" manager should behave, both on and off the job, though these may vary greatly from one situation to another.

In the giving of orders, for example, authority may be emphasized or underplayed. As we discussed earlier, North Americans tend to resent the outward display of authority, and often feel it proper that their bosses go through the forms of consulting with them. Engineers, scientists, and professors seem to hold this expectation particularly strongly. Australians seem to resent authority

---

[21] Temple Burling, Edith Lentz, and Robert Wilson, *The Give and Take in Hospitals* (New York: Putnam, 1956), p. 266.

[22] Herbert Simon, "Authority," in Conrad Arensberg, *et al.,* eds., *Research in Industrial Human Relations* (New York: Harper & Row, 1957), p. 106.

even more than do North Americans. But there are many other cultures in which a boss is expected to be firm and to know his own mind.

Of course, all supervisors are expected to be fair and to treat people in a "nice way." But the nice way in the university would be very out of place in the Army. An officer, for example, is expected to have a "military bearing," and a professor to display a "scholarly attitude." Some groups expect their supervisor to "act like a boss," and the men take advantage of him if he doesn't rule with an iron hand; in other groups it is a great compliment to say that the supervisor "doesn't act like a boss." In some situations a good boss is expected to "let his men alone"; in others he should be available every minute of the day—that is, he should be "in there pitching and providing leadership." In some situations a manager will lose face if he swears and loses his temper. In others he is a "softy" if he does not.

This much is clear: A manager should become familiar with his subordinates' expectations as soon as possible. The manager may eventually wish to change these expectations, but he must recognize the likelihood of resistance (see Chapter 13).

Social distance. Perhaps the most subtle of these expectations about managerial behavior concern the social distance (or status differentiation) which the boss should keep from his subordinates: Military officers should be aloof from their men; deans should invite all new faculty to dinner; plant managers are expected to make "howdy rounds" in the plant and to be good fellows at the company picnic (but perhaps only there); supervisors should show interest in their subordinates' home life (and in some plants go out drinking with their men on pay day). In most situations a boss is expected to "be friendly" (and this is particularly true where the American tradition of equality prevails), but the meaning of friendliness varies greatly from one situation to another. To violate these expectations may well lead to trouble.

A wide variety of factors is relevant here. Life insurance agents feel under great pressure from their job and their boss, and as a consequence, according to one study, fear that if he gets too close to them he will criticize them.[23] At sea there has been a traditional social gap between officers and men. This distance is maintained by means of separate uniforms and separate eating and sleeping arrangements. Yet, on smaller ships this traditional formality tends to break down. Moreover, there is more formality in the navy, where men are subject to danger, than there is in the merchant marine. And there is a decidedly different attitude in the American merchant marine, where most men rise from the ranks, than on European ships, where officers and the men they supervise usually come from different social classes.

The question of expected social relationship is closely tied in with techno-

---

[23] L. G. Wispe and K. E. Lloyd, "Some Situational and Psychological Determinants of the Desire for Structured Interpersonal Relations," *Journal of Abnormal and Social Psychology*, Vol. 55 (1955), pp. 57-60.

logical considerations. In a scientific laboratory a premium is placed on widespread communication of information and widespread participation. Here status differences are expected to be played down, and social relations are close. But in military organizations where the "technology" requires instant obedience, social relations are kept distant. Indeed, it is feared that if enlisted men become socially close to their officers and learn of their personal inadequacies, they may begin to question the officers' orders.[24]

When businessmen and government officials go to foreign countries they run into all sorts of unanticipated problems of social distance. An anthropologist describes how: [25]

> "British respect for rank and maintenance of formal distance seems to have fit well with chieftainships and aristocracies in some parts of traditional Africa and the caste system in India. American equalitarian biases, on the other hand, have seemed to fit poorly in some parts of Oceania, where rank and social distance seem important. . . . With secularized Hindus, nationalist change-oriented Africans and others sensitive about the possible social connotations of superiority in the maintenance of social distance, American informality—even "backslapping"—have been seen as desirable traits in the relationship. Some Latin Americans have even felt Americans to be cool and remote by their standards —more like the image we would have of the stiffly correct Britisher."

The manager must be concerned with his off-the-job contacts as well as those on the job. In a small community, for example, there are bound to be many unplanned after-hours encounters, and a manager's failure to meet the normal community standards of friendliness and politeness will not be excused. In a large city, however, off-the-job meetings must be arranged in advance by the manager. If he goes out of his way to be "one of the boys," he may set up a pattern of expectations that cannot be maintained on the job.

Social distance is intimately connected with the manager's style of leadership. If he maintains informal, permissive relationships off the job, it will be hard for him to exercise autocratic supervision on the job; on the other hand, if he avoids all social contacts not directly connected with work, he will find it difficult to develop a free-and-easy relationship in discussing job-related problems. Certainly, snubbing people, particularly those with whom one has frequent work contacts, violates our democratic standards.

Work customs.   A manager should also be sensitive to the indirect effect of his actions on work customs. Take status, for example. Assigning younger workers to the newest equipment may enable them to earn higher bonuses than their seniors, thereby splitting the work force into two hostile groups.

---

[24] Technological change, however, has largely outmoded the brave infantrymen of Tennyson's day, whose job was "not to reason why," and put in his place a technician who is expected to make decisions on his own. Along with this the social aloofness of the officers has tended to decline. See Morris Janowitz, *The Professional Soldier* (New York: The Free Press of Glencoe, 1960).

[25] Robert N. Rapoport, "Some Notes on Para-Technical Factors in Cross-Cultural Consultation," *Human Organization*, Vol. 23, No. 1 (Spring 1964), pp. 8-9.

Innocent decisions about parking lots or the arrangement of tables in the cafeteria may upset delicate social relations, and may lead to turmoil and antagonism.

Time-honored work customs sometimes conflict sharply with management's formal rules. In a gypsum board plant, for example, it was a well-established practice for workers to take "extra" boards home with them for personal use. When a new manager decided to enforce the rules against "stealing," he helped precipitate a wildcat strike.[26]

WORK DEMANDS

On most jobs there is felt to be an implicit contract between boss and subordinates which governs what the boss may legitimately demand in the way of work.[27] If he restricts his demands to those that are believed legitimate, then obedience is almost automatic. On the other hand, if he makes demands that are felt to be excessive, he must be prepared for resistance. Implicit bargaining plays a very important role here.[28]

Most employees realize that they assume certain obligations when they accept a job, and acknowledge that the boss has a right to insist on a "fair day's work." In effect, they feel, "Since I work here I must obey orders and try to do a job. I realize that it is the boss's job to get work out and the company's job to make money. So I'll do my *fair* share."

But employees have definite expectations of what constitutes their "fair share," a notion often embodied in a "bogey." They resent what they regard as "being taken advantage of." As we saw in the train marshaling case, they resist doing more than their bogey, and those who do so are subject to punishment by their peers.

Employees generally question working outside the limits of their customary job description (whether written or not), particularly if the boss's demands seem to threaten their status. Regardless of the union contract, for example, a group may consider it unacceptable for a maintenance man to be asked to do production work—or vice versa.

As we have seen in Chapters 2 and 3, craftsmen and professionals tend to have well-developed internalized standards of how they should do their jobs. Craft and professional pride lead them to turn out work which is of generally high quality and in at least fair quantity. On the other hand, they vigorously resist efforts by managers without the requisite craft or professional skills to interfere in what they feel is their area of craft or professional autonomy.

---

[26] Alvin Gouldner, *Wildcat Strike* (Yellow Springs, Ohio: The Antioch Press, 1954).

[27] Some readers may recognize that this is related to what Chester Barnard calls the "zone of indifference" (*The Functions of the Executive*, Cambridge: Harvard University Press, 1950), and Herbert Simon calls the "zone of acceptance" (*Administrative Behavior*, New York: Macmillan, 1947, Chap. 7).

[28] Simon, *op. cit.*, also suggests that the existence of the "zone of acceptance" is made possible, in part, by subordinates' inertia—their reluctance to make decisions on their own.

A manager's instructions are more likely to be accepted if they seem to be concerned with getting the job done, rather than with the arbitrary exercise of authority for authority's sake. Employees object to being given busy work after their "fair day's work" is done. In general, subordinates reject orders as unfair if they are not reasonably related to the purpose for which they were hired.

Indoctrination leads men to resist inappropriate assignments. The more strongly an individual is indoctrinated in the organization's objectives, the more willing he is to accept work assignments which he feels are helping to achieve those objectives, and the more strongly he resists assignments which he feels are irrelevant to them.

On the other hand, technical instructions concerned with the job are considered legitimate—unless the individual making them is felt to be incompetent. Similarly, subordinates accept orders which are obviously required by the situation. They resent rules that are imposed for no apparent reason. Thus, no-smoking rules are hard to enforce unless employees are convinced there is a real fire hazard. The manager must be able to justify rules as essential to getting the job done, maintaining plant safety, and so forth.

Conversely, subordinates often feel that their boss is remiss when he fails to enforce legitimate regulations. Mine workers in one situation placed the blame for accidents on a foreman, since it was his job to see the rules are followed.[29]

> [Employees] know that, as a group, they are incapable of making quick decisions; if the organization is to function effectively, there must be leadership in making decisions and putting them into effect . . . They have no respect for the supervisor who gives orders timidly and with uncertainty. And, strange, as it may seem, they like discipline—when they see that it is important in getting the job done.[30]

Employees often expect the boss to show *leniency,* to ignore minor or technical violations of rules as long as the job is getting done. As we have seen they also expect that under unusual conditions (say, when they have bad days) the boss will give them a break and not insist even on the fair day's work. As we have seen, this expectation involves a form of implicit bargaining, for in exchange for this "good turn" the employee may feel some obligation to work extra hard in genuine emergencies.

A SYSTEM IN EQUILIBRIUM

To conclude, we have seen that legitimacy is largely determined by subordinate expectations, and that these expectations in turn are established

[29] Alvin Gouldner, *Patterns of Bureaucracy* (New York: The Free Press of Glencoe, 1954), p. 195.
[30] William F. Whyte, *Human Relations in the Restaurant Industry* (New York: McGraw-Hill, 1948), p. 259.

and enforced *in part* by the various forms of implicit bargaining discussed in Chapter 6. At first, the bargain established in this fashion may be little more than an armed truce, but over time, expectations arise that the bargain *should* be observed by both parties. Gradually, expectations "harden" and acquire what anthropologists have called the "crust of custom" and the "aura of legitimacy."

Thus, the manager-subordinate relationship can be conceived of as a system in equilibrium: There are strong forces operating against all parties to restore them to equilibrium should they ever stray away. The manager is confined and restricted by his subordinates' expectations. As long as he is content to accept them, his job is rather easy. The manager who ignores or flouts these expectations does so at his risk, though sometimes—if the organization is to deal successfully with external challenges—the risk must be taken. Before doing so, however, the manager should pause and consider what he intends to do, or perhaps devise an approach that will achieve his objectives without a frontal attack on what subordinates feel to be right and proper.

It should be emphasized that expectations arise through other means besides implicit bargaining. Some expectations are established by the culture generally and efforts to change them solely through the group are doomed to failure. The manager's task is made even more difficult because his subordinates may belong to a number of different groups, each with its own set of expectations. Indeed there are times when expectations are quite difficult to determine. Certainly a manager is misconstruing his function if he is trying to win a popularity contest.

Conclusion

Although delegation may reduce a manager's need to exercise authority, he cannot abandon it altogether. The boss remains a boss. In fact, there are some people who, because of personality or background, expect their boss to provide firm, detailed leadership, and there are situations where delegation is not enough to get the job done. Knowing *when* (and when not) to use firmness is one of the critical criteria for effective leadership.

It is also important to know *how* to use authority: The manner in which it is used may spell the difference between resentment and acceptance. The effective supervisor maintains good communications with his subordinates. He develops personal relations which indicate that he accepts and values them as individuals. Although he may make decisions which his subordinates don't like, he endeavors to consult with them, to listen to their suggestions, to provide them with wanted information, and to treat them fairly. Even the handling of mistakes may provide an opportunity to strengthen supervisor-subordinate communications. Such methods may not generate positive enthusiasm for management's objectives, but will reduce resistance to authority. At the minimum they provide the hygienic supervision discussed in Chapter 6.

Subordinate acceptance of authority (though not necessarily enthusiasm) is facilitated when the manager's right to a job, his behavior on the job, and the demands he makes on subordinates—all are accepted as legitimate. His claim to legitimacy is judged in a group and cultural setting, however, and expectations may vary substantially from one situation to another.

Though subordinate expectations (or concepts of legitimacy) do place limits on a manager's discretion (limits which he may at times wish to expand), within the "zone of indifference" he often has a considerable degree of freedom. Certainly a manager should not show exaggerated concern for what his subordinates think. Effective leadership requires an understanding of social pressures, but a true leader does not become a prisoner within them; instead he makes use of them to work toward organizational objectives. In the next chapter we shall consider the relationship between the manager and the subordinate work group within which many of these social pressures are generated.

The Manager and the Group

9

Our discussion so far has been concerned primarily with the relationship between the manager and individual subordinates. But as our analysis of legitimacy demonstrated, boss-subordinate relations do not occur in a vacuum. Men belong to groups, and these greatly influence their expectations and behavior. Thus, this chapter will consider some of the problems involved in developing the work group into a team which works effectively for management objectives. We will consider the desirability of building cohesive groups and the methods by which this can be done, the development of group participation (and the controversial question of group decision-making), and how the manager can work through the informal organization.

Building a Work Team

Not long ago a nationally known concern distributed to its supervisors a pamphlet entitled "Deal with Individuals, not Groups." Its message was simple: Individuals, if properly handled, will work for management's objectives; groups will inevitably oppose management. Cater to the worker's competitive spirit, reward his individual efforts, and break up his attachment to the group, the argument ran, and you will be surprised how much work he puts out.

The fostering of competition is not the only means that management can use to break up group cohesion. As we saw in Chapter 4, groups can be made so large and heterogeneous that "team spirit" becomes difficult to develop. Similar effects can be obtained by modifying technology and work arrangements. In restaurants even the height of the counter separating waitresses from countermen affects their ability to work together.[1]

But is it wise for management to try to splinter the informal organization? There is no absolutely clear answer to this question. To be sure, cohesive groups show greater teamwork. Its members gain greater social satisfaction from working together. Morale is higher. Turnover and absenteeism are frequently lower.[2] Further, it may be easier to supervise a closely knit group, since the supervisor need not repeat information and orders to every member; the informal leader will act as an effective channel of communication to and from the supervisor. A quarreling, disorganized group finds it hard to work together and may direct its aggressiveness against management in the form of poor workmanship, sabotage, grievances, and wild-cat strikes.[3]

On the other hand, certain dangers arise when the work group becomes too tightly knit. Such a group may be reluctant to accept new employees as members and, though there may be more cooperation within the group, cooperation with outsiders may suffer. Thus, competition and ill feeling may develop among rival groups.

But does cohesion increase productivity? Several studies suggest that cohesive groups produce either substantially more than the average or somewhat less.[4] Particularly where the job requires close cooperation among the members of a work team, the mere existence of cohesion makes work more efficient. In general, however, cohesion results in higher productivity only if the group accepts management's demands for higher production as legitimate. If the group is unified for the purpose of protecting itself against management, then greater cohesion will mean less production. All cohesion means is that the members will adhere more closely to the group standards, whatever they are.

---

[1] William F. Whyte, *Human Relations in the Restaurant Industry* (New York: McGraw-Hill, 1948), Chapter 6.

[2] Elton Mayo and George F. F. Lombard, *Teamwork and Labor Turnover in the Aircraft Industry of Southern California* (Boston: Graduate School of Business Administration, Harvard University, 1944).

[3] Cohesive groups may do the same thing, but their efforts are better coordinated, more carefully thought through, and less erratic than those of the disorganized group. Leonard R. Sayles, *Behavior of Industrial Work Groups* (New York: Wiley, 1958), pp. 7–40.

[4] Stanley Seashore, *Group Cohesiveness in Industrial Work Groups* (Ann Arbor: Survey Research Center, University of Michigan, 1954); Daniel Katz and Robert Kahn, "Human Organization and Worker Motivation," *Industrial Productivity*, L. Reed Tripp, ed. (Champaign, Ill.: Industrial Relations Research Association, 1951), pp. 161–162; Morton Deutsch, "The Effects of Cooperation and Competition on Group Process," *Group Dynamics*, Dorwin Cartwright and Alvin Zander, eds. (Evanston, Ill.: Harper & Row, 1953), pp. 319–353.

Where management finds that there is no possibility of developing groups with goals that are compatible with the objectives of the organization, it may become necessary to resort to measures that will weaken or eliminate informal groups. Continuous movements of personnel, particularly those showing leadership potential, and supervisory patterns that stress dealing with the individual are two possible ways of keeping strong groups from developing.[5] In most instances, however, given a sound over-all program of human relations, it is in management's interest to promote teamwork.

What can the supervisor do to develop teamwork? Most important, he can develop a sensitivity to the facts of group life discussed in Chapter 4. He can familiarize himself with the social geography of the group he supervises and learn to identify the patterns of status, leadership, friendship, and cliques that exist within it. Understanding relations can help in a host of ways:

1. He can avoid putting enemies together by carefully assigning men to work positions—thus reducing the possibility of personal friction.

2. He can put friends together. True, this arrangement may lead to more talking on the job, but the evidence suggests that more work will be done too, particularly where the work requires cooperation. One study showed that carpenters and bricklayers who were allowed to choose among themselves whom they would work with outproduced those who were not permitted this choice.[6] Similar results were obtained when laundry workers were assigned on the basis of sociometric preference,[7] and where air-force pilot-training groups were selected in this fashion.[8] (On the other hand, sociometric selection of work teams may be inconsistent with an organizational policy of racial integration.)

3. He can provide special help and attention to isolates—the lonely workers who make no friends. Careful recognition of the position of such employees and the use of clique leaders to help them win acceptance may do much to improve their performance and to prevent them from quitting.

4. He can assign men in such a way as to avoid the growth of competing subgroups.

> A study of social organization in the merchant marine suggests that watches (work teams) were most effective when (a) the entire group came from the same social background, or (b) every member of the group came from a different background. When two sharply different cliques formed, efficiency was impaired.[9]

[5] These were among the techniques used by the communists during the Korean War to break down the morale and cohesion of American prisoners.

[6] R. H. Van Zelst, "Sociometrically Selected Work Teams," *Personnel Psychology*, Vol. 5, No. 3 (Autumn 1952), pp. 175-185.

[7] John H. Jacobs, "The Application of Sociometry to Industry," *Sociometry*, Vol. 8, No. 2 (May 1945), pp. 181-198.

[8] L. D. Zeleny, "Selection of Compatible Flying Partners," *The American Journal of Sociology*, Vol. 52, No. 5 (March 1947), pp. 424-431.

[9] Stephen Richardson, *The Social Organization of British and United States Merchant Ships* (mimeographed; New York State School of Industrial and Labor Relations, 1954), p. 54.

5. He can cut down on excessive transfers *between* departments, within the limits of union seniority rules.

6. He can rotate jobs within the group in order to strengthen each employee's identification with the team as a whole rather than with his individual job.

7. He can try to set up situations in which the employee can make his job easier by cooperating with others.

> In restaurants we studied, management trained the waitresses to work together and help each other. They were taught to consider two, three, or more stations as a unit and to divide the work among themselves in the most efficient manner.
>
> . . . The waitresses are told to help only those girls who will return the favor. . . . The girl who helps nobody can get nobody to help her, and she drops behind and has trouble with her service. The girl who gives help gets help in return.[10]

8. He can provide financial incentives: Group incentives may do more to encourage cooperation than individual bonus plans.

9. He can make sure that new workers are carefully introduced to the group. Many companies have a "big brother" system in which every new employee is assigned an older employee to help him become familiar not only with the formal requirements of the job but also with the informal mores of the group. In his social contacts with the group, the supervisor should be careful not to exclude the new employee.

10. He can provide employees such as maintenance men or internal auditors, who are constantly moved from department to department, some opportunity to work together as a common group and to feel they have a home.

Developing Group Participation

Many high-production supervisors have discovered that they can obtain better results by giving a group an opportunity to participate in decision-making, either through consulting with the group or by allowing it to make and implement decisions by itself.

> Industrial engineers in a metal-plating department had been trying for a long time to figure out an equitable way of dividing up the girls' work. The operation was unusually complex and erratic, and every time the engineers made a suggestion the girls were quick to prove that it was unfair to someone. The engineers were about to give up in disgust when the girls asked, "Why not let us decide?" In a short while they had worked out job allocations that even the engineers agreed were superior to theirs.

Naturally everybody gains from this sort of participation. The girls win the satisfaction of exercising greater control over their work environment, as

---

[10] Whyte, *op. cit.*, p. 214.

well as the feeling of success from having accomplished something by themselves. Management gains in that better decisions are often made by people
close to the job. There is less need for the supervisor to exercise authority or
to follow the philosophy of "be strong"; individual employees are more likely
to obey rules they themselves have established.

Employees who are given the freedom to regulate themselves are far more
capable of making sound decisions when emergencies arise. Since they make
the decisions by themselves, there is less need for them to refer every problem
to the manager. As a consequence, he can concentrate on long-term planning
and handling relations with other departments.

When subordinates are given the necessary freedom, they often do an
impressive job of working out their own methods of scheduling, quality
control, and so forth. They may even set production goals for themselves and
discipline those who fail to live up to expectations. Sometimes these goals are
surprisingly high.

> Groups that participate in setting goals for themselves often make higher
> demands for themselves than supervisors and methods engineers consider prac-
> tical. A furnace cleaning job was cut from four to two days; tardiness was set
> at less than 3 per cent when formerly it was 10 per cent; service calls were
> reduced from one in 14 to one in 21 . . . repairs per man per day rose from
> 8.5 to 12.5 when the crew planned the service; and over a period of three years
> men worked more days when they decided whether or not the weather was
> inclement than when the supervisor made the decision.[11]

The mere fact that the group is given the power to enforce and implement
rules increases the likelihood that they will accept the rules, even rules to
which they might otherwise object. In other words, whether or not a group
accepts management's objectives depends not only on *what* is demanded but
also on *how* it is demanded.

> The superintendent of a machine operation was convinced by his Safety
> Department that long-sleeved shirts were a safety hazard even when rolled up.
> So he posted a notice that beginning the next Monday morning wearing long-
> sleeved shirts on the job would be prohibited.
> Monday morning four men showed up with long sleeves. Given the choice
> of working without shirts or cutting off their sleeves, they refused to do either
> and were sent home. The union filed a sharp grievance, asking for back pay
> for time lost.
> Then the Personnel Department stepped in. The rule was suspended for a
> week and a special meeting was called with the union grievance committee.
> The safety director explained that if a worker got his sleeve caught in a machine
> his whole arm might be ripped off. The union agreed to the rule provided that
> it was extended to include management (who originally had been exempt on
> the grounds that they didn't get close enough to the machines).
> Next Monday the rule went back into effect. A few men, forgetfully, arrived
> in long sleeves. The other men handed them a pair of scissors and insisted that
> the offending sleeves be cut off on the spot. Later in the afternoon a union vice-
> president and a company time-study man were treated in the same way.

---

11 Norman R. F. Maier, *Principles of Human Relations* (New York: Wiley, 1952), p. 172.

Summarizing, these examples suggest that permitting the group to participate in decisions—through actually making the decisions, enforcing them, or being consulted about them—may result in genuine advantages for management. Employees take more responsibility for minor problems without constantly running to the supervisor with questions, they set production goals (at times at higher levels than would be set by management), they enforce their own rules, and they even modify their group standards in a way they might not otherwise do. In addition, of course, members of the work group gain many satisfactions from participation: a chance to be creative, to feel a sense of accomplishment, to show leadership, to let off steam, and so forth. Furthermore, there are situations where the group expects management to consult with it; if management fails to do so, subordinates may feel that management is behaving illegitimately.

How can the manager stimulate participation of this sort? To some extent he can permit it to develop naturally, merely by refraining from close supervision. However, if he goes too far, and simply says "Take over," fumbling and confusion are bound to result. In the following two sections we shall see that managers can encourage the group to develop effective participation through (1) holding meetings with subordinates to consider mutual problems, and (2) working through the informal organization of the group.

Holding Meetings

Many an effective manager calls his subordinates together whenever he has a problem of common interest. Of course, individual problems can be discussed and worked out in private conversations, but *group* problems require *group* discussion. Such meetings need not be formal. Indeed, meetings range all the way from a regular session of the board of directors to an informal discussion between a foreman and a couple of mechanics around a machine that has been causing trouble.

Meetings of this sort may be used for three different purposes:

For information-giving.   This meeting is simply a substitute for posting a notice or speaking to subordinates one by one. Obviously, taking the whole work force away from their job is an expensive procedure, but it insures that everyone will be notified of new directives or information which are important to the whole group. Furthermore, such meetings give subordinates a chance to ask questions, raise objections, and discuss the implications of the announcement.

For consultation.   Just as a manager can ask individuals for suggestions on how to solve a problem (see p. 192), so he can call a meeting for the same purpose. Though the manager will make the final decision on whether or not the suggestions are accepted, people derive great satisfaction from knowing that their ideas are being considered and even more if they are used. A group of individuals exchanging opinions and experiences often comes up with better suggestions than any one person working alone. A suggestion that has evolved from the contributions of many members of the group is more likely to be implemented with enthusiasm by the entire group than is a suggestion that is the brain child of one person, whether he is the manager or an individual subordinate.

For group decision. Just as a supervisor can delegate authority to individual subordinates to handle problems that involve them alone, so he may call a meeting and delegate authority to a group to handle problems that involve the group as a whole. Of course, there is little difference between a meeting called to solicit suggestions and a meeting called to enable the group to make decisions on its own. But, by waiving its veto power, management thrusts upon the group the responsibility for choosing between alternatives.

GROUP DECISION-MAKING: SUBJECT FOR CONTROVERSY

Most business meetings are called for the first two purposes mentioned above—for information-giving or for consultation. Yet, the greatest amount of interest and conflict about group meetings centers on the third purpose, group decision-making.[12] Some observers seem to feel that group decision-making is almost a cure-all for every business ill. There are books on human relations and supervision devoted almost entirely to this one process. The controversy revolves around three basic questions: (1) whether group decision-making will lead to decisions which from management's point of view are proper, (2) whether group decision-making is a form of unfair manipulation, and (3) whether group decision-making is more effective than individual decision-making.

Can meetings be trusted? Critics make this objection: "Very well, group decision-making has some value, but can you be sure the group can be trusted to make what is from management's point of view the right decision? Won't subordinates avoid responsibility and try to get out of work? If given the power to make decisions, won't they wander over into areas that are none of their business?"

Actually, there are many areas in which management does not care what decision is made, so long as there is no excessive dissension. For example,

---

[12] For example, see Alfred J. Marrow, *Making Management Human* (New York: McGraw-Hill, 1957); Maier, *op. cit.;* W. H. Whyte, Jr., *The Organization Man* (New York: Simon and Schuster, 1956); Chris Argyris, *Personality and Organization* (New York: Harper & Row, 1957); Herbert Thelen, *The Dynamics of Groups at Work* (Chicago: University of Chicago Press, 1954). Rensis Likert, *New Patterns of Management* (New York: McGraw-Hill, 1961); George Strauss, "Some Notes on Power Equalization," in Harold Leavitt, ed., *The Social Science of Organization* (Englewood Cliffs, N.J.: Prentice-Hall, 1963), pp. 41-84; Robert Dubin, "Business Behavior *Behaviorally* Viewed," in Chris Argyris and others, *Social Science Approach to Business Behavior* (Homewood, Ill.: Irwin-Dorsey, 1962).

management is unconcerned with how men divide up the dirty work so long as the work is done—or how rest periods or vacations are scheduled, so long as the time allotted is not exceeded. Since no vacation schedule can satisfy everybody, hard feelings are bound to result. The manager who can pass the responsibility on to the group saves himself a major headache.[13]

In other areas the manager's objectives coincide with those of the group—in matters of accident-prevention or avoiding jam-ups in the parking lot, for example. Possibly management should reserve a veto power over decisions in such matters, although it is unlikely that the group will make decisions that are, from management's point of view, far wrong.

The manager, of course, is interested not only in getting a sound decision but also in getting one that is accepted by the group. An *adequate* solution that is enthusiastically implemented by the group may well be better than a *perfect* solution that meets with stubborn antagonism. Thus, the group-decision process is of particular value when management is more concerned with getting *acceptance* of a decision than with its *quality*.

How can a manager keep a meeting from encroaching on areas of decision-making that are not its proper concern? One way is to set clear *limits* to the group's area of freedom. (These limits are similar to the authority-delegating limits we discussed in Chapter 7.) Suppose management is interested in re-furnishing the ladies' lounge. The experienced manager might say, "We have $500 allowed us. How should we spend it?" rather than "What should be done?" or, even worse, "How much should we spend?" Similarly, instead of asking "How much vacation time should you get?" the manager might ask, "How many people can we spare at any one time during vacation and still maintain production? Who should go when?"

If there is no agreement on basic objectives, however, even the setting of limits provides no absolute safeguard against what management might regard as irresponsible decisions. Children balk at being asked, "Which do you want, milk of magnesia or castor oil?" and their parents also object to being asked to make that sort of choice. Normally a group will refuse to make a decision on "We've got to lay off 20 men. Who should they be?" unless there is some previous agreement among the parties that *someone* will be laid off. There must be a mutual acceptance of objectives before a group decision is possible.

Ideally, management provides broad areas of freedom in which subordinates can regulate their own behavior (this is simply teamwork). However, there are bound to be areas of basic conflict between superiors and subordinates, between the organization and its members. In approaching these areas, the most a manager can do is explain why he has made a particular decision and perhaps ask for questions. At one time or another, every supervisor must face the inevitability of making and announcing distasteful decisions.

---

[13] Note, however, that the manager still must preside over the process by which the men make the decision. If the manager merely says, "You decide," without helping to establish a procedure by which the decision can be made, there will be endless bickering and confusion. It is the manager's responsibility to help the group resolve its internal disputes.

Manipulation?   Some observers feel that group decision-making is nothing but manipulation or even brainwashing—a device by which management imposes its will upon the group without the group's realizing what is happening. Certainly, many managers look upon participative techniques as a means of getting subordinates to accept decisions which are not in the subordinates' interest, or as a way of making them feel that there is no real conflict between their interests and those of management.[14]

Much of the argument is exaggerated. Group decision-making works best in those areas where management is really willing to accept the group's free decision. True, management may pretend that the group has more freedom than it really has. And it may try to manipulate the discussion process so that employees seem to agree when they really do not. But experience suggests that subordinates quickly see through "mock democracy" of this sort. Such attempts at brainwashing may be successful at first, but in the long run in a free society they are likely to backfire, giving rise to mistrust and resentment.

It must be remembered that group decision-making is a form of delegation and is subject to the limitations we discussed in Chapter 7. It works best on jobs which are of intrinsic interest to those who do them, and it works much less well with those whose central life interest is away from the job. Similarly, it works best where participation is encouraged consistently throughout the organization and less well where the objects sought by participation are inconsistent with the subordinates' basic values.

For example, since academicians, professionals, and members of higher management are likely to have roughly the same objectives as do their bosses, participation with these groups may well be effective over a wide range of subjects.[15] On the other hand, among workers who lack intrinsic interest in their work, participation may be effective only over a narrow range. Thus, group discussion among secretaries about when to hold a coffee break may lead to acceptance of the agreed-upon time and perhaps to fewer breaks at other times. It is more problematical, however, whether such a discussion will lead to their working harder.

Genuine group decision-making on the low levels of an organization may well be confined normally to what may seem to be rather trivial matters, which are, nevertheless, often of considerable importance to those directly involved. Group *consultation* may have a wider role at this level, provided the manager makes it clear at the outset that the final decision will be his.

Group vs. individual decision-making.   Even apart from possible differences in objectives, is group decision-making more effective than individual decision-making? The answer seems to depend on the nature of the group, the problem being considered, and what is meant by "effective." Groups sometimes turn out higher-quality solutions than do individuals, although this isn't always

---

[14] Raymond E. Miles, "Human Relations or Human Resources?" *Harvard Business Review,* Vol. 34, No. 4 (July 1965), pp. 148-163.

[15] Participation may be particularly effective for academicians and professionals, since these groups value highly the concept of "colleagueship."

the case. In solving problems where there is one definite solution, a group is more likely to be accurate than an individual. Furthermore, group problem-solving has the advantage of enlisting a variety of backgrounds and experiences; thus, the range of solutions is usually greater, and the group solution is more likely to represent a balanced point of view. Meetings are particularly useful when the participants represent various departments whose coordination is required to implement the final decision, for the discussion tends to force the departmental representatives to look at the problem from an organizational rather than a departmental point of view.[16]

Individual decision-making, on the other hand, is more likely to be firm than to represent a compromise. Individuals are more capable than groups of handling subtle relations—whether in threading a needle or in developing a complex theoretical formula.[17] Great works of art are almost without exception the products of single individuals. "Could *Hamlet* have been written by a committee," it has been asked, "or Mona Lisa been painted by a club?" [18]

In addition, meetings are awfully time-consuming. Decisions reached in them take longer than do those of individuals, particularly if time is computed in terms of total man-hours expended. Sometimes, of course, the higher quality and easier acceptance of decisions reached through meetings makes them worth the extra time involved. On the other hand, managers on occasion pass the buck to meetings when they are psychologically unprepared to make decisions themselves. Meetings under these circumstances rarely accomplish much.

There is the risk, too, that presenting a problem to a group to discuss may lead to greater conflict than existed before—and skillful leadership is required to prevent this [19] (as we shall see in Chapter 12). The danger of conflict is particularly great where vested interests are involved (for example, when a group is deciding whether "soft jobs" should be rotated or assigned on the basis of seniority). The less cohesive the group, the greater the difficulty in reaching agreement, though experience in making decisions of this sort may help cohesion develop.

The advantages and disadvantages of group decision-making through com-

---

[16] But, one experienced executive warns, the over-all manager who chairs the meeting should still make the final decision, for by his very position he is best suited to look at the problem in terms of the needs of the organization as a whole. Wilfred Brown, *Explorations in Management* (London: Tavistock Press, 1960).

[17] Thus, groups may be more efficient than individuals in solving crossword puzzles, but individuals are better at devising them.

[18] Donald W. Taylor, Paul Berry, and Clifford H. Block, "Group Participation, Brainstorming, and Creative Thinking," *Administrative Science Quarterly*, Vol. 3, No. 1 (June, 1958), p. 27.

[19] In addition, there is the problem that if the boss consults with his subordinates regarding one area of management, they may establish expectations of being consulted in regard to other areas, too. Since it may not be possible to consult everybody in a large organization, perhaps it might be better not to start a process which is difficult to control. See Robert Dubin, "Psyche, Sensitivity, and Social Structure," in Robert Tannenbaum, Irving R. Weschler, and Irving Massarik, *Leadership and Organization* (New York: McGraw-Hill, 1961).

mittees are effectively summarized in contrasting remarks by well-known executives from two companies with vastly different attitudes toward the use of committees:

> "If you can name for me one great discovery or decision that was made by a committee, I will find you the one man in that committee who had the lonely insight—while he was shaving or on his way to work, or maybe while the rest of the committee was chattering away—the lonely insight that solved the problem and was the basis for the decision." [20]
>
> "It stands to reason that if you get five men together and one man is wrong, the mistake will be picked up. Or if one man has a good idea, the others will contribute to it and develop it. And if they have good ideas, what comes out may be better than the separate ideas added together." [21]

GROUP CONSULTATION ON A DAY-TO-DAY BASIS

The preceding discussion may have given the impression that the use of meetings involves a drastic change from traditional management practice. Quite the contrary. In some companies most major decisions have long been made by committees, particularly at the higher levels of management. (Sometimes this practice is called "multiple management.") And at lower levels it is now accepted practice for supervisors to hold regular meetings at which subordinates can raise questions, discuss common problems, and consider new developments. Increasingly, such meetings are being held even on the hourly-paid level, though they are still probably more common in service organizations such as restaurants,[22] hospitals, stores, schools, and libraries than in manufacturing plants.

Some organizations require that regular meetings be held as a standard practice at all levels. Unfortunately, supervisors may call these compulsory meetings merely because they are told to do so: They go through the motions but never become involved in the spirit of consultation. An office girl once described her experience to us:

> "We have meetings once a month. The office manager asks us if we have any questions or suggestions. Sure we have lots of complaints, but no one has the courage to bring them up. Once in a while one of the girls who is looking to make a good impression asks some silly question, although she already knows the answer.
>
> "Most of the meeting is spent by the office manager telling us we ought to cooperate more, we ought to be neater in our work, and so forth. Frankly, I always resent these meetings—they take you away from your work. And I hate the way the office manager talks about our smooth-working loyal group when I despise her and so do the other girls."

---

[20] Ralph J. Cordiner, former Chairman of General Electric, as cited in Justin G. Longenecker, *Principles of Management and Organizational Behavior* (Columbus, Ohio: Merrill, 1964), p. 206.

[21] Frank Abrams, former Chairman of Standard Oil of New Jersey, as cited in *ibid.*

[22] For a good description of such a meeting in a restaurant, see Whyte, *op. cit.*, pp. 236-240.

Actually, the mere act of holding formal meetings is less important than the manager's willingness to consult with subordinates informally when problems arise. Status differences create less of a barrier to communication when consultation takes place around the drawing board, over the machine that has broken down, or in the cafeteria—than at a formally called meeting.

Working Through the Informal Organization

It would be impractical for a manager to call a meeting every time he has a problem to solve. Often he can work out a solution by himself, taking into account the standards and expectations of the group. But at other times the successful manager will make use of the informal organization of the group.

INFORMAL LEADERS

As we mentioned in Chapter 4, groups evolve their own leadership. Informal leaders play key roles in every organization, and without their cooperation management must face an uphill battle against sabotage and apathy.

W. F. Whyte tells the story of two settlement-house recreational directors who handled the same problem in different ways.[23] The problem was this:

> The younger boys were to use the play center till 9 o'clock, then they were to leave and make room for the older boys. But, instead of going home, the younger boys would hang around the door, bang on the windows, and generally create a nuisance.
>
> Again and again the first recreational director asked the boys as a group to go away—but with no results. Faced with the same situation, the second director turned to one member of the group and merely said: "Listen, Joe, the time's up. Be a good fellow and take your gang out of here." Joe, who was the informal leader, complied immediately and the group left.

Why was the second director so successful? He recognized the informal leader's special status, and gave him an opportunity to gain still more status through proving his power to the director. Under the first director's approach, the informal leader could exhibit his power only by opposing the director's will; had the group obeyed the director, the informal leader would have lost status.

The situation is very much the same in business and industry. A supervisor can either fight the informal organization and its leaders or work with them. If the informal leaders fail to win recognition by working *with* management, they will get it by working *against* management.

Management is often heard to complain, "All our trouble is caused by a

---

[23] William F. Whyte and Burleigh B. Gardner, "The Man in the Middle: Position and Problems of the Foreman," *Applied Anthropology*, Vol. 4, No. 2 (Spring 1945).

few ringleaders. If we could only get rid of them, our trouble would disappear, morale would rise, and our employees would be loyal once again." Unfortunately, these "ringleaders" are often informal leaders; the trouble they cause reflects the desires of the group. It is particularly important to work with informal leaders of *strategic* groups (see p. 122). In dealing with them, a certain amount of bargaining is often required. Eliminate the informal leaders, though, and the group may become still more antagonistic to management, morale may fall even lower, and new ringleaders will step to the fore. In a nonunionized situation it may be possible to eliminate ringleaders one by one till finally nothing is left but a cowed, disorganized mass of individuals who docilely obey orders. However, such individuals never show a gleam of initiative or teamwork.

What is the alternative to firing ringleaders? Working with them. There are numerous ways in which a manager can build up good relations with the informal leaders working under him. Among other things he can pass information along to them first, ask their advice on technical or human-relations problems, and assign them to train others.

There are, however, several dangers that the manager must guard against:

1. The informal leader is often hard to identify. The outstanding man who does the best work and cooperates most readily with management may *seem* to be the informal leader, whereas these characteristics may actually make him a social isolate. On the other hand, the "loud-mouth" may serve as the group's *spokesman* rather than its actual *leader*. The group may even have different leaders for different purposes. Sometimes the members of the group will follow one individual when they act in cooperation with management and another when they are antagonistic. Finally, there may be no identifiable informal leader at all.

2. The very fact that the informal leader works closely with management may result in his losing status with the group: He will be known as a "company man." This danger is particularly acute when there is antagonism between the manager and the work group generally and the informal leader is asked to do things that the group does not accept as legitimate.

3. Carried too far, cooperation becomes favoritism. It is one thing for the manager to give the informal leader information and to ask for his advice. It is quite another to give him easier work or special favors. Nothing could be more effectively calculated to drive him from his leadership position.

THE WORKING SUPERVISOR

The working supervisor is a group member to whom a manager may show special attention without giving rise to charges of favoritism. There are two kinds of working supervisor. The most obvious is "the straw boss," sometimes called the working foreman, leadman, keyman, or group chief. He is the leader of a group of men who do roughly the *same* sort of work. He shares their work and performs certain quasi-supervisory duties as well.

The other sort of working supervisor exercises his authority by virtue of his technical position on the work team, because his work is *different* from that of the others and requires more skill. Working supervisors are common in process industries and also in some of the older, more traditional industries in which craft skills still prevail. For an example from a traditional industry:

> In glass-blowing shops where high-quality crystalware is manufactured for the luxury market, each work team is headed by a gaffer. The gaffer, the top man in a six-step hierarchy, is a craftsman of considerable skill and long seniority in his trade who does more intricate work than either members of his team. He is accountable to management for the quality and quantity of the ware produced by his team and has almost complete authority over their work performance.

The supervisory power of these top-status crew members rarely receives such formal recognition from management. Instead, it exists because of tradition and because supervisors have found these men to be effective assistants in running the department.

Since the working supervisor often gains status because of his seniority and technical proficiency, subordinates will be more willing to accept orders from him than from the foreman himself. This is particularly true where the foreman has not come up from the ranks himself, where coordination of the work force requires a high degree of technical skill that can be acquired only through years on the job, or where constant attention and order-giving are required, as with a fast-paced steel-mill crew.

We have observed situations in which management has impaired output and demoralized the work group by deliberately or inadvertently taking away some of the working supervisor's power and prestige.[24] This often happens when a college-trained foreman pays too much attention to the formal organization chart and not enough to traditional relationships between workers and management.

Actually the relationship between foreman and working supervisor is a highly personal one and cannot be established simply by top-management edict. In many cases, the supervisor can substantially increase his effectiveness by consulting with the working supervisor and channeling orders through him.[25]

THE UNION STEWARD

The union steward is ordinarily an informal leader who commands respect outside union matters. Provided the over-all union-management relationship is friendly, the manager may wish to pass on information to the steward first,

---

[24] See George Strauss, "The Set-Up Man: A Case Study of Organizational Change," *Human Organization*, Vol. 13, No. 2 (Summer 1954), pp. 17-25.

[25] Charles R. Walker, Robert H. Guest, and Arthur N. Turner, *The Foreman on the Assembly Line* (Cambridge: Harvard University Press, 1956), p. 45.

use him as a sounding board for proposed changes, and even ask his
Again if relations are good, this consultation can be handled outside u.
text of formal collective bargaining and in a way that will not lead to the los.
of the manager's power or the establishment of precedents that management
may later regret. Such consultation has the great advantage of permitting the
steward to participate in solving technical and human-relations problems in a
constructive, positive fashion; otherwise, in order to display his status, the
steward has to resort to the essentially negative activity of processing grievances. In a strongly unionized situation, the supervisor will never be able to
develop cooperative relations with his subordinates if he bypasses or ignores
the union.

Promoting an Informal Leader into Management

In selecting a supervisor, is it better to promote an informal leader from
the ranks or to hire someone, presumably a college graduate, from outside? [26]
An examination of this question may help us tie together some of the matters
discussed in this chapter.

It is often argued that the opportunity to be promoted from the ranks provides motivation for men to work harder. Further, it is argued that the informal
leader is likely to have developed both technical ability and an ability to
lead the people with whom he has worked. On the other hand, the necessity
for both technical ability and informal leadership has been challenged.

Let us look at the technical question first. In recent years the need for the
manager to possess technical ability has been de-emphasized. Since the
manager's primary job is to motivate others to work, his own technical proficiency is secondary. As one personnel director put it, "A supervisor's job is to
manage *people,* the people take care of *things.*" Increasingly, management is
looking for generalists rather than specialists for supervisory posts.

Symptomatic of this change has been the growing tendency to hire college
graduates as foremen, thus substantially reducing the hourly-paid worker's
chance to advance into management. The so-called "jet programs" for college
graduates emphasize broad experience rather than specialization. Even in
engineering, the best opportunities for getting ahead lie in administration
rather than in jobs that require professional skill.

There are good reasons for this shift in emphasis. Certainly the evidence we
mentioned in Chapter 7 suggests that it is the poorer supervisor who does
the same sort of work as his men and who concentrates on the technical aspects
of his job. The better supervisors are more concerned with long-range planning
and development, and tend to delegate petty responsibilities. It is clearly short-

---

[26] For an excellent discussion of the dilemma, see William F. Whyte, *Men at Work*
(Homewood, Ill.: Irwin-Dorsey, 1961), pp. 379-385.

sighted to promote people to supervisory positions purely as a reward for technical performance if they have shown no evidence that they can lead people.

And yet, as we have seen in this chapter, technical ability helps the manager legitimatize his authority. In addition, such background obviously makes it easier for him to communicate with his subordinates, and it helps him make better technical decisions (unless, as is happening in many industries, technological change is so rapid that the man from the ranks cannot understand new developments).

How about the argument that the best way of insuring that a supervisor will be well accepted by the group is to appoint an informal leader who is already well liked? This raises a difficult and much-debated question: Should a man be asked to supervise his former equals? Among the problems to consider in deciding on such a step are:

1. Is the leader really respected by the group? Our research shows that in some disunited groups, particularly those that reject most of management's objectives, the apparent leader is often only a mouthpiece who has been selected for his ability to cause trouble, but who commands no real respect from the group.

2. Is there a basic conflict between the group and management? If the informal leader is promoted to a supervisory position and asked to work for objectives and enforce regulations that the group rejects, either (a) he will flatly refuse to do so, or (b) he will agree to work for management's goals and be considered a traitor by his former friends. In any event he will be faced with a painful moral dilemma. If the question "Which side are you on? Management's or labor's?" is asked too insistently, it is obvious that the formal leader cannot also be an informal one.

Another problem, one which creates a great deal of anxiety for the new supervisor who has risen from the ranks, is whether to continue to fraternize with his former friends—or to try to maintain a social distance from them. A newly appointed supervisor cannot help asking himself: "Can I maintain discipline and command respect if I keep up my old friendships? If I cut them off, won't the men think I am high-hatting them? But how can I keep up my old Friday night poker games with Jack and Joe unless I am equally friendly with Bill and Gus? How do I break off my old game with Jack and Joe?" (Family ties make things even harder. One foreman stated his hardest problem this way: "How do you discipline your sister-in-law's uncle?") One thing seems sure—it is as unwise for a man who has come up from the ranks to cut off his ties arbitrarily as it is for a superintendent who is new to a department to create artificial ties.

We have observed many situations in which informal leaders have stepped into formal leadership with hardly a change in their relationship to the group. The manager remains "one of the boys," and becoming boss does not cost him the respect of his new subordinates. A highly respected foreman told this story about what happened when he was promoted:

> "A lot of young fellows who came in my department after the war came from my neighborhood and I always helped them learn their jobs. I guess since I was the oldest man in the department they always came to me with their questions. *When I became foreman I kept on doing just what I did before. My relations haven't changed since I became foreman.*"

This type of adjustment occurs most frequently on jobs where subordinates enjoy a great deal of freedom and where high technical skill is required—in maintenance work, for example, or among professional engineers.[27]

There is some evidence that employees are more likely to accept a manager who has worked his way up through the ranks in a department where there is a well-defined status hierarchy than in one where all the employees are on the same status level. In a department where there is a step-by-step progression from unskilled to skilled jobs, all workers have a chance to move up, and the manager's job is just the logical top rung of the ladder. Moreover, the manager has legitimatized his position by demonstrating high technical skill. In departments where all the workers do the same job, however, the jump from worker to supervisor makes one, in a way, a "traitor" to his class and is more than just the logical last step toward which everyone has been aspiring.

Conclusion

The manager rarely interacts with his subordinates in isolation. Usually this occurs in a group setting. In handling group problems the effective manager will consult with subordinates before taking action and in some areas will encourage them to make their own decisions. He may meet with the group as a whole or channel his activities through the group's informal structure. He may work with informal leaders, working supervisors, and union stewards. He may even wish to promote informal leaders into management.

A strong case can be made for participative-management, in which the manager makes a practice of encouraging his subordinates as a group to discuss a wide variety of significant work-related problems. Ideally, participation of this sort will lead both to greater cohesion and to greater acceptance of management's objectives. To the extent that such a cooperative relationship can be established, the gains are substantial for both employees and for management. An atmosphere of cooperation provides essential need satisfactions for subordinates: the social satisfaction of working together, a feeling of identification with the group and the over-all organization, and a pride in

---

[27] In research laboratories and in construction work, individuals are constantly switching back and forth from being a supervisor to being a subordinate. The individual who is momentarily a supervisor cannot afford to antagonize his subordinates, since he may be "given the works" when he is in the position of a subordinate again.

accomplishment. Belonging to a group reduces the feeling of anonymity and provides a sense of identity.

For the manager, such cooperation, if achieved, makes life a lot easier. There is less need for him to check on his men, for they make their own rules, take care of emergencies by themselves, and may even discipline their own team members. Participation is particularly useful during periods of change.

There is a danger of being Pollyanna-ish, however. We have tried to suggest the limits of participative management. There are many areas in which there are conflicts of interest between subordinates and management. Subordinate acceptance of the legitimacy of management's demands and behavior does not necessarily mean that these subordinates will "internalize" and work enthusiastically for management's objectives. It may only mean that they will put in a "fair day's work." What is such a fair day's work is largely determined through implicit bargaining and may be fairly low. To the extent that subordinates expect to be consulted, participative techniques may provide merely hygienic management (see Chapter 6) rather than positive motivation to work.

In a sense, strengthening group cohesion through participation may make management's task harder, for the group will now develop expectations that its acquiescence is required for what management does. Meetings take up a lot of time. If they are given genuine freedom to make important decisions, there is no guarantee that the decisions will be those which management wants (and the very process of discussion may lead to internal friction among group members). If the meeting is manipulated so as to come to the "right" conclusions, the members will eventually see through such mock democracy. In fact, many of the benefits of participation can be obtained without formal meetings, merely through working with subordinates on an informal basis.

LEADERSHIP: A LAST WORD

In our discussion of leadership we have tried to emphasize that there is no one pattern of management that is universally appropriate. Instead, the pattern of management that is most appropriate to a given situation depends on a number of factors:

1. The personality and background of the manager. *Example:* A manager who is brought in from outside the organization will almost of necessity maintain a greater social distance from his new subordinates than will one who has risen from the ranks.

2. The personality and background of the subordinates. *Example:* Professional engineers expect and require a higher degree of delegation than do older nurses with a rural background.

3. The type of work. *Example:* Assembly-line workers, who have relatively little opportunity to obtain need satisfaction from their work, may require closer supervision than do maintenance men.

4. Urgency of getting results. *Example:* If quick results are required, there may be no time to develop a cooperative, cohesive work group.

The sensible manager will take all these factors—and many more—into account before he decides how to behave in a particular situation. Even in a given situation, however, there is a broad range of leadership approaches that will be successful if properly implemented. For instance, in Example 1, a manager brought in from outside might very quickly develop close social relations with his subordinates and thus increase rather than decrease production. Or, in Example 3, a maintenance supervisor might get excellent production in complete violation of the principles of general supervision.

It is important to remember that many successful businessmen have violated all the principles discussed here. They have been successful in spite of their human relations—or perhaps because they have so inspired their subordinates to identify with the company and its success that employees have given their all in spite of supervisory actions that would be resented in almost any other context. (We are talking here about what some sociologists call the difference between "instrumental" and "expressive" leadership.)

In fact, the ability to supervise is only one of the many characteristics of a good manager. The company president, for example, must be effective in dealing with his subordinates. But this is only one part of his duties: He also makes plans, evaluates the recommendations of others, represents the company to outsiders, and so forth. He must have technical and administrative as well as human-relations abilities. In fact, as we shall discuss in later chapters, getting along with still higher management may be more important for him than getting along with subordinates. It has been suggested that the primary function of any top executive is to adjust the goals of his organization to the needs of his times.[28] The ability to sense the main current was the central genius of Washington, Lincoln, Franklin Roosevelt, Queen Elizabeth I, and Churchill. It is also the genius of the business executive who decides at the opportune moment to switch his company's operations from wholesaling to direct sales— or the man who steals a march on the market by making plans for the mass production of a new chemical though the laboratory tests are far from complete.

Certainly we would admit that the executive's ability to make critical decisions of this order is more crucial to the survival of the organization than his particular skill in dealing with people.[29] An organization permeated with inappropriate [30] human-relations practices, however, is unlikely to remain profitable for long, regardless of the personal brilliance of the man at the top. An organization can be successful even if some of the individuals in it, even those at the very top, lack important skills, *provided* there are others in the organization who can fill in for them. The president may be inadequate in dealing with people, but the organization will be little harmed provided he

---

[28] Philip Selznick, *Leadership in Administration* (Evanston, Ill.: Harper & Row, 1957).

[29] Though we would argue that major critical decisions must be made in the field of personnel administration just as frequently as in such fields as marketing, production, or finance.

[30] Note we use the term *inappropriate*. The appropriate practice for the given situation may be the unrestrained use of authority.

channels his contacts through someone high in the management hierarchy who is skilled in this area. Available evidence suggests that the quality of supervision in itself is often relatively unimportant in determining levels of productivity—particularly where production rates are determined by technology or by group standards.[31]

Similarly, on lower levels it would be unrealistic to expect management to promote men entirely on the basis of their leadership abilities. What is important is not that every manager be a good leader, but that the structure of the organization and management policies be such as to encourage sound human-relations practices.

At this point you may complain, "A few chapters ago you seemed to state a strong preference for delegation. Now, many hedges later, haven't you worked yourself into a position where it doesn't seem to make much difference what kind of supervision is used?" By no means. We think that the healthiest, soundest, most profitable organization will be the one in which delegation can be used effectively. But to make it possible to use delegation effectively, it may be necessary to revamp the whole organization through changes in organization structure, delegation, improved communications, and even, as we suggested in Chapter 2, substantial changes in the technological processes of production. Changes of this sort may well create cumulative changes in the over-all organization that will make general supervision possible.

As a consequence, the face-to-face relationship between supervisor and subordinate cannot be considered in isolation from the other factors that we will consider in later chapters. First, however, we should define more closely some of the skills required by the supervisor.

PROBLEM ONE

The President's Letter

The following letter was sent to the *Harvard Business Review* by the president of a medium-sized insurance company. The president is explaining why his company has so few immediate personnel problems in its Home Office (which, we may assume, houses about 500 employees, most engaged in routine, clerical operations.) [32]

The reason lies not in the attitudes of workers but in the attitude of management. It is true that lavish offers of fringe benefits give no assurance of mollified workers. This company has gone far in the fringe area, but I have never felt that what we did accounted for the remarkable *esprit de corps* our people show. I feel it is how we do it.

By that I mean that for eleven years since I came to head this company my first objective in dealings with our people has been to dignify them as individuals and to express a feeling of pride in them which quickly won their recognition. This is the pattern followed by my staff. Supervisory attitudes—management's real intent—

---

[31] Robert Dubin, "Supervision and Productivity: Empirical Findings and Theoretical Considerations," and George Homans, "Effort, Supervision, and Productivity," in Robert Dubin and others, *Leadership and Productivity* (San Francisco: Chandler, 1965).

[32] Vol. 32, No. 6 (November 1954), reproduced by permission of the author and publisher.

are quickly observed and evaluated by employees. My company takes this seriously.

Alex Osborn of B.B.D.&O. is an old friend of mine. You may have seen his two recent books, one captioned "Your Creative Power," and the other more recent one entitled "Applied Imagination." These books have been widely circulated among our officers and supervisory people, and many things have come out of them. For example, we took a longer look at our suggestion plan and approached it on the basis that whatever the quantity or quality of suggestions, the Suggestion Committee must deal, not only with an open mind, but liberally, with suggestions in the first year. While we get many suggestions that cannot be given dollar awards, we make sure that occasionally a good suggestion gets a walloping return. We now invest a rather substantial sum in suggestion awards, and I submit we get a great deal of genuine interest and benefit. Our plan works well and it costs us about the same as one qualified clerical person.

I am interested in the local orchestra, and a few years ago it was brought to my attention that there were several unsold boxes. I hit upon a plan evolved from Osborn's thinking that pays off three ways, and it has been most successful. Our people are encouraged to bring flowers from their garden to decorate the lobby of our building. They are given a credit line for so doing and feel good about it; secondly, our hobby is as attractive as any you will find; and thirdly, those who add to its beauty are rewarded by pairs of tickets to the concerts. The orchestra benefits as do our people. The plan appealed to every bank and insurance company in this town, save two, and there are no unsold boxes. Parenthetically, I maintain a box adjacent to that purchased for the employees. I am usually there and find an opportunity to visit either before the concert or during intermission with my people and their husbands and wives and friends.

Perhaps the most significant thing we have done is one which has given dignity to every person in the building and it happens to be in the field of philanthropy. In 1947, I was General Chairman for the Community Chest Campaign, and the slogan adopted by the company's employees committee that year was "PAR FOR E.A.R." [E.A.R. is the president], and in that year there was 100% giving. The company became pleasantly notorious throughout the city for this 100% accomplishment; and believe it or not, with a constantly changing personnel, the record of 100% giving—every officer, every employee, every cafeteria and building maintenance worker—has been maintained through the years since. Every year the drive is completed on the first day and a telegram sent to the general chairman. In the public meetings which follow, our people are photographed and feted. Every individual feels personally responsible for the result.

Our pay scales are measured by objective job analysis and careful performance rating. Our hours are the best, our working conditions as good as any, and there is a constant effort to be humane in all matters.

We have had interesting conversations with the group acting as the Board of Governors of the "Employees' Club" over the years, and we have met every reasonable request they have made. Biweekly pay was one of the requests which we adopted costing us about 8% more in salary, smoking in work areas which we permitted, music in work areas which we maintain. We are always willing to listen to our people. If they want something that will help them in their work and in their happiness here we will go far to supply it.

Ours is not a perfect shop, and I may be lulled into thinking it is happier than I suggest, but of one thing I am sure, while most of our officers have had collegiate experiences, there isn't one who came into the world with a gold spoon in his mouth, and that may account for their interest in people and their problems.

I have a great feeling of intimacy with our employees. I write dozens of longhand letters to those who do me and this company favors, and I write a specially dictated letter to each person on his reaching a fifth, tenth, etc., anniversary.

We make a good deal of a Christmas Party that is really a family affair. There is no drinking in connection with it, though we are not opposed to drinking as such. We bring in the families and children of all people who wish to come. It is a very successful affair.

Similarly we take an interest in our retired people and annually give them the finest dinner and entertainment in the best place available. We encourage them to visit the office and to attend the functions held by active employees.

If our people should become upset about anything I am prepared to say it would be my fault, because there is nothing reasonable they could urge that we could afford to do, that we aren't doing, or be willing to do. If we could not do it my experience with them has been that we could spell out the reasons convincingly and acceptably.

We take good care of our older people and pay an extra service allowance for length of service which is quite considerable in the case of the older and in some cases, less productive people. We have meetings in which the dignity of the individual is advanced with deliberate care.

Morale cannot be won in a day or purchased at any price. It takes a long time to develop good morale and it takes constant planning to preserve it. On the other hand, I could lose it all in one day's misbehavior. All I would need to do would be to walk through a work area and complain about the posture of a couple of people and ask whether it was necessary to burn as many lights. It would help to turn on lights but it would never do to turn one off.

The important thing is that the work be congenial; and if that is not so, liberal rules and wage scales become of less importance. Care must be taken in the employment of people and more care in the treatment of them later. We try to take that care and that I think is why we apparently do so well in our company.

1. Evaluate the effectiveness of this company's program.
2. How are the various forms of motivation, which were discussed in Chapter 6, utilized in this company?

PROBLEM TWO

The Tool Crib Attendant Who Reads

Bill Smith works as a tool-crib attendant at the Acme Company. A tool-crib attendant has a fairly responsible job: He has to keep tabs on who gets what tools, keep the tools in order, make minor repairs, and order new tools when the stock runs low. At the beginning and end of each shift there is a lot of work to do, but most of the time the men have relatively little to do, especially on the night shift. Nevertheless it is one of the highest-paid nonskilled jobs in the plant. (To work up to a skilled job, a man has to start as an apprentice in his twenties.)

Until last year Bill held an important union office and used his free time and the strategic location of the tool crib for political purposes. Last year he was defeated; those who opposed him felt his aggressive attitude toward the company was merely provoking trouble.

Shortly thereafter Bill was caught by his foreman reading a newspaper on the job. The following exchange took place:

Foreman: You're supposed to be working now. We're not paying you for reading.

Bill: I'm doing my job. I've got nothing to do now. How does it hurt you if I read?

Foreman: If I let you read, then the men on production will want the same privilege. If I stop them, they will say I'm discriminating against them. You pushed a grievance case just like that yourself. In fact, since I'm dealing with a legal eagle like you, I'll give you a written warning just to cover myself 100 per cent.

Bill: Why do I get the warning? I'm not the only one who's been reading papers. You're picking on me just because I made you eat a lot of dirt when I was a union official.

Foreman: No, I'm warning you because you're the first man I caught. I'll warn everyone else I catch too.

Bill: You can't give me a warning. There's nothing in the plant regulation about reading newspapers. We've never received any notice and you're punishing me for a rule you've just set up. That's poor personnel policy.

Foreman: OK, I'll post a written order too—and this warning is just to make double sure you know about it.

Bill: OK, I'm filing a grievance. By posting the notice you're admitting this is a new order. I don't want any warning in my file that you can hang over my neck from now till doomsday.

Bill filed his grievance, but his steward, who was a political opponent, never "found time" to push it. Shortly afterward, Bill's wife got a job as a night telephone operator on the 11:30 P.M.-7:30 A.M. shift. Bill's own shift ran from 8:00 A.M. to 4:00 P.M. Bill's plan was to pick his wife up after she finished work, then drive down to the Acme Company, where he would turn the car over to her and go to work himself.

Acme and the phone company were on opposite sides of town and Bill began to come in late for work. After this occurred several times, his foreman gave him a written warning that if he came late again, he would be fired. From then on, whenever he saw he couldn't get to the plant by the starting whistle, he went home, reported sick, and took the rest of the day off. Technically, management could have required a doctor's certificate from him, but this was never requested unless a man had been out of work for several days.

Finally, the situation got to be too much for Bill and he requested a transfer to the midnight shift in accordance with the seniority provisions of the union contract. The foreman turned him down on the grounds he did not possess sufficient "fitness and ability" to work the night shift since there was provision for only one tool attendant on the night shift and Bill's poor tardiness, absentee, and newspaper-reading record would mean that the company would often be caught short.

Bill did not explain the real reason for his absenteeism, fearing that it might bring him punishment. Instead, he caught the plant manager at the plant gate and said to him:

Bill: Mr. Struthers, I just asked my foreman to give me a transfer to the "mid" shift and he turned me down. I got the seniority, but he said I couldn't make the move because I've been absent too much. That's true: My wife's been sick once in a while and I've had to stay home to take care of the kids. If I can work the night shift, my sister can take over when my wife's not feeling good.

Mr. Struthers: OK, Bill, I'll see what I can do.

Next day Struthers had the following phone conversation with the foreman:

Mr. Struthers: Is it true you turned down Bill's transfer application because of his absentee record?

Foreman: Yes I did. I don't think he can be trusted on the job.

Mr. Struthers: Well, I'm willing to take the chance.

The following day Struthers told Bill his transfer would go through shortly. Meanwhile the day-shift foreman told the night-shift foreman, "You're going to get a guy named Smith who will give you a pack of trouble. Watch him like a hawk."

Six o'clock the first morning of Bill's new shift, the foreman dropped in on him, sure that Bill would be asleep. Instead Bill had spent the whole evening washing down the walls and building a new cabinet for his equipment. Since that time the foreman has checked on him only at infrequent intervals. Bill is fairly satisfied with the new work:

> "Of course, it is just as boring as can be. I had out about ten tools a night. I've repainted and completely straightened out the crib, but you can't do that forever. I can't read my paper in the spare time, so lots of times I go to sleep, often for six hours. I have an arrangement with the fellows in the shop that if anybody from management comes they'll make some noise and wake me up."

1. Was management wise in instituting the no-newspaper-reading rule? List the arguments that could be presented *for* and *against* this course of action. (Assume management may not increase Bill's job duties.)
2. What was wrong with the way the order was issued? What would you have done?
3. Suppose you were night-shift foreman and word came to you through the "grapevine" that Bill was sleeping on the job. Would you have done anything? What? Why?
4. Go through the rest of the case and point out other mistakes made at different levels of management.

PROBLEM THREE

Filling a Vacancy for Foreman

Management has been having a great deal of trouble in the cone-making department in the Ashford Plant. Cone-making used to be done entirely by hand and required considerable skill. Today much of the skilled work is handled by machinery, but the cone-makers still put in a good deal of physical effort in feeding the machines, and the work process involves heat and fumes. The department is isolated from the rest of the plant in an older, rather dilapidated building.

For years management has pretty much let the cone-makers have their own way, though, on occasion, the men have gone on slow-downs or wildcat strikes over petty grievances. Their foreman, Mike Malone, has looked upon his job chiefly as that of protecting his men from management pressure. In recent years, productivity has tended to fall and costs in this department are considerably higher than in comparable departments in other plants. In part because of anticipated employee resistance, management has been reluctant to install new production methods and it is giving some thought to shutting down the department eventually. Malone is ready to retire and management must find a successor. Among the possibilities are:

a. *John Callahan,* age 50, who has been with the department for 33 years. He knows cone-making backwards and forwards, is well liked by the men, and has been union steward for years.

b. *Gus Nowak,* college graduate, age 32, who has done an outstanding job in cutting costs as foreman of the assembly department, a department of low-skilled workers which includes many women and has always had considerable turnover.

1. Is this a cohesive group?
2. Why might it resist change?
3. What are the relative strong and weak points of each candidate for foreman? Which one would you select?
4. Assuming Nowak is selected, what advice would you give him?
5. Assuming Callahan is selected, how should the plant manager try to handle him?

PROBLEM FOUR

The Safety Guard

While walking through your department, you notice that one of the operators a couple of aisles over seems to be working with the safety guard up. However, as he catches your eye, he fumbles with a piece of stock and knocks the safety guard into place—at least that is how it looks to you. This is a serious offense. When an employee commits this violation (often in order to speed up his operation and make it a little easier), the usual penalty is a three-day layoff. Several people have been seriously injured by failure to use the safety guard.

1. How would you approach the employee?
2. What would you say?
3. What would your objectives be in your discussion with him?

PROBLEM FIVE

The Poor Work of Jane Smith

Jane Smith has been a slightly better-than-average employee, though not an outstanding worker. Recently, the quality of her work has been declining, for no apparent reason. You have just checked some of the parts she has been working on and decide that nearly half of them are unsatisfactory. This is about the worst performance you have ever spotted.

1. How would you approach Jane?
2. What would you say first?
3. Should you first compliment her on her work?

PROBLEM SIX

A Close Haircut

"Our work load in stock control has increased enormously in the past few months. I liked the job and even started taking work home, just one or two nights a week at first, but even more later on so that we wouldn't fall behind. I knew the boss was anxious to make an outstanding record and I was anxious to show him that I could hold up my own end.

"Then one day I extended my lunch hour to get a haircut. Probably no one would have noticed it, but the barber gave me a real close cut. When my boss came by my desk later on he bawled me out for taking company time for personal business, asking me what I thought I was paid for. He pointed to the company policy book which said that employees were forbidden to take time off during work hours. I started to tell him how much time I had been putting in extra, on my own, but he cut me short, saying that he was referring to company time."

1. What did the boss do wrong here?
2. How is the subordinate likely to react?
3. In view of the company policy, what would you have done if you were the boss in this case?

PROBLEM SEVEN

Inflammable Material

Through the years your company has had a no-smoking rule that has been largely ignored. Recently some of your departments have begun working with rather inflammable material, though there is still almost no fire danger in most of the departments. You are plant manager.

1. Describe the steps you would take to handle the danger of fire and yet maintain sound human relations.
2. Why would you take these steps rather than others?

PROBLEM EIGHT

Hospital Orderlies

Hospital orderlies are often homeless older men who accept hospital work in spite of its low pay because it offers them free room and board. Their duties normally include various sorts of dirty work, such as moving beds and carrying stretchers—work that is too hard for women.

A. In some hospitals each orderly is assigned to a ward or group of wards where he works under the direction of the head nurse and does any work that the nurses, student nurses, practical nurses, and nurses' aides on the floor request. When he is through with one assignment, he waits around for another.

B. In other hospitals all orderlies work out of a central orderly room. When a head nurse wants an orderly for a specific job, she calls the head orderly, who dispatches men as needed. When an orderly finishes his assigned task, he reports back to the orderly room.

1. What special human-relations problems would you find in situation A which you wouldn't find in situation B and vice versa?
2. Compare the two situations in terms of the special skills required by the head nurses to deal with orderlies.

PROBLEM NINE

Time to Sleep

The Merrimac Corporation sells, rents, and services electronic data-processing equipment and employs a large staff of servicemen to keep its customers' equipment in order. The 30 servicemen who work out of the St. Louis district office (which covers most of the Midwest) all live in the St. Louis area and are often required to travel to customers in distant locations; usually they travel by air. A given trouble call may take several hours or even days of work.

A problem has arisen from the fact that, when an assignment is completed, the men fly back to St. Louis and often arrive home late in the evening or even after midnight. Under these circumstances management has always allowed the servicemen to take a few hours extra sleep and not report to the office the first thing in the morning. Recently there have been signs that the men have begun to abuse this privilege. A few men have developed the habit of taking the entire morning off after every out-of-town trip, even if they arrive back at their home by 5:00 the previous evening. And other employees are beginning to wonder whether they might do the same.

Management has considered imposing a hard-and-fast rule that all servicemen must report for work at 9:00 A.M. regardless of what time they got in the night before. But in some cases this would impose an obvious hardship, and it might encourage the servicemen to spread their work out so that instead of finishing their job in the afternoon and returning home late they would slow down and work through the next morning, returning home in the afternoon.

Above all, management is anxious not to disturb the employees' high morale and interest in their work. These servicemen are paid a salary, receive liberal fringe benefits, being treated almost like members of the management.

Advise management on how to handle this problem.

PART THREE

MANAGERIAL SKILLS

In this section we shall look more closely at some of the skills that the effective manager must possess. Obviously, before a manager can supervise his subordinates he must be able to communicate with them. Yet communication is not a simple matter. The words uttered by the sender of a message may have a different meaning for him than for the man who receives them. Particularly when subordinates are insecure, hostile, or suspicious of their superiors, they may ascribe unintended meanings to messages from above. To prevent misunderstanding, the senders of messages, at all levels of the management hierarchy, must be careful to fashion them so that their meaning is clear to the receiver. This is the problem we shall discuss in Chapter 10, "Communications."

Effective communication is a two-way process. The good manager must also be a good listener. Interviewing, which is merely deliberate listening, is an essential skill if the manager is to get to know his subordinates. In addition, merely by listening the manager may help subordinates solve their own problems or at least induce them to become more receptive to what he has to say (Chapter 11, "Interviewing: The Fine Art of Listening").

Because the manager must deal with groups as well as individuals, committee meetings and informal conferences are becoming increasingly important as a means of communication in industry. As we shall see, the skills of conference leadership are closely akin to the skills of interviewing (Chapter 12, "Conference Leadership").

Chapter 13, "Introducing Change," considers a problem that is directly influenced by the quality of communications within the organization. As we shall see, it is the meaning that is communicated by a proposed change that most often leads to resistance. Effective use of communications, interviewing, and conference leadership—as well as of some of the managerial skills discussed earlier—helps insure that change will be readily accepted.

What happens when change is rejected? When subordinates refuse to obey new rules—or, for that matter, old rules too? Then discipline is required (Chapter 14,

"Discipline"). In a way, discipline is also a form of communication: The message management is trying to transmit is that it really intends to enforce certain rules. To make discipline accepted and meaningful, the rule and its penalty must be carefully communicated, and the offender must be made to understand that the reason for his being disciplined is the fact he broke the rule, not personal animus on the part of the manager.

Considered together, these are some of the skills that an effective manager uses in implementing the philosophy which we discussed in the preceding section of this book.

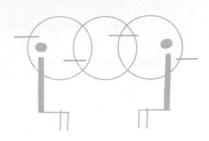

Communications

10

"But I didn't think you meant I was to inspect *every* unit."
"How did I know he was serious about quitting?"
"Our employees are always misinterpreting what we say...."
"You can't trust management to tell the truth."

There is hardly an aspect of management's job that does not involve communications. Serious mistakes are made because orders are misunderstood. Casual kidding leads to anger. An off-hand remark by the big boss leads the plant manager to adopt a get-tough attitude with the union. All spring from a breakdown in communications.

.In this chapter we shall be concerned largely with face-to-face communications between individuals. In Chapter 15 we shall look at communications in terms of the over-all organization.

On the surface, face-to-face communications would seem to be simple. Have you ever listened to two old friends talking together? Rarely do they use complete sentences; often a single word, a grunt or a groan, or a raised eyebrow communicates as much meaning as lengthy speeches would convey between casual acquaintances. A few syllables go a long way.

But successful communication does not necessarily take place automatically whenever two people get together. Let's examine a situation more typical of business life. The shop-clerk tells his boss with pride, "This is the heaviest day we've ever had." But the boss thinks the clerk is lazy and looking for an excuse not to unload new stock. So he answers angrily and the subordinate concludes that the boss is an overbearing, ungrateful so-and-so.

The basic problem in communications is that the meaning which is actually received by one person may not be what the other intended to send. The speaker and the listener are two separate individuals living in different worlds; any number of things can happen to distort the messages that pass between them.

The human sensory apparatus does not transmit an exact duplicate of reality from the outside world into the mind of the observer. Our needs and experiences tend to color what we see and hear. Messages we don't want to accept are repressed. Others are magnified. Still others are created out of thin air (for example, the "faults" in a person we dislike) or are hideously distorted from their original reality.[1]

What are the causes of breakdowns in communications? What can be done to overcome them? We shall consider each of these questions in turn.

Why Communications Break Down

HEARING WHAT WE EXPECT TO HEAR

What we hear or understand when someone speaks to us is largely shaped by our own experience and background. Instead of hearing what people tell us, we hear what our minds tell us they have said. These may be the same things—or very different. We all tend to have preconceived ideas of what people mean; when we hear something new we tend to identify it with something similar that we have experienced in the past.

> The manager tells an employee that the company has lost some important orders. Now this employee has had other jobs, and whenever a company has lost business he has been thrown out of work. So he "hears" the manager's statement as, "You can expect to be laid off in the near future." When the man announces that he has quit to work elsewhere, the supervisor may be surprised to learn that the man thought his job was in danger.

Psychologists have said that individuals are motivated to obtain information which is consistent with their conception of themselves.

An extreme form of letting expectations determine communication content

---

[1] Our discussion is greatly influenced by Alfred Korzybski, *Science and Sanity* (Lancaster, Pa.: Science Press, 1933).

is *stereotyping*. For example, we may expect athletically inclined, big-muscled people to be rather dull, and when they say something we say to ourselves, "Well there is another typical remark made by someone who is all brawn and no brain." We grow up believing that Rarutanians (or some other group) are shiftless and lazy. Bill Jones is a Rarutanian. When Jones comes up with an intelligent short cut on his job which took a great deal of time and energy to develop, we take it as proof that "he's always looking for a chance to loaf, just like all the rest of them." Though ridiculous, such stereotypes are stubbornly preserved even in the face of conflicting evidence.

Although this is short-cut thinking, "one of the most time-consuming pastimes of the human mind is to rationalize sentiments and to disguise them as logic."[2]

IGNORING INFORMATION THAT CONFLICTS *(Cognitive dissonance)* WITH WHAT WE ALREADY "KNOW"

Most of us resist change. We tend to reject new ideas, particularly if they conflict with what we already believe. In some ways our communications-receiving apparatus (sense organs and brain) works like an efficient filter. When we read a paper or listen to a political speech, we tend to note only those things that confirm our present beliefs. We may even comment that it is "good to get that additional information." On the other hand, we tend to ignore anything that conflicts with our beliefs; sometimes our filters work so efficiently we don't hear it at all. And even if we do hear it, we either reject it as a fallacious notion or find some way of twisting and shaping its meaning to fit our preconceptions. Because we hear and see what we *expect* to hear and see, we are rarely disappointed.

Communications sometimes fail to have the desired effect because they run counter to other information that the receiver possesses. Management may insist that the company must reduce costs if it is to survive. Everyone is urged to work harder and cut expenses to the bone. But some of the employees shrug off the announcement, for they know that salesmen still receive lavish allowances for "entertainment expenses." These expenses may be justified as a means of obtaining orders, but this is something the employees are in no position to appreciate. The same reaction would set in if they saw wasteful methods of manufacture countenanced week after week without being corrected.

Similarly, statements that hard work leads to promotion are likely to be ignored in a company where promotions in fact often are made on the basis of seniority or favoritism. A guarantee that "the company never cuts an incentive rate because employees are earning too much" is disregarded if rates have in fact been cut as a result of minor engineering changes. Even if the company

---

[2] Fritz Roethlisberger and William Dickson, *Management and the Worker* (Cambridge, Mass.: Harvard University Press, 1939), p. 88.

is perfectly justified in retiming a job after the method or product has been changed, the employee may be convinced that this is simply an excuse for cutting the rate.

> The story has been told that, while the U.S. was able to break the Japanese top-secret code before Pearl Harbor and thus had information concerning the projected attack, this data was ignored because it did not fit into the working hypotheses of some key government officials. The record of World War I is filled with similar examples of information being ignored that was inconsistent with plans and policies that had been drawn up by the French and German General Staffs.[3]

EVALUATING THE SOURCE

"The first time I met Bill Smith he tried to impress me that he was a big shot. Ever since, I have discounted everything he says because I know what kind of blowhard he is."

Not only does the receiver evaluate what he hears in terms of his own background and experience, he also takes the sender into account. How reliable is he as a source of information? Does he have an axe to grind?

Often the receiver ascribes nonexistent motives to the sender. This is particularly true in labor-management relations. Many union members, convinced that management is trying to weaken the union, interpret every company statement as an attempt to deceive them. Similarly, management often regards every union grievance as a political maneuver designed only to win votes. Both sides are sometimes right, of course. But this mental set makes mutual understanding and agreement more difficult.

One experimenter clipped a cartoon from a union publication illustrating "The Four Goals of Labor" and pasted it up with a caption indicating that it had come from a publication of the National Association of Manufacturers. When the clipping was shown to union members, they were overwhelmingly critical of it as an unfair, biased representation of labor's goals. Having accepted the source as antilabor, they automatically drew the "obvious" conclusions.[4]

This sort of bias is one of the reasons why company newspapers (so-called "house organs") find it difficult to gain worker acceptance. Once employees become convinced that the paper is just a management mouthpiece, many will believe nothing it prints, no matter how objective or verifiable. So, too, with pamphlets and other give-aways. If these are tagged as propaganda, all the information they contain becomes suspect, even useful information about health and household safety.

Similarly it is hard for a manager to shed a reputation for being hardboiled or unfair. Suppose he goes through a training program and emerges with every intention of turning over a new leaf. Subordinates may well be extremely

---

[3] Barbara Tuchman, *The Guns of August* (New York: Macmillan, 1962).

[4] William H. Whyte, Jr., *Is Anybody Listening?* (New York: Simon and Schuster, 1952), p. 223.

suspicious of his motives and assume that his new approach is just a trick. If so they will distort and misconstrue every move he makes. He is now unpredictable.

A manager who receives a suggestion from a colleague or subordinate may assume one of two things: (1) Here is an alert, intelligent employee who is anxious to make a contribution to the efficiency of the organization, or (2) here is somebody who is trying to show me up by suggesting something he figures I was too foolish to think of myself. And which of the two motivations he attributes to the subordinate will have a substantial effect on what he actually "sees" in the suggestion.

In short, it is extremely difficult for us to separate what we hear from our feelings about the person who says it.

HALO EFFECT

One aspect of stereotyping and evaluating the source is the tendency to ignore the "greys" and to react in "black or white" terms. Thus, when someone is speaking who has gained our trust or who begins a speech by saying something with which we agree, we will hear nearly everything he says as good and correct. On the other hand, someone we distrust will be ignored or heard to say nothing worth attending to. The failure to make appropriate discriminations between the "good" and "bad" that may be intermixed within a single person and his comments is often called the "halo effect."

DIFFERENT PERCEPTIONS

People interpret the same stimulus in different ways, depending on their previous experience. Take the case of a supervisor who is watching a group of employees laughing.

1. To the manager who believes that work must be painful in order to be productive, the laughter communicates to him that time is being wasted, and perhaps assignments are too easy.
2. To the manager who believes that contented employees work harder, the laughter communicates that he is succeeding as a manager.
3. To the manager who is personally insecure, the laughter communicates that the men are ridiculing him.

Clearly, the group with which we identify ourselves—the "reference group," as psychologists call it—tends to build in a bias. As advertisers discovered long ago, an individual rarely changes his mind by himself. His attitudes toward politics, music, recreation, work pace, and all his other activities and interests are largely colored by the group with which he identifies. As we mentioned in Chapter 9, the supervisor is wasting his time trying to convince an individual employee to work harder when there is a strong group standard to the contrary. The employee would be risking ostracism if he went along with the supervisor's request. Management often uses slogans and posters to indoctrinate workers with the ideas of promoting safety, cutting scrap losses, making suggestions, or engaging in good housekeeping. They even send personal letters to employees' homes. The trouble with these efforts is that they are directed to the *individual,* whereas the basic attitudes and convictions are determined by the *group.* Thus, if an employee's fellow workers see the supervisor as harsh and unfair, chances are he will feel the same way.

Even the categories of thought used by different groups may be widely divergent. It may well be that trying to convince an hourly employee to improve his *industriousness* will be less effective than trying to convince him to improve his *skill.* Employees can distinguish differences in skill but can't always distinguish differences in industriousness.[5]

In a large organization, the difficulties of perception are compounded. An announcement may go to dozens of groups with different occupational and status interests. What each group "hears" depends on its own interests. An announcement that the company has purchased the plans for new products that will be manufactured in a new plant on the West Coast may be heard in these different ways:

> *Design engineer:* "This may be an indication that the company prefers to go outside the organization for new ideas, and that is bound to hurt our status."
> *Production engineer:* "This new product will mean more work for us. Some of us may have a chance to move out West."
> *Worker:* "The new products aren't going to be manufactured in the home plant. That means if business should get slack, we're likely to get laid off. A bad trend."

Or take this example.

> The head of marketing has recently spent a great deal of time convincing the company president that they are losing business because competitors' prices are lower. Thus, when the president requests new cost-saving efforts, the marketing manager hears the news as a significant policy statement. On the other hand, the production manager, who does not contact customers, "hears" this as another platitude.[6]

This is one of the most serious sources of friction in industry. With all the sincerity in the world, we try to frame a message that will break the communications barrier and carry an appropriate meaning to those to whom it is directed. But in many instances we know too little about their point of view, and our efforts miscarry.

The trouble may be simply that a subordinate doesn't understand what sort of information his boss wants him to supply. Consequently, the subordinate

---

[5] Harry Triandis, "Categories of Thought of Managers, Clerks and Workers about Jobs and People in Industry," *Journal of Applied Psychology,* Vol. 43, No. 5 (1959), pp. 338-344.

[6] For more cases of how organizational location and prior experience determines perception see Margaret Chandler, *Management Rights and Union Interests* (New York: McGraw-Hill, 1964), p. 298.

has no way of knowing what he should tell his boss, or when or where he should speak. Inevitably, the boss complains that vital facts have been kept from him or that he is being deluged with useless information.

The reverse situation is just as troublesome. In training a subordinate, a superior often tries to communicate information before the subordinate is ready to understand it.

In conclusion, it is very difficult to understand information that is outside our experience, no matter how simply and clearly the information is presented by the sender.

WORDS MEAN DIFFERENT THINGS
TO DIFFERENT PEOPLE

This is the so-called "semantic" problem. Essentially, language is a method of using symbols to represent facts and feelings. Strictly speaking we can't convey *meaning;* all we can do is convey *words.* And yet the same words may suggest quite different meanings for different people. The meanings are in the people, not in words.

When management says that profits are essential if the business is to survive, it is thinking of profits as a means by which the company can buy new equipment, expand, and provide more jobs. To management, profits mean a successfully operated, growing enterprise. But to employees, the word profit sometimes suggests a picture of excess funds piled up through paying inadequate wages. No matter how often management explains the need for profits, employees may persist in attaching the meaning of "excess," "unearned," or "unfair" to the term. Any attempt to communicate about profits must surmount the barrier of established meanings attached to the word.

We find this problem arising in the "economic education" programs conducted by many companies. These programs try to give workers an understanding of how profits and productivity are related to job security and high wages, and an awareness of the advantages of our economic system over others. It has been estimated that companies are investing $100,000,000 each year in such attempts.[7]

Here again the difficulty is that the management which sponsors these programs and the employees for whom they are produced live in different worlds. Abstractions like "profits," "capital," and "productivity" have real meaning in the world of management, but they may have little meaning to the employee (or very negative associations).

In addition, the "psychological distance" that separates the rank-and-file worker from top management impedes understanding. They have little experience in dealing directly with one another. When they do interact, the contact tends to be highly restrained, formal, and artificial—unsuited to real communication.

---

[7] Whyte, *op. cit.,* p. 7.

This problem is especially acute with abstract terms. But even simple concrete words and phrases often lead to trouble; again because the sender and receiver live in separate worlds. For instance:

> The foreman spots oil on the floor and tells a machinist, "Get that oil wiped up as soon as you can; it's a real safety hazard." The machinist nods that he will. Ten minutes later an inspector slips on the very same spot.
>
> The supervisor is enraged by this needless accident. When he prepares to penalize the machinist for failing to follow instructions, he is told, "But I was going to do it *as soon as I could,* as you told me. I thought you could see that I was working on a delicate cut, and I had to finish that first."

To the supervisor "as soon as you can" meant immediately; to the operator it meant as soon as it could be done without endangering his work. It is foolish to try to decide who was right. Here we see the fallacy of the simple "tell them what you want them to do" approach. Simply telling people isn't enough when the sender and the receiver give the words different meanings. Confusion arises even when words are selected with great care.

Symbols. For some people, a particular word or phrase may have a symbolic meaning that others overlook. When we use words of this sort, we may find ourselves communicating things we had no intention of saying.

> When the manager tells a new supervisor that the parking lot is too crowded for him to have a parking sticker, something more is being communicated than simple information on parking conditions. What the new supervisor hears may be this, "You are not accepted as a member of management, and everyone will soon know it."

The manager's reference to parking stickers carried far more meaning than he had intended.

Observers of collective bargaining have noted that violent antagonism develops in discussions about "management prerogatives" or the "union shop." Again, these are terms that have great symbolic significance. While the manager is talking about prerogatives to the union, he is really trying to say that the very basis of the managerial function and perhaps of the free-enterprise system is involved. Similarly, the union leader arguing for the union shop feels that acceptance or rejection symbolizes the real place of the union in the plant —is it a permanent, accepted institution or merely a temporary nuisance that is being tolerated? Compromise on such issues is difficult, for both parties feel that their vital interests are at stake.

ARGOT

Occupational groups and sometimes social groups tend to develop their own special language, called "argot." Sometimes group members forget this when they are talking to an outsider who doesn't share these "insider" meanings.

The new supervisor was dismayed when a subordinate told him that a customer's shipping request had been "pickled in oil." The men used this term to mean giving an order extra-special treatment.

Although argot simplifies in-group communication and provides a sense of belonging and sometimes status to those who use it, there may be other motivations involved in its use. Individuals may seek to impress people with their complex technical knowledge—for example, by talking about "I/O" (input-output) equipment instead of computer printers. In a sense, they use words that will communicate something about themselves by not communicating about the subject under discussion!

Similar to argot is the use of special techniques of speaking and acting that only insiders understand. For example, Americans often tease each other, feigning extreme criticism when it is not meant seriously. Someone not used to this joking style might take seriously, with disastrous results, a comment like this maintenance supervisor's (to one of his mechanics): "That certainly is the crummiest piece of work that ever took a man so many wasted hours to get done!" Overseas, such joking is often not appreciated.

Of course, teasing and joking perform another function in communication that is often forgotten. Many people learn to impart in this fashion delicate or sensitive information that would be unacceptable (or cause an antagonistic reaction) if it were said straightforwardly.

NONVERBAL COMMUNICATION

In trying to understand what another person is trying to say to us (and thus to predict their future behavior) we use many *cues* beside language. Looking at the eyes, the shape of the mouth, the muscles of the face, even bodily posture may tell us more about what the other person really thinks than the words he uses. The reverse is that we ourselves often communicate things unintentionally. Arriving at the office angry because of a traffic jam, a disgruntled manager may be "telling" his subordinates by his general appearance that he is dissatisfied with their work, although that was never intended.

Styles of dress, tone of voice, even our manner of speaking often communicate a good deal about us. The noncollege-trained employee may have a difficult time adjusting to a company in which most employees have degrees because he always seems "different." He must learn a number of subtle bits of behavior that are assimilated during college and that communicate to others that one is sophisticated, or well educated, or reasonably high in status. It is not easy to learn all these hidden cues, which communicate even more than what we think we are saying.

EFFECTS OF EMOTIONS

When we are insecure, worried, or fearful, what we hear and see seems more threatening than when we are secure and at peace with the world. Rumors of all sorts spring up when management makes a change of any kind without adequate explanation, even a change as simple as moving desks around the office. This is particularly true during an economic recession. Then statements and actions that under less trying circumstances would have passed unnoticed become grounds for fear. "Yes, Joe might be right, they are going to double the work load." "I saw the foreman looking at the seniority list; I guess the rumors are right, a lot of men will be laid off because of the new equipment."

By the same token, when we are angry or depressed, we tend to reject out of hand what might otherwise seem like reasonable requests or good ideas. Our gloom and despair color everything we do and see. Similarly, when elated, we may not "hear" problems or criticisms.

NOISE

Living in a world of words and being deluged by sounds all the time, individuals learn to "tune out" many things. While a mother usually hears her child crying, the father often sleeps through, although he would hear his wife call. Many things a manager says are ignored, actually never heard, because they sound so much like what he always says: "Work efficiently," "This order is very important," "Save materials," "The company is depending on us." Thus, before individuals can hear a message, they must learn to discriminate between background noise (that is, what is always being said) and what is significant new information.

SUMMARY

Barriers to communications among members of an organization cause breakdowns, distortions, and inaccurate rumors. They plague the daily life of the' manager who must depend on accurate transmission of orders and information for efficient operation. The implication is clear: Don't assume that every message that you send will be received in the form you intended it to be.

Overcoming Barriers to Communication

Up to this point we have purposely presented a discouraging, one-sided picture: pervasive problems and no solutions. But the picture need not be this bleak. We now know many techniques for improving communications, even though—it should be emphasized—none is a cure-all. Perfect understanding between people is impossible.

Among other things, good communications requires solving simultaneously two quite different problems. The manager must learn to improve his *transmission*—what words, ideas and feelings he actually sends to the other person. At the same time he must cope with his own *reception*—what he perceives the other person's reactions and statements to be. We shall devote the rest of this chapter to a discussion of several methods by which a manager can maximize his success in communicating. At first glance, these techniques may appear mechanical substitutes for mutual trust and understanding. However, a wide variety of research confirms the efficacy of considering communications as a type of engineering problem—the problem of transmitting information from one point to another.

UTILIZING FEEDBACK

Perhaps the single most important method of improving communications is *feedback*. This term, adopted from engineering,[8] refers to the ability of certain complex machines (technically, systems) to check on their own performance and to correct it if necessary.

We all use this principle of feedback in our human communications—perhaps without realizing it. Even in casual conversations we are constantly on the alert for cues to whether we are being understood (such as attentive nods from the other person). Similarly, a good teacher is always interested in audience reaction among his students. If they seem confused or drowsy, he knows his lecture isn't getting across. The good supervisor is equally conscious of the need to determine his subordinates' reactions to what he is trying to communicate.

An interesting study illustrates the importance of feedback. Two students were placed in different rooms and one was asked to communicate to the other the position of an interconnected series of dominoes placed on a grid. Both had identical grids in front of them. The sender was permitted to explain to the receiver, in any way he saw fit, the relative positions of the dominoes. Yet it was impossible to complete the task successfully when the receiver was forbidden to respond—that is, when communications were entirely one-way. No matter how painstakingly the sender explained the pattern, the receiver never understood all of it. Apparently some opportunity to ask for further information, at least to answer "yes" or "no" to the questions of the sender (e.g., Did you understand what I said?), is essential if complex information is to be communicated. Without feedback, false perceptions creep in, and even a small error that goes uncorrected may become magnified into a major distortion.

This experiment also revealed that communications gain in speed and efficiency as more and more feedback is permitted. Limiting the receiver to "yes" or "no" responses is less effective than allowing him to expand his comments to whatever he deems appropriate.

---

[8] For sophisticated analyses of how principles of electronic communications may be applied to human communications, see Norbert Wiener, *Cybernetics* (Cambridge, Mass.: Technology Press, 1954); Colin Cherry, *On Human Communication* (New York: Wiley, 1957); Claude E. Shannon and Warren Weaver, *The Mathematical Theory of Communications* (Urbana: University of Illinois Press, 1949).

USING MANY COMMUNICATION CHANNELS

How do we know if the person to whom we are communicating understands, agrees, or sympathizes with us, or is indifferent, hostile, or confused? There are several techniques for maximizing feedback.

Observation. In a face-to-face situation, we can observe the other person and judge his responses by his total behavioral set. We can watch for nonverbal cues—the expressions of puzzlement, anger, or comprehension that flicker across the face of the listener, or the subtle body motions that reveal impatience, animosity, or agreement. These cues give eloquent expression to attitudes that the receiver may be reluctant or unable to express in words.

Indeed, by their posture and facial expression, the set of their lips, the movement of an eyebrow, people often tell us more than they do in hours of talk or scores of written memoranda. A subordinate is seldom eager to challenge the orders of his superior. But in the course of informal, face-to-face discussion, an alert supervisor can detect the subordinate's lack of enthusiasm by his tone of voice and his general physical behavior.

Few of us appreciate just how much valuable information these nonverbal cues transmit. As one social scientist has observed, "When communication is at peak efficiency, in the most intimately shared situations, words are often superfluous. Good examples of this are the hospital operating room, the jazz band, and some small interdependent work teams in industry." [9] The close coordination necessary for these groups to achieve their goal is attained exclusively through occasional nods and glances.

Listening with a "third ear." We must listen carefully if we are to discover what a person is trying to say. Though few of us can qualify as psychiatrists, we can learn to listen with a "third ear" by asking ourselves such questions as: "What did Joe really mean when he told me he was 'fed up'? Was it his assignment? His family? His chances for promotion? Me, as his boss? Why did he remain silent when I asked him for details?"

There is a hidden content in many communications that can only be inferred by the listener. (This underlying element is frequently referred to as the *latent* content as distinct from the *manifest* content.) Although the listener should keep his imagination in check, he should try to go beyond the logical verbal meaning where there is some evidence that emotional feeling is involved. Most communications are in fact a combination of fact and feeling.

A good example of this hidden content is provided by the word "communications" itself. An office manager complains to the personnel director that all his human-relations problems stem from "poor communications." If the personnel director wants to be of assistance, he will try to get behind the man-

---

[9] From a lecture by Dr. Robert N. Wilson, University of North Carolina.

ager's use of the word "communications." The manager might mean that there are divisive cliques that tend to distort his orders or that he, the boss, never hears the "real truth" about what is going on in the office. He might be using the word communications to mean that cooperative teamwork is lacking, or to mean many other things. The point is that the words used by a speaker may not be very informative until we have an opportunity to question him on what he really means in terms of actual observable behavior. The listener must try to get back to the *referents* of the speaker and to avoid the easy assumption that both people are attaching the same meaning to abstract words.

Adjusting rate of speaking. To facilitate communications it is important to become aware of differences in speaking patterns. Some people, for example, speak with long-drawn-out pauses between thoughts or sentences. If such speakers are interrupted by someone who becomes impatient sitting passively so long, they will often fail to reveal all of their original ideas. Also, interruptions can cause anger, which impedes communication, as already noted.

In conversation, a listener's attention is often lost by a speaker who insists on talking too long a time without allowing the other person to respond. Many individuals have such verbal energies that the words come out like a torrential downpour, and, in the process, they lose their audience. On the other hand, the natural style of speaking for some people is in short bursts. These people are only comfortable and able to say all that they want to if the other individual replies each time they stop.

Failure to adjust, to synchronize, to the speaking patterns of the other person causes breakdowns in communications because of lost ideas as well as the discomfort and emotional reactions associated with interruptions or long silent periods.[10]

USING FACE-TO-FACE COMMUNICATIONS

Face-to-face communications are superior, under most circumstances, to written orders, printed announcements, or business letters. Only when the sender is able to experience direct feedback from the receiver can he really know what the receiver is hearing and what he is failing to hear. How else can the sender become aware of the hidden meaning—the symbolic significance the receiver is ascribing to his words? How else can he bring out into the open contradictory information already in the receiver's mind that may cause him to reject or ignore the communication?

Another reason for the greater effectiveness of voice communications is that most of us communicate more easily, completely, and frequently by voice.

---

[10] A more precise explanation and description of how people differ in the physical pattern of their interaction is provided by the researcher who has done most of the studies in this field. *Cf.* Eliot Chapple and Leonard Sayles, *The Measure of Management* (New York: Macmillan, 1961) pp. 114-141.

Probably the greatest advantage of voice communications is that they provide immediate feedback. Merely by looking at the audience, the skillful speaker can judge how it is reacting to what he is saying. If necessary he can modify his approach or vary the intensity of his voice. (The human voice can provide a wider variety of emphasis and pace than any printed page, regardless of the number of type fonts used.)

Even better feedback is possible if the recipients of the message are allowed to comment or ask questions. This gives the supervisor an opportunity to explain his meaning or to consider unexpected problems. (Printed material can provide explanations, but few writers can anticipate all the questions that might be asked.)

For example, it is almost impossible to criticize someone's performance in writing without their taking serious offense. The cold type or words always sound more harsh and condemnatory than they may have been intended, and such written criticisms often provoke strong emotional counterreactions. The result is that the recipient tends to reject the entire message as having come from a hostile source. The same criticism discussed in a face-to-face exchange can be made much more acceptable and thus will be heard.

Furthermore, we usually ascribe more credibility to what we hear someone say than to words attributed to him in print. Employees conditioned to the "slick" releases of public relations offices tend to discount many of the printed announcements they read. Actually hearing the boss say that the company is in serious trouble, however, may carry a great deal more weight than would a statement in the house organ, particularly if employees have an opportunity to ask the boss direct questions.

A Secretary of State explained why he frequently left Washington:

> "Well, I fly because I go to meet heads of government, foreign ministers of other countries, and in a few minutes or at most a few hours of personal consultation you can achieve a much better understanding than you can possibly achieve by working through notes and writing to each other." [11]

Does all this mean that written messages have no place in the organization? Not at all. In fact, they are often indispensable. Lengthy, detailed instructions must be put in writing so that the person to whom they are addressed can have a chance to study them at leisure. The spoken word exists only for an instant, and then vanishes. The written message provides a permanent record to which the receiver can refer to make sure he understands what has been said, and to which the sender can refer as evidence that he has in fact said it. Frequently, too, the relative formality of written communications gives the message greater weight than it would have if it were delivered orally.

For very important messages, both the spoken and written word may be used in combination. For instance, if a new procedure is to be introduced,

---

[11] Dana Adams Schmidt, "Instant Diplomacy and the New Diplomats," *Columbia University Forum* (Fall 1958), p. 36.

the supervisor might call a meeting of his subordinates to give them a rough outline of the change. At this point he could (1) explain why the change is necessary, (2) answer their questions, and (3) perhaps make adjustments to meet objections. Once general agreement has been reached, the new procedure can be reduced to writing for future reference.

SENSITIVITY TO THE WORLD OF THE RECEIVER

It is extremely difficult to get through to a listener when what you are trying to communicate contradicts his expectations and predilections. If your typist has been in the habit of preparing only a single carbon, you must *stress* a request for two carbons. If being sent to the front office is regarded by employees as a sign of impending discipline, you must take pains to communicate that this is not the reason, if in fact it is not.

In short, you must be sensitive to the private world of the receiver, try to predict the impact of what you say and do on his feelings and attitudes, and tailor your messages to fit your receiver's vocabulary, interests, and values. Managers who work with a variety of groups in the organization must learn techniques of "simultaneous translation" to avoid misunderstandings. The greater the gap between your background and experience and that of the receiver, the greater the effort you must make to find some common ground of understanding. If the supervisor really wants to communicate with the sweeper, for example, he must find a way of (a) fitting his remarks to the sweeper's attitudes and beliefs, (b) making some appeal to the needs of the sweeper, and (c) constantly testing (via feedback) whether his message is being received.

The Detroit Edison Company has adopted an interesting approach. Its house organ features a "rumor clinic" in which top management deals candidly with questions raised by employees on such subjects as: alleged pay and vacation inequities, why some employees receive company-bought clothing and others do not, the quality and price of cafeteria food, and the reasons for layoffs or overtime. In answering questions submitted by workers, management has an opportunity to communicate information about the company's economic conditions, engineering and sales problems, and so on—and in terms of direct interest to employees.

Sensitivity training. Recognizing the crucial role of communications and the widespread incidence of misunderstanding, many organizations have sought to improve the ability of managers to *empathize*. Empathy is defined as the ability to put yourself in someone else's place and thus to understand better what they feel and are trying to say. One of the best ways of doing this is to learn the impact that your own way of speaking and behaving has on other people. Although associates, and certainly subordinates, are understandably timid about candidly revealing how they react to a manager's style of interaction, special training groups assess openly one another's interpersonal shortcomings. This procedure has been given a name, *sensitivity training*.[12] The objective is not only to minimize distracting and disturbing behavioral characteristics but to help managers see how individual differences affect communication. As the poet Robert Burns once said: "The giftee ... to see ourselves as others see us."

AWARENESS OF SYMBOLIC MEANING

As we have seen, symbols play a vital role in the "private world" of the listener. Here is a case in which effective communication was blocked until symbolic meanings were taken into account:

> To help in the preparation of market analyses the District Sales Manager asked the salesmen to compute correlation coefficients from their records. These coefficients could be calculated quite simply and painlessly by use of a simple formula. But the salesmen refused to do what they were asked. One excuse followed another: The computations were too complicated, it was clerk's work and not part of their job description, the coefficients were really useless, and so on. There seemed to be no way to convince the men to perform this simple task, and their persistent refusal seemed out of all proportion to the issue at hand.
>
> Why was this modest request greeted with such stubborn resistance? The very degree of the salesmen's reaction was the key to the problem. Investigation revealed that coefficient correlations had been tried three years earlier, when the department was headed by an inept supervisor who had earned the universal dislike of his subordinates. Among other things, he had tried to revamp all the departmental procedures and in the process had introduced this statistical technique. Ever since, the salesmen had associated the term "coefficient correlation" with autocratic supervision. To them it had become a symbol of oppressive management. Once the company had plumbed this seemingly irrational attitude, it was a simple matter to develop a different terminology for the operation, to conduct training in how the computations should be carried out, and to gain ready acceptance for the whole activity.

The moral of this story is clear: If there is extraordinary, unexpected resistance to a proposal, try to find out whether some symbolic meaning is associated with it.

TIMING MESSAGES CAREFULLY

We have already noted that our current beliefs often distort the meaning we ascribe to what we hear or see. There is an analogy here to the concept of "noise" as used by the communications engineer. The supervisor must recognize that when he is trying to tell his subordinate something, other things are being heard simultaneously that may distort his message.

One way of limiting the amount of noise or distortion is to communicate

---

[12] For an extensive treatment of this subject see Leland Bradford, Jack Gibb, Kenneth Benne (eds.), *T-Group Theory and Laboratory Method* (New York: Wiley, 1964).

your message before those other beliefs or attitudes come into play. Then the communication will meet less resistance and your chances of getting it accepted will be greatly increased.

> Management announced that Foreman Green would retire in a few months and would be replaced by a man named Williams from another department. One of the men felt that Williams had done him an injustice years ago, and spread the word among his fellow employees that Williams was a tyrant who played favorites.
>
> Long before Williams set foot in the new department, a petition was sent to top management requesting that a different foreman be assigned. And once Williams showed up, everything he said and did was fitted into the picture the employees had already established. Every job assignment he made was scrutinized for favoritism. Even harmless statements were often interpreted as threats.

A situation like this is an ideal breeding-ground for misunderstanding and unrest. Yet management could have minimized the problem by taking positive action before the picture of the new supervisor got established, perhaps by having the employees meet him as soon as the announcement was made.

In other words, a message is more likely to be understood when it is not competing with other, potentially conflicting messages. Of course, this was the basis for "brainwashing" during the Korean War. Some of our captured soldiers were isolated from their buddies and exposed to repeated anti-American stories. A more moderate application of the concept of minimizing *noise* would involve the isolation of a group of executives at a mountain-top conference center. Without the interference of normal communications they would be more likely to "hear" a major departure in corporate policy that was being announced.

It is worth remembering that people listen when they are motivated to hear. As many staff experts have discovered, fellow managers actually tend to hear the good ideas that the expert has only when the manager has a problem for which the idea might provide a solution. Training sessions similarly are most effective, for example, *after* an employee has been faced with the kind of problems which would cause him to recognize the need for additional training. Earlier "messages" may be ignored or not heard because they are competing with so many other stimuli reaching the individual.

REINFORCING WORDS WITH ACTION

Words by themselves are suspect. Employees are more likely to accept new propositions when they observe an actual change in behavior or participate themselves in the process of change. For example, supervisors in one company were told that they would have the final say in granting individual pay increases. This was a radical departure from past practice. Most of the supervisors were skeptical about whether management really meant what it said. But this feeling disappeared when they began filling out recommendation forms themselves and sending them to the Personnel Department (a minor clerical job that in the past had been done in the superintendent's office). The consistent reinforcement of verbal announcements by action increases the likelihood that the communication will be accepted.

Employees learn that their supervisor, not the Personnel Department, controls pay increases when they see him taking this action and hear directly from him that they are to receive the increase. Where Personnel does the notifying, they perceive otherwise.

Management must be careful not to allow supersalesmanship techniques to dominate its thinking in communicating to employees. Because employees are able to judge for themselves the quality of the relationship they enjoy with a company, sustained repetition of slick slogans will not be effective. One cannot advertise one type of personnel program and deliver another. In the same vein, low-pressure statements are probably more effective than high-pressure pronouncements. Instead of telling workers how generous their pension benefits are, it may be more effective to give them the facts (comparative data on pension plans for the industry or community) and let them draw their own conclusion. It is difficult if not impossible to communicate "values"; facts can be transmitted with some success, but even facts are subject to distortion.

Once management has acquired a reputation for accuracy and reliability in its communications, it can do a more effecive job of communicating information on new problems. The British learned this lesson during the war.

> Early in World War II, when the radio stations of most countries were widely suspected of distorting the war news, the British Broadcasting System adopted a policy of frankly reporting Allied setbacks. This gave the British an advantage in morale and tactics over their enemies when the tide turned in favor of the Allies, for Europeans of all nationalities were ready to believe the news of the German rout—simply because it came from a source that had proved itself trustworthy.

USING DIRECT, SIMPLE LANGUAGE

Written communications should be as intelligible and readable as possible. Rudolf Flesch, one of the foremost proponents of simple, clear, direct writing and speaking, urges that multisyllable and erudite words be avoided, that lengthy sentences be broken down into more manageable units, and that metaphors, irony, and other indirect devices be shunned.[13] He has developed various scales by which the readability of material may be related to the education and comprehension level of different groups of readers.[14] Flesch and others who have specialized in research of this sort also advocate the use

---

[13] Rudolf Flesch, *The Art of Plain Talk* (New York: Harper & Row, 1946), and *The Art of Readable Writing* (New York: Harper & Row, 1949).

[14] For instance, the Flesch index for this section is 5.45 or difficult. According to Flesch, it should have a potential audience of 24 per cent of all readers, *op. cit.*, p. 205.

of words and phrases that personalize the material and make it more concrete and immediately intelligible.

Every manager must insure that his announcements, public statements, and directives are couched in simple, direct language. Government agencies have been the favorite butt of jokes about "gobbledegook," but many private organizations also are guilty of torturing simple statements into complicated puzzles, and of using specialized and complex jargon. Low readability is undoubtedly a factor in the breakdown of communications. (And since most people talk more simply than they write, it is another reason for using face-to-face communications whenever possible.) High readability, however, is not an answer in itself to the fundamental barriers to communication that we have discussed.

INTRODUCING A PROPER AMOUNT OF REDUNDANCY

Communications engineers have developed techniques for measuring the amount of "redundancy" in a message—roughly the amount of repetition it contains. The supervisor who wants to give a direct order or transmit technical information should make sure that his message includes substantial redundancy. Then, if any word or phrase is misunderstood, there are other elements in the communication that will carry his point. To give a very simple example:

> A firm manufacturing several thousand varieties of chemical compounds used a numerical coding system to refer to each of the products. Increasingly, management found that mistakes were creeping into the ordering system. When a supervisor requested a shipment of compound #28394, a clerical error would occasionally result in a wasted shipment of #23894. Each digit was crucial, and the slightest mistake was costly. Eventually the firm adopted individual names for each compound and these words had a great deal of built-in redundancy, as do nearly all words. If a clerk ordered "calitin" instead of "calithin," the shipping department knew what he meant.

If each word is crucially important, it pays to say the same thing in several ways. In giving complicated directions, for example, it is wise to repeat them several times, perhaps in different ways, to guarantee successful transmission.

At times, however, a manager may want to avoid redundancy, and concentrate instead on introducing novelty or originality into his communications.[15] We tend to ignore many of the messages we receive simply because they sound so familiar. Most of us are guilty of repeating our favorite clichés to the point where people no longer listen to what we say because it is all so predictable. ("I know what the boss is going to say the minute he starts on that line about us all being one big happy team.")

There is some need for surprise, in modest doses to be sure, if we are to gain the attention of those with whom we wish to communicate. This is particularly

---

15 Cherry, *op. cit.*, p. 14.

true when our message contains something that contradicts expectations. For instance, to repeat our previous example, if your typist has been in the habit of preparing only one carbon, you must stress your request for two carbons.

Thus, the supervisor needs to balance carefully the redundancy and surprise elements of his communication.

Conclusion

Nearly every aspect of human relations and of supervisor-subordinate relations involves communications. When a selection policy is geared to admit people with similar backgrounds and interests, some of the problems we have discussed in this chapter are minimized. Similarly, carefully planned training

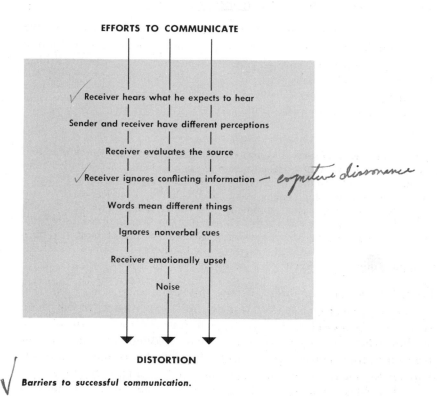

EFFORTS TO COMMUNICATE

✓ Receiver hears what he expects to hear

Sender and receiver have different perceptions

Receiver evaluates the source

✓ Receiver ignores conflicting information — *cognitive dissonance*

Words mean different things

Ignores nonverbal cues

Receiver emotionally upset

Noise

DISTORTION

✓ *Barriers to successful communication.*

and orientation programs help establish a common point of view and reduce misunderstandings that arise from differing frames of reference. Even the structure of the organization—affecting as it does status relations and the number of levels between top management and the worker at the bottom—has a most significant effect on the ability of people to communicate easily and quickly.

The swiftest, most effective communication takes place among people with common points of view. The supervisor who enjoys a good relationship with his subordinates has much less difficulty in explaining why air-conditioning equipment cannot be installed for another year than does the supervisor who is not trusted by his men. When people feel secure, they can talk to one another easily. Where discontent is rife, so is misunderstanding, misinterpretation, rumor, and distortion. In this sense, communication is a dependent variable. Where there is mutual trust and human relations are good, it is easy; where there is distrust, it is almost impossible. Therefore, the communications area is *not* the place to start improving supervisor-subordinate relationships.

Nevertheless, the problem of communicating accurately and effectively in each contact makes a supervisor's job more difficult. He must guard against the natural inclination in our highly verbal society to assume that simply *telling somebody* is enough to insure successful communication. Fortunately, as we have seen, the supervisor can resort to a number of techniques to facilitate the transmission of understanding between people in their day-to-day activities.

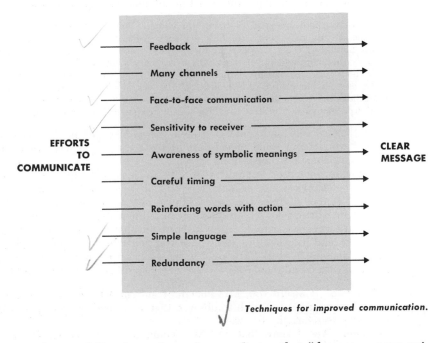

EFFORTS TO COMMUNICATE

- Feedback
- Many channels
- Face-to-face communication
- Sensitivity to receiver
- Awareness of symbolic meanings
- Careful timing
- Reinforcing words with action
- Simple language
- Redundancy

CLEAR MESSAGE

Techniques for improved communication.

One must be careful and not draw the conclusion that "the more communication the better" is always true. There are limits to how much an individual can absorb and be responsive to. Employees need to be protected from needless information so that they concentrate on important data. Also, there may be private fears, hopes, and hostilities within an organization that ought not to be communicated because they would only engender adverse reactions.

Communications is a matter of both transmitting and receiving. This chapter has emphasized transmitting. In Chapter 11 we will consider one of the most useful techniques for receiving information: interviewing.

PROBLEM ONE

"Welcome Aboard"

This was Joe Phelan's first day on the job, and he was anxious to learn as much as possible about what was expected of him and what kind of company he was going to be working for. He had been hired as a technical writer primarily to prepare manuals to help customers operate the complex industrial equipment the company manufactures.

He was somewhat apprehensive since this was the first time he had ever worked for a large corporation, and this company had a reputation for being impersonal and bureaucratic.

No one greeted him when he came in a few minutes before nine this Monday morning, but remembering the man's name he was replacing, he found the office that he assumed was to be his. The desk still contained a few candy bars and a rather worn blotter. There was also a note to call his supervisor, Cal Thompson.

He followed instructions, and in a few minutes Thompson appeared:

"We certainly are glad to have you aboard, Phelan. Hope you like your new office. By the way, here are half a dozen manuals we issued during the past few months; I think if you read them you'll learn a lot about the work we do. Later this morning my secretary will bring over a lot of background material on the new Series 18 machine which you'll be working on, and tomorrow you'll meet the engineer in charge of the project. Oh, yes, don't forget to go down to the Medical Office sometime today; they want to complete your records. If you have any questions don't hesitate to call me, but I've got to go to a meeting now myself."

Joe thanked him and said he looked forward to getting into the project. "Also, I wonder if I could meet some of the sales people who work with the kind of customers I will be writing for?"

Although Thompson thought that Phelan seemed a little over eager to make a good impression, he only replied, "In due time," and left the room. Thompson's tone of voice convinced Phelan he had spoken out of turn.

Just then Thompson's secretary called to tell him that the normal lunch hour for the department was from 12:30 to 1:30 and that if he had any typing to do he should send it to her and she would transmit it to the typing pool. Phelan, without thinking, replied, "I thought lunch was at noon and I've already agreed to meet an old friend then. And, by the way, could I see the Series 18 file?"

Secretary: "I assure you, Mr. Phelan, I am correct when I say 12:30, but whether or not you wish to observe that, of course, is up to you. I am not your secretary, by the way."

Phelan: "Yes, I know that, but Mr. Thompson said you would have those materials."

Secretary: "If he said that, he must have forgotten to give them to me. When he does, I assure you that you will get them immediately."

1. Note all the communications breakdowns that occurred and in each consider what misconceptions each party received.
2. How much of this could have been avoided if Joe Phelan had been less apprehensive?

P R O B L E M   T W O

The Case of the Disappearing Furniture

Carlin Mailaway specializes in reproductions of New England antiques and sells them by means of a nationally distributed catalog. The company, located in Great Barrington, Massachusetts, has won a dominant position in the market it serves.

Recently, Carlin instituted a more formal inventory system. The results were appalling to the General Manager, James Coffin. According to the second quarterly inventory, at least $2,000 worth of merchandise had disappeared "mysteriously" during the preceding three months. Almost simultaneously the warehouse supervisor found several pieces of merchandise wrapped as trash in a refuse barrel—as though they had been placed there by someone who intended to retrieve them later.

As soon as the figures were confirmed by a sample rechecking, Coffin dictated a letter to the Warehouse Supervisor, and sent copies out to every one of the 28 employees working in the warehouse. The letter read as follows:

> Our auditing procedures have just disclosed a shocking loss of goods in our warehouse. In the future, no unauthorized personnel are to be allowed into the warehouse section of our building and all employees working in the area will be expected to refrain from carrying packages in or out of the department and permit close scrutiny of their persons as they leave work.
>
> In no sense should any of our loyal, faithful employees interpret this as a slur against their characters. We know that they would want these stern provisions to be introduced to eliminate any possibility that they might be implicated.
>
> We will appreciate your cooperation and thank you for your help in the past.

1. As a long-service employee in this department, how would you "interpret" this letter? Would others interpret it differently, do you think? Which ones and why?
2. What would you think the General Manager's motives were in writing this letter?
3. What alternative procedures might have been considered? What would their shortcomings and advantages be?
4. Might the Manager's letter have been better conceived and written?

P R O B L E M   T H R E E

Fair Employment Policy

For many years the Brace Machine Works had employed Negroes only in menial jobs. After deliberation, and in part as a result of the passage of new state legislation, top management decided to adopt an unambiguous policy of offering equal employment opportunities for members of all nationality, racial, and religious groups.

The president of the company called in the personnel director for his counsel on how to announce this new policy in a way that would not only assure Negroes of equal employment opportunities but would also guarantee that they would not be discriminated against in opportunities for promotion to better-paying, more skilled positions.

1. If you were the personnel director, what advice would you give the president?
2. In helping him frame his approach, what questions would you ask, what information would you need, and what knowledge about the company would be useful to you?

Interviewing:

The Fine Art of Listening

11

"My boss doesn't give a hoot about me. As far as he is concerned I am another piece of machinery."

"I'll say this about my boss: No matter what your problem is, he'll hear you through."

"Though I'm supposed to be in charge of this department, it's my people who do the work. I try to remember that to himself each person is absolutely different from anyone else. He wants special recognition. So I try to pay attention to him, listen to his problems."

Effective communication requires effort both by the sender of the message and the receiver. The last chapter was devoted largely to the sending of messages. In this chapter we shall be concerned with an important aspect of receiving them—with listening.

Listening is one of the most important of all management tools. Yet even though people learn to listen before they learn to talk, relatively few listen well—few have learned the art of *interviewing*.

What do we mean by "interviewing"? Most people think of interviewing in the sense of the formal interviews connected with getting a job. By interviewing we intend much more than this: we mean deliberate, active listening whose purpose is to draw the other person out, to discover what he really wants to say, and to give him a chance to express himself fully.

Historical Background

Management first became aware of the value of interviewing in industrial relations during the 1920's as a consequence of studies conducted at the Hawthorne plant of the Western Electric Company.[1] These studies were primarily concerned with the determinants of morale and productivity. However, in their attempts to uncover basic feelings regarding these factors, the researcher found that direct questions designed to find out how the subjects felt about specific aspects of their jobs resulted in superficial, "lifeless" answers. Even worse—or so it seemed at the time—instead of giving "straightforward" responses, some of the people interviewed tended to talk about what interested them most at the moment.

Following this clue, the interviewers tried a radically new experiment: They sat back and decided to let the interviewees direct the interviews. Now they discovered that people began to express their *feelings* as well as give factual answers. Employees launched into long tirades (to which the interviewers patiently listened) revealing attitudes that might otherwise have been kept carefully guarded. In fact, some employees expressed attitudes that they had not been consciously aware of themselves. As a consequence, the interviewers got a much better picture of the psychological geography of the plant. They discovered surprising relationships about which they would never have learned by asking direct questions.

More important: The employees benefited greatly as well. Just by talking freely in the presence of a sympathetic listener, they got their problems off their chest and felt better. They experienced what psychologists call *catharsis* (from the Greek: to make pure). In addition, merely by talking things over, the employees began to gain insight into the nature of their own problems. Once they had relieved their feelings by speaking openly in a receptive environment, they were able to look at their problems more objectively. And their clearer understandings, supplemented by further discussion, often enabled them to work out solutions (at least to those problems that they were in a position to solve themselves).

Impressed by the value of the Hawthorne experience, Western Electric

---

[1] For the most thorough review of these studies, see F. J. Roethlisberger and W. J. Dickson, *Management and the Worker* (Cambridge: Harvard University Press, 1939). For a critical analysis of these studies in the light of later research, see Henry Landsberger, *Hawthorne Revisited* (Ithaca: New York State School of Industrial and Labor Relations, 1958).

instituted a program of formal counseling. Specially chosen counselors were trained in the use of *nondirective* interviews. (By nondirective interviews we mean—as we shall explain later—a type of interview in which the interviewer encourages the interviewee to express his own thoughts with considerable freedom—as contrasted to _directive_ interviewing, in which the interviewer asks direct questions and tries to keep the discussion within predetermined limits.)

These "free-floating" counselors were given no regular supervisory duties; they were completely separate from the normal management hierarchy. Their function was merely to listen to employees' problems without giving advice or taking action. Other companies rapidly followed Western Electric's example. Particularly during World War II counseling was very popular. Many employers assigned "free-floating" counselors throughout the company, especially to help women workers.

The counselors faced a tough ethical problem of what to do with the information they received. If they repeated to management what they had been told, the workers would no longer trust them. On the other hand, if they could use their information in a discreet manner, they might be able to eliminate the causes of trouble. Often the counselors compromised by giving management general reports without revealing details that might identify individuals.

In recent years the use of such counselors as a personnel tool has declined. It was discovered that this technique has many drawbacks, including the following:

1. Although counseling might help an individual make a better adjustment to a poor environment (say to an inept supervisor), it didn't improve the environment itself. Employees often began to feel that they were wasting their time talking to a counselor who could do nothing for them, and ended up almost as frustrated as before.

2. Counseling is directed almost entirely toward changing *individual* attitudes and behavior, in spite of other evidence from the Hawthorne study itself that group attitudes are often more important than individual attitudes.

3. The counseling system gave subordinates a chance to bypass and tattle on their supervisors. Naturally, the supervisors objected.

4. In some cases employees began to compare the "good" counselor with the "bad" supervisor. Supervisors felt they were entitled to the undivided loyalty of subordinates.

5. The counselors discovered that they were spending most of their time with a few disturbed individuals who really needed deep psychotherapy rather than counseling.

The basic trouble with "free-floating" counseling was its separation from line management. Line management emphasized downward communication. Counseling provided upward communication. But the two forms of communication went along different channels.

Management began to learn that effective communications must go both

ways. Upward communication and downward communication, listening and
order-giving, are both more effective if done by the *same* person. Furthermore,
if they are merged into the same process, something new and better emerges.
Thus, there has come the realization that counseling or interviewing or listening
(which are really all the same thing) is not a special technique for use by
personnel experts only, but a vital aspect of good management generally.

Listening as a Management Tool

To list the circumstances where interviewing is useful would be almost
like listing the functions of management itself. Indeed, all through our discussion of general supervision and methods of correcting mistakes we constantly emphasize the importance of listening. The following example indicates
what might happen when this approach works at its best.

> Suppose you are a division manager and you want to introduce a new system
> of quality control. Although you have not as yet consulted with the production
> supervisor, you have heard through the grapevine that he has strong objections
> to the new system. Yet his cooperation is essential if the system is to succeed.
> You feel pretty certain that your plan is good and that the production super-
> visor's objections are not well grounded. You are the boss, of course, and you
> could give him a direct order to put the plan into effect. (Question: How would
> the supervisor react to this order? How loyally would he carry it out?)
> Instead, you decide to listen to his point of view. In spite of the grapevine
> you can't really be sure you know what his objections are until he has spoken
> to you personally. If you are at all sincere, you must admit to yourself that his
> objections may have some merit. (Question: What would happen if you had
> already made up your mind, and just went through the formalities of listening?)
> So you explain the proposed change to him, being careful to emphasize that
> you still have an open mind, and ask him to comment. You listen attentively
> and encourage him to express himself fully. As he speaks, he relaxes and ex-
> plains his point of view with more balance and restraint than he would if he
> felt he were on the defensive. Instead of trying to answer his arguments, you
> encourage him to tell you everything he thinks and feels about the change.
> When he finishes, you briefly summarize what he has said to make sure you
> understand—and also to indicate *to him* that you have understood.
> After speaking his piece, the production supervisor feels free to listen to your
> point of view—which may have changed since you heard his objections. You
> fill in some of the areas where you feel he was mistaken, indicate the points on
> which you have changed your own thinking, and explore with him any adjust-
> ments that seem necessary. Even if he is still not fully convinced of the wisdom
> of your plan, he is more willing to try it out and probably feels pleased that
> you consulted him and listened to his objections.

The above example suggests the flexibility of the interview technique
(though we must emphasize that the results are frequently not as good as we
have pictured). It is obviously well suited to formal interviews, such as those
used for hiring, exit, and requests for transfer. But it is also appropriate in less
formal situations, such as the following:

Low morale: finding out the cause of employee dissatisfaction, turnover, or absenteeism.

Discipline: discovering why employees are performing unsatisfactorily and helping them to evolve means of correcting themselves.

Order-giving: getting reaction to and acceptance of orders, to see that the person who receives the order really understands it.

Resistance to change: gaining acceptance of new techniques, tools, procedures.

Merit rating and evaluation: helping an employee correct his weaknesses.

Training: finding out how much an employee knows and what difficulties he experiences in learning.

Grievance-handling: finding out the real causes of a union grievance and getting the union officers to agree to a constructive solution.

Settling disputes: finding out the causes of the disputes between employees and getting them to agree to settlement.

The interview approach is not something to be applied only when dealing with specific problems. It is a general attitude which the manager can apply day in and day out in his dealings with fellow supervisors, subordinates, and his boss. In a nutshell, it is a matter of always being ready to listen to the other fellow's point of view and trying to take it into account before taking action oneself. If this attitude is absent, then communications may become blocked, as they did in one company:

> The most frequent complaint was that although orders and instructions about work traveled easily enough, it was difficult to take up ordinary feelings, especially if they were critical about the job or about life in the factory. The main stumbling block in getting such feelings resolved was the reticence about communicating them upwards. The reticence was said to be due to the fact that if a person tried to express to his superior his feelings about the job, or about the superior himself, it was all too likely that the superior would argue with him and try to show him that his feelings were unreasonable and that they did not tally with the facts. Having the existence of one's feelings denied in this way only made things worse. The person was not only left with the original feeling but in addition had a resentment against his superior for not understanding him and not helping him get at what was disturbing him.[2]

ESTABLISHING CONFIDENCE

The supervisor must take the initiative in encouraging subordinates to come to him with their problems (see our discussion in Chapter 8). He must show that he is willing to hear them out. Otherwise minor irritations may grow to tremendous proportions, even before the manager has become aware of the danger. For example, the manager does something the subordinate doesn't like. The subordinate doesn't feel free to talk about it. Gradually his irritation grows and he begins to see his superior in a new light. Everything the supervisor does may now seem threatening and unfair. The subordinate's antagonism grows stronger and stronger, until at last there is a serious breakdown in his relationship with the supervisor.

---

[2] Elliot Jaques, *The Changing Culture of a Factory* (London: Tavistock, 1951), p. 133.

If the initial interview is a pleasant experience for the subordinate, he will come back more freely and more regularly when new problems arise. If it has been an unpleasant experience and if he feels he has been "put on the spot," he will be reluctant to reveal what is on his mind in the future.

The manager should be aware that some of the men who report to him will be easier to get to know than others. Some will talk to him quite freely and easily. Others will hold back because of fear or natural timidity. The manager must be careful not to spend all his time with those to whom it it easy to talk.

To avoid the charge of favoritism, and to insure that he is able to deal with the problems of all his employees, the supervisor must go out of his way to make contact with employees who are reluctant to come to him. The manager must recognize that there is an invisible barrier which separates him from his subordinates. For some, this status difference is of little importance, but for many it makes effective upward communication much harder.

OFF-THE-JOB PROBLEMS

Managers sometimes use interviewing to help employees solve personal off-the-job problems. Normally stable individuals may have unexpected trouble and seek to use their supervisor as a wailing wall. However, the manager should be careful not to give advice or get himself saddled with the responsibility for running his subordinates' personal lives.

The manager should be particularly cautious when sensitive areas are reached in the course of an interview. In situations like this, what most people want is a sympathetic, understanding listener rather than an adviser. They may ask for advice, but actually they want only a chance to talk. Even when advice-giving is successful, there is the danger that the employee may become over-dependent on his manager and run to him whenever he has a minor problem.

The manager should be still more careful when deepseated personality problems are involved. In such a case it is wise to refer the person to a professionally trained specialist rather than to play amateur psychologist. The average manager is not equipped to do counseling, nor is this part of his job. The patient-psychiatrist or client-counselor relationship is just not consistent with that of subordinate and boss. And the subordinate may resent being conned by the nondirective technique into blurting out confidences which he later regrets having revealed.

The Use of the Nondirective Approach

The type of interviewing we shall discuss here has been called "non-directive" because it emphasizes permitting the interviewee (rather than the interviewer) to direct the interview, at least in the early stages. What can this approach accomplish? The nondirective interview has three functions:

1. From the point of view of the interviewer, it helps provide clues to what the interviewee is really thinking and what lies at the root of the problem. Thus, for a manager, the interview is a means of getting information on which he can base decisions.

The first answer an employee gives to an involved question may not be the whole truth. He may not be exactly lying, but he finds it difficult to express just how he feels. True, if the manager starts to fire direct questions, he will usually get direct answers, and they may *sound* reasonable. But they may represent only a small, inaccurate sample of the interviewee's total feelings.

Most of us have trouble expressing our real feelings to others. In part this is so because we are fearful or ashamed of what the other person will think. We want to make a good impression. This reluctance to reveal our true attitudes is also a product of our inability to understand our own complex, often conflicting, and even unconscious feelings. Consequently we often say things we don't really mean.

Patient, prolonged, skillful listening is required to help another person express his feelings. Good interviewing, then, is essentially a technique to encourage expression which is uninfluenced either by the preconceived notions of the interviewer or by the need of the interviewee to make a good impression.

2. It helps the interviewee achieve catharsis, a feeling of relief. There are many sources of frustration in modern industry, and unless frustration is relieved it may lead to aggression, regression, and other undesirable responses. The interview provides a channel through which frustration may be partly drained away, even though the causes of the frustration remain.

3. Nondirective interviewing helps a man develop greater insight into his own problems. Turning his questions back and encouraging him to talk enables him to answer them himself. We often think better when we think out loud—when we have to organize and weigh our thoughts—than when we are thinking to ourselves.

In arranging his thoughts before presenting them to a sympathetic listener, the interviewee may bring his problem into sharper focus and, without additional help, actually change his own attitudes. At this stage one hears comments such as, "You know, the more I talk about this, the more I think I have been on the wrong track." Solutions reached in this fashion are much more likely to be implemented with enthusiasm than are those suggested by the supervisor.

STAGES IN AN INTERVIEW

In understanding how the nondirective approach should be used, it is helpful to think of the interview as running through three stages: feelings, facts, solutions.

1. *Feelings.* The interviewee is encouraged to release his feelings; the interviewer is concerned with helping the interviewee express himself. This stage is the most purely nondirective, for the interviewer still has little idea where the discussion will go.

2. *Facts.*   Having blown off steam, the interviewee is now ready to look at the facts rationally. In this stage the interviewer can be more directive and may even use "probes" (to be discussed later) to bring out information that the interviewee has not already volunteered. In fact, the interviewer may contribute additional information on his own.

3. *Solutions.*   Once the facts have been assembled, the interviewee is in a position to weigh alternate solutions and pick the best one. As we have mentioned frequently, it is preferable to help the interviewee work out his own solution; however, the supervisor may have to be rather strongly directive to make sure that the solution is consistent with the needs of the organization.

These, then, are the three major stages of the interview, although it may switch back and forth from one stage to another as different problems are considered. Still on a given problem the interviewer should stick to the order indicated: feelings, facts, solutions. Certainly he should avoid the common human tendency to jump to a solution before getting all the facts.

Equally important, he should not waste his time trying to isolate the facts before the interviewee has had a chance to express his feelings, to blow off steam. Why? Because feelings color facts, and as long as a man is emotionally excited he is unlikely to approach problems rationally. Furthermore—and the point is subtle—the feelings of the people concerned in the situation are themselves facts that must be considered. For instance, the office manager has been having trouble getting Mary to do a full day's work. The most important fact in this solution may be the manager's intense dislike of Mary as a person. Until the manager's feeling is recognized as a complicating element, "facts" he presents will be distorted by his antagonism toward Mary.

Does this mean that the interviewer should never express himself—that he should never try to correct the other person if he is wrong, or try to change his opinion? Of course not. It may be enough for the psychiatrist or the professional counselor merely to listen. The supervisor must also take action. But in most cases, before he takes action he should wait until he has heard the interviewee's whole story.

Suppose a subordinate comes to you and says, "Boss, you've got to transfer me from this job. I can't stand it any more." If he insists on his request, you will have to give him some kind of answer. Only antagonism will result if he gets the impression that you are trying to put him off. But there is no need for you to commit yourself before you have heard him through.

The nondirective approach is not a magic solution to all human-relations problems, of course. There are times when a supervisor may have to be quite firm and directive in the solution stage of the interview to make sure that the solution is consistent with the needs of the organization. For instance, the supervisor may listen patiently to the subordinate's objections to a new system; the subordinate may persist in his resistance; and the supervisor may still have to overrule him, explaining why, and insist that the system be used. However, the subordinate will have had the satisfaction of being consulted, of knowing that he had his day in court to present his side of the story.

Interviewing Techniques [3]

Skillful interviewing is an art, and like all arts it requires training and experience. It can be learned better by practice than by reading a book, especially when the practice is supervised by an experienced instructor. Fortunately, one can gain unsupervised practice every day of the year.

Each interviewer must develop a system that is comfortable for him and that fits his personality, but he should avoid using the same technique with all people and for all purposes. An interview held for disciplinary reasons will naturally be different from an interview held for the purpose of order-giving.

Regardless of the form of the interview, here are a few hints that may prove useful.

ENCOURAGING THE INTERVIEWEE TO TALK

Your primary objective is to get the interviewee to talk freely, *not to talk yourself*. The best way to find out what the other person wants to say is to listen, and the best interview is usually the one in which the interviewer talks least.

But listening is not easy, for our natural impulse is to talk. This is particularly true when we feel threatened by what is being said to us—for instance, when we are being criticized. Under these circumstances our normal impulse is to defend ourselves rather than to listen.

Listening is more than just not talking, however. It requires an active effort to convey that you understand and are interested in what the other person is saying—almost that you are helping him say it. A friendly facial expression and an attentive but relaxed attitude are important. A good interviewer also makes use of phrases such as "Uh-huh," "I understand," "That explains it," or "Could you tell me more?"

Even silence can be used to keep a man talking. When he pauses in his discourse, he is either being polite and giving you a chance to talk, or else he wants you to comment, to evaluate what he is saying. Merely by not taking up his challenge, by waiting through his pause, you indicate that you have nothing to say at the moment, that you want him to continue talking.

Even if you plan to use the nondirective approach, it is vital to set the stage properly, to indicate to the interviewee what you want the interview to cover. For example, if you wish to talk to a worker about sloppy work, you might start with, "Bill, you seem to be having a little trouble with the blue-edge gadgets."

---

[3] Three excellent and very different treatments of interviewing are: Carl Rogers and others, *Client-Centered Therapy: Its Current Practice, Implications and Theory* (Boston: Houghton Mifflin, 1951); Robert L. Kahn and Charles E. Cannell, *The Dynamics of Interviewing* (New York: Wiley, 1957); Stephen Richardson, Barbara Dohrenwend, and David Klein, *Interviewing: Its Forms and Functions* (New York: Basic Books, 1965).

REFLECTIVE SUMMARY

One of the most effective devices to encourage the other person to talk is the *reflective summary*, in which you try to sum up the feelings a man has expressed, disregarding the factual details and incidentals. For example: "The reason I want to quit is that so-and-so foreman keeps pestering me. He won't give me a chance!" Then he stops, wondering whether he has got himself into trouble by saying too much. Your response, "He won't give you a chance?" encourages him to tell the rest of his story, but it does not commit you in any sense. Such a summary serves a number of purposes:

1. It shows the worker that you are giving his ideas careful consideration and that you understand him—in other words, that you are being fair.
2. It gives him a chance to restate and elaborate his attitudes if he feels that you haven't quite grasped his point.
3. It serves to highlight what he has really been saying. Often people are surprised to learn what their words have meant to someone else, and are rewarded with deeper insight into their own attitudes.

The reflective summary is particularly effective if you reflect not only what the man has actually said, but can somehow put into words what he has tried, unsuccessfully, to express. Be careful, however, not to hear more in his words than he intends to put into them. For if he finds you reading things into his words that he did not mean to be there, he will be doubly careful to watch what he says.

Your summary should indicate neither approval nor disapproval of what the interviewee is saying. It should simply indicate that you are listening attentively. For instance, he says, "It's got to the point where I may lose my temper and take a poke at the foreman." If you were to say, "Well, that's quite understandable," you would almost be inviting him to carry out his threat! A far more satisfactory response would be, "You are really sore at him because. . . ."

PROBES

The "free-floating" counselor is interested primarily in getting at the interviewee's underlying feelings. And as a supervisor you too are interested in the feelings of your subordinates. But if you know that you must act on the basis of what you learn in the interview, you will also want to get all the facts, the whole story.[4] This means that after the feeling stage has passed, you should to some extent direct the interview. Tactfully and calmly, you should steer the conversation, but without forcing the interviewee into an area he does not want to enter, and with no hint that you have already made up your mind.

---

[4] In other words, your interviewing is "organization centered" not "client centered." See Rogers and others, *op. cit.*

One way to direct the interview is to build on what the interviewee has already said. By repeating certain words selected from what he has said, you can indicate that you would like him to talk more about this particular area. This device is called a "probe." For example, in explaining how a fight started between himself and another employee, the man being interviewed says, "Joe was always riding me. When he picked up my lunch bucket, that was the last straw." Now if the supervisor wants to find out more about what Joe has done to arouse this man, he has a good chance to insert a probe: "You say Joe was always riding you?" Then he stops and waits for the man to go on. Notice that the interviewer does not say: "What did Joe do to make you so sore?" Rather, he simply repeats the employee's own words. Chances are this approach will encourage the man to tell more about the "riding" than he would if he had been asked a direct question.

Less subtle probes are: "Could you tell me more about...?" or "I am interested in what you said about...."

WEIGHING ALTERNATIVES

Sometimes it is enough if the interview helps you find out how the employee feels about the situation and what the essential facts are as *he* sees them. In other instances, however, you may wish to help him devise a solution. How can you do this without seeming to impose your own ideas on him? The following approach may be useful both in individual interviews and in group meetings:

Let us assume one of your managers wishes to discipline severely one of his employees who has been a troublemaker. The manager's first suggestion, for example, may be that he should go right out to the shop and fire the troublemaker. If you keep asking for additional suggestions, he may suggest lesser penalties. Finally, he may even come around to suggesting certain changes in his own behavior.

Now, after the manager has offered all these suggestions, you would attempt to get him to examine each one:

> What would its probable effect be?
> How would the men react?
> How would it help him solve his problem?

By helping the interviewee think through his problem, you may succeed in having him come to a conclusion that is *his*, not yours. And if it is his, he will be much more likely to act on it with enthusiasm.

COMPLEMENTING THE OTHER'S
INTERACTION PATTERN

People speak more easily when the other person complements their own "interaction pattern." That is, most people have a characteristic way by which they balance off talking and listening periods. When they are talking, they want the other person to be still and not interrupt them; when they have finished, they find it uncomfortable to wait for a reply. Thus, a good interviewer learns to adjust to the other person's pattern his own tendencies to talk and to be silent. He is careful not to interrupt with a question or even an "uh-huh" until the other person has finished. Similarly when the other person does stop talking, the good interviewer comes in with a response. The one exception to this is when the interviewer thinks that a short silent period will encourage the interviewee to continue talking.

DIRECT QUESTIONS

One of the most frequent errors made by inexperienced interviewers is transforming the interview into a game of "twenty questions." A man has fallen into the habit of coming to work late and his supervisor is anxious to straighten him out before discipline becomes necessary. Having had some training in human relations, the manager suspects that a home problem is involved. His end of the conversation may run something like this:

> "Do you have trouble starting your car?"
> "Is there any trouble at home?"
> "Does your alarm clock go off on time?"
> "Did you have a drink too many last night?"

To each question Bill replies, "No, it isn't that." And to himself he says, "That's none of his business." And then another question is shot at him.

Here the manager, not Bill, is directing the interview. Note that every one of these questions is phrased in such a manner as to put Bill immediately on the defensive and make him over-cautious in what he says. Some of the questions, such as, "Did you have a drink too many last night?" he may feel are insulting.

The interviewer rarely knows the right questions to ask; if he did, he would probably know the answers as well. The interviewee's problem is usually more complex than it seems at first glance, and direct questions tend to narrow it down too quickly.

To complicate matters, most subordinates try to say what they think will please their supervisor. Direct questions often imply the kind of answer the supervisor wants, or at least give the subordinate an "out." For instance, the question "Did you have trouble starting your car?" provides a ready excuse for a tardy worker.

If the supervisor wants to find out what the subordinate really has on his mind, he should leave the situation as free as possible to permit the subordinate to emphasize the things that are important to *him*.

If possible, the interviewer should avoid questions that can be answered with a simple yes or no. "Well, do you like your job?" "Do you think the tools are in bad shape?" Questions of this sort shut off discussion because they can be answered by a relatively meaningless "Oh, I guess so," "I suppose you might say that."

Things to Avoid

TOO MUCH WARM-UP

Many people feel that before getting down to the subject of an interview, particularly if it is an unpleasant one, they should try to place the interviewee at ease by discussing some irrelevant topic—baseball, fishing, the traffic problem, or what have you. Thus, a foreman calling a man in to lay him off may chat about the Dodgers for a few minutes before settling down to the nasty task.

This approach may relieve the foreman's anxiety, but it intensifies that of the worker, particularly if he has some idea of why he has been called in. While he is on the "hot seat," he may be thinking, "Why doesn't this character get down to business? Why does he have to play cat-and-mouse? What's this building up to?"

Such "warming-up" is useful at times; however, the interviewer should be careful to use it only when it actually reduces anxiety. Often when the supervisor initiates the interview, "beating around the bush" merely increases the suspense. Similarly, if the employee comes to the supervisor with a problem, he probably wants to get down to business without delay.

PREMATURE JUDGMENT

The interviewer should avoid giving any indication that what the subordinate says either pleases or displeases him. In other words, he must refrain from passing judgment before all the facts are in. This restraint is extremely important because subordinates look for verbal or facial cues that will tip them off to what the superior wants or does not want to hear. (Of course, unconsciously we are always forming impressions, even on the most meager facts. However, the supervisor should be aware of his predispositions and try to keep them from warping his judgment or his communication.)

Criticizing or moralizing puts the interviewee on the defensive. Even if he does not argue back, he will begin to edit what he says in order to win the interviewer's approval. He will concentrate on proving that he is right rather than on giving an honest explanation. Certainly putting a man on the defensive makes is harder to find out what he really thinks.

Even praise or sympathy should be avoided until the end of the interview, for it makes the interviewee think his present approach is correct and encourages him to avoid the hard work of thinking the problem through.

ARGUING

Little is gained from argument, at least in the early stage of the interview. Yet everyone has a strong human tendency to correct the other person when he says something that is obviously wrong. Moreover, if the interviewer himself is attacked personally, he must exercise tremendous restraint not to answer back.

For example, an employee says he is having trouble doing the work because the stock has been changed. "The company must be buying cheaper material these days." Now if you know that there has been no change whatsoever in the materials, you will be strongly tempted to "set the employee straight" on this point, although his complaint may be a symptom of something much more basic. If you give way to this temptation, you may simply transform the interview into a fruitless argument. If you just continue to listen, however, the employee may move on to more basic problems and difficulties that he finds more troublesome to discuss.

EXCESSIVE PSYCHOLOGIZING

Sometimes managers abuse the nondirective technique by shifting the discussion from the technical aspects of the question at hand to the subordinate's motives in dealing with it.[5] Such abuse occurs most commonly when the manager has a psychology or social work background. For example, a subordinate may have a sound practical objection to something his boss may want to do. Instead of listening to the objections themselves, the excessively psychologically-oriented boss may look upon the subordinate's attitude as an example of hostility and may seek its emotional basis. Obviously such an approach often adds to the hostility it is designed to alleviate.

ADVICE-GIVING

When you finally get the complete picture as the employee sees it, you may be able to provide advice or information that has not previously been available. But again it is often better to help him work through his own problems. In any event, you should hold off giving advice until *after* the interviewee has told his entire story—until you have all the facts.

MASTERMINDING

Many people go through the motions of the nondirective interview but violate its spirit. They hope by asking shrewd questions to manipulate the interviewee into believing that he is thinking through his problem by himself, though the way questions are worded inevitably forces the interviewee to arrive at the interviewer's own predetermined conclusion.

Masterminding is used with various degrees of sophistication. One of the less subtle forms makes constant use of the leading question, the "don't you feel?" approach: "Don't you feel it would be better for the company and your own future if you came to work on time?"

---

[5] For a good discussion, see Peter Blau and W. Richard Scott, *Formal Organization* (San Francisco: Chandler, 1962), pp. 188-89.

Questions like this usually permit only one answer. They are thinly veiled forms of advice, judgement, or just plain bawling out. They are even more directive than an overt, straightforward statement. The interviewee is often free to reject outright advice, and even if it is clear that he must accept it (in other words, when the advice is really an order) he may be unhappy about it, but willing to be a good soldier. Masterminding, however, not only requires the interviewee to do what the interviewer wants, but also to say that he likes it. The interviewee is treated like a child and the alleged interview degenerates into a form of brainwashing.

There are subtler forms of brainwashing in which the interviewee may actually feel convinced of something at the time of the interview, only to realize that he has been duped after he has had a chance to think things over. Conversion at a forced rate seldom lasts. As the poet Robert Burns once said:

> He who is convinced against his will,
> Is of the same opinion still.

People change their attitudes slowly, and only when they are ready to do so.

Conclusion

Interviewing is a form of communications, and like other forms of communications it is most effective when it is two-way. A good interview is more than a one-way process in which the interviewee tells his story to the interviewer; the interviewer must in turn be constantly communicating his interest in the interviewee as a person and in what he has to say.

It is not enough for the manager to understand his employees; he must also give them the feeling that he is sincerely trying to help them. The manager must not only listen, but must also communicate the feeling to his employees that they are being listened to.

The basic purpose of nondirective interviewing is to enable the interviewer to find out how the individual sees the problem or situation at issue, and then to help him think and, above all, *feel* his way through to a solution. The goal of this whole philosophy is for the supervisor to be perceived as a source of help—as a man who can assist the subordinate to develop and do a better job.

It has been argued that the interview approach would be fine if a manager had nothing else to do all day except serve as a wailing wall, but that in practice he just doesn't have time to do much listening. Realistically, pressure and other demands may make him abrupt and unsympathetic in his dealings with subordinates. And yet the manager who "makes time" to listen may find not only that his human relations are better, but that in the long run he will save enough time by having fewer personnel crises to deal with.

The nondirective interview is not a cure-all for every situation. Effective interviewing requires considerable skill, and even a good interviewer discovers that many people find it difficult to discuss their problems. Moreover, many problems involve several people and require group discussion. Finally, certain problems cannot be decided at the manager-subordinate level. Still, in spite of these reservations the interviewing technique is a general-purpose tool for every manager.

PROBLEM ONE

Interviewing Drill

In each of the following cases, which of the responses suggested would be more likely to lead to a constructive solution of the problem? Remember that these represent the opening of the interview.

1. You have come home from a hard day and your wife greets you with:
    "What a day I've had. The baby was crying all morning. The washing machine broke down and I had to do the things by hand. Then I went downtown to buy a hat and had to wait twenty minutes for a bus. I couldn't find a thing I liked and everybody was so pushy and the store was so crowded. When I got back the baby-sitter had let the stew burn—and I'd worked on it so hard. I'm so mad I could cry. And I've got to go downtown tomorrow again to look for a hat."
    a. "You must have had an awfully hard day."
    b. "Your old hat looks pretty good to me."
    c. "I'm tired too. You should hear what happened to me. First. . . ."
    d. "Don't say another word. Put on your glad rags and I'll take you out for dinner and don't mention it."
    e. "You know, maybe we ought to get another baby-sitter."

2. A worker has been late three times in the last two weeks. You ask him why and he replies:
    "I just can't seem to get up in the morning. Frankly, I've lost my enthusiasm for the job. It doesn't interest me any more. So when I do get up I've got to rush like mad to get here."
    a. "Don't you think you are letting the company down?"
    b. "Do you have an alarm clock?"
    c. "You've got to lick this problem or I've got to lay you off and give you some time to think it over."
    d. "The job doesn't interest you any more?"
    e. "Are you having any trouble at home?"
    f. "Have you thought of going to bed earlier?"

3. A worker who has been making little progress tells his boss:
    "I just can't seem to get the hang of things. I try to find out what I'm supposed to do, but no one tells me. The other guys don't pay any attention to me and I can't figure it out by watching. Maybe I ought to quit."
    a. "Why don't you give the job a chance? Most people take a while to learn it."
    b. "Why don't you try harder? You can't get ahead without hard work."
    c. "If I were you I would ask the other fellows to help you."
    d. "Do you have any ideas why the other fellows don't help you?"
    e. "I'll assign one of them to instruct you."
    f. "You feel that the other fellows don't pay any attention to you?"
    g. "Let me show you how to do it."

4. A toolmaker tells his foreman:

"I've had ten years' experience and no one ever told me I did a bum job. Sure I make a few mistakes, but why do I get all the blame?"

a. "All I want you to do is be a little more careful in your work."
b. "You feel the standards are too high?"
c. "I'm not saying it is your fault. I am just asking you to please do the piece over."
d. "You feel you are unfairly blamed?

PROBLEM TWO[6]

The Extra Half Plum

Scene I

Mary, a salad girl, is seated at a table backstage by herself, thumbing through a magazine. She is off duty. Miss Jones walks on stage from the right and stops at Mary's table.

Miss Jones: Mary, may I speak to you for a moment?

Mary: All right.

Miss Jones: It's about your work. I feel that you're a hard worker but there are times when you seem to grow a bit careless. I've noticed lately that sometimes your salads are a trifle sloppy in appearance, and you don't always check your recipes carefully enough. For example, the fruit salad calls for two halves of plums. I saw you putting three on some of the salads today. If you just check up on things like this, you'll do the job I think you're capable of.

(Mary does not answer. She shuts the magazine, gets up, and walks away. Miss Jones looks startled, then walks toward the office of Mr. Black, the manager, downstage left, and knocks on the door.)

Scene II

Black: Come in. (Miss Jones walks in and sits down.) Hello. What is it, Miss Jones?

Jones: I'm worried about Mary Stevens. I thought maybe you'd want to talk to her.

Black: What seems to be the trouble?

Jones: Well, she's a hard worker, but sometimes she just doesn't seem to have her mind on her work. Now that wouldn't be so bad if she'd let us correct her, but the girl won't take criticism. I just asked her to be a little neater in putting up her salads and I checked her on putting an extra half plum on the fruit salad. I put it just as tactfully as I know how, but she wouldn't even answer me. She just sat still until I was finished and then walked right out on me. It was a deliberate insult.

Black: Yes, that's bad. . . . Do you think she is quitting?

Jones: Well, I don't know. But I don't see how I can use her when she behaves that way.

Black: Do you want to get rid of her?

Jones: Well, you know how short we are at that station. I can't really spare her and she can do a very good job when she wants to. Maybe it's some

---

[6] We wish to express our thanks to Professor William F. Whyte for permission to use this case, which was prepared by him.

trouble at home. I don't know. But I thought you might be able to help her.

Black: I'd be glad to talk to her for you. She'll be coming in for her pay-check tomorrow. I'll see her then.

Jones: Thanks. That'll be a big help to me.

Scene III

(Black's office. Black at desk; Mary comes in.)

Black: I was hoping you'd come in to see me. Won't you sit down, Mary?

Mary: (hesitates, then sits down) Well, I suppose you know all about it.

Black: Miss Jones told me something about it, but I want to get your side of the story. After all, we want to be fair with you. I've always done my best to see the employee's point of view. We want you to feel satisfied with your work here, and if there is some problem I can help out on, I want you to feel free to talk things over with me.

Mary: Well, I don't suppose I should have walked out, but I just couldn't take it.

Black: You mean, you can't take criticism?

Mary: Well, not exactly. But this is such a nerve-wracking job. And Miss Jones is always picking on you. She doesn't seem to appreciate the work you do.

Black: Mary, don't you think you're being a little unfair to Miss Jones? Now, I happen to know that she thinks very well of you. She wants to help you.

Mary: She doesn't act that way. I mean—well I know she has to see that the work gets done right, but it seems she's always looking over your shoulder to catch you or something. And such little things, too, she—

Black: Mary, you have to remember that the little things add up together to make something pretty big. If we neglected the little things, we wouldn't be in business very long. Now that extra half plum—it may seem like noth-ing at all to you, but we have to work out the prices and portions to make a small profit on that salad. If we put in an extra half plum, we're really giving it away. If we sell 100 of those salads a day, that mounts up. We're doing all the work for nothing. Now, I'm not criticizing you, but I just want you to understand the importance of these things. Do you see what I mean?

Mary: Well, if I did put on an extra half plum, it was only on 2 or 3, not 100. I don't remember every one, but I know it was only 2 or 3.

Black: Sure, that's what I'm getting at. You were just a little careless. That's all. Miss Jones was trying to correct you. Now, you don't blame her for trying to see that the work is done right do you?

Mary: Sure, she wants it done right, but she doesn't realize what we're up against. It's one thing to know just how to make a salad. It's another thing to have to make hundreds of them in a rush, like I have to. If Miss Jones had ever worked behind the counter like the rest of us, she'd know what it's like.

Black: But Miss Jones did work behind the counter when she was getting her training.

Mary: That's different. You weren't so rushed then like we are now.

Black: Yes, that's true. But I'm not trying to defend Miss Jones to you. I'm just trying to help you to get this thing straightened out. Now, you didn't like the way Miss Jones criticized you. But let's look at both sides of it. Do you think you were fair to her?

Mary: I know what you think. You think I wasn't polite to her. All right, I wasn't. I lost my temper. If I had said anything, I would have told her what I thought of her. So I thought it would be better not to say anything. Well, what of it? It's done, and I'm through now. Give me my paycheck and let me out of here.

Black: Your check is here for you, Mary, but let's not be hasty about this. Remember your aunt has worked here a long time. She hoped you'd fit in too. If you just walk out this way, it'll be quite a blow to her.

Mary: I don't care about her or Miss Jones or you either. I've got my own life to live. I'm tired of having people always pick on me and tell me what to do. I know what I want to do now. I want to get out of here. Give me my check!

Black: Well, if that's the way you feel about it—(hands her the check).

1. Comment on how Mr. Black handled his conversation with Mary.
2. How should he have handled it?
3. What mistakes did he make?

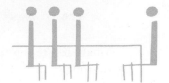

Conference Leadership

12

Among the most valuable skills of the modern executive is the ability to function as an effective conference leader or committee chairman. In fact, meetings have become so common in modern business that many observers are worried lest "group think" replace individual initiative. In some companies all important decisions are based on group consensus. A standing joke is, "All we do is meet all day and never get time for work."

Why this emphasis on meetings? As we have seen (in Chapter 9), one reason is the growing realization that people are more enthusiastic about carrying out plans that they have helped draw up than they are about implementing plans that are simply announced from above. Moreover, as business activities grow increasingly specialized it becomes more urgent to coordinate departments and encourage subordinates to volunteer advice.

Conference skills are useful, of course, even when the participants are not sitting around a table at a formal meeting. The manager needs these skills in his day-to-day activities whenever he is talking to a group of subordinates or equals and trying to reach some sort of agreement. Suppose three workers are quarreling over their vacation schedules and come to the foreman for a solution. He could listen and play judge. But it would be better if he could somehow get them to work out a schedule themselves that they could all accept.

In Chapter 9 we distinguished three types of meetings: those called for the purpose of giving information, those called to elicit suggestions, and those called to arrive at decisions. Although we shall be primarily concerned with decision-making meetings in this chapter, the skills we discuss are useful in the other types of meeting as well.[1]

Let us start with an example:

> The Plant Manager has called a special meeting of his top staff to consider whether a new cafeteria should be built. The present cafeteria is 40 years old and too small for current needs.
>
> It is 2:45 p.m. and the meeting is getting nowhere fast. It has been in session since lunchtime and the participants have been alternately bored and annoyed with each other. There has been a lot of hot air but little real progress. Everyone has his pet point of view and so far there has been no semblance of agreement.
>
> Of course the Plant Manager could put a stop to all this talk by proclaiming his own opinion, but at least on this issue he doesn't want to act without the close support of his staff. To this moment he has failed as a conference leader. Yet unless he can induce the group to accept a common solution there will be no new cafeteria.

Why all this trouble? What are the pitfalls that make running a meeting such a difficult art to learn? For one thing, there are invisible currents (sometimes called the "hidden agenda") in every discussion that must be recognized and mastered if agreement is to be reached. It is the ability to identify these currents and to direct them into proper channels that constitues the strength of a good conference leader.

The success of any meeting, particularly one called for the purpose of decision-making, depends largely on three interrelated factors: (1) the development of unity and teamwork within the group, (2) the chairman's ability to handle the meeting, particularly his skill in maintaining the proper degree of looseness or tightness of control, and (3) the participants' observance of an agenda designed for the orderly consideration of the problem at hand.

Many of the concepts we shall discuss in the following pages were developed by R. Freed Bales of the Harvard Laboratory of Social Relations,[2] by the Research Center for Group Dynamics, and by the National Training Labora-

---

[1] For an excellent discussion of conference leadership generally, see Norman R. F. Maier, *Problem Solving Discussions and Conferences* (New York: McGraw-Hill, 1963).

[2] Over the years Professor Bales, using a room with one-way glass to permit observation of meetings in session, has developed ingenious devices to measure interaction among committee members. See R. F. Bales, *Interaction Process Analysis* (Cambridge: Addison-Wesley, 1950), and R. F. Bales, "In Conference," *Harvard Business Review*, Vol. 32, No. 2 (March 1954), pp. 44-50.

tory for Group Development [3] (sometimes called the "Bethel group," after Bethel, Maine, where the Laboratory conducts an intensive summer training program).

Internal Unity and Teamwork

In addition to carrying out their formal tasks, the members of every meeting carry on an informal social life among themselves; if this informal life is unsatisfactory, the formal tasks will not be performed successfully. In other words, before we can have a smoothly working committee we must have a smoothly working social group.

As we discussed in Chapter 4, a new group is a collection of strangers, each of whom is anxious to establish a position that meets his personal needs.

> When people are confronted with each other, they must first find the place where they fit in. This involves being in or out of the group, establishing oneself as a specific individual, and seeing if one is going to be paid attention to and not be left behind or ignored. This anxiety gives rise to individual-centered behavior such as overtalking, extreme withdrawal, exhibitionism, recitation of biographies and previous experience.[4]

Much of the early history of a group consists of attempts to establish pecking orders or status hierarchies. Only when these relationships have coalesced and a well-defined informal organization has been established can the group settle down to work. Gradually the members of the group develop friendships and teamwork, and the aggregation of self-conscious individuals grows into a real group.

The success of the conference depends a great deal on the needs and interests of the people who take part in it. "The problems on the conference table are really not as difficult to deal with as the people around the table." [5] Let us look at some of these needs and interests, using as an example the cafeteria meeting we mentioned earlier.

Outside commitments of the members. It is just human nature for committee members to think first about how a new proposal will affect them and the people with whom they work. Mr. A, the assistant controller, is worried lest he give the impression that he has committed his boss (who is not present) to spend money on the cafeteria.[6] Mr. B, from the main office, wants the

---

[3] See Leland Bradford and John R. F. French, eds., "The Dynamics of the Discussion Group," *Journal of Social Issues*, Vol. 4, No. 2 (April 1948).

[4] William C. Schultz, "The Interpersonal Underworld," *Harvard Business Review*, Vol. 36, No. 4 (July 1958), p. 132.

[5] William M. Sattler and N. Edd Miller, *Discussion and Conference* (Englewood Cliffs, N.J.: Prentice-Hall, 1954), p. 149.

[6] In a situation like this it is sometimes a good idea to adjourn the meeting for a few days before trying to reach final agreement—or else make it clear that "representatives" do not bind "principals."

cafeteria located near where he works. Even though the arguments for building it elsewhere are very persuasive, he is worried about how those who work for him will react to having to take a long walk to lunch.

Differing perceptions of the issue. Mr. C has been sold on the desirability of a new cafeteria for a long time and feels that the only question left is how to design it. Mr. D, on the other hand, feels pressured by any discussion of design, since he hasn't been convinced that a new cafeteria is needed in the first place. Mr. C and Mr. D have obviously started out with different assumptions as to the purpose of the meeting. These differences will undoubtedly lead to friction.

Equally troublesome are the differing perceptions of the assistant controller and the personnel director. One thinks purely in terms of cost, the other in terms of improving morale. Moreover, different commitments are likely to cause differing perceptions, so that people see the same "facts" differently.

Obviously, what is needed at the outset is an agreement on the basic nature of the problem (or, in most cases, problems) and the setting up of an agenda so that each problem will be considered in turn. Certainly the chairman should refrain from stating baldly, "Gentlemen, *this* is the problem," for his perceptions may differ from everyone else's. Instead, he should find out from the participants what *they* think the fundamental issues are and then try to establish a common basis for discussion.

Personal needs. People do not stop acting like people just because they are at a meeting. They abandon neither their personal idiosyncrasies nor their status position in the organization. Mr. E has just had a fight with his wife. Mr. F is an assistant division manager and *expects* to receive respect. Mr. G wants to show up well in the discussion so that he will be promoted. Mr. H enjoys an argument of any kind. Mr. I is just shy.

Reactions to individuals rather than to ideas. Mr. J talks too much; consequently the group habitually rejects his ideas. Mr. K is disgusted by all this chatter and keeps his mouth shut. Mr. L, who is on the opposite side of the political fence from Mr. M, is almost automatically against whatever Mr. M is for and would love the chance to make M look silly. L and M are leaders of opposing cliques. When cliques develop in a group, the members tend to evaluate a new idea on the basis of how it will affect their prestige rather than on the basis of its real merits.

Thus, members bring to the meeting what sociologists call their respective roles—their points of view and patterns of behavior. It is the chairman's job to handle these various roles in such a way that individual viewpoints are dovetailed for the good of the group—in other words, so that teamwork develops.

So long as a committee has an unsatisfactory internal life, the members will go out of their way to look for matters of substance on which they can disagree, to make mountains out of molehills. On the other hand, a closely knit group will not be disrupted even by differences of policy. Each member feels assured of the acceptance and respect of colleagues. Social activity and good-natured kidding help build solidarity. Furthermore, once a matter has been fully aired, the minority is willing to go along with the majority, for there is group pressure to conform. At the same time, the majority respects views that are strongly held by the minority and is reluctant to override them. Mr. J's need for security no longer forces him to talk all the time. Mr. I's shyness no longer prevents him from offering suggestions. All the members show willingness to listen to each other's points of view, and to accept each other's foibles.

Once the members begin to experience the subtle transformation that marks the emergence of an effective team, they begin to take on new roles related to the functioning of the meeting itself. Some of these roles have to do with the *content* or subject matter of the meeting. Others have to do with the *process* by which the discussion is carried out. Here is a suggestive, though by no means complete, list of these roles (note that not all of them are constructive): [7]

CONTENT ROLES

Initiator—makes suggestions
Information-seeker—asks questions
Blocker—objects to other people's suggestions for action
Expert—knows the facts
Destructive critic—tears other people's ideas apart

PROCESS ROLES

Summarizer—summarizes where the group stands
Task-setter—tries to get the group to move on, emphasizes what
  still has to be done
Decision-announcer—announces decisions after the group has
  reached agreement
Traffic cop—decides who talks when
Encourager—encourages others to contribute
Mediator—tries to narrow differences
Playboy—kids around (and sometimes reduces excess tension)

(In addition to the roles we have mentioned, there are also inactive roles, such as follower, listener, and daydreamer.)

Does this mean that every member of the group plays only one role at a time? Not at all. Members frequently switch from one role to another and may play several roles simultaneously. Similarly, any one role may be played by several people at once.

If certain key roles are neglected--that of initiator or summarizer, for

---

[7] See "Training in Member Roles," *Adult Leadership,* Vol. 1, No. 8 (January 1953), pp. 17-23; and Kenneth D. Beane and Paul Sheats, "Functional Roles of Group Members," *Journal of Social Issues,* Vol. 4, No. 2 (Spring 1948), pp. 41-50. Although we use the same types of role as Beane and Sheats, we categorize them differently.

example—the whole meeting will suffer. But overemphasis on any single role should be avoided. Clearly, everyone cannot serve as an initiator or a harmonizer. In fact, a meeting in which everyone is careful not to step on anyone else's toes never accomplishes anything. Similarly, "rigidity of role-taking" [8] is undesirable, for team spirit is shattered when one person insists on always acting as destructive critic or demands parliamentary procedure regardless of the situation.

One of the responsibilities of the chairman is to help people fit their roles together for the good of the group. He wants to insure that the meeting will enjoy the full benefit of Bill's skill as a summarizer, Joe's expert knowledge, or Dick's special skills by calling on each at the *proper* time.

In summary, a successful meeting requires that members subordinate roles based on personality needs, outside commitments, and so forth, and accept roles, both content and process, which will help the meeting move toward its objectives. In other words, from an aggregation of individuals a work group arises which both satisfies the social needs of its members and works in reasonable harmony in solving problems.

The Chairman

The chairman himself plays a variety of roles: traffic cop, mediator, decision-announcer, and so forth. Indeed the success of the meeting depends to a large extent on the skill with which he plays these roles.

The so-called "autocratic" chairman plays both content and process roles: that is, he acts as an advocate of one point of view and also tries to get the meeting to reach agreement. His "democratic" counterpart is concerned primarily with process and tries to remain neutral when it comes to a question of content. But even the democratic chairman will be flexible in how he uses process roles, depending on the kind of problem being considered, the nature of the group, and the amount of time available. At times he must keep tight control over the meeting (that is, keep many of the process roles for himself); at other times he may exercise only loose control and try to spread responsibility throughout the group.

With this brief introduction, let us look more closely at various approaches to the chairman's responsibilities.

SHOULD THE CHAIRMAN ASSUME CONTENT ROLES?

It has been argued that the chairman's job is to help others express their point of view while keeping his own to himself. His function has been defined as "interviewing the group," helping it work through its own problems and reach its own decisions. Like the interviewer, the chairman needs to be per-

---

[8] Beane and Sheats, *op. cit.*, p. 47.

missive and unbiased. He is a catalyst who serves to bring out ideas already present in the group.

Certainly it is true that if he takes sides or expresses his own opinions other members may hesitate to take issue with him (particularly if the chairman happens to be the boss). In fact, any value judgment offered by the chairman may inhibit or distort communication.

> We have observed this problem at union meetings where the local president serves as presiding officer. The president seems to have a split personality. During most of the month he must act on his own initiative, like the commander of an army. Here his success depends on personal forcefulness, ingenuity, and ability. But in the meeting he is expected to be completely impartial even when his policies are under attack. Such switches in role are extremely difficult to make. The members are confused too. Bob Jones starts to criticize the president's activities as chief executive at the wrong point in the agenda—and is then called out of order. Bob can hardly avoid suspecting that the president is being less than impartial.

It is frequently unrealistic, however, for the chairman to remain completely neutral. Naturally, it would be foolish for the chairman of a three-man committee to keep his opinions completely to himself (although at times this is what a mediator does in labor relations). And if the chairman is an expert on the subject under discussion, it would be senseless for him to withhold his factual knowledge and his informed opinions—though if the subject is touchy he should be careful to distinguish his role as expert from his role as chairman.

What about the meeting in which the chairman is also the boss and has already made up his mind about what he wants to do? Should he pretend to remain impartial throughout the meeting, even though he knows very well that he may ignore the group's recommendations as soon as the session is over? Or should he try to mastermind the group into thinking that his ideas are really their own? Experience suggests that it rarely pays for the chairman to play cat-and-mouse with the group, for people resent being manipulated. Nor is it wise for him to exaggerate the amount of freedom that is actually being bestowed on the group. In such a situation, it is probably best for the chairman to open with something of this sort: "I'm thinking of doing so-and-so. What are the loopholes in this plan? Will it or won't it work?" The chairman should then try to answer questions and objections and must be willing to accept constructive suggestions.

In meetings where the members in fact enjoy a wide range of freedom, the chairman should normally try to stay neutral. However, it is often hard for a chairman to restrain himself, particularly where he is also boss. Feeling that he is expected to act as a vigorous initiator and decision-maker, the boss may fear that if he were to sit back and listen his behavior would be interpreted as a sign of weakness and indecision. And so, if the chairman is really anxious to let his subordinates make their own decision, he must learn to control his desire to take a dominant role.

With the important exceptions noted, then, the chairman is usually wise to avoid assuming content roles. What about process roles?

SHOULD THE CHAIRMAN ASSUME PROCESS ROLES?

It has been argued that the chairman should not assume process roles. When the field of group dynamics was first explored, there was a great deal of interest in what are known as "leaderless groups." It was felt that in a really mature group there would be no need for a formal chairman. Instead, every member would share the responsibility for steering the meeting and would automatically exercise the self-discipline needed to make the meeting a success. Strong leadership, it was argued, is undemocratic and tends to prevent the group from reaching its maximum potential.

Leadership groups have proved useful in psychotherapy, as a technique for selecting leaders, and in what is known as sensitivity training. And almost every day we all participate in groups that get things done with only informal leadership or with no apparent leadership at all. Nevertheless there is strong evidence that if a group must meet over a period of time,

> there is need for a stable structure of group organization if the group is to move ahead on the tasks before it. . . . When the leadership is in doubt, the members will become preoccupied with the leadership problem and with their relations with each other in general, and they will not be able to move ahead towards their goal until progress can also be made in the development of a regular pattern of interaction.[9]

In other words, the chairman performs an essential function in developing a pattern of teamwork that will lead to the efficient handling of problems. Sometimes an informal leader, acceptable to all the members of the group, will emerge naturally—though there is always the danger there will be a long, nasty struggle for power. But usually, time will be saved if a chairman is formally elected or appointed.

One study has suggested that groups without formal leaders are less effective in solving mathematical problems than groups with leaders.[10] Apparently the significant difference between such groups is that the formal leaders give minority opinions a chance to be expressed, and often it is the minority opinions that lead to a correct solution. In leaderless groups, however, minorities have less opportunity to speak up. Another study showed that as leaders become better trained, the quality of group discussion improves.[11]

Thus, it seems that the chairman makes an important contribution to making discussion effective. Now let us look more closely at what he does.

---

[9] William F. Whyte, *Leadership and Group Participation*, Bulletin 24, New York State School of Industrial and Labor Relations, pp. 19-20, 25.

[10] Norman R. F. Maier and A. R. Solem, "The Contribution of the Discussion Leader to the Quality of Group Thinking: The Effective Use of Minority Opinions," *Human Relations*, Vol. 5, No. 3 (August 1952), pp. 277-288.

[11] Norman R. F. Maier, "The Quality of Group Decisions as Influenced by the Discussion Leader," *Human Relations*, Vol. 3, No. 2 (June 1950), pp. 155-174.

THE CHAIRMAN'S DILEMMAS

The chairman is beset by dilemmas. The goals of a meeting are (1) to devise what seems the best solution to the problem under consideration, (2) with the greatest amount of unanimity, (3) in the shortest period of time. Obviously these three goals sometimes conflict.

1. The quality of the final decision depends both on the amount of time devoted to hammering it out and on the degree of freedom the members enjoy to make comments and suggestions. Too much haste or too zealous an attempt to work out a compromise acceptable to everyone may result in an unsatisfactory solution.

2. It is wise to give everyone a chance to participate in decision-making, particularly when the committee members are expected to implement their own decisions. "A few words [on each member's part] will serve to express and solidify his involvement, and to avoid his subsequent dissatisfaction." [12] The chairman should try to persuade the minority to go along with the majority, or, at times, try to induce the majority to accommodate objections that the minority feel to be extremely important. But this takes time and may result in a less satisfactory solution.

3. Most business meetings run under a time limit—either implicit or explicit. Even where there is no limit, the members become bored or frustrated if the meeting lasts too long. However, time can be saved only at the cost of less participation and a less carefully considered solution.

These conflicts among the basic goals of the meeting present the chairman with some perplexing problems. He must somehow manage to obtain general participation, but he must *also* keep the discussion relevant and directed toward the agenda, and he must *also* insure that the meeting will move steadily along toward its ultimate purpose—the making of a decision. How can the chairman keep all these balls in the air at the same time?

OBTAINING GENERAL PARTICIPATION

Probably the chairman's hardest job is to encourage nonparticipants to speak up and to persuade those who talk too much to give others a chance to be heard. The man who sits cloaked in silence all through the meeting is often either apathetic or secretly opposed to the solution being discussed. Bring his objections out into the open and they may either be answered or the program may be modified to gain his support. Only through active participation can he get the feeling that *we* made the decision.[13]

---

[12] Bales, "In Conference," p. 46.
[13] E. Paul Torrance, "Function of Expressed Disagreement in Small Group Processes," *Social Forces,* Vol. 35, No. 4 (1957).

This does not mean that the conference leader should strive for absolutely equal participation by all members. Naturally, on any given subject some people are likely to be better informed or to have stronger feelings than others. Even though each member of the meeting has a single vote, the members are rarely equal in fact. "In bureaucracy, ideas do not stand on merit alone. It is not only an opinion or an idea which wins but also a man." [14] Furthermore, evidence suggests that the man who talks most in a conference tends to have the best ideas and tends to approach problems in the most constructive manner.[15]

How can the conference leader stimulate participation? His general attitude is important. He should accept everyone's contribution without judgment and should seem to want everyone to participate. He should try to ask questions that are specific enough to stimulate a spirited response, even controversy. Once discussion is underway, he can use the reflective response to keep it going: "Jack thinks we can afford new equipment only if we can count on a large increase in sales. What do the rest of you think?" As in interviewing, here the reflective response serves to acknowledge Jack's contribution and to spur the others to join in.

A more elaborate technique for involving everyone in the discussion is the so-called "buzz session," in which the conference is broken down into small committees, each meeting in a separate part of the room. Each committee is instructed to discuss an assigned question and report back to the meeting as a whole after a specified period of time. Among the advantages of the buzz session are: forcing people to think for themselves, getting people to talk who would remain silent in a larger group (in fact, it is the only way in which all the members of a very large group can participate), and, often, saving time because a lot of discussion gets boiled down into a brief report. Buzz sessions are particularly useful in a larger conference.

Another technique of eliciting discussion is for the chairman to start at one side of the room and ask each conferee in turn to give his thoughts about the problem at hand. This device is particularly useful at the beginning of the meeting.

STICKING TO THE AGENDA

The chairman must also keep the meeting from wandering off into a discussion of irrelevancies. Otherwise progress will be slow and morale will fall.

One of the most effective techniques for keeping the discussion moving along in the right direction is to record on a blackboard or flip chart both the original agenda and the essential steps that are taken as the meeting progresses. Keeping a visual record of the unfolding discussion serves three functions:

---

[14] Victor Thompson, "Hierarchy, Specialization and Organizational Conflict," *Administrative Science Quarterly*, Vol. 5, No. 4 (May 1961), p. 503.

[15] R. F. Bales, "How People Interact in Conferences," *Scientific American*, Vol. 192 (March 1955), p. 18.

(1) It acknowledges contributions and encourages people to speak up, (2) it prevents repetition of what has already been said, and (3) it encourages participants to ask themselves whether their contribution will be relevant before they start talking.

Other, more specific techniques (besides the blunt "You are out of order") may be used by the chairman to keep the session marching along at a brisk pace:

> ... Comment, "That's a good point. Do you mind if we take it up later?" (And perhaps point to the appropriate spot on the posted agenda.)
> ... Repeat or write down only the relevant part of each contribution.
> ... Ask, "How does this fit in with what we are discussing?" (Perhaps you yourself are at fault for not recognizing its relevancy.)
> ... Summarize what the group has accomplished and what still must be done, so that the participants can decide for themselves what is relevant at the moment.
> ... Ask a member to do the summarizing, thus spreading responsibility for keeping the discussion on the track.

The chairman should not be too dictatorial in ruling people out of order. After all, what seems irrelevant to the chairman may seem perfectly relevant to the majority of the members. And even an apparent irrelevancy may spark a completely new approach to the problem. In fact, to the man who made it, the contribution must have seemed relevant or at least associated in some manner with the problem under discussion. If the chairman cracks down on a member now, he may inhibit this member's contribution in the future. Moreover, some irrelevancies, such as wisecracks or funny stories, actually help relieve tension and create a relaxed atmosphere.

KEEPING THE CONFERENCE MOVING
TOWARD ITS GOAL

As we have pointed out, the chairman faces a dilemma in keeping the conference moving toward its proper goal. If he moves too fast, some of the participants may feel pressured and resentful, and may not feel involved in the group's decision. On the other hand, if he moves too slowly, some members may grow restless and apathetic. The fact that most conferences operate under the pressure of a time limit helps the chairman keep the discussion moving, but it also obliges him to be less permissive than he would otherwise be.

As we shall see, a carefully prepared agenda helps the group progress, particularly when it is supplemented by periodic summaries to remind the group of what is still to be accomplished. A blackboard listing of matters still to be covered can gently coerce participants to move faster.

Through experience, the chairman learns to sense the opportune time to move on to the next point. Certainly it is time when the members start repeating gossipy irrelevancies. Having decided that the discussion has stalled, the chairman may resort to various techniques to motivate the group to move on. Note the difference in urgency between "Does anybody want to add anything" and "Unless someone has something else to say, I'd like to take up...." A short summary also helps close off one topic and lead the way to another.

THE CHAIRMAN'S TIGHTNESS OF CONTROL

How tight should be the chairman's control over process? To refer back to our discussion of process roles, certainly the chairman must perform the function of traffic cop. In addition, he may decide to assume all the other process roles: mediator, encourager, task-setter, and so forth. But if he does, he must realize that he will be exercising extremely tight control over the meeting, and he will run the risk of appearing dictatorial. Even if he does this in a highly benevolent fashion—by drawing others out, acknowledging contributions, and so on—the members may become resentful under his paternalistic rule.

Perhaps the best solution is for the chairman to try to induce the members to accept a share of the procedural responsibilities. The more fully the members share in the work of making the decision, the more likely they will be to carry it out with determination.

The comparison shown in the illustration on the opposite page suggests some of the differences between groups in which the leader exercises tight control and groups in which the leader exercises loose control.

The Agenda

The chairman is responsible for steering the group step by step toward the final decision.[16] Before the meeting gets under way he should give careful thought to his over-all strategy—to his agenda. But he must not insist that his plan be followed rigidly, for he cannot predict exactly how the members will react to the questions that come up. Consequently he must be flexible enough to adjust his strategy to the ever-changing demands of the group. He must remember that what may seem to him the most efficient way to analyze a problem may not meet the psychological needs of the group.

The chairman who exercises tight control normally decides on his over-all plan in advance, even though he may apply it with flexibility. He may even circulate copies of the agenda before the meeting as a means of helping the members prepare for the discussion. The chairman who exercises loose control may let the group itself decide on the agenda. Or he may listen to a preliminary discussion of the problem and then propose an agenda that seems to cover the main issues raised.

---

[16] One experiment showed that groups which follow "developmental" plans for discussion (that is, agendas) came up with higher-quality decisions than groups which permitted "free discussion." Norman R. F. Maier and P. A. Maier, "An Experimental Test on the Effects of 'Developmental' v. 'Free' Discussion on the Quality of Group Decisions," *Journal of Applied Psychology*, Vol. 41, No. 5 (October 1957), pp. 320-323.

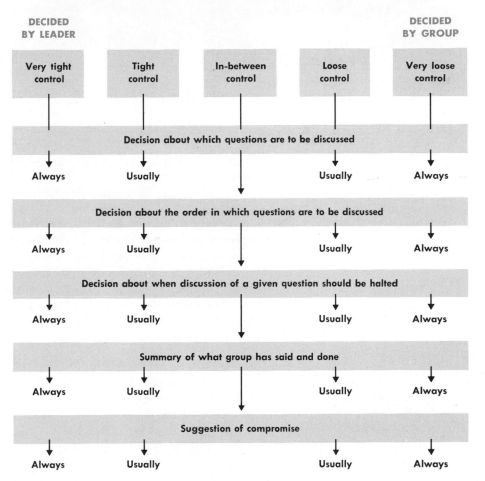

The chairman can exercise *tight* or *loose* control in a number of different ways.

The productive meeting seems to pass through successive stages of development. If these stages are ignored or taken in the wrong order (for instance, if there is an attempt at decision-making before the facts are evaluated), the meeting will take longer and be less productive.

There are certain standard procedures for analyzing problems, such as (1) assembling facts, (2) evaluating them, and (3) making a decision. But such neat formulas are often too simple to be of any real value. Instead, the course the discussion takes should be determined by the chairman's (or the group's) evaluation of what the crucial issues are. Here, for example, are three alternative agendas for a discussion of the problem of tardiness.

Agenda I

1. Should we have a firm rule against tardiness?
   a. What advantages?
   b. What objections?
2. How could such a rule be enforced?

Agenda II

1. Why are people late?
2. What can be done to handle each reason for lateness?
3. How can these suggestions be put into effect?

Agenda III

1. How much of a tardiness problem do we actually have?
2. What can be done about it?
3. What are the advantages and disadvantages of each suggestion?
4. Which one should we adopt?

Note the differences among these three agendas. Agenda I concentrates on one solution of the problem: a definite rule. Agenda II tries to find the basic causes of the problem and makes it possible to explore alternative solutions. Agenda III goes even deeper by exploring whether a serious problem really exists. Each of these agendas will lead to a different kind of discussion. Which agenda is best, of course, depends on the immediate situation.

With this warning against the dangers of too standardized an approach, let us sketch roughly the steps through which a typical problem-solving meeting might progress. (Note that we do not say *must*.)

Preparation. There is no need to repeat the standard injunction that the chairman should make sure of his arrangements beforehand—a suitable room, a blackboard, and so forth. But it is just as important for him to remember that advance briefing of the members on the main topics that are likely to be covered may stimulate them to do some thinking before the meeting. A preliminary caucus of those who are most concerned with the problem may be useful, provided it does not suggest to the others that the meeting has been rigged.

Social warm-up. Remember that a committee cannot become an effectively functioning work group until it has first become a comfortable social group. An opportunity must be given for new members to be introduced and for old members to go through the standard social ceremonies of banter and kidding (though when the participants see each other regularly, this period may last only a few seconds). To regard such social activities as disruptive or extraneous is to misunderstand completely what happens within a normal group. If the opportunity for socializing is not given before the meeting, chances are that it will occur during it.

Statement of the problem. The chairman's initial statement of the problem sets the stage for what is to follow. If there have been earlier meetings, he may simply summarize what has transpired so far. If it is the first meeting on a particular problem, the chairman's opening statement may cover: the general nature of the problem, its importance, its background and history (if necessary), the range of freedom the group will have in making a decision, and, possibly, a tentative agenda.

Free discussion. There is real value in having a free, unrestricted discussion before settling down to the systematic analysis necessary for decision-making. By free discussion we mean a chance for the participants to talk about those aspects of the problem that seem most important to them, regardless of whether the comments have any logical relevance to each other. In our tardiness conference, for example, A may brag that there is no lateness in his department; B may insist that he can't stop tardiness in his department until the other supervisors do something to put their deparments in order.

Many a member comes to the meeting burning with a pet idea that he *must* get off his chest before he starts listening to anybody else. He is bound to bring it up at the first opportunity, even when it is obviously not relevant to the topic of the moment. (Thus, even if the chairman tries to start the discussion by asking, "Why are people tardy?" Mr. C would insist on talking about the side issue of how to enforce rules.)

Unrestricted discussion of this sort makes it easy for people to warm up to the problem and to start participating. It gives the chairman a chance to survey the psychological atmosphere, so that he can plan his strategy and anticipate the crucial issues. Finally, the free-discussion period provides an opportunity for participants to get to know each other's position; it is in every sense a warm-up before people start "keeping score."

Adopting the agenda. When the free discussion has served its purpose, it is time for the chairman to propose an agenda or ask the group to suggest one. In either case it is important that the agenda be made explicit.

Getting the facts. Too often meetings flounder because members are arguing from conflicting factual premises. Facts may be hard to obtain but at least they are subject to objective inquiry, and it is usually easier to get agreement on facts than it is to get agreement on opinions. Actually, one may lead to the other.

> A rich background of common facts lays the groundwork for the development of common inferences and sentiments, and out of these common decisions can grow. No decision rests on "facts" alone, but there is no better starting point.[17]

Listing alternative solutions. Logically, the next step is for the group to suggest alternative solutions to the problem at hand. The chairman will normally want to elicit as many suggestions as possible, to insure that no good idea is overlooked and that no participant feels neglected.

In recent years a technique known as "creative thinking" has come into use as a means of stimulating suggestions. Although it has had its most enthusiastic following in advertising and public relations, its principles are sometimes useful in other fields. The advocates of this approach insist that all alternatives should

---

[17] Bales, "In Conference," p. 47.

be listed before any attempt is made to evaluate them, since premature judgments may interfere with getting the maximum range of ideas.[18]

The heart of creative thinking is "brainstorming," a process in which the members throw out ideas as they occur to them. No attempt is made to evaluate the suggestions at this point. Instead, the chairman writes them down as fast as they are made. The emphasis is on unorthodox, "free-wheeling" ideas, or on "hitchhiking"—that is, using another person's ideas as a springboard for a completely different one of your own. On a question such as "What can be done to stimulate sales of government savings bonds?" a good group can think of as many as a hundred ideas in five minutes. "Brainstorming" has been compared with free association in psychoanalysis, where the patient is expected to give expression to everything that comes into mind. Brainstorming has been criticized, though, as leading to fewer suggestions than would be produced by the same number of people working alone.[19]

Evaluating alternative solutions. Having listed the alternative solutions, the next step is to evaluate them. Although the method of evaluation will naturally depend on the nature of the problem, evaluation normally proceeds by stages. One approach is to discuss the advantages and disadvantages of each proposal in turn (along with suggestions on how to overcome difficulties), and then to compare one proposal against another.[20]

Notice how this approach differs from typical parliamentary procedure, in which each suggestion is considered separately and accepted or rejected in turn with no explicit consideration being given to possible alternatives.

During this evaluation period the chairman should try to help the group guard against the normal human tendency to think only of objections without trying to figure out how they can be overcome, or to take a black-and-white position for or against each idea, without trying to weigh alternatives realistically.

Narrowing the alternatives.[21] The group's function is to narrow down the many conceivable alternatives to the one or more on which general agreement can be reached. Normally, the more adequate the evaluation has been, the easier it will be to reach agreement. Yet the process is not automatic.

The first step is to determine which alternatives can be eliminated by unanimous consent. The remaining alternatives, which presumably have some sup-

---

[18] The creative-thinking movement is largely the brain-child of Alex Osborn, co-founder of the advertising firm of Batten, Barton, Durstine and Osborn. See his *Applied Imagination* (New York: Scribner's, 1953).

[19] For an excellent review of the research in this area, see Marvin Dunette, "Are Meetings Any Good in Solving Problems?" *Personnel Administration,* Vol. 27, No. 2 (March 1964), p. 12.

[20] This is an elaboration of the "risk technique," which is discussed in Norman R. F. Maier, *Principles of Human Relations* (New York, Wiley, 1952), pp. 62-73.

[21] Note that the techniques suggested here are the same as those listed by successful labor-management mediators.

porters in the group, can then be narrowed down (1) by their proponents becoming persuaded that they are wrong, (2) by mutual concession—that is, by a negative compromise in which everyone gives up something, or (3) by synthesis—that is, by a constructive or positive compromise that incorporates what every member regards as significant and that leaves out nothing that anyone feels is important. Probably the third alternative is the best, and the second the worst.

In the process of working out a solution, the chairman may take entirely upon himself the function of conciliator or "middleman." But there will be greater acceptance of the final decision if there are other "middlemen" in the group who assist in finding a constructive synthesis or compromise.

One of the chairman's most difficult problems is to help the minority surrender its position without loss of face. Agreement is easier to achieve if the chairman is able to convince each of the factions that the final decision incorporates some of their ideas and that each has won a partial victory.

At times agreement is not reached because the members misunderstand each other's position, or because they disagree over the facts themselves. To forestall unnecessary stalemates, the chairman may ask "Is this what you mean?" There are enough clear-cut problems to be settled without letting semantics cloud the issues.

> People often think they disagree when actually they simply are not talking about the same experiences. In such cases they do not draw each other out enough to realize that, although they are using the same words, they are talking about different experiences.[22]

The chairman can also invite the protagonists to restate their position in a constructive, positive form (avoiding criticisms of their opponents), by asking clarifying questions, or perhaps by summarizing the various positions in a way that will emphasize the areas of agreement. If none of these work, it may pay to refer the problem to the committee, or to recess while the members think things over.

One observer has proposed a "procedure for coercing agreement" to be used when the chairman feels the conference is bogging down in emotional argument. Here the chairman takes a firm stand and entertains only questions and answers designed to ascertain facts, to clear up details, and to distinguish one proposal from another.[23]

Taking a vote.   Should the chairman insist on working through to a unanimous agreement no matter how long it takes, or should he terminate the discussion by taking a vote? Traditionally, voting has been regarded as the

---

[22] Bales, "In Conference," p. 49.
[23] See Irving J. Lee, "Procedure for 'Coercing' Agreement," *Harvard Business Review*, Vol. 32, No. 1 (January 1954), p. 39. For criticism of this approach as being autocratic and mechanical, see Harold P. Zelko, *Successful Conference and Discussion Techniques* (New York: McGraw-Hill, 1957), pp. 152-153.

democratic way to make decisions, and the practice has taken on almost ceremonial overtones. In fact, a vote is often taken even where there is no opposition, just to show the group's solidarity.

And yet it can be argued that voting sometimes makes agreement more difficult to attain, since it plays up the differences among members and makes side-taking unavoidable. The trouble is that once a man has publicly committed himself to a position it becomes awkward for him to change his mind. Moreover, the man who is flatly overruled by a vote may be less likely to carry out the group's decision with enthusiasm. The public recording of each member's position tends to split the group into opposing factions, and encourages the members to pay more attention to the arguments of those who are on "their side" than to the arguments of the opposition.

It can even be argued that in a sense majority rule is actually undemocratic, since it shows no respect for the minority. The Quakers, for example, insist on unanimity, and any member can block a decision until he is convinced of its validity. Consequently, whenever action is finally taken it enjoys unanimous support.

> If [the group] can reach unanimous consent . . . the effort is well worth while, for there will be no disgruntled minority which refuses to support or reluctantly supports group action. The search for unanimity places a premium on trying to understand a person rather than arguing him down.[24]

Insistence on absolute unanimity, however, has certain disadvantages: (1) It makes for unduly long meetings and delays essential action, (2) in a sense it lets the dissenter make the decision (since he decides whether there will be a decision or none at all), and (3) the common-denominator compromise that suits everybody is rarely bold, imaginative, or capable of arousing enthusiasm. The unanimity rule may work well enough in a religious community (particularly one in which the members have a strong sense of social values),[25] but in industry quick decisions are often of the greatest importance.

The chairman should seek unanimity whenever possible, of course, and on most issues this is not too hard to obtain. The chairman can usually sense when agreement has been reached, and then he needs only to state the "decision" and ask if everyone agrees. Unanimity should not become a fetish, however. If the cost in time and frustration promises to be too great, the leader should call for a vote. A minority that loses after having had ample opportunity to sway the majority frequently accepts the results without too much ill feeling. To do otherwise in our society is considered poor sportsmanship.

Releasing tension. Arguments, decision-making, and undertaking commitments naturally result in the building up of tension within the group. The

---

[24] Frank S. Haimon, "Group Think or Group Thinking," *Adult Leadership,* Vol. 1, No. 10 (March 1953), p. 12.

[25] Even Quakers, however, sometimes feel frustrated because of a hold-out objector. See Whyte, *Leadership and Group Participation,* p. 35.

Bales study has suggested that after a decision has been reached it is important to give people a chance to release this tension by relaxing and engaging in informal social activity. The chairman who ignores this need by rushing the members back to work will find that until they let off steam they just won't settle down to business.

Self-evaluation

Successful group cooperation does not occur spontaneously. Group members must learn to work together. This process can be speeded up if the group sets aside some time to examine the effectiveness of its own activities—in other words, to learn from itself. Self-evaluation enables the group to improve its performance constantly.

Evaluation of this sort is usually more successful if there is some sort of feedback.[26] For example, one member of the group may be designated as a "process observer." He takes no active part in the meeting; instead, he makes a series of running notes on what is happening and then reports his observations during the evaluation period. "The observer can act as the eyes for the group leader, who because of his own responsibility for discussion, is unable to attend as closely to the difficulties in the group process and to be as objective about his own feelings." [27] A typical observer's report might start this way:

> "Discussion was slow at first. No one was sure what the problem was. Then Bob presented his ideas and almost everyone started contributing. Jack sidetracked us a bit by talking about . . . and the rest seemed bored until Jim (the chairman) very tactfully suggested that Jack defer his comments until later. I notice that Gus and Mike have been very quiet."

Even this small segment of the report would provide plenty of meat for self-evaluation:

1. How could the problem have been stated better at the beginning?
2. How did Jack feel about being called out of order? (When discussed in the evaluation session, this would permit Jack to let off steam, might persuade him to show more self-discipline next time, and would help the chairman evaluate his handling of Jack's irrelevancies.)
3. Why were Gus and Mike so quiet?

Indeed, the chairman can interrupt the meeting for a special report from the process observer whenever he thinks discussion has bogged down. The role of the observer should be rotated in order to give everybody a chance to observe the group from outside.

---

[26] See David H. Jenkins, "Feedback and Group Self-evaluation," *Journal of Social Issues,* Vol. 4, No. 2 (Spring 1948), pp. 50-60.
[27] *Ibid.,* p. 57.

Another aid to self-evaluation is a "post-meeting evaluation form," which is filled out by each of the members. A simple form might include questions such as these:

1. On the whole, how did you regard the meeting?
   Excellent—— Very Good—— Good—— Fair—— Poor——
2. What was good about the meeting?
3. What was bad about the meeting?
4. Was the chairman too strict? Too easy?
5. Do you feel you had sufficient opportunity to talk?

Parliamentary Law [28]

Parliamentary law is a formalized procedure designed for large deliberative bodies. Consequently it rarely has much value in small committee meetings, and even in large meetings it should be applied with flexibility. If a group tries to follow the letter of the law, it will fall into interminable, meaningless wrangles, resulting in the frustration of everyone concerned.

Strict observation of parliamentary law demands that the group vote for or against each proposal, with no provision for making a systematic comparison of alternatives. Parliamentary procedure is supposed to save time and to produce a more orderly meeting, but its rigid rules often do just the opposite, particularly since few people understand their intricacies.

Nevertheless, parliamentary procedure does have one major advantage for large meetings: It keeps control over process firmly in the hands of the members themselves. Only the group as a whole can decide when to stop debate, to make a decision, or to move on to the next question. The chairman's power is restricted to recognizing speakers and calling members out of order (and even this is subject to appeal).

Conclusion

The ability to act as an effective chairman or a productive committee member is becoming increasingly important in management. The same basic rules of conference leadership apply when the company president sits with the board of directors in mahogany and velvet surroundings as when the foreman calls his men together in the locker room to discuss a production technique.

Good meetings don't "just happen." They require skillful leadership on the part of the chairman and sincere cooperation on the part of the members.

---

[28] For a sharply contrasting view on the value of parliamentary law, see Malcolm Knowles, "Move Over Mr. Robert," *Adult Leadership*, Vol. 1, No. 2 (June 1952); Robert W. English, "General Robert Replies," *Adult Leadership*, Vol. 2, No. 2 (June 1953), p. 29; and Zelko, *op. cit.*, pp. 151-152.

When the members are unable to integrate their individual needs and roles, meetings tend to degenerate into futile wrangles. A feeling of solidarity and common purpose is required before members will evaluate ideas on their merits rather than in terms of self-interest.

The chairman plays a variety of roles, depending on the purpose of the meeting. The more effective chairman minimizes content roles. If he is a strict chairman, he will assume strong process roles; if he is a loose chairman, he will not. *maximizes process roles*

The chairman faces a constant dilemma in deciding how tight a rein to keep on the discussion. Too tight control may frustrate the natural development of ideas, force people to conclusions before they are ready, and generate resentment. Too loose control may result in a feeling of aimlessness and confusion.

The chairman must constantly keep in mind that the goals of meetings (high-quality decisions, general acceptance, and economy in time) often conflict with one another. He must encourage participation and yet at the same time keep the discussion both relevant and moving toward a conclusion.

The successful meeting proceeds smoothly from stage to stage. The chairman senses the invisible currents at work within the group and decides on the proper moment to move on.

If a meeting is to achieve its objective there must be a carefully devised agenda to insure an orderly, efficient procedure for discussion and decision-making. An effective agenda takes advantage of the natural stages through which a meeting passes, and is flexible enough (1) to meet the needs of the particular problem, group, and time limit, and (2) to be modified during the course of the meeting as the need arises. An agenda that has been accepted by the members serves many purposes: It insures that every point of view has been considered; it allows for maximum participation, and (hopefully) it enables the meeting to make its decision within the time allowed.

In a broad sense, the first three chapers of this part have been concerned with communication problems: those involving transmission of messages (Chapter 10), the reception of messages (Chapter 11), and improving the flow of messages among members of a meeting (Chapter 12). In each of these areas, as the following table illustrates, certain principles have emerged which dovetail neatly with similar principles from other areas.

Communicator	*Interviewer*	*Conference Leader*
1. Directs message to the world of his audience.	Tries to understand how interviewee sees problem.	Helps each member understand how others see problem.
2. Pitches remarks in terms audience can understand; takes into account what words mean to the audince.	Tries to understand what the words of the interviewee mean to him.	Helps members understand what each other's words mean.

Continued page 300

Communicator	*Interviewer*	*Conference Leader*
3. Tries to discover the audience's emotional state and takes this into account in framing message.	Helps interviewee release feelings before getting down to consider facts.	Allows group to express feelings before getting down to decision-making.
4. Tries to indicate to audience that he understands their problem.	Tries to indicate that he understands interviewee's problem.	Tries to indicate that he understands conference members' problems.

PROBLEM ONE

Staff Meeting

Role play a meeting of the Dooley Division Staff (Chapter 16, p. 417) discussing a proposal by the new purchasing agent to introduce a formal requisition or inventory-control system. Various members of the group may take on the roles of Dooley, Wallace, the chief engineer, the controller, the general foreman, and the purchasing agent. Assume that Dooley has no strong preference, either for or against the new system, but that he is anxious to get a fairly unanimous agreement within his staff.

Introducing Change

13

We live in a world of change. We Americans in particular have learned to expect change as part of our everyday life. We pride ourselves on being modern and up-to-date in our habits and behavior. Still we may be more traditional than we think. To be sure, we accept and even welcome changes in terms of material things, such as household gadgets or cars. But we tend to resist changes in our interpersonal and job relations, because these changes threaten the security of the orderly and familiar ways we have known in the past, and often our status as well.

If a company is to survive today, it must be able to react to changing conditions by changing itself. In fact, it *must* anticipate environmental changes by altering its own policies and structure in time to meet these new conditions as they arise. The ability to introduce change with a minimum of resistance is a key managerial skill. In this chapter we shall discuss (1) why there is resistance to change and (2) what can be done to deal with it.

Types of Resistance to Change

Of all the types of resistance to change, perhaps the one most commonly recognized is the resistance of many employees to technological change—to automation, for example. Such resistance is readily understandable. In some instances, technological change means that employees must agree to work on faster machines with increased workloads. In others, it requires the acquisition of new skills and even a new approach to work; for example, the worker must learn to watch and adjust equipment rather than to operate it manually.[1] In still others, as in the case of locomotive firemen and flight engineers, it may mean the loss of work altogether.

But there are many other forms of change which are also resisted: changes in organizational structure, methods of compensation, and so forth. Take the case of a clothing store, once famous for its high-quality merchandise, which is located in an area from which high-income customers have moved. A new owner resolves to introduce a lower-priced line and to induce his salesmen to engage in high-pressure salesmanship. The salesmen are likely to react violently to changing well-established patterns.

Resistance to change is sometimes as deep-rooted at the managerial level as it is at lower levels. In many companies one hears constant complaints about "old fogies" who are hampering progress. As we explore elsewhere,[2] there are problems involved in re-educating managers to improve their supervisory practices, to give higher priority to accident prevention, and so forth. Indeed, managers tend to resist the introduction of almost any new personnel practice. They may regard a new system of job evaluation as a threat to existing status relationships, or the introduction of tests in hiring as a threat to their traditional prerogative to hire whomever they wish.

Resistance to change may show itself in unexpected ways, for instance in aggression, regression, and in all the negative reactions discussed in Chapter 6. It may appear as absenteeism, resignations, requests for transfer, and as "the expression of a lot of pseudo-logical reasons why the change will not work."[3] One clear sign of resistance is a series of apparently "emotional" or "irrational" objections to minor changes; these often indicate that more deep-seated problems are involved.

It should be emphasized that not all change is resisted. Some forms of change are welcomed (such as pay increases). Aerospace companies, for example, engage in constant technological and organizational change with

---

[1] See Charles R. Walker, *Towards an Automatic Factory* (New York: Harper & Row, 1957).

[2] George Strauss and Leonard R. Sayles, *Personnel* (Englewood Cliffs, N.J.: Prentice-Hall, 1960), Chapter 24.

[3] Paul Lawrence, "How to Deal With Resistance to Change," *Harvard Business Review*, Vol. 32, No. 3 (May 1954), p. 49.

relatively little resistance. It is not change itself which causes the resistance, but the meaning of the change for the people involved. Thus, one should expect greater resistance to change in a company which is contracting or stationary in size than one would in a company which is expanding, even though the expanding company has a larger number of changes—the reason being that in the expanding company the changes are less likely to threaten employees' social or economic status.[4]

What Causes Resistance to Change?

ECONOMIC FACTORS

The most obvious reason is economic. Workers resist automation when they fear they will lose their jobs; they are unimpressed by arguments that in the "long run" there will be more jobs in other parts of the country. What concerns them most is the economic welfare of themselves and their families.[5]

Similarly, a craftsman may fear that new developments will reduce the economic value of his skill. In the same way, managers themselves oppose a change that helps the company as a whole but hurts their individual promotional opportunities.

Sometimes the economic factors underlying resistance to change are obscure and not immediately apparent. In one plant the employees began to damage parts they were sending to a new plant overseas; formerly the parts had been shipped to a domestic plant. Was this blind resistance to change? Not at all. Investigation revealed that the employees were afraid the company was shifting more and more of its operations to the overseas plant and feared that eventually they would lose their jobs.

We must, however, guard against the common misconception that workers generally—and particularly their unions—blindly resist all forms of technological progress. The Hat Workers and Clothing Workers unions, for instance, have developed special programs designed to encourage management to introduce such changes. They recognize that only through rising productivity can their wages be raised. Similarly, John L. Lewis and the United Mine Workers cooperated with coal-mine owners in an extensive mechanization program which has resulted in substantially fewer jobs in the coal fields, but higher earnings for those who remained. Foreign visitors to this country express surprise at the extent to which American workers have learned that technological change redounds to their benefit and is the source of rising wages. There is, however, a significant gap between the intellectual recognition of this relationship and the acceptance of change in a particular case.

---

[4] Michael Stewart, "Resistance to Technological Change in Industry," *Human Organization,* Vol. 16, No. 3 (Fall 1957), pp. 36-39.

[5] For similar reasons, workers may object to bigger workloads, even when there is no demand for greater physical effort. They reason that they may work either themselves or their friends out of a job or that management is getting "something for nothing."

INCONVENIENCE

Equally understandable is the resistance to change that threatens to make life more difficult. A worker fights the assignment of extra duties; he has learned his old job so well that it requires no attention any more, while the new job requires surface attention. Similarly, executives dislike the inconvenience of being reassigned from one location to another. Even if the company pays their expenses, there is the bother of buying and selling houses, packing, and readjusting to new work and a new environment.

All of us develop a vested interest in our usual way of doing things. Our everyday habits provide us with a certain security in our life. Some of these are quite trivial: We drive to work by a fixed route every day, even though other routes are equally good; when our usual route is temporarily blocked, we are annoyed by the inconvenience of having to change our pattern.

Learning new ways requires the expenditure of energy, and human beings are generally lazy. Even for the simplest job there are "tricks to the trade" that take time to learn. When a man is thrown into a new situation his tricks no longer apply and he loses the security of the familiar.

UNCERTAINTY

The new way is always strange, threatening, and laden with uncertainties—even if it is an improvement over the old. We have a chance for a new job at higher pay. Should we take it? Maybe not. How hard will it be? How long will it take to learn? Will we be able to meet the challenge? Who will our friends be? The opportunity may be very good indeed, yet there is a strong tendency to let well enough alone.

One reason for this fear is the lack of factual information. We know our present circumstances; we don't know what the new ones will be. Some people are gamblers by nature, but the average person hesitates to venture into uncharted waters. The uncertain is always threatening.

New equipment is introduced into the plant. What will it mean to our job, our status, our security? A new boss is assigned to the department. What will his policies be? How will they affect us? Often the rumor mill exaggerates the potential threat of a change. Until management clarifies the impact of the change, such rumors can panic a group of employees.

Uncertainty caused by lack of information may be corrected simply by providing answers to questions—assuming that management is aware of what questions are being asked. But there is another kind of uncertainty that cannot be dissipated by providing information: the anxiety that springs from the individual's fears about how *he himself* will react to the new situation. Every draftee is assailed with doubts the night before his induction. What will army life be for me? Every veteran is delighted to provide information, but no one can predict how *I* will react. For this sort of uncertainty there can be no quick remedy.

SYMBOLS

Symbols raise special problems. Remember that a symbol is something which stands for something else. The flag symbolizes one's country; the Bastille, pre-revolutionary oppression in France; the supervisors' parking lot, their special status; the restaurant's white table cloth, its general excellence. A symbol cannot be eliminated without threatening in people's minds the things for which it stands. Note, for example, the widespread emotional reaction to the change in the Canadian flag, or the following case from industry:

> The new manager of the Integrity Insurance Company had little difficulty with his "modernization" program until he decided it was a waste of money to print policies on high-quality parchment paper. His proposal to substitute a cheaper but still durable paper led to a storm of protest from the company's insurance agents: The new paper wouldn't look or wear well, it didn't look right, the customers would think it cheap. Investigation revealed that to the agents the parchment paper was a symbol of Integrity's reputation as a leader in the industry. They began to fear that these changes would mean that Integrity would be just like any other insurance company.

Small changes may symbolize big ones, particularly when employees are uncertain about how extensive a program of change will be. When a situation begins to shift, subordinates search for indications of what lies ahead. For Integrity's agents, the cheaper paper was a convincing sign that management intended to degrade the company's prestige. A symbol represents a whole framework of treasured relationships and values; subordinates unite to protect it against attack just as if everything it represented were actually in danger.

THREATS TO INTERPERSONAL RELATIONSHIPS

As we mentioned in Chapter 4, anything that disrupts the customary social relationships and standards of the group will meet with strong resistance. In particular, employees oppose changes which threaten their status or their painfully acquired, socially valued skills.

> For example, vests and coats in one clothing center are made by separate groups of tailors, though to an outsider their skills seem readily interchangeable. Over the years the demand for vests has fallen off while an acute shortage of skilled coatmakers has developed. Yet in spite of the combined urging of union and management, the vestmakers refuse to transfer to coatmaking. As a result the vestmakers lose over $30 a week. Why do they persist in this apparently illogical attitude?
> The vestmakers are a small, tightly knit clique of friends who are proud of their skill. They have a long-established union local of their own. They fear that if they were transferred to coatmaking their clique would be broken up, they would become the *least*-skilled coatmakers rather than highly skilled vestmakers, and they would lose the protection of their local. Thus, the change is a threat to their prestige, their ability to meet their social needs, and their union protection.

Even when no change in physical location is involved, most changes tend to upset interpersonal relations. Take the situation in a small firm that had just hired a new purchasing agent.

> Previously each department head had ordered his own supplies. Now the department head merely filled out a purchase order and the purchasing agent decided on the supplier and negotiated the price. Though this policy saved the department heads from being pestered by salesmen and saved the company money, the department heads were highly antagonistic. They missed the feeling of importance that came from dealing directly with salesmen; the purchasing agent was far less obsequious to them than the salesman had been, and he threatened their authority by suggesting at times that they might use cheaper, lower-quality material. This fact may help explain why they began complaining about red tape and about how the purchasing agent made their jobs harder, not easier.

Every supervisor develops patterns of informal relations with his subordinates. And every new supervisor requires a long period of initiation before he is accepted by his subordinates as their legitimate leader (see Chapter 8), in part because they fear that he may not follow his predecessor's patterns of informal relations. In fact, *any* new member of a group has a hard time until he develops satisfactory relations with his colleagues—and one of the reasons why people resist being transferred to new jobs is that they dislike the disruption of old relations and the work of establishing new ones.

Other changes may threaten a man's opportunity to provide leadership. For instance, before automation a crew chief on a press directed the men who worked with him; after automation there was less need for teamwork and less opportunity for him to issue orders. Or the change may mean that the man who used to call the signals waits passively for someone else to take the initiative. Under the old scheme the maintenance man scheduled his own work; under the new scheme he must wait until someone calls him, thus reducing his discretion and status and substantially changing his social relationships with others.

Individuals adjust their pattern of social relations to fit their own special personality needs, just as they adjust other elements of their life in the formation of habits. Over a period of time, assuming an employee is not anxious to quit his present job, he has probably developed a good fit between his personality needs and the requirements of the job. The man who wants to boss others around, even if he is not officially a supervisor, has probably found a position in the work group that permits him to initiate activity; the worker who wants to avoid social pressures has probably found a job where no one can push him, not even the man who works next to him. Changing work procedures and systems, and introducing new equipment, upsets these convenient, pleasant job patterns. The sequence of work may be so drastically changed that the man who was formerly isolated must now work with a high-pressure colleague, and the leader is left with no one to lead.

**RESENTMENT TOWARD NEW ORDERS
AND INCREASED CONTROL**

Whenever management institutes change, it must substantially increase the number of orders it gives to subordinates. This results in a change in interpersonal relations, and this second change, in turn, may well lead to resistance.

Some people resent taking any orders at all. Others have become accustomed to a certain level of control from higher management but resist any attempt to strengthen than control. On routine jobs or on jobs where employees are used to being their own boss, direct orders from management are relatively rare. When change occurs, they become subject to all sorts of unusual pressures from supervisors, engineers, and the big boss. Suddenly they find that someone is checking up on them and barraging them with far more orders than usual. This sharp increase in control reduces their feeling of autonomy and self-reliance. It emphasizes their dependence on management.

Similarly, members of management often resist change when it is initiated by staff people who normally have little control over (or even contact with) the line people who must carry out the change. Staff people have a strong incentive to promote change because it increases their prestige and influence; for almost these very reasons, however, line people have a tendency to resist change.

Resistance of this sort occurs even in the relations between staff groups. Engineers, for example, often resist suggestions by purchasing agents to utilize new materials which have come to the purchasing agents' attention through salesmen. Engineers feel that they should have exclusive authority to specify the material used, and that they should tell the purchasing agent what sorts of material should be used—not vice versa. So when purchasing agents try to influence the engineers, they are reversing the usual channel of communication. (We shall discuss this problem at greater length in Chapter 17.)

When told that they *must* change their behavior, people sometimes become stubborn. They seek to defend themselves and become more committed than ever to their old attitudes. As we shall see, change is easier when the people who are to be changed are consulted beforehand or have a chance to participate in making the decision—and thus do not feel pushed.

It has been argued that one of the main problems in introducing change is to keep it from being introduced in an intermittent fashion. The organizations that have greatest difficulty are often those that make changes only once in a while. The trick, it is claimed, is to make change almost continuously, to make change for the sake of change, even if there is no compelling reason for change at the moment. Perhaps this suggestion is too extreme. Still it does emphasize the point that living under change is very different from leading the same placid existence day after day.

UNION ATTITUDES

Unions are also likely to resist change unless management consults with them, either formally or informally. It is not enough to inform individuals or consult with them. Every union has certain institutional needs that must be met if it is to retain its members' loyalty. If management makes a point of working with the union, the union may cooperate in introducing the change. If management ignores the union, the only way the union can preserve its status is by opposing management.

What happens when management decides to introduce new equipment that will require men to learn new jobs and assume new responsibilities? The typical approach in some companies is for the industrial engineer to make all the necessary plans, perhaps in consultation with the foreman. When the equipment arrives, the foreman assigns men to the new jobs and the personnel department computes the new pay rates. Almost inevitably, the union will find something wrong with the change and will file a grievance—and perhaps even sponsor a slow-down or wildcat strike. Why? If the union were to accept management's action passively, it would in effect be abandoning what it regards as its proper role. The only way to save face is to fight the proposed changes.

In other companies, management customarily informs the union of proposed changes long before they are made, asks for suggestions on how the seniority clause should operate when men are transferred, and bargains over wage rates for the new job. The union's status is preserved, and it assumes responsibility for resolving what might be a bitter dispute over who will be assigned to the new jobs. Of course, in bargaining over wages the company may have to make concessions, but the over-all cost may be less than the expense of trying to force the change over the union's objection, for workers are in an ideal position to insure that unwelcome change will prove unsuccessful or costly.

CHANGE AND THE OVER-ALL ORGANIZATION

So far we have dealt with change as if it occurred in a vacuum. Obviously, this is not so. "Since every group is a social system, any change in one of its component parts is likely to require or result in alteration or rearrangement of other parts." [6] Apparently simple changes may involve a host of people who at first may not seem concerned. For example, a change may appear to affect only Mr. A, but it affects his relationship with Mr. B, who becomes upset, thus hurting his relationship with Mr. C. Mr. C in turn deals with Mr. A in a less friendly fashion than usual, which further upsets Mr. A. Eventually, a comparatively minor change touches off a major crisis.

Change must be seen in organizational terms. Rarely are a manager and his

---

[6] Paul C. Agnew and Francis L. K. Hsu, "Introducing Change in a Mental Hospital," *Human Organization*, Vol. 19, No. 4 (Winter 1961), p. 199.

immediate subordinates the only ones involved. Very often the need for change develops first: Profits decline, competition adopts new products or production processes, equipment begins to wear out and get out of date, and so forth. Management may cling to its traditional ways at first, even though to an outsider the need for adjustment may be obvious. Eventually, one group within management (usually a staff department) may become aware of the problem and propose a solution. Now it must sell its solution to other groups within management. Line personnel may resist because they have the difficult task of implementing the change. Other staff men may resist also: the controller, for instance, because the change is too expensive, or the personnel director because it would disrupt a tricky union relationship.

While the plan is under consideration, rumors fly, restlessness increases, and sometimes exaggerated fears arise. When the plan is finally tentatively adopted at higher levels, management must now try to win the acceptance and co-operation of those at lower levels, and sometimes from the union. Often the change may have widespread and unexpected ramification and may disrupt precariously balanced relationships.

The process should not be considered entirely a one-way street which runs, for example, from staff to line to subordinate employees. Line management will seek additional information from staff, it will raise objections, and it will suggest modifications in the proposed plans. Staff people may now be the ones who are resisting the changes proposed by line. Subordinates will react in the same way, openly if they are permitted to speak out, otherwise on an undercover basis. (For example, they may "modify" management's plans through outright sabotage.) Often subordinates propose change which higher management will "resist" in turn.

In organizations where human relations are sound, however, change is usually taken in stride. But in organizations where tensions and dissatisfactions are high, changes will be more difficult to accomplish. For example:

> The high degree of [social] integration, the relative lack of conflict, and the level of job security in the chemical industry provide an atmosphere in which technological change is more accepted by workers and management than in the automobile industry, where, because of its history of labor-management strife and its irregular employment patterns, workers are naturally suspicious of the motives and effects of technological innovation.[7]

In some situations, stresses which are not obvious in ordinary circumstances become evident when change is introduced, almost as if the change is the straw which breaks the camel's back. Consider the following ingenious study conducted at General Electric:[8]

---

[7] Robert Blauner, *Alienation and Freedom* (Chicago: University of Chicago Press, 1964), p. 153.

[8] Stanley Schacter and others, "Emotional Disruption and Industrial Productivity," *Journal of Applied Psychology*, Vol. 45, No. 4 (August 1961), pp. 201-213. The above description of the experiment is somewhat oversimplified, but gives the essential picture of what was done.

The experiment was concerned with two sets of groups of workers, all doing repetitive, no-attention work. First these employees went through a "manipulative period" of several weeks. One set of employees, the "Favored Groups," received praise and friendly help from their bosses and were protected from disruption. The other set, the "Disfavored Groups," were nagged and pestered by management in a number of annoying ways. As might be expected, the Favored Groups developed positive attitudes toward their treatment while the Disfavored Groups expressed feelings of considerable aggravation. Nevertheless, neither treatment seemed to have a significant effect on the various groups' output rates.

At the end of the manipulation period, all special treatment stopped, except that shortly thereafter slight changes were made in each group's production methods. In both sets of groups both quantity and quality of output went down but the effect was very significantly greater in the formerly Disfavored Groups than it was in the Favored Groups.

The lesson for management here is that, although morale may have little impact on productivity under normal conditions, it may well have the effect of making change more difficult.[9] The impact of change upon an existing organization is always difficult to predict.

VIOLATION OF EXPECTATIONS

One concept may help summarize much of what we have said about resistance to change. In previous chapters we suggested that in most well-established groups there are generally accepted (legitimate) norms about the rights and responsibilities of both managers and subordinates—and that the nature of both these rights and responsibilities are established by implicit bargaining. Change, however, violates the implicit bargain. Unless the manager is careful in how he introduces change, his action is likely to be regarded as illegitimate, and subordinates, through resisting the change, will seek to restore the previous equilibrium.

Reducing Resistance to Change

Let us examine the problem of introducing change in still another framework. Take a situation in which workers are producing at 70 per cent of the efficiency that might be expected on the basis of purely technical considerations. Obviously, certain forces are operating to hold the rate down. For instance:

1. Dislike of work.
2. Fear of working oneself out of a job.
3. An informally set "bogey."
4. Dislike of the supervisor.

---

[9] For another study which leads to the same conclusion, see Chris Argyris, "Organizational Effectiveness Under Stress," *Harvard Business Review*, Vol. 38, No. 3 (May 1960), pp. 137-146.

Yet another set of forces must be operating to keep the rate *as high as* 70 per cent. These may be:

1. Fear of losing one's job—or at least fear of losing special privileges.
2. Pressure exerted by the supervisor.
3. Financial incentives (if there is piece work).
4. Fear of being caught idle.

Presumably, at the 70 per cent rate of production, the two sets of forces have reached a balance which has been called a "quasi-stable equilibrium." [10] That is, a system has been established in which one set of needs is balanced off against the other. (See A in the diagram.)

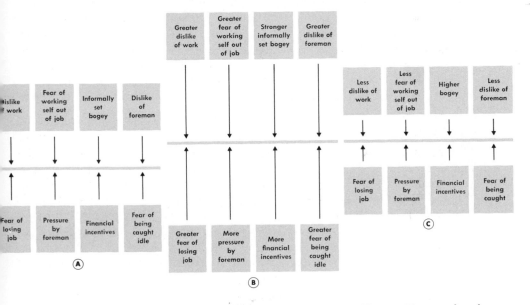

A shows quasi-stable equilibrium; B shows higher equilibrium with strengthened upward forces; C shows higher equilibrium with weakened downward forces.

Now, if management wants to increase production, the typical approach is to strengthen the upward forces (B in diagram), perhaps by having the foreman apply even more pressure or by installing piece work. This method of introducing change we shall call *overcoming resistance*. Of course, the higher production climbs, the more workers' resistance is raised, until finally a new equilibrium is reached where the two sets of pressures are once more in balance. However, and this is a crucial point, at the new equilibrium, stronger forces are operating on each side, and tension is at a higher level. Frustration

---

[10] This concept of quasi-stable equilibrium was developed by Kurt Lewin. See his "Frontiers in Group Dynamics," *Human Relations*, Vol. 1, No. 1 (1947), pp. 5-42.

is greater, and employees are more likely to devise techniques to insulate them-selves from the pressures acting on them. From management's point of view this is an inefficient way of doing things. It is like trying to stop a car by using the brakes without taking one's foot off the gas.

Fortunately, there are more efficient ways of accomplishing the same ob-jective. Instead of strengthening the upward forces, management can weaken the downward forces (C in diagram), perhaps by making the work less dis-agreeable, or by inducing workers to change their bogey, or by reducing their dislike of the foreman. This method we shall call *reducing resistance*. Here, too, a new equilibrium will be reached at a higher level of production, but at a lower level of tension. It is like stopping a car by taking one's foot off the gas, but by not using the brake.

Though method 2 (reducing resistance) frequently cannot be used without some of method 1 (overcoming resistance), the former places the least strain on human relations.

In overcoming resistance, management seeks to apply enough pressure on a man to induce him to do what is expected. For instance, the most obvious way to overcome resistance to change is simply to threaten to fire a man if he doesn't adjust, or promise to pay him more if he does.

But this threatening approach leads to all the problems we discussed in Chapter 6 under "be strong." A man may respond to threats either by quitting altogether, by sabotaging the change once it has been introduced, or by implementing it in a half-hearted manner.

What about trying to deal with resistance by promising a man an economic reward if he will accept the change? If the reason for resistance in this case is largely economic—and in many cases it is—obviously an economic reward is a good answer, for it helps reduce the cause of resistance and thus helps get the change accepted with less tension.

On the other hand, economic rewards are less successful if the reason for resistance is noneconomic. For instance, an executive may be offered a salary increase to move to a new location. Let us assume that the executive's im-mediate reaction to this offer is that the new location is very unpleasant and that he has misgivings about the type of work he will be doing and the type of men he will be associating with.

Confronted with such a choice, the executive will probably experience painful indecision. Indecision is always frustrating even between attractive alternatives. He may even try to get the salary increase without leaving town, perhaps by going to work for another company. And regardless of what he decides, for years to come he may resent having been forced into the decision. If he stays, he may deplore his economic sacrifice every time he pays a bill. If he goes, his attitude may make it difficult for him to adjust to the new situation.

A large chemical company used quite a different approach in manning a new laboratory in a remote section of the country. Their approach emphasized reducing causes of resistance. First, the company publicized the importance and challenge of the new laboratory's work and hinted broadly that assignment there would offer great opportunities for promotion. Then it invited a small core of experienced engineers to accept positions in the new lab and told them that they could invite less-experienced men to join them. However, management made it clear that those who were invited were free to reject the invitation. The potential candidates and their families were brought together from all over the country at the site of the new lab and were given a chance to get to know one another and to investigate housing possibilities. As a consequence, the firm had little trouble recruiting able men to work in the new location.

In the discussion that follows, we shall seek to emphasize methods of reducing, rather than overcoming, resistance.

THROUGH ECONOMIC INCENTIVES

As we mentioned earlier, much of the resistance to change has an economic motivation. Either men hear that the change will result in an immediate loss of job or earnings, or else they fear that it will affect their long-run job security or chances for promotion. The easiest solution in such a case is simple but expensive: Guarantee that these fears are groundless. For instance, if a man refuses to work on a new machine merely because he fears a loss of piece-work earnings, management might guarantee him that his earnings will be no lower on the new machine. It is quite common in union contracts today for management to guarantee that no one will be displaced by technological change. Certainly, too, if new equipment is to be introduced that will displace men, the change should be made in a period of expanding employment when the displaced employee can be offered another job that offers equally good security and pay.

Such guarantees are extremely useful in smoothing over change. The difficulty is their expense. The very reason for change may be the desire to cut costs because of economic necessity. Even in such a case management may reduce resistance if it can truthfully show that the change will be an improvement in the individual's own (not just the company's or the other workers') economic prospects in the long run.

Though the bulk of this chapter is concerned with noneconomic means of handling resistance, you should not draw the wrong impression from our allocation of space. *Economic motivation is very important in our society.* And when the cause of resistance is economic, all the noneconomic techniques that we are about to discuss will be meaningless. True, an employer may successfully manipulate an employee into acquiescing to a change that is not in the employee's best interest. But in the long run, in a free society such attempts at brainwashing tend to backfire against their instigators. We emphasize this point because there are employers who feel that if proper "human relations" are applied, employees will be willing to do without a fair wage. Such misuse of human relations is, in our opinion, highly immoral; fortunately, it is rarely successful.

THROUGH TWO-WAY COMMUNICATION

Resistance to change that springs from fear of the unknown can be reduced simply by providing appropriate information. This information should explain not only *what* is to happen but also *why*. And it should be sent to the whole organization, to those both directly and indirectly involved.

This question of communications raises all the problems that we discussed in Chapter 10, particularly: (1) Is the information really understood? And (2) does it answer the questions actually being asked? Here, as in most areas of human relations, only *two-way* communication will serve the purpose. When major change is contemplated, supervisors and subordinates should sit down and discuss the proposed plan in a way that will bring doubts and questions out into the open where they can examine and answer them. After all, even though management's ideas may work in theory, employees may have the know-how to make them work in practice. Indeed, what management diagnoses as *employee* resistance to change is sometimes really management resistance to listening to employee suggestions.

THROUGH GROUP DECISION-MAKING

We have seen that most people have a strong desire to participate in decisions that affect them directly. Group decision-making involves subordinates actively in the process of introducing change and enhances their sense of control over the environment.[11]

> One group-decision experiment was made with girls who were learning machine-paced work and who were failing to keep up with the required pace.[12] In discussions with their foremen, the girls requested that they be allowed to determine the pace themselves. A dial was installed that allowed them to set their own speed. It was discovered that the girls set up a work pattern which varied with the time of day, but that the *average* speed was considerably higher than the *constant* speed previously set by engineers. Yet the girls reported that their work was easier, and their total output was between 30 and 50 per cent higher than expected.

Unfreezing attitudes. People often resist change because they hold certain fixed attitudes or stereotypes to which they adhere in spite of all

---

[11] See, for example, Lester Coch and John R. P. French, "Overcoming Resistance to Change," *Human Relations*, Vol. I, No. 4 (1948), pp. 512-532; Kurt Lewin, "Studies in Group Decision," Dorwin Cartwright and Alvin Zander, eds., *Group Dynamics* (Evanston, Ill.: Harper & Row, 1953), pp. 287-301; and various articles in *Journal of Social Issues*, Vol. 1, No. 3 (1945). It should be noted that not all the "group-decision experiments" have been able to be duplicated. For an example of failure, see John R. P. French, Joachim Israel, and Dagfin Äs, "An Experiment in Participation in a Norwegian Factory," *Human Relations*, Vol. 13, No. 1 (February 1960), pp. 3-20.

[12] William F. Whyte and others, *Money and Motivation* (New York: Harper & Row, 1955), Chapter 10.

evidence to the contrary. Group decision-making helps them *unfreeeze* these attitudes so that they can be re-examined.

> An example occurred in a pajama plant.[13] During World War II the company's staff psychologist tried to persuade management, in view of the general manpower shortage, to abandon its policy of not hiring workers over 30. The top-management group immediately opposed this suggestion, insisting that older women took too long to train, had a higher absenteeism rate, and never worked at top speed. When the staff psychologist mentioned the good performance of older women currently employed, management dismissed them as exceptional cases.
>
> Shifting to another approach, the psychologist tried to involve management in a minor research project to find out how much money the company was losing through employing older women. Management itself determined the criteria to be used (production rates, turnover, absenteeism, and learning speed) and also decided how the data were to be gathered. In short, management became actively involved in the project. To management's surprise, the data showed that older women were better on all counts. Highly excited by these findings, management changed its policy and even spread the word of its shift to other companies.

Notice that the psychologist failed when he tried to attack management's stereotypes head-on. But he succeeded when he induced management to unfreeze its old attitudes by engaging in the research study. By doing this, management opened its mind to objective evidence. In a sense the approach used was like double-clutching. Instead of shifting directly from one attitude to another, the group went first into "neutral" before taking up its final position.

Establishing new group standards. In Chapter 4 we mentioned that groups develop certain standards of proper conduct and that individuals who fail to live up to these standards are subjected to pressure to conform. When an individual member of a group decides to accept a change imposed from above, he fears that his fellow workers will criticize him for playing along. But when the entire group is involved in the decision leading to the change, just the opposite occurs: The man who *refuses* to accept the change is pressured into accepting the group decision. In effect, group decision-making may lead to the establishment of new group standards that are rigidly enforced.

Commitment. Group decision-making commits each member of the group to carry out the decision that is agreed on. Even if a member has reservations or second thoughts, he is under strong pressure to implement the decision. Providing employees with information and arguments may influence them one way or another, but they themselves must decide whether to accept or resist a proposed change if they are to experience any commitment to the ultimate decision.

---

[13] A. J. Marrow and John R. P. French, "Overcoming a Stereotype," *Journal of Social Issues,* Vol. 1, No. 3 (1945), pp. 33-37.

Though group decision-making may serve as a useful tool in reducing resistance to change, it is by no means a cure-all for management's problems. It works effectively in areas where management is relatively indifferent to what the group decides; for instance, management may not care how the work is divided up so long as the job is done. Group decision-making may also prove effective when management and employees have overlapping but not conflicting interests. But when no community of interest exists, or when participation is foreign to a group's experiences, group decision-making is of little use in reducing resistance to change (see Chapter 9).

THROUGH BARGAINING

How does bargaining differ from group decision-making? In group decision-making, management gives the group freedom to make its own decisions (though within limits). Bargaining implies a willingness to talk things over and to make compromises in an effort to get the group's approval of proposed changes. However, management does not agree in advance to accept any decision made by the group. Normally, it accepts only some of the group's proposals and only as a *quid pro quo* in exchange for the group's accepting the rest of what management wants.

Sometimes bargaining is implicit (as we mentioned in Chapter 6)—that is, unspoken understandings are reached on how much management will demand in the way of change, and subordinates in effect agree to accept a limited amount of change as long as management is "reasonable" in its demands.

Often, explicit and open bargaining is more useful, particularly in a unionized situation. As we have seen, unions insist on being consulted on every matter that affects the welfare of their members. Some changes, such as pay cuts, may clearly require union approval. In other instances, management may have the power to make a change on its own, but may be caught up in a swarm of grievances if the union does not approve of what was done. When workers are transferred from one job to another, for example, the union may charge that the seniority clause of the contract has been violated. When workloads are increased, the union may charge that there is a violation of the health and safety clause of the contract or of established past practices.

Many managements insist on their "prerogative" to make all decisions by themselves. When the union attacks their actions, they try to limit the discussion to the strictly legal question of whether the contract was in fact violated. They feel that once the union is given a say, it will be difficult or impossible to operate efficiently or to make any decisions at all.

There are times when management probably should stand on principle, particularly to show that unrelieved obstinacy on the part of the union can provoke equal obstinacy on the part of management. But management should set an example of reasonableness—at least to the extent of listening to the union's point of view.

Management loses little of its essential power when it informs the union well in advance of proposed changes and shows a willingness to listen to objections. But these gestures may not be enough in themselves. The union is seldom satisfied just to be informed or to be given an opportunity to air its objections, if these objections always prove fruitless. If management wants to win the union's support in introducing change, it must give careful open-minded attention to grievances brought up by the union. And it may even let the union participate in the decision-making process itself.

Regardless of whether management lets the union participate in decision-making, management must be prepared to make concessions and to accept union suggestions that it may not feel fully desirable, on the theory that a reasonably adequate solution enthusiastically supported by the union is better than a perfect solution strongly opposed by the union.[14]

Many of these same principles apply to dealing with nonunion groups. The interests of management and subordinates often conflict. Regardless of how assiduously management uses the techniques of consultation and group decision-making, there will be occasions when subordinates are unwilling to accept everything management wants. Under these circumstances it is only common sense for management to make some concessions to the subordinates' strongest objections, if only as a means of winning more complete acceptance of other aspects of the proposed change.

Collective bargaining is difficult with nonunion groups, for there is no established mechanism to rely on. With small nonunion groups, however, it is at least possible to discuss problems with the group as a whole, and with larger nonunion groups management can deal with informal leaders or specially selected committees. It should be emphasized, though, that such meetings are useless unless all participants feel free to express their objections openly.

Management is under no obligation to bargain over every change it wants to initiate. On occasion it must push proposals through without regard to the objections of subordinates. But whenever management acts this way, it should be fully aware that it may be preparing the way for costly resistance later on.

HANDLING SYMBOLS

How can management minimize resistance when it becomes necessary to change or eliminate some feature that has acquired symbolic meaning? First, management should indicate clearly that changing the symbol is not the same as attacking the values for which the symbol stands. Thus, in switching from parchment paper for insurance policies (see case on p. 305), the sales manager

---

[14] This is not the place to enter into a full discussion of the techniques of collective bargaining. We might observe, though, that in dealing with a union it is rarely wise to adopt a take-it-or-leave-it attitude. In fact, if the union is to survive politically it must win some sort of "concession." Management may sometimes adopt an extreme position at first, just to give the union a chance to win an apparent victory. Also, management should not insist that the union give immediate answers to its proposals; rather, it should give the union leadership a chance to consult with its rank-and-file membership.

might emphasize that the change will help create the modern, up-to-date atmosphere that customers of the Integrity Company expect.

Sometimes it is possible to replace one symbol with another: When a new state is added to the Union, the old flag is discarded, but a new one takes its place. Similarly, if it becomes necessary to move foremen's cars from the front to the rear parking lot, special areas might be reserved for them, marked with special signs.

> We have been told of an interesting example of this technique used by the administrative staff of a hospital.[15] Members of the resident medical staff often had guests in the hospital cafeteria for Sunday dinner. Due to crowded conditions they often found it impossible to find a whole table for themselves. They had the cafeteria director place a sign on a group of tables: "Reserved for Medical Staff." Immediately several other high-status groups asked for similar consideration. To avoid the inflexibility and embarrassment that would arise if a majority of tables were specially reserved, the director changed the notices to read: "Medical Staff Are Requested to Use These Tables." This request could be justified on the grounds that it would make doctors easier to reach in case of emergency calls—and it also minimized the feeling that this was an additional symbol of the doctors' higher status.

MAKING CHANGES TENTATIVE

When the individuals concerned are permitted to participate in making the final decision on whether or not to accept a change, it is sometimes useful to ask the group to go along with the change on a tentative, trial basis at first. This approach has two advantages:

1. It enables employees to test their own reactions to the new situation, and provides them with more facts on which to base their decision.

2. It helps to "unfreeze" their attitudes and encourages them to think objectively about the proposed change. A change introduced on a trial basis is less threatening and generates less resistance than a permanent change.

However, where the individuals concerned do not participate in making the final decision, tentative changes may be unwise. They prolong the period of uncertainty and tension and the length of time in which the group is supervised closely. And there is always the chance that employees will in effect "participate" in the final decision—by resisting it or sabotaging it.

SLOW CHANGE OR QUICK?

Should change be introduced slowly or quickly? The answer is not clear. Many people believe in "making haste slowly," on the grounds that slow changes are less disruptive than fast changes and provide greater opportunity for adjustment. Given time, the new will blend with the old—as, for example, in the British constitution.

---

[15] We are indebted to Dr. Robert Wilson for this case.

Fast changes, if forced on people, may lead to violent resistance, and the resulting shock may disrupt the entire organization. There may be some resistance to slow change, but it will be less intense at any given time. Indeed, if the change is introduced slowly enough, it may not even be perceived—or else the organization may become accustomed to constant, gradual change as a natural process, as the fashion industry has.

Slow change entails certain dangers of its own, however. Every change has widespread ramifications, and it is bound to be less effective if it is just patched onto the existing set of practices. In introducing change it is far better for management to consciously re-examine the entire process to determine what adjustments should be made. Unfortunately, however, when management introduces slow change, total re-evaluation is rare (often because management wants to avoid "trouble"), and practices are continued that become increasingly inappropriate to the changed situation.

> The story is told of how during World War II the British army ordered a time study of their standard procedure for firing artillery.[16] Most of the operation seemed efficient enough, except that just before the gun went off two men came to attention. When the time-study man asked why, he was told, "We've always done that." Only after considerable research did he discover that the original purpose was to keep the horses from jumping (though horses had not been used for years).

When change is so gradual that people do not recognize that it has occurred, they may well continue to behave in a way that was appropriate only to the old situation.

> We observed this tendency in a factory where management sought to strengthen the power of the foreman. Formerly the set-up men were the ones who gave orders to the operators; the foreman had little direct contact with his men, concerning himself chiefly with over-all administration. It was decided to make this change gradually, "so they won't realize what is happening," and the foreman began giving all the orders on his own and to refuse to support the set-up men's decisions.
>
> As time passed, both the set-up men and the operators became increasingly confused. The set-up men tried desperately to maintain their traditional prestige and resisted the foreman every inch of the way. They met each new slight to their authority with growing indignation. Production gradually slumped until the foreman himself gave in and began once more to channel his orders through the set-up men.

If change is to be made slowly, management would be wise to give everyone concerned an over-all picture of what is eventually intended. Otherwise employees will begin to wonder, "Something is happening, but we don't know what," and exaggerated fears will arise about where the change is leading.

Actually, if employees fully understand and accept the change, there is little

---

[16] Elting Morison, "A Case Study of Innovations," George Shultz and John R. Coleman, eds., *Labor Problems: Cases and Readings,* 2nd ed. (New York: McGraw-Hill, 1959), p. 264.

reason not to make the change rapidly. Adjustment is required only once, and there is small likelihood of anachronistic holdovers from a former period. Fast change eliminates the need for the constant series of adjustments which are required by slow change and which leave the organization in an endless state of turmoil.

OTHER TECHNIQUES

One of the most common and most difficult problems in introducing change is that of bringing in a new manager to head up an existing department in an established company. Ordinarily, if the old manager has been well liked, the new one will have two strikes against him, for none of the employees will believe that he can be as good as his predecessor. At the outset, everyone wonders what changes the new man will make. His most inconsequential acts are carefully examined for clues to his future policy, and may be exaggerated into foreboding of future disasters. His subordinates may resent him as an outsider and prepare themselves to reject everything he does.

Let us examine this problem and how it was handled in a specific situation; our example will illustrate several techniques that may be helpful in introducing change in a wide variety of situations. W. F. Whyte describes how a new supervisor was introduced into a large restaurant: [17]

> Since the old supervisor had developed warm relations with her subordinates, the restaurant manager was afraid that her departure might have a bad effect on the morale of the whole organization. Consequently he prepared the way for her successor with great care. First, he discussed the problem of a replacement with both the old supervisor and the chef, her chief assistant. The chef proposed a candidate for the job; though this candidate had to be rejected, the reasons for the rejection were fully explained to the chef.
>
> When the new supervisor was finally selected, she was introduced to her subordinates at a general meeting. The manager announced that the old supervisor was leaving and went on to say how much she meant to the restaurant. The old supervisor spoke with great emotion about how sorry she would be to leave her associates. Then she introduced the new supervisor, extolled her virtues, and asked her employees to show the new woman the same cooperation they had given to herself. Finally, the new supervisor promised to do her best to follow in her predecessor's footsteps.
>
> For the next few days the new supervisor followed the old one around, getting to know people and trying to learn the supervisor's routine and methods of dealing with people. On the old supervisor's last day, the whole kitchen staff gave her a farewell party.
>
> Although the new supervisor decided that she would eventually make certain changes in the operation, she spent her first few weeks trying to follow the human-relations pattern established by her predecessor. Only after she was fully accepted by the group did she begin making changes.

---

[17] Adapted from *Human Relations in the Restaurant Industry* (New York: McGraw-Hill, 1948), pp. 319-331. For another example of a successful handling of what sociologists call a "succession crisis," see Robert Guest, *Organizational Change: The Effect of Successful Leadership* (Homewood, Ill.: Dorsey-Irwin, 1962).

What techniques were used here to win acceptance for the new supervisor? How might these techniques be used in other situations?

Consultation.   The manager respected the key position of the chef in the informal organization and requested his opinion on the change. When he felt the chef's opinions had to be rejected, he was careful to explain why.

Other organizations may use similar techniques to involve key subordinates in the selection process and thus substantially increase their acceptance of the final decision. Universities, for instance, typically appoint faculty members to the committees that choose presidents or deans.

Induction.   The old supervisor was careful to introduce the new supervisor to all key personnel and to explain the customs of the organization. Doubtless this did much to save the new supervisor from making social *faux pas*, to help integrate her into the social pattern of the organization, and to minimize the amount of disruption caused by the change in command.

Ceremony.   The meeting at which the new supervisor was introduced, and the farewell party for the old supervisor, both served a ceremonial or symbolic function. They formalized the fact of change and helped the old supervisor pass on some of her prestige to the new.

There is a tendency in our cynical society to play down the importance of ceremony. Yet it is no coincidence that throughout history every strong, stable institution—be it church, state, university, or company—has been noted for the ceremonies by which it helped focus individual loyalty on the organization as a whole.

Ceremonies are particularly important in time of change. Take, for example, the traditional ceremonies observed at the crucial moments of our life: birth, graduation, marriage, and death. The presence of relatives and friends and the giving of gifts and flowers help symbolize friendship and the unity of families. By involving ourselves in the formalized rites of the ceremony, we somehow protect ourselves from some of the fears and pains of moving from one stage of life to another. The heightened emotional atmosphere helps prepare individuals for major changes in their relationships with others. Indeed, we have learned to expect really important changes to occur in this way.

Probably more important, the use of ceremony is a public proclamation that in spite of apparent change the basic values remain the same; the new pays obeisance to the old. The English cry, "The King is dead; Long live the King." The French say, "Plus ça change, plus c'est la même chose." In primitive countries, oil companies may hire medicine men to sprinkle holy incense on new oil wells—thus showing their willingness to come to terms with the other culture.

Avoiding change until acceptance is assured.   The new supervisor avoided making changes until she had developed informal, social relations with her subordinates. This is in conflict with the old adage that a new broom should sweep clean—or that a new manager should make all his changes at once. True, as we suggested earlier, it is sometimes (but certainly not always) desirable to complete change quickly rather than to let it drag on. Even so, it is usually wise for a new manager to wait before taking action until he knows more about the organization and the people with whom he is dealing.

In earlier chapters we distinguished between the supervisor's formal and informal authority, pointing out that the first arises from his official position, the second from the respect accorded his technical and leadership skills. The man who has both informal and formal authority can win acceptance of his ideas more easily. But the new manager has only formal authority and in effect must force his ideas on his subordinates. After a few months he begins to accumulate informal authority; as he becomes trusted as an individual, his ideas meet with less resistance.

Building on the past.   In the restaurant case cited above, the new supervisor made it clear that she had no intention of throwing out past practices wholesale. As anthropologists and missionaries long ago discovered, it pays to learn the customs of the people with whom one works, particularly their ceremonies, symbols, and expected ways of doing things. Changes can be introduced more easily if an adjustment is made to the past. There are times, of course, when one may wish to cast out all the old patterns of behavior and start completely from scratch. However, in doing so one also casts out the good with the bad, the baby with the bath.

Conclusion

Change is among the most common of management problems. Yet management suffers from selective perception: Too often it is so concerned with the technical aspects of change that it fails to consider the human-relations problems which many changes generate. It fails to recognize that even a seemingly small change may have profound ramifications and that people sometimes resist change even when it is in their economic interest. They have vested interests in the old ways; they fear the uncertainties of the new. They give strange meanings to change, and dislike having their traditional customs, symbols, and patterns of dealing with people violated. People seldom resist change just to be stubborn; they resist it because it hurts them economically, psychologically, or socially.

Management often regards resistance as something essentially irrational, forgetting that apparently irrational attitudes or behavior may be symptoms of deep-seated problems. Or management may seek to overcome signs of resistance without knowing why the resistance exists. Too often management assumes that winning acceptance of change merely requires good salesmanship or one-way communications. Just as management plans the technical aspects of change, so must it consider in advance the impact on human relations. It must seek to find out how change will affect the people involved, and particularly how it affects their interrelationships.

The first step in dealing with resistance is to bring the real problems out in the open, to establish genuine two-way communication. After all, management has the responsibility not only of generating new ideas, but also of getting them accepted. Those who are seeking to initiate change would be wise to listen carefully to questions, objections, and suggestions for modification. Questions should be answered. Some objections and proposed modifications may be useful and their acceptance will improve the over-all quality of the proposed change. Other objections and modifications may not be of high quality themselves, but their acceptance in the spirit of bargaining may make it easier to win acceptance for the over-all change. Symbolic meanings must be considered and an intelligent judgment made on whether change should be introduced quickly or slowly.

P R O B L E M   O N E

Small Fashionable Store

A small, fashionable clothing store with about 25 long-service employees has always catered to the wealthy classes. Traditionally it has closed at 5:00 P.M., but a new manager is considering whether it might be more profitable to stay open two nights a week until 9:00.

He is concerned about how he would distribute evening work, particularly since each salesclerk has her own clientele. Also, he is far from sure whether any of his present customers would prefer to come in during the evening. The salesgirls work on commission.

1. Advise him on what he should do about the employee-relations aspect of his projected change. In particular, discuss why the employees might resist this change and what might be done to reduce each form of resistance.

P R O B L E M   T W O

New Marketing Manager

You have recently been hired by the Winspear Corporation as Marketing Research Director with instructions to rejuvenate the entire research program. When your predecessor started the program 30 years ago, he had advanced ideas, but in the years prior to his retirement he seemed to slow down both physically and mentally. He handled a few projects himself, but the rest of the staff (12 employees) gradually began to look for guidance to Heath Bailey, Assistant Marketing Research Director. Bailey ran the department in a competent but unimaginative manner.

Your talk with your new subordinates indicate that they are quite capable, and in general get along together well. However, two of the youngest men in the department, Bob Hertel and Jim Delevan, seem restless and anxious to try out new ideas.

At present Bailey handles all administrative matters himself. Following the practice developed under your predecessor, the staff reports to him, he hands out assignments, makes decisions, and then at long intervals tells you what he has done.

By now you have a number of research projects that you would like your research staff to begin. Some are quite different from anything the staff has done before, and several require a good deal of travel—which is also new.

1. Are the human relations in this department sound?
2. Should you try to change Bailey's key position in the organization? Why? How would you go about making the change?
3. What sort of relationship would you like to develop between yourself, Bailey, and the rest of the staff?
4. How should you handle Hertel and Delevan?
5. How do you intend to introduce the new research programs?

Discipline

14

We have purposely left discipline to the end of this part so that we could discuss other problems first. Discipline is required only when all other measures have failed. Suppose you have clearly instructed an employee on his duties, have listened to his problems, have tried to help him to do better, and have tactfully criticized his performance (as discussed in Chapter 8)—yet he still fails to meet standards. Then what? Then, reluctantly, you are forced to resort to discipline.

But can discipline be made consistent with what we have said about general supervision? We think it can.

In the first place the best discipline is self-discipline, the normal human tendency to do one's share and to live up to the rules of the game. Once people understand what is required of them, they can *usually* be counted on to do their job effectively and with good cheer. Yet some people (perhaps most of us) find that the possibility of discipline lurking in the background helps our "better selves" win out over our "lazier selves." As one man put it:

"If you can get away with small things you keep trying to get away with bigger and bigger things until, finally, you are caught and you are in trouble. Just for example, if you can sneak nuts and bolts out of the plant in your lunch box, you start trying to take spare parts and accessories out next. . . . It's much better if you know that they are going to check your lunch box every night and you can't even take out the smallest thing. Then . . . you don't get into bad habits." [1]

Ordinarily, if employees feel that the rules by which they are governed are reasonable, they will observe them without question. That is to say, they will respect the rules not because they fear punishment, but because they believe in doing things the *right* way. Coming to work on time; following the supervisor's instructions; avoiding fighting, drinking, and stealing at work; punching the time clock—all these are accepted by a majority of workers as reasonable rules, as necessary conditions of work.

Standards accepted by the group are frequently enforced by the group. (See, for example, our story on page 213 of how machinists enforced the rule against long-sleeved shirts.) Still, it is useful for management to back up the group when it is seeking the same objectives as management. The following quotation from a worker on an automobile assembly line illustrates a common feeling:

"If a man is late all the time, the guys just try to avoid him. They have no use for a guy like this. He just makes it hard for us all because the utility man [the substitute for all jobs on the lines] cannot do the work as well as the regular man, and so we have to work harder just to keep the work up. Of course, if a guy is just trying to give a smart aleck foreman a hard time, we are all for him. . . . But if the fellow is just a slacker, the foreman should straighten the man out for the sake of everybody." [2]

Most employees are tolerant when a man has an occasional off day, provided he does his part the rest of the time. But they resent seeing someone else "get away with murder" while they are doing a full day's work. As one man said:

"[Management] should be able to trust men, not have to watch them all the time. But you don't like to do your best and work hard while the other guy goofs off, loafs, and is always busy while you swing the job. It burns you." [3]

In fact, unless the culprit is disciplined the rest of the group may adjust to his low level of performance.

Thus, consistent proof that all rules are being enforced serves to strengthen the informal group's efforts at correction. Clearly, good supervisory practices will vastly reduce the need for discipline. But if employees realize that infractions of rules will be disciplined, good supervision will become even better.

When new rules are introduced, management must make every effort to

---

[1] Daniel M. Colyer, "The Good Foreman—As His Men See Him," *Personnel*, Vol. 28 (September 1951), p. 142.

[2] *Ibid.*, p. 143.

[3] *Ibid.*

convince employees of their reasonableness and legitimacy.[4] For instance, as we mentioned in Chapter 9, management should avoid introducing too many rules or rules that seem unrelated to doing the job at hand. No organization would survive if its only means of winning acceptance of correct procedures was to discipline all violators. Our disastrous experience with Prohibition shows the futility of trying to enforce a law that the majority feels to be unreasonable. In other words, management should try to establish what has been called "positive discipline," an atmosphere in which subordinates willingly abide by rules which they consider fair. In such an atmosphere the group may well exert social pressure on wrong-doers and reduce the need for the "negative" punitive discipline discussed in this chapter.

Types of Discipline

How severe should the penalty for wrong-doing be? In recent years many companies have provided what is called "progressive" or "corrective" discipline, which calls for increasingly severe penalties each time a man is disciplined. Except for very serious wrong-doings, an employee is rarely discharged for a first offense. This is particularly true if the firm is unionized, since arbitrators insist that a man be given a second chance unless the offense is particularly bad. Ordinarily, the sequence of penalties under "progressive" discipline is as follows:

1. Oral warning.
2. Written warning.
3. Disciplinary layoff.
4. Discharge.

Oral warnings, as a form of correction, were discussed in Chapter 8. When a man fails to maintain standards, or has broken a rule, a clear oral warning that repetition may eventually call for discipline is in order. The supervisor should, of course, concentrate on helping the subordinate figure out ways to prevent his troubles from recurring.

Written warnings are the first formal stage of progressive discipline. Psychologically, perhaps, they are not different from oral warnings, but they are made part of the employee's record—and they can be presented as evidence if more serious penalties follow or if the case is taken to arbitration. Written warnings, sometimes called "pink slips," are often prepared in four copies—one each for the foreman, steward, personnel department, and the disciplined individual.

---

[4] One of the problems of introducing new industries into underdeveloped areas is that the new industrial employee, fresh from the farm, has no conception of factory "etiquette." In India, for example, employers find it difficult to teach employees that they have to report to work regularly.

Disciplinary layoffs (to be distinguished from layoffs caused by lack of work) are next in severity. Usually they are for several days or weeks; layoffs in excess of a month are uncommon. Some companies skip this stage of discipline altogether, particularly when it is hard to find a trained replacement, on the grounds that it is too cumbersome to replace a man for just a few weeks. Moreover, the disciplined employee may return from his layoff in an even nastier mood than when he left.[5] On the other hand, there are some employees who pay little attention to oral warnings, but to whom actual punishment, such as loss of income, is convincing proof that the company means business. For them a layoff may be the shock that serves to bring them back to their sense of responsibility.

Discharge remains the ultimate penalty, and one that is being used less and less commonly. The expense of training a new employee makes the loss of an experienced man very costly to the company, and the hardships that face a man who has been discharged make arbitrators and unions increasingly unwilling to permit its use. Many arbitrators, indeed, refer to discharge as "industrial capital punishment"—and for good reason.

> Consider the impact of a discharge on a man of say 55, with 30 years' seniority. In the first place, he may lose pension rights worth $15,000 or more, plus substantial vacation benefits. Few high-paying employers would be willing to hire a man of his age, especially after they check his references and discover his discharge. Certainly he can expect less pay than he was getting from the job to which his 30 years' service had carried him. Further, as a low-seniority man, he is now fully susceptible to all the winds of economic misfortune. Assuming he loses $1.50 an hour for the rest of his life, his financial loss may be as high as $50,000.

No wonder one arbitrator told us: "I am very reluctant to let a man be fired unless I feel the company's grounds are justified, both morally and legally. I think the employee should have every chance to mend his ways." Faced with this attitude among arbitrators, companies are being forced to place greater emphasis on their selection and training programs. Workers who are discharged today are often individuals who simply don't care for their jobs, younger employees with no family responsibilities, or persons with severe behavior problems, such as alcoholics or psychotics.

Because of the serious implications of discharge in the modern economy, some companies authorize their foremen only to "suspend" employees for a five-day period, and reserve to higher management the final decision on whether they are to be discharged.

Demotion is seldom used as a disciplinary measure; it is ordinarily reserved for situations in which an employee has been mistakenly promoted or is no longer able to perform his job. As a disciplinary measure, demotion has a

---

[5] For the argument in favor of eliminating layoffs as a step between warnings and dismissal, see John Huberman, "Discipline Without Punishment," *Harvard Business Review,* Vol. 42, No. 4 (July 1964), pp. 62-68.

number of disadvantages. Losing pay over a period of time is a long, slow form of constant humiliation, as compared with the sharp slap of a layoff. Also, if a company is going to retain a trained man in any capacity, it makes more sense to use his highest skill.

Managers whose performance is below standard are rarely given layoffs or formal demotions. Instead, they are often quietly transferred without cut in pay from responsible jobs with substantial promotional opportunities to dead-end jobs with little or no opportunity for salary increase or promotion.

Most firms find that it is best not to treat either managerial or hourly paid employees so harshly that they give up hope or lose motivation.

The "Hot-Stove Rule"

Inflicting discipline puts the supervisor in a dilemma. How can he expect his subordinates to continue to regard him at a source of help, when discipline is by nature painful? Can he impose discipline without generating resentment? We think so—through what Douglas McGregor called the "hot-stove rule." This rule draws an analogy between touching a hot stove and undergoing discipline. When you touch a hot stove your discipline is *immediate*, with *warning, consistent,* and *impersonal.*

Let's look at these four characteristics as applied to discipline. When you burn your hand you are angry with yourself. Sometimes you are angry with the stove too, but not for long. You learn your lesson quickly, because:

1. The burn is immediate. There is no question of cause and effect.
2. You had warning. Particularly if the stove was red hot, you knew what would happen if you touched it.
3. The discipline is consistent. Everyone who touches the stove is burned.
4. The discipline is impersonal. A person is burned not because of who he is, but because he touched the stove.

In short, the act and the discipline seem almost one. You are disciplined not because you are bad, but because you have committed a particular act. The discipline is directed against the act, not against the person. There will still be resentment against the source of the discipline, but the more automatic the discipline becomes, the more this resentment is reduced. As one worker put it: "I really had it coming to me. I was looking for trouble. I can't blame the foreman. His job was to enforce the rules. That's what he is paid for."

Put another way, "the purpose of discipline should be to obtain compliance with established rules of conduct—that is, to correct improper conduct. It should not be punitive in nature, that is, to discipline solely for the purpose of getting even with the employee." [6]

Let us see how the "hot-stove rule" works out in actual practice.

---

[6] H. D. Garrett, *Building a Responsible Work Force* (Ann Arbor, Mich.: Bureau of Industrial Relations, University of Michigan, 1955, multilith).

IMMEDIATE DISCIPLINE

The supervisor should begin the disciplinary process as soon as possible after he notices a violation of the rules. (Of course, if he has lost his temper he should wait until he has cooled down.) Note what happens if he delays action:

> Joe Jones has a bad tardiness record. He comes in a half-hour late, but thinks the supervisor hasn't noticed it. By noon, Joe decides he has nothing to worry about.
>
> The supervisor *has* noticed it, but he is busy on another problem and he figures it might be a good idea to let Joe "stew awhile." Late in the afternoon, just before closing time, he calls Joe into the office to give him a two-day layoff.

Naturally, Joe feels he has been treated unfairly and resents both the discipline and the supervisor. He assumes the supervisor has been saving his grudge instead of "having it out like a man." In the future, he will never feel secure with the supervisor and will always wonder, "What's he going to pull on me next? Why does he have to play this cat-and-mouse game with me?"

Further, the more quickly the discipline follows the offense, the more likely it is that the offending person will associate the discipline with the offense rather than with the person imposing the discipline—that is, the more automatic the discipline will seem.

Of course, immediate discipline does not mean that a man should be judged without full investigation. But it does mean that the supervisor should take notice of the offense as soon as possible and push the investigation with all due speed.

> For instance, a man comes in to work after two days' absence. According to your records, he never called in to report sick, and, therefore, he is subject to discipline. "Immediate discipline" requires that you call him into your office for an explanation as soon as he gets to work. However, if he claims he was unconscious under a doctor's care during this period, you obviously are not going to discipline him until you have a chance to investigate. Even here you should push your investigation as rapidly as possible.

When the facts of a case are not clear, and yet immediate action is necessary, many companies provide for suspension. The employee is told that he is "suspended" and that he will be informed later about what discipline will be imposed. This technique may be used where tempers are so high that calm appraisal is impossible, or where the guilt is obvious but the amount of penalty can be determined only after further investigation. Suspension also makes possible a consultation among various levels of management before the final penalty is determined. Since suspension is a form of layoff, however, it should not be used unless the offense calls for at least a layoff. If the suspension is longer than is justified by the offense, arbitrators will usually order back-pay.

ADVANCE WARNING

If discipline is to be accepted without resentment, both the man who is being disciplined and his fellow workers must regard it as fair. And *unexpected* discipline is almost universally considered unfair. This means that (1) there must be clear warning that a given offense will lead to discipline, and (2) there must be clear warning of the amount of discipline that will be imposed for a given offense.

Assume that a rule has been posted for several months but that the supervisor has never disciplined anyone who violated it. Clearly, no one expects that the rule will be enforced in the future either. Now the supervisor grabs one man and makes an example of him. The victim might well cry, "Why me?" Discipline without warning violates the workers' expectations of fair supervision.[7] Further, if the case were taken to arbitration the company might lose.

Does this mean that once an order is laxly enforced the company can never again enforce it? Perhaps, in a unionized situation, for an arbitrator may rule that a *precedent* of no enforcement has been established. If, however, there has been at last some enforcement of the rule (that is, if the company has not given clear evidence of its acquiescence to nonenforcement), the company can begin strict enforcement once it has issued clear warning of the change in policy.

> Suppose, for instance, the company has been very lax in requiring men to be at work on time. Before starting to penalize tardy workers, the company should give clear warning that it is tightening up on enforcement. The foreman might call the men together and, after appropriate discussion and explanation, say "From now on I'll expect you to come to work on time. Anyone who is more than five minutes late without adequate excuse will receive a written warning. If you receive more than two written warnings in any 30-day period, you will get a day's layoff."

We have already discussed the need for effective communications within the organization. Once more, let us emphasize management's responsibility to make sure that all employees really know what the rules are and how they are to be enforced. A failure to communicate such information deprives employees of clear warning. A communications program might include, among other things, the following:

1. Upon induction, the immediate supervisor can explain the rules to all new employees, perhaps with the help of the personnel department.

2. Notices can be posted on the bulletin-board, and handbooks distributed to employees.

3. In some cases, lists of penalties can be included in the union contract.

---

[7] See Alvin Gouldner, *Patterns of Bureaucracy* (New York: The Free Press of Glencoe, 1954), p. 170.

4. When rules are changed, the immediate supervisor can call a group meeting or notify individuals informally.

5. When a rule is about to be violated, or actually is violated (provided it is a minor, first offense), the supervisor can issue an informal warning.

Many arbitrators, interpreting the legal meaning of the contract, might say that posting a notice on a bulletin board constitutes clear warning. But from the point of view of human relations, this is not enough. Written communications should be supplemented by oral communications. The better job management does of explaining a new rule and why it is necessary, the easier it will be to enforce it—simply because workers will be more likely to accept it as reasonable. Regardless of the legal requirements of arbitration, management is clearly to blame if the men unwittingly violate rules because they don't know what is expected of them. Good communications pay off by significantly reducing the amount of discipline that must be imposed.

CONSISTENCY

If two men commit the same offense and one man is more severely disciplined than the other, naturally there will be cries of favoritism. One of the quickest ways for a supervisor to lose the respect of his subordinates and to lower the morale of the work group is to impose discipline in a whimsical, inconsistent way. Consistent discipline is considered fairer and is far more likely to be accepted by the workers involved. Indeed, consistency is basic to good human relations.

Management must always keep in mind the educational function of discipline (and also of nondiscipline). Consistent discipline helps to set limits (that is, to inform employees what they can and cannot do); inconsistent discipline inevitably leads to confusion and uncertainty. Consistent discipline is essential if the work environment is to be kept stable. When some rules are permitted to go unenforced, employees may either (1) decide to ignore all rules, or (2) become confused about what is really required of them.

> Whenever we are speeding on the highway, we must feel this same sort of anxiety. After all, we are breaking the written rule; on the other hand, it isn't often enforced. Maybe this is a place, or a set of policemen who don't take the rule seriously, and we can speed a little. But still there is a lurking insecurity, because the police may, at any time, decide to enforce this particular rule.[8]

For instance, one day the boss lets Mary, his secretary, get by with handing in a report that is full of erasures. The next day he bawls her out for a sloppy report that is actually less sloppy than the previous day's. Under the circumstances, it is hard for Mary to know what standards are expected of her. She may well decide that the discipline has nothing to do with her act and "learn" only that the boss has a personal grudge against her. Not only won't she learn the rules, but she will be resentful as well.

---

[8] Mason Haire, *Psychology in Management* (New York: McGraw-Hill, 1956), p. 60.

Every individual wants to know the limits of permissible behavior, and one way to establish these limits clearly and dramatically is to punish those who exceed them. We all tend to be unhappy and insecure in a situation where we are not sure what is expected of us. Child psychologists, for instance, have learned that children are not necessarily happier when they are given absolute freedom. One reason they get into so much mischief is that they are trying to find out how much they can get away with, at what point Daddy will spank. Grown-ups are the same way. They want to know "How far can I go? What can I do? What can't I do?"

Consistency is hard to maintain. Some people we like—others we don't. Sometimes we see a rule violation as a personal insult, a direct challenge to our authority. Other times, prompted by our natural instinct to be understanding and kindhearted, we are tempted to tell the rule-breaker, "Well, I'm going to let it go this time, but don't do it again."

Dissatisfaction may arise over excessive leniency as well as over excessive harshness.

> The office had a rather strictly enforced rule that employees could not leave without permission until the end of the work day. Braden was caught by his supervisor in the hall heading for the exit about ten minutes before quitting time. Upon review the normal penalty of a two-day layoff was suspended because the following week was Christmas. However, a petition was signed by the other employees protesting this decision as showing favoritism and thus being discriminatory! They felt that since he was obviously guilty, he should receive the same penalty others had received.

One source of inconsistency is management's tendency to be stricter in slack times and to ignore rule violations when manpower is short.

> Crawford had a terrible absenteeism record. He missed work for two days without a legitimate excuse. Normally, given his record, his offense would justify an immediate two-week layoff. However, Crawford's services were badly needed on a rush job. No one else could take his place. So the supervisor added the incident to Crawford's personnel record and warned him that a further violation would lead to discharge.

Keeping Crawford on solved the immediate problem of maintaining production. But the long-term effects might have been more serious. What did Crawford and the other workers learn from this incident? One of several things: (1) The absentee rule was not to be enforced strictly, (2) the supervisor was playing favorites, or (3) strict discipline in time of slack work was merely a dodge to get around the seniority provisions of the contract. In any case, the employees' respect and trust for their supervisor probably took a nose dive.

Often a supervisor finds it easier to transfer a problem employee to another department than to face the hard task of disciplining him. In one case a man who had consistently failed to live up to company rules had been transferred 11 times without any record of disciplinary action appearing in his personnel folder. This employee could hardly be blamed for not knowing what standards of behavior were expected of him. No one had taken the trouble either to help salvage him or to rid the company of a constant expense.

Consistency in enforcing discipline may be expensive in terms of lost production, but inconsistency may be even more so. Although the evidence is incomplete, it would appear that automobile plants which are most hesitant about enforcing rules against wildcat strikes (work stoppages not officially authorized by the union) have had the worst record of such strikes. Yet if a whole department goes on strike, it may be very costly to discipline everyone. Not only will the company lose the production of that department, but the men in other departments may walk out in sympathy.

Wildcat strikes are set off by a variety of causes (frustration with the work or slow handling of grievances, for instance). Obviously it is better to eliminate the causes than to punish the symptoms.[9] Still, if no discipline is imposed, the men "learn" that they can engage in such strikes with impunity. Companies that have been willing to sustain the short-run costs have found that wildcat strikes have decreased. Further, when management takes a firm stand, the union finds it easier to discourage its members from taking matters into their own hands. Many union leaders have told us candidly that they find it hard to observe the "no-strike" provisions of their contracts when management doesn't take the initiative in disciplining violators. "We can't be more against strikes than management."

Consider another problem involving consistency of discipline. We have heard foremen say, "I can only catch a small proportion of the rule violators, but those I catch I punish severely." Is this fair? Many men consider it a form of "Russian roulette." Adventurous souls may make a game of this procedure and try to see how much they can get away with. Furthermore, scattered instances of discipline hardly constitute clear warning.

If a rule is on the books, the supervisor should make an effort to enforce it (and enforce it uniformly). If he finds it impossible to do so, the rule may have to be revised or dropped altogether. Sloppy enforcement of one rule encourages employees to disregard other rules.

In some situations, of course, 100 per cent consistency is impossible. For instance, unless everyone is searched as he leaves the plant, stealing may be impossible to stamp out. However, such searches are expensive and deeply resented by employees. The company may have to rely on stern punishment of anyone who is accidentally caught stealing. Since workers generally accept antistealing rules as reasonable, there will be little resentment of this policy, inconsistent though it seems.

Does consistency require that the penalty should be determined entirely by the offense, regardless of the personal history and background of the person who committed it? Of course not. We have already said that it is common

---

[9] Indeed, if workers are prevented from wildcatting they may release their aggressions in other ways—through slowdowns and absenteeism, for example.

industrial practice to be more lenient on first offenses. Arbitrators are reluctant to let "industrial capital punishment" be imposed on a man unless a reasonable effort has been made to rehabilitate him. Certainly each case should be considered on its own merits. As a top industrial-relations executive put it:

> "There is no precise mechanical formula. . . . Each instance of misconduct must be viewed . . . individually. . . . This, of course, is a matter of judgment, but . . . four principal factors should be taken into consideration . . . first, the seriousness and circumstances of the particular offense; second, the past conduct record of the employee and his length of service; third, the lapse of time since his last misconduct for which disciplinary action was taken; and fourth, the plant practice in similar cases." [10]

For example, three employees are caught gambling. One has been disciplined for the same offense before, the other two have not. The first man is discharged, the other two are given written warnings. This, we would argue, is being consistent as it may first appear. Although each case should be considered on its own merits, the over-all disciplinary program must be kept consistent. Certainly if two individuals with the same personal histories commit the same offense, they should be treated equally.

How long should a rule violation be held against an employee? Current management practice tends toward disregarding offenses committed more than a year or two ago. Thus, an employee with a poor absenteeism record would start afresh if he maintained a good attendance record for a year.

The rules of fair warning and consistency require that discipline be neither greater nor less than expected. If the degree of discipline comes as a surprise, the company may have failed to give adequate warning; if it is less than expected, the company will have difficulty in gaining acceptance of a more serious penalty in the future. When there is uncertainty and misunderstanding about whether the offense is to be punished and how much the punishment is to be, then the policy is inconsistent. If the rule-breaker sees the supervisor as wielding arbitrary discretion, then he may blame the supervisor for his discipline rather than himself.

There has been considerable discussion in industrial-relations circles about whether or not good personnel policy requires the posting of all rules and the setting of standard penalties for violations. For example: "Rough-house: First offense, warning. Second offense, one-day layoff. Third offense, one-week layoff. Fourth offense, discharge."

Those who favor such lists argue that they provide effective warning and greater consistency. Those who oppose them feel that they make it harder for management to distinguish between various degrees of guilt. Mandatory discharge for stealing would mean that the employee who is seen taking a box of safety clips would receive the same penalty as one who was caught robbing the safe. One company with a rigid series of penalties was obliged to impose only a one-week layoff on an employee who had altered his output records—this

---

[10] Garrett, *op. cit.*, p. 5.

was the standard penalty for inaccurately reporting production figures. Actually, the employee had been doctoring his records for years and had received hundreds of dollars in unearned incentive payments as a result. Had the company not set up a specific penalty in the rule book, it could have imposed a far more severe penalty.

Some companies insist that unless they maintain a uniform list of penalties they are unable to justify discipline to the union. Others say that such lists enable the union to force the company into excessively legalistic decisions on discipline. For instance, if the company had no specific rule against loafing, legally it couldn't discipline a man no matter how lazy he was.

IMPERSONALITY

We have said that a good supervisor encourages his subordinates to express themselves freely and tries to play down differences in status. He tries to build up the feeling that he and the worker are on the same team. Doesn't the imposition of discipline seriously endanger this relationship? It may. In fact, the disciplined employee might easily murmur, "That so-and-so. I thought he was my friend. I'd rather have a foreman who wasn't such a hypocrite and then you'd know where you stand."

It is not easy to impose discipline without causing the person disciplined to feel resentful and aggressive. But the supervisor can minimize the danger to the relationship by imposing dicipline in as impersonal a way as possible.

> Discipline is most effective and has least negative effect on individuals, if the individual feels that his behavior at the particular moment is the only thing being criticized and not his total personality.[11]

In its opening stages, the disciplinary interview is not much different from most other forms of interview. First, state the problem as you see it; then encourage the subordinate to state his point of view. Let him tell you his story. Ask *how* it happend, not *why*. Give him every chance to explain himself. Try to avoid this sort of exchange:

> *Foreman:* Late again, I see. Didn't I tell you yesterday, if you were late once more this month, I'd give you a layoff. . . .
> *Employee:* But . . .
> *Foreman:* (ignoring him) Well, you've had your last chance. You better go home.
> *Employee:* But I did get here on time—only the superintendent called me in to his office to discuss the Savings Bond drive.

Instead, do your best to draw the man out and try to discover the real story. Use the interview technique. Don't ask him for his excuse, but concentrate on the *basic* reasons for his rule violation. Is he having trouble at home? Has he been poorly instructed on the job? Has he lost his motivations? Why? (Of

---

[11] Chris Argyris, *Executive Leadership* (New York: Harper & Row, 1953), p. xiii.

course, you should have asked yourself some of these questions long before the employee's misconduct led to discipline.)

Sometimes your interview will give you all the facts you need. In other cases you may need to investigate further, perhaps by checking with other members of management. Avoid making a decision until you have the whole story, but reach your decision as soon as possible.

Once you have decided what discipline is appropriate, impose it quietly and impersonally. For example, suppose in a lateness case that the employee shows general irresponsibility, and that his only excuse for his latest tardiness was that he forgot to set his alarm clock.

> *Supervisor:* Well, I can see how it happened. But from the company's point of view, not setting your alarm clock is not an adequate excuse, particularly since this has happened three times this month.
> (Pause—in which to listen to objections.)
> You have already received two written warnings this month and the rules now require that you receive a day's layoff.
> (Pause—again for objections.)
> Jim, you've got to figure out a way to get here on time. You do a fine job when you are here, but the rule (and I think it is a fair one) is that if this occurs again within 30 days you will receive a week's layoff and if it occurs again you will lose your job. I don't want this to happen. Now what can be done about it?
> (Then discuss positive means of avoiding trouble in the future. Try to get him to suggest a workable plan—or suggest one yourself. Even if this doesn't work, end with:)
> Jim, will you try harder to get here on time in the future?
> (The answer is bound to be "yes" and you have, for what it is worth, a positive end to the interview and a positive commitment to do something.)

Note that the discipline here has been imposed impersonally and the employee has been given every chance to express his objections. After imposing discipline the supervisor reverts to his role of *helping*. The interview ends on a positive note.

After disciplining a subordinate, you may understandably tend to avoid him or to alter your attitude toward him in subtle, hardly noticeable ways. But these shifts in attitude are particularly dangerous, for they generate corresponding alterations in the subordinate's attitude. He concludes, "You hurt me and you know it." Eventually, the whole relationship may be destroyed. By contrast, if you treat the man as you always have, you indicate that by-gones are by-gones, that it was the act that was punished, not the man.

Simple as this advice may seem, it is hard to carry out in practice. Both parties are upset by what has happened. It is easy to understand why the person who has been disciplined is resentful, but the act of imposing discipline is also emotionally distasteful to the person who imposes it. Most of us hate to hurt other people, and when we do so we feel guilty—even when such a feeling is not justified. To protect ourselves from guilt feelings, we have to build up a feeling of anger. But, since we fear the anger of the person we have disciplined, we become unapproachable and cold after we have imposed the penalty. As a result, we seem to be disciplining the other person *as a person,* rather than as the violator of a specific rule. Naturally his response is, "He doesn't like me."

Two mistakes are common in imposing discipline: the supervisor either apologizes or bawls the offender out.

APOLOGETIC DISCIPLINE

Supervisor: Jim, I'm sorry I have to do this, but the rule says I must. How would the other fellows feel if I didn't do something?

Subordinate: (to himself): Even the boss doesn't think it's a good rule. Boy, I sure have tough luck. *Or:* He doesn't have guts enough to back up his own rules. *Or:* Why does he worry about the other fellows? I know they won't care if I get off. *Or:* Who's he kidding?

PERSONAL BAWLING OUT

Supervisor: I've given you every chance, gone out on the limb for you, and you haven't helped at all. You told me last time that you would really make sure you'd leave home early, and you broke your promise. Well, I've done all I can for you. You are letting the company down. You aren't being fair to them or to the other men. You've got to wise up or you'll really be in trouble, and I won't bail you out.

In the second case, the superintendent is being overpersonal, possibly because he feels a little guilty. There is no need to remind the employee over and over again of what he has done, to rub his nose in the dirt. Instead, it is much better for the supervisor to make it clear that he wants to let by-gones be by-gones and that he assumes the man will mend his ways.

It requires a great deal of maturity to approach discipline without a sense of guilt or hostility, particularly if you feel that a man's disregard of the rules is a reflection on your own supervisory abilities.

The Role of the Union

As yet we have said little about the role of the union in matters of discipline. We have observed in our research that unions rarely object strongly to discipline provided it is applied consistently and provided the rules are clearly publicized and generally considered reasonable. Of course, union officers may go through the motions of filing a grievance at the request of a disciplined member, much as a lawyer defends a client even though he is wrong. But in doing this, they often feel as this union officer did:

"I've got to go to this grievance meeting and fight for that so-and-so. He had it coming to him and got what he deserved. How can he think he is so much better than anyone else he doesn't have to follow the rules?"

Management should not expect the union to discipline members who violate the contract.[12] When the union does impose discipline, it is abandoning its

---

[12] There are a few exceptions in the building and clothing trades, where powerful unions may discipline members who violate the contract.

traditional role as the worker's defender, and management is failing to assume its responsibilities. A management spokesman makes this point:

> "The union cannot maintain its proper function of representing the employee and protecting his interests if it assumes any part of management's function of setting disciplinary penalties. If the union agrees with management as to what a proper penalty should be in a particular case, it forecloses its right to protest the penalty. Union representatives should be in a position to protest any disciplinary action taken by management against an employee on the grounds that the discipline is unfair, unjust, discriminatory, lacks cause, or is too severe. Any procedure which forecloses the right of the employee to have his case aired in the grievance procedure is basically unsound." [13]

Management must also be realistic about the union leader's political position. Often union leaders feel obliged to defend members whom they themselves think are guilty; to do otherwise would be to risk defeat at the next election. Once management recognizes that union leaders must often perform what is for them an unpleasant job, life becomes a good bit easier for both management and the union.

Management may be able to reduce the number of grievances prompted by disciplinary action by bringing the union into the earlier stages of the disciplinary procedure.

> Bill Jones has been absent frequently. According to accepted plant practice, after five no-excuse absences, he can be laid off for a month. Jones' foreman informs the department steward that he intends to enforce the rule against absenteeism and that the steward might try to "straighten Jones out" before he gets into real trouble. Where the foreman-steward relationship is a good one, the steward will often warn the man informally that continued violations may lead to a penalty that the union will find difficult to get reduced.

In this way the union is given an opportunity to play a constructive role without being burdened with the responsibility for applying discipline.

QUASI-LEGAL PROCEDURES

The presence of a union need not impair management's efforts to maintain a satisfactory disciplinary policy. But it may force management to adopt what might be called a "quasi-legal" procedure.

Most union contracts require (1) that the company may discipline employees only for "just cause," and (2) that any employee who feels he has been unjustly disciplined may appeal to higher management through the grievance procedure, and, if management's answer is unsatisfactory, to arbitration. The arbitrator makes the final decision on whether the discipline was for just cause. He may be able to sustain the company's action completely, or reduce the penalty, or decide the penalty was entirely unwarranted and eliminate it altogether.

The grievance procedure provides a valuable protection to the individual

---

[13] Garrett, *op. cit.,* p. 1.

worker, awkward though it may be for management. Since Magna Carta, an established principle of Anglo-Saxon law has been that an individual shall not be judged by his accusers. Management has the right—one might even say the *duty*—to establish the rules under which the organization shall operate. But a channel of appeal must be kept open from management decisions on whether or not these rules have been violated. Thus, the grievance procedure operates as a means of enforcing consistency.

In our Anglo-Saxon tradition, a man is assumed innocent until proved guilty, and in establishing guilt the burden of proof is almost entirely on management. For instance, to prove that a man has been loafing on the job, more than the supervisor's unsubstantiated word is required. Management must be able to produce objective, factual data which show that other employees on comparable jobs consistently produce more than the alleged offender. And it must show that the worker's low production was not due to poor material or faulty equipment. Similarly, the union may challenge any rule that has not been clearly communicated to the employees or consistently enforced.

As a consequence, disciplinary matters must sometimes be handled in a legalistic, courtroom manner, particularly when they reach the arbitration stage. Unfortunately, both union and management may find themselves devoting more energy to legal intricacies than to dealing with the human problems involved. Each side tries to build up an air-tight case and to poke loopholes in the case of the opposition. The billowing clouds of legal technicalities often serve as a smoke screen that obscures the underlying human problems. Fortunately, the company that maintains a generally fair disciplinary policy as part of its standard procedure is less likely to become involved in the legalisms of arbitration.

The existence of the grievance procedure means that the supervisor's disciplinary penalty may be reduced or eliminated, either by higher management or by an arbitrator. It is even possible that a man, who the supervisor is sure has flagrantly violated the rules, may be totally exonerated. Under these circumstances the supervisor naturally may feel frustrated when his decision is not "backed up." However, such possible miscarriages of justice are the price that must be paid for development of a judicial system which permits every accused employee to have his "day in court." A basic tenet of our society is that it is better for a guilty man to go free than for an innocent man to be convicted.

The reason why "guilty" employees are acquitted at higher stages of the grievance procedure is usually that the supervisor has failed to gather evidence, to be consistent in his application of discipline, or to communicate the requirement of the job to employees. Hence it is important for higher management to train and advise supervisors on the requirements of a sound disciplinary policy.[14]

---

[14] For a good analysis of the problems of effective disciplinary policies in unionized companies see Orme Phelps, *Discipline and Discharge in the Unionized Firm* (Berkeley and Los Angeles: University of California Press, 1959). Also see Lawrence Stessin, *Employee Discipline* (Washington, D.C.: Bureau of National Affairs, 1960).

Conclusion

Basically, discipline is a form of training. When disciplinary problems arise, it may be as much management's fault as the workers'. Many disciplinary problems grow out of management's failure to inform employees what is expected of them.

On the other hand, effective discipline depends on more than one-way communication in which the supervisor tells employees what to do and punishes them if they don't. Employees may be aware of a rule, yet refuse to accept it. For instance, if there are large numbers of employees taking extra-long lunch hours or using sick leave as a vacation, the problem is not to punish the guilty but to get group acceptance of a new standard. We must initiate discipline by winning acceptance of the standard (a process discussed in Chapter 9). Once this has been accomplished, discipline will be provoked only by the small minority of recalcitrants.

For discipline to be accepted, the rules must be effectively communicated and the penalties inflicted must be consistent. Discipline helps employees learn the requirements of their job; and if discipline is applied impersonally, without personal animus, the respect shown the supervisor by his subordinates may actually be increased.

PROBLEM ONE

Discussing Mistakes

Suppose an employee has been making a series of small mistakes. Is it better for the supervisor to (1) discuss each mistake with him as it occurs, or (2) discuss his *over-all* record with him from time to time?

PROBLEM TWO

The Drunkard

Dave Thatcher comes to work drunk. The foreman sends him home with another man, intending to speak to him when he is sober. As soon as Dave comes in the door the next morning, he drunkenly picks up a high-pressure hose and squirts the foreman in the face. The company discharges him for insubordination, assault with a deadly weapon, intoxication, and violation of company rules. There are no posted rules or penalties.

The union doesn't deny that Dave was pretty high. However, it alleges that (1) he has been having trouble with his wife, (2) his record has otherwise been excellent, (3) he was sent home but not otherwise given a warning on the first day, and (4) in other cases of drunkenness that occurred this year the men were referred to Alcoholics Anonymous.

The company answers: (1) The wife trouble is irrelevant, (2) Dave's work has not been good, even though he has not received previous formal discipline, (3) he was in no condition to appreciate a warning on the first day, and (4) the men referred to Alcoholics Anonymous were quiet drinkers who hadn't committed major violations of company safety rules. It adds that Alcoholics Anonymous is for alcoholics and, aside from the two-day spree, there is no evidence that Dave is an alcoholic.

1. Was the company's position correct?
2. What sort of penalty should be imposed?

PROBLEM THREE

Absenteeism and the Troubled Employee

The Turner Company has struggled to get supervisors and employees alike to accept the principle that the organization cannot and will not tolerate absenteeism. Persistent absenteeism is now consistently considered grounds for discharge. For the past year, James Allen, a highly skilled maintenance repairman, has been absent without notice once or twice a month. With the company for six years, he has the reputation for high-quality work, for accepting almost any assignment unquestioningly, and for working overtime when necessary.

When confronted with the facts (and he has received one disciplinary layoff already), he always promises to do better. Although he is a very quiet, uncommunicative man, it is known that he has family problems. His wife is a rather disorganized homemaker; they have six children, one of whom is always ill.

The company does not like to contemplate losing this skilled man, yet fellow employees are beginning to talk, and whenever he fails to show up for work, one hears comments like "Old Jim is out again doing the housework."

As this man's supervisor, how would you handle this problem? Make your objectives and methods explicit.

PROBLEM FOUR

The Auto Thief

The company's employment application says "Falsification of this form will be grounds for immediate discharge." Among the questions on the form is this one: "Have you ever been convicted of a crime?" Howie Bowman was employed three years ago and has a perfect record. Suddenly the company finds out that 15 years ago, when he was 17, Howie was convicted of stealing an automobile and given a suspended sentence. He had not mentioned this fact on his application.

1. Should Howie be disciplined?
2. How long should the company hold this rule violation against him?

PROBLEM FIVE

Fight

The foreman catches two men fighting. Smith had been kidding Jones about his hillbilly background. Jones took a poke at Smith. Smith hit back. Both have had a good record in the past.

While some companies try to determine who really started a fight, others feel they will get nowhere trying to settle personal feuds between workers, but should exercise discipline only when one party resorts to his fists to settle differences. What do you think? Should both men receive equal punishment? Should Jones be punished more severely for starting the fight—or Smith for provoking it?

PROBLEM SIX

No Gambling

A foreman says, "We have rules posted against gambling. Of course, we don't enforce them against small bets and there is some card-playing for money in the washroom at lunch break. However, we have the rules posted as a standby measure if things get out of hand."

Do you agree with this foreman's approach?

PROBLEM SEVEN

The Bookies

A company has a posted rule against gambling. Six months ago two men were given written warnings about shooting dice. One day the local police arrest two other men on plant property for bookmaking. There is evidence that they have been collecting bets on horses in the plant. The men plead guilty before the judge, who gives them a suspended sentence. When they return to the plant they are discharged. To date, both men's records have been perfect.

If this case were carried to you as an arbitrator, what would you decide?

ORGANIZATION

Up to this point we have been talking about some of the components of the organization: individual workers and their jobs, supervision, informal groups, and unions. Each of these is an integral part of the organization, but there is a missing element still to be considered: the organizational system itself, within which all these components interact. In this section, therefore, we consider the impact of the organization on human behavior.

As long as people work in small groups where they see each other almost continuously, little thought need be given to defining in advance how they are to relate to one another. They develop patterns of relationship almost spontaneously: Few formal plans need be made except to insure a high quality of supervision.

As more and more people are added to the organization, however, the management of personnel becomes more complex. In order for work to be done efficiently, an orderly pattern (or system) of human relationships must be evolved. This pattern is commonly referred to as *organizational structure*. A company such as General Motors, for example, must coordinate the activities of hundreds of thousands of people doing thousands of different tasks in dozens of locations. In large organizations, merely giving consideration to the needs of *individual* workers and the requisites of face-to-face supervision is not enough.

Our primary questions, then, are these: What patterns of human relationships enable an organization to function most efficiently? What problems arise in the attempt to establish these patterns? What type of organizational structure is most likely to motivate people to work toward management's objectives? How can structure be evaluated in human-relations terms?

In a very real sense, an organization is a set of human relations. Every organization has a hierarchy of authority. The men at the top give orders to the men beneath them and so on down the line. The purpose of the hierarchy is to make it possible for a large number of people to work under the over-all control of a relatively small number of managers.

Organizations also spread out horizontally. Rather than having one person do the total job—for example, designing a new machine—many people are brought together and their activities are coordinated so that, although each does only a small part of the total job, finished engineering drawings are produced. This is the familiar principle of division of labor. By assigning only a limited number of tasks to each specialist, the organization hopes to attain greater productivity than when each person does the whole job by himself.

These two principles—(1) control exercised from the top down through successive levels of hierarchy, and (2) specialization of function—are the source of a host of challenging human-relations problems that management must somehow solve. Indeed, failure to develop an adequate organizational structure may nullify the benefits of effective supervision. Careful planning in this area must precede any other management program.

Within the broad field of organization, we shall concentrate our attention on several types of problem. Perhaps the most obvious one, but certainly not the simplest, concerns the ability of a many-leveled organization to control itself—the ability of upper levels of management to direct the efforts of employees whom they never contact directly and probably do not even know. Chapter 15 ("Hierarchy") discusses these "vertical" relationships, the passing down of orders and information through a series of levels, and the efforts of management to develop systems by which information from below will flow upward to these same levels.

Many organizations that resort to the use of specialists in their attempts to achieve maximum productivity find that the alleged benefits of specialization are simply not forthcoming. Coordinating all the specialized parts so that they fit together neatly into a productive organization gives rise to many human-relations problems. These problems of coordination are described in Chapter 16, "Specialization."

Within management itself and for work involving the collaboration of many specialized, trained professionals, it is often impossible to construct small autonomous work groups within the organization. Successful completion of their respective missions requires a large number and wide variety of "lateral relationships" that cross department and functional lines. By looking at two extended cases, one involving the role of purchasing agents in manufacturing organizations, the other, the difficulties encountered by a development engineer in getting other groups to cooperate with him, we hope to portray realistically the difficulties inherent in lateral relationships. (Chapter 17, "Case Studies of Lateral Relationships.")

A number of answers have been proposed to the human-relations questions associated with large organizations. These proposals are analyzed in Chapter 18 ("Minimizing the Human Problems of Larger Organizations"). We shall devote particular attention to efforts to provide greater decentralization, whereby lower levels of the organization are assigned self-contained tasks that limit their need for contact with other levels of the organization.

Hierarchy

15

Heretofore we have dealt with the human problems of organizations under a somewhat unrealistic assumption. Our discussion has concentrated on a two-level organization: an employee and his supervisor in direct face-to-face contact with one another. Although we complicated the picture by dealing with the impact of different types of technology and work groups, the problems still fit into this simple form of organization.

It should be apparent that as the size of an organization increases, there will have to be more than two levels.[1] No longer can a single manager supervise everyone. With the addition of a number of managers comes the need for supervising and coordinating the work of the managers themselves: managing the managers. Thus, another level is introduced into the organization, and with it relationships which do not involve face-to-face contact. More and more levels will be introduced as the organization grows in size.

---

[1] However, as we shall see on page 352, there is no simple relationship between the number of people and the number of levels; a 10,000-employee organization will not necessarily have twice the number of levels of management as a 5,000-employee organization.

In this chapter we shall be looking at the human problems associated with multi-level organizational structures. First we shall want to consider what these organization structures look like in the real world. Then we shall examine in turn the distinctive problems of leadership and communication in this type of organizational setting.

Characteristics of Hierarchies

The term hierarchy refers to this multi-leveled, vertical structure. A hierarchy tells us who outranks whom within the organization, who must defer to whom; in other words, the formally prescribed status differences. The result can be summarized in the familiar organization pyramid.

For coordinating the activities of large numbers of people, some form of pyramidal organization is inevitable, simply because there will always be fewer people with very high status than with moderate or low status. Only in this way can order be maintained:

> In all organizations of any size at all, the flows of materials, people, and messages quickly fall into patterns, or "channels." One has only to make a circle of a hundred points and to connect each point with all the others by a straight line to realize how quickly an unpatterned flow of communications and transportation would break down; even in a small organization, this has the makings of a colossal traffic jam. The simplest way to order these flows is to establish a chain, so that each individual only communicates with two others, but this is both slow and highly vulnerable to breakdown that paralyzes the entire organization. It is safer, faster, and more economical to divide the members of the organization into groups having individual spokesmen through whom all flows into and out of the group nominally pass, and to gather the spokesmen into groups with spokesmen of their own, thus establishing the familiar pyramidal hierarchical form. This arrangement permits comparatively fast contacts from top to bottom without overburdening anyone, for it reduces the number of contact points considerably, yet it permits most of the organization to continue operations even when part is cut off. The pyramidal distribution pattern of most large organizations develops, in short, because it has significant advantages over the alternatives to it.[2]

Thus, it is easy to understand the emergence of a pyramidal structure when the efforts of more than a small number of people must be coordinated. However, there is disagreement about what its actual shape or form should be.

Those students of management whose views have been labeled "scientific management"[3] or "bureaucracy theory"[4] conceive of a very regularly shaped

---

[2] Herbert Kaufman, "Why Organizations Behave as They Do: An Outline of a Theory," Papers Presented at an Interdisciplinary Seminar on Administrative Theory, University of Texas (Austin, Texas, 1961), p. 47.

[3] *Cf.* Luther Gulick, "Notes on the Theory of Organization," in Luther Gulick and Lyndall Urwick, *Papers on the Science of Administration* (New York: Institute of Public Administration, 1937), pp. 1-45.

[4] For a brief description of the bureaucratic, or rational, model of organization, see Victor Thompson, *Modern Organization* (New York: Knopf, 1961), pp. 73-77.

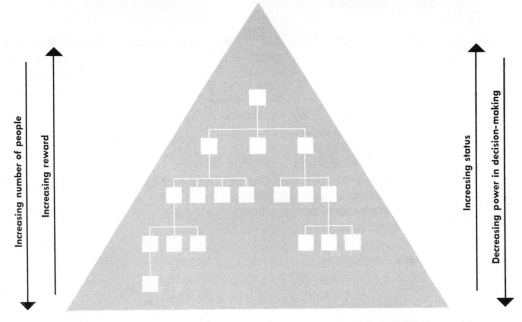

The organizational pyramid.

pyramid. The table of organization or organization chart that is so familiar (see the figure above) represents this pyramid. The actual relationships among members of organizations are presumed to be consistent with this structure with the results that:

1. Nearly all contacts take the form of orders going *down* and reports of results going *up* the pyramid.
2. Each subordinate must receive instructions and orders from only one boss.
3. Important decisions are only made at the top of the pyramid.
4. Each superior has only a limited "span of control," that is, he supervises only a limited number of individuals.
5. An individual at any level (but the top and bottom) has contact only with his boss above him and his subordinates below him.

Under the impact of recent research, this traditional view of the organization pyramid is undergoing modification. Let us look at each characteristic of the pyramid theory and compare it with recent research findings.

UP AND DOWN CONTACTS

Traditional view. The only significant contacts in an organization are those between superiors and subordinates: giving orders (downward) or reporting back on results (upward) or requesting information (up or down).

Recent research. Researchers are becoming increasingly aware of the importance of horizontal or lateral contacts in activating organizational goals (see Chapter 16). For some time, organization theorists referred to these horizontal contacts as the "informal organization," implying that they were not really required or anticipated by management when it designed the "formal organization" (or the pyramid). To be sure many "informal" relationships are primarily social contacts that take place largely within informal groups (Chapter 4), yet other contacts are work-oriented, such as: [5]

1. Work-flow contacts among people who must collaborate to get a job done.
2. So-called "staff-line" relationships (see Chapter 16), which can be envisioned as diagonal contacts.
3. Appeals to higher management by those on lower levels for modification of decisions made by their direct bosses.

ONE SOURCE OF ORDERS

Traditional view. The manager or boss is viewed as the one source of *legitimate* power to which subordinates should respond. Other sources (such as informal groups) are viewed as illegitimate.

Recent research. Since staff groups are in a position to reward friends and to make life less pleasant for enemies, they too exert power. Though staff's requests may be called "advice," line learns that this is advice which it is perilous to ignore. In addition, fellow employees with roughly the same status in the organization exert pressure and even give orders. For example, when an engineering group requests some drawings from drafting, engineering is giving what amounts to an order, even though the two departments may be of equal formal status.

DECISIONS MADE ON THE TOP

Traditional view. All important decisions are made by top managers since these are the best informed and most competent people in the organization and so can set broad policies for the organization as a whole. The policies they make are passed down through successive levels of the organization and, as they are passed down, are spelled out in increasing detail and transformed into operating instructions.

Recent research. The traditional view may have been realistic when companies comprised a small number of trained (and educated) managers and a large number of relatively unskilled, untrained workers. Today, organizations hire many managerial, professional, and technical personnel. Since they are

---

[5] One of the earliest analyses of these nonpyramidal contacts is provided by Conrad Arensberg. See his "Behavior and Organization: Industrial Studies," in John Rohrer and Muzafer Sherif, eds., *Social Psychology at the Crossroads* (New York: Harper & Row, 1951), pp. 324-352.

often better informed on technical subjects than their superiors, the latter must abdicate certain key decisions to them. This view has been expressed as follows: [6]

> . . . the business enterprise of today is no longer an organization in which there are a handful of "bosses" at the top who make all the decisions while the "workers" carry out orders. It is primarily an organization of professionals with highly specialized knowledge exercising autonomous, responsible judgment. And every one of them—whether manager or individual expert contributor—constantly makes truly entrepreneurial decisions which affect the economic characteristics and risks of the entire enterprise. He makes them not only by "delegation from above" but inevitably in the performance of his own job and work.

As companies move toward process automation, the relative number of managerial personnel increases dramatically. There may be three to four times the number of managers for a given number of nonsupervisory employees in companies employing this type of technology, compared to those with older methods of production! [7] The existence of relatively large numbers of staff personnel and department heads can produce pyramids that are quite "middle heavy" (or that bulge in the middle) as distinct from the rather tall, thin structures envisioned by traditional theory.

Further, the modern organization is not a unified, homogeneous entity directed toward one set of objectives. As we shall see in Chapter 16, individual departments and groups compete with each other for status and recognition. Each group develops its own special objectives which may sometimes conflict with the goals of the larger organization.

LIMITED SPAN OF CONTROL

Traditional view. An effective organization requires tight control. The supervisor is responsible for coordinating the work of his subordinates. To do this he must have a very limited span of control. The fewer subordinates, the better the management. This point of view results in quite steep pyramids. In large companies it is not unusual to find ten levels separating the hourly employees from top management.

Recent research. As we have already seen, under many circumstances subordinates perform more effectively with limited supervisory order-giving and controlling. Also, coordination can often be enhanced if employees contact one another directly (that is, through lateral not hierarchical relationships). "Flatter" organizations, involving broad spans of control, thus are often desirable.

---

[6] Peter F. Drucker, "Long-range Planning, Challenge to Management Science," *Management Science*, Vol. 5, No. 3 (April 1959), p. 242.

[7] Joan Woodward, *Industrial Organization: Theory and Practice* (London: Oxford University Press, 1965), pp. 56-57.

Whereas traditional management theorists assumed that there were fixed maximum numbers of subordinates who could be supervised effectively, new research suggests that the desirable number varies, depending on the basic technology of the enterprise. A study of 90 English companies showed the following differences: [8]

KIND OF TECHNOLOGY	MEDIAN SPAN OF CONTROL OF FIRST-LINE SUPERVISORS
Unit or small-batch production (fabricating "one of a kind" products such as custom-designed suits or electronic equipment)	23 subordinates for each supervisor
Mass-production and assembly-line work	49 subordinates for each supervisor
Process production (continuous processing of chemicals and other fully automated "flow type" manufacturing)	13 subordinates for each supervisor

These striking differences in span of control are maintained at higher levels of the organization. For example, the most successful *process-production* companies in the above study all had ten or more subordinates reporting to the chief executive. However, in *mass-production* plants only half this number reported to their respective chief executives.[9]

Another way of predicting the "span of control" of supervisors is to observe the frequency with which the manager has to check how operations are proceeding, issue new instructions, and answer questions, or in any way get involved in the work process. The more routinized are operations or the more responsibility that can be delegated to subordinates, the greater the number of subordinates that can be supervised.[10]

NO BYPASSING

Traditional view. Contacts in the organization are supposed to follow the table of organization. An individual restricts his relationships to his immediate boss and his immediate subordinates. As a result every manager has full information about the activities and people he is responsible for.

Recent research. For reasons that will become clear in the latter parts of this chapter, timely communication often requires bypassing certain steps in the hierarchical chain. Also, every organization needs an *appeal channel,* a

---

[8] *Ibid.,* p. 69.

[9] *Ibid.,* p. 71.

[10] See Robert Dubin, "Leadership and Productivity: Empirical Findings and Theoretical Considerations," in R. Dubin, G. Homans, F. Mann, and D. Miller, *Leadership and Productivity* (San Francisco: Chandler, 1965), pp. 14-17.

mechanism by which subordinates can go over their boss's "head" when they feel a serious injustice has been done to them.

Special Problems of Extended Hierarchies

Although we have been critical of the simple, traditional view of organizational hierarchies, it would be a serious error to ignore the importance of rank differences. There clearly are successively higher levels in the modern organization, with fewer occupants of the levels as one moves upward. And clearly, too, status differences make leadership and integration possible, and promise rewards that encourage employees to seek advancement by effective performance.

These differences also pose some rather special problems, however, particularly for extended hierarchies (that is, structures with many levels). We shall first want to look at the impact of the hierarchy on the position and problems of the immediate supervisor and on his relationship with subordinates. Secondly, we shall assess the impact on the efficiency of operations and communications.

THE MANAGER AS A MAN IN THE MIDDLE

Our emphasis in earlier chapters—and the emphasis in current research, training, and management thinking—has been on the relationship between supervisors and their immediate subordinates. In actual day-to-day activities, however, many supervisors spend less time with their subordinates than they do with superiors, staff, and others at their own level. And as we saw in Chapter 7, there is empirical evidence that the effective supervisor spends a greater proportion of his time on upward and horizontal contacts than the ineffective supervisor does.

Every manager, except for the company president, belongs to two groups: the work group of which he is the leader, and the higher-management group of which he is the immediate representative. The manager is thus a man in the middle, endlessly beset by conflicting loyalties and demands. The ineffective manager allows himself to be squeezed by these conflicting pressures; the effective supervisor resists them and serves as a communications link between those above and those below him.

The pattern of leadership utilized by the manager will be influenced, even determined, by the "styles" practiced by his superiors. The reactions of his subordinates to his leadership will also depend on his ability to balance off loyalty to his subordinates (by fighting for their interest with higher management) and loyalty to his own boss above (by accepting his desires and objectives and transmitting them downward to all subordinates). As we shall see, this is easier to say than to perform, and there are many temptations to do differently.

Transmittal of supervisory styles.[11] Supervisory styles are "handed down" from level to level; good supervision at the top is reflected by good supervision at the bottom. The evidence suggests that those who receive general supervision are more likely to practice general supervision themselves, and that those who are supervised closely will supervise their subordinates closely.[12]

It is perfectly natural for a manager to reflect the supervisory style of his boss, for the boss is the one who hands out rewards. His actions are looked upon as clues to the behavior he expects from his subordinates. "To a greater or lesser extent, any assigned job becomes, in this medium, two jobs: one job is to carry out the assignment; the other (but not always the secondary) job is to please the superior." [13] The subordinate imitates his boss's work hours, his sense of humor, perhaps even his car, and certainly his style of supervision.

If a supervisor is subjected to pressure by his own boss, he has a strong tendency to pass it on to those below. Transmitting pressure—and perhaps increasing it a bit in the process—is a time-honored way of relieving frustration and soothing a wounded ego. Moreover, when the boss applies pressure on the man directly below him, he is saying in effect that he wants immediate results regardless of the long-run effects on subordinates farther down the line. As a consequence, many supervisors decide:

> "I can't afford to have any mistakes made in my department or my boss will get me in trouble. He's likely to quiz me on everything that happens. So I better check up on everything and have all the facts and explanations at my finger tips. This means I have to keep close tabs on my men."

Yet "keeping close tabs" on the men may generate widespread frustration, aggressiveness, and other negative reactions. One general foreman made this shrewd observation:

> "Some people . . . have got to recognize the fact that by putting too much pressure on the foreman, you are only going to drive him to do things that lead

---

[11] See Rensis Likert and Daniel Katz, "Supervisory Practices and Organizational Structure as They Affect Employee Productivity and Morale," Personnel Series 120 (New York: American Management Association, 1948); Daniel Katz, Nathan Maccoby, and Nancy Morse, *Productivity, Supervision, and Morale in an Office Situation,* Part I (Ann Arbor: Institute for Social Research, University of Michigan, 1950); Robert Kahn and Daniel Katz, "Leadership Practices in Relation to Productivity and Morale," in Dorwin Cartwright and Alvin Zander, eds., *Group Dynamics* (New York: Harper & Row, 1953).

[12] See Edwin Fleishman, "The Description of Supervisory Behavior," *Journal of Applied Psychology,* Vol. 37, No. 1 (February 1953), pp. 1-6; Edwin Fleishman, "Leadership Climate, Human Relations Training, and Supervisory Behavior," *Personnel Psychology,* Vol. 6, No. 1 (Summer 1953), pp. 205-222; Charles R. Walker, Robert Guest, and Arthur N. Turner, *Foreman on the Assembly Line* (Cambridge: Harvard University Press, 1956), p. 25.

[13] Harold Leavitt, *Managerial Psychology* (Chicago: University of Chicago Press, 1958), p. 264.

to friction on the job. . . . As for myself, I have a thick skin, and I absorb a lot of the pressure and only pass on what I think should be passed on." [14]

Ineffective supervisors often "develop into pompous, petty bureaucrats. . . . Their outstanding trait is a Janus-like subservience to their superior—combined with a thirst for unrestricted power over their subordinates. . . . They are extremely status conscious, they prefer subordinates who are boot-lickers." [15]

Furthermore, no supervisor can permit his subordinates to exercise freedom in areas in which he does not have freedom himself. Some top managements, for instance, issue strict rules which describe in detail what they want sub-ordinates at all levels to do in almost every conceivable situation. Under such circumstances the supervisor has little discretion himself and cannot delegate any at all.

On the other hand, the supervisor who receives general supervision from above feels free to let his subordinates make decisions by themselves. Know-ing that he will be judged by over-all results, he encourages his subordinates to experiment and does not penalize them for making unintentional mistakes. He is confident that his own boss will back him up when his judgment is questioned, whether by subordinates, by other supervisors, or even by top management. He recognizes that as long as he produces results his boss will back him up and refrain from meddling with petty details. Imbued with a sense of confidence and freedom, he operates in what we have called an "atmosphere of approval." Here we have an extension of the principle of delegation of authority. In effect the boss is saying, "I really mean it when I tell my subordinate that I am giving him authority. I won't interfere with his decisions so long as the final results are good."

One reason for an ineffective manager's poor performance is his personal insecurity. Uncertain about where he stands in the eyes of his boss and his company, fearful that the axe will fall any minute, and anxious to avoid the boss's displeasure, it is little wonder that he is reluctant to experiment or to encourage his subordinates to develop their own ways of doing things.

Representing subordinates.   Employees are quick to recognize that their immediate supervisor has limited powers. The levels above make many crucial decisions that will affect their welfare.

> "I can't describe how angry I get every time those managers in mahogany row make the kind of decision I know they wouldn't make if they really knew what was going on in our division."

Therefore, the effective supervisor must act as a spokesman and protector for his subordinates, and must represent their interests to higher management.

14 Walker, Guest, and Turner, *op. cit.*, p. 25.
15 Robert N. McMurray, "Recruitment, Dependency, and Morale in the Banking Industry," *Administrative Science Quarterly*, Vol. 3, No. 1 (June 1958), p. 90.

(You will remember that, in our discussion of informal leadership in Chapter 4, we mentioned that the informal leader functioned as "an outside contact man" for the group. The effective supervisor fills a similar role.)

In a sense, the effective supervisor serves as a shock-absorber, shielding his men from outside influences that jeopardize their welfare and productivity. As one foreman put it:

> "If I treat a man right and he figures a way of doing a job which gives him a little rest, then so much the better for him. My boss doesn't understand that, so that you might say I am a concrete wall between the general foreman and the men. I have to take it one way, but not give it out the same way." [16]

He accepts responsibility when things go wrong. When someone on a higher level asks for explanations, he does not say, "That's Joe's fault; I'll speak to him." Instead, he takes the "rap" himself rather than involve Joe with higher-ups. (Whether Joe knows about this specific favor is irrelevant; the group will know the results of the policy, and that is what is important.) He tries to ameliorate the rigid requirements imposed by higher management, in an attempt to make life easier for his subordinates.

Moreover, he speaks out for the interests of his men when he thinks that management has made a wrong decision. He acts as spokesman for subordinates who have little opportunity to contact higher levels of authority. Note what one worker said:

> "My present foreman is the nicest guy I ever worked for. The other foremen respect him also. I saw him stick his neck out with the general foreman over work loads. . . . He'll argue a point with the general foreman if he thinks he is right." [17]

What this means in practice is dictated by the situation. To the average soldier or sailor, a good commanding officer is a man "who will look out for his men." One observer described a typical case in the Navy:

> The personality of the captain was an important factor maintaining morale and efficiency despite the tensions among the enlisted men. The captain was extremely popular with the men who looked upon him as their active protector against higher authority. . . . Although many of the 3,000 men aboard seldom saw their captain, there was a growing body of lore concerning his disregard of naval formalities and his concern for enlisted men. [18]

In other cases, acting as spokesman for the group may mean fighting for promotions, cutting red tape to get an employee immediate benefits under an

---

[16] Walker, Guest, and Turner, *op. cit.,* p. 26.

[17] *Ibid.,* p. 27.

[18] James F. Downes, "Environment, Communications and Status Change Aboard an American Aircraft Carrier," *Human Organization,* Vol. 17, No. 3 (Fall 1958), p. 14.

insurance plan, or pointing out to the time-study engineers that their controls are too "tight."

However, the manager cannot fight for his men or take a critical attitude toward management decisions if his boss forces him to be a "yes man." In battling for the interests of his group, the manager may have to tread on a lot of toes; he may even have to disagree with the boss himself. But he can behave in this way only if his boss permits him to do so, if the boss in turn listens to his suggestions and backs him up when he gets into trouble with other departments.

Much depends on the supervisor himself, of course. Being a spokesman for the group is not enough. The supervisor must be successful in getting results.[19] This means he must have the skill to make effective presentations to his boss and to other departments: he must be a good listener and a good communicator. And, since it takes time to develop good relations, he must be able to plan his work and train his men well enough so that he doesn't have to be constantly present in his own department.

Thus, the effective supervisor has what has been called "influence"[20]—that is, other levels of management respond to his requests. When the supervisor is successful, the confidence of his men is reinforced. When he is perpetually turned down, his men become disillusioned with his effectiveness in exerting influence.

In fact, general supervision *without* influence may lead to poorer results than close supervision *with* influence (or at least to more dissatisfaction).[21] Why? Take the case of the general supervisor who commands no influence. He calls a group meeting to discuss a common problem. Then he takes the group's suggested solution up to higher management, only to find that it is rejected out of hand. A group that goes through this experience several times sinks into frustration and cynicism; it becomes antagonistic toward the company and disrespectful of the supervisor. Subsequent attempts by the supervisor to practice general supervision will be interpreted merely as weakness. Finally, the men may decide that, since trying to work *with* management has failed, they might as well try working *against* it. They may choose to by-pass the supervisor altogether and seek to challenge higher management directly, either through their union or through an independent wildcat strike.

The effective supervisor, on the other hand, is able to persuade management to satisfy the group's legitimate requests. This kind of activity helps build reciprocal loyalty between supervisor and subordinates. "Since our supervisor stands up for us, we'll stand up for him." As a consequence, the subordinates are more likely to comply with his requests.

[19] At an insurance company, supervisors of the less productive departments were more likely to recommend promotions; but supervisors of the more productive departments won the promotions. From Katz, Maccoby, and Morse, *op. cit.*, p. 27.

[20] Donald Pelz, "Leadership within a Hierarchical Organization," *Journal of Social Issues*, Vol. 7, No. 5 (1951), pp. 48-55.

[21] Nancy Morse, *Satisfactions in White Collar Jobs* (Ann Arbor: Survey Research Center, University of Michigan, 1953), p. 164.

Conflicting loyalties. Do effective supervisors feel greater loyalty to their subordinates or to their boss? Often members of management complain, "We've got to make our supervisors feel they are company men. They're always taking the employees' point of view." This may not be too regrettable a situation. There is evidence that at least on the first level the good supervisor identifies as closely with his subordinates as he does with management.[22]

In a study of the Prudential Insurance Company, supervisors were asked questions designed to determine whether they identified more closely with the company or with employees. As the following table indicates, employee-identified supervisors had the more productive sections: [23]

	IDENTIFIED WITH	
	EMPLOYEES	COMPANY
High-production supervisors	9	2
Low-production supervisors	4	8

This same company had separate dining rooms set aside for supervisors. The high-productivity supervisors, reflecting the attitude of their employees, objected to this form of segregation. The low-productivity supervisors went along with it.[24]

Still, the employee-oriented supervisor's loyalty is not undivided. He is also loyal to upper management—or, to be more precise, he is motivated to carry out the assignments that have been delegated to him. As a result, he may sometimes find himself in conflict with the men he supervises and have no choice but to act restrictively. And yet he must somehow manage to keep his dual role intact, for he will sacrifice his effectiveness if he becomes too interested either in meeting management's production demands or in safeguarding the interests of his men.

> If management fails to recognize this duality and attempts to enlist a supervisor's undivided loyalty, he may lose his ability to act as a representative of his employees and eventually his effectiveness in helping management gain its objectives.[25]

Although personality and experience differences affect loyalty too, there is some tendency for lower-level managers to be more downwardly oriented

---

[22] Katz, Maccoby, and Morse, *op. cit.*

[23] *Ibid.*, p. 23.

[24] *Ibid.*, p. 25. High-producing foremen in a tractor factory were more critical of company policies and their bosses than were low-producing foremen. Kahn and Katz, *op. cit.*, p. 222. Higher-rated Forest Service supervisors were more likely to be critical of their superiors than were lower-rated supervisors. A. L. Comrey, J. F. Pfiffner, and H. P. Beem, "Factors Influencing Organizational Effectiveness: The U. S. Forest Service," *Personnel Psychology*, Vol. 5, No. 4 (Winter 1952), pp. 307-328.

[25] F. C. Mann and J. K. Dent, "The Supervisor: Member of Two Organizational Families," *Harvard Business Review*, Vol. 32, No. 6 (November 1954), p. 112.

than their higher-level counterparts.[26] This divergence can be explained by the likelihood that the farther down you go in the hierarchy, the more cohesive the work groups are. As we have seen in Chapter 4, the greater the cohesiveness, the more effective is the group in being able to pressure their superior.

The special problem of the first-line supervisor. First-line supervisors probably suffer more from being men-in-the-middle than do the members of any other supervisory group. Their subordinates, whether they are production workers, office girls, or engineers, do the actual work of the organization. These subordinates have no one to supervise and often little chance for promotion. As a consequence, even if they are paid salary or commission, they are less likely to identify with management. In fact, since they normally do not compete with one another, they have a tendency to join together in defense against higher management.

The first-line supervisor can ignore this potentiality for revolt only at his own peril. His subordinates, as a group, are in a strategic position to embarrass him. By following his instructions too literally and by failing to use common sense, they can spoil work, damage equipment, and waste materials. By slowing down in unison they can prevent him from meeting schedules; through a hundred different subterfuges they can increase his costs and make him look bad in the eyes of his superiors. Thus, though the first-line supervisor is subject to many pressures from above, he cannot pass these pressures down to lower levels; if he tries to do so, he will only make matters worse.[27]

The inevitable result is that the first-line supervisor must somehow come to terms with his subordinates. He must be particularly careful to insure strong, continuing motivation, primarily through bargaining and on-the-job need satisfaction. Often, too, he must make deals with the union steward involving special concessions to the men in return for their implicit agreement to keep production high.

As might be expected, expedient arrangements such as these are rarely acceptable to higher management. Consequently supervisors sometimes become "two-faced," turning one face to management and another to their subordinates. Caught inescapably in the middle, they must cope with all the problems of higher levels of management and at the same time resolve all the problems that are peculiar to their own position in the hierarchy.

PERSONAL CONTACT BETWEEN HIGHER AND LOWER LEVELS

Even with effective representation, there is evidence that employees like to have some personal contact with higher managment. Some such contact facilitates identification with the total organization.

---

[26] For an empirical exploration of some facets of this problem, see Peter Blau and W. Richard Scott, *Formal Organizations* (San Francisco: Chandler, 1962), pp. 159-163.

[27] For a description of the reaction of foremen in a situation where higher management imposes pressures which they cannot pass on, see Chris Argyris, *Executive Leadership* (New York: Harper & Row, 1953), Part II.

We are all familiar with generals, kings, and presidents who on occasion mingle with the "people." An actual view of the leader, perhaps hearing his words directly, even touching his hand or coat, is meant to impart confidence in his human or organizational qualities. Particularly if the head of the organization has a strong personality, he can impart a sense of identification with himself; he in turn personifies the total organization. In an effort to recreate the personal intimacy between hierarchical levels that characterizes small organizations, many managers try to cultivate the feeling of "one big happy family." They resort to such devices as:

> Personal appearances by top management before employee groups.
> Special, personal letters from the company president to employees on anniversaries with the company, or after special accomplishments (*e.g.*, a new patent).
> Christmas parties, bowling teams, golf tournaments, and other events at which various levels of the organization meet informally.

All these efforts are designed to counteract the impression that the company is impersonal, to give the feeling that top management consists of flesh-and-blood individuals who are wise decision-makers and genuinely interested in the welfare of the people who work for them. But two factors seriously limit the effectiveness of this approach as a means of communication:

1. As we noted in our discussion of communications, lower levels of the organization may suspect or distort management's motives. Here are two not untypical comments made at a lavish annual company picnic: "Today is 'Be Nice to the Children Day.'" "Look at the big boss over there, surrounded by apple polishers. He really thinks he's one of the boys. Ha!"

2. This type of communication is directed primarily downward. Printed messages or talks before large groups provide little opportunity for feedback. Even picnics and bowling leagues are poor devices for eliciting a sampling of employee opinion.

> The manager of one large plant made a daily recording of a "management-to-management message of the day" which any supervisor could listen to by dialing a special number in the plant phone system. One foreman said, "That's the typical kind of conversation we have around here: *they* tell *us*. But when that so-and-so finishes, I always cuss him out. I sure hope that really is just a recording."

Nevertheless during crises (for example, when labor relations are strained) these direct "lines" to the top may be utilized extensively.

As with other aspects of supervisory behavior, such personal contacts by higher management cannot be evaluated in isolation; they take on meaning only in the over-all context of human relations. If the president's "personal" birthday card fits into the employee's previous perception of his relation to the president, fine. If not, the birthday greeting may seem hypocritical.

Similarly, it is waste of effort for the boss to be a mass of smiles at the annual picnic if he is completely unapproachable at other times of the year. Under such circumstances, gestures that are intended to be warm and personal may well be perceived as merely mechanical or hypocritical.

On the other hand, at times the absence of direct contact can assist in maintaining an aura of omnipotence, of more-than-average human qualities, even of what bureaucracy theorists have called "charisma." [28] Frailties and blunders are more easily perceived among those with whom one is in close working proximity.

Multilevel organizations have certain advantages over smaller organizations in reducing tension over the exercise of authority. Depending upon an individual's needs, upper levels—far removed from his immediate experience—can be seen as composed of either saints or sinners. If immediate supervision is unsatisfactory, subordinates can say: "If only the old man (the president of the company) really knew what was going on he would straighten things out." On the other hand, many blame unpopular decisions on top management rather than the immediate boss. (However, supervisor who maintains good relationships with subordinates by always blaming his superiors is not doing his job effectively.)

Patterns of Downward Communication

If we turn from the impact of hierarchy on leadership to day-to-day operations and communications we shall discover still other human-relations problems.

At the beginning of the chapter we concluded that a hierarchical form of structure is necessary to move directions and information efficiently through a large body of people. It would be incorrect to assume, however, that this dissemination is the same process as communication within the small group. The multiple levels introduce problems, for orders are not simply passed downward through one subordinate manager and then another until they reach the lowest level in the structure.

Unfortunately, when we draw boxes and connect them with lines, we have a tendency to believe that the system we design will function like a physical model—that is, we think of an organization as though it were a system of interrelated pipes and reservoirs. Water starting at the top always reaches the bottom in exactly the same quantity and quality as when it started out—if everything is connected correctly, that is. Thus, the model suggests that someone at the top issues an order or makes a policy decision, and the next person in the hierarchy passes the instructions along to the men who report to him, and so on down the line.

---

[28] Magical qualities which cause followers to obey instructions and even to make extreme sacrifices without question; the response is distinguished from rational evaluations of a leader's superior technical ability.

Similarly, significant information from "down the line" is reported upward through the same system of "pipes" so that those at the top will have at their finger tips all the information they need to administer the affairs of the organization. This constant circulation of information up and down the chain of command provides the lifeblood of the organization and keeps it in a healthy state of alertness and efficiency. Each employee at the bottom is supposed to respond in some predictable way to plans originated at the top, regardless of the number of linkages through which orders must flow before reaching him, and regardless of how many layers his ideas and experiences must pass through before reaching the top again.

But an organization is not made up of mechanical parts or pipes. It consists of *people*, whose attitudes and behavior are affected by the system of human relations in which they function. These people upset the simple mechanistic working of the hierarchical model. They introduce distortions in both the downward and upward transmission of information. Here we shall concentrate our attention on these distortions and on the human-relations problems they create.

DISTORTION IN DOWNWARD COMMUNICATIONS

In a sense, we are now dealing with the problem of exercising good supervision where there are more than two levels of authority. As we shall see, the supervisory practices we recommended previously appear simple in contrast to the complexities of motivating and directing people in a multi-level structure.

Let us start with an example. Top management decides that racial discrimination in employment shall be eliminated. What happens as this policy is passed down the line through successive stages of the hierarchy? By the time the policy reaches the individuals who do the actual hiring, it may have been

Prescribed channels of communication.

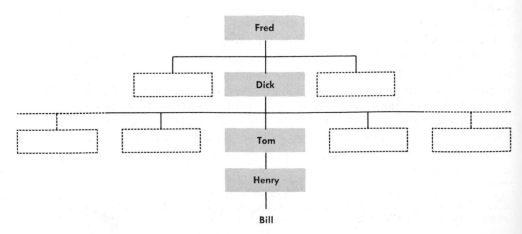

transformed almost beyond recognition, for example: "Hire *some* Negroes at each location, so that the company appears to be nondiscriminatory."

In part, this sort of distortion is caused by the communications problems we discussed in Chapter 10. People may "hear" the new policy in ways unintended by top management. The result is wide differences in interpretation, which grow increasingly wider the more broadly the policy is communicated.

But the organization itself complicates matters further. The order-giver is a long way from the final recipient. You may have played the game in which a story is passed from person to person in a group. Each person alters the facts slightly to fit his own needs and preconceptions, often without intending to do so. When the story finally re-emerges, it has been distorted beyond recognition. Information passing through many status levels can be more confused.

Complex statements of policy, whose accuracy depends on subtle shades of meaning, are particularly vulnerable to distortion as they move "down the line." A fairly simple company decision to grant every employee with more than six months' service a two-week vacation with pay could probably be communicated down through several levels without major alteration. But an announcement of policy on union matters, or on promotions, is often badly mangled or downright misleading by the time it filters down through the levels of the organization.

Two sorts of distortion are particularly common. The first is *exaggeration.* Every subordinate is highly dependent on his boss's goodwill, for the superior has countless ways of making his job either easier or harder. Consequently, most subordinates are highly sensitive to the boss's every whim and seek to anticipate his desires, sometimes before they are expressed. This constant search for clues to what the boss wants often leads to strange results.

> Nearly every company is familiar with what happens when one of the members of top management makes a visit to an outlying installation. If local management hears through company gossip that the visiting dignitary is likely to be impressed by the physical appearance of the organization, a sudden redirection of effort takes place. Employees are taken away from their regular jobs to do housekeeping chores which are normally neglected. Equipment and buildings take on an unusual "shine."

Many a subordinate asks the boss's secretary, "What is he gunning for today? Is it safe for me to mention . . . ?" The authors once observed a personnel department hectically preparing to run a morale survey (though the department doubted that it was a good idea) purely because a top official had read a short article in a popular management magazine and had remarked to the personnel director, "This looks like a good idea for us."

The second common type of distortion is just the opposite: the *playing down* of directives. Lower management drags its feet in carrying out an order, or follows the letter but not the spirit. For example, we once observed the reaction of middle and lower management to a top-management directive to install a supervisory performance-evaluation program. This program required each superior to rate his subordinates every six months, and then to discuss his ratings with them. With few exceptions, the managers were reluctant to adopt this new program, which they felt would breed more antagonism than good will. So they procrastinated, in the hope that the program would gradually be forgotten by all concerned.

Distortion of this sort occurs when the subordinates as a group feel strongly opposed to a new policy and feel that top management is not really serious about implementing it. Many subordinates show sheer genius in endlessly evading directives without becoming overtly insubordinate, making sure that nothing can be "pinned on" them (that is, feigning acceptance).

In short, employees frequently receive mystifying directives that have been passed down from higher levels of the organization. For example, managers are told costs must be cut. But how should a priority be placed on this order compared to other instructions that have been issued? Should other objectives that have been established—for example, smooth labor relations or safe working practices—be ignored? Or modified? Or given a lower priority? When directives appear to conflict, as they often do, or priorities are unclear, as they often are, employees spend a great deal of time and energy "researching" the problem: What is top management really thinking now and what group has the most influence on the president's thinking?

Obviously, in small organizations, where orders come from immediate supervisors with whom the subordinate has almost continuous contact such problems are minimized. Over time the manager's scale of values and personal priorities become clear and his changing preferences are easy to interpret.

To summarize, the larger the organization, the more difficult communications are, and top management finds it harder and harder to maintain firm control over the lower levels of the hierarchy simply by issuing orders. Top executives are never really sure of what is happening below, and those at lower levels become uncertain about what is expected of them. As a result, management's decisions often become vitiated or distorted as they move down the line.

SHORT-CIRCUITING THE LINES OF COMMUNICATIONS

Going through channels: the red-tape problem. The typical large company has not one but a number of separate hierarchies with parallel lines of upward and downward communication. Each hierarchy represents a specialty. Since, in theory, these specialties are completely independent of one another, except for coordination at or near the top, one might think that there would be very little need for contact between them. Nothing could be further from the truth.

Take a typical problem: A group of plumbers are working on the air-conditioning equipment in the accounting office. The men stop work a half-hour before quitting time and engage in extensive "clean-up" operations. After this has been going on for several days, the clerks begin to grumble that they should have the same privileges.

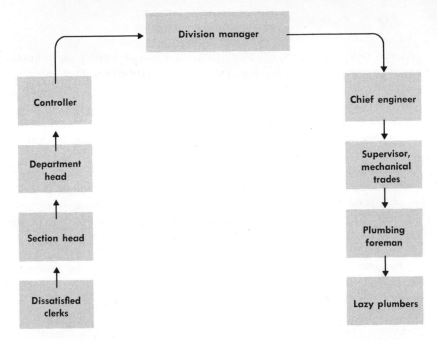

Accounting and maintenance hierarchies.

How can the accounting supervisor handle this problem? In theory, he must report the matter to his supervisor and so on up the line until it reaches the common boss over both accounting and maintenance. Then the matter descends down the maintenance chain of command till it hits the plumbers.

In this case it might take six supervisory contacts before the problem could officially come to the attention of the supervisor who is directly responsible. If there were a need for frequent adjustments between the accounting section head and the plumbing foreman, the number of contacts would soar astronomically.

In one sense, this cumbersome procedure is desirable. If the accounting supervisor were to start giving orders directly to the plumbers, the plumbers would be subject to all the evils of "too many bosses." A clearly defined sequence of supervisory contacts, by contrast, helps to bring order into interpersonal relations.

But in emergencies the need to go through channels can be costly in terms of managerial time and may only complicate the problem. Days and weeks may pass before a serious problem can be attended to. Think what would happen in a hospital: "... Suppose a piece of oxygen equipment goes out of order. If the nurse were to report it to the head nurse, she to the chief engineer, and he to the repairman, the patient would probably be dead before the equipment was fixed." [29]

---

[29] Temple Burling, Edith Lentz, and Robert N. Wilson, *The Give and Take in Hospitals* (New York: Putnam, 1956), p. 323.

As you can see, it becomes more difficult to move swiftly and effectively on challenging problems within the specialized organization. Particularly in large companies, the burden of going through channels, in terms of the sheer number of interactions that must take place for every problem, tends to slow the organization and creates endless frustrations and conflicts. It is under these circumstances that one hears that "red tape" or bureaucracy is defeating the purpose of the company.

As a result, there is a widespread temptation to short-circuit the chain of command. In the case above, the accounting supervisor might go directly to the plumbing foreman. But those who are left out—those who get "short-circuited"—are understandably resentful of such violations of the chain of command and feel their leadership position threatened.[30]

Bypassing.   A manager may become so frustrated by the time-consuming process of going through channels and the apparent inability of subordinates to carry out instructions precisely as they were intended, that he bypasses intermediate levels and goes straight to the men involved. For instance, the superintendent goes directly to an employee to find out why a new machine is producing so much scrap, or the division manager calls in a salesman to tell him to give special attention to a customer who is threatening to take his business elsewhere. Often top-management expediters are sent as temporary replacements for lower managers who are in trouble. Here is a description of a top executive (former President of Curtiss-Wright) who is particularly well known for taking direct action and cutting through red tape:

> Hurley is chief expediter at C-W and chief executioner of good ideas with bad cost records. He seldom "moves through channels." He figures that the division manager doesn't have any more idea than he has of what is wrong or the figures would not have been negative in the first place. So instead of waiting for a briefing, Hurley moves directly to the spot, right down to the machine on the floor if that is the heart of the problem. Many a division manager has discovered hours later that the boss has been in his department and long since moved on. And many department heads have discovered that an important job has been given to an employee they hardly know, and without consulting them. Hurley spots a man who seems bright and says, "You do it." That the job may be completely unrelated to the employee's work is of no concern to Hurley.[31]

Attractive and dramatic though bypassing may seem, we must remember that sticking to the formal channels has one great advantage: It insures that everyone who is supposed to be informed actually is informed.

Mass communications.   In many companies the word *communications* refers not to the transmission of orders and information through normal

---

[30] *Cf.* George Homans, *The Human Group* (New York: Harcourt, Brace, and World, 1950), p. 430.

[31] William B. Harris, "Curtiss-Wright Throws Away the Book," *Fortune*, Vol. 57, No. 1 (January 1958), p. 115.

hierarchical channels, but to what we would call mass communications: the company newspaper ("house organ"), bulletin-board announcements, direct mailings to employees, fillers in pay envelopes, movies, a loudspeaker system, and so forth. Almost every large company has a special staff assigned to preparing material of this sort.

Mass communications are seldom used by themselves to convey messages that are really important. When management wants to raise production or cut costs, it sends clear, unmistakable orders down the line, and makes sure that every subordinate understands them. Mass-communications techniques are used chiefly in areas that are peripheral to management's main job of getting the production out—areas such as safety, personnel policies, suggestions, and the company's financial position.

Why are mass-communications techniques used so widely in these areas? There are several reasons:

1. Often the information to be transmitted is of a technical nature. If details of a new insurance scheme, for example, are transmitted by word of mouth from top management through the various levels of supervision, they are bound to be badly distorted by the time they reach the rank and file. Further, management may feel that the supervisors are not qualified to explain such involved matters as why depreciation must be deducted from profits to give an accurate picture of the company's financial position, therefore top management must communicate directly with employees.

2. Since messages of this sort do not have A-1 priority, management wants to insure that they will not be distorted or forgotten by lower supervision. Lower supervision is chiefly interested in getting out production, and messages relating to "fringe" areas may be laid aside or given perfunctory attention. The supervisor tells his men at the end of a meeting, "And, of course, as you know, I'm supposed to tell you once a week to be sure to wear your safety hats."

Many of the messages sent through mass-communications channels are sponsored by staff departments, such as finance or personnel. And these departments have learned through sad experience that if they have to trust line management to carry their messages, the information will never reach lower-level employees.

3. Finally, in contrast to what we said earlier, some messages are so vitally important that it is essential that details not be distorted by transmission through channels.

> A large, geographically dispersed corporation, recently made a number of vital changes in salary policy affecting every one of its 75,000 employees. To insure uniform and simultaneous reception, loudspeakers were installed in every location and work stopped for 15 minutes to permit the company president to address the entire workforce.

As is probably already clear, it is unwise for management to rely excessively on mass communications. With the exception of movies and loudspeaker announcements, mass communications involve the printed rather than the spoken word; they are always one-way rather than two-way. You will remember from our discussion in Chapter 10 that printed one-way communications lack flexibility and the opportunity for the feedback of the face-to-face spoken word. A man can't ask questions of a bulletin board, nor does a letter repeat itself if the reader is drowsy or inattentive.

If the message is of any importance at all, the use of mass communications tends to reduce the status of the immediate supervisor. In effect, top management is saying, "We don't trust you to explain complicated problems." Often, too, if the message is of importance, the subordinate has questions to ask about it. If his boss can't answer them, then the subordinate's respect for him will drop even more.

On the other hand, the fact that messages are sent through mass communications channels rather than through the line may indicate to the employees that the message is really not important. If the boss says "work faster" and the bulletin board says "work safer," the subordinate will be more likely to pay attention to the boss than to the bulletin board.

Improved mass-communication methods.   In order to overcome these difficulties, many companies are using mass communications with greater finesse. For example, top management may (1) give higher supervisors advance notice before relaying messages to lower levels, (2) urge the immediate supervisor to add a few words to supplement the formal message, and (3) encourage subordinates to address questions concerning these materials to their immediate boss. Such efforts preserve the advantages of specificity and uniformity, enable the immediate supervisor to retain his status, and encourage feedback from subordinates.

Of course, these procedures also mean that management must devote more time and effort to its attempts to disseminate information through the normal hierarchical channels of communication. As an expert in this field put it:

> If the general manager is planning a direct-mail letter to all employees, explaining the new working requirements resulting from the defense program, the foreman should know about it before some employee on the morning shift brings it to him with a question. The foreman or immediate supervisor should know in advance, not only that certain information is about to be given to employees, not only the mere content of the letter or article or bulletin, but a substantial amount of explanatory and supplemental data to make him a respectable source of answers for questions employees may raise.[32]

Let us look at an example of how this works in practice.

> In an effort to explain past performances and future prospects, some companies have experimented with movies to dramatize the annual financial report. These often fail to accomplish their objectives since there is little tie-in between

---

[32] Alexander B. Heron, *Sharing Information with Employees* (Stanford, Calif.: Stanford University Press, 1942), p. 191.

the accomplishments of the company as a whole and those of any particular department. In an effort to provide this tie-in, some companies have supplemented the movies, with a verbal report by the immediate supervisor on prospects for the department for the coming year. (Naturally he must be briefed to answer questions on company finances.)

Notice that mass communication was effectively supplemented by personal contacts by the immediate supervisor. The supervisor's status was enhanced rather than impaired.

The grapevine. Though not consciously designed by management, the grapevine is frequently an extremely effective means of communication. "Being flexible and personal, it spreads information faster than most management communications systems operate. With the rapidity of a burning powder train, it filters out of the woodwork, past the manager's office, through the locker room, and along the corridors." [33] Often subordinates learn of top management's decisions through the grapevine long before anything is put into writing. And when formal messages are transmitted, rumor "helps" explain and interpret them. Since the grapevine is personal, spoken, and permits feedback, it often has a far stronger impact on the recipient than do other forms of communication.

Many times the grapevine is surprisingly accurate; in fact, exaggeration is less common than simplification and abbreviation.[34] Of course, individuals in a position to initiate the process—for example, a key executive secretary—gain status and influence in the informal organization.

Many managers feel that rumors should be stamped out, on the grounds that they are often false, exaggerated, malicious, and even give away management secrets. Yet the grapevine performs a very useful function: It tends to correct some of the shortcomings of formal communication. Bill and Joe are in totally different divisions of the organization, but their work is closely tied together. A change is made in Bill's department that will vitally affect Joe. It may take weeks for the message to go up through the formal channels of communication and then reach Joe—possibly much distorted. But if Bill passes the word along to Joe on the job, the message is transmitted efficiently and accurately.

Actually it is unrealistic to expect that rumors can be stamped out. The grapevine fills a vital human need. Gossip gives people a social outlet and a chance to exercise their imagination. It gives an opportunity to relieve fears of the unknown by expressing anxiety in the form of stories. Above all, it allays curiosity.

The grapevine is bound to exist in any organization. If facts are available, it will transmit them effectively, though often with some distortion. If facts are

---

[33] Keith Davis, *Human Relations in Business* (New York: McGraw-Hill, 1957), p. 244.

[34] *Cf.* Theodore Caplow, "Rumors in War," in *Some Theories of Organization*, Albert Rubenstein and Chadwick Haberstroh (eds.) (Homewood, Ill.: Dorsey, 1960), pp. 280-287.

not available, the grapevine may invent them. From a few clues, vastly perverted images may be constructed. Rumors rarely cause trouble where facts are readily available.

The best way to minimize undesirable rumors is to improve other forms of communication. Untruthful rumors rarely get started if the boss announces his intentions in advance, and if his subordinates feel free to ask him questions.

We have been talking about three somewhat different techniques used to short-circuit formal downward channels of communication: bypassing, mass communications, and the grapevine. More generally, we have been discussing the whole process of downward communication as a means of coordinating people in the organization, the reasons why this communication sometimes fails, and what can be done to improve it.

COMMUNICATION AND SUPERVISION

It is useful, for a moment, to look at the relationship between hierarchical communication and patterns of supervision. The aggressively authoritarian manager may have difficulty even in communicating *downward*. Sometimes subordinates seek to impress the boss by doing more than he has requested and thus exaggerate his orders. Alternatively, they may object to the boss's order, yet fear to express their objections openly. Instead, they "play down" the order and systematically sabotage it or give it only token compliance. Subordinates may be afraid to ask their boss questions even when they fail to understand what he has said. In the last two instances, it should be noted that the boss's failure to encourage upward communication makes downward communication more difficult.

Often, this type of manager has little confidence in his subordinates, so he discourages downward communication, particularly through the regular channels. He doesn't trust subordinates to convey information or orders and, not trusting them with information, he doesn't see why they need more than the minimum amount required to do their job. His idea of good communication frequently is in terms of what we have called mass communications.

Patterns of Upward Communication

A healthy organization needs effective upward communications as much as it needs effective downward communications—and for two primary reasons:

1. *Obtaining information.* Top management depends on a steady stream of information from subordinates in order to make intelligent decisions. How well are we doing on Line 7? Is that new quality-control man working out

OK? Are we going to have to hire some more junior engineers? Without some sort of reporting system, top management can never find out what orders are needed or how effectively its orders are being carried out. Effective upward communication furnishes management with quick and accurate reports on what is happening at lower levels.

Successful upward communication requires that management's questions be truthfully answered. More than this, it requires that vital information be transmitted upward even if management has never requested it; it requires that *management be willing to listen to unsolicited messages.* The men on the top do not always know the right questions to ask or the right instructions to give. Subordinates frequently have useful suggestions to make, questions to ask, or problems of which their supervisors are ignorant. Unless subordinates feel free to communicate these matters upward, management will lack some of the data essential to sound decision-making.

2. *Maintaining morale.* It is psychologically unsound for the initiation of contacts to run in only one direction—always from superiors to subordinates. No one is happy when he is always on the receiving end. We all want some opportunity to express ourselves, particularly to those who control our activities and welfare. When we are disturbed or under pressure from others—for example, when an earlier deadline has been unexpectedly imposed, or another department is demanding speedier service from us—the need to express ourselves becomes even more urgent.

DIFFICULTIES IN UPWARD COMMUNICATION

Effective upward communication is difficult to obtain, particularly in larger organizations. In a small firm, the informality that usually prevails between the employees and the top boss produces a feeling of intimacy and personal satisfaction. Indeed there is a certain amount of censorship at each level in a large organization. Let us examine this difference in detail.

Covering up. Subordinates have a natural tendency to withhold unfavorable information from their superiors, or to filter the information as it is passed up the line. Often middle- and lower-level managers conspire with subordinates to hide from higher levels serious mistakes, deviations from standard procedures, or unsolved problems. Sometimes these deceptions are deliberate falsehoods to avoid blame; sometimes they just take the form of failure to report self-incriminating information. (For example, because an operator was not properly instructed, an entire batch of chemicals had to be thrown out, but the waste was disguised as garbage.)

The subordinate's fear of sending unfavorable information upward also reflects his lack of certainty concerning what top management wants. Recognizing the imperfection of downward communication, and not sure of what is expected, he tries to avoid reporting anything that might give an impression of failure. (Thus, poor downward communications often make upward communications harder.) [35]

Status problems. In an effort to maintain his superior position, and to ration his scarce time, the manager may isolate himself from his subordinates by setting up barriers. An advance appointment, appropriate dress, passing the scrutiny of an officious secretary—all may be necessary before a man can ask the boss a modest question.

A department head calls in one of his subordinates to give him special instruction on handling an important project. The instructions are confusing, but the subordinate makes no attempt to ask clarifying questions. Why? Simply because he is afraid that the supervisor will interpret his questions as evidence of slowness or stupidity. He is not sure that the questions he will ask will be "good ones"—that is, the kind of question an intelligent, competent man is supposed to ask. So rather than risk hurting his reputation, he remains silent.

Strangely enough, this common cause of breakdown in upward communication is also one of the easiest to remedy. The solution is simply for the supervisor to encourage questions, indicating that they are expected and appropriate —in fact, giving the subordinate the feeling that asking questions indicates a high degree of alertness.

PRESSURES FOR UPWARD COMMUNICATION

In a small organization the manager can see for himself how his decisions are being carried out. In the large organization, managers can "see" only through the eyes of others. Top management normally relies on "auditors" and the reports of managers at the next level in the hierarchy, who in turn must rely on those reporting to them, and so on down the line of command. But top management finds it very difficult to discover what is really happening on the levels below. One often hears executives asking, "We wonder what is really going on at the work level."

Quite revealing are the apocryphal stories about the efforts of navy captains to learn what is happening below decks. In the typical tale the captain disguises himself as a seaman and wanders through the ship, or invites a seaman to his cabin for drinks and talk.[36]

On the other hand, employees are often anxious to bring their problems to the attention of higher management. Joe feels that his manager is discriminating against him and wants a fair hearing from someone higher up on why he has been denied a promotion. Jack has thought up a new fixture that he is

---

[35] One would expect upward communication to be much more effective in a company that practices general supervision. Here subordinates are more likely to feel free to discuss problems with their bosses without fear of being bawled out for mistakes. The close supervisor, on the other hand, tends to build a wall of suspicion between himself and his subordinates.

[36] Downes, *op. cit.*, p. 17.

sure will cut machining time by one-third, but his foreman brushes him off with a curt rejection. Bill feels at ease with his immediate supervisor, but realizes that it is pointless to complain to him about his salary when someone higher up makes the decisions. In effect, all these men are saying, "If only someone in top management would listen to us!"

APPEAL CHANNELS AND BYPASSING TECHNIQUES

Appeal channels. Most organizations have some form of appeal channel by which a member can challenge his immediate superior's decision.[37] Some procedures are quite formalized, as with the establishment of a union in a company or with the use of the Inspector General in the armed forces. Since a superior has so much power over his subordinates, it is not surprising that these channels have been carved out. They give subordinates a greater sense of security and provide higher management with useful information.

However, organizations have also been successful in using less formalized procedures. Many companies have experimented with the "open-door" policy whereby every employee is guaranteed the privilege of walking into the office of any manager at any level in the organization to voice his complaints. In some companies this policy has succeeded in opening up a worthwhile channel of appeal. More often, however, subordinates take advantage of the privilege only rarely. Why? One reason, of course, is the deterrent of social distance—the fear that keeps the buck private from complaining to his colonel that he has been assigned to KP too often, even though the colonel makes himself available. More than this, the subordinate realizes that once he exercises the privilege of appeal, he will have jeopardized his whole future with his immediate superior.

A subordinate knows intuitively how his supervisor feels about the open door. He calculates that if he walks through this portal he has only a slim chance of winning anything and a good chance of losing a great deal. After all, the immediate superior controls many things that the complainant holds important—job, salary level, work assignments, and so forth. The risk is too great, so the open door is rarely entered.

In at least one very large and successful American corporation the formal open-door policy works. There is a well-publicized series of appeal steps, almost like a grievance procedure, that ends in the president's office, which is many hierarchical levels above the average employee. Each year a significant number of employees get to see the president with their personal "grievances." He has so frequently supported them and reversed decisions of lower levels of supervision that, not surprisingly, there has been a morale problem among supervisors! Nevertheless, it should be stressed that this is not the typical case,

---

[37] A very interesting analysis of appeal systems in business, the military, the U.S. Government, the UAW, and the Catholic Church is contained in William G. Scott, *The Management of Conflict* (Homewood, Illinois: Richard Irwin and Dorsey Press, 1965).

but it does indicate what a management can do in creating a viable appeal channel.

Understandably, a supervisor is upset when a subordinate decides to go over his head with an appeal to a higher level in the organization—this behavior spotlights his own deficiencies. The supervisor also begins to worry lest the subordinate reveal practices or mistakes that he has carefully tried to cover up. And he recognizes that if the top boss does decide to grant the complainant's demand, a steady stream of complaining subordinates may carry appeals over his head, and thus seriously endanger his leadership position.

In spite of what we have just said, a boss can always, if he wishes, encourage employees to bring problems directly to him, bypassing their direct supervisors. Many times a higher-level manager will be contacted informally—perhaps while he is walking through the office—by an employee who has a special request or protest. The frequency with which this occurs depends more on the attitudes of higher management than on any announced open-door policy.

What is a boss to do when the subordinate of one of his supervisors comes to him with a problem? If such bypassing is encouraged, the effect on the supervisors' morale may be disastrous. Yet if it is completely banned, the effect on the workers' morale may be equally harmful. Probably the best approach is to listen to at least a summary of the problem and then to suggest tactfully that the subordinate see his immediate superivsor.

But suppose the man has already seen his supervisor? One solution would be for the boss to call the supervisor and subordinate together and hear them out. Such a meeting, however, might aggravate the tension between them, and inhibit both of them from talking freely. The supervisor might have had confidential reasons for taking the disputed action. Above all, the fact that the subordinate is implicitly making charges against his supervisor tends to make the supervisor feel that he is on trial, that he must defend his every action. To make a meeting of this sort successful would required unusual human-relations skills on the part of the boss.[38]

Probably a better approach is for the boss to listen carefully to the subordinate's problem, without committing himself one way or the other, and then promise to discuss it with the supervisor. In his meeting with the supervisor, the boss should try to minimize his interference with the supervisor's freedom to make decisions within the limits of his delegated discretion. If the problem is serious enough, the boss may use the nondirective technique to help the supervisor talk through his difficulties. If possible, however, he should leave the final decision to the supervisor. In the event that he feels compelled to reverse the supervisor's decisions, he should be careful to give the reasons why. Further, in order to preserve the supervisor's prestige, he, not the boss, should be the one to explain the final decision to the subordinate.

---

[38] For an example of a boss who was able to make such meetings successful, see William F. Whyte, *Human Relations in the Restaurant Industry* (New York: McGraw-Hill, 1948), pp. 298-300.

Attitude surveys. Many companies use morale or attitude surveys as a means of finding out how their employees feel about their job, their supervisors, specific policies, or the company as a whole.

Today the making and interpretation of such surveys is a growing but specialized field. Psychologists in colleges, in management consulting firms, and in individual companies have become highly skilled in preparing, administering, and evaluating questionnaires.

Some experts argue that standardized surveys (which can be purchased from firms specializing in psychological services) are the best, for they make it possible to compare firms and departments and to point out significant deviations from "norms" that have been developed on the basis of experience elsewhere. Other experts argue that special questionnaires should be devised to meet the needs of each particular company.

Most surveys consist of written questionnaires that may be filled out on the job or at home. (As might be expected, a high percentage of the "take-home" questionnaires are never returned.) In either case, care is taken to preserve the anonymity of the respondent.

Many questionnaires require the employee to indicate the degree of his feeling in regard to each point. For example:

I feel fairly well satisfied with my present job:

_____ strongly agree	_____ disagree
_____ agree	_____ strongly disagree
_____ undecided	

Other questions may invite the employee to choose among various alternatives:

The following items describe different conditions that may be bothering you in your work. Check the ones that need to be improved: [39]

Ventilation	( )	Unpleasant noise	( )
Lighting	( )	Faulty unsafe equipment	( )
Too cold	( )	Dirty work station	( )
Too hot	( )	Lack of sanitation	( )
Drafts	( )	Too far from rest room	( )
Sun glare	( )	Unpleasant dust	( )
Dampness	( )	No union	( )
Unpleasant odors	( )	Other _____	( )

Some surveys try to elicit more detailed (and perhaps deeper) answers through so-called "open-ended" questions, such as, "What would you say are your most serious dissatisfactions with your present job?" A modification of this technique is the sentence-completion procedure, in which the respondent

---

[39] Roger M. Bellows, *Psychology of Personnel in Business and Industry,* 2nd ed. (Englewood Cliffs, N.J.: Prentice-Hall, 1954), p. 155.

is requested to complete sentences like "The most serious complaint I have about my present job is _____."

Because employees are sometimes reluctant to reveal their deeper feelings and may not even be able to express them, attempts have been made to adapt psychiatric techniques to industrial use. For example, rather than using verbal questions, the respondent may be shown cartoons of people in the organization talking, but with the traditional little "balloons" over their heads left empty. The respondent is asked to fill in the balloons with what he thinks the people are saying to each other. These more sophisticated forms of survey are far more expensive to score than the check-your-answer forms, and are less frequently used.

Once the forms have been filled out, the results must be tabulated and analyzed. Simple, so-called "straight runs" (e.g., 70 per cent of the men like their jobs) are usually less useful than cross tabulations, such as:

	AMONG MEN WHO LIKE THEIR JOBS	AMONG MEN WHO DISLIKE THEIR JOBS	TOTAL
Foremen speak to them often	85%	15%	100%
Foremen speak to them rarely	45	55	100

The survey results are then presented to top management, which sometimes disseminates them to lower levels. Indeed, some companies use survey results as a springboard for supervisory training.[40] On occasion, the results are specific enough to dictate immediate action, as in the case of a survey which revealed that many employees misunderstood the details of a new pension plan. More often the results are ambiguous. They raise a host of questions but the answers, if any, must be found through careful re-examination of policies and behavior in the affected areas.

Thus, surveys point up broad problems, but rarely suggest solutions. They are a rather artificial form of upward communication and their findings are subject to serious forms of distortion. Employees may purposely or unconsciously misinterpret questions and give misleading answers. By their very design, these surveys make no provision for communicating the specific problem of specific employees. Often they are expensive and time-consuming. For all these reasons, attitude surveys are a valuable adjunct to, but not a substitute for, more unambiguous, direct means of upward communication.

---

[40] For an interesting example of the use of feedback from morale surveys to change supervisory attitudes (as they learn what their subordinates believe and perceive), see Floyd Mann, "Studying and Creating Change: A Means to Understanding Social Organization," in Industrial Relations Research Association, *Research in Industrial Human Relations* (New York: Harper & Row, 1957), pp. 146-167. A more complete analysis of the theory behind the use of survey data as a means of upward communication is contained in Rensis Likert, *New Patterns of Management* (New York: McGraw-Hill, 1961).

Committees. Management sometimes sets up special conference groups or committees to find out what is on the minds of employees. These committees give lower-ranking personnel a chance to express their attitudes directly to top management, thus bypassing intermediate levels. For example, the first-line supervisory group may elect representatives to meet weekly or monthly with the general manager to discuss current problems. The representatives are encouraged to ask about the rumors floating about on their level, ask questions, ventilate gripes, and give management some ideas of the unsolved problems in their departments.

Some companies have used similar devices for hourly-paid personnel.[41] Here caution needs to be exercised to insure that these committees do not conflict with existing unions or violate the provisions of the National Labor Relations Act, which prohibts employers from assisting in the formation of employee organizations with union-like functions.

Other techniques. Suggestion systems are used by many companies as a means of collecting specific ideas for improving company efficiency. Ordinarily, suggestions are presented in such a way as to bypass the intermediate levels of management.

> The experience of one company highlights the manner in which suggestion plans bypass normal communication channels. An employee suggested that the installation of a coin-operated coffee machine would reduce the half-hour coffee break to a few minutes. The employee wrote out his proposal and dropped it in the "Suggestion Box." It was the first indication top management had ever had that half-hour coffee breaks were being permitted at lower levels.

In a sense, a union itself provides a very important channel of upward communication by bringing the average worker's problems directly to the attention of top management. Many cost-sharing union-management cooperation plans bring committees of workers face to face with top management in discussions of production problems.

Staff specialists provide another upward channel because of the ease with which they can contact higher management. They may hear of good ideas that have been smothered by unsympathetic superiors or good men who have not received adequate recognition. (Of course, their "mobility" can be a source of conflict between these specialists and the line manager.)

Summary. Effective upward communication is essential both to organizational efficiency and to individual job satisfaction. Top management needs to know what is happening on lower levels, and subordinates feel helpless unless

---

[41] For a description of how one company makes use of overlapping committees that blanket the entire organization, see Elliott Jaques, *The Changing Culture of a Factory* (New York: Holt, Rinehart and Winston, 1952).

they have some opportunity to talk freely to their own bosses and to make direct contact with the decision-makers at higher levels.

Of course, a great deal of information passes upward through the ordinary channels of the hierarchy. This is particularly true when supervisors at the various levels (1) encourage subordinates to speak freely about their problems, and (2) make a vigorous effort to represent their employees' problems to higher levels of management. As we have suggested, the effectiveness of communication through an organization is directly related to the supervisory practices of the individual managers. With general supervision pervading the entire organization, each subordinate feels free to talk to his own boss, and communications tend to flow upward more efficiently and with less distortion than under close supervision.[42]

Even with highly effective supervision, however, upward communication through many levels of hierarchy is inefficient and subject to some degree of distortion. For this reason some sort of short-circuiting or appeal channel is required to permit individuals to give vent to their feelings and to preserve the health of the organization. Since excessive short-circuiting tends to undermine the position of intermediate management, however, these techniques should be considered chiefly as auxiliary aids. It is more important that each supervisor be sensitive to the problems of those on the levels below him.

In summary, there are at least three reasons why supplementary channels like appeal channels are important for an organization:

1. Upper management can get additional feedback on the results of its own decisions and activities beyond that carried by the chain of command. Serious sore spots may be detected.

2. Individuals at lower levels who might feel oppressed and powerless to do anything about it gain a means of protecting themselves, to a degree, from the arbitrariness of the hierarchy.

3. New ideas which might otherwise get lost may reach key decision-making areas.

This last is worth expanding on briefly. The weight of the hierarchy, of tradition, and the impact of controls that we shall be discussing next may be all on the side of preserving the status quo. Individuals with a great deal of initiative and new ideas may be discouraged from doing or saying things that would "rock the boat"—would in the short run create new problems for their supervisor. As organizations come to depend more and more on new technical knowledge, on research findings and ideas, they must protect themselves against the possibility that originality will be summarily rejected. Often the supervisor cannot judge the intrinsic quality or usefulness of a man or his idea, and both need to be exposed to higher levels of the hierarchy.

---

[42] See our discussion of the General Electric case in Chapter 6.

Statistical Controls

Now let us explore what is probably management's most effective means of upward communication—statistical controls. Normally, management introduces statistical controls in order to further coordination, pinpoint responsibility, and find out what is actually happening at the operating level. Since figures are harder to distort than subjective reports, higher management insists on receiving a constant flow of data on production, sales, costs, quality, grievances, salary increases, turnover, and so forth.

FUNCTIONS OF STATISTICAL CONTROLS

Through cost accounting, for example, "standard costs" are developed for every item produced or service rendered. If the standard cost of an item is 35 cents and the foreman can make it for 33 cents, he is making a "profit" (part of which may accrue to him, personally, as a bonus). If he spends 37 cents to make it, he is incurring a "loss." These departmental profit and loss accounts, called *variance accounts*, provide standards by which higher management can measure departmental efficiency. Other standards may be set in terms of quantities produced, man-hours expended per unit, sales, scrap loss, turnover, and so on.

To insure that these data reach headquarters rapidly and without distortion, they are ordinarily collected by staff departments, such as accounting, quality control, and personnel. Because these departments operate at least semi-independently of the line, the data can be reported directly to the top without being filtered through intermediate steps of management that may have reputations to protect. Computers enormously increase the amount of data that can be assembled and the speed with which they can be transmitted to top management.

In addition to providing top management with the information it needs for decision-making, statistical controls serve many other functions described briefly below.

Supervision by results. Statistical controls eliminate the necessity for close, detailed supervision, and provide the evidence needed for supervision by results. Through reports on profits, sales, and so forth, top management can evaluate the effectiveness of subordinate departments without checking on every detail of their work. Without satisfactory statistical controls, decentralization is difficult.

Standards. Statistical controls also make it possible for management to set standards for achievement and to emphasize areas that require special attention. For instance, if top management is anxious to focus attention on a scrap-reduction program, it will begin asking all subordinate departments to report each month how much they have reduced scrap losses over the preceding month. Thus, statistical *controls* are a means of downward communication and exerting pressure.

Personnel evaluation. In turn, they help develop goals and provide motivation and measures of success for those whose work is measured by controls. Statistical controls that measure individual performance provide a means for selecting, appraising, and compensating employees.

DIFFICULTIES IN MEASUREMENT

Yet statistical controls should not be considered as a magic cure for all organizational ills. Improperly handled, they may create as many problems as they cure. Elements like department costs, efficiency, and productivity are difficult to measure fairly, while the very act of measurement may distort effort.

Naturally if employees are to be evaluated largely in terms of their success or failure in meeting these goals, it is important that the goals be fair and reasonable. Establishment of such goals is a highly technical and often inaccurate procedure. It is all too easy to set standards that are too "tight" or too "loose." (It should be obvious, too, that the greater the reliance on statistical measures of efficiency, the greater becomes the power of the staff departments which prepare them.)

Many types of work are so general and intangible that it is almost impossible to devise an adequate technique for measuring them. How is one to measure the effectiveness of the personnel department? [43] Surely not in terms of cost, because low cost may simply mean that nothing is being accomplished. Not in terms of turnover, number of strikes and grievances, productivity, and so forth, for all these things are related to over-all plant policy or the organization as a whole. Roughly the same sort of objections can be raised against any direct rating of staff departments. And there are other departments, such as research, where meaningful results become apparent only in the long run.

In talking to engineering supervisors in a large research organization, we heard this common complaint: Supervisors had a hard time evaluating their subordinates, and subordinates didn't know what was required to get a pay

---

[43] Or how does one measure the efficiency of a university professor? By the number of students who take his courses? But this may depend on whether the professor makes it a "snap course" or on the nature of the subject matter (witness the rise of physics). By student rating? Perhaps, but teaching ability is more than being a good showman. By relative scores on an identical exam which is jointly graded and given to all students in the same course? Possibly—but note the motivation this gives the professor to cover only those points likely to be on the exam. In many colleges promotion is largely based on the number of scholarly articles published, with an obvious effect on the relative time spent on research as against teaching. How does one compare the relative efforts of a classics professor with one in chemistry? Obviously, direct measurement has its limitations in the university as well as in industry.

raise or promotion. One supervisor put it this way: "An engineer is constantly making decisions in which he is balancing time against efficiency against cost. It is practically impossible to know whether his judgment is good. Also, if a man doesn't get results, how are you to know whether he has been 'goofing off' or been up against a streak of bad luck?"

Even more severe problems arise in attempts to make a comparative rating of various departments. How does one rate costs in division A, which makes the same product year after year, against division B, where the product is always undergoing change? Some department stores try to measure departmental efficiency in terms of sales and profit, but the level of sales in any department may depend on its location in the store, the weather, and the business cycle more than on the individual efficiency of the department manager.

Unfortunately, the measures selected to evaluate performance may be a reflection of what is easy to measure, rather than the real criteria of effective performance.[44] Because of the problems of dealing with short-run and long-run factors, situational exceptions, the combination of personnel, production, financial and marketing effectiveness, one often sees organizations using overly simplified controls, devices which are not much different from worker incentive plans that just measure raw output.

DISTORTING BEHAVIOR

If excessive emphasis is placed on statistical controls, compared to other forms of upward communication, the very act of measurement may lead subordinates to distort their efforts and work less efficiently.

Overemphasis on the items measured.   Departments will normally concentrate on the items that are being measured rather than on the job as a whole. Successful banks realize that good customer relations are vital and that a very poor impression is created when a teller refuses to serve a customer until he has finished adding up his figures. Yet "the teller has found all his rewards in the past for careful balancing of the books. . . . He has never been rewarded or punished for his treatment of customers." [45]

Top management rarely realizes how alert subordinates are to adapting their behavior to the reward and punishments implied in the controls being used. Very slight changes in what is measured are magnified into very substantial changes in behavior.

In the past the development engineers in the ABC Chemical Company had devoted themselves to helping line managers solve day-to-day production problems. A new head of Engineering for the company was very interested in the

[44] *Cf.* Kenneth Arrow, "Control in Large Organizations," *Management Science*, Vol. 10, No. 3 (April 1964), p. 400.

[45] Mason Haire, *Psychology in Management* (New York: McGraw-Hill, 1956), p. 17.

new mathematical techniques of operations research and "model-building" techniques. As the "word got around" that he appreciated very sophisticated analytical reports, most of the engineers gave up their efforts to aid line managers and began working on quite advanced "theoretical" research projects. This changed drastically the relationships the engineers had with production, and they were no longer perceived as a source of assistance.

Token compliance. Supervisors may greet statistical control with token compliance—that is, by striving to *look* as if they were meeting their standards. Unfortunately, the effect of keeping up appearances may well be to lower overall performance.

As part of a drive to cut excess inventory, the divisional superintendents in one company were required to give a monthly report of supplies on hand. What happened? There was a scramble to use up all the stock before the end of the month and to insure that no new supplies were delivered until after the beginning of the next. But the average inventory over the month remained just about the same.

Inefficient scheduling of work. Sometimes the existence of standards results in a long-run deterioration of real performance, *even on the items being measured.*

> Because management in one company paid so much attention to end-of-month efficiency ratings, department supervisors left no stone unturned to get as many units into finished stores as possible. They even resorted to such expensive and disruptive processes as "bleeding the line"—that is, stopping operations in order to complete more units by the deadline. This process is summarized by what another foreman said:
> "For the last two weeks of the month we're driving hell out of the men. We have to get pieces out and we are always jammed up at the end of the month. . . ." [46]

Even where employees are not subjected to such hectic pressures, the mere existence of standards may induce them to schedule work less efficiently. A claims adjuster once told us, "Of course, some claims are harder to handle than others, but as far as the quota is concerned they all count the same. So I always try to keep a few easy cases aside to handle at the end of the month if it looks like I won't be able to meet the quota without them. I try not to turn in too many cases in any month or they'll always expect me to work that hard." Pieceworkers also build up "banks," to equalize their earnings over the week.

Emphasis on short run rather than long run. The use of statistical controls often produces short-term results at the expense of the organization's long-term

---

[46] Frank Jasinski, "Use and Misuse of Efficiency Controls," *Harvard Business Review*, Vol. 34, No. 4 (July 1956), p. 107. This problem is even more serious in Russia where "storming" (as it is called there) during the last week of every month is done at high pressure. David Granick, *The Red Executive* (Garden City, N.Y.: Doubleday, 1960), pp. 267-270.

good. Managers often complain that supervisors are "department-centered" and show no loyalty to the organization as a whole. For instance, department managers in retail stores are rewarded for high sales and profits in their *own* departments. By pushing shoddy merchandise they can sometimes get high sales for themselves at the expense of the goodwill of the entire store. Yet under these circumstances, what other sort of motivation could be expected? Similarly, salesmen, conscious of the importance of an impressive sales record, may ignore the store's public relations—showing themselves unwilling to spend time with indecisive or dissatisfied customers—in favor of the easy, free-spending customer.

Supervisors are supposed to maintain both high morale and high productivity. Morale is intangible and difficult to measure, but productivity and costs can presumably be measured to a tenth of a decimal place. As a consequence, productivity comes first; good employee relations are a luxury to be enjoyed only when there is nothing wrong with output. Measuring factors such as costs, output, and scrap alone may encourage short-sighted supervisors to overemphasize short-run production results at the expense of human assets and longer-run efficiency. One authority suggests: "There is only one solution to this situation: obtain adequate periodic measurements of the character and quality of the human organization ... which will penalize managers financially and otherwise when they permit the quality of the human organization under them to deteriorate." [47] And many companies do attempt to measure the state of their human relations through turnover figures, morale surveys, and other techniques.

Covering-up. Faced with the necessity of having to look good on paper, the natural impulse of employees is to try to "adjust" the reported statistics. At times plain lying is sufficient, but sometimes it is necessary to hide the evidence. In one department the men put defective parts in refuse cans and covered them over—with the foreman's full knowledge. In another, the foreman himself came back to the department at night to pick up damaged equipment and drop it in the local quarry.

Thus, controls may injure upward communications, or what is called "the intelligence function." Ironically, the more reliance is placed on control measures, the less top management may find out about what is really happening.

> In the midst of a safety campaign, one employee suffered a slight injury at the end of his shift which might have kept him home for several days. The foreman begged him:
>
> "If you can possibly come to work tomorrow I will guarantee you will not have to do a lick of work until you really feel up to it. I'll pick you up at home and drive you back. But for the love of Mike, let's not have a lost-time accident on our record."

---

[47] Rensis Likert, "Measuring Organizational Performance," *Harvard Business Review,* Vol. 36, No. 2 (1958), pp. 41-50.

Passing the buck.   Another unfortunate by-product of excessive emphasis on standards is an added inducement to pass the buck. If parts turn out defective, there is always an argument about which department should be charged with the cost or repair. Similarly, there may be endless haggling over whether time spent in training new employees, or in the handling of grievances, should be charged against the particular department or against the personnel department.

In a well-known national company, accident-prevention is so strongly emphasized that regular tribunals have been established to determine whether an accident will be "charged" against the foreman of the department in which it occurred. In one case, all sorts of internal political pressures were used to influence the panel members in their decision. These tribunals seem more concerned with fixing responsibility than in determining and eliminating the causes of accidents.

Impaired teamwork.   Statistical controls and supervision by results rest on the assumption that each individual supervisor should be held responsible for the efficiency of his own department. Within limits it is healthy to encourage individual responsibility. Yet overemphasis on individual performance may lead to excessive individualism and selfishness, particularly in departments that are highly interdependent.

> In one large company, maintenance and repair charges assessed against production departments were "adjusted" by management. Departments that were "friendly" to maintenance received low charges, while unfriendly departments received not only their own charges, but those left over after the special reductions.[48]

Reduction in discretion.   Insofar as statistical data are used as the basis for evaluating the success or failure of managers and departments, they serve to reduce the discretion of the immediate supervisor. As one researcher has noted:

> The evaluation of subordinates is a major responsibility of supervisors. If this evaluation were based entirely on statistical indices, this responsibility would be reduced to a clerical task, the application of a mathematical formula to a set of data. This would not only make the job of supervisor less interesting for him but also undermine his authority over subordinates.[49]

Another expert points out the need for preserving supervisory discretion:

> The practical effect of this high-handed behavior [excessive reliance on statistical controls], oddly enough, is not to make top management the boss, rather, the accountant with his rows of figures becomes the dominant voice in the company. He becomes a manager by default, as it were, because knowledge is

---

[48] Melville Dalton, *Men Who Manage* (New York: Wiley, 1959), p. 37 ff.
[49] Peter Blau, *The Dynamics of Bureaucracy* (Chicago: Univ. of Chicago Press, 1955), p. 41.

power, and the knowledge on which action is based is what the accountant puts into his reports.

The fact is that the day accountants can devise a balance sheet or graph which encompasses total reality, we can do away with executives—but not until then.[50]

Effect on centralization.   The introduction of electronic data-processing apparatus has a similar effect on the position of the supervisor. Such equipment makes available to top managers vastly more data than they have ever had before, and permits them to make detailed decisions affecting the smallest department in the company—thus completely bypassing middle management.

Some observers, however, believe that improved processing of statistical control data can strengthen the decision-making ability of lower levels of the organization. Used properly, computers can also process information that communicates directly to first- and second-level supervisors rather than to higher management. One manager of data-processing operations described the situation in his company:

> [In the old days] many decisions were of necessity made at the plant manager's level because the superintendent didn't have the local facts.
>
> Now the superintendent makes the decisions and they're better decisions because information is more complete, more accurate and available when the manager needs it.
>
> Take the foreman. Decisions he used to make about stock each day were based on not much more than experienced intuition. Now that he knows the answers these decisions are easy—almost automatic. He can concentrate on areas like personnel relations, performance, on schedule and operating efficiency.[51]

Standards as a form of pressure.   Without question, management uses standards as a means to apply pressure. The techniques, of course, vary with the supervisor, as these contrasting quotations indicate:

> "I go to the office and check the budget every day. . . . If it's OK, I don't say anything. But if it is no good, then I come back here and give the boys a little—well, you know, I needle them a bit."

> "You know, it is a funny thing. If I want my people to read the budget, I just lay it on my desk and leave it alone. They'll pick it up without doubt." [52]

Notice that both approaches use standards as a form of pressure. Basic to both is the assumption that failure to meet a quota is prima-facie proof of falling down on the job. In effect, the standards are transformed into an extremely arbitrary boss. Many a supervisor says, "I don't want excuses, just get the job done." It does little good for the subordinate to reply, "But I did get

[50] Jasinski, *op. cit.*, p. 111.

[51] *For Line and Staff Supervisors* (New York: National Foremen's Institute, July 1959).

[52] Chris Argyris, *The Impact of Budgets on People* (New York: Financial Executives Foundation, 1952), p. 24.

the job done—only the profit figures don't give the complete picture." When standards are boss, all explanations are regarded as excuses.

> Perhaps one of the [supervisor's] greatest criticisms of budgets was the fact that they never included the reasons *why* they were not achieved.... Supervisors disliked intensely the fact that their departments would look "sick" in the budget while the reasons for the "sickness" were never published along with the results.[53]

Controls are not omnipotent.   In most organizations there are other pressures at work "balancing off" the pressures exerted by the use of standards. As we have observed, the work group, unions, and colleagues have standards or norms of their own which may conflict with the requirements being imposed by top management. Then the supervisor, charged with the responsibility of making a good showing in the eyes of his boss, finds himself caught "in the middle."

This phenomenon even occurs in totalitarian states, where consumers, community groups, and employees can exercise some influence because of their ability to withhold or give enthusiastic cooperation. For example, a notable study shows that in Russia the factory manager tends to resist standards imposed from *above* because of informal pressures being exerted from *below:*

> These informal pressures constitute standards of which the manager must take cognizance, pressures to which he must adjust, in order to maintain such relations with his "working community" as will permit him to meet standards directly set and enforceable by superiors....
>
> [The manager reacts to pressures from above by] providing for a safety factor; simulation, or feigning the meeting of standards, and *blat,* or the use of personal influence to obtain favors.[54]

IMPROVED USE OF CONTROLS

The use of control measures is an essential part of management's job in any large organization. No top manager can know everything he needs to know without quantitative data that summarize what is happening and that compare actual results with expected or planned results. When carefully presented, these data enable him to detect trouble-spots almost instantly, without reviewing every facet of day-to-day operations. All he need do is look for the variances, the departures from the quantitative limits that he has set for his subordinates—the number of units to be processed, the amount of permissible overtime, the number of merit increases, and so forth.

The challenge for the manager is also to develop methods of using control channels of communication that do not have the serious drawbacks described

---

[53] *Ibid.,* p. 11.

[54] Andrew G. Frank, "Goal Ambiguity and Conflicting Standards: An Approach to the Study of Organization," *Human Organization,* Vol. 17, No. 4 (Winter 1958-59), p. 9.

above. If he is successful, the rewards can be substantial—greater autonomy, job satisfaction, and better performance for subordinates at each level.

Since the controls themselves often originate with staff specialists who are not the direct superiors of the managers being appraised, conscious attention must be directed to their relationship. One study urges that accountants and line managers establish a human-relations pattern of give and take:

> On the other hand, if a definite program is set up, involving regular assignments for accounting personnel requiring them to contact operating supervisors for information, the accountant may begin to arouse the interest of the operating executives in possible uses of accounting data. They may also obtain a better understanding of these executives' needs for data. When this occurs, the operating heads will generally encourage or seek out more frequent contacts with the accountants. Each begins to gain a more thorough understanding of the vocabulary, problems and methods of the other. This cycle continues until a fairly high degree of communication and use of accounting data is attained.
>
> This provides the controller's department with an opportunity to show that it really intends to provide data in useful and usable form, in terms of operating departments' need, so that when it is asked for help, it meets such requests promptly.[55]

One test of good usage is the organization's response when a man fails to meet standards. Is his failure regarded as evidence of incompetence, perhaps meriting discipline? Or is it just a cue for management to find out how badly he has fallen down, to help him find out why, to stand ready to give him whatever assistance he needs? Management must decide whether to use controls as a means of "catching" people, or as a means of identifying problems and allocating the resources of the organization to provide assistance. Management's choice is dictated in part by its approach to setting standards in the first place. Standards are probably most effective when they are set by the supervisor and subordinate working together. They are least effective when they are imposed by staff officials or top managers who have relatively little understanding of the specific department. Standards are particularly troublesome when they are used as a basis for setting compensation (as in a bonus system) without appropriate appeal channels.

In summary, statistical data do not necessarily give a complete picture of "results." Failure to achieve "results" should always raise the question "*Why?*" "What has happened to cause this departure from what we anticipated?"

> In the words of the old saw, "Figures don't lie." Maybe they don't lie, but that doesn't mean that they are capable of dictating action without the aid of managerial judgment bolstered by information gleaned from multiple sources.[56]

Such comments become even more important in an age of computers.

---

[55] Herbert Simon, *et al.*, *Centralization vs. Decentralization in Organizing the Controller's Department* (New York: Financial Executives Foundation, 1954), pp. 49-50.

[56] Jasinski, *op. cit.*, p. 106.

Conclusion

Organizational structure is more than a series of interconnected boxes and lines on a chart. It is a pattern of human relationships—planned and unplanned—that has evolved over a period of time in response to the human and technical problems of the firm.

As organizations grow in size they also grow in "height," in the number of managerial levels they contain. On paper these hierarchies look quite simple and logical, but they do not function as simply as many theorists have stated. Recent research suggests that:

1. There are many important human relations that contribute to the operation of the organization that are not "hierarchical." (These will be discussed in greater detail in the next chapter.)

2. In the modern organization, individuals receive instructions and pressures from other people besides their boss.

3. With complex technology has come the greater likelihood that important decisions will be made at relatively low levels of the structure.

4. There is no simple formula for determining the right "span of control" for a manager and it is *not* true that the smaller the number of subordinates, the better.

5. Bypassing, meaning skipping levels in communications in both upward- and downward-direction contacts, is a relatively common occurrence.

The manager of any large organization faces a most difficult task of getting all employees (frequently including many levels of supervision as well) to coordinate their efforts and to follow his leadership and direction. To accomplish this objective he must make use of both downward and upward channels of communication—he must both give orders and assess their effectiveness. Yet the systems of human relations that he depends on for transmission are far from foolproof. Organizations often do not function as planned. Serious distortions are introduced by the necessity of communicating through many levels; interpersonal contacts inevitably are limited and restrained between employees at different levels.

The individual supervisor also has his problems in dealing with the hierarchy. The leadership techniques he can use are limited by the methods of management used by his manager and his manager's manager. He must learn to balance the conflicting demands of those over him with those underneath. If he succumbs completely to either (for example, by failing to represent vigorously the interests of his subordinates to higher levels), his leadership position is weakened, if not destroyed.

In an effort to duplicate some of the communication advantages of the smaller organization, modifications are introduced in the hierarchical structure. These include, among others, techniques for bypassing and short-circuiting, such as mass communications, attitude surveys, and special committees. Multi-leveled organizations have special needs for protected appeal channels by which those at lower levels who feel an injustice or believe they have been unfairly treated can get a hearing at key decision-making levels without depending on their immediate supervisor to represent them. Unions and open-door techniques help to fill this need. However, there is a danger that these modifications can be as injurious to the organization as the problems they are supposed to remedy. Usually they threaten the leadership position of the immediate supervisor.

Large organizations cannot depend upon the ability of management to oversee everything directly. Therefore, a variety of control measures are developed which serve to both measure and motivate performance. While they are supposed to communicate to upper management accurately and impartially what lower levels have accomplished they are susceptible to a variety of distortions. Perhaps more than any other factor, the problems surrounding the utilization of controls typifies the complexities for human relations associated with multi-leveled hierarchies.

Two distinctive features of large, many-leveled organizations are the use of rules (or policies) and quantitative controls. Poorly administered rules and controls can throttle initiative, destroy job satisfaction, and create debilitating inflexibility. However, they can be used to advantage by the administrator who is sensitive to their impact. Rules and controls developed with care insure that employees will know what is expected of them, what criteria they will be judged on, and what discretion they have to make decisions. All the way up the line, supervisors are relieved of the time-consuming and morale-damaging necessity of interfering in the work of subordinates in order to make sure it is going as planned. (Rules and policies were discussed in Chapter 7.)

PROBLEM ONE

Bad Fixture

Telephone Conversation—(Plant Manager phones, somewhat excitedly, to one of his superintendents)

PM: "Say, this morning when I was walking through one of your departments, one of the setup men, Joe Smith in Department X, stopped me and said the fixture he was using on his machine was no good. It had to have a couple extra clamps on it which slowed production down on his machine by 10%. What are you doing about this?"

Supt.: "I don't think I know anything about the situation you're talking about. I'll have to check into it."

PM: "But the setup man said that this has been going on for two days now. Haven't you heard anything about it?"

Supt.: "No, I guess I wouldn't hear anything about it unless it involved a problem that the foreman out there thought he couldn't handle."

PM: "Well, get on it as soon as you can, and let me know what you find out as soon as you do."

In Superintendent's Office

Supt.: (to Foreman) "I've called you in to ask whether we are having any serious trouble with the fixtures over in Joe Smith's area."

Foreman: "Well, I've been with Engineering on this. They're designing an entirely new-type fixture, so we're getting along with this the best we can in the meantime. I know it's costing us something to limp along this way, but I figured it was cheaper than ordering a replacement for the old fixture at a thousand dollars and have it become obsolete in the couple weeks it would take them to develop the new one. I feel this new design is going to really save us some money. Why, is there anything wrong?"

Supt.: "Yeah, the boss wants to know what we are doing to take care of it. Maybe this is something I should have known about since the boss was so interested."

Foreman: "Oh yeah, I remember yesterday when the boss came through; Smith and he started talking. I guess I should have gone over to see what was up. And the next time, on something like this, I'll check with you immediately."

Supt.: "Did the setup man know what was being done with Engineering about the fixture?"

Foreman: "Sure. I told him yesterday. He knows the whole story. I wonder what he's trying to pull—griping to the boss."

Supt.: "Well, I'll call the boss and you take care of Joe."

Foreman: "O.K."

1. Why was the PM disappointed that the Superintendent did not know about the malfunctioning fixture? Should he have been upset?
2. What effect did the PM's call have on the methods of supervision that would be used in the future? Describe the probable changes in the relationship between the PM and Superintendent, between Superintendent and Foreman, and between Foreman and setup man.
3. Did the Foreman handle Smith correctly? Is there anything the Superintendent can do to review this problem with the Foreman that will not discourage the Supervisor in taking responsibility and initiative?
4. Assume that the whole incident could be repeated. What should the PM do after learning about the operating troubles in Department X? Be specific in describing what should take place in the contacts between:

    PM and set up man
    General Superintendent and Superintendent
    Superintendent and Foreman
    Foreman and setup man

5. What might Smith's motives have been in this case?

PROBLEM TWO

The Assistant's Dilemma

Bill Adams was hired to fill a new job as assistant to Alfred Grozia, the laboratory head and research director. Adams' assignment was to handle all the administrative details for a very busy executive-scientist.

After about six months on the job, Adams was on good terms with nearly everyone in the lab. In the course of a conversation, Adams learned that one of the ablest metallurgists, Isaac Carroll, was seriously considering quitting. Carroll's boss, Felt, a project director who reported directly to the research director, had been giving Carroll a great deal of extra routine work to do. Not only was Carroll finding it difficult to complete his regular research activities and earn recognition for the quality of his performance, but he also found the additional work tedious and unsatisfying. Carroll had asked for a technician to serve as an assistant, but this request had been turned down.

Adams was unsure of what to do. He was convinced that Felt was unaware of Carroll's extreme dissatisfaction. Felt had a reputation for "pushing" people, although he was technically competent. But Adams was reluctant to broach the question to Felt; the two had never hit it off, and Felt had made it clear that he wanted no interference from the boss' assistant. Moreover, Adams was reluctant to speak directly to Grozia, for fear that he might be regarded as a "spy," and cause Carroll serious embarrassment. If word got out, Felt would feel that Carroll had gone over his head. At the same time, Carroll's resignation would be a serious and needless loss to the organization.

How would you handle this situation if you were Adams?

PROBLEM THREE

Quitting Time

Eggert is the general manager of a large Eastern department store, with responsibility for directing most of the operating departments. For years, two of these departments—packaging and merchandise-marking (ticketing)—have been afflicted by a high turnover rate, failure to meet deadlines, and employee grievances.

Recently the situation in marking has improved significantly, although it is still far from satisfactory. Apparently the present supervisor in the marking department, Elsohn, is doing a good job—at least the selling departments are no longer complaining about incorrect ticketing or failure to have merchandise ready for floor display on time.

Recently Colson, the head of the packaging department, complained to Eggert that all sorts of disciplinary problems were being created by the way Elsohn was running his department. The two departments were physically adjacent, and Colson's employees noticed that the people in marking consistently stopped work 15 to 25 minutes before the end of the day to freshen up, gossip, and relax. There was a clear store rule that all personnel were to work until the closing bell had rung; ample time was provided during the day for employees to take breaks.

Colson said he could hardly enforce this rule in his own department so long as it was being flagrantly violated next door. Eggert promised to "look into the situation."

1. What would you do if you were Eggert? What information would you need? What criteria would you use in evaluating new data?
2. What are the dangers here?

PROBLEM FOUR

A Letter to the President

The company president has received a long letter from an employee in the shipping department, complaining that he did not get a promotion to which he felt himself entitled. The reason, claims the employee, is that his supervisor has a grudge against him. Moreover, he claims, the supervisor's judgment cannot be relied on. In his letter, he discloses a number of violations of company policy that the supervisor has countenanced, and a number of private deals that have been worked out in the department.

What should the company president do with this information?

PROBLEM FIVE

The Friendly Division Manager

"I'm the manufacturing superintendent of the Snyder Division of the Amherst Corporation. I've been on the job in this plant for six months and I have a big problem—my boss, Clarence Akron, who has been Division Manager for about fifteen years. Clarence loves his job and he loves people. He knows all 700 employees in the Division by name and he spends a great deal of time wandering about, listening to people's problems and helping supervisors out of trouble. He's even pitched in on the assembly line when we've had a tight schedule.

"All this is fine—except for two things. He spends so much time talking to individual employees and to first-line supervisors that he never has time to spare for his office work and the long-range problems. And his whole approach makes my job—keeping the manufacturing end of the Division going—much harder. I never know what he has told the men—so in a way he's more on top of *my* job than I am. I'm just a figurehead. Frankly, I'm ambitious. I'd like to do a good job here, but his attitude makes it hard—though he's always been friendly and personally helpful to me. The other men on my level, the chief engineer, the sales manager, and the office manager, all have the same troubles I have, though they've been here longer and have got used to it.

"What should I do? Should I talk to Clarence alone? What should I say to him? Should I try to get the rest of management to see him as a delegation? Should I talk to the Vice President (I know him rather well) next time he pays us a visit from Corporation headquarters? Or is there some other approach?"

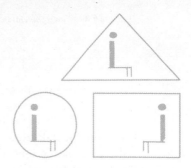

Specialization

16

Seldom is an organization composed of people who all do the same type of work. The typical pattern is for individuals and groups to *specialize* in one function or activity, leaving other functions to their colleagues in other departments or divisions. In fact, specialization has become so common in contemporary life that we tend to take it for granted. In this chapter, however, we shall see that the use of specialization as a means of increasing output and efficiency has many repercussions on the patterns of human relations in the organization.

Specialization creates two kinds of problems:

The first you should be familiar with, based on the discussion in Chapter 2—the effect on job satisfaction.

The second effect, to which most of this chapter will be devoted, is the problem of coordination.

Specialization and Job Satisfaction

Actually, we can think of two kinds of specialization: specialization by task and specialization of people.[1] Task specialization, the most familiar, involves breaking jobs down into their finest components (as suggested by Taylor and his disciples). Task specialization requires *less* training. The concept behind task specialization is simple enough: It is more efficient to have each employee perform a single function than to have everybody do a little of everything. For example, as soon as a service station has enough volume of business, one man concentrates on selling gasoline, another on lubrication, and others on repairs.

More specifically, task specialization has these clearly recognizable advantages:

1. It reduces training costs, for a worker learns more quickly when he concentrates on a single function.
2. It avoids the waste of time involved in shifting a man from one kind of job to another, and enables each man fully to develop his skills for a particular job.
3. It makes unnecessary the duplication of equipment that would otherwise be used on only a part-time basis.
4. It enables the company to purchase more specialized equipment.
5. It simplifies the problem of developing job controls.
6. It reduces wage costs by making it possible to hire less-skilled workers.

People specialization, on the other hand, involves hiring employees with high levels of training: product designers, reliability engineers, market researchers, and the like.

Task specialization, as we saw in Chapter 2, can create serious morale and motivational problems. In the typical white- or blue-collar factory, many employees have little sense of accomplishment, autonomy, or identification with work; their fragmented jobs yield both monotony and drudgery. Further, these workers realize they can be easily replaced.

Individual specialists, on the other hand, often work on depth-attention jobs, identify strongly with their work, and may even enjoy professional status. And they enjoy substantial job security, as we saw in Chapter 3.

Each has a specialized task to do which is not the result of breaking down some larger, more complex task. Indeed, some of these jobs did not exist before new activities and responsibilities in business required their addition.

---

[1] Victor Thompson, *Modern Organization* (New York: Knopf, 1961), pp. 25-27.

The Need for Coordination

Managers sometimes believe they can get something for nothing. They can get the advantages of increased specialization by dividing up more complex jobs into simpler jobs or by hiring additional trained specialists. But they ignore the possibility that the problems of coordination so created may more than outweigh the advantages gained. Dividing up work is easier than putting the parts back together again. The purpose of any organization is to complete work: the production of goods or services. Individual task performance is only useful insofar as it serves to facilitate the attainment of the over-all objective of the enterprise. No matter how hard an employee works, his efforts are wasted unless they integrate with those of his fellow workers.

> Acme Distributors used telephone operators to take phoned-in customer orders. The operators formerly typed up the forms for use by central billing and the warehouse. The company recently added a group of special typists to transcribe the operators' pencilled notes. Now there is conflict because some operators use abbreviations and have poor handwriting. Also, some operators fail to look up in the catalogs the serial numbers of special items, thus requiring the transcribers to do extra work. None of these problems existed, of course, when one girl did a total job.

How specialization creates unproductive work has been described in a popular spoof on the internal workings of large organizations, *Parkinson's Law.*

Parkinson's Law. Parkinson argues with adroit satire that the number of people employed in a given department within an organization has no relationship to the amount of work that needs to be done. In order to improve their own position vis-à-vis others in the organization, managers are motivated to expand their staffs needlessly: "An official wants to multiply subordinates, not rivals." However, this grand strategy for self-aggrandizement rarely reveals itself because the new personnel make work for one another—with the organization's strong propensities for division of labor. Parkinson describes how seven officials can keep busy doing work that was formerly handled by a single employee of an English ministry, Mr. A.

> For these seven make so much work for each other that all are fully occupied and A is actually working harder than ever. An incoming document may well come before each of them in turn. Official E decides that it falls within the province of F, who places a draft reply before C, who amends it drastically before consulting D, who asks G to deal with it. But G goes on leave at this point, handing the file over to H, who drafts a minute that is signed by D and returned to C, who revises his draft accordingly and lays the new version before A.
>
> What does A do? He would have every excuse for signing the thing unread, for he has many other matters on his mind. Knowing now that he is to succeed

W next year, he has to decide whether C or D should succeed to his own office. He had to agree to G's going on leave even if not yet strictly entitled to it. He is worried whether H should not have gone instead, for reasons of health. He has looked pale recently—partly but not solely because of his domestic troubles. Then there is the business of F's special increment of salary for the period of the conference and E's application for transfer to the Ministry of Pensions. A has heard that D is in love with a married typist and that G and F are no longer on speaking terms—no one seems to know why. So A might be tempted to sign C's draft and have done with it. But A is a conscientious man. Beset as he is with problems created by his colleagues for themselves and for him— created by the mere fact of these officials' existence—he is not the man to shirk his duty. He reads through the draft with care, deletes the fussy paragraphs added by C and H, and restores the thing back to the form preferred in the first instance by the able (if quarrelsome) F. He corrects the English—none of these young men can write grammatically—and finally produces the same reply he would have written if officials C to H had never been born. Far more people have taken far longer to produce the same result. No one has been idle. All have done their best. And it is late in the evening before A finally quits his office and begins the return journey to Ealing.[2]

TECHNOLOGY AND HUMAN RELATIONS

Buried here is an important principle of organizational behavior: The division of labor is responsible for a predictable pattern of human relations. Anything that changes the specialization is going to change human relations. For example, if we give A some additional assignment it is likely to change *whom* he sees, *when* he sees them, *how often,* and *what* he must do in relation to other people he contacts.

Managers are often insensitive to how profoundly rather small changes in technology, by altering jobs, can change human relations. Take, for example, the division of labor in a restaurant.[3] Generally, a single bartender prepares drinks in response to the verbal orders of waitresses who have just come from their customers. The result is usually a group clustered around the hapless bartender asking when their order will be ready. To complicate matters, there may be misunderstandings concerning what combination of drinks was ordered by a specific waitress. Is it the fault of the inadequately enunciated requests of the waitress or the poor memory of the bartender?

Now look at the changes in the pattern of relationships if the restaurant changes technology by insisting that all waitresses write their orders and place them on a spindle to await the bartender:

1. Contacts between waitresses and bartenders are reduced by the buffer action of the spindle and written orders.
2. The bartender can now exercise more initiative by rearranging and

---

[2] C. Northcote Parkinson, *Parkinson's Law* (Boston: Houghton Mifflin, 1957), pp. 5-6.

[3] William F. Whyte, *Men at Work* (Homewood, Illinois: Dorsey Press), pp. 128-129. The analysis here has also benefited from Elias Porter, *Manpower Development* (New York: Harper & Row, 1964).

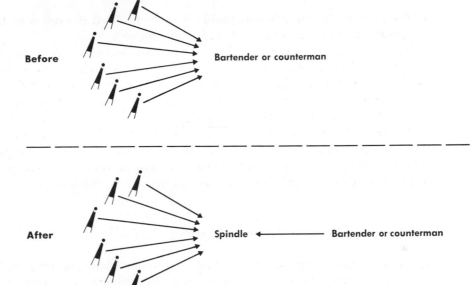

Before   Bartender or counterman

After   Spindle ◄──────── Bartender or counterman

Change in technology provides change in human relations.

combining waitresses' orders in such a way as to make his own job easier or more pleasant (for instance, mixing all the Manhattans at the same time). (In the words of modern computer theory, serial-order events have been transposed by providing a display device with possibilities of random access, the spindle.)

3. Waitresses no longer have to wait in line to place their orders; the spindle becomes a "queuing device" for holding their orders in place.

4. Disagreement over who ordered what can be resolved by written evidence rather than more fallible individual memories. Furthermore, differences in voice characteristics and in ability to demand service are cancelled and greater equality among waitresses is maintained.

COORDINATION AMONG SPECIALISTS

Management anticipated that, if well-trained, highly motivated specialists could be hired or trained and if each did his job correctly, coordination would take care of itself. But if we watch these staff and technical specialists at work, we see the same human-relations problems in coordination that we glimpsed both with the operators and transcribers and the bartenders and waitresses.

Clearly, the problems of coordination have increased as more specialists have been created, more tasks subdivided, and thus more human relations created. Coordination is a human-relations problem: How to get A to do his job so that it fits into the way B and C are doing their work. The modern organization is characterized by ever greater interdependence, at all levels of the hierarchy.

There are more human-relations problems to be resolved if work is to be accomplished and over-all organizational goals attained.

To express it another way: Specialization has increased the relative importance of lateral relationships, as distinct from hierarchical (superior-subordinate) relationships. Both managers and nonmanagers alike spend a great deal of their time in contact with other people in the organization (and some outside the organization, as well, such as with government, unions, suppliers, customers) who are neither their boss nor their subordinate. Many of these relationships involve people at roughly the same status level. In one organization, for example, managers had to maintain close working relationships with as many as 70 or 80 people who were not superiors or subordinates.[4]

Basic Patterns of Lateral Relations

But we can go further than noting simply the lateral-relations explosion that characterizes the modern organization. By watching the interaction of managers, professionals, technicians, and blue-collar people in large, complex organizations, we can identify certain recurring patterns of relationship. These patterns encompass the ways in which specialists in the organization come together, the recurring problems they face, and the feelings these problems generate.

Research suggests that there are at least five distinctive patterns: [5] Work flows, service flows, advisory flows, audit flows, and stabilization flows. Each poses problems that are distinct from the supervisory problems already dealt with. These relationships will be described in turn.

WORK-FLOW

Nearly every employee is in an intermediate position in the flow of work: He depends on those who precede him to prepare supplies, papers, or semifinished parts for him to work on; those who follow him similarly depend on him. For example, a factory clerk may collect and summarize production data; he then sends it on to an accountant who processes the data further. Or, the waitress gives her order to pantry personnel; they in turn are served by runners from the kitchen; the cooks and their assistants in turn prepare the food for the runners. Each of these is an example of a work-flow sequence. Note that employees who must time their actions to coincide with the needs of others

---

[4] Leonard Sayles, *Managerial Behavior* (New York: McGraw-Hill, 1964), p. 43.

[5] The discussion here draws on the work of George Strauss in "Tactics of Lateral Relationship: The Purchasing Agent," in *Administrative Science Quarterly*, Vol. 7, No. 2 (September 1962), pp. 161-186, and "Work Flow, Interfunctional Rivalry and Professionalism," *Human Organization*, Vol. 23, No. 2 (Summer 1964), pp. 137-149, and of Leonard Sayles, *op. cit.*, pp. 93-103.

may not work near one another; they may not even have a common supervisor. Naturally these relationships generate problems.

Who is at fault? Friction is normal on any job, for work rarely goes as planned. And when things go wrong in a specialized organization, people are tempted to avoid accepting responsibility and to pass the buck to others involved in the work sequence. For example:

> A shortage of material develops on the night shift. When asked why, the night-shift workers protest that the day shift failed to keep the material bins full. They insist the day shift never does its share; they just used up the stocks provided by the night truckers.
>
> The accounting department is criticized for failure to meet its schedule for making reports. It blames the production department for failing to provide needed data on time.

This natural tendency of each person to defend his own interests hurts the organization as a whole. Employees sometimes devote more energy to proving that another is at fault for some problem than in trying to solve the problem. This difficulty is accentuated when higher management pressures subordinates for results at any cost, and imposes heavy penalties. Thus, the system of rewards built into the organization frequently motivates its members to think only of their own personal interests. In so doing, they make it more difficult for others to do their job.

Status complications. Normally, higher-status employees give orders to lower-status employees, and not vice versa. This is true throughout life. We expect to have to respond to persons of higher prestige than ourselves; in fact, we are often very reluctant to try to approach them first. We wait to be ap-

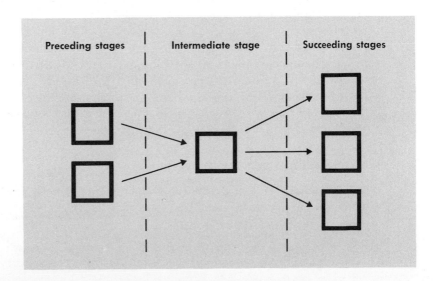

Work-flow contacts.

Preceding stages   Intermediate stage   Succeeding stages

proached, and similarly we expect to initiate action to people we feel occupy positions of less prestige than ourselves.

Sometimes the work-flow patterns *reverse* this normal relationship. We have all seen situations such as this:

> A clerk or office boy is sent by the department head to ask a skilled crafts-man in another group if it would not be possible to speed up his work on a particular job. The employee bristles when approached in this manner by a mere "clerk" and may, if anything, slow down his operation.

This is a critical source of human-relations difficulties in the restaurant industry. Whenever female waitresses give orders to male bartenders, or when young pantry personnel give orders to veteran chefs, periodic blow-ups hurt productivity as well as job satisfaction.[6]

Uneven patterns. Most people want to achieve some equilibrium in their dealings with others: They don't want two people asking them to do something one day and 25 the next. Employees are willing to tolerate a certain amount of variation in this contact pattern from day to day as the work load varies; however, this range of tolerance can be exceeded only at the expense of much tension and discontent. Unfortunately, work rarely flows evenly through an organization. There are usually periods of crisis when everyone feels under tension, tempers are short or nonexistent, and normally suppressed conflicts break out into open hostility.

Some of the crises are periodic. At the end of the month clerks in the billing department work under high pressure; store clerks rush to spruce up their display before the monthly visit of the district manager. Many organizations go through annual cycles. In a toy company, for instance, design changes must be made in the spring; production works hardest from July to October, while shipping is under greatest pressure till the first of December. Other crises are unplanned. A vital piece of equipment breaks down, a rush order comes in from an important customer, the "brass" from the main office arrives on a surprise inspection trip.

In each of these situations the normal level of contacts is left far behind as members of the organization scurry around to get other individuals and groups on whom they depend to get their work out faster, cheaper, or more impressively. When work routines are interrupted, management becomes worried, and frequently many levels of the hierarchy descend simultaneously on some small group of employees, thus making matters even worse.

DESIGN AND DEVELOPMENT DECISIONS

Sometimes problems between specialized departments arise not from the actual flow of work but from the need to coordinate decisions. Here we are

---

[6] William F. Whyte, *Human Relations in the Restaurant Industry* (New York: McGraw-Hill, 1948), pp. 105-108.

faced with many of the problems we have already discussed, plus some others that we have not as yet considered.

Increasingly in modern industry, the work of each department is so closely coordinated with that of the other departments in the organization that each department's decision affects all the rest; and yet no department can make a decision without knowing what the others are doing. Problems of this sort resemble simultaneous equations, where no one part of the problem can be solved without solving all the rest. In industry, such problems often arise in large engineering laboratories that design new products, or in "job shops" that are constantly planning the production of items to the customer's special order. Each department or group controls a part of the "answer"—but these parts must be assembled before the organization's problem is solved.

> To see these problems in action, let us look at the process of designing a new-model TV set, as we observed it in one company. The Engineering Department is, of course, the one most directly concerned, and it consists of five sections. *Electrical* determines in theoretical terms how the set will be made (technically: what the over-all "system" will be). *Mechanical* tries to fit the components together; it often finds that Electrical's theoretical plans are impractical or even that one Electrical engineer's theoretical suggestions are incompatible with those of another. *Chassis* designs the cabinet; close coordination is required if the components are to fit into the cabinet. This is not as easy as it sounds, since Electrical and Mechanical are constantly designing improvements which give better reception, but which conflict with the company's over-all goal of producing an ever-thinner, lighter set.
>
> *Automation* designs the machinery which makes the printed circuits and attaches the tubes to it; in contrast to Electrical, which wants an ever-more "sophisticated" set, Automation wants one that is simple enough to be reduced to printed circuitry and put together mechanically. *Industrial Engineering* determines the techniques by which the set will be manufactured (other than the operations that are 100 per cent automated). Like Automation, it seeks to eliminate what it feels to be unnecessary frills.
>
> Further complicating over-all coordination are the pressures brought by outside departments: Sales wants an attractive product that will sell easily, and Manufacturing wants a set that is easy to put together. And management as a whole is interested in keeping costs low, profits high.

Note that in this case no one section can make modifications without affecting all the others. A change in cabinet, for instance, may require adjustments by every other section, yet each adjustment may in turn require further compensating adjustments elsewhere. Each section has its own vested interest. Electrical, with its goal of technical perfection, conflicts, for example, with Industrial Engineering's goal of manufacturing ease.

Since a new model must be designed each year, intergroup conflicts tend to reach a crescendo as the time for a final decision approaches. During the early part of the year there is little pressure to resolve agreements, and each section is free to work on its own pet projects. As the deadline draws near, an increasing number of compromises and adjustments must be made, tempers grow raw, and human-relations problems begin to complicate the technical ones.

Each engineer likes to feel that he has *completed* his end of the job and hates to reconsider his position just to please another section. No engineer likes to sacrifice his own brainchild.

Complicating all these problems are the changing status relationships between departments. When TV was new, the major problem was to design a workable set, and Electrical was the highest-status section. Today the emphasis is on sales appeal and manufacturing ease. Electrical still thinks its function is the most important one, but management seems to favor other sections when it makes critical decisions and hands out promotions.

We have gone into the problem of this TV engineering department at some length because we think its problems are typical of many in management. When an organization is small, and specialization at a minimum, the problem of coordination can be solved by one man who keeps all the details in his head and can predict by himself all the possible ramifications of each possible change. Once the organization passes a certain size, however, no one person can keep track of all the variables. At this point, good communication among the specialists becomes all-important—both to enable each person to get all the information he needs to make a decision, and also to help preserve organizational morale.

SERVICE RELATIONSHIPS

Often an organization centralizes auxiliary functions such as maintenance, purchasing, laboratory analysis, and computer processing. These "service relationships" between the suppliers of services and their in-company "customers" involve distinctive human problems.

Bottleneck operations.   Intergroup competition may manifest itself in a struggle to corral as much as possible of a "scarce resource." The incident below involving interdepartment competition for scarce maintenance facilities, as described by a departmental supervisor in a large industrial plant, will help illustrate what we mean:

> "Whenever we need equipment repaired, we put a tag on it saying what we think is wrong and send it to the Repair Department. We have a series of different-color tags which we can use. We use a white tag for a routine job. Yellow tags mean important but not top priority. A red tag means the repair is highly urgent and production will be held up until the piece is returned. Well, we suddenly burned out one vital unit and I sent it down with a red tag because we needed it back desperately. When I didn't hear from them for several days, I really got mad and decided to check on what was holding us up. Well, you can imagine how burned up I was when I entered the Repair Department to see that every piece they had down there was red-tagged."

This approach, of course, simply makes scarce resources become scarcer. When one supervisor decides that he may not have all the supplies or repair facilities available that he might need in the future, he takes steps to build up an ample reserve. When other supervisors follow suit, a potential shortage becomes an actual scarcity and the whole priority system breaks down.

This kind of situation strains relations among the individuals and groups that are competing for the scarce resource, and each accuses the other of selfishly trying to grab more than its share. Needless to say, the common supervisor to whom these groups report constantly will have to mediate among them and resolve intergroup disputes.

Unbalanced pressure.   In organizational terms, pressure springs from the efforts of *others* to originate action for you when you are unable to originate for others. Pressure is great when one person repeatedly and consistently attempts to do so (the supervisor who comes back constantly to ask why a certain job has not been completed), or when a relatively large number of people come to you with conflicting demands (as was the case in the repair department described above, and in most service departments).

In either instance, the endless pressure is bound to keep you in a state of unrelieved discomfort. Look back to the "Case of the Red Tags" from the point of view of the repair department. Imagine the pressure the repairmen are under who control the scarce resource! Here is an example of a job subjected to constant pressure, as described by the supervisor in charge:

"We are part of a special purchasing division that services the engineering department. It is our job to order parts and materials for the various research projects the engineers undertake. Well, it has gotten so that nothing is routine anymore. The engineers are always engaging in rush projects—you know, some-

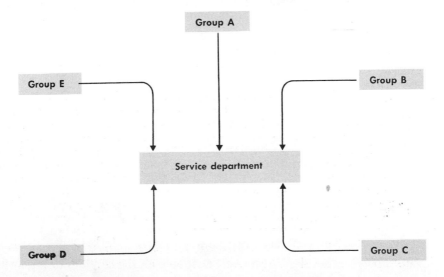

Pressure resulting from conflicting demands.

one gets a brainstorm and they want to get it under way immediately. So they come down with the orders they want filled. First they try to get you to tell them it will be done within an hour. By the next morning they're calling the boss to complain you are not working on it fast enough, and by the next afternoon they are in the office themselves trying to get you to put their order ahead of someone else's. They can't seem to understand that it all takes time and we've got lots of other rush jobs. It seems as though we are always under pressure; someone is always asking for greater speed than we can give them. Let me tell you, I have never experienced such tension; I don't know how much longer we can take it."

Reaction to pressures. The tensions created by these pressures take their toll in departmental efficiency. The rate of personnel turnover is often high, while those who stay usually resort to one or the other of the following patterns of defense or adaptation:

1. Some workers affect an air of resignation, though they may be seething inside; they work off their tensions on their families, friends, or themselves (in terms of psychosomatic illness).

2. Others fight back. They give vent to their frustration by dealing with their tormentors in an aggressive fashion. One observer has related a classic case of how a group defends itself against excessive pressure from other groups:

> The Ship's Store department on a large ship found that certain groups were always demanding rapid service on complicated requisitions. The Ship's Store workers, moving with speed and efficiency, merely announced that these offending groups would have to fill out in perfect detail the multicopy, excessively complicated formal requisition sheets that were required by an official, but rarely observed, rule. These same pressuring groups also were denied their share of the personal items that were distributed, in part, at the discretion of the Stores department: stationery, film, etc.

Unfortunately, this response may further reduce organizational efficiency and lead to additional pressure.

3. Still others develop a cordial personal relationship toward the offending groups in the hope of cutting down the pressure. The expert at this approach uses a mixture of kidding, sympathetic listening, and sincere concern. This is the approach followed by the men's store that hires a delectable blonde to handle complaints.

4. Finally, some workers establish their own system of priorities and firmly resist all efforts to violate it. This is what the rushed butcher does when he asks his customers to take a number and wait until it is called.

Employees who work side by side day after day often work out their own systems for accommodating the demands they make on one another. These systems may be reinforced by group norms that forbid fellow members to push or pressure one another. Large, specialized departments, however, even when they are located close together, seldom develop such informal patterns of accommodation.

The supervisor's responsibility. The alert supervisor is sensitive to the impact of the organization on his subordinates. What can he do when this is the source of trouble? Here is one easy solution:

> Joe Santini was in charge of the central offices of a diversified manufacturing company. As one of their miscellaneous duties, some of his men were assigned the job of moving office equipment when departments were relocated. Santini discovered that one of his most loyal subordinates, in charge of this operation, was about to quit, claiming that he couldn't take the "strain of his job any more." After investigation the supervisor discovered that the man who was ready to quit had been subject to a series of conflicting pressures. The company had been undergoing rapid change and expansion. In the process everyone wanted their facilities moved at the same time, each claiming that their job had priority and that the "President is vitally interested in our getting into our new quarters as soon as possible." This man had no way to resist their demands—he was many levels below all the managers who came into his office to get service. Santini's solution was a direct one. He got top-management approval for a new policy: All requests for moves were to come directly to his office and he would assign a priority to them based on date of submission and company needs. Because of Santini's relatively high position in the organization, he could not be intimidated as his subordinate had been, and in turn, the subordinate found that there was no longer so much pressure in his job.

This solution represents just one small example of reorganizing the pattern of interpersonal contacts required by the division of labor as a means of solving certain morale problems.

ADVISORY RELATIONSHIPS

Modern organizations employ many technical experts to provide advice. An internal advisor can help solve questions such as the following. To the plant engineer: "We seem to be getting more machine breakdowns on line 24 than on any of the others; what's wrong?" To the company lawyer: "Our largest customer is threatening to shift to a competitor; is it legal for us to give him a special price advantage?" To the packaging department: "We're getting a lot of breakage in shipments; what's wrong with our packing methods?" Note that most of these questions concern recurring problems that the normal organizational procedures have not been able to cope with successfully.

The personnel department has a typical advisory relationship (although it may have other nonadvisory functions, as well). Using this department as a case study, let us examine some of the human problems inherent in the advisor's role.

What is "advice"? Many theorists draw a sharp line between line and staff. The staff man is expected to provide technical information or advice and counsel (because he is an expert in the field), but he does not make decisions. In practice, however, these theoretical distinctions are blurred, and the technical expert performs all three tasks.

When providing information, the personnel manager simply furnishes the facts that will help the manager make sound, well-informed decisions. For instance:

1. The disciplinary clause of the union agreement means thus and so.
2. The "going rate" for engineers like Jones in our present labor market is $850 per month.
3. Other companies in the metropolitan area require their carpenters to move small machinery when necessary in the course of their work.

Or he may play a more active role and furnish advice:

1. You are likely to provoke a wildcat strike if you give Bill Williams a disciplinary layoff.
2. On the basis of the record, Jones looks like a better bet for the promotion, since the man on the job will have to assume a good deal of initiative without close supervision.
3. If you hire Smith at that salary, you are going to have some dissatisfied older employees in your departments.

Finally, he can make decisions:

1. Don't discharge Brown; give him a warning slip.
2. Hire Green to replace the man who left.
3. Pay White $100 per week for that new job.

Sometimes there is a very narrow line between providing facts and providing advice. Thus, by selecting his facts carefully, the personnel manager can actually sway the line manager's decision one way or the other. Also, what is given as "advice" may be interpreted by the recipient as a decision.

The temptation to exceed the advisory role. Historically, management has tended to turn over more and more functions to well-trained experts who have specialized knowledge in a relatively narrow field. When experts were first used to supplement the skills of line supervisors, the distinctions between information, advice, and decision-making were rarely made. Further, management showed a readiness to accept expert advice uncritically. Often, since management was very anxious to avoid trouble with the unions, for example, the industrial relations department actually *told* supervisors whom to hire, what to pay them, and how to answer their grievances. The result was often disastrous to the prestige and status of supervisors.

Nor is it surprising to find that advisory groups seek to broaden that range of influence. A personnel man may be hired just to give expert advice on employment and training problems. But it would be a safe prediction that he will soon seek to have his expertise applied to a wide variety of matters, such as wage and salary questions, grievances, and reorganization problems. In practice, it takes a strong-willed personnel manager to resist the temptation to become a decision-maker. Once he has grown accustomed to providing advice and counsel, he may find it irresistible to take the next step and actually make decisions.

Even when the personnel manager is careful not to usurp the line supervisor's responsibility, his actions may still be misinterpreted. The following case illustrates this problem:

> A grievance was filed against Gus Homes, a departmental supervisor, for failing to divide overtime equally. Homes argued that employees who failed to meet production standards on regular work should not be given overtime. The union contract said nothing about overtime, although general plant practice sanctioned equal division. The personnel director of the company, anxious to avoid any union bargaining on the overtime issue, urged Homes to change his mind. Homes refused. Some weeks later, Homes was transferred to a less desirable job. The plant grapevine reported that the manager had "given him the axe" on the recommendation of the personnel director. The truth of the matter was that the manager had believed for some time that Homes should be removed from his department. The overtime situation was just one among many reasons that seemed to justify the move.
>
> From this point on, other supervisors thought twice about refusing the personnel director's "advice." His recommendations had become cloaked with line authority; he had become another boss.

When the manager wants more than advice.   Line managers, themselves, may encourage staff experts to broaden their range of activities. The willingness of the personnel man to help out on a difficult problem, for example, may provide the supervisor with welcome relief from burdensome responsibilities. In effect, he says to the personnel man, "Good, you handle the personnel and I'll take care of all the technical problems." Then, if a decision backfires, the line supervisor can simply point out that he was following personnel's advice. What a pleasant relief this excuse provides!

And so it is easy to understand the line supervisor's reluctance to question the expertise of the specialists whom top management has hired. The subordinate manager who challenges their ability runs the risk of making a bad decision for which he will have to bear all the responsibility. He may even prefer to interpret "advice" as a decision in order to avoid assuming responsibility and in order to pass the buck to the expert.

Paradoxically, a manager may resent an advisory group's power and at the same time grumble that it is failing to take responsibility for decisions. As one supervisor expressed it:

> "We stay away from the industrial relations department as much as possible —they're always trying to sell you on some new program that makes more work for you. But then when you go to them with a problem you can't get a straight answer from them; they won't tell you how to handle it. They give you a lot of pros and cons and stuff that leaves you more confused than when you went in."

Broader contacts.   Staff advisors are in position to short-circuit the usual chain of command and to communicate with people at all organizational levels. Frequently they have *top* management's ear, and this fact increases lower management's reluctance to disregard staff's advice. Staff men may also develop close relations with men at the *lower* levels of the organizational ladder. For example, personnel people often provide a more sympathetic ear for the disturbed employee than does his own supervisor, and he may prefer to take his troubles to them. If this happens too often, the line manager will lose contact with his employees and their respect as well. For instance, a manufacturing superintendent once told us, "My foremen have learned that they can get action a lot faster if they go to staff than if they see me. Except when there is trouble I am pretty much a figurehead—and then I am the one who has to bear the blame."

Caught in this dilemma some managers take the easy way out—they pass the buck to higher management and to staff. In effect, they say, "Don't blame me. Blame the other guy."

Sometimes this device is necessary and useful. But used to excess it becomes a crutch for weak supervision. It makes subordinates lose respect for their supervisor and breeds distrust in the organization as a whole.

Conflicting advice.   We have simplified, of course, by implying that at one time only one advisor (the personnel man) is involved. In fact, in the modern organization, expertise is distributed among many specialized groups and a given problem can call for knowledge of engineering, standards, methods, personnel, and finance. The boundary lines are never clear and each group feels that theirs is the real "answer" to the difficulty. Thus, a manager may be deluged with helpers, many of whom are inclined to remind him of their associations with higher management in order to encourage his adoption of a particular solution to the problem.

AUDIT RELATIONSHIPS

In traditional theory a manager watches everything his subordinates are doing to be sure that they are not violating the rules or standards of the organization and that they are achieving their work goals. In large organizations, however, it is often difficult for the manager to make these observations directly. For one thing, where the work is highly technical, the manager may not be trained to evaluate its adequacy.

For example, even an engineering manager who is not a specialist in circuits may be unable to answer the questions: "How good is the new design for that circuit?" Lack of adequate technical knowledge may also prevent the manager from assessing the adequacy of subordinates' financial and personnel skills.

Similarly, the rules, procedures, and standards of an organization may be so complicated and extensive that no single manager can administer all of them. Just imagine how many personnel, engineering, and financial procedures alone there may be in the typical large manufacturing company. Such procedures have been developed over the years to facilitate coordination among departments and jobs on the assumption that carefully circumscribing the jobs of specialists will make it less likely that they will do things that handicap the work of others.

Finally, the manager has difficulty overseeing the observance of standards because of the tendency of subordinates to hide or distort unfavorable information (see Chapter 15). Not being able to evaluate everything himself and not fully trusting all that he sees and is told, the manager in the large organization must use specialists who help him appraise and evaluate the work of subordinates. Yet their work, in turn, creates a host of human-relations problems.

Standards are ambiguous.

> The engineers inspecting a finished piece of electronic equipment claimed that it would not operate in a room kept at 100 degrees temperature. The department that built the equipment argued that the humidity was too high in the room and that if the air had been dryer it would have held up, as the standards require, and operate at 100 degrees.

Standards conflict.

> The inventory control department told the supervisor he must get his people to work overtime because his output is below scheduled requirements. However, the accounting office has issued an ultimatum that all overtime work must cease since the budgeted overtime allowance has already been exceeded for this particular accounting period. The supervisor spends a good deal of time going back and forth between these two "audit" groups, trying to get one or the other to concede.

Auditing generates suspicions and distrust.

> Quality-control inspectors often say that bad work is hidden so that it won't be discovered and reported, thus making the job of checking quality that much more difficult. In trying to do a thorough job and overcome the hurdles that are put in their way, the inspectors appear to be overly eager to find trouble. Many operators and their managers assert, "Inspectors have to find a certain number of errors to justify their existence and their fancy budgets."

Additional problems are created because these relationships are often so sporadic that there isn't an opportunity to develop regularized patterns of interaction.[7]

---

[7] A good analysis of these problems with some solutions is presented by Herbert Simon and others, *Centralization vs. Decentralization in Organizing the Controller's Department* (New York: Financial Executives Institute, 1954).

STABILIZATION RELATIONSHIPS

Somewhat similar to the audit pattern is the stabilization relationship, except that the contacts are more frequent and regular. These relationships grow out of the need to coordinate the separate parts of an organization, each of which pursues its own objectives. As with auditing, this function would have been performed by the manager himself before the age of specialists. Let us look at some typical examples:

> A manager would like to reduce his output tomorrow because two machines will be down for repairs. He can't make this decision himself, however, because it will obviously affect other departments in the flow of work, departments that rely on those parts for their assembly requirements.

> A manager wants to give an employee a large raise to keep another employer from bidding him away. The raise is an unmixed blessing for the particular manager, but it could hurt other managers who have to explain why their best employees are not getting comparable increases.

In the first case, the manager will have to have his production schedule checked with production-control department. In the second case, a salary administrator will have to give approval. Thus, stabilizing relationships involve getting approval for certain critical decisions from experts who are supposed to keep the total organization's needs in view. As in auditing relationships, the needs are often not absolute and fixed; there is much room for differences of opinion. What will actually happen may be the product of the respective negotiating skills of the individuals involved. Possibly, as some have argued, in the future computers will determine the true optimal course of action, thus eliminating any need for haggling.[8]

A persistent problem is that both auditing and stabilization relationships force managers to contend with multiple sources of influences all pulling in various, often inconsistent directions. For example, the personnel department may urge managers to utilize lower-skilled employees because they are easier to hire in a tight labor market while at the same time the engineering department may be demanding more exacting work. The astute manager learns to sense which requirements are the most dangerous to ignore and adjust his behavior accordingly. At times, personnel considerations predominate, then engineering, and perhaps later on financial.

Organizational Implications of Increasing Specialization

As noted before, many people think of the organization as a pyramid with all decisions being made at the top and all orders passing down from

---

[8] Harold Leavitt and Thomas Whisler, "Management in the 1980's," *Harvard Business Review*, Vol. 36, No. 6 (November 1958), p. 47.

the top, to be obeyed by the subordinates below. But reality is more compli-cated. As specialization has increased, so has the need for obtaining effective cooperation and coordination between specialized work groups, if work is to move smoothly through the various stages of production, if service groups are to be spared overloading, and if advisors, auditors, and stabilizers are to be used properly.

With hierarchical relationships it is clear who is boss and who is sub-ordinate; but lateral relationships are less clear since no one is clearly superior to another. Hence, lateral relationships lead to much intergroup friction and competition for status and influence. Unless managers are effective in mitigat-ing these conflicts, great inefficiency results.

Specialists often identify more with their respective groups than with the organization as a whole. One reason, of course, is that the members of each group interact with one another more frequently than they do with persons outside the group. This identification with an informal group provides an important need satisfaction for employees who might otherwise feel lost in the larger organization (see Chapter 4). It enables them to relieve themselves of pent-up hostility and bolsters their self-confidence. These satisfactions can contribute to over-all efficiency, but, as we know, a price must be paid for these advantages.

What happens when groups of specialists concentrate on their own narrow interests rather than on the interests of the organization as a whole? Each group is intent on growing as influential as it can. Each seeks to impress its own point of view on the total organization. Each wishes to enhance its relative status or prestige. Though the competitive struggle may help keep each group on its toes, it may also get out of hand, leading to destructive friction between groups, and doing serious injury to the organization as a whole.

DEPARTMENT IN-BREEDING

As time goes by, each specialized group—the accountants, the production men, the engineers—comes to adopt a distinctive point of view or "organiza-tional character." [9] Each develops a certain dominant value or goal that shapes its entire way of doing things.

The "in-breeding" that develops within these specialized units makes it difficult to hammer out common agreement on interdepartment problems. Since representatives of each specialty have been conditioned to think in a characteristic way, they find it hard to work together with others as a team. (As we discovered in Chapter 12, these outside commitments present the com-mittee chairman with one of his most difficult problems.) Here is a good description of what happens:

---

[9] For an excellent discussion of this point, see Philip Selznick, *Leadership in Administra-tion* (New York, Harper & Row, 1957), pp. 38 ff.

We've refused to recognize or admit that the various components of our industrial machine are driven by different people with different motives. Sales, for example, is always looking for something to add to the product in order to gain competitive advantage . . . sales presses for changes to get an edge over competitors. Engineering wants changes too, but for an entirely different reason. They're always fighting for easier, cheaper production. Where Sales wants to add to the product, Engineering wants to simplify it. Production has a totally different idea. They know that their salvation lies in keeping the men at the machines doing the same thing over and over again. Any production man will tell you how and why repetitive work is the secret of mass production. And he'll fight changes at the drop of a suggestion.

Thus we have three major divisions of one business looking at the same product from three conflicting points of view. Each of them tries to impress on top management that its contribution is the most important and in the process it pushes under the rug anything that might lower its own status, and slyly points up the faults of its "competitors."

Is it any wonder that we have friction? And, mind you, this friction exists when people are working together with the best intentions.[10]

A sociologist looking at the same problem draws a similar conclusion, but in somewhat different terms:

The over-all managerial problem has become more complex because each group of management specialists will tend to view the "interests of the enterprise" in terms which are compatible with the survival and the increase of its special function. That is, each group will have a trained capacity for its own function and a "trained incapacity" to see its relation to the whole.[11]

Specialization and the Foreman's Role

Earlier we noted some possible sources of conflict between advisory groups such as personnel departments and line management. This was but one example of a more general problem affecting the status particularly of first-level supervisors or foremen. Let us look at the impact of specialization on the foreman. Although we shall be discussing foremen in the following pages, most of the observations are just as relevant to office supervision at the first level.

Fifty years ago. A half-century ago, the foreman had almost absolute power. He did all the hiring (there were no personnel departments in those days) and he expected his men to show gratitude for being selected. If he

---

[10] Bernard Davis, "The Pill's Grim Progress," *Esquire,* British edition, Vol. I, No. 3 (August 1954), p. 55; cited by Lt. Col. Lyndall F. Urwick, "The Span of Control—Some Facts about the Fables," *Advanced Management* (November 1956), p. 11.

[11] Reinhard Bendix, "Bureaucratization in Industry," in A. Kornhauser, R. Dubin, and A. Ross, *Industrial Conflict* (New York: McGraw-Hill, 1954), p. 170.

picked friends or relatives, no one was in a position to object. The workers were completely dependent on him and naturally catered to his every whim. Often they even felt obliged to give him Christmas presents. As one old-timer put it:

> "In the old days the foreman used to be King—he really *was* a big shot—he'd walk down the plant floor like he really owned the place and you better do what he wanted fast—or you'd be looking for another job."

He had the sole power to discharge employees, for unions were rare and personnel standards nonexistent. If the stories of old-timers are to be believed, it was not uncommon for a foreman to fire a man "just to show who was boss and to keep people on their toes." Single-handed, he took care of all the activities that are now called scheduling, methods, safety, wage administration, and quality control (though many foremen of those days would not have known what the terms meant).

Superintendent

Foreman

Worker

Foreman fifty years ago.

Scientific management. The first blow to the foreman's prestige was the scientific-management movement. The doctrine of specialization preached by its apostle, Frederick Taylor, meant that the foreman's job would be broken up into functional specialties. By 1930 many of the foreman's functions had been taken over by staff departments. *How* men worked was decided by the methods department; the *sequence* in which they handled products was decided by production control. Quality-control inspectors came into the foreman's shop to check on quality. A special organization arose to handle safety, and another was set up to take care of maintenance. In many cases even the hiring of workers—the foreman's traditional prerogative—was taken over by the personnel department, thus usurping one of the foreman's main sources of prestige and loyalty.

The union. During the 1930's the union made its first appearance in many plants. No longer was the worker obliged to humor the foreman in order to protect himself from being fired. Union membership sapped the loyalty of employees to their immediate supervisor, making it harder for him to make his orders stick. A radically new style of supervision was required, to which it would take the foreman years to adjust.

Worse, another official was added to those who could give the foreman "orders"—this official was the union steward, who was technically the foreman's subordinate.

Further, largely as a means of protecting itself against the union, management began to centralize the functions of discipline, promotion, and salary administration in the personnel department. Management's reasoning went this way: The union filed grievances whenever the foreman violated the contract or showed favoritism; and whenever a foreman in one plant made an unfortunate decision, the union regarded it as a precedent that could be used against the company in its other plants. Very well, said the company, we will centralize all these functions in the hands of experts, to insure a uniform, consistent policy.[12] What little power the foreman had left was now restricted by specific rules.

As a consequence, the foreman was exposed to conflicting orders and pressures from all sides. His fall from power was almost complete.

Loss of opportunity for promotion.   The next blow fell when the foreman was deprived of his opportunity for promotion into higher management. More and more companies now began to recruit their future executives from among college graduates. In some companies the foreman was faced with a dead-end job.

The war.   Next came the war period, with its frantic pressures to perform miracles with untrained help. And then the final blow: The advent of wage controls meant that in many cases the foreman's wages fell below the wages

---

[12] Even nonunion companies adopted this policy, in an effort to eliminate possible causes of unionism.

The growth of staff.

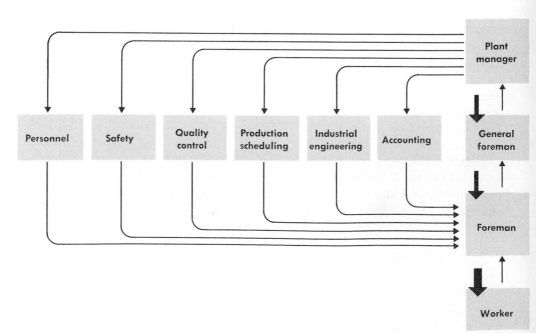

of some of the men he supervised, particularly the men on piece work. By the end of World War II, foreman morale was at an all-time low.

The foremen join a union.   To protect themselves against this steady erosion of their prestige and power, a number of foremen decided to establish a union of their own. The Foreman's Association of America spread like wild-fire.[13] The foreman reasoned that if other workers could bolster their position by joining a union, he would be foolish not to do the same thing himself. He felt himself excluded from management, relegated to the status of a mere messenger boy.

Management rediscovers the foreman.   The rapid spread of the Foreman's Association came as a traumatic shock to management. It was bad enough to lose workers to the union; if the first-line foremen were to defect as well, how could management hope to control its men?

Management's first reaction was an all-out attack on the Foreman's Association. The biggest battle was at Ford, where after a lengthy strike the Association was completely crushed. (Some companies are still suspicious of foremen's clubs of any kind, even those run by the YMCA.[14])

On a more constructive level, measures were taken to induce foremen to feel once again as though they were members of management. One measure was largely social: Management clubs, management dinners, and other activities were arranged at which foremen could mingle on a supposedly equal level with their superiors. Management also made an effort to improve downward communications by means of newsletters and meetings designed to help the foreman feel that he was "in the know" on company developments—hopefully, before the union learned of them.

But management's major efforts to rehabilitate the first-line foreman were in the area of training. At the least sophisticated level, the newly instituted training programs consisted of trite exhortations to feel and act like management (though, as one foreman put it, "it is more important to be treated as management than to be told that you are management"). The better-conceived programs helped to equip foremen with the attitudes and skills necessary to lead men rather than drive them.

More substantial than any of these measures was the decision taken by some companies to cut down on the power of staff and restore it to the foreman. In many instances foremen were given the final say over hiring, discipline, and promotion. Some of the safety and quality-control departments, along with

---

[13] This was the period during which the National Labor Relations Board gave it the same status as other unions, a condition that was reversed by the Taft-Hartley Act. Foremen joined unions also to obtain the advantages of the wartime wage and salary stabilization programs.

[14] At times with reason: we were present at one foreman club's "annual gripe session," to which management was invited. The interchange sounded remarkably like collective bargaining.

much of personnel, became advisory, with the foreman exercising actual control in these areas.

A few large companies have experimented with creating a kind of super-foreman. The number of employees reporting to the foreman have been doubled or tripled but he has been given a number of assistants and an advisory staff who report directly to him. Thus, for example, he has his own industrial engineer and personnel assistants. They assist him in setting work standards, dealing with grievances, scheduling, and so on. With his own staff the foreman no longer has to negotiate with outside staff departments.

All these efforts reflect a recognition that the foreman leadership role cannot be fractioned. If the foreman is to have the confidence, loyalty, and respect of his subordinates, he must have some significant control over those areas of decision-making that most affect his people. Surely work standards, grievance handling, and wage increments and similar subjects are examples of such crucial subjects. As we have seen elsewhere in this chapter, the challenge is to provide the advantages of specialization (and expert knowledge) without destroying the human relations necessary for a well-functioning organization.

Conclusion

Organizational human-relations problems often are mistakenly thought of solely as a by-product of autocratic supervision or uninteresting jobs. But normal frictions between specialist groups also contribute to human-relations problems. With increased emphasis on specialization in the modern organization and on "lateral relations" have come increasingly difficult problems of coordination.

We do not question the contribution of specialization to productivity. However, this chapter has emphasized that a manager's problems do not end when he has broken a single job into parts that can be handled by specialists. Managerial success depends on being able to put these parts together again and on developing coordinated cooperation among various individuals and subgroups so that the total organizational goals can be achieved.

The division of labor and the technology prescribe a pattern of human relations; change one and you change the other. Management typically underestimates the human relations consequence of even slight changes in specialization or layout or equipment. Yet these have an immediate impact on who must do what with whom, when, and where, and thus ultimately on the total job.

Employees learn to identify with their own specialty and frequently lose sight of the over-all organization. Specialists tend to develop close ties with members of their own specialty and to develop distinctive points of view that clash with the points of view of other specialties. Employees who are supposed to integrate their work activities so that ideas, materials, or papers pass smoothly from department to department often engage in struggles for their "fair share" of rewards and prestige. Very often these clashes are not resolved by fixed rules or by top management decision but by bargaining. The weapons used in these intergroup struggles are techniques that enable men to avoid responsibility, to "pass the buck." Extreme specialization increases the likelihood of bottlenecks in the work flow, and those who are caught in the bottlenecks are subject to heavy pressures from fellow employees, such as mutually conflicting demands from other departments for quick service. All this pressure leads to bickering between departments and a breakdown of morale.

On the positive side, the increased emphasis on negotiations, the multiplicity of relationships that have to be maintained (compared to just dealing with superiors and subordinates) also gives much greater challenge to managerial jobs in the modern organization.[15]

We examined in some detail the relationship conflicts inherent in five different patterns of on-the-job relationship prescribed by the division of labor. These were the work-flow, service, advisory, auditing, and stabilization patterns. We noted that any given manager must spend as much, if not more, of his time and energy engaged in these lateral types of relationship as he does dealing directly with subordinates and superiors. Over the years, the position and status of the first-line supervisor has been endangered by these new specialists, and new organizational arrangements have become necessary to avoid further deterioration.

We have suggested certain "short-term" remedies that may help to ameliorate some of the pressures arising from specialization. In Chapter 18 we shall consider the possibility of making basic changes in the organizational structure designed to eliminate some of the underlying causes of discontent.

P R O B L E M   O N E

The Dooley Case

You were just promoted from a buyer at headquarters to the job of Purchasing Agent of the newly acquired Dooley Division of the General Products Company. In most companies the job of P.A. is to negotiate for the purchase of needed equipment and supplies on the basis of requisitions submitted by user departments. Most P.A.'s feel that at the plant level they should report to the plant manager.

As you left your old boss in central purchasing, he cautioned you,

"Be careful now. Remember, that division was pretty much a one-man firm till we bought them out. Bill Dooley would never have sold out if he didn't need capital for expansion. His outfit is a big money-maker and as Division Manager he is still the boss there. As long as he brings in the profits, no one from headquarters is going to interfere with his decisions. He's never had a P.A., and you are the only man sent from headquarters except the controller. The Big Boss [company president] persuaded him that having a P.A. was the fashionable thing to do, but I'm not sure if Dooley knows what purchasing is all about."

You arrived at the new plant—miles away from the main office. Dooley turned out to be a likable bundle of nerves of about 45. He showed you around, or tried to, because it seemed that he couldn't take a step without someone run-

15 *Cf.* Leonard Sayles, ed., *Individualism and Big Business* (New York: McGraw-Hill, 1963).

ning to him for a decision—mostly on technical questions. The administrative problems he seemed to push off on Bob Wallace, the manufacturing superintendent.

As you went around, you noticed a sanding belt that was not of the latest design. So you commented that one supplier had developed a new product that was both cheaper and better. Dooley seemed delighted: "Well, get us the new product. That's what we have you here for." Wallace seemed a little unhappy but said nothing.

You were shown your new office, next to Wallace's and personnel's in the factory building; Dooley, the accounting office, and engineering were in the new building.

When Dooley left, Wallace sat down with you and began to speak haltingly. "To tell you the truth, I'm not sure how we will be able to use you. We never had a P.A. before. Dooley brought you in because headquarters said you might help out here. We are really a very small outfit with only 200 people, and we just don't believe in paper work. We have always worked so well together that we really don't need it. Now as I see your job, it is to keep the salesmen off Bill's and my shoulders—except for the few with whom we have developed very good relations—and to buy our supplies at the lowest possible cost."

Before you could comment, he was off on an errand, having instructed a general foreman to show you around. You asked what you felt were shrewd questions about costs and output, some of which the general foreman seemed reluctant to answer. You noticed several parts that it would seem better for the company to buy rather than make. When you suggested this, the general foreman answered, "This is a small firm, mister, and a lot of people depend on this work."

You tried to talk to the chief engineer. He showed a lot of interest in your background, your family, your housing arrangements, but he seemed to freeze up when you mentioned his work.

"It's highly technical . . . making big advances which are hard for a layman to understand. . . . Yes, we make up the blueprints and tell the shop what to make. They're a good lot. All local boys, been with us a long time, take care of the troubles before they come up. . . . Specifications? Well, insofar as we have them, we draw them up with Dooley; he tells Wallace what to buy . . . I guess you'll be helping Wallace on that. He handles all the paper work. He needs help. Things have been getting pretty busy recently."

The controller gave you a different picture.

"I'm going crazy here. Been trying to get some sort of cost analysis, but don't make any progress because there are no records kept of anything. If I want specific information, I can usually get it from Dooley or Wallace—they keep it in their heads—but I can't develop anything systematic. If I try to pin Dooley down on a new system of some type, he seems to listen, but he's off on a new problem before I get an answer. I just can't get cooperation from anyone."

Next day Wallace started giving you instructions. "Get in touch with some of the coal firms in town and see what price you can get. Maybe we can buy cheaper. Call up Louhurst Bros. and ask them to send over 10 gallons of Sherman-Williams white paint."

You asked if a purchase order was needed. He answered, "No. When the bill comes in, Mary in the office will call Jack in receiving, and if it came in OK, she'll send out a check. . . Oh, Tom or I sign it."

Just then the phone rang. It was Wallace again. "I'm sending over a salesman from the MM Company, who is going to make some widgets for us and it's a big order, so make up some kind of contract with him—he'll tell you what we agreed on—and send it to me to check over and sign."

1. How much could you realistically expect to accomplish during the next three months?
2. What problems would you face in getting acceptance of a real purchasing program?
3. How is your problem complicated by the personalities and vested interests of these people?
4. How do the various parties—Dooley, Wallace, the general foreman, the chief engineer, and the controller—view you?
5. What plans could you make for handling each of them?
6. What mistakes did you make at the outset?
7. How has the absence of specialization, rules, procedures, and so forth helped or hindered the Dooley Division?

PROBLEM TWO

Making Quota

Just before their pre-Christmas business reached its maximum, the Cantor Toy Company installed a new conveyor line which provided a more mechanized means of spraying and drying their toy soldiers. Simultaneously they placed the operation on a three-shift, round-the-clock basis to meet the heavy influx of customer orders.

A group of six sprayers worked on individual fixtures and placed the sprayed soldiers on a conveyor belt which went into a drying chamber. The drying cycle took about two hours, so that the same sprayers were able to take off dried units and box them. The job description and the incentive plan under which the sprayers worked took into account the fact that each sprayer was both a sprayer and a packer. There were continuous shifts so that the next shift would package soldiers that had been sprayed during the last couple of hours by the previous shift and so on.

Management observed that during the first hour or so of each shift the sprayers always seemed to be in trouble and behind their quota (if they were to actually make a bonus for the day). On closer examination it became apparent that each shift was normally careful to place sprayed soldiers on the conveyor belt in such a way that they could easily be removed for packaging without interrupting the spraying operation. However, toward the end of the day, when the sprayed units would no longer be packed by themselves (because the drying cycle ran over into the next shift), they grew careless in their haste to make their own quota. The next shift would then find them bunched and unevenly spaced, would fall behind, and, in turn, would take a careless attitude toward the spacing of the pieces they rushed through to make their quota during the last couple of hours.

1. To what extent is this production problem due to poor attitudes toward work and to what extent is it the result of the technology—the organization of work?
2. Have you any suggestions for eliminating this problem?

PROBLEM THREE [16]

Technician Pool

The Bellows Chemical Laboratories were engaged in the development and production of a number of organic chemicals used in the printing and textile industries. As a result of the growing acceptance of the company's product line, the research laboratory experienced a major expansion.

In this company the job classification of "laboratory technician" referred to persons who performed routine tests at the direction of professionally trained employees. A variety of tests was involved, and many of the tests required considerable skill to execute. All the technicians had completed high school and several had attended college for one or two years. Several technicians had also worked in the factory and had been transferred to the laboratory at their own request. The professionals in the laboratory were all graduate chemists or engineers.

The work of the laboratory was organized under the "project" system. The work was authorized by management, as required, and assigned by the head of the laboratory to one or, at the most, two professionals for execution. When the work was completed, the chemists or engineers involved were given new assignments.

Until recently, the size of the laboratory (both professional and technician groups), was small enough so that frequent interaction among the entire staff was possible. Desks of all personnel were located within a single "conversational" area, and everyone had fairly accurate knowledge of the goals and work requirements of the various active projects. When a chemist or engineer had a series of tests to be run, he would ask the technician who seemed least burdened with work at the time to undertake the assignment. On the whole, this arrangement worked smoothly. Delays in the work and manifestations of discontent among the personnel were infrequent.

Recently the demands on the laboratory have increased markedly. The number of active projects has increased by a substantial margin, and the number of professionals employed has approximately doubled. Also, several additional technicians have been assigned to the laboratory.

When it became apparent that the informal arrangement for scheduling technician time would not function adequately with the larger group, a "technician pool" was created and put in the charge of a senior technician. Professionals who desired tests run were to route their requests through the head technician, who in turn would assign technicians from the "pool."

The new arrangement has had two unexpected results. First, the number of technicians per professional employee has had to be increased to get the required work completed on schedule. Second, a considerable degree of discontent has developed among the technician group and to a lesser extent among the professionals. Not infrequently, conflict arises over priority in the use of equipment. Availability conflicts between the head technician and the chemists over technicians are becoming more numerous. One of the technicians has requested that he be transferred out of the laboratory. Whereas the old informal scheduling of technician time had become cumbersome and inefficient, the new technician "pool" has resulted in still further loss of efficiency and in open conflict.

---

[16] We are indebted to one of our former students, Mr. E. W. Coleman, for the outline of this case.

1. To what extent were the new problems involving the allocation and as- signment of technicians an inevitable product of expansion in the labora- tory?
2. Why didn't some of these conflicts over priorities emerge when the laboratory was smaller? It is unlikely that there was a surplus of tech- nicians, even then, and there must have been times when a chemist or engineer could not obtain personnel when they were needed.
3. "Pools" are used to conserve many scarce resources in the organization. They are supposed to insure that everyone has an equal opportunity to use facilities and that the facilities are not wasted. Why doesn't this reasonable explanation enable everyone in an organization, like the laboratory, to accept temporary shortages and inconveniences, since the total group is probably benefiting by the arrangement?

PROBLEM FOUR

A Drop in Quality

The Wilton Company manufactures a small replacement part sold by automo- bile accessory dealers. The company is in a highly competitive industry, and recently has been losing ground to other manufacturers whose product sells for slightly less than that manufactured by Wilton. The Executive Committee of the company has decided to try to decrease their unit labor costs. The plant manager has indicated to the two division heads who report directly to him (the superintendent for fabrication and the superintendent for assembly) that they will be held responsible for tightly adhering to new output standards, which require about 5 per cent more work for approximately the same wage cost.

During the first week after the application of the tighter standards and the closer checking of department cost figures, a major disagreement arose between the two division heads. Since the matter of quality standards was also involved, the plant manager invited the head of the inspection department to attend the meeting. The chief inspector also reports to the plant manager, and serves in a staff capacity to the production departments.

The following exchange took place during the meeting:

Plant Manager: "I have called this meeting to find out what we can do about this awful production situation. As you know, it was just a week ago that we decided to try to up our output by about 5 per cent. I am certainly shocked at the results of our program. As you probably know by now, the figures for the week indicate that instead of some increase in output we actually suffered a 9 per cent decline over our average for the past two months. Apparently, a large share of this poor performance is due to low-quality work and scrap. How do you explain this?"

Superintendent for Fabrication: "I know what's holding us up! It's simple. Jack, here [superintendent for assembly] is sending back nearly one out of five parts that we send to him, claiming that they are not perfect, and he can't use them in his assembly operations. This is ridiculous; we are utilizing the same tolerances we've always utilized. There is no such thing as perfection, as he knows, but all our parts are within limits."

Superintendent for Assembly: "All I know is that we can't continue to meet our old output standards, no less meet these new ones, if we're going to have to use parts that are finished like these have been. If my foremen are going to be able to insist that each employee work along at 100 per cent efficiency, those employees have got to have parts that don't jam when they try to fit them together. Sure, if we had all the time in the world, we could fuss around with them to make them fit—they wouldn't have to be remachined—but we don't have all the time in the world and we've got to have good parts if we're going to have any decent level of output."

At this point the plant manager asked for an opinion from the chief inspector. His response was brief, and somewhat unexpected.

Chief Inspector: "All I want to say is that in the past week my inspectors have been under more pressure from both of your foremen than they have ever endured. Both in fabrication and assembly the inspectors have been pressured to pass work that was really borderline, if not below standard. I can assure you that we haven't succumbed to any of these pressures, but our job has just been made that much more difficult. I don't see why your production foremen can't stick to the standards and leave it up to our inspectors to find out whether or not the parts fit."

1. How do you explain the sudden drop in quality at the fabrication stage?
2. What is likely to be the effect on interdepartmental relations of this attempt to increase output?
3. What do you see as the basic problem in the manufacturing organization of the Wilton Machine Company? Do you have any suggestions for improving the organizational structure?

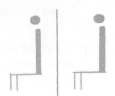

Case Studies
of Lateral Relationships

17

A good way of comprehending the significance of lateral relationships is to look at some jobs through the eyes of the persons who actually handle them. This approach can also provide a realistic view of how much one's own work depends on other people, some or all of whom may be in other departments. As we know already, specialization creates a flow of work which must be maintained by effective human relations patterns.

From this approach we can see how difficult it is to gain acceptance for one's own point of view in the face of opposition from members of other work groups. Although a job description may require working with others, it does not instruct an individual in persuading those others when they have contrary points of view.

In the cases that follow, try to observe how jobs are expanded or contracted in order to meet both individual needs (for additional status and job satisfaction) and group needs (for preserving intact the jurisdiction and customary procedures of the work group). Note how these professional and managerial jobs require negotiating skills, powers of persuasion, and a great deal of inter-actional energy. Although a member of any of the groups described would insist that he is working for the total good of the organization, in fact each group has a rather narrow view of the total goal and is often seeking to improve its own position (at the expense of some other group).

According to traditional organization theory, of course, none of this should occur. All problems should go through the boss-subordinate hierarchy, and specialists are available only to advise. In practice, however, the modern organization depends on lateral relationships precisely because there are so many specialized points of view and so many required contacts that no single manager could handle the communication flow alone.

The first case, Production Engineering, is the simpler one. Through the eyes of a young engineer we observe the difficulties encountered in attempting to improve the functioning of a quality-control gauge. The engineer must gain the cooperation of many persons to whom he cannot give orders; but even though his work is supposed to benefit the entire organization, various groups see him as threatening their own welfare.

The second case is more complicated. Based on an extensive field study of one of the authors, it examines the organizational position of the purchasing agent, the man who orders materials and parts from outside-the-company suppliers.

As you will observe, the purchasing agent spends much of his time inter-acting with the people inside the organization who help determine how "purchasing work" is to be carried out and its status. This group includes engineering, production, and financial personnel among others.

Production Engineering: A Case Study of Failure [1]

I am George Brague, an electrical engineer formerly on the staff of the Plant Technical Department, headed by Roy Phelps. The department is part of the management of an aluminum foil manufacturing plant (see the organization chart).

My special assignment was to complete the design and installation of a sophisticated control device called a U.V. Gauge. Because the product some-times varies in thickness, this gauge has been designed to measure the thickness of the foil as it comes off the coating machines. If the tolerance varies by as little as .0001 of an inch the control would stop the machine until proper adjustments are made.

Actually the original work on the U.V. Gauge was done by my predecessor, Gus Phillips. He had worked with it for two years in the pilot plant facility

---

[1] We should like to express our appreciation to Ralph Franke, a former student, who prepared the original version of this case.

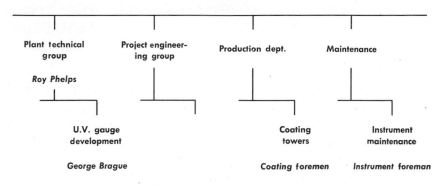

Plant manager

Plant technical group — Roy Phelps — U.V. gauge development — George Brague

Project engineering group

Production dept. — Coating towers — Coating foremen

Maintenance — Instrument maintenance — Instrument foreman

Foil plant organization.

and had begun to install it on the production equipment when he took another job. At that point work on the gauge ceased.

WORKING WITH MAINTENANCE

After acquainting myself with the project, my first step was to write a work order to Instrument Maintenance. The work order said, "Please check all components of the U.V. Gauge installation to assure that it is in operating condition. If there are any questions please contact George Brague ext. 237." I assumed that this maintenance work was within the capabilities of any instrument mechanic. The purpose of the work order was to have the tubes, connections and other components on the equipment checked to make sure they were in operating condition. The equipment had been unoperative for a number of months and it had been poorly cared for. For example, one of the tubes had been taken for someone's TV set.

A few days after writing the work order, I met the instrument foreman in the hall. "I saw your work order on the U.V. Gauge," he said. "You know if you want to get things done around here you have to push them," and then he walked on. I didn't understand the significance of his comment, but not knowing the man and not feeling very secure as a new member of the organization, I said simply, "Oh! That's interesting."

After about a month and a half nothing had yet been done on the work order. By this time I was more familiar with the project so I went to talk to the head of maintenance. When I asked, "What's happening on my work order to check out the U.V. Gauge on D tower?" he became quite agitated. "What you are asking us to do even an electronics engineer couldn't do. Your predecessor couldn't get the damn thing to work," he replied. "How in the blazes do you expect a plain instrument mechanic to do it?"

I thought to myself that here was an unfortunate communications problem. Maintenance had interpreted my work order as saying: "Fix the U.V. Gauge so that it performs the job of accurately measuring coating thickness." These were not my intentions. I only wanted to have all the tubes and other components checked so that the instrument would be in working condition. I didn't expect them to solve all the problems of making it a usable device for production.

I recalled that the current head of maintenance had been assigned to the production department when Phillips had been working on the gauge. Phillips' activities probably had made his work harder. And here was a new engineer apparently trying to give maintenance the responsibility for an instrument which might never work.

I said, "You misunderstand. All I want the instrument mechanic to do is . . ." Two days later a man was assigned to the job.

The only instrument mechanic who was familiar with the equipment had worked with Phillips. I explained to him that I was quite unfamiliar with the equipment and needed his help. I tried to build up his pride in being the only man qualified to work on this instrument. Although he was not eager at first to become involved in my problems, he soon was helping me quite willingly. I also provided him a sympathetic ear for the trouble he had previously encountered in keeping the gauge in operation.

Of course, I needed his services many times, and I found it much easier and faster to find him myself than to go through proper channels. My instrument was not officially within his jurisdiction, but since he worked under loose supervision and we became good friends, it was not difficult to persuade him to spend time on my problems. (This had another desirable feature: His time was never charged to my budget.)

I found that it paid to go through channels only on big jobs (that is, those you couldn't get done any other way) and jobs which you were in no rush to accomplish (which unfortunately were very rare). Often when I needed a major part, I had the Purchasing Department buy it from an outside supplier rather than have it constructed internally. You could get it much faster that way with much less personal inconvenience. Furthermore, I believed that if you limited your requests within the plant, you were more likely to get help when you were *really* caught in a jam.

[Note the violations of company rules and policies!]

WORKING WITH THE PROJECT ENGINEERING GROUP

The Project Engineering Group also gave me trouble. P.E.G. spent most of its time drafting the drawings necessary for new equipment.

Let me backtrack: The Plant Technical Group, my department, works closely with Production on both their short- and long-range problems. They are supposed to be the problem-solvers: Find out what's wrong, decide what to do about it by running necessary tests, etc., and then write specifications for equipment changes or additions which then go to the P.E.G. for detailed design and drafting. These specifications are a constant source of conflict between the two groups. P.E.G. would often send them back saying we had failed to include sufficient information; we would then claim, "P.E.G. wants us to do their work for them!" Or P.E.G. would complain that Technical didn't know what they were talking about, or they hadn't run enough tests to justify the installation. Then Technical would claim that P.E.G. was trying to avoid its responsibility for incompetent design work. Charges and counter-charges flew.

There are several reasons for the conflicts between these departments. The P.E.G. engineers are older and more experienced than the Technical engineers and may well have resented younger, less experienced engineers telling them what to do. Since the Technical engineers are primarily consultants, they have wide contact with all levels of supervision in the plant and are well known by the people that count—thus increasing P.E.G.'s resentment. In fact, Technical people grab most of the promotions. Finally, the two groups are separated physically as well as organizationally, so it is difficult for the engineers to get to know each other socially in the plant.

My own experience was much the same as that of my colleagues. P.E.G. seemed supercritical, always sending my plans back to be redone. At one point the head of P.E.G. raked me over the coals, saying, "A college freshman engineer could do better work than this." Knowing that materials would be scrutinized by such a hostile group made me jumpy and caused me to make many mistakes. These, in turn, confirmed the P.E.G. manager's low opinion of my work.

WORKING WITH PRODUCTION

The U.V. project's urgency was not related to Production needs. The plant could operate quite satisfactorily·without it, although costs would be slightly higher and quality somewhat lower than with it. The real push came from Phelps, my boss, the Technical Superintendent who wanted to make sure that his plant would be the first to develop it successfully. Being new to his position, he wanted to make a good showing for the corporate headquarters technical staff. This project was also of special interest to him since before his promotion he had been personally responsible for it.

As for the production people, they recalled the number of shutdowns and delays that they had experienced when Phillips had worked on the gauge. Accordingly, they seemed convinced that it was a waste of everybody's time to play around with a gauge that would never work. In addition, coating had become a bottleneck, and the plant manager was applying a tremendous amount of pressure to get production up. All of the managers were working under great pressure.

The installation of my equipment required a shutdown of one-sixth of the area for a two- or three-day period. A shutdown of the coating tower was already scheduled for other construction work, but they were reluctant to have production delayed even longer while the gauge was being installed.

I talked to the coating foreman a number of times about the value of the system but got little positive response. Phelps, however, did a great deal of pressuring and bargaining on higher levels. I have no idea what went on there, but permission finally was given to have the equipment installed.

It was not, however, electrically wired; therefore, the gauge was still inoperative. Over two months elapsed without the wiring being connected. I would talk to production, and they would say, "See maintenance; they are the ones that have to do the work." And maintenance would say, "Talk to production; they won't shut down the equipment so that we can do the work." Phelps would then put the pressure on me, "What's holding up that project?" Each day he grew more impatient.

Apparently, Phelps kept after the production manager. Finally, one week the plant manager said, "That equipment had better be in operation by Friday or everyone involved will stay here until it is running!" The equipment was wired that Thursday. Friday morning, the plant manager wanted to know why it wasn't running yet. I explained to him what I still had to do to calibrate the instrument and check out the wiring. To myself I said: "You idiot; it took four months to get the thing put in, but I don't even get four hours to do my work!" By spending the whole weekend at the plant, I did get it into production by Monday morning.

During the next couple of months I spent at least 60 hours a week in the plant. The pressure formerly put on production to get the equipment installed was now turned on me to keep the equipment in operation. A great amount of trouble persisted with the measuring part of the system. Hence, the production foreman was unwilling to take charge of the system and operate it as a piece of production equipment. The usual phone call would come at 10:00 o'clock at night and I would hear, "Your equipment is not working, come in and take a look at it." The test equipment gave the foremen a wonderful scapegoat on which to blame all their operating troubles.

This was a common problem for engineers. Test equipment would be blamed for everything under the sun, and good ideas would often go down the drain for no other reason. Engineers found it difficult to explain their equipment to foremen and operators, particularly since production involved a three-shift, seven-day operation. Further, most of the engineers believed that the foremen wouldn't understand very much of the explanation since none of them were technically trained. Thus, an engineer would often come in one morning to find equipment on which he worked three months to design and get installed removed because "It gave us . . . trouble." Usually the trouble they experienced on the run seemed totally unrelated to the new equipment.

FURTHER TECHNICAL PROBLEMS AND FAILURE

For about two months we seemed to make progress. The gauge seemed to be improving coating quality, and the foreman was becoming "sold." Then a real blow: The chemical formula for the coating was changed. The U.V. Gauge didn't really measure the thickness of the coating, rather it measured the amount of ultraviolet light absorbed by the coating. (The absorption was proportional to the thickness.) This change in one fell swoop threw out our calibration; we were back to where we started six months before.

The tremendous pressure placed on the coating section by the plant manager was also beginning to have its repercussions. Operators were bidding out of the area into other jobs in the plant (often lower-paying ones). Even a foreman asked to be returned to the position of a machine operator, and the union began to complain about the pressure in production.

Then the plant manager turned his attention to the U.V. Gauge. This instrument, he reasoned, may be responsible for our problems in this area. The next thing I knew, the plant manager called Phelps in to ask why production runs should be rejected on the basis of these readings, considering all the technical troubles the engineers were having. I am sure Phelps put up a good defense for his pet project, but it apparently was not good enough, for an order was issued that the foremen would *not* reject stock according to the thickness readings of the U.V. Gauge.

Shortly afterwards I left the company. The U.V. Gauge was still in ill repute, nothing was being done about investigating different equipment, and no coating-thickness control system was in use in the production area. Although I suggested several different ideas to Phelps for accomplishing the same continuous type of control, he rejected all of them, being deeply committed to the U.V. Gauge.

The Purchasing Agent:
Tactics of Lateral Relationship

Most companies of any size have Purchasing Departments. P.A.s deal with other departments—engineering, production scheduling, quality control, and the like.[2] Thus, the P.A., like most *staff* members of management, predominantly engages in *lateral relationships*, not hierarchical, or superior-subordinate, relationships.[3]

CAUSES OF FRICTION

The P.A.'s original functions were: (1) to negotiate and place orders for materials with outside suppliers at the best possible terms—but only in accordance with specifications set by others; and (2) to expedite orders, that is, to check with suppliers to make sure that deliveries are made on time. This

---

[2] For convenience, we shall use the abbreviation P.A. to represent the Purchasing Agent. Technically speaking, the head of Purchasing is usually called the Purchasing Agent and the men under him who actually place orders with suppliers are called "buyers."

[3] The material following is derived from George Strauss, "Tactics of Lateral Relationship: The Purchasing Agent," *Administrative Science Quarterly*, Vol. 7, No. 2 (September 1962), pp. 161-186, with some material added from the author's article, "Work-Flow, Interfunctional Rivalry, and Professionalism," *Human Organization*, Vol. 23, No. 2 (Summer 1964), pp. 140-141.

arrangement gave the P.A. broad power in dealing with supplier salesmen, but he was little more than an order clerk within the company.

An ambitious P.A. feels that placing orders and expediting deliveries are but the bare bones of his responsibilities. He looks on his most important function as that of keeping management posted about developments: new materials, new sources of suppliers, price trends, and so forth. And to make this information more useful, he seeks to be consulted before any requisitions are drawn up, while a product is still in the planning stage. He feels that his technical knowledge of the supply market should be accorded recognition equal to the technical knowledge of, for example, the engineer and accountant.

Specifically, the ambitious P.A. would like to suggest (1) alternative materials or parts to use, (2) changes in specifications or redesign of components which will save money or result in higher quality or quicker delivery, (3) more economical lot sizes, and (4) "make or buy" decisions.[4]

---

[4] Some companies calculate carefully whether they should manufacture a part or some needed material themselves or contract out the production to an outside vendor. This is called a "make or buy" decision.

The purchasing agent's world.

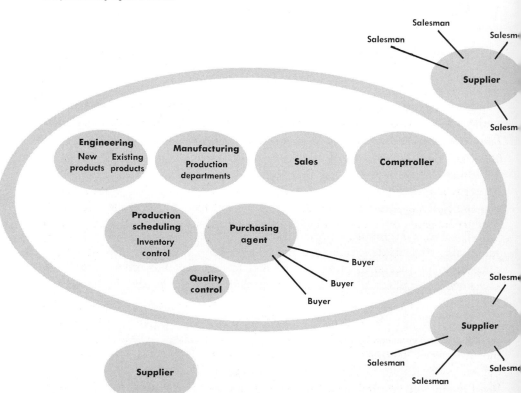

One way of looking at the P.A.'s desire to expand his influence is in terms of work flow. Normally, orders flow in one direction only, from engineering through scheduling to purchasing. But the P.A. is dissatisfied with being at the end of the line and seeks to reverse the flow. Such behavior may, however, result in ill feeling in other departments, particularly engineering and production scheduling. [Compare this with TV design case, p. 401.]

CONFLICTS WITH ENGINEERING

Engineers write up the *specifications* for the products which the P.A.s buy. If the specifications are too tight or, what is worse, if they call for one brand only, P.A.s have little or no freedom to choose among suppliers, thus reducing their social status internally and their economic bargaining power externally. Yet engineers find it much easier to write down a well-known brand name than to draw up a lengthy specification which lists all the characteristics of the desired item. Disagreements also arise because, by training and job function, engineers look first for quality and reliability and thus, P.A.s charge, are indifferent to low cost and quick delivery, qualities of primary interest to purchasing. Let's consider a few specific types of conflict.

The P.A. charges the engineer with being a perfectionist and with making specifications so restrictive as to give him little freedom in choosing the best value.

> "[An engineer in our company] rarely sees the price and cares less. . . . The chief trouble is his lack of cost consciousness . . . [his] tendency to gold-plate, to order a Cadillac where a Chevy would do."

The engineer may insist on a product which has a life of ten years when the product as a whole may have a life of only three years. He insists on getting parts with extremely fine tolerance, although looser tolerances would be satisfactory. [Note the significance of group norms and values here.]

Further, P.A.s are particularly anxious to prevent "backdoor selling," which occurs when an outside salesman bypasses them and seeks to influence someone else in the organization (usually an engineer) to requisition the salesman's product by name or—more subtly—to list specifications which only this product can meet. Backdoor selling threatens the P.A.'s status in two ways: (1) It encourages specification by brand, and (2) it makes both salesmen and engineers less dependent on him.

All these problems are aggravated by the "completion barrier." Usually the P.A. seeks to change specifications only after the engineer has already committed his plans to blueprints and feels he has completed his work—in fact, he may be starting another project: The P.A.'s interference inevitably threatens the engineer's feeling of accomplishment and completion. In any case, engineers are jealous of their professional status and often resent the efforts of the P.A. to suggest new techniques or materials. These are areas in which the engineer feels that he is uniquely competent. One P.A. complained of the conservatism and professional jealousy of the engineer, his unwillingness to be told by anybody not an engineer. Part of this is clearly a status problem. Engineering is an accepted profession; purchasing, if a profession at all, is still fighting for recognition. As a result, the P.A. has something of an inferiority complex, particularly if he does not have a college degree. One complained bitterly:

> "Engineers are a special breed of cat that think they know everything, including purchasing. They feel I am just a clerk."

CONFLICTS WITH PRODUCTION SCHEDULING

The size of the order and the date on which it is to be delivered are typically determined by production scheduling. The P.A.'s chief complaint against scheduling is that delivery is often requested on excessively short notice—that schedulers engage in sloppy planning or "cry wolf" by claiming they need orders earlier than they really do—and thus force the P.A. to choose from a limited number of suppliers, to pay premium prices, and to ask favors of salesmen (thus creating obligations which the P.A. must later repay). Schedulers, on the other hand, claim that short lead-times are not their fault but the fault of departments farther up the line, such as engineering (which delays its blueprints) or sales (which accepts rush orders). In addition, P.A.s claim that schedulers order in uneconomic lot sizes and fail to consider inventory costs or the savings from quantity discounts. In some instances, as we shall see, the P.A. seeks to solve these problems through combining production scheduling, inventory control, and purchasing into one "materials handling" department, which he hopes he will head.

P.A.s often feel more friendly towards production schedulers than they do towards engineers. There is less of a status barrier, for schedulers are not likely to be college men and they have little claim to being professionals.

TECHNIQUES FOR HANDLING LATERAL RELATIONS

Normally, the P.A. attempts to fill requisitions as instructed. The majority of interdepartmental contacts are handled routinely and without friction in accordance with standard operating procedures. Yet many difficult problems cannot be easily programed. Other departments are constantly placing pressures on the P.A., who must take countermeasures, if only to preserve his status and position in the organization. And if the purchasing agent wishes to expand his power aggressively, as many do, he will inevitably run into conflict.

Understandably, then, successful P.A.s have developed a variety of techniques for dealing with other departments, particularly when they wish to influence the form and contents of the purchase requisition they receive from other departments. As an example, let us look at some of the techniques which might be used if production scheduling submits a requisition with a very short lead time.

1. Rule-oriented tactics
   a. Appeal to some common authority to direct that the requisition be revised or withdrawn.
   b. Refer to some rule (assuming one exists) which provides for longer lead times.
   c. Require the scheduling department to state in writing why quick delivery is required.
   d. Require the requisitioning department to consent to having its budget charged with extra cost (such as air freight) required to get quick delivery.
2. Rule-evading tactics
   a. Go through the motions of complying with the request, but with no expectations of getting delivery on time.
   b. Exceed formal authority and ignore the requisition altogether.
3. Personal-political tactics
   a. Rely on friendships to induce the scheduling department to modify the requisition.
   b. Rely on favors, past and future, to accomplish the same result.
   c. Work through political allies in other departments.
4. Education tactics
   a. Use direct persuasion, that is, try to persuade scheduling that its requisition is unreasonable.
   b. Use what might be called indirect persuasion to help scheduling see the problem from the purchasing department's point of view. (In this case it might ask the scheduler to sit in and observe the P.A.'s difficulty in trying to get the vendor to agree to quick delivery.)
5. Organizational tactics
   a. Seek to change the work flow pattern—for example, have the scheduling department check with the purchasing department about the possibility of getting quick delivery *before* it makes a requisition. (This puts the P.A. into a *stabilization* role.)
   b. Seek to take over other departments—for example, to subordinate scheduling to purchasing in a new integrated Materials Department.

Let us look at these tactics in greater detail.

RULE-ORIENTED TACTICS

The tactics listed below are *rule-oriented* in the sense that the P.A.'s approach is perfectly legitimate under the formal rules of the organization.

Appealing to the boss. According to traditional organizational theory, whenever two executives on about the same level cannot agree, they should take the problem to their common superior for solution. Yet most P.A.s look upon this as a drastic step, to be taken only when other means have failed. In other words they do not make much use of the hierarchy.

The general feeling, particularly among stronger P.A.s we studied, was that too frequent reference to the superior would weaken their relations both with the superior and with their fellow employees. ("After all you've got to live with them.") To bring in top management too often would, in effect, be an admission that the P.A. could not handle his own problems. Moreover, there is a myth in many corporations of being "one great big happy family," and, as a consequence, it is difficult to bring conflicts out in the open. Furthermore, since the P.A. is usually the aggressor, in the sense that he is seeking to expand his power beyond its formal limits, he is unlikely to go to the boss unless his case is unusually good.

On the other hand, the threat of going to the boss loses its effectiveness as a weapon if the threat is never carried out. The following quotation summarizes a common position:

> "It depends on how much fuss you want to make. If it is really important, you can tell him you will discuss it with his boss. But, I don't want you to get the wrong impression. If you have to resort to this, you are probably falling down on the job. By and large, we have a good relationship with our engineers. However, there are times when you have to take a tough position. You aren't doing your job if you always go along with them in a wishy-washy fashion."

One agent explained how he "educated" engineers to accept substitute products instead of insisting on one well-known name brand.

> "We prepared our evidence and we were all set to take it to the top—and then, at the last minute, we backed down and told them it was too late in the game. But we indicated that in the future we would take similar issues to the top and they knew we would. So there has been much more understanding. . . . You have to risk making a few enemies once in a while."

Reference to rules.   A second traditional bureaucratic means of dealing with other departments is to cite applicable rules or to rely on a formal statement of authority (such as a job description). For instance, a P.A. may circumvent pressure to place an order with a given company by referring to company rules requiring competitive bidding on all purchases in excess of $10,000. When asked, most P.A.s agreed, in theory, that rules of this sort are useful weapons, but they varied greatly in the extent to which they relied upon them in practice.

Some P.A.s went very much "by the book," day in and day out. In general, these were men without college training, and they worked for large, rule-oriented companies that were slow to change. In answer to questions, these men often said, "This matter is governed by corporate policy," or made references to manuals and procedures. The latter spelled out the specific authority of the purchasing department in relation to internal company customers.

If flexibly used, procedure manuals provide the P.A. with an added bargaining weapon in dealing with other departments. Even though he may permit rules in the manual to be ignored most of the time, he can always do so as a favor in return for which he may ask favors. And the rules put a legal stamp on his efforts whenever he decides to ensnarl another department in a mass of red tape.

Many P.A.s, however, were anxious to expand their influence and authority beyond that granted them in the procedures of the formal organization. (They wanted to be able to help write specifications, determine order sizes, and so on.) The expansionist P.A. must be careful not to become too rule-oriented. After all, his goal is to expand his influence beyond the areas over which the rules give him definite authority—not to retreat behind them.

Requiring written acceptance of responsibility. Another bureaucratic technique used by many P.A.s is to require others to justify their decisions in writing. For example, if a production scheduler orders a part for delivery with very short lead time, the P.A. can ask him to explain in writing why there is such a rush. He hopes the scheduler will be embarrassed unless he has a good excuse—and in any case, the effort will make him reluctant to make such last-minute requests in the future. Certainly this helps expose the scheduler who constantly cries "wolf."

P.A.s may ask for written explanations to clear themselves of responsibility for having ordered parts at high prices. Just as often, however, this play is used to make others hesitate or to have evidence against them later. In insisting that such reports be written, the P.A. can refer to company rules or to possible audits. Thus in asking for such a statement, P.A.s often say, "I need it to document my records."

Again, it is the weak, noncollege P.A. who makes the most persistent use of such tactics. Many seem to feel that an approach of this sort is cowardly and defeatist. As one put it, "If you are trying to get a man to say 'yes,' I don't see any value in forcing him to put his 'no' in writing. Then he will never move." And another said, "I suppose you do punish an engineer by forcing him to give you a long written explanation, but that's hardly the way to win friends or advance your point of view." Furthermore, "You can always ask an engineer to give you a formal test result, but if he wishes he can always make the test fail" (thus proving that the less expensive part the P.A. wished to order will not be satisfactory).

Financial charges. Cost-accounting procedures may also be used as a lever. A number of P.A.s made comments like this:

> "Whenever I get a request for a rush delivery, I ask the department which wants it whether they are willing to authorize overtime [5] or air freight. Since this gets charged against their budget, they usually hesitate a bit. If they go along I know they really need it. And if they have too many extra charges the auditor starts asking questions."

---

[5] That is, the vendor is authorized to make an extra charge for having his men work overtime.

This tactic resembles the one previously discussed, particularly when the agent enters a statement into his records that the product would have been cheaper had the requisition been received on time.

RULE-EVADING TACTICS

Literal compliance. In dealing with pressures from other departments, the P.A. can always adopt a policy of passive resistance—that is, he can go through the motions in hope of satisfying the demands. This tactic of feigned acceptance [6] is often used with production scheduling. For example, after completing a lengthy phone call in which he half-heartedly tried to persuade a vendor to make a very quick delivery, a P.A. commented, "My buyer tried already and I knew that they just weren't going to be able to deliver that soon. Still, production scheduling was screaming and they threatened to go to the plant manager. So I tried to handle it in such a way as not to hurt my relations with the vendor. They knew why I had to call."

This game of passive resistance can be skillfully played in such a way as to set a trap for the other department.

> One P.A. told how he dealt with an engineer who had placed a requisition for one company's products after having been lavishly entertained by its salesman. The P.A. wrote a long memo explaining why he felt this to be a poor choice and presented it to the engineer in a fashion which he knew the engineer would reject. The P.A. then placed the order. As he had predicted, the products arrived late and were totally inappropriate. The subsequent investigation led both to this engineer's transfer and demotion and to other engineers' having greater respect for the P.A.'s advice. [7]

It should be noted, however, that these tactics were reported only by "weak" P.A.s. Instead of passively seeming to accept unreasonable requests, the stronger P.A.s actively oppose them.

Exceeding authority. Occasionally P.A.s may revise the term of requisitions on their own initiative, even though they have no formal authority to do so. For instance, a P.A. may extend a lead time if he knows the production scheduler has set the delivery date much earlier than is really required. Where a requisition calls for a given brand, he may purchase a substitute which he feels sure is an equivalent. Or he may buy a larger quantity than requested in order to take advantage of quantity discounts.

When a P.A. revises requisitions in this manner, he may or may not tell the requisitioning department what he is doing. In either case he is exceeding his formal authority. In effect, he is daring the requisitioning department to make an issue of it. This requires considerable courage. No sensible P.A. will expose

---

[6] Melville Dalton, *Men Who Manage* (New York: Wiley, 1959), p. 232.

[7] A tactic like this can always backfire, of course. The agent himself may be blamed for the failure. Much depends on the whims of the "auditing" group.

himself in this way unless (1) his over-all political position is secure and (2) he feels the terms of the original requisition were clearly so unreasonable that the requisitioning department will hesitate to raise the issue and expose its mistake.

Most P.A.s queried were reluctant to use this tactic. Even if they could safely change orders in a given case, continual flouting of the requisitioning department's desires would create too much antagonism in the long run.

PERSONAL-POLITICAL TACTICS

Friendships and exchange of favors are used in almost every organization to get things done and to oil the wheels of the formal organization. None of the tactics which follow are contemplated by the company's formal scheme; all involve the use of personal relations.

Friendships.   Most P.A.s prefer to deal with friends. Friendships help reduce the kinds of tensions to which agents are commonly subject. Even where friendship is not involved, it is easier to deal with people when you know their idiosyncrasies and special interests. Not surprisingly, comments like this were common:

> "[In handling problems] friendships count a lot. Many of the people here started when I did 25 years ago. We are all at about the same level and most of them are pretty good friends of mine. A lot is a matter of trust and confidence."

P.A.s seem to rely on friendship contacts as a means of communication and of getting quick acceptances of proposals that could be justified on their merits in any case. Rarely do P.A.s rely on friendship alone. As one put it, "You can accomplish some things on the basis of friendship, but you can't do too much or you will strain your friendship."

Exchange of favors.   To some extent P.A.s operate on the principle of "reward your friends, punish your enemies," and are involved in a network of exchange of favors (what sociologists call "patterns of reciprocity")—and sometimes even reprisals. Favors of various sorts may be given. Most P.A.s are under pressure to make personal purchases, for example, to help someone in management buy a set of tires at wholesale rates. Since there are usually no formal rules against such extracurricular purchasing, the P.A. has a strong incentive to help those who help him most. Similarly, a P.A. is in a position to suggest to a salesman that it might be strategic to take a "cooperative" engineer to lunch. And there are always people in management who would like him to do a favor for a friend or relative who is a salesman or who owns a small business.

Other favors are more work-related. An agent may expedite delivery for a production scheduler who normally gives plenty of lead time for his orders but who now has a real emergency on his hands. Or he may rush parts for an engineer who is building a prototype model. "If a man is reasonable with me," one P.A. commented, "I'll kill myself to get him what he wants." The P.A. is less likely to exert himself for the man who has been uncooperative in the past.

The use of reprisals can be seen most clearly in dealing with salesmen. As one P.A. put it, "I play ball with those who play ball with me. If a salesman operates behind my back (and goes directly to our department heads), he's going to have a hell of a time getting me to give him an order." Reprisals are more risky in dealing with management.

> One assistant P.A. told how he "delayed" getting catalogs for "uncoopera-tive" engineers and gave "slow service" to engineers who habitually cried "wolf." However, both this man's supervisor and his personnel director ex-pressed concern over his poor human relations and his tendency to antagonize others.

The typical P.A. observed, however, seemed to feel that if he used such techniques he ran the risk of permanently impairing his relations with others. Furthermore, these techniques might always backfire; for example, if produc-tion were delayed because components were delivered late, the P.A. might be blamed.

Interdepartmental politics.   In addition to their personal relations with people, P.A.s inevitably get involved in interdepartmental power struggles. Indeed, as the following quotation suggests, the P.A. like the supervisor is often a man in the middle, subject to conflicting pressures from all sides:

> "Production scheduling wants quick delivery, engineering wants quality, manufacturing wants something easy-to-make, accounting wants to save money, quality control has their own interests. And then you've got to deal with the supplier—and present the supplier's position back to your own organization, and only the agent sees the over-all picture."

Much of the P.A.s time is spent seeking informal resolution of such problems —and he often acts as a mediator. The following is a common situation:

> Production scheduling has been pushing hard to get early delivery of a par-ticular component (because the sales department has been pressing for in-creased production). In response to this pressure the supplier puts new, inex-perienced men on the job. But when the components are delivered, quality control declares the work is sloppy, rejects it *in toto,* and wants to disqualify the supplier from doing further work for the company. Production scheduling and the supplier are naturally upset; the supplier insists that the defects are trivial and can be easily remedied; and purchasing is placed in the difficult position of trying to mediate the issue.

If the P.A. is not careful in situations like this, he may become a scapegoat; everyone may turn on him and blame him for the unhappy turn of events. On the other hand, the successful P.A. is able to play one pressure off against another and free himself—or he may enlist the support of a powerful depart-ment to back him. If he is shrewd, he can get both sides to appeal to him to make the final decision and thus gain prestige as well as bestow favors which he may later ask returned.

Like it or not, P.A.s of necessity engage in power politics. In doing so, they necessarily develop allies and opponents. Each department presents a special problem.

1. Engineering: Unless the relationship with engineering is handled with great tact, engineering tends to become an opponent, since value analysis invades an area which engineers feel is exclusively their own.[8] Purchasing is at a disadvantage here. Engineers have the prestige of being college-trained experts, and engineering is much more strongly represented than purchasing in the ranks of higher management.

2. Manufacturing: There is often a tug of war between purchasing and manufacturing over who should have the greater influence with production scheduling. These struggles are particularly sharp where purchasing is trying to absorb into its own department either inventory control or all of production scheduling.

3. Comptroller: The comptroller is rarely involved in the day-to-day struggles over specifications or delivery dates. But when purchasing seeks to introduce an organizational change which will increase its power—for example, absorbing inventory control—then the comptroller can be a most effective ally. But the P.A. must present evidence that the proposed innovation will save money.

4. Sales: Sales normally has great political power, and purchasing is anxious to maintain good relations with it. Sales is interested above all in being able to make fast delivery and shows less concern with cost, quality, or manufacturing ease. In general, it supports or opposes purchasing in accordance with that criterion. But sales is also interested in reciprocity—in persuading purchasing "to buy from those firms which buy from us" (in order to increase sales, of course!).

5. Production scheduling: Relations with production scheduling are often complex. Purchasing normally has closer relations with production scheduling than any other department, and conflicts are quite common. Yet these departments are jointly responsible for having parts available when needed and, in some companies, they presented a common front to the outside world. Unfortunately, however, production scheduling has little political influence, particularly when it reports relatively low down in the management hierarchy.

The shrewd P.A. knows how to use departmental interests for his own ends:

> "Engineering says we can't use these parts. But I've asked manufacturing to test a sample under actual operating conditions—they are easy to use. Even if engineering won't accept manufacturing's data, I can go to the boss with manufacturing backing me. On something like this, manufacturing is tremendously powerful."

---

[8] In "value-analysis" programs, purchasing agents seek to evaluate parts that are ordered by the company to see if cheaper or simpler parts might be substituted.

EDUCATIONAL TACTICS

Next we come to a set of tactics designed to persuade others to think in purchasing terms.

Direct persuasion. Direct persuasion—the frank attempt to sell a point of view—is, of course, the agent's typical means of influencing others. Successful persuasion means "knowing your products backwards and forwards ... building your case so that it can't be answered ... knowing what you are talking about."

Most P.A.s feel it essential that they have complete command of the facts, particularly if they are to bridge the status gap and meet engineers on equal terms. As one of them said, "The engineer thinks he is the expert; the only way you can impress him is to know more than he does." Thus, many P.A.s go to considerable lengths to acquire expertise; they spend a great deal of time learning production processes or reading technical journals.

Yet some of the stronger P.A.s pointed out that too much expertise can be dangerous in that it threatens the other man's status. "Never put a man in a corner. Never prove that he is wrong. It doesn't pay to be a know-it-all." Thus, some P.A.s look upon themselves primarily as catalysts who try to educate others to think in purchasing terms:

> "Actually it is an asset not to be an engineer. Not having the [engineering] ability myself, I've had to work backwards. I can't tell them what to do but I can ask questions. They know that I'm not trying to design their instrument. ... You have to give the engineer recognition. The less formal you are in dealing with them the better. It doesn't get their dander up."

Indirect persuasion. Recognizing the danger of the frontal approach, P.A.s often try forms of indirection—manipulation, if you like—which are designed to induce the other departments to arrive at conclusions similar to those of the agent but seemingly on their own. For example:

> "We were paying $45.50 a unit, but I found a vendor who was producing a unit for $30 which I felt would meet our needs just as well. There was a lot of reluctance in engineering to accept it, but I knew the engineer in charge of the test was susceptible to flattery. So I wrote a letter for general distribution telling what a good job of investigating he was doing and how much money we'd save if his investigation was successful. ... That gave him the motivation to figure out how it could work rather than how it could not work."

Indirect persuasion often involves presenting the facts and then letting the other person draw his own conclusions. The P.A. may ask an engineer to run a test on a product or even simply attach a sample of the product to an interoffice buck slip, asking, "Can we use this?" Similarly, by choosing which salesmen may see engineers, he can indirectly influence the specification process. (In fact, once a P.A. decides that a product should be introduced, he and the outside salesman will often coordinate their strategies closely in order to get it accepted by others in management.)

Most P.A.s feel that engineers should have no part in negotiating prices; they fear encroachment on purchasing's jurisdiction. But one successful agent we met encourages engineers to help out in the bargaining because "that's the best way I know to make these engineers cost-conscious." Another arranges to have foremen and production schedulers sit in while he negotiates delivery dates with salesmen. "In that way they will know what I'm up against when they give me lead times which are too short for normal delivery."

MODIFYING THE ORGANIZATION

Above we have described a variety of tactics by which a Purchasing Department may seek to introduce changes in the organization. For the most part, these are efforts to get others to adopt behavior and attitudes that will facilitate the objectives of the purchasing group itself. There is another method of introducing change in organizations which is often more powerful than these techniques of persuasion and pressure. When the job of people and their positions in the organization change, their behavior is likely to change. This tactic means changing the division of labor: who does what with whom, when, and where.

Below we shall only look at a few examples of this modification of the structure of the organization. In the first, job patterns are changed so that purchasing does not have to initiate as much to outside departments. The second example involves a change in purchasing's departmental boundaries or formal jurisdiction.

Inducing others to initiate action.   In most of the examples discussed here, the agent seeks to initiate change in the behavior of other departments. He is the one who is trying to change the engineer's specifications, the production scheduler's delivery schedules, and so forth. The other departments are always at the receiving (or resisting) end of these initiations. As might be expected, hard feelings are likely to develop if the initiations move only one way, just as they do in one-sided, superior-subordinate relationships.[9]

Recognizing this, many of the stronger P.A.s seem to be trying to rearrange their relations with other departments so that others might initiate changes more often for them. Specifically, they hope to induce the other deparments to turn instinctively to purchasing for help whenever they have a problem—and at the earliest possible stage. Thus, one P.A. explained that his chief reason for attending production-planning meetings, where new products were laid out,

---

[9] Actually, of course, initiations do occur in both directions. The production schedulers initiate for the P.A. when they file requisitions and the engineers initiate when they determine specifications. But the participants seem to distinguish between the direction of routine initiations and the direction of initiations designed to change some decision or procedure.

was to make it easier for others to ask him questions (to develop advisory relationship.) He hoped to encourage engineers, for example, to inquire about available components before they drew up their blueprints. Another P.A. commented, "I try to get production scheduling to ask us what the lead times are for the various parts we order. That's a lot easier than our telling them that their lead times are unreasonable after they have made commitments based on these."

Some purchasing departments send out what are, in effect, ambassadors to other departments. They appoint "purchase engineers," men with engineering background (perhaps from the company's own engineering group) who report administratively to purchasing but spend most of their time in the engineering department. Their job, again an advisory one, is to be instantly available to provide information to engineers whenever they need help in choosing components. They assist in writing specifications (thus making them more realistic and readable) and help expedite delivery of laboratory supplies and material for prototype models. Through making themselves useful, purchase engineers acquire influence and are able to introduce the purchasing point of view before the "completion barrier" makes this difficult. Similar approaches may be used for quality control.

Work assignments within purchasing are normally arranged so that each buyer can become an expert on one group of commodities bought. Under this arrangement the buyer deals with a relatively small number of outside salesmen, but with a relatively large number of "client" departments within the organization. A few purchasing departments have experimented with assigning men on the basis of the departments with which they work rather than on the basis of the products they buy. In one case work assignments in both purchasing and scheduling were so rearranged that each production scheduler had an exact counterpart in purchasing and dealt only with him. In this way closer personal relations developed than would have occurred if the scheduler had no specific individual in purchasing to contact.

Even the physical location of the P.A.'s office makes a difference. It is much easier for the P.A. to have informal daily contacts with other departments if his office is conveniently located. Some companies place their P.A.s away from the main office, to make it easier for salesmen to see them. Although this facilitates the agents' external communications, it makes their internal communications more difficult. Of course, those companies that have centralized purchasing offices and a widespread network of plants experience this problem in an exaggerated form. Centralized purchasing offers many economic advantages, but the P.A. must tour the plants if he is not to lose all contact with his client departments. Of course, the alternative is to decentralize purchasing, putting a purchasing group under each plant manager.

Value-analysis techniques sharply highlight the agent's organizational philosophy. Some agents feel that value analysis should be handled as part of the buyer's everyday activities. If he comes across a new product which might be profitably substituted for one currently used, he should initiate engineering-feasibility studies and promote the idea ("nag it" in one agent's words) until it is accepted. Presumably purchasing then gets the credit for the savings, but resistance from other departments may be high. Other agents, particularly those with college training, reject this approach as unnecessarily divisive; they prefer to operate through committees, usually consisting of engineers, purchasing men, and production men. Though committees are time-consuming, communications are facilitated, more people are involved, more ideas are forthcoming—and, in addition, the purchasing department no longer has the sole responsibility for value analysis.

To the extent that he allows others to take the initiative, the agent himself must take a passive role. Not all agents are emotionally prepared to do this.[10] Some feel that it smacks too much of the "order clerk." A number commented, in effect, "I don't want to be everyone's door mat."

Formal organizational change. The final approach is for the agent to seek to expand the formal grant of authority given his department (which might mean a larger budget too), as, for example, to place other functions such as traffic, stores, or even inventory control and production scheduling in one combined Materials Department. Agents who exert their energies in this direction generally reject the "human-relations" or "participative" approach to management. They like to resolve problems through memoranda ("it helps keep emotions down") and are not particularly optimistic about the possibilities of converting other departments to think in purchasing terms ("after all every department has its own point of view—that's natural"). They spend considerable time developing statistical controls to measure their own efficiency and that of their subordinates, and they are more likely to be in companies that have similar philosophies. For example, one agent explained why value analysis in his organization was concentrated in the purchasing department: "(Our company) doesn't believe in joint assignments or committees. If a man isn't competent to do the job himself, then we find another man. We don't want weak sisters." And another argued. "The responsibility must be concentrated in one department or another. It can't fall between two stools."

CHOICE OF TECHNIQUES

The foregoing list of tactics is presented merely to illustrate the *range* of techniques available to the agent. Most agents use all of these techniques at one time or another, depending on the problem. Different techniques might well be used in introducing a major policy change than in handling routine orders. All these techniques illustrate the complexities involved in lateral relations.

---

[10] After all, a certain type of active, initiating sort of personality is required if the agent is to bargain successfully with suppliers; it is hard for the same individual to adopt a passive role within the organization.

Purchasing agents and the buyers who work for them come into conflict with a number of other departments for whom they are supposed to provide essential purchasing services. Although in theory they are in the organization to provide help, the purchasing agents also have their own objectives, which they believe are consistent with the total goals of their companies. More specifically, we can observe the efforts of purchasing personnel to become a recognized professional group and to get other departments to treat them as professionals. A whole arsenal of techniques is employed by the agents both to gain status for their departments and to develop viable relations with the groups with which they must work. All of the methods, however, relate to concepts with which you should now be familiar: using rules, employing statistical controls, exchanging favors, using the hierarchy, and introducing organizational changes.

They also illustrate the contrast between techniques that emphasize face-to-face human-relations and communication skills and those that emphasize the use of authority, power, and the hierarchy.

PROBLEM ONE [11]

Systems and Procedures vs. The Branch Office

Many companies have set up departments to analyze such paper-work activities as billing operations, interoffice correspondence, inventory-control problems, and various file systems. This type of department is usually placed on a staff level and is called the Methods Department or Industrial Engineering Department.

In the Rajah Comptometer Company, this department is called the Systems and Procedures Department. On a staff level, it is directly responsible through its department head to the vice president in charge of marketing. As Systems and Procedures increased in size and in scope of activities it undertook, line personnel began to regard it as in the same category as the company's financial auditors. Depending on what line people you talked to, Systems and Procedures was called everything from a bunch of "idiotic college-bred snoopers" to "a necessary evil." Almost every branch manager, salesman, and plant foreman has heard by word of mouth that the department raises havoc with normal work techniques when it undertakes investigations, that its remedies cause more work than the original method employed, and that the cost of maintaining it outweighs the cost "cutbacks" that result from its work. "Maybe we are even paying their salaries by our efforts," has been a frequent comment.

When department employees went out into the "field" to conduct an investigation, the local branch manager decided with whom they could talk and work. This rule inhibited the Systems and Procedures people, since the branch manager did not always let them talk to the personnel who were close to the problem they were investigating. Moreover, since their visits were always announced in advance, line personnel met them with a "hale fellow, well met" attitude. And yet line had a great many misgivings, feeling that the investigation would be an inconvenience and that the resultant suggestions would be "half-baked" at best.

Recently, two men from the Systems and Procedures Department were ordered to make a cost analysis of the paper work involved in receiving and

---

[11] We are indebted to a former student, Stuart Pennels, for the outline of this case.

answering a typical comptometer service repair call in the Columbus, Ohio, District Branch. They arrived early one Monday morning to spend the week with the repairmen who did the work. The first morning they spent with the manager, who had been forewarned by a letter from the comptroller's department and another from the home office general service manager. The local manager was not too happy to see people from the home office, simply because their presence implied some deficiency in his managerial ability. (Branch offices operate on the theory that no news from the home office is good news.) After a long lunch, paid for by the "visiting firemen" because they were on an expense account, the manager spent the afternoon trying to discover what the Systems and Procedures men were "really" trying to do. After they had assured him that his office had been selected for the investigation only because it typified small district offices and for no other reason, the manager told them that he did not want his service department upset, and that his foreman had been there fifteen years and was very touchy about criticism. "The men in my service department are the best in all the Midwest." Then the manager said that it was getting late and he felt he would like to talk to the service foreman first before the Systems and Procedures men did, so that he could "smooth the way."

Tuesday morning the Systems and Procedures men finally were able to see the service foreman. He seemed very reluctant to listen to their explanations of the investigation, let alone cooperate with them. The six servicemen who worked for him were equally unresponsive; they had obviously been warned not to give away any branch "secrets."

The servicemen of Rajah Comptometer are talented, skilled mechanics. The speed and efficiency with which they respond to service calls has won them an enviable reputation in the trade. Few of them have college degrees; most are high-school graduates. And they look askance at anyone who is (1) a college man and (2) doesn't know how to repair a comptometer.

The Systems and Procedures men spent the second day vainly trying to justify their trip to the service foreman, and trying to communicate with the group as a whole. The third day was almost equally unsuccessful, although their casual revelation that there would be a new comptometer model in the spring did alleviate some of the tension.

The two Systems and Procedures men spent Wednesday night trying to figure out how they could gain access to the service department group. They realized that they were hampered by the fact that they were newly hired, college-trained employees who didn't know how to repair a comptometer or even know the names of its parts. So they spent three hours memorizing the names of various parts out of a service linebook they happened to bring along. To win acceptance from the foreman, since all the servicemen seemed to take their cues from him, they also decided to appeal to his interest in gardening and rare flowers.

1. How would you evaluate the situation faced by the two Systems and Procedures men in the Columbus branch office?
2. Given your evaluation of the situation, what alternative courses of action are open to them? What do you think of the course they chose?
3. Can this problem be worked out in the "field"? Or is it an over-all company problem that cannot be solved by staff representatives?
4. What objectives should these men set for themselves in their field work?

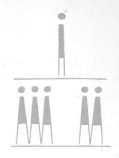

Minimizing the Human Problems of Large Organizations

18

We have been looking at some of the problems that stem from extended lines of authority and the division of labor in the contemporary organization. By this time you may have decided that the "game is not worth the candle"—that too heavy a price must be paid in terms of human relationships to win the advantages of large-scale organization. There are those who look back nostalgically to the "good old days" when companies were small, when the boss knew all his employees intimately, when everyone worked together and did a whole job, when problems of coordination and communication were at a minimum. Neither horizontal nor vertical cleavages were particularly significant, and the work group and the company were synonymous. Many studies have shown that employee morale is higher in small groups than in large ones.[1] Supervision and job satisfaction are all easier to achieve in the more intimate setting.

---

[1] See R. W. Revans, "Industrial Morale and Size of Unit," in Walter Galenson and Seymour Lipset, eds., *Labor and Trade Unionism* (New York: Wiley, 1960), pp. 295-300. See also Mason Haire, *Psychology in Management*, 2nd ed., (New York: McGraw-Hill, 1964), p. 28. Professor Haire also has included a stimulating section on the interrelationships of organization size, shape (structure), and functions (pp. 223-228).

The technological and economic advantages that come with size, however, mean that large organizations are here to stay. Size makes possible many of the economies of specialization (*e.g.*, mass production) and the introduction of expensive equipment (*e.g.*, electronic data-processing machines). As the organization grows, it usually gains what economists call "economies of scale"—that is, money can be borrowed at lower interest rates, supplies purchased in larger quantities, and so on.

Even from a human-relations point of view, large organizations possess advantages. Larger companies have pioneered in introducing personnel programs designed to eliminate many of the sources of unrest common to smaller companies. They have sought to regularize employment, to develop training and promotion programs stressing merit rather than nepotism, to introduce equitable wage and salary administration programs that adjust income to job responsibility, and to provide retirement and insurance programs to reduce the fear of illness and old age.

The basic problem is this: How can organizations gain the advantages that come with size and specialization without paying a heavy price in terms of reduced employee and managerial effectiveness? In the small organization where face-to-face relationships predominate, a manager of goodwill who likes and respects people may prove highly successful. In the large organization, good intentions are not enough; human relations needs to be *planned* to insure an environment conducive to productivity.

How can organizational structure be designed to minimize human friction? In answering this question, we shall try to show that the manager who plans his organizational structure intelligently and realistically can:

1. Reduce the number of levels in the organizational hierarchy, even though he does not reduce the total number of employees.
2. Improve the efficiency with which the immediate work group solves the difficult work-flow problems of coordination and cooperation.
3. Improve cooperation between groups within the organization.
4. "Factor-in" the personality variable into the design of jobs.

Fewer Levels of Supervision

In Chapter 15, we mentioned that the existence of many levels within an organization complicates the problems of management. The individual employee feels lost because he is many steps removed from the key decision-makers who control his welfare, and both top management and the worker feel isolated from one another. Orders and information have to pass up and down through so many levels that there are countless possibilities for break-downs and distortions in communication.

It is not uncommon for large corporations to have ten to twelve levels intervening between the hourly-paid employee and top management. And yet the number of levels required by the organization is *not* automatically determined by the number of employees. For instance, Sears Roebuck reported in 1950 that with 110,000 employees in their retail division, there are only four levels of supervision *between* the president of the company and the salespeople in the stores.[2] This "flat" structure is not accidental; it is a reflection of deliberate management policy to maximize the number of subordinates (the span of control) reporting to a given supervisor. The result is that the levels of supervision in the organization are kept to a minimum.[3]

IMPACT OF FLAT VS. TALL ORGANIZATIONS
ON HUMAN RELATIONS

Fortunately, the Sears Roebuck Company has analyzed the effect of its organizational setup on human relations within the company. Sears operates many stores that have an almost identical number of employees doing highly similar jobs. In some of these stores, 32 department managers report directly to the store manager; in others, the department managers report to 5 or 6 division managers, who in turn report to the store manager.[4] Obviously, the first is a relatively *flat* type of structure; the second, a *tall* type. What has Sears observed in the operations of these two quite different organization patterns?

The tall organization tended to encourage close supervision. With a relatively small number of subordinates, each supervisor, whether he was the store manager or the division manager, was able to give very detailed instructions to and exercise strong control over every one of the people in his unit. But in the flat organization the relatively large number of subordinates made this type of supervision physically impossible. Each supervisor was obliged to rely on general supervision and good training; he just didn't have the time to keep a close watch on everyone. The delegation of responsibility in these stores encouraged subordinates to work on their own initiative and learn from their own mistakes. Since the supervisor could not make a decision on every problem that arose, subordinates achieved a high degree of self-reliance. The results showed themselves in the higher profits, better morale, and greater number of promotable executives produced by the flat organization.

Another obvious advantage to the fewer-leveled organization is the saving of managerial time: Problems are handled more quickly. Equally important are the better human relations associated with fewer levels. Communication is

---

[2] James C. Worthy, "Factors Influencing Employee Morale," *Harvard Business Review*, Vol. 28, No. 1 (January 1950), p. 69.

[3] There are other organizational techniques for reducing the number of supervisory levels, which we shall not detail here. The interested reader will find a description of them in an excellent case study of reorganization at the International Business Machines plant in Endicott, N. Y.: F. L. W. Richardson, Jr., and Charles R. Walker, *Human Relations in an Expanding Company* (New Haven, Conn.: Labor and Management Center, Yale University, 1948), pp. 32-48.

[4] A good summary of the Sears experience may be found in William F. Whyte, *Men at Work* (Homewood, Illinois: Dorsey Press, 1961), pp. 88-93.

expedited; the individual employee finds it easier to identify with the work of his part of the organization.

Not every organization, of course, can arbitrarily increase the number of subordinates reporting to each of its supervisors. The ability of Sears to make use of a relatively "wide" span of control is a function of the following factors:

1. It was possible to develop efficiency measures (controls) for the various departments so that a manager could be left to make nearly all his own decisions and only have to account for the final results: in other words, supervision "by results."

2. Department store personnel receive a good part of their compensation in the form of commissions and bonuses based on sales performance. These incentives provide them with a high degree of motivation and decrease the need for close supervision.

3. No great amount of coordination between department managers was required in these stores. In effect, each department could be operated relatively independently of the others, thus reducing the amount of supervision required by the store manager.

One other interesting facet of the Sears study is worth mentioning since it relates to what we shall say later about personality. The Sears organization found that certain managers *preferred* the "tall" organization and its attendant close supervision. Given their personalities, that was the way they wanted to manage. Others, if they were shifted into that kind of store, immediately set about to increase the number of people reporting to each supervisor. Their personality was such that they trusted people and didn't want to exercise close supervision.

Building Integrated Work Teams:
A Systems View

Which jobs should be put together under a common supervisor? This is often called the departmentation decision. Naive managers assume that the answer is obvious:

> The drill presses and the punch presses have *always* been in separate departments.

> The sales engineers report to the manager of engineering; after all they're engineers, aren't they?

But, of course, such decisions are not obvious. Whereas many organizations rely on functional boundary lines (grouping together employees with similar job titles or "functions"), others are showing an increasing interest in a *systems view* of organization. In this approach, the manager looks at what people actually have to do in their relationships with one another if work is to flow smoothly. Those people who must coordinate their task are then placed together under a common supervisor.[5]

The significance of this approach was underlined by the problems associated with producing highly complicated military equipment like the Polaris submarine. A large number of separate tasks had to be integrated perfectly. If task No. 32 wasn't done, No. 33 couldn't begin—and there were thousands of these distinguishable design, manufacture, and assembly tasks. Further, the sophistication of the technology required that each task be done in such a way as to intermesh perfectly with the others in terms of dimensions and operating characteristics.

Given these kinds of problems, new organizational procedures had to be invented. New *control* techniques like PERT (Program Evaluation and Review Technique) were given to managers to enable them to watch the progress of the work through its various stages and to identify where bottlenecks threatened. More importantly, managers were given responsibility for the development of a total weapons system rather than being divided up according to functions (such as design, development, manufacture, testing, and so on). This was the same "task force" procedure that had been utilized in the Manhattan Project, which developed the atomic bomb.[6]

In civilian work, this systems approach reflects itself in increasing emphasis on organization by *product* manufactured or service rendered rather than by *process* or function. But this distinction will be clearer if we look at an example.

THE AJAX COMPANY: CUSTOMER-ORDER PROCESSING DEPARTMENT

To illustrate how this reorganization can be accomplished, we shall describe a case in which changes in organization substantially altered the human relations of the situation. Notice particularly that the original emphasis on functional specialization, a characteristic of modern organizations, as emphasized in Chapter 16, was the chief source of the difficulty. The division of labor employed *before* the change looked logical and reasonable on paper; but when real people filled the jobs that had been created, continuous personnel conflict and inefficiency arose. Management's mistake was in assuming that people behave like the rectangles and lines of an organization chart.

Before

The Ajax Company manufactured small home appliances which it sold to retail outlets. Every order sent in by salesmen in the field had to be processed by four different groups of employees in the home office.

    a. *Customer contact clerks* communicated with the customer if the salesman's order was unclear, if the merchandise ordered was unavailable, or if price changes had taken place.

---

[5] For a more complete and precise definition of these criteria, see Eliot Chapple and Leonard Sayles, *The Measure of Management* (New York: Macmillan, 1960), pp. 18-45.

[6] *Cf.* Richard Johnson, Fremont Kast, and James Rosenzweig, *Theory and Management of Systems* (New York: McGraw-Hill, 1963).

b. *Billing clerks* checked the arithmetic on the order and entered correct charges and credits on the customer's account.
c. *Inventory checkers* checked to make sure that goods ordered were available for shipment.
d. *Credit approval clerks* examined the customer's credit status in order to authorize shipping.

The Ajax Company placed each "functional" group of employees under separate supervisors, as in the diagram below.

Thus, each customer order passed through four distinct departments (and two divisions). Each specialist belonged to the organizational unit to which his function was *logically* related.

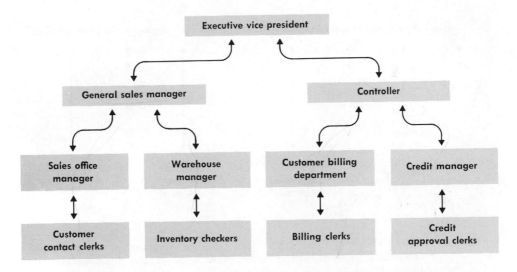

You can probably predict what happened. The design of the organization made no provision for the cooperation and communication required to complete the *total job* of customer-order processing. There was constant conflict among employees. Inventory checkers complained that they had to track down merchandise that might later be dropped from the order as a result of the discovery of a salesman's clerical error or inadequate customer credit. Customer contact clerks were in a constant dither because their letters were rendered obsolete by the work of the credit clerks or the inventory checkers. Responsibility for delays in processing orders were "passed" from one group to another. The billing clerks complained that the inventory checkers were always late with their information, and the inventory checkers retorted that their delays were the result of faulty information from customer contact clerks.

Higher management was always being called in to settle disputes. When conflict arose between an inventory checker and a customer contact clerk, for example, each would contact his superior, who in turn would take the battle up to the General Sales Manager. When the billing clerk complained that he couldn't get up-to-the-minute information from the customer contact clerks (and thus made embarrassing errors in customers' accounts), the problem might have to go to the Executive Vice President, who was their common supervisor. Even the Sales Manager and the Controller were constantly blaming one another for difficulties in each other's departments.

After

In a reorganization of these functions, all employees processing customer orders were placed under a single general office supervisor, who in turn had first-line supervisors for the various geographic areas served by the company. The new organization looked like this:

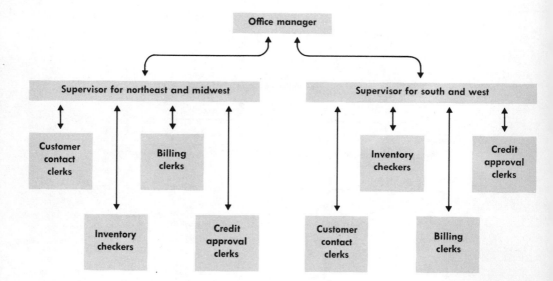

Under each of these supervisors, the same specialists continued to do much the same job they had done before. Now, however, any dispute could be settled face-to-face within the immediate work group, or, in exceptional instances, by the first-line supervisor. No longer was it necessary to channel complaints up the line through two or three levels of management. The new scheme saved a great deal of executive time, and made it possible to settle most problems by horizontal work-flow contacts between the employees themselves. The arrangement increased output enormously by eliminating many petty frictions.

We have omitted from our description the changes that took place in the new staff responsibilities of the sales, warehouse, and credit managers. Each manager became responsible for establishing standards of performance for the clerical employees who did work involving their respective special interests, and for auditing to be sure that these standards of performance, that is, controls, were being observed.

REDUCTION IN NUMBER OF LEVELS

In the past, Ajax had spent a great deal of management time and energy trying to solve the coordination problems that inevitably arose *between* its functional specialists. The sales office manager, the warehouse manager, the head of the customer billing department, and the credit manager were constantly becoming involved in work-flow problems. Further, many questions had to go even higher, to a third level in the hierarchy: to the general sales manager and the controller. In this type of "functional" organization any difficulty in one group is immediately communicated to every other group.

Under the systems arrangement, on the other hand, most decisions, and all information that has to be communicated, is handled either at the work level, among the employees themselves, or between them and their immediate supervisor: one of the two geographic office supervisors. The organization of this part of the business now consists of two relatively autonomous divisions, each of which can function almost entirely on its own. In effect, this unit has become much "flatter"—that is, the lowest level of the hierarchy is much closer to the highest level.

In short, what happened at Ajax was this: (1) Management reduced the number of levels of supervision that had to participate in the solution of normal, daily work problems. And (2) it created more inclusive work teams that could handle problems on a face-to-face basis with a minimum of friction.

IMPROVED COMMUNICATIONS AND COORDINATION

Recall the recurring struggle and frictions among the customer contact, billing, and credit approval clerks and inventory checkers. There was little of the mutual help, loyalty, and protection that we described as characteristic of the informal work group in Chapter 4. Why? The employees who had to interact with one another in order to complete the assigned work of processing customer orders did *not* belong to the same group. The billing clerks, for example, may have had a fine relationship with one another, but unfortunately the people they had to work with were not other billing clerks. They were working with employees in other departments: inventory checkers, customer contact clerks, and so on.

The manner in which work activities are organized influences the quality of communications within the work group: People who work near one another and identify with the same group find it far easier to share the information they need to coordinate their jobs than do people who have infrequent contact with one another. In fact, much of our earlier discussion of flow-of-work problems could just as logically have appeared in a discussion of "communications problems." When two work groups have so much trouble understanding each other that communications are misinterpreted or go astray, or when top management complains that lower levels fail to understand the needs of the business—these are usually indications that the groups that make up the organization are too far apart. Because they report to different supervisors, they develop unique interests. Their separate worlds, their special skills, their special desires and activities, create barriers to effective communication.

Vast quantities of information are required to perform many of the jobs within the large organization, and the superior-subordinate relationship cannot possibly carry the burden of communicating all of it. If every employee had to rely exclusively on his immediate superior for information about the company and his particular function within it, the supervisor would have to spend full time "communicating" information.

Students of organization are often surprised by the amount of work-oriented information that is communicated during what appear to be social contacts. During a coffee break it is not unusual to hear a conversation of this sort:

> "Say, Joe, just out of curiosity, tell me what your guys are doing to mangle those parts we're supposed to put together in a minute and a half in our assembly operation."
>
> "Bill, you've got the wrong villain. Orders came down from the plant manager's office to loosen up on our tolerances. They figure we were rejecting too many out-of-limits parts and wasting money. In fact, they claim that you guys have been having it too soft with our perfect parts; now you'll have to just work a little harder to put 'em together."

These semi-social contacts, which are normally a product of membership in the same group, are an indispensable supplement to the more formal channels of communication.

RESEARCH STUDIES OF ORGANIZATION CHANGE

Mining.[7] Let us examine what happened when a natural work team in a coal mine was broken up. At one time all the operations at the mine face were performed by a small team which worked together on a single shift. Since they were in close contact with one another, it was easy to devise solutions for problems as they arose. Each member of the group felt responsible for the entire operation.

In the mistaken belief that it would increase efficiency, management combined these small groups into much larger ones working over larger areas. For example, one crew did nothing but prepare the new "face" for blasting. Others handled the recovery of the coal that came down after the dynamite had been set off; another crew worked on timbering and moving rail lines. This new division of labor was carried out on a three-shift, 24-hour cycle: Each shift performed a different function. Each worker became a specialist. As a result, no single group of workers felt responsible for the total operation; as problems arose, each shift developed the habit of shrugging them off and passing the buck to the next shift. Communications, which at best are very troublesome in a mine, were further complicated by the workers' being separated from each other in time and space. Previously, the small groups were almost self-supervising (motivated as they were by a group incentive plan); now, coordinating the various individual workers, none of whom had much motivation, became a complex management task. Even new equipment did not compensate for production losses due to work-flow problems.

---

[7] E. L. Trist, G. W. Higgin, H. Murray, A. B. Pollock, *Organizational Choice* (London: Tavistock Publications, 1963).

Similar problems arise even when employees are not separated into different time shifts, as the next case suggests.

Textile mill.[8]   An Indian textile mill, which had undergone intensive "job re-engineering," did not attain satisfactory output levels. Each occupational group in the mill was assigned a work load based on a careful study of all the job components. For example, in one room containing 240 looms, the following assignments were made to the 12 types of specialist:

1. Each weaver tended approximately 30 looms.
2. Each "battery filler" served about 50 looms.
3. Each "smash hand" was assigned some 80 looms.
4. Each of nine different categories of maintenance men was responsible for from 120 to 240 looms.

All these occupational tasks were highly interdependent, and the utmost coordination was required to maintain productivity. But the assignment of work loads militated against coordination. In effect, each weaver came into contact with five-eighths of a "battery filler," three-eighths of a "smash hand," and even smaller fractions of the other nine workers on whom he was at least partially dependent to keep his looms operating.

When the work was reorganized so that all interdependent workers were made part of the same work group, production soared. Work groups were reconstructed so that a single group of workers was responsible for the operation of a given bank of looms. The new interaction pattern produced regular relationships and communications among workers and led directly to the increase in output.

An automated power plant.   With good fortune a team of social researchers were able to study the introduction of automation into a large steam power plant. Automation, with its integrated controls, served to break down the organizational boundaries between the independent boiler, turbine, and electrical departments. These groups of men had been responsible separately for steam generation, turbine operation, and the distribution of the resulting electricity. Automated processing permitted management to put a single foreman over the entire operating force and eliminate intergroup problems. In the research, the employees also reported:

> . . . being significantly more satisfied with the amount of information they got about both the plant and the company [than a comparable work force in a nonautomated plant]. Reducing the number of people between the top staff and the employees appears to have eliminated one of the communication barriers between these . . . groups . . .[9]

---

[8] A. K. Rice, "Productivity and Social Organization in an Indian Weaving Shed," *Human Relations,* Vol. 6, No. 4 (1953).

[9] Floyd Mann and L Richard Hoffman, *Automation and the Worker* (New York: Holt, Rinehart and Winston, 1960), p. 56.

Summary of cases.   The conclusion to be drawn from these studies is that in designing the organization the administrator should provide each work group with a relatively autonomous task. Only under such circumstances can competent *internal* leadership and group responsibility develop.

Ideally, the individual worker should be permitted to coordinate his activities by himself (that is, through job enlargement). If the same girl does both the typing and the filing, problems in integrating the two processes are unlikely to arise. The next best thing is to have the coordination take place within the immediate work group, where each individual feels loyalty and responsibility to his fellow workers and is willing to adjust his pacing, the quality of his work, and his over-all efforts to the needs of the others.

DEVELOPING IDENTIFICATION
WITH THE TOTAL JOB

The type of organization rearrangements we are considering have another valuable by-product. The new groups that are created are more likely to have high morale than are large, highly specialized work groups.

The structure of a work group has profound effects on the job satisfactions derived by its members. An employee who is just one of many, all doing the same operation, which operation in turn is only a small part of some larger activity, feels little sense of accomplishment or identification with the larger unit. However, in the semi-autonomous groups we have been describing, in which people who do complementary tasks are brought together:

> Employees have a much better opportunity to know each other, so that cooperation between individuals and departments can develop on a more personal, informal basis and not be so largely dependent on impersonal systems and administrative controls. Employees can see much more readily where they themselves "fit" into the organization and the significance of their jobs in the whole scheme of things.[10]

You will recall that this is one of the major sources of satisfaction under process automation as contrasted to mass-production technology (see Chapter 3). Employees see themselves as responsible for a total process, something with an observable output, and their jobs are designed to mutually facilitate the total effort rather than a fractional part.

When large numbers of people doing similar work are brought together in a single department, particularly if their work is unchallenging, personnel difficulties are likely to multiply. Typing pools, departments filled with hundreds of draftsmen or engineers doing identical tasks, all are sources of serious morale problems. To be sure, such a scheme may mean that the work can be scheduled more efficiently and that complex and labor-saving equipment can

---

[10] Worthy, *op. cit.*, p. 68.

be used to handle the work of the entire organization. Yet the concentration of a large number of people, all doing the same job, tends to isolate them from the total organization. These groups become conscious of areas where their needs conflict with the rest of the organization. We have seen an occupational group that was satisfied with its pay and working conditions become a sore spot in the organization when the entire group was concentrated in the same department.

> In one large automobile manufacturing company, the draftsmen became a source of friction after they were all moved into one department instead of being scattered around among the departments that used their services. The new department became known as "Siberia."

Improving Coordination Between Groups

It would be unrealistic, however, to assume that completely autonomous work groups can be developed. In the modern organization, work groups and departments have to cooperate with one another if the objectives of the enterprise are to be attained. Consequently, management has a responsibility to innovate organization changes that further intergroup cooperation.

LAYOUT

Excessive physical distance among groups almost invariably reduces their opportunities to cooperate.

> "As accountants, our job is to help department heads improve their procedures and records to make their jobs easier and the results more effective. Oftentimes, however, we are not called in early enough when a new project gets started or some change is contemplated. The fault lies in our location—the laboratory accounting office is located in a small rented building several miles from the nearest research or development group. Being far away they never get around to calling us until their plans are already fixed; it takes so much longer to undo things than to get in on the ground floor. When we used to be located in the same building, these problems never occurred."

One way to improve opportunities for contact between groups that need to coordinate is to revise office and work-floor layouts. At the same time, the manager may also want to separate groups that do not need such intimate contact. Too easy access between such groups may encourage them to make unnecessarily frequent demands on each other.

Where for one reason or another such physical shifts are impossible for the manager to arrange, he may be able to devise special procedures to bring groups together that have to coordinate their activities but that are part of separate organizational families. We observed one company in which such procedures were hit on by chance. Two groups of engineers who reported to separate departments but who were working on interrelated drawings found that they needed to see each other more frequently than the normal flow of work allowed. Since there was no company cafeteria, the members of the two groups developed a car-pooling arrangement for traveling to and from lunch so that they could discuss their problems on the way.

COMMITTEES AND COORDINATORS

Special committees are useful in facilitating exchange of information between groups that normally have little contact with one another:

> The members of one department were upset by another group's habit of sending in requests for "rush orders" that put tremendous pressure on everyone to do the impossible. They couldn't understand why these last-minute needs could not be predicted earlier in the day. It was only when cross-department staff meetings were held that they learned about certain inherent technical problems in processing that made additional supplies necessary at the last minute.

Under the direction of a skilled chairman, committee meetings provide an opportunity for systematic, face-to-face discussion of problems and dissemination of information.

Increasingly, large companies make use of coordination or liaison specialists. For example, *product planners* have the responsibility for getting development engineering, manufacturing, and sales to work together. They work between each of these groups, persuading them to modify their efforts for the common good, that is, the design, production and distribution of a new product.

TRAINING

As we have seen, many of the problems of coordination in specialized organizations arise out of the fact that each group has its own "vested interest," its own typical point of view or approach to problems. The engineer is interested in quality, for instance; his training and the nature of his work give him little interest in cost reduction. The accountant has just the opposite point of view. Such differences are inevitable (in fact, properly utilized by management they contribute to organizational strength).

An effective training program can help the engineer put himself into the accountant's shoes. It can show each group how its own actions sometimes cause unwitting but unnecessary affronts to other groups. It can show each group how it can communicate with others in understandable terms.

Clearly, then, provision must sometimes be made for communicating across department lines even though the departments normally have little in common, and even though they report to separate parts of the organization. Realistically, of course, this type of communication can never be as effective as face-to-face communication between members of the same work group.

SUPERVISION

The good manager evaluates the status of intergroup relationships as part of his regular supervisory pattern. He seeks to identify potential and actual points of friction in the organization and to determine whether they are the result of poor organization design, personality problems, bad placement, or temporary operating problems.

The Meaning of Decentralization

Some of the types of reorganization we have been describing might approximately be called shifts toward greater *decentralization*. Large, amorphous organizations in which nearly every decision must go up through many levels are highly *centralized*. They are the ones cursed with the problems of many-leveled hierarchies and specialization described in earlier chapters (like the Ajax Company before it was reorganized).

And yet centralization is not just a product of a particular managerial or supervisory philosophy, such as: "Close supervision is useful because people can't be trusted." Centralization also results from the design of the organization itself. When operations are highly specialized and departments finely sub-divided, decisions *must* be made by higher levels in the organization, and rigid rules *must* be employed. The reason, of course, is that no supervisor, any more than a single employee, is in a position to be "on his own." Because only a small part of the total job is done by any one employee or department, upper levels of management must step in to insure cooperation and coordination.

> Where the work of the organization is broken up into so many functional divisions again, cooperation can no longer be achieved spontaneously. After all, each functional unit was set up as a distinct entity in order that it might achieve a more efficient system. Each unit, therefore, tends to operate primarily in terms of its own system rather than in terms of the needs of the organization as a whole. Each unit becomes jealous of its own prerogatives and finds ways to protect itself against the pressures and encroachments of others. Conflict develops on the employee level as well as the supervisory level, thus forcing an extra administrative load on higher levels of management because of the need for constantly reconciling differences.[11]

Under decentralization, by contrast, management often considers a very different set of variables in deciding on organization structure. Rather than grouping employees together because they do similar work, management assesses the number and type of contacts required to complete a total operation. It designs work groups to facilitate coordination and cooperation between people who must interact frequently. When interrelated jobs are carefully

---

[11] Worthy, *op. cit.*, p. 71. Harold Leavitt titles an interesting description of this dilemma "The Jigsaw Puzzle of Responsibility," in his text *Managerial Psychology* (Chicago: University of Chicago Press, 1958), pp. 266-269.

grouped together, the supervisor can be left pretty much to his own devices. He can serve as an effective leader, since he has autonomy himself and can in turn delegate some autonomy to his subordinates.

There is some evidence that American industry is moving in the direction of greater decentralization. The Vice President of Manufacturing in a large oil company has described the organization of one of the company's new refineries in systems terms much like the automated power plant on p. 455:

> In this refinery all the men except the accountants and laboratory technicians are part of a single operating team. There is only one department—the Operating Department. The men have been trained somewhat as the crew of a submarine, in that every man can fill almost any breach. They are not concerned whether someone is doing their work, or whether they are doing someone else's work. Their interest lies, as a team, in keeping the operation going. All of the operating work is their work.
>
> There are ten on each shift. They run the entire refinery, including crude distillation, catalytic cracking and reforming, product testing, blending and shipping of products, and the utilities.[12]

Under this philosophy of management some of the large concentrations of staff groups that create problems of coordination for the line manager are being dispersed. Middle managers and sometimes even first-level managers may be assigned their own staff specialists (to assist in methods work, personnel, finance, tooling, and so on). That they can directly control the activities of the specialists makes coordination much simpler and helps train the supervisor to do his own control and planning work. In turn, as a manager gains skill and experience in these tasks which had been taken away from him (see Chapter 16, p. 413), his self-confidence and status are built up. This helps him deal more effectively with his immediate subordinates and superiors.

Decentralization means shifting "downward" the point at which all the employees necessary to do a complete job come together and report to a common supervisor. Again, this shift means that more responsibility can be delegated to the supervisor. Building the organization structure around the flow of work permits the large company to enjoy the human-relations advantages of the small company. All the operations that need to be integrated come under a common supervisor at the lowest possible level. This supervisor is able to communicate directly with everyone who has any impact on his ability to meet the goals assigned him. Workers and managers who must coordinate their activities are made members of the same team. Each employee is able to contact directly his real boss—the man who makes the important decisions.

In other words, an organization should consider its needs for *horizontal* communications before constructing its *vertical* or *hierarchical* lines of communication.

---

[12] Clarence H. Thayer, Vice President in Charge of Manufacturing, Sun Oil Company, Philadelphia, Penn., "Automation and the Problems of Management" (address to the Wilmington, Delaware, Chapter of the Society for the Advancement of Management, delivered on October 14, 1958).

LIMITATIONS OF DECENTRALIZATION

This technique of decentralization is not a cure-all for human-relations problems, however. While companies like General Motors, Sears, duPont, General Electric, and others are enthusiastic about its virtues, others, like Chrysler, have tried it and moved away.

One of the reasons for this difference in experience may be that decentralization requires unusually able personnel—managers and employees who can accept delegation and general supervision and the responsibilities these entail. This means that management must devise good selection procedures by which it can accurately identify supervisory talent and must also provide for effective on-the-job training. Decentralization demands that all managers in the company share a common understanding of the methods and objectives of the organization; otherwise autonomy may lead to anarchy.

There are other limitations that make decentralization something less than a cure-all for organization ills. Decentralized organizations may not be as effective in making quick decisions or in adjusting to rapid environmental changes. For example, it may be hard to get separate units to agree to manpower cutbacks unless the change is imposed from above. Many organizations are composed of parts that are too interdependent to allow for a great deal of autonomy—the opposite of the Sears Roebuck case described earlier. Interdivisional cooperation may prove deficient when each division concentrates primarily on its own objectives rather than on those of the organization. One division may be unwilling to share scarce technicians with another, although the needs of the latter are more pressing. A research laboratory that is completely autonomous may fail to coordinate its activities with the needs of the manufacturing divisions. In turn, the manufacturing divisions may fail to appreciate how they can make use of research. Finally, decentralization has many added hidden costs arising from duplication of specialized staff work and the costs of operating the necessary controls to keep top management informed.[13]

Personality and Organization Structure

In the previous section we have observed how job performance is affected by organization structure decisions (for instance, work-group boundaries). Billing clerks at Ajax handled their jobs differently *after* the Customer-Order Processing Department was reorganized.

---

[13] For an excellent criticism of decentralization from the point of view of the accounting and finance functions, see John Dearden, "Mirage of Profit Decentralization," *Harvard Business Review*, Vol. 40, No. 6 (November 1962), pp. 140-148. Dearden details the extra costs associated with decentralization, particularly the increasing number of financial specialists that must be maintained and their costly battles with line officials over the "true" profit figures for each decentralized unit.

Another key influence on job performance is personality. Particularly on jobs with a high human-relations content, where most of the working day is spent interacting with other people, personality is a major determinant of what will be done and how it will be done. This statement holds for store clerks and superintendents and industrial engineers as well as many other white-collar jobs. The role of personality is hardly surprising, however, since an important component of personality is an individual's capacity for dealing with other people.

Let us first look more specifically at how personality shapes job performance and then consider what can be done about the personality factor in order to improve organizational performance.

HOW PERSONALITY SHAPES THE ORGANIZATION

Traditionally, personality was ignored in organizational decision-making because jobs were dealt with in isolation. It was assumed that a job could be defined in terms of abstract "responsibilities" without giving much thought to the relationships between jobs, what behavior was expected of the individual in relation to other people in the organization. Thus, it should make no difference whether the position "Product Engineer for Special Fabrics" is occupied by Mr. Ross or by Mr. Jones. Each should do it in exactly the same way, because that is the way the organization is designed to function.

But practice differs enormously from theory. The organization will undoubtedly not function the same way when Ross has the job as it did with Jones. Each man's personality will reveal itself in the way he works with his colleagues, his boss, his subordinates, and other departments. As a result, when the incumbent on a job changes, everyone has to adjust to a whole series of changes in the way work is accomplished.

In spite of organizational theory, it is naive to assume that employees fit themselves into the straitjacket of the job specification. As they try the job on for size they begin squirming a bit, pulling in here and pushing out there, until the job begins to fit their personality needs. The result is that the organization functions differently from the way the designers of the structure envisioned.

> Brown as purchasing agent is supposed to spend about half his time analyzing sources of supply and negotiating terms of purchase, and the other half managing the employees in the purchasing office. Brown enjoys negotiating, but is unhappy handling what he calls these "darn petty personnel problems." So he spends less and less time supervising and more time buying. Gradually the job of running the office is assumed by his chief assistant, since the employees need someone to turn to with their problems.
>
> In contrast, Smith is supposed to spend nearly all his time drawing up engineering specifications. However, he has a flair for dealing with people, and he soon finds that other engineers are coming to him with their personnel problems. He begins to represent them directly in contacts with the division

head. As his reputation as a "fixer" grows, upper management uses him as a trouble-shooter. He does less and less engineering and more and more human-relations work. At the same time, his own boss, the section head who prefers puzzling over blueprints to worrying about employee relations, is by-passed and gradually loses authority.

Research suggests that waitresses whose personality includes certain leadership attributes perform very differently from those who lack these characteristics. For example, the latter can't deal with pressuring customers or rush periods when the kitchen falls behind.[14] They break down and cry!

What an organization *really is* reflects the personalities of those who hold key jobs. The personality of the chief executive officer permeates the entire company, and as we noted earlier, personal preferences of store managers at Sears determined whether "tall" or "flat" organizations evolved.

Similarly, supervisory styles, how subordinates are dealt with, is often a reflection of personality make-up. Here is one example: [15]

> Berg believed that a good supervisor should delegate as much responsibility as possible to subordinates. He couldn't understand why he was always being criticized for failures to delegate. If one watched him supervise the answer was clear enough. Yes, he would give orders that would allow the individual to assume a great deal of responsibility. But he was very impatient and never took the time to train a subordinate thoroughly before giving a new assignment. Often the employee didn't know the background of the problem he was expected to handle and how it related to other activities for which he was responsible. Lacking complete information and adequate training, he either went very slowly or made serious mistakes. When Berg observed this behavior he hastily moved in and handled the job himself, always saying "It's easier to do it myself; no one wants to take real responsibility any more." Thus, his method of handling order-giving (arising from his fast-paced personality), frustrated his own intellectual belief in delegation.

USING KNOWLEDGE OF PERSONALITY
TO SOLVE HUMAN-RELATIONS PROBLEMS

When personality problems arise, a manager has three principal choices. He can endeavor to get people to modify their behavior to make their job performance more consistent with the needs of the job, or he can change the job, or he can replace the person. The last, of course, is the most drastic and frequently the most painful decision.

Modifying behavior. If the manager knows the proper behavior in a given situation, he may be able to persuade or train employees to adopt this pattern. Unfortunately, though, many managers are content just to tell their

14 William F. Whyte, *Human Relations in the Restaurant Industry* (New York: McGraw-Hill, 1948), pp. 131-133.

15 This and the cases following are adapted from Eliot Chapple and Leonard Sayles, "The Man, the Job, and the Organization," *Personnel* (March-April, 1958), pp. 72-79.

people, "delegate more," for example, rather than actually to observe how subordinates are dealt with.

In the Berg case cited above, Berg's manager was able to get him to recognize that he, in fact, did not delegate. Working with his personnel director, Berg became aware of his own propensity to "move in" too rapidly. He learned the importance of spending adequate time in giving assignments, to spend at least a half hour consecutively with a subordinate when a new project came in, and to wait several days before going back to the subordinate after making an assignment.

An extensive study of a supermarket chain illustrated much the same technique.[16] Middle managers (district managers) had to learn a whole new set of behavioral patterns to make effective a shift to a decentralized method of operation. In other words, they had to learn to handle their subordinate store managers in a different way if the subordinates were going to assume more responsibility for store operations and be less dependent on their boss for decision-making. Those district managers who were successful in making the transition learned to talk less in their contacts, letting the store manager talk more. In doing this they also had to

1. Ask fewer questions
2. Give more information
3. Give opinions less frequently
4. Give many less directions and suggestions

Some personalities found this new pattern easier to adopt than did others, for whom it went against their basic propensities.

Many times conflicts occur between specialists who are supposed to collaborate. Because of personality problems, the jobs don't intermesh as they should as each comes to distrust or dislike the other. Here is an example of a conflict in industrial engineering:

> Two section heads in the industrial engineering department of a medium-sized company had been feuding almost since the day—two years before—when they both promoted to their present positions. One was the installations engineer. The other was a methods engineer whose primary responsibility was to develop new operations, to test them out in the experimental shop maintained in the department, and to turn the processes over to the installation section for testing. Whenever trouble broke out between him and the installation engineer, the methods man was convinced that the latter had changed the process or hadn't followed the method as he had spelled it out, while the installation engineer was equally convinced that the basic idea was wrong or that the methods engineer hadn't taken into consideration the practical requirements of the shop.
>
> The methods engineer found making contacts with others difficult. He was

---

[16] Paul Lawrence, *The Changing of Organizational Behavior Patterns* (Boston: Division of Research, Harvard University Graduate School of Business Administration, 1958).

slow to take initiative, easily upset by criticism, and tended to withdraw into his shell and become increasingly petulant. The installation engineer was a man with a great deal of energy and initiative. He liked to get things done quickly and usually had little difficulty dominating others.

Since both men were good engineers and did their job well, the chief engineer was unwilling to transfer either one out of the department. On the other hand, he became increasingly aware that the backbiting wasn't helping his relations with production since each man was enlisting others outside the department in the feud.

With the aid of the training director, the chief engineer took a hand in this situation. First, the two of them discussed with the installation head how he disturbed his opponent by being too quick to take the initiative and by dominating every time he tried to raise an objection. The installation engineer came to understand that it was his natural way of behaving, effective though this made him in the shop, which brought out these instinctive reactions in the other man. It would help matters, he was advised, if he genuinely tried not to jump in when the methods engineer was attempting to formulate an idea and if he could refrain from taking over the discussion until the methods engineer had finished making his point.

To the methods engineer, on the other hand, it was suggested that he should refrain from seeing the installation engineer on a day when he had too many other contacts or had been upset by other problems. The chief engineer also worked out a schedule whereby each man could plan his contacts instead of leaving it up to the installation engineer to take the initiative every time he thought he might have a problem.

In recent years management has been experimenting with a variety of other techniques such as "sensitivity training" [17] to get key personnel to modify their behavior when it is upsetting to other people and jobs.

Redesigning jobs. Many times it is easier to change the job than to change the person. Many behavioral attributes are too deeply ingrained to modify easily. Thus, parts of a job that are difficult for the individual to perform or on which he conflicts badly with other people may have to be removed. Jobs can, in fact, be viewed as flexible packages of component parts, at least some of which are shiftable in order to tailor the job to the needs and competencies of the individual personality who will be manning it.

A large aircraft firm employed a training director who had long years of experience and many skills in designing both programs and materials. However, he lacked the ability to develop effective working relationships with the managers of other divisions. Within his own department he was competent, but he was unable to make himself initiate contacts with the divisional managers often enough to build up effective relations with them. Nor was he able to put over his program in the face of any opposition. Though management believed that training should be carried out at the divisional level, the training director found every excuse to stay in the central offices. Top management then evolved a plan to shift the "selling" parts of his job to an assistant and give the training director additional responsibilities for company publications.

---

[17] *Cf.* discussion of sensitivity training in Chapter 10.

Selection and rejection.   Many times the types of problems we have been describing are avoided by considering the behavioral requirements of the job in advance and selecting an appropriate personality to fill the job. Of course, when the selection turns out to be a poor one, when the individual is unable to develop satisfactory relations with subordinates or colleagues, he may be shifted to another job or leave the company. This course of action can be embarrassing and costly to all concerned and thus is used as a last resort. Thus, changing people (personalities) changes the operating characteristics of organization just as does any structural change.

Conclusion

If we want to understand how an organization functions and what sources of personnel problems lie within it, it is not enough to look at the formal organization chart. We need to observe the actual operation of the organization: who comes into contact with whom in the course of getting the work done—at whose initiation and how frequently and for how long. These interpersonal relationships are the life blood of the organization.

Unfortunately, some managers believe that the prime requisite for a smooth-running organization is a clear-cut, symmetrical organization plan which shows each man who his boss is and what his responsibilities are. Or they assume that the most logical scheme is to bring together under a common supervisor all employees who do similar work—that is, to organize personnel according to a "functional" pattern.

The results of such approaches to organization may have a disastrous effect on efficiency and human relations. They consume a great deal of managerial time simply because many levels of supervision are regularly involved in the day-to-day problems of getting work done. They encourage intergroup struggles and make it difficult or impossible for supervisors to use the techniques of general supervision. Supervisors are compelled by the difficulties inherent in the organization structure to resort to close supervision and rigid rules; they cannot afford to delegate much responsibility. But the mere piling up of pressures, rules, and controls does not guarantee that all the parts of the organization will do "as they are told" and coordinate their activities effectively.

We have endeavored to show how some of the problems stemming from large, impersonal hierarchical structures based on the principle of division of labor can be ameliorated or solved. Care needs to be taken to insure that both work groups and department jurisdictions encompass as many as possible of those jobs that are closely interrelated. Cooperation that arises spontaneously out of the structure of the organization is far easier to maintain than that which is imposed by rigid rules, control, and close supervision. Furthermore, such decentralization leads to an enormous saving in managerial time and energy. It means that more of the day-to-day work problems can be solved by the immediate supervisor, rather than having to be carried up through one or even several levels to a common supervisor.

In short, organizations should be constructed from the *bottom up,* rather than from the *top down.* In establishing work-group boundaries and supervisory units, management should start with the actual work that must be performed, an awareness of who must coordinate his job with whom, when, and where. Making work groups as inclusive as possible discourages close supervision and fosters downward delegation. Rather than an amorphous institution in which people cannot understand the relationship of their jobs to the objectives of the business, the organization then takes on some of the desirable characteristics of the informal group, an organic human system.

In a somewhat analogous fashion the manager endeavors to build effective personality-job combinations. Jobs are analyzed in terms of what patterns of human relations will be required of the persons filling the job. An effort is made to find personalities compatible with the behavioral requirements of the job and to modify ineffective relationships. This can sometimes be done by transforming elements of the job (for instance, the training director helping the individual to observe where his activities are inadequate—such as the manager, Berg.)

We have traveled a rather long road to prove our point. At the outset, you will recall, we emphasized that to a substantial degree the human relationships in an organization are a product of its structure, as well as of the type of people, jobs, and supervision that make it up. In outline form, this is the pattern we have tried to develop:

Structure of the organization

> Personality
> Number of levels
> Type of specialization and controls
> Degree of centralization

↓

Shapes the pattern of human relations or interaction

> Social (informal group) contacts
> Up- and down-the-line contacts
> Flow-of-work (horizontal) contacts

↓

Whose product is

> Quality of teamwork
> Degree of cooperation
> Type of leadership
> Personal motivation

Traditionally in the field of human relations, these variables have been divided into those that compose the "formal" organization and those that make up the "informal" organization. The term "formal" connotes that these elements are specified or contrived by top management, whereas "informal" organization refers to those patterns of human relations that evolve out of day-to-day experiences. The diagram below may make this distinction clearer:

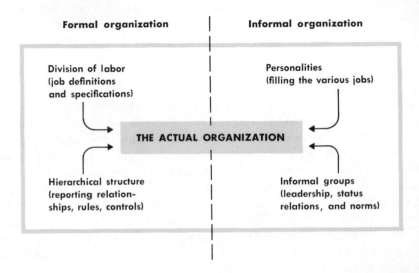

The formal and informal elements interact to produce the actual pattern of human relations that can be observed: how work is actually performed in terms of who does what with whom, when and where, as well as who defers to whom, who initiates to whom, and what implicit rules of behavior govern these contacts. This structure of human contacts and communications provides the framework within which problems of personnel policy and decision-making can be realistically understood and dealt with by administrators.

PROBLEM ONE [18]

Alternative Organization Structures

You head a division of your company that will perform three primary functions or operations; "A work," "B work," and "C work." Since no major equipment is involved (*i.e.*, there are no economies of scale), each of these types of work is divisible into any size; however, the finished service or product requires one unit each of "A," "B," and "C." (One example might be machining, assembling, and inspection.) The total volume of output required of the department is such that there is need for three units of "A work," three of "B work," and three of "C work."

The organization could be structured in one of two different ways:

---

[18] This case is taken from material presented by James Worthy in his paper, "Some Aspects of Organization Structure in Relation to Pressures on Company Decision-Making," *Proceedings of Fifth Annual Meeting, Industrial Relations Research Association*, L. Reed Tripp, ed. (Madison, Wis.: Industrial Relations Research Association, 1953), pp. 72-76.

1. All of each type of work could be placed under a common supervisor, one unit having all the "A work," one all the "B work," and one all the "C work." Each of these supervisors would report to a common second-level supervisor, a superintendent.

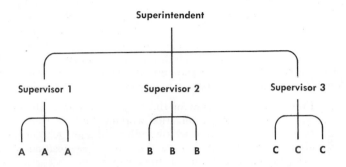

2. Alternatively, these nine units could be placed under three supervisors, each of whom managed one unit of "A work," and one unit of "B work," and one unit of "C work." Again, these supervisors would report to the superintendent.

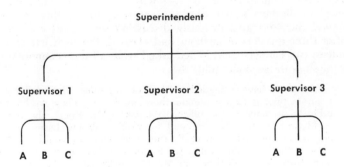

Compare the relative advantages of these two systems of organization. Consider the impact of each on the problems of supervision, coordination, the ability of the superintendent to delegate to his subordinates, the quality of personnel required for the various supervisory jobs, the amount of management development that would be accomplished.

PROBLEM TWO

Fresh Produce

The Freshway Supermarkets prided themselves on their policy of decentralization. Each store manager's bonus depended on the profit performance of his store. In general, each manager controlled his own purchasing, advertising, display, and clerical activities. The corporate offices of the chain provided certain essential services through pooled purchasing and staff assistance in technical areas: equipment selection, employee testing, techniques for reducing food spoilage, suggestions for improving advertising copy, and so forth.

Harry Alpert, the manager of the South Dayton store, earned the highest bonus of any of the midwestern managers. To a large extent this was the result of Alpert's technical ingenuity. By means of several inventions he was able to reduce the cost of his refrigeration equipment and to keep his fruits and vegetables looking fresher longer (thereby avoiding the waste of markdowns). He also developed a stock-handling system that was a significant improvement over the method recommended by the central-staff industrial engineering department. In fact, Alpert violated several of the routine procedures that had been established by central staff groups. However, he was careful not to disclose his techniques or deviations to others for obvious reasons.

1. From the point of view of the organization as a whole, how was Freshway's policy of decentralization working out?
2. Is there any way of rewarding individual managers for their initiative and ability that will not deprive the whole organization of innovations developed in any single unit of the system?
3. Is a central staff consistent with decentralization?

PROBLEM THREE

A New File Cabinet

Jane Hall, Director of Market Research for the Summertime Fabrics Company, looked out of her office to see why her secretary had not responded to the telephone-flashing signal. She was surprised to see three executives hovering around the secretary, obviously discussing some matter of great importance. After three-quarters of an hour had elapsed, the men left and Miss Hall was able to call her secretary. When asked what all the commotion was about, this is the story the secretary told:

"Since we have expanded the use of our sales office customer questionnaires, I am beginning to accumulate them in droves. They no longer fit in the file cabinets we have in the office, so I asked Mr. Frank, the office manager, if I could have another file. He said he would call Purchasing, and request that a new one be ordered. Apparently they told him they could not authorize the purchase without the approval of the Systems and Procedures Department. Mr. Frank then called them and they sent Mr. Otto over with a slide rule and lots of tables that tell you what shapes and sizes are most efficient for storing things. As Mr. Otto and Mr. Frank were interviewing me on just what items I wanted to keep in the files, their size, and how often I would be using them, Mr. Helpton came down from Purchasing. He said that frequently the most scientific file either wasn't readily available or was much higher in cost, and he usually found it moved matters along if he could get the Systems people to compromise on a unit they regularly order from a reliable supplier. Mr. Frank stayed in the conversation because he said that while he didn't want his budget to be charged with any fancy, unnecessary equipment, he wanted me to have the right file cabinet now, when I needed it. It took the three of them the good part of an hour to come to an agreement on what kind of file I should have."

1. What organization problems do you see here?
2. What is their source?
3. What organization changes could be introduced that would eliminate or minimize this type of situation?

MANAGEMENT'S
RESPONSIBILITIES

It may seem strange to elevate a single chapter to the level of a "part" of our book. But it seemed appropriate to us to "step back" from the pressures of day-to-day human-relations problems to ask some broader questions. Although it would be presumptuous of us to refer to this last chapter as a philosophical treatment of "management's responsibilities in dealing with people," we have at least tried to suggest some of the long-range implications of these responsibilities. At some point the administrator has to ask himself what *values* he will observe in making human-relations decisions. How should he weigh "human" against "profit" considerations? Should he even try to weigh them? What is the meaning of "social responsibility" and what are the organizational problems of giving effect to these responsibilities? These are not easy questions to answer, although many critics of business, and many businessmen themselves, are quick to criticize contemporary trends in the personnel and human-relations field. Many of these criticisms are reviewed here.

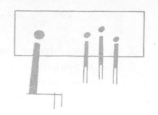

Management's Responsibilities in Dealing with People

19

Unlike such specialties as electrical engineering or finance, management involves *human beings*. The engineer, for instance, need never give a thought to the impact his maintenance program will have on the "personality" of his equipment. The accountant busies himself with tractable, obedient figures. But the manager must keep himself constantly alert to the impact of his personnel administration on the employee as an individual and as a citizen. And he must understand the subtle relationships that prevail between corporate efficiency and employee satisfaction.

Historical Perspective

PRIVATE CHARITY

For hundreds of years, managers have been aware of their special obligations to employees. The early New England textile manufacturer, for example, often provided elaborate opportunities for his "charges" (typically young girls) to worship and to gain an education. Some owners, of course, were flagrantly paternalistic—eager to extend benefits in order to receive praise for their generosity. Rockefeller and Carnegie are today better known for their philanthropy than for their often ruthless business practices. Even the worst of the "robber barons" might provide housing facilities, grant Christmas gifts, and distribute other forms of largess to those who worked for him. Yet much of this philanthropy was personal (rather than corporate) charity, and benefits were given as gifts, not rights. By the 1920's many companies had institutionalized these obligations by establishing a special department—the personnel department—to deal with the legitimate needs of their employees. ("Legitimate" needs, as we have seen, can be defined in many different ways.)

The personnel department was sometimes regarded as a buffer between management and workers, as the workers' "representative" that could be counted on to intervene on their behalf. Although management often encouraged this attitude simply to keep the unions out, there was also a sincere feeling that every organization needed a "conscience," someone who could speak for employees and who would be responsible for their welfare. Many managers genuinely believed that their decisions should be guided by concern for human beings as well as by a desire for profit maximization. In making layoffs, companies often gave special consideration to men with families or with long service, even though they might be less efficient than the men actually dismissed.

Gestures of good will and efforts to be just were haphazard and erratic. John Jones, whose needs happened to come to the attention of top management, received excellent treatment; Gus Smith, who was not quite so lucky, lost his job, even though his claim for consideration was as valid as Jones's. Some personnel directors proved effective spokesmen for employees; others had neither the interest nor the ability to do so.

Cynics argued that these humanitarian policies were only a reflection of management's deep-seated opposition to unions, or evidence of a selfish desire to raise morale in order to boost productivity. Clearly, however, some managers went beyond dollars-and-cents considerations and were genuinely altruistic.

HOW CONTEMPORARY MANAGERS VIEW THEIR ROLE

Management attitudes have become more complex in recent years. Top managements of many corporations have become self-perpetuating groups who own relatively few shares of stock in the corporations they control. Since management's control can no longer be legitimatized purely on the basis of ownership, many managers are now seeking other bases on which to justify their powerful economic role. Increasingly managers look upon themselves as professionals, and as we saw in Chapter 3, professionals traditionally concern themselves with the ethical basis of their actions.

Corporate objectives are less clear than they once were. Growth, share of the market, company (and managerial) prestige are partially supplanting the goal of maximizing profits, and some managers claim that their function is to act as trustees for a number of interests (some of which admittedly conflict). It is not uncommon for managers to talk of being mediators among stockholders, employees, customers, and the community rather than solely representatives of the stockholders.[1]

On the other hand, many sincere businessmen feel that business should not pose as the guardian of the general welfare. They, too, argue on practical and moral grounds.[2]

First, they claim that management cannot mediate among the competing claims of stockholders, employees, suppliers, and the community. The businessman owes his first responsibility to the owners of the business, which means that he must devote primary attention to profits and efficiency. When he takes other interests into account, he abdicates that responsibility. In fact, only by concentrating on profits and efficiency can he bestow the greatest benefits on the community as a whole. These observers argue that only then will he make economic use of the company's personnel and material resources, with maximum production and minimum costs.

Yet the close interrelationship between business and society seems more clearly recognized by businessmen today than it was before the Great Depression and World War II—and this is true even in industries not closely affected by government purchasing and government regulatory commissions. Many businessmen—more commonly in some circles than in others—are beginning to develop a sense of having, as a class, a special responsibility (call it *noblesse oblige* if you like) to behave in the interests of the national welfare, to function as good citizens.

There is also a more practical motivation. With improved and widespread public education and effective mass communication media, public opinion is a more potent pressure on business. The alert business leader recognizes that if he is to maintain reasonable autonomy in decision-making, he must maintain public good will. As the Celanese Corporation announced:

> The company proudly cherishes its freedom to innovate and considers that corporate self-discipline, like personal self-discipline, is the chief condition of retaining that freedom.[3]

---

[1] Earl F. Cheit, "The New Place of Business: Why Managers Cultivate Social Responsibility," in Earl F. Cheit, ed., *The Business Establishment* (New York: Wiley, 1964), pp. 152, 156.

[2] In a letter to *The New York Times* (Western Edition, Nov. 8, 1963, p. 8), Roger Blough, Chairman of the Board of U.S. Steel, explained his attitude towards the suggestion that his company should play a positive role in solving racial problems in Birmingham, Alabama:

"As individuals we can exercise what influence we may have as citizens, but for a corporation to attempt to exert any kind of economic compulsion to achieve a particular end in the social area seems to me to be quite beyond what a corporation should do, and quite beyond what any corporation can do ... I believe that any attempt by a private corporation like U.S. Steel to impose its views, its beliefs and its will upon the community by resorting to economic compulsion or coercion would be repugnant to our American constitutional concepts, and that appropriate steps to correct this abuse of corporate power would be universally demanded by public opinion and by Government."

[3] As cited in Cheit, *op. cit.*, p. 188.

Ever since Taylor's scientific management, executives also have been endeavoring to increase their rationality. Objectivity is also another hallmark of professionalism. For example, it is felt that promotion and salary increase ought to be awarded on the basis of merit, not friendship,[4] since this policy is rational in terms of the welfare of the business. The emphasis on behavioral sciences as a guide to solving human-relations problems is, in fact, an emphasis on what is presumed to be an orderly, scientific way of approaching problems in contrast to an emotional, personal-preference mode of solution.

Another aspect of this rationality is the greater use of rules and general policies. Both devices avoid the complexities of deciding each individual case by itself and the difficulty of justifying such decisions. In the broadest sense, it is a shift towards the rule of law. Leaves of absence and vacations tend to be granted in terms of general rules rather than managerial whim. Of course, union and government pressure for written contracts and better record-keeping have both been spurs in this direction.

Finally, professional managers tend to take a longer-run point of view. Although good human relations may not show up immediately in lower costs and higher profits, it is asserted that over the long run, investments in a more satisfied work force will show a return, just as do capital investments in any other area.

Unfortunately, these various sources of increased managerial awareness of human-relations responsibilities may not always provide mutually consistent answers. Decisions that could be justified by asserting that management has certain *social* responsibilities as a good citizen may not be justifiable in terms of long-run profitability. But such problems will be less abstract if we look at some actual cases. As we shall see in the two cases following, however, a more professional concept of the managerial role does not provide any automatic solutions to the complex problems of human relations in the modern organization.

Here are two examples of the problems of applying the concepts of management's responsibility for human relations. In the first, larger problem, the field of race relations, we shall view some of the organizational realities that make difficult the translation of broad policy into practice. In the second, the Duffy Case, we shall see that decision-making in what first appears to be a small problem is made difficult by the large number of tough questions that have to be answered (questions on which data and behavioral principles are not easy to find).

---

[4] The sociologists call this shift from personal to impersonal decision-making a move from *particularism* to *universalism*.

Management's Responsibilities
in the Field of Race Relations [5]

What is management's responsibility in the area of race relations? Does management in a free enterprise system have any responsibility other than to stay within the law and to maximize profits? And if management does have an added responsibility, is it enough to be scrupulously color-blind and always to select and promote the best man? Or should management go further, actively seek Negro applicants, and offset the previous discrimination against Negroes with reverse discrimination which favors them? If so, by how much?

Most managers will tell you that the company policy is to treat people *objectively,* not to allow race (or religion or national origin) to be a determinant of how individuals are treated by the organization. Further, many have a sense of *social responsibility* to do something in the race relations field to further the public good. Although these beliefs have existed for a number of years in many organizations, there is rather impressive evidence that Negroes have been widely discriminated against. To explain this gap between ideology (belief) and practice, we must apply some of our knowledge of how organizations function. We shall also review some of the problems of implementing policy decisions in this area.

WHY THE DISCREPANCY?

At least three reasons can be given for management's failure to translate its feelings into action.

1. Obligations towards Negroes are relatively low on management's perceived list of obligations.
2. Few managers see themselves as discriminating or treating Negroes unfairly.
3. In some cases top management's policy is not translated into action at lower levels.

Low priority of obligation. Though management does recognize moral and social obligations, purely business obligations usually come first. Until recently, management tended to keep its obligations toward Negroes primarily on the eleemosynary level (for example, grants to Negro Colleges), and to compartmentalize these obligations from purely business ones. Though many managers—particularly in personnel departments—may have felt a moral obligation to hire Negroes, they also felt a practical obligation not to stir up present

[5] The material in this section is drawn from a research project conducted by George Strauss in the San Francisco Bay area in 1964. It is adapted from an article by George Strauss, "How Management Views Its Race Relation Responsibilities," to appear in Arthur Ross and Herbert Hill, eds., *Employment, Race and Poverty* (New York: Harcourt, Brace & World, 1966).

employees or customers. And in this case the practical obligation came first, since there were real fears (some justified) that introducing Negroes would lead to "trouble."

Modern organization theory has rediscovered the old saw that it is the squeaking wheel which gets the grease. Though management may try to solve problems on a rational basis, it doesn't attempt to solve all problems at once; instead, it tends to go from crisis to crisis and the span of attention given to any one problem may be fairly short. Obtaining acceptance of Negro employees requires that management give up some of its limited supply of time and energy; in the past other problems seemed more urgent.

Management's concept of social responsibility is strongly influenced by its perception of what the public wants. Management would like to be socially responsible, but normally only to the extent that its actions are noncontroversial. Managers want to be considered good citizens, but being a good citizen is often viewed as adjusting to the community's values rather than trying to change them. Until recently, managers believed that, on the whole, the community wanted discrimination.

No perception of discrimination.   Few managers perceived themselves as being discriminatory or irrational and nonobjective in their selection policy. Many were surprised to discover that their firms hired no Negroes. Management just did not see the Negro applicant as a potential skilled tradesman, salesman, or executive. Stereotypes (see Chapter 10) such as these were easy to maintain because in many cases very few qualified Negroes would apply for such jobs—both because there were in fact very few qualified Negroes and because those who were realized there would be little point in applying.

Poor communications.   In some cases, discrimination has occurred because a sincerely felt top-management policy not to discriminate has not been implemented at operating levels. In a hierarchy, certainly such policies are not self-enforcing. In most cases they represent sharp contrasts with past practices and many employees will tend to resist them if they can. Since there is such a sharp conflict between creed and deed in this area and pious platitudes are frequently uttered, it is understandable that many employees are uncertain about what is being communicated, about whether these new policies are to be taken seriously.

Lower management is subject to a great deal of pressure: to maximize production, to minimize labor expense, to maintain quality, to eliminate grievances, to prevent accidents, and so forth. Many of these pressures exerted by various staff groups as well as upper management are mutually inconsistent: For example, an increase in production is usually attained at the cost of higher labor expense, more accidents, and so forth. The smart subordinate learns what is really important, emphasizes these matters, and tries to "get by" in other areas. In a sense every executive is like a juggler, tossing balls so fast that he cannot stop. Some of these balls are heavy balls and if he drops them it really hurts his toes. Other balls are light and it doesn't matter what happens to them. The supervisor learns that if he drops the ball marked "production" or "costs" he quickly gets into trouble. But in the past no one really cared if he dropped the ball marked "equal employment."

Thus, when management really wants to get something accomplished, it must do more than issue a policy statement or make a token gesture. It must adjust the rewards and punishments, the pressures within management, to be consistent with these goals. It must change *controls*.

THE IMPACT OF RECENT CIVIL-RIGHTS PRESSURES

The foregoing should help us understand the impact of recent pressures from Negro action groups and the government.

These pressures have brought the problem to the forefront of management's attention, for it is hard to ignore a chorus of chanting pickets at your front door. Pressures help translate moral obligations into practical necessities and raise the Negro question quite a few notches higher in management's scale of priorities.

These pressures and associated governmental actions have spelled out in much greater detail the social and moral obligations of businessmen. Those businessmen who believe that their only obligation is to stay within the law, now know that the law outlaws discrimination. Those who wish to remain "good citizens" now know that the obligation set for them by the more articulate representatives of society calls for them to hire an appreciable number of Negroes at all levels of the organization.

In addition, there is a certain tendency to follow the leader among management groups. Once the pattern is set by leading firms, other companies may follow because it is the thing to do.

The requirement of government-contract agencies (and Negro action groups) that employers take a periodic census of the number of Negroes employed, by level and occupation provides management with "statistical control data." Executives can no longer plead lack of knowledge of what is happening in their own organization. And management always pays greater attention to a problem once it can be stated in terms of numbers, as we saw in Chapter 15.

There is also considerable feeling that business should not botch up the Negro question the way it did the union question in the 1930's. It is felt that if business does not take the lead in this area, then the government and civil-rights groups will be able to place restrictions on business policy which business will never be able to remove. A top executive was blunt: "If we don't take the responsibility here and handle it our way, we will create a monster which we won't be able to handle in the future."

Thus, we have seen how a sense of responsibility does not translate itself automatically into organizational change. But even when resistance to change is breached, a number of difficult policy questions remained to be solved. These pose dilemmas for which there are no easy answers.

COLOR BLINDNESS OR AFFIRMATIVE ACTION?

Let's look more closely at the problem of translating nondiscrimination into management action. Management can be neutral and "color-blind" in its policies. It can step up efforts to recruit Negroes without lowering hiring standards. It can pick Negroes for job vacancies even though they are not the *best*-qualified applicants, just as long as they meet minimum standards. It can provide special training for those who don't meet minimum standards at the moment, but might eventually be qualified. And it can lower its present minimum standards to accommodate those who will never meet them.

Generally speaking, the argument focuses on two alternatives. Some believe that it is enough to be color-blind and scrupulously impartial. Others feel their companies should take affirmative steps to recruit and hire Negroes.

Color blindness. Those who believe in color blindness, or neutrality, recognize the legitimacy of the nondiscrimination argument (and some will admit that perhaps they had been inadvertently discriminating in the past), but they feel that reverse discrimination in favor of Negroes is just as unfair as discrimination against them.

Affirmative action. Affirmative action is demanded because color blindness rarely results in integration. "You can post an equal-employment sign for a hundred years," the director of an employers' association remarked, "and a hundred years from now, there will still be no change in the work force."

The traditional recruitment channels—word of mouth, relatives of present employees, union hiring halls, better (that is, white) schools and colleges—rarely reach Negroes. Even when Negroes hear of vacancies they seldom apply for jobs which past history has taught are not open to them.

For a number of jobs now opening up for Negroes, there are few, if any, trained, qualified candidates. If Negroes have never had the opportunity to gain experience or training, obviously there will be no experienced or trained Negroes available. Educational requirements tend to preserve racial imbalance because of the relatively low proportion of Negro high school and college graduates. Even so-called objective intelligence and aptitude tests may contain built-in cultural bias which tends to reduce their effectiveness as a predictor of Negro ability.

Thus, if a company is to hire any Negroes at all for some jobs, it must lower or drop its requirements of experience, education, or training, revamp or eliminate its testing procedures, and—if qualified Negroes still cannot be found—provide training so that Negroes can obtain these qualifications.

Does affirmative action mean reverse discrimination? This is largely a semantic question. Those who are committed to the principle of integration normally use the euphemism "affirmative action" in public, but in private admit that this involves reverse discrimination, at least in the sense that opportunities are granted to Negroes which are not made available to whites and that where two candidates are equally qualified, the Negro will get the job.

Which is the socially responsible, the long-run profit-maximizing course?

Satisfaction vs. Profitability

Rules, contract clauses, and even behavioral science findings often do not furnish a ready answer to two critically important questions: What are the legitimate needs of employees, and when is it justifiable to put those needs aside in favor of the profit needs of the company? Unfortunately, most personnel problems still cannot be resolved simply by reading the company manual or the union contract. And the most important problems of all have a dismaying tendency to crop up between the rules, in the uncharted territory where there are no clear precedents, no obvious "right" or "wrong" answers.

THE DUFFY CASE

Bill Duffy is the head of a clerical department in a large brokerage office. Most of the work is relatively routine though of considerable importance to the company. Duffy's department has always been known for its high morale and for its ability to maintain work schedules.

Duffy started with the company right after finishing high school. Although he is just celebrating his 50th birthday, he has already accumulated about 30 years of seniority. In many ways, he seems much older than his years. He lacks stamina and his thinking processes are slower than those of many of his older colleagues.

Over the past year, the responsibilities of managing the department have been pretty much taken over by the assistant department head, Joe Jenkins. When a difficult problem comes up, the clerks now turn to Joe for an answer. Duffy continues to sign papers that need the signature of the department head, and he is consulted as a matter of form on all major policy questions. But Jenkins has become the real head of the department.

Top management considered Duffy's case at a recent meeting. A couple of the men present thought that the company should encourage him to accept early retirement, although they recognized that this would be a serious psychological and financial blow to him. His retirement benefits would be less than half of what they would be if he continued to work until 65. It might be possible to demote him to a less responsible position, but there were no jobs open that would fit his capacities. After reconsidering the matter, management decided to retain Duffy in his present position, feeling that too "harsh" an approach to the problem would prompt substantial dissatisfaction in the organization.

NAGGING QUESTIONS

The Duffy Case presents us with a number of more explicit questions than did the question of employment policies in the racial area. These are questions involving all sorts of intangibles, conjectures, and risks.

Equity Considerations and Individual Satisfaction.

1. How much does the company "owe" an employee who has given 30 years of loyal service? What obligation does it have to him?
2. Can this obligation be met in financial terms? What is the relationship between Duffy's dissatisfaction, on the one hand, with being only a "figure head" and his satisfaction, on the other hand, with maintaining his salary and title?
3. Should management adopt a more liberal policy toward early retirement for long-service employees who become "disabled"?
4. Is it fair to Jenkins, whose salary is approximately 30 per cent lower than Duffy's, to let him assume the responsibilities of a managerial job without granting him the prestige and economic rewards that normally go with it?

Organization and Profit Considerations.

1. What effect would Duffy's forced retirement have on the morale and performance of other long-service employees? Would it be more harmful than their realization that inefficiency and ineptness are protected by the fiction of having a formal department head and a real one? What impact will management's decision have on employees' attitudes toward opportunities for promotion?
2. What would be the long-run costs of establishing more liberal early-retirement benefits? How would these costs compare with the apparent savings offered by the present policy?
3. What is the effect on department efficiency of having two managers? Can Duffy's salary be justified in terms of the contribution he is making?
4. Will management's decision have any effect on the company's ability to recruit highly motivated young men?

These are only a few of the highly complex short- and long-run questions raised by this case. There are two fundamental problems: (1) How much importance should management ascribe to efficiency as against human satisfaction, and where does one draw the line? And (2), assuming that management can resolve this first problem, what are the best ways of achieving optimal efficiency and human satisfaction?

What at first glance appears to be a single organization problem is normally intertwined with a whole host of other policy problems. This case, for example, is tied in with the company's promotion policy as well as with its policies on fringe benefits (pensions and severance pay). Also involved are job evaluation, recruitment, organizational structure, individual needs and motivations, and the attitudes of the work group.

The manager must constantly seek to resolve the diverse and conflicting claims of individuals and groups both in the short run and in the long run. And yet, since he cannot ascribe exact weights to each factor, or predict the future with any real accuracy, he must rely heavily on intuition, personal judgment, and probability.

Nor do employee needs and company needs fit into neat, separate compartments. There is no simple answer to what course of action is "equitable" or what decisions will improve "efficiency," for the two objectives are intimately associated. There are very few decisions that affect employee satisfaction which do not also have a direct bearing on work efficiency.

The Contemporary Scene: How Much Human Relations?

Management in recent years undoubtedly has begun to show greater concern for the welfare of its employees. True, strong unions, government regulations, and labor shortages have contributed heavily to this shift in attitude, but enlightened executives are sincere in their acceptance of human relationships as a vital part of managerial responsibility. In fact, the human-relations movement has profoundly altered the qualities that have traditionally been associated with the successful business leader. No longer is he judged solely on his drive, ambition, decisiveness, or ability to make money. Now he is also expected to develop cooperative, satisfying relationships within the organization.

Both the economic position and the psychological position of subordinates have improved tremendously over the last generation. The emphasis on human relations has tended to take the bite out of authority and the harshness out of arbitrary rules; it has promoted compassion and dignity at the work place. There is less likelihood of arbitrary discharge, less discrimination in handing out rewards. Work loads are easier and supervision is fairer. At least in larger companies, employees have considerable opportunity to protest inequities through union or company grievance procedures. No one would pretend that we have achieved Utopia, but tremendous progress has been made.

In recent years, however, the human-relations approach to management has been subjected to a sustained and unexpectedly strong attack from observers who stress efficiency and productivity above all other management objectives. These criticisms, which have come from many sources, reduce themselves to the following charges:

1. The human-relations approach tends to complicate what are essentially very simple problems. All that is required in dealing with people is honest common sense and the application of the golden rule.

2. Computers will solve the problems, not managers.

3. The human-relations approach leads management to interfere in the personal life of employees, to take over community functions, and to encroach on areas that are outside the province of the business organization. It manipulates people and dupes them into accepting changes that really are against their best interests.

4. By overemphasizing people at the expense of productivity, the human-relations approach may prove disastrous to the organization.

Let us look briefly at each of these charges. Since they are so commonly leveled, the student of management—whether in the university or the business firm—must expect to run across them in one form or another.

DOES THE HUMAN-RELATIONS APPROACH COMPLICATE SIMPLE PROBLEMS?

Recently in a talk before a group of businessmen, one of the authors tried to explain how complicated human relations really are; he emphasized all the factors that the manager should take into account before making a decision involving people. He felt reasonably proud of the presentation, but complacency was shattered during the discussion period by the following comment from the floor: "Professor, doesn't everything you say boil down to the golden rule? I've had 40 years' experience in industry and I've found that the important thing is to be honest and sincere with people. Show an interest in them and you'll never have any human-relations problems."

But are sincerity and good will and even common sense enough? We think not.

The findings of modern psychology suggest that applying the golden rule is just too simple an approach, mainly because it assumes that everyone has identical needs. In the Duffy case, for example, a great deal of insight into the total organizational situation would be required before management could make a truly ethical decision. Is it more ethical to transfer an older employee to a lower-paying job, or to terminate his employment and give him early-retirement benefits? What does common sense tell you?

Unless management is aware of the impact of each decision on the individual and on the group, it cannot know whether it is acting to the advantage or to the detriment of the members of the organization. It is not enough to apply the golden rule or to ask, "How would I want to be treated in a similar situation?" This projection of oneself into the position of the other person may lead to unwise and highly unjust actions.

Many disastrous mistakes are made with the best of intentions. A kind-hearted supervisor decides not to penalize an employee who has family troubles even though he is persistently late and fails to meet production standards. The situation grows worse and worse until finally the employee is discharged. Were the supervisor's intentions good? Of course they were. But they led him to injure both the individual and the organization. No business-man really lets concern for others control everything he does. Were he completely motivated by charity and altruism, he would never try to take business away from a competitor and he would never discipline a subordinate. What the ethically motivated businessman *does* believe is that he should take into account the welfare of others *along with* other factors.

WON'T COMPUTERS SOLVE THESE PROBLEMS?

With recent developments in the management sciences and computer technology, it is widely believed that many subjects which now take mana-gerial resources and time will be handled in routine fashion by data-processing and operations-analysis techniques.[6] It has even been argued that many human-relations problems are complicated needlessly by unthinking managers or those seeking to make work for themselves to justify larger staffs.

However, in reviewing the previous two cases, it does not appear that these problems lend themselves to the decision-making techniques that are useful in deciding what size batch of a variety of components to manufacture or where to locate a warehouse. There were such a multiplicity of considerations, each of which is laden with value judgments, and such heavy requirements for personal skill in the execution of any decision reached (or even in securing adequate data) that it is unlikely machines will ever do the job. In fact, in the future, because computers will handle effectively some other technical aspects of the managerial job, it is likely that an increasing proportion of the managerial work load will be in the human-relations arena.

DOES THE HUMAN-RELATIONS APPROACH
INVOLVE MANIPULATION AND INTERFERENCE?

Managers are often charged with trying to manipulate their employees.

> In many cases human relations has been used or is intended to be used, to manipulate, to adjust people to what the boss thinks is reality, to make them conform to a pattern that seems logical from the top down, to make them accept unquestioningly what we tell them.[7]
> The . . . evil of the "human relations" fad is its repeated violation of the dignity of the individual. It becomes a technique for manipulating people. There are certain areas that should be free of the boss's review and his stand-ards of performance. Today, we stick our noses into other people's business,

---

[6] For a sophisticated view of the impact of these new techniques on the managerial job see Herbert Simon, *The New Science of Management Decision Making* (New York: Harper and Row, 1960).

[7] Peter F. Drucker, "Human Relations: How Far Do We Have to Go?" *Management Record* (March 1959).

> analyzing their motives and judging their lives. We should be able to take a man at face value and not always fret about what he really means. Too many of us are trying to be little tin Freuds . . . consciously trying to be a gentleman. If it doesn't come from the heart, it is phony.[8]

It is claimed that such techniques as nondirective interviewing and group decision-making are designed to get employees to do things they don't want to do, or at least that they don't realize they are doing. A familiar example is the supervisor who pretends to be interested in his subordinates and to consult with them, but only in order to disguise his essentially authoritarian approach (see Chapter 8).

Also, these critics insist, excessive concern over the individual usually leads to paternalism, with all its attendant evils. Attempts to plumb the employee's personal feelings and attitudes thrust the company into areas that are properly the province of the individual, the family, and the community. (The union adds that only an organization which is directly responsible to workers—that is, the union itself—can protect the individual's welfare consistently and vigorously.)

Fortunately, most employees are quick to spot insincerity. Gimmicks and deceit are soon exposed, as some companies have learned to their sorrow. The only group that is duped is management itself, which has underestimated the intelligence of its employees.

We see little danger that brainwashing, mass persuasion, or subliminal suggestion will win much acceptance in organization administration. The power of suggestion may be quite effective in persuading a customer to buy one brand of cigarettes rather than another—but this is because cigarette brands are not very different and because most customers have no vested interest in which brand they smoke. Brainwashing may change basic attitudes in prisoner-of-war camps where the individual is isolated from alternative sources of information. In the typical work situation, however, personnel decisions are of immediate importance to the people involved; employees do have a vested interest in what happens to them on the job. Further, few companies can isolate their employees from other points of view. Whatever the company or the individual supervisor says and does, it is discussed and criticized by employees on the job, by the union, and by other groups in the community. Management's pronouncements can always be checked against the viewpoints of others. Clearly, the employee is not likely to succumb to propaganda; indeed, his suspicion is often so great that it is hard for management to get the truth across to him (see Chapter 10), let alone falsehood.

Some critics argue that the supervisor is resorting to manipulation whenever he tries to minimize conflict and gain acceptance for a point of view or for some change. But is there anything objectionable about efforts to weigh alternative courses of action and to select the one that avoids personnel problems? Is it not, rather, highly desirable for management to enlarge its perspective to include rational solutions to its human-relations problems? In

---

[8] Malcolm P. McNair, "Too Much 'Human Relations'?" *Look* (October 28, 1958).

short, are not human relations deserving of as much careful attention as engineering and finance?

DO HUMAN RELATIONS
IMPAIR MANAGERIAL EFFICIENCY?

> "Management has been sold a bill of goods by human relations. In the process of coddling people it has lost sight of its major objective—getting work accomplished profitably. Management's job is to get the work done and to let employees worry about themselves."

This is the considered view of many critics of the human-relations movement in management.[9]

To assess the validity of this charge, we must place the problem in historical perspective. Only a short time ago business was being accused of neglecting personnel problems. Now it is being accused of ignoring business objectives in its attempts to "coddle" people. Why this remarkable shift?

Many companies discovered only quite recently that they had "people" problems. Years ago, when businesses were much smaller, most managers (who were also the owners) knew their employees personally and were able to handle problems informally. Turnover was not particularly worrisome, for good replacements were readily available. Unions were weak. Perhaps most important, there was no professional concern with the job of management— certainly not with personnel administration. Businessmen busied themselves with buying and selling in the marketplace and gave little thought to organizational problems. No manager considered himself inept or ineffective simply because he had high turnover or labor strife—this was the fault of weak foremen or troublemakers in the work force.

Today, businesses are large and impersonal. Trained employees are harder to replace, and alert unions are ready to transmute management's mistakes into costly grievances. It is generally accepted that all levels of management have a continuing responsibility for solving human-relations problems—that these are not just transitory phenomena or the result of bad luck.

In the course of this rapid transformation of the executive into a professional, and this rapid acceptance of personnel administration as a general management responsibility, it is not surprising that many mistakes have been made. Naive managers seeking quick and easy solutions have been victimized by charlatans. Companies have purchased expensive suggestion systems, engaged enthusiastic speakers, prepared expensive give-away brochures, and have footed the bill for whole kits of supervisory gimmicks in the mistaken belief that there were simple, quasi-mechanical techniques for solving employee-

---

[9] Many criticisms of this sort have appeared in the *Harvard Business Review;* for instance: Malcolm McNair, "Thinking Ahead: What Price Human Relations?" Vol. 35, No. 2 (March-April 1957), pp. 15-39; Robert N. McMurray, "The Case for Benevolent Autocracy," Vol. 36, No. 1 (January-February 1958), pp. 82-90.

relations problems. Rather than try to understand the functioning of organizations, the nature of groups, and the importance of individual differences, some companies have gone overboard in embracing such cure-alls as "participative management" or "public speaking for everyone." There has been a regrettable follow-the-leader fashion-conscious acceptance of anything called "human relations."

Some managers have simplified human relations to the point of absurdity. They insist that good management is just a matter of liking people and inducing them to like you. "Getting to know your people" is the sure guarantee of success, perhaps tempered by this warning: "Don't get pushy about production; it annoys people."

The principle of two-way communication has been particularly abused. Some authorities seem to assume that all trouble within the organization is purely and simply the result of "misunderstanding." Jones misinterprets Brown's motives and Brown fails to realize that Jones is operating within a different frame of reference. The moment the communication dam is broken, understanding will flood through the organization.

Given this simple definition of the management problem, one might well ask why improvement has been so long in forthcoming. A ready answer is that the human being is recalcitrant, hard to change. Some ardent "human-relationists" throw the whole problem right onto the psychiatrist's couch. There has been a mushrooming of quasi-therapeutic cures for insensitive, uncommunicative people: role-playing, group therapy of one kind or another, sensitivity training, nondirective counseling. Apparently the hope is to change the manager's personality, to make him show more "consideration," to induce him to be less autocratic.

Many of these techniques have a useful role to play, but they may be overemphasized. What is wrong with this approach? At least three things, in our opinion:

1. True, some problems are created and others are magnified by poor communications. But many problems cannot be solved by better understanding alone. They can be solved only by carefully wrought changes in technology, work procedure, organizational structure, or personnel policies.

2. True, counseling and training may improve communications and may even help people develop skills—and that is all to the good. But changing personality itself is an expensive, arduous job, with a poor prognosis.

3. Human relations is not an end in itself. The purpose of business is not to make people happy (though some have argued otherwise) but to achieve its over-all goals of productivity and profitability. And the purpose of *human relations* is to help management elicit the cooperation of people in working toward those goals.

Although we decry the uncritical acceptance of human relations as a magic cure, we feel that it is a mistake to go to the opposite extreme. The manager cannot be concerned about getting work done without also being concerned about people. Even in the fully automated factory or office, important jobs must still be done by human beings. Their willingness to coordinate their efforts with those of other people and with the system and equipment developed by engineers is an essential component of a successful organization.

In his efforts to conquer disease, man has resorted to charms, incantations, and witch doctors. But no one would suggest that just because he put his faith in gimmicks and myths in the past he would be better off today to ignore the problems of illness and concentrate on "living."

The manager cannot ignore the human-relations problems of his organization and concentrate exclusively on getting the work out. Getting the work out depends on getting cooperation out of people both inside and outside the formal boundaries of the organization. The future will see increasing, not decreasing, attention paid to the human-relations problems of the organization.

Conclusion

We hope you have not been discouraged by our survey of the human problems inherent in the organization. As most managers have learned, there are no perfect, final solutions to these problems. Every area we have explored is rich in challenges to the decision-making skill of the executive.

Only when we place these problems in the larger context of American life does their full significance become apparent. The individual human being, and his opportunities for development and satisfaction, have a high value in our culture. We expect our institutions to provide him with a chance to express and satisfy his needs and to fulfill his capabilities. The evolution of private organizations that are consistent with and complementary to our democratic political institutions is a high achievement in itself. Throughout the ages, man has struggled to achieve individual freedom without jeopardizing the safety and welfare of others, and to engage in productive work that will satisfy the economic and physical needs of himself and society. Not unexpectedly, severe conflicts arise between the needs of the individual and the needs of the groups and organizations that make up society. As the administrator makes choices between organizational efficiency and the satisfaction of individual needs, he is acting as a mediator in this inevitable, and, we believe, socially useful, divergence of interests.

PROBLEM ONE

Mary's Ailments

The Ames Department Store prides itself on the excellence of its Medical Department. All new employees are required to take a rigid pre-employment physical. Because of an error, Mary Fillipi came to work as a salesgirl several days before completing her physical exam. She was a charming person and immediately made fast friends among everyone in her department including the buyer and assistant buyer.

Thus, everyone was disturbed when Mary received a notice from the Personnel Department that she could not be hired because the medical examination had disclosed two rather serious internal ailments.

The buyer represented the department in requesting that Personnel make an exception in this case because (1) the girl had already been working a week and (2) she promised to become, not only one of the most well-liked employees, but also an excellent salesgirl. Further, the employees, whose sympathies had been aroused, felt that Mary was being discriminated against because of a health problem when, in fact, Ames should assist handicapped people in finding gainful employment.

Personnel turned down the request on the grounds that the hiring requirement of passing the medical examination was a fixed, long-established company policy. Also, as the Director of Personnel put it,

> "The employees should be told that the store's ability to pay unusually generous fringe benefits, including the best sickness plan in the city, is due to our selectivity in hiring. Should these standards be eroded, over time, the employees will receive less favorable fringe benefits."

Evaluate the decision of Personnel in this case.

PROBLEM TWO

Inadequate Performance

Bill Carter had been hired by a former general manager as an administrative clerk, originally at a salary of $40 per week. His work had never been good, and several times during the past thirteen years his immediate managers had considered discharging him. But Bill was a pleasant, mild-mannered person who never committed any serious errors, although he lacked energy, perseverance, and intelligence. Also, he had a big family, was often heavily in debt, and aroused the sympathies of many who knew him. His assignments, however, were performed perfunctorily and often had to be redone by others. Although his work had been criticized, no serious penalties had ever been assessed. His case recently came up for review since his annual salary was now $15,000 and his present boss refused to continue him on his budget. During the course of the discussion among the top management group, the following points were made:

1. There was no way to justify his present salary. The work of the department had become more complex over the years at the same time that Carter's work had become more slovenly. He was not even suited for any lower-level positions, and such a demotion would be likely to aggravate his already marginal performance.

2. On the other hand, Carter was now 49; other jobs at his age and with his record would not be easy to find, and management was at fault for sustaining him over years of inadequate performance.

What should be done in the Bill Carter case? Consider, among others, the following two positions:

   a. Why should present management be penalized for the errors of omission and commission of an earlier management?

   b. At least some, if not all, of Carter's behavior is the product of what he learned in the company, namely, that marginal effort is quite enough and that one can get by with little accomplishment. His former supervisors taught him this.

PROBLEM THREE

Scandal

Hollis Corfu's name appeared in the local paper in connection with a rather scandalous event. Corfu was a young man in his early twenties who had been working in a modest clerical position for the Carp Insurance Agency for several years. His work had been considered very satisfactory, and he was a pleasant person, so everyone was shocked to see his name in print.

Some weeks later it was learned that Corfu had pleaded guilty and received a suspended sentence. By this time the manager of the Agency had received a large number of telephone calls from parents of other young people who worked for the firm. All indicated they were surprised that Carp employed people of questionable moral character, and many said they would urge their sons or daughters to resign unless Corfu was discharged. In one case, a job applicant turned down a position when it was offered, mentioning the case as her reason.

When the manager interviewed Corfu, he learned that the case was by no means clear-cut. There were real doubts that the lad had been involved in the incident, but he had received poor advice from his attorney and had pleaded guilty simply to avoid the cost and embarrassment of a court case. Of course, to the community at large he now *was* guilty.

1. How would you weigh the equities in this case?
2. What responsibilities does the firm have in this case?
3. If there is additional information you believe is required, make your own assumptions and consider the impact of these on your decision.

PROBLEM FOUR

How Good Should a Neighbor Be?

The Foremost Aluminum Company has a clear antidiscrimination employment policy. However, the company also subscribes to what it calls its "good neighbor" policy. It endeavors to behave in a way consistent with local mores and customs and to "fit" into each community in which it operates.

Thus, in plants located in Southern communities, Foremost has been less forceful in recruiting Negroes than it has at plants in other locations.

1. How do you evaluate these somewhat contradictory policies?
2. Would your assessment vary if you knew that the local union in a specific location (a) agreed with management's position or (b) disagreed?

Index

Name Index

Subject Index